Contemporary Educational
Psychology: Concepts, Issues, Applications

Contemporary Educational Psychology: *Concepts, Issues, Applications*

ROBERT CRAIG
WILLIAM MEHRENS
HARVEY CLARIZIO
Michigan State University

JOHN WILEY & SONS, INC.
New York · London · Sydney · Toronto

Library of Congress Cataloging in Publication Data:

Craig, Robert C
   Contemporary educational psychology: concepts, issues, applications.

   Bibliography: p.
   1. Educational psychology. I. Mehrens, William A., joint author. II. Clarizio, Harvey F., 1934-   joint author. III. Title. [DNLM: 1. Psychology, Educational. LB1051 C886d]

LB1051.C698   370.15   74-13462
ISBN 0-471-18350-4
ISBN 0-471-18351-2 (pbk.)

Printed in the United States of America

10 9 8 7 6 5 4 2 1

Preface

In this text we present the concerns and conclusions of educational psychologists in ways that will help teachers make better educational decisions. The range of topics is great because the range of teachers' responsibilities are broad. Teachers must make decisions affecting the welfare of students and of society in each of the five major areas in the book: (1) goals and objectives, (2) development, (3) learning and instruction, (4) classroom dynamics, and (5) measurement and research. These divisions are also principal topics of the typical course in educational psychology for which this text was written.

What distinguishes our book from other texts in educational psychology? Why is another text needed? There are other books with some of the features we believe necessary in an effective text, but none of them contain the combination we desired. An explanation of this statement requires an examination of the characteristics of other texts. For this purpose we believe nearly all fall into three general categories.

(1) *Scholarly texts that are difficult to read and often impractical.* Such texts have been traditional in educational psychology. They are often good science, but many fail to bridge the gap between the scholar and the student, the laboratory and the classroom, or the laboratory and society. Even the books that do this best are considered "hard to read" and "uninteresting" by students.

(2) *Readable, well-illustrated, and timely texts that are somewhat superficial and unorganized.* As a result of student reactions to standard texts, the authors of some books woo student interest with an easy style, many classroom examples, and the generous use of color and illustrations. Unfortunately, such books are shallow and unorganized. They fail to communicate a consistent orientation or strategy with respect to developmental problems, learning and instruction,

measurement and evaluation, or any other educational concern. A variety of developments and attempted applications are reviewed, but these are not integrated into an organized, usable strategy or model. Rarely is any recommendation or approach given priority over any other, nor is there a description of circumstances where it would be the choice. True responsibility for application is evaded with a kaleidoscopic camouflage of illustrations, sensible-sounding suggestions, and anecdotes.

(3) *Systematic texts limited to the achievement of a narrow range of instructional objectives.* The third type of text is also a reaction to shortcomings of standard texts. Its authors have sought greater relevance and practicality through the detailed development and illustration of a model for classroom instruction. We share their concern for thoroughness, system, and usefulness, but we are unwilling to sacrifice comprehensiveness in an introductory text or course. The arena for educational decisions is much broader than the achievement of classroom content objectives. One function of an introductory text is to introduce students to the range and variety of educational concerns.

This text is the result of our efforts to write a book that would be (1) comprehensive and authoritative with a well-balanced treatment of diverse psychological views, like better standard texts; (2) up-to-date with respect to educational and social concerns, like more recent comprehensive texts; (3) attractive and helpful to students, also like recent general texts; and (4) systematic and explicit with respect to strategies of application, like the narrower texts about instructional models.

More concisely, this book is different because it is current, readable and practical, as well as comprehensive, systematic, and scholarly. In our judgment this combination of qualities is not found in the same degree in any other text.

Our attempt to be practical and systematic as well as comprehensive required a special effort to select and relate the most appropriate content. Our foremost criteria for the inclusion of content were (1) *relevancy:* the concepts or data had to deal with problems related to educational practice; (2) *authority:* preference was given to concepts supported by evidence from well-designed research, established scientists, or experienced practitioners; (3) *meaningfulness:* the ideas or materials had to be interpretable by students; (4) *recency:* in keeping with a contemporary focus, preference was given to issues and concerns of the present.

This task required the skills of all three authors. Our different training, experience, and resources helped us to develop each topic more effectively than one person could independently. Each of us, for example, had practical and university teaching experience in the particular areas for which he assumed primary responsibility. These area responsibilities were: Craig—learning and instruction; Mehrens—objectives, measurement, and individual differences; and Clarizio—developmental aspects of readiness and classroom dynamics. Each author had previously published text materials and research papers related to his area. In addition, we have collaborated on a comprehensive book of readings, *Contemporary Issues in Educational Psychology* (Allyn and Bacon, 1970, 1974) for which the division of responsibilities was similar.

Our debt to the many scientists and educators whose ideas we borrowed and adapted to our purposes is great. We have tried to acknowledge this frequently, albeit inadequately, by the use of references.

Grateful acknowledgment is also due our colleagues and students at Michigan State University who willingly or unwillingly, wittingly or unwittingly, served our needs for the tryout of ideas and preliminary materials.

We thank Myrna Russell and Lillie Crowley for their help in preparing the manuscript.

Robert C. Craig
William A. Mehrens
Harvey F. Clarizio

Contents

PART I
INTRODUCTION

CHAPTER 1
Educational Psychology:
An Overview

"Well, Mr. Decision Maker! We're waiting."
(Drawing by Modell; © 1972 The New Yorker Magazine, Inc.)

Surely education is the most important enterprise in our society. The nation is currently spending over $50 billion a year for education, and more than one third of the nation's population attend school. As a reader of this text, you are evidently interested in this important enterprise. It is likely that you intend to make education your profession. Congratulations! It is a stimulating, challenging, and rewarding profession.

You may ask whether a course in educational psychology will make you a better educator. To use the language of the day: Is educational psychology relevant to the educator? We (and practically all other educators) think so. In this chapter and the next we hope to explain why.

OBJECTIVES FOR CHAPTER 1

1. Understand the relationship between teaching, learning, and educational psychology.
2. Recognize the complexity of the field of educational psychology.
3. Relate the model of the teacher as a decision maker to the field of educational psychology.

WHAT IS TEACHING, LEARNING, AND EDUCATIONAL PSYCHOLOGY?

Teaching

When a person is introduced to a new field of study he usually has one important question in mind: "What is the field all about?" This question is not always asked in education. Too many people think they know the answer. Yet even professional educators do not agree on the definition of teaching. Eisner (1964, p. 119), for example, defines teaching as ". . . what occurs when teachers by virtue of their instructional activities succeed wholly or in part in enabling pupils to learn." Smith (1960, p. 230) defines teaching as ". . . a system of actions intended to induce learning." The difference in the two definitions is in whether the teaching only *intends* to induce learning or whether it *succeeds*.

When we speak of teaching here we mean the task, not the success use of the word. This seems preferable since a child must, in the final analysis, do his own learning. No one can do it for him. The success of teaching depends on the teachers, the setting, the students, and how the three factors interact. Teachers do not have complete control over all these variables. Defining teaching in its intentional sense still allows us to focus on learning as a goal of teachers and to point out that a teacher is not working with just subject matter, but also with the students' reactions to subject matter (Hyman, 1970, p. 4). Learning can occur without the learner being taught, and teaching does not necessarily lead to learning.

Learning

What is learning? Learning is typically defined as a relatively permanent change in the behavioral tendency of the learner. We infer learning from observed behavior. If a student can recite the multiplication tables, we infer learning. If he can make hydrogen sulfide in a laboratory, we infer learning. This will be enlarged on in Chapter 6. In this chapter we just emphasize the relationship between learning and behavior.

Educational Psychology

Psychology is the science of behavior. The goals of psychology as a science are to understand, predict, and control behavior. We thus have a logical relationship between teaching and psychology. In teaching we are concerned with the behavior of the learner and the teacher and the relationship between them.

Educational psychology is a special branch of psychology. This is more than saying it is the application of general psychological principles to the educational setting. Like industrial, clinical, experimental, or social psychology, educational psychology ". . . possesses an independent body of applied theory explaining the distinctive phenomena in its own field, in addition to being related in a more general way to its parent discipline." (Ausubel, 1969, p. 2) The subject matter of educational psychology can be inferred from the questions and problems facing the educator. Several examples of these questions and problems follow.

1. At what age should students be expected to learn to read? Why do some youngsters learn so much earlier and easier than others?

2. Why are some youngsters so dependent—or so anxious—or so aggressive—or so shy? What can, and should, teachers do about these different behavioral patterns? Are these behavioral tendencies learned or innate?

3. What intervention or remedial strategies are most effective in educating the disadvantaged?

4. How can we motivate the pupils?

5. What is the best way to teach a subject so that forgetting is minimized and transfer is maximized?

6. How can one best teach for problem solving or creative thinking?

7. How can educators best provide for the individual differences of the learners? How should we teach the slow learners or the gifted?

8. What are the factors that influence group effectiveness? Can peer group influence be used to enhance learning?

9. How can educators change the inappropriate attitudes of some students?

10. What is mental health? What is the school's responsibility regarding mental health?

11. How can a teacher maintain effective classroom control?

12. How can we determine the effectiveness of a particular instructional sequence?

13. How can we accurately measure Girder's understanding of history?

14. How can we interpret intelligence test scores?

15. What is the best way to evaluate and report the progress Shelly made in third grade?

Because the answers to such questions are complex, educational psychology is a complex subject, and because of the complexity, there is considerable controversy in the field (see Clarizio et al., 1974). However, this should not make one pessimistic or encourage the conclusion that the study of educational psychology is fruitless. In spite of the complexity, educational psychologists do have at least tentative answers, answers on which there is often a high level of agreement, to questions such as those listed.

The complexity of the questions and the tentativeness of many answers mean, however, that somehow teachers must be infused with a spirit of scientific inquiry. Education and educational psychology are dynamic, not static. Teachers cannot simply be skilled craftsmen who, once they have learned the trade, need to learn no more. They must be professionals, instilled not only with dedication, but with an attitude that allows them to continue to grow in effectiveness as the sciences, such as educational psychology, which contribute knowledge to the art of teaching, grow.

The general objectives of a course in educational psychology can be summarized as follows: (1) to provide teachers with some basic skills related to teaching; (2) to give teachers tentative action guidelines to perplexing questions regarding the teaching-learning situation; (3) to help teachers to understand the scientific knowledge that supports the guidelines; and (4) to instill in teachers a spirit of inquiry so that they may continue to grow in knowledge.

TEACHING-LEARNING MODELS

Psychologists often speak of models. Models are "as if" representations of how systems may work. Several teaching-learning models have been presented by educational psychologists. It cannot be said with assurance that any one of them "fits the facts" better than another. A model is useful to a teacher to the extent that it helps him conceptually organize and understand his teaching tasks. A very useful and popular model, which suggests the underlying theme of the book, is to consider the teacher as a decision maker.

The Teacher as a Decision Maker

Decision making is the act of choosing among various courses of action or alternatives. Decision making is certainly not unique to teachers; all individuals make choices. But a look at how decisions are made—which alternatives are chosen—should assist us in understanding the educational process and the importance of educational psychology in this process.

Psychologists, economists, political scientists, and others have been studying the whole process of decision making and have built various models describing the process. Although these models vary somewhat in detail, they have several things in common.

1. Decision making is defined as the act of choosing among various courses of action or alternatives.

2. Good decision makers are aware of the various alternatives.

3. Each alternative (or course of action) has several possible outcomes, and good decision makers are aware of these outcomes.

4. Each outcome has, at least theoretically, some given probability of occurrence.

5. Each outcome has a certain utility value (or desirability).

6. The more information one has about various alternatives, outcomes, and the probabilities and desirabilities of the outcomes, the better the decision (choice of alternative) is likely to be.

Expanding the decision-making model somewhat to tie it closer to education, we can classify an educator's activities into the following areas:

1. Deciding what goals or objectives are to be sought.

2. Gathering information on present characteristics of the learners, the teacher, and the educational and social settings.

3. Gathering information regarding the probability of achieving one's objectives given the input data mentioned in point 2 above for each of several educational approaches.

4. Reconsidering the objectives in view of the probabilities.

5. Choosing a course of action or alternative.

6. Appraising continuously during the course of action to determine whether conditions have changed and whether objectives are being realized.

7. Revising the course of action and/or the objective if failure appears imminent.

Another commonly used term similar to "decision maker" is "problem solver." A teacher solves many problems—or makes many decisions every day. Many times the decision must be immediate, almost automatic. Thus, these decision-making tasks cannot all be approached through extensive data gathering and weighing of evidence procedures. Knowledge of educational psychology can assist both in the teacher's immediate decision making and in the longer range, more deliberate decisions.

The following is an example of a problem that calls for a decision.

> A kindergarten student would never remain in his seat but would just wander around the back of the room.

What should the teacher do? (1) He must first consider his immediate goals or objectives. Of course, the longer-range goals would include a consideration of the total cognitive and affective development of both the wandering child and the rest of the class, but the immediate objective may be to increase the child's "remaining in the seat" behavior. (2) If the teacher has some knowledge of educational psychology (like the material on classroom discipline discussed in Chapter 14), and some information on the present characteristics of the student and the rest of the class, he could (3) make a judgment about the probability of achieving the desired objective for each of several possible responses, (4) reappraise the objective in view of the estimated probabilities, and (5) choose a course of action. During this course of action the teacher should (6) appraise continuously to see if the objective is being realized and (7) revise the action and/or objective if failure appears imminent.

In the particular situation presented above, the teacher decided to increase the students' "remaining in seat" behavior by allowing the student to browse in the back of the room as a reward for previous "sitting" behavior. A timer was set and would ring softly after the student spent 5 minutes in his seat. He was then allowed to browse in the back of the room. After 3 minutes, the bell would ring again and the student was told to take his seat. Gradually, the in-seat time required to earn the "travel time" was increased. Using this procedure the student could wander at times without defying the teacher's authority and the teacher no longer rewarded the student's misbehavior by paying attention to him. The teacher found that granting of privileges for in-seat behavior was an effective means of modifying the student's unacceptable behavior. This is an illustration of the use of the psychological principle of reinforcement.

Many principles and techniques of classroom management are presented more fully in Chapter 14. The principles of educational psychology discussed in this text will provide teachers with useful guidelines about the probability and desirability of various outcomes. Knowledge of principles in areas such as readiness, learning, motivation, individual differences, and classroom manage-ment all help a teacher with both his immediate and long-range decision making. For example, the principles of readiness should influence when a teacher starts to teach a unit. The principles related to motivation, transfer, discovery learning, and the hierarchical nature of learning all assist in setting strategies so that teachers can attain their goals most efficiently.

Glaser's Instructional-Technology Model

Although the decision-making model is the one we feel most generally useful, there are other popular models. Glaser (1962) has suggested a basic teaching-learning model that is simple to remember and understand but, more important is a reasonably accurate model of the steps that should be taken in an *instructional* process.

The model is presented in Figure 1-1. It has four parts: (1) specifying the objectives, (2) preassessment, (3) instructional procedures, and (4) evaluation. To effectively instruct in a particular unit we must (1) know what we want to teach, (2) determine whether the students already know it, do not know it but have prerequisite abilities to learn it, or cannot learn it without maturing and/or learning prerequisite material first, (3) determine instructional procedures that will allow the students to attain the goal, and (4) evaluate whether or not the goal has been at-

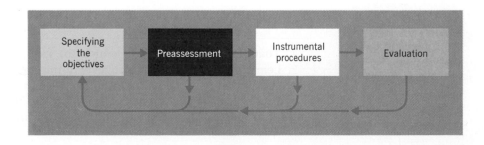

Figure 1.1
A teaching-learning model.

tained. The arrows suggest that the model is circular. Evaluation helps in revising both the objectives and the instructional procedures.

A limiting feature of the Glaser model is that it best fits instruction (or training) as opposed to the broader concept of education. Instruction, as Glaser defines it, is a set of very specific procedures leading to very specific behavioral outcomes. The model is best suited to the steps one takes in a technological, programmed sequence of instruction where the outcomes are cognitive and can be specified in advance. However, educators are often educating (if not carrying on instruction) in less structured and formal settings, and their objectives are usually both cognitive and affective in nature.

In developing the organizational framework for a text in educational psychology one could (and some do) choose to more or less rigorously follow a single teaching model. However, we agree with Gage (1964) that no single model is appropriate or sufficient.

Not all of the material that follows in the remainder of the text can be neatly pigeonholed into one of the four boxes of Glaser's model or into one of seven activities mentioned in the decision-making model. It seems futile and misleading to force such an organization. For example, the material presented in all the chapters will relate to determining realistic objectives. Many chapters, such as the one on the disadvantaged, contain material relevant to all seven activities related to decision making. In evaluation, it is hard to separate preassessment (step 3) from postassessment or evaluation (step 6). A particular achievement test (or interest inventory) that may be used as a preassessment measure to tell us where to begin instruction may well have been used as a postinstructional evaluation device for the preceding unit. Certainly the principles of measurement are very similar in both instances. To break these evaluative subareas apart and place them in different units to accommodate a rigid following of the seven decision-making activities would result in a less organized topical presentation and would be using the model inappropriately to organize a textbook. Also, teachers often engage in the seven processes almost at the same time. That is, decisions at all seven stages must be made every day.

This text is organized by content topics; we believe this presents things more efficiently than following a teaching process outline would. We feel that each chapter contributes information that will assist the educator in the seven general educational activities specified above. Therefore, the underlying theme of this text is that a teacher is a decision maker and that the material in this text provides guidelines to assist teachers in making good decisions.

Summary

1. Teaching is an activity in which the goal is to induce learning.

2. Learning is defined as a relatively permanent change in the behavioral tendency of the learner.

3. Psychology is the science of behavior and the goals of psychology are to understand, predict, and control behavior.

4. The subject matter of educational psychology can be inferred from the questions (problems) facing the educator.

5. Because these questions are complex, educational psychology is a complex subject and there is considerable controversy in the field.

6. In spite of the complexity and controversy, educational psychologists do have at least tentative answers to many questions.

7. Teaching cannot be adequately explained by a single model.

8. A general decision-making model is helpful to educators in conceptually organizing and understanding the teaching task.

CHAPTER 2
Educational Psychology and the Goals of Education

(Redrawn from *ESTABLISHING INSTRUCTIONAL GOALS* by W. James Popham and Eva L. Baker. Copyright © 1970 by Prentice-Hall, Inc., page 48)

Educational Psychology and the Determination of Educational Goals

Educational Psychology and the Communication of Educational Goals

Educational Psychology and the Attainment of Educational Goals

Educational Psychology and the Evaluation of Educational Goals

In both the generalized model of decision making and Glaser's teaching-learning model, goals (objectives) are an essential step. In this chapter we will present an overview of the ways in which educational psychology influences educational goals.

OBJECTIVES FOR CHAPTER 2

1. Know various sources that can serve as guidelines in developing educational goals.
2. Appreciate the necessity for communicating educational goals.
3. Recognize the various ways of communicating goals and the advantages and disadvantages of each.
4. Judge whether an objective has been written in behavioral terms.
5. Recognize the value of educational psychology in devising methods of meeting educational goals.
6. Accept the responsibility of gathering and disseminating accurate information to aid in decision making.

EDUCATIONAL PSYCHOLOGY AND THE DETERMINATION OF EDUCATIONAL GOALS

The first task (or decision) of educators is to determine the goals of education. It is absolutely necessary to establish goals; without them we have no way of determining in which direction to head. Do you recall the exchange between Alice and the Cat?

"Would you tell me, please, which way I ought to go from here?"

"That depends a good deal on where you want to get to," said the Cat.

"I don't much care where—" said Alice.

"Then it doesn't matter which way you go," said the Cat.

"—so long as I get somewhere," Alice added as an explanation.

"Oh, you're sure to do that," said the Cat, "if you only walk long enough." (Carroll, 1916, p. 60)

What, and how much, do we want students to learn? Educational goals are not easy to specify or agree on. Indeed, educators have long been faced with choosing between competing, if not conflicting, goals. All worthwhile goals will not be attained, nor should they be striven for with equal fervor. Should schools strive for excellence or equality, diversity or conformity? Are schools to be more concerned with teaching the three Rs, developing character, or instilling good self-concepts in their pupils? Should schools be a vital force in promoting social change? If so, can they also completely accept the various value systems held by different American subcultures? Is it democratic to spend more time, money, and energy on those who come to school from impoverished environments?

These competing goals involve questions of value, and educational psychologists do not necessarily have the answers. In fact, educational psychology is concerned more with the techniques to effectively attain and measure goals than with determining these goals and setting priorities. But we submit that there is a relationship between educational psychology and the selection and specification of educational goals. Psychological knowledge of individual differences, for example, can help us determine the degree to which we should expect and strive for conformity in our students. Research evidence on attitude change can help us to determine to what extent we should expect and strive for certain attitudes in our students. Educational psychology can help determine the appropriateness of goals and, indeed, plays a role in discovering new goals.

Goal Appropriateness

Two considerations in setting objectives are the relevance of the goals and the feasibility of attaining them.

RELEVANCE OF GOALS

Goal relevance depends on both the needs of society and the needs of the learner (Tyler, 1950). In the satirical story of *The Saber-Tooth Curriculum* (Peddiwell, 1939), a society was described in which the major tasks necessary for survival were catching fish to eat, clubbing horses, and scaring away the saber-tooth tigers. The school set up a curriculum ideal for the society's needs: teaching a course in each of those three areas. But the environment changed; the stream dried up, and the horses and tigers went away. The new society had different tasks necessary for survival, but strangely enough, the school curriculum did not change!

Teachers, school districts, and the entire "educational establishment" must continually reexamine the goals of education in view of society's needs. For example, the perceived needs of society are different now than they were immediately following the launching of the first Russian satellite, the "Sputnik." What kinds of marketable skills must modern students be taught? Should education be job oriented or more general in nature? Do we need to teach individuals what to do with their "leisure" time? At this particular time in our society should we be stressing competition or cooperation?

The needs of the learner must also be considered when specifying relevant goals. The motivation to achieve, for example, is related to the probability of success. That is, a student's aspirations will vary depending on how he perceives his chances of success and whether or not he was successful on a previous task. Chapter 7 will consider this issue in further detail.

The term "needs assessment" is popular among those who advocate the "systems approach" to education. (See Sweigert, 1968a, 1968b.) Needs assessments are formal attempts at determining what should be done and learned in schools. Needs assessment is based on the notion that the relevancy of education must be empirically determined and should identify the discrepancy between "what is" and "what should be" (Kaufman, 1971). For example, suppose we decide that every eighth grader should be able to read well enough to understand the daily newspaper. If, through some type of measurement, we find some eighth graders cannot read this well, then we have detected a discrepancy, or need.

Not only is noting the discrepancy between "is" and "should be" helpful in educational planning, the knowledge of what education has achieved may be useful for determining what education should achieve. As Dyer (1967, p. 20) points out: "People are more likely to get clear in their minds what the outcomes of education *ought* to be if they first get clear in their minds, what the outcomes actually *are*." In other words, knowledge of present outcomes may help in setting *realistic* objectives.

REALISM OF GOALS

Setting unrealistic goals is a sure way to discourage both students and teachers. The psychological nature of individuals delimits to a large extent what teachers should and should not expect. If a kindergarten teacher had as a goal that his five-year-old students should sit quietly and attentively during the school day, he is sure to be disappointed because he is setting an unrealistic goal, a goal that is almost sure not to be attained because of the psychological nature of children!

Much of the material in this text should assist you as teachers to set realistic goals. In Part II we discuss various aspects of readiness. A teacher should know what is reasonable with respect to dependency and character development. Knowledge of the Piagetian stages of development leads us to certain expectations regarding the levels at which we can reasonably expect students to acquire certain cognitive characteristics. Some understanding of the differential rates of development and the effects of heredity and environment on development should also assist a teacher in establishing realistic goals. In Part III the material presented on topics such as motivation, knowledge learning, retention, transfer, strategies for teaching principles and problem solving, and individual differences will assist in goal setting. One should not expect, for example, that students will remember all they learned in first-year algebra, or that all the knowledge retained will transfer to problem solving in physics. The psychological facts of individual differences should lead us to have different expectations for different students and differential expectations for a single student across different subjects. The material presented on classroom dynamics in Part IV should assist a teacher in setting realistic goals of classroom behavior. The material in Part V should help teachers realize that it is unrealistic to expect above-average achievements from every student.[1]

---

[1] If you are unsure as to why this is unrealistic, look up the definition of median given in Chapter 15.

In short, goals should be established that are in harmony with what educational psychologists know about how children develop, how they learn, and how they differ from each other in these two respects. Knowledge of educational psychology can assist teachers in educational decision making regarding the goals of education.

Discovering New Goals

As knowledge progresses in the field of educational psychology, new educational goals are being discovered (or at least older goals become sharpened). Concepts such as teaching for transfer, learning to learn, teaching problem-solving skills, teaching to encourage creativity, and teaching to improve a student's self-concept have not always been explicitly stated in education. These goals arise out of research in educational psychology and add new dimensions to the educational process.

Guidelines in Selecting Goals

We have discussed some general ways in which educational psychology can assist in specifying educational goals. An educator in the process of specifying his goals should, among other things, ask himself if the goals are relevant and realistic. The material presented in this text should help to answer those questions. However, goal selection is a difficult process, and an introductory course in educational psychology (or any other course) cannot teach you all you should know about such a process. We can, however, introduce you to some sources of information about goals—sources we hope you will delve into in greater detail when you become a teacher.

SOURCES OF INFORMATION ABOUT GOALS

Establishing objectives for a school, a group, or an individual student is made easier with the use of published guidelines. Some of these, such as the "Seven Cardinal Principles of Secondary Education" (Commission, 1918) help in explaining why schools exist in a very general or philosophical sense, but they are too vague to be much help for the specific purpose of guiding instruction. The principle of "Good Citizenship" does not really help us to know what or how to teach. However, other published objectives are more detailed and therefore more useful for this purpose. Two such examples are the *Elementary School Objectives* (Kearney, 1953) and *Behavioral Goals of General Education in High School* (French et al., 1957). The National Assessment of Educational Progress (NAEP) has published separate booklets of objectives for 10 subject matter areas: art, career and occupational development, citizenship, literature, mathematics, music, reading, science, social studies, and writing. Still other sources of objectives are the Instructional Objectives Exchange Center (see Popham, 1970) and the Westinghouse collection (Flanagan et al., 1971).

One limitation of the published catalogs of objectives is that they do not in and of themselves necessarily provide for local options. There are obviously other objectives, not listed in these sources, toward which school districts, classrooms, and individual pupils should strive. We wish to stress, however, that this limitation is not an argument for not using the aforementioned publications. They can be very useful. However, educators in various localities should not perceive them as complete statements. Local educators still have the obligation of stating, teaching toward, and evaluating objectives that may be unique. As Popham (1970, p. 175) has pointed out:

"Objectives should increase the educator's range of alternatives, never decrease his self direction."

Educational psychologists have advocated various techniques of stating objectives, but before we consider that topic we should discuss one more general source of ideas concerning the objectives—the taxonomies.

TAXONOMIES OF EDUCATIONAL OBJECTIVES

Educational psychologists have used taxonomies as a means of specifying (as well as communicating and evaluating) goals. These taxonomies classify the goals of education and are useful both as a means of communicating goals and of understanding some relationships among them. Classification systems for the cognitive (Bloom et al., 1956), the affective (Krathwohl et al., 1964), and psychomotor (Harrow, 1972) domains have been published. Derr (1973) has published a taxonomy on the social purposes of public schools. Chapters 8 to 10 present illustrative applications of the classes of the cognitive taxonomy.

EDUCATIONAL PSYCHOLOGY AND THE COMMUNICATION OF EDUCATIONAL GOALS

In the last section we discussed how knowledge of educational psychology assists in setting goals. In this section we will discuss some ways in which educational psychologists advocate communicating goals. Not all ways of wording goals communicate equally well. For example, in 1947 the report of the President's Commission on Higher Education

(1947, p. 9) contained the following paragraph:

"The first goal in education for democracy is the full, rounded, and continuing development of the person. The discovery, training, and utilization of individual talents is of fundamental importance in a free society. To liberate and perfect the intrinsic powers of every citizen is the central purpose of democracy, and its furtherance of individual self-realization is its greatest glory."

As Dyer (1967) points out, this is an example of word magic, an ideal many Americans would enthusiastically support without knowing what the words mean. Educational goals, no matter how appropriate, are worthless, if they do not communicate.

How Should Goals Be Communicated?

There are different points of view concerning the best way to communicate educational goals. Actually, there is no one best way to state goals; it depends on who you are communicating with and the purpose of the communication. For example, goals should be stated differently for the purposes of helping plan instructional strategies than for informing taxpayers. They must be stated differently to aid in evaluation than to explain the school's objectives at a PTA meeting. In the following pages we discuss some of the issues regarding methods of communicating goals.

IMMEDIATE VERSUS ULTIMATE GOALS

The welfare of our nation depends on what people can and will do during their whole life. The only reason we have for teaching anything in school is because it is intended to have a permanent effect on the learner. We, as educators, are interested in the ultimate behavior of our students. In our society they should, among other things, be informed voters, able to handle their own finances, and capable of holding jobs.

It is certainly appropriate to state these general ultimate goals. But this is not sufficient for several reasons. First, these ultimate goals are very difficult to measure. Second, these ultimate goals are not sufficient guidelines for the teacher or the student. We should also talk about immediate goals. When setting these immediate goals we should have considered how their achievement will relate to the ultimate goals and we should communicate this relationship (see Lindquist, 1951).

GENERAL OR SPECIFIC

Educational goals can be written at very general or very specific levels. The quotation by the President's Commission presented earlier would be an example of an extremely general goal—one so general as to be vague and therefore almost meaningless. A goal that Johnny will answer "two" when asked "What is 1 + 1?" is a very specific goal. That goal is certainly not vague, but the degree of meaning is also very limited. Certainly it would ordinarily be inefficient to *communicate* goals to anyone—student, parent, or other teacher—at that level of specificity. It would be much better to state that Johnny should be able to add all combinations of single-digit numbers, or two-digit numbers, and so on.

Of course, when *evaluating* Johnny's ability to add we will ask him to add several specific combinations. The tasks we ask Johnny to perform in a test are the most specific way of stating objectives, and we are not denying that specific objectives are relevant. But what we wish to do is to generalize Johnny's ability to add other combinations from observing his performance on a limited number of combinations. If we had *communicated* to Johnny

which specific combinations we were going to test, his ability to add these would not be good evidence that he had learned to add other combinations as well.

This point is not always well understood by educators. Years ago it seemed wrong to most educators to tell students what questions would be on the test and to teach for those specific questions. But the philosophy of stating goals, teaching toward them, and then assessing their attainment (see the teaching-learning model in Figure 1-1) has confused some people. They argue as follows. "If we really want students to know certain things we should tell them which specific things we wish them to learn, teach those things, and then test over those same things." This is an accurate way of looking at the teaching-learning process, and an accurate way to communicate objectives *only* if those objectives stated are all inclusive. Otherwise students will concentrate on the goals communicated to the exclusion of others. This is one concern of educators regarding performance contracting. If teachers or students know which specific performances are to be required, they can concentrate on those particular ones and learn them. However, in such a situation we cannot generalize from the achievement of those specifics to what the students know about the subject matter in general.

We should not attempt to express *all* our objectives in very specific terms unless those specifics are absolutely essential or when we have such a small set of goals that all specifics can be communicated. Otherwise we should talk in more general terms. Learning the letters in the alphabet is an example of a task where communicating specific objectives would be appropriate. In such a training process it may be quite beneficial to tell a student, or his parents, that by a certain day you wish him to be able to recognize the first five letters in the alphabet. Actually, communicating specific objectives may be appropriate for almost any training program of limited duration. Hopefully the goals are essential and probably few enough in number so that they can all be specified. However, when education—as opposed to training—is taking place, the number of specific kinds of goals that may be appropriate is too large. All specific objectives cannot be communicated. In a course such as ninth-grade social studies or an introductory course in educational psychology one must communicate at a more general level. Giving examples or samples of specific goals is appropriate, but the student must be told that these objectives are only sample ones and his learning is not to be restricted to those specifics.

Of course, it is easy to be too general in the communication of goals. To say that a student should understand mathematics or understand music is not adequate. More detail than that is necessary. In a later section we describe a way of writing objectives that should be "general enough to provide direction . . . and specific enough to be clearly defined by the behavior that students were to exhibit when they had achieved the objectives." (Gronlund, 1970, p. iii) The writing of both general and specific objectives for different learning outcomes is illustrated in Chapters 8 to 10.

TEACHER OR LEARNER FOCUSED

Goals can be stated either in terms of what teachers are going to do or in terms of the outcomes they expect from their teaching. When goals are stated in terms of teacher activity, they are more apt to be referred to as aims or directions; when stated in terms of student outcome, they are more apt to be called objectives. Most educational psychologists (including us) feel that it is more fruitful to state the goals in terms of expected student outcomes of the instruction instead of the teaching activity or process. This is in keeping with our definition of teaching as an activity where the goal is to induce learning (or change behavior). As Popham states:

"The only sensible reason for the educator's engaging in instruction is to modify the learner's behavior; therefore, these intended changes must be described in terms of measurable learner behaviors." (Popham, 1969, p. 35)

Not all educators believe that *all* goals must be stated in terms of student outcomes. Eisner (1969) argues for the legitimacy of what he terms expressive objectives. An expressive objective

". . . identifies a situation in which children are to work, a problem with which they are to cope, a task in which they are to engage; but it does not specify what from that encounter, situation, problem, or task they are to learn. An expressive objective provides both the teacher and the student with an invitation to explore, defer, or focus on issues that are of peculiar interest or import to the inquirer." (Eisner, 1969, pp. 15–16)

He uses a teacher who may wish his suburban class to visit the slums as an example. The teacher may prefer expressive objectives, being either unable or unwilling to anticipate the outcomes of each of the many learning experiences the youngsters might have. Strong believers in the value of stating all objectives in terms of student outcomes might argue that the teacher should not provide the students with that experience unless he is willing to specify the anticipated, desirable behavioral changes of the students.

Whether or not one believes that all objectives should be stated in terms of student outcomes, there is agreement that, in general, educators should move in that direction. The focus in educational goals should be on the student outcomes, not the teaching process. We believe that teachers should strive to express as many goals as possible in terms of student outcomes but that, *on occasion,* the wish to expose students to an experience may, in and of itself, be a legitimate objective even though outcomes of the exposure may not be able to be specified or even evaluated.

Thus, we are, in general, arguing *against* objectives such as

> "The teacher will lead a discussion on ecology."

A better wording would be

> "The students will describe the present situation in our country with respect to air and water pollution."

BEHAVIORAL VERSUS NONBEHAVIORAL OBJECTIVES

One of the controversies of recent years with respect to goals is whether or not they must be stated in behavioral terms. A behavioral goal (usually called an objective) is one that specifies what the learner will be *doing* when we evaluate whether or not he has attained the goal. (Thus one would state a behavioral goal by saying "the student will add" instead of "the student will understand how to add.") The difference in the wording of the goal is that behavioral objectives use action verbs while nonbehavioral objectives do not. There is no disagreement that when we evaluate whether or not students have met certain goals we must evaluate the students' behaviors. There is some disagreement about whether we should, prior to the evaluation, communicate our goals in behavioral terms and whether all goals we have must be amenable to evaluation. Behavioral objectives tend to be more specific than nonbehavioral objectives and this has contributed to the controversy over them. For example, a nonbehaviorally worded objective may be as follows.

1a. The students will understand arithmetic manipulations.

More specifically we might state that:

1b. The students will understand how to take a square root.

Even more specifically we might state that:

1c. The students will understand how to take the square root of sixty-nine.

Behavioral counterparts using an action verb that focuses on what the learner will be *doing* would be as follows.

2a. The students will perform arithmetic manipulations.
2b. The students will compute square roots.
2c. The students will compute the square root of sixty-nine.

Most advocates of nonbehavioral objectives would suggest that point 1b above is specific enough. Many (but not all) advocates of behavioral objectives might argue that point 2c is *not* specific enough. They would prefer even more detail, such as

2d. The students will compute the square root of sixty-nine without the use of tables, slide rules, or any other mechanical device. They will use paper and pencil, show all work, finish within 60 seconds, and be accurate to the nearest hundredth.

Again, conditions and criteria must be specified during evaluation, but many educators do not feel it necessary to communicate specific behavioral objectives prior to instruction or evaluation. We should keep in mind, however, that the debate about whether or not one communicates in behavioral terms is often intertwined with the debate about how specific our communication of goals must be.

If your instructor tells you that you are to "understand" the concept of "transfer of training," what does he mean? Does he want you to be able to define it, give an example of transfer, or list teaching techniques that lead to transfer? If he wants you to understand correlation, does he wish you to be able to compute a correlation coefficient, interpret one, determine its statistical significance, derive the formula, or list common errors of interpretation? If the teacher means all of these, he should say so. If he only means certain ones, he should make this clear. A student has a right to know, in general, what types of behavior the teacher expects him to exhibit when being evaluated. However, if we expect a student to derive an equation, it is not likely that the derivation *per se* is our goal. Instead, we probably wish to infer some "mental process," such as understanding, from that act. If we teach a particular derivation and the student memorizes it, we may end up assuming he understands it when he doesn't.

A GENERAL APPROACH TO GOAL COMMUNICATION

Gronlund's (1970) small (58 page) text was designed specifically as an aid in stating objectives for classroom instruction and, in our opinion, is the most useful guide for the practicing classroom teacher, although other guides are also available (see Kibler et al., 1970; Burns, 1972). Gronlund (1970, p. 6) suggests that stating objectives is a two-step process:

1. To state the instructional objectives as general learning outcomes.

2. To list, under each instructional objective, a representative sample of the specific types of behavior that indicate attainment of the objective.

One should teach toward the general objective, not the specific samples. Gronlund's general summary guidelines for writing objectives are as follows (Gronlund, 1970, p. 17):

1. State the general instructional objectives as *expected learning outcomes*.

2. Place under each general instructional objective a list of specific learning outcomes that describes the terminal behavior students are to demonstrate when they have achieved the objective.

a. Begin each specific learning outcome with a verb that specifies definite, observable behavior.

b. List a sufficient number of specific learning out comes under each objective to describe adequately the behavior of students who have achieved the objective.

c. Be certain that the behavior in each specific learning outcome is relevant to the objective it describes.

3. When defining the general instructional objectives in terms of specific learning outcomes, revise and refine the original list of objectives as needed.

4. Be careful not to omit complex objectives (e.g., critical thinking, appreciation) simply because they are difficult to define in specific behavioral terms.

5. Consult reference materials for help in identifying the specific types of behavior that are most appropriate for defining the complex objectives.

One more point is that writing educational objectives behaviorally is a difficult task. Most educators do not do this task nearly as well as the theorists suggest (see Ammons,

1964). As a partial aid for teachers who recognize the need for behavioral objectives but who have neither the time nor talent to develop a comprehensive list of their own, the sources listed earlier (Popham, 1970; Flanagan et al., 1971) can be very helpful.

An Example of Stating Objectives For Instruction and Evaluation

In writing behavioral objectives following Gronlund's (1970) suggested procedures, one begins by stating a general learning outcome. For this statement such nonaction verbs as applies, comprehends, knows, understands, and so on, are permissible. Examples of objectives for this section in this chapter stated as general learning outcomes would be:

1. Knowing sources of information about objectives.

2. Understanding the importance of behavioral objectives.

3. Comprehending that goals are stated differently depending on the purpose of the statement.

4. Appreciating the value of making objectives behavioral.

Once all general outcomes are stated the next task is to make a *representative* list of explicit student behaviors that can be used as evidence that the general objective has been achieved. Since making affective objectives behavioral is the most challenging, let us try to specify some behavioral objectives for the general statement 4 above.

a. Completes a nonrequired assignment on writing behavioral objectives.

b. Gives a report on one of the texts mentioned on behavioral objectives.

c. Enrolls in a 1-hour seminar devoted solely to writing behavioral objectives.

d. Proselytizes for the need for behavioral objectives with other students.

e. Completes favorably a rating scale on the importance of behavioral objectives.

This sample of specific learning outcomes could be made much more complete. Only time, divergent thinking, an understanding of the word "appreciates," and an awareness of the multiple ways to measure are necessary. These behaviors, if performed under natural conditions, are ones from which we can reasonably infer positive affect.

At the beginning of both Chapters 1 and 2 you were presented with sets of objectives. Following Gronlund's approach, these were stated as general outcomes instead of as specific behavioral objectives. You will find such a general list at the beginning of each chapter in this text.

Unanticipated and/or Unmeasurable Outcomes

Most educators will admit that stating objectives behaviorally is not a panacea for existing weaknesses and limitations of education. The list of objectives will always be incomplete. There will be unanticipated outcomes of instruction and these, too, should be evaluated. Also, while every objective is, in principle, measurable, we must admit that in practice it is not so.[2] Eisner's example of a teacher taking her suburban children to visit the slums is a good illustration of an educational

---

[2] This can be seen if learning is defined as the predisposition to respond in a certain way under certain environmental conditions. The evaluator may simply not have the environmental conditions sufficiently under control to make an evaluation of whether learning has occurred.

procedure that will have both unanticipated and unmeasurable outcomes. The same holds true of *any* encounter with students. There will always be unanticipated and unmeasurable outcomes. Regarding the unanticipated outcomes, educators should be alert to them and try to evaluate as many as possible. However, to do this one must obtain some clues as to what they might be so that they can be evaluated. These clues can be obtained in many ways, such as interviewing students or parents and careful classroom, lunchroom, and recess observations. The unmeasurable outcomes can and should be minimized by educators employing a variety of measurement techniques. Certainly there are a fair number of outcomes that cannot be measured by the traditional paper-pencil achievement test. Procedures such as observations, anecdotal records, sociometric devices, and attitude inventories are essential to obtain evidence for many outcomes.

EDUCATIONAL PSYCHOLOGY AND THE ATTAINMENT OF EDUCATIONAL GOALS

While the field of educational psychology has assisted educators in determining and communicating goals, it has probably been of greater assistance in devising methods of meeting those goals. There are some individuals who display doubt about the usefulness of educational psychology to teaching. After all, they argue, teaching is an art and psychology is only a science. Some feel that science not only does not contribute to the art of teaching but that indeed ". . . it is very dangerous to apply the aims and methods of science to human beings . . . ." (Highet, 1950)

There is no doubt that teaching was successfully being conducted prior to the time psychology became a field of scientific inquiry. Thus, teaching is not absolutely dependent on psychology. But most educators feel that psychology, as a science, can contribute to the art of teaching. As pointed out previously, teaching is an activity where the goal is to induce learning, learning is inferred from behavioral change, and psychology is the study of behavior.

The fear of science as a tool of education stems from the belief that science will reduce education to a rigid formula. This is an unwarranted belief that even the most rudimentary study of the field of individual differences (a subarea of psychology) would dispel. As Dewey (1929) pointed out many years ago, reducing education to a formula would be a departure from science rather than a use of it. He suggested that science can contribute to teaching just as it does to engineering and that "It is not the capable engineer who treats scientific findings as imposing upon him a certain course which is to be rigidly adhered to: it is the third- or fourth-rate man who adopts this course. Even more, it is the unskilled day laborer who follows it."

The principles, tentative or firm, of educational psychology do present some important guidelines for educational decision makers regarding which, in what sequence, at which ages, and in what fashion activities can best be presented to induce learning. Of course, knowledge of principles unaccompanied by judgment will not be effective. Good judgment (common sense) without knowledge of psychological principles will not be very efficient, either. A good teacher should be both artist and scientist.

The principles of educational psychology discussed in this text regarding topics such as readiness, learning, motivation, individual differences, classroom management, and evaluation can all assist the teacher's decision making and explicate the attainment of educational goals.

EDUCATIONAL PSYCHOLOGY AND THE EVALUATION OF EDUCATIONAL GOALS

Whether one thinks of education in terms of a decision-making model, a teacher-learner model such as Glaser's, or some other model, it is obvious that information gathering and evaluation are integral parts of education. To do an effective job of educating we must gather data on our goals and evaluate both the appropriateness of our goals and the degree to which the goals are being achieved.

There are many decisions that educators must continually make, and countless more that they must assist individual pupils, parents, and the general public in making. As we mentioned when introducing the decision-making model, the more information on which a decision is based, the better that decision is likely to be. In fact, many decision theorists define a good decision as one that is based on all the relevant information.

Teachers have the important responsibilities of obtaining accurate information to assist in their own educational decision making and gathering and imparting accurate, relevant information (in readily understood terms) to others, such as pupils, parents, or other teachers who are also engaging in educational decision making. The last unit in this text discusses information gathering and dissemination techniques, which should help teachers fulfill these particular responsibilities. There are principles and techniques of measurement that, if applied, increase the likelihood of the information gathered being both accurate and useful. There are numerous existing tests and inventories that can be used to gather important data. There are some definite limitations of all measurement data of which educational decision makers should be aware. Finally, there are various ways of recording and disseminating information — each having some advantages and disadvantages — of which teachers should be cognizant.

Summary

1. One of the important tasks of educators is to help to determine the goals of education.

2. Two considerations in setting goals are their relevance and the feasibility of attaining them. Knowledge of educational psychology helps to determine both this relevance and realism.

3. There are many published statements that can serve as guidelines for the teacher involved in determining goals.

4. The taxonomies by Bloom and Krathwohl et al., have also helped educators determine and communicate about goals.

5. There is no one best way to state educational goals; it depends on who you are communicating with and the purpose of the communication.

6. We should state both immediate and ultimate goals, and the relationships between them.

7. Most educational goals can be more efficiently communicated in somewhat general terms. At times, however, as in specific training

programs within an educational setting, it is appropriate and expedient to communicate very specific objectives.

8. It is generally better to state goals in terms of the student outcomes instead of the teaching processes.

9. A behavioral objective is one that specifies what the learner will be *doing* when we evaluate whether or not he has attained the goal. Thus, statements of behavioral objectives make use of action verbs.

10. Stating objectives in behavioral terms is mandatory if we are to evaluate those objectives. Such behavioral statements are also typically helpful in planning instructional strategies.

11. One potential problem of stating behavioral objectives is that one can confuse the behavior with the objective. At times, the behavior is the objective. At other times, it is only an indicant of an objective.

12. Gronlund's approach of stating objectives in a two-step process is recommendable. He first states general learning outcomes—often in nonbehavioral terms. He then lists under each of those a representative sample of the specific types of behavior that indicate attainment of the objective.

13. Unanticipated and/or unmeasurable outcomes do occur as a result of education. If there are too many of these, though, it may well indicate that insufficient thought went into specifying the original objectives and planning the instruction and evaluation procedures.

14. The principles of educational psychology are very useful in helping educators to devise methods of attaining educational goals. This text will discuss such principles and explain their usefulness in educational decision making.

15. The more information on which a decision is based, the better that decision is likely to be.

16. Teachers have the important responsibilities of obtaining accurate information and disseminating that information to pupils, parents, and others making educational decisions. The last unit of this text should be helpful to teachers in fulfilling those obligations.

PART II
READINESS:
DEVELOPMENTAL ASPECTS

CHAPTER 3
Cognitive Readiness

(Drawing by Edwin Lepper, from Today's Education, NEA Journal, 1970)

Readiness: Past and Present
Two Aspects of Cognitive Readiness
Determinants of Developmental Readiness
Natural versus Accelerated Cognitive Readiness
Piagetian Theory: Basic Concepts
Piagetian Theory: Educational Implications

Every culture has convictions about when youth are ready for certain activities. In our society, for example, youth is regarded as ready to be toilet trained around eighteen months old, to ride a tricycle about age four or five, to be held responsible for their actions according to certain religious beliefs at age seven, to cross busy streets alone or ride a bicycle to school at age ten, to drive a car during midadolescence, to fight for their country, drink alcoholic beverages, vote in elections, and get married sometime during late adolescence.

Societies also have some basic beliefs about the readiness of youth for formal education. For instance, in the United States one is "ready" to enter first grade if his sixth birthday occurs before a certain cutoff date in the fall of that school year. Or one is "ready" for college after having accumulated a given number of credits during four years in high school. If anything, the concept of readiness (or entry behavior) is probably attracting more attention from educational psychologists, curriculum planners, teachers and subject-matter specialists (mathematicians, biologists, chemists, physicists) than it has in the past. In addition to their concern with the "what" and the "how" to teach, there is confusion about "when to teach." (Tyler, 1964)

This chapter deals with the topic of intellectual readiness, that is, with the problem of "when to teach" intellectual skills. By intellectual readiness, we mean the adequacy of the student's present ability to benefit from new learning tasks. In practice, a student is said to show readiness when his scholastic achievements are reasonably commensurate with the amount of effort and practice required (Ausubel and Robinson, 1969).

·OBJECTIVES FOR CHAPTER 3

1. Describe the ways in which the notion of readiness has changed during the past two decades.
2. Differentiate between "developmental readiness" and "subject matter readiness."
3. Identify the three components or determinants of readiness and give an example of how these components interact in a complex way.
4. List arguments in favor of a "natural" approach to readiness and those in favor of a "produced" readiness approach.
5. Present an example of a readiness program that does not rely on an either-or philosophy.
6. Describe the basic concepts and stages in Piaget's theory.
7. Describe the specific ways in which a teacher might assess a student's level of intellectual development and ascertain the proper placement of subject-matter content.
8. Identify the teaching methods that are most suitable to students at different levels of intellectual development.

READINESS: PAST AND PRESENT

The readiness issue is far from being settled; it yields "answers" today that contrast greatly to those advanced even as late as about 1950. Although admittedly oversimplified, the following list summarizes the contrasts between the concept of readiness in the 1950s and in the 1970s.

Readiness in the 1950s	*Readiness in the 1970s*
1. Readiness is more or less understood as reading readiness.	1. A more unified, comprehensive, multidimensional concept of readiness exists that takes into account the mental, personal, social, and physical aspects of development.
2. Preschool instruction by parents is not desired because it would only lead to problems when the child enters formal instruction in school.	2. Parents are encouraged to provide as much intellectual stimulation as possible for their children.

3. The prevailing belief is that maturational factors are most important in readiness and that one cannot do much about these. We cannot produce readiness. We have to wait. We must be patient. Do not push the child.

4. Readiness is of no central public or governmental concern.

5. Readiness means readiness of the child for the school. The school sets the standards and the child has to work up to them. If he cannot, he will fail the class (or be promoted "regardless," depending on the school's promotion policy).

6. Schools are basically subject-matter centered, not child centered.

7. There is a beginning concern with the gifted child, and, although to a lesser extent, an increasing concern about the mentally retarded and emotionally handicapped.

3. The belief exists that children can learn more earlier and faster than in the past. There is a push for more and better learning.

4. Education and government are keenly concerned about the issue of readiness, particularly among the educationally retarded. Widespread government programs are in evidence.

5. It is assumed that the school must be ready for the child.

6. Although intellectual goals continue to be valued, there is a felt need for a more humane education that allow for spontaneity, openness, and the coordination of feeling and thinking.

7. While an "education for all children" is still at best a lofty ideal that has found no realization in practice, there is an expressed concern over the plight of the lower class student and the causes leading to differences in readiness and school achievement.

What events led to a reexamination of the concept of readiness? The factors are multiple, from political pressures to psychological theory. All the factors below resulted in a demand for increased academic excellence at all levels of the educational ladder.

1. In the early 1950s, charges were made that students were not being adequately prepared for a scientific age. The launching of the first Russian satellite in 1957 seemingly gave credence to the criticisms about the intellectual aimlessness of our schools and triggered a strong demand for the development of untapped scientific talent. Science, mathematics, and foreign languages were designated as critical areas in the curricular revisions of the late 1950s and early 1960s.

2. Educators and psychologists stressed the role of early experience in intellectual development and changes in belief regarding a fixed or unchangeable IQ. The theories of Piaget and Montessori were rediscovered and, at times, reinterpreted. Whereas psychologists had previously emphasized the importance of the preschool years for intellectual development, psychologists were now stressing the significance of the early years for intellectual development. The child's "mind" had been rediscovered.

3. The Civil Rights Movement with its war on poverty became a potent impetus for change. The fact that many youngsters were not prepared for the kind of schooling given them led to the Great Cities, Higher Horizons, Head Start, and Follow-through Programs.

By the late 1960s, it became painfully clear that the major crises confronting education were not solely ones pertaining to subject-matter proficiency. The revolt against the military-industrial complex soon spread to the educational establishment. The violence and destruction in the cities and on the university campuses bore little relationship to one's mastery of the structure of physics or mathematics. Student activism was carried out by individuals of varying intellect and educational level. The common factor was alienation from society; intellectual level appeared irrelevant. "The attitudes of these persons toward themselves and others are such that they find it difficult to achieve happiness in our society. Their attitudes, motives, and emotions make it difficult to contribute to society and actualize themselves within its framework." (Zigler, 1970)

The responsibility for the alienation of youth, said the critics, can be traced to the lack of flexibility and relevance in the curriculum and the depersonalization of the student. The result was an about-face in educational philosophy. The importance of a favorable identity and a healthy self-concept received additional emphasis as the prob-lems of the educationally disadvantaged were explored. Earlier revision of the curriculum had been unsuccessful. A more fundamental restructuring of the entire educational system seemed in order.

As we entered the 1970s, the goals of the schools remained intellectual in nature, but these goals were to be accomplished through teaching methods and a curriculum that did not ignore the individual or the problems facing mankind. The revolutional events of the preceding years led also to a reexamination of the theories and practices bearing on readiness at all levels of education.

TWO ASPECTS OF COGNITIVE READINESS

General Developmental Readiness

Readiness in the developmental sense of the term reflects general cognitive maturity, which in turn depends on several age-level changes related to intellectual functioning. These changes in intellectual functioning are especially worthy of interest by educators and psychologists because they influence learning, retention, and thinking processes. Age-level changes have been identified in the following areas of cognitive functioning.

1. *Perception.* While preschool children concentrate or "center" on a single feature of an object or event to the neglect of other important aspects, the elementary school child attends to the essential features of events and is not misled by centering on superficial aspects that attract attention.

2. *Subjectivity-objectivity and egocentricism.* As children advance in age there is a decline in egocentricity and subjectivism, as illustrated by their increased ability to view situations from the standpoint of others and to pay

greater attention to the informational requirements of the listener.

3. *Structure of knowledge.* With increasing
age, the child organizes his world more in
terms of verbal propositions and abstractions and less in terms of perceptual and
concrete experiences with a given phenomenon.

4. *Problem solving.* Students are better able
to engage in hypothesis formation (if-then
thinking) as they grow older (Ausubel and
Sullivan, 1970).

Certain of the trends that reflect general
developmental readiness have definite implications for curriculum planning, particularly
when breadth or depth of subject-matter
readiness are at issue. At the elementary
school level, when thought is concrete
and intellectual ability still relatively undifferentiated, breadth (or horizontal enrichment)
instead of depth of subject matter (or vertical
enrichment) should be emphasized. At the
high school level, however, an opposite kind
of developmental situation emerges. As intellectual abilities and interests are now becoming more crystallized and thought is becoming more and more abstract, it is now
developmentally feasible to place added emphasis on the depth of one's knowledge. The
most important of the general developmental
trends for educational programming—the
trend toward greater ability to comprehend
and manipulate abstractions—will be discussed more fully when we discuss Piaget's
stages of intellectual development.

Subject-Matter Readiness

There is another less developmental kind of
readiness, of course, that depends on having
previously learned the specific knowledge or
skills prerequisite for success or a new task.
One cannot learn to speak until he knows the
alphabet, for example. Readiness of this type
is a matter of sequence in learning, and this
is an important topic covered in Chapters 8
and 9.

DETERMINANTS OF DEVELOPMENTAL READINESS

For purposes of discussion, developmental
readiness will be analyzed in terms of its
three component parts: maturation, prior
learning, and instructional strategy. Although discussed separately, the student
should bear in mind that in everyday life,
all three factors interact and their respective
contributions to the learning of any particular skill are difficult to isolate.

Maturation

Maturation refers to any instance of development that occurs in the demonstrable absence of specific practice (Ausubel and Sullivan, 1970). In contrast to earlier definitions,
the concept of maturation now allows for the
influence of genetic factors as well as the effects of incidental experience. By incidental
experience, we refer to experiences that are
spontaneous, undirected, and unexplained
(in contrast to formal learning experiences).
Evidence supporting the occurrence of maturation comes from three kinds of studies:
those involving restriction of practice, premature practice, and delayed practice.

Studies involving *restricted practice* suggest that phylogenetic traits—those essentially
identical for all members of the species, such
as walking—are essentially independent of
experience. For example, strapping infants
to a cradling board does not delay the onset
of walking (Dennis, 1940), smiling occurs
in the absence of social example (Dennis,
1941), and facial expressions of laughter,

fear, and anger develop no differently in blind than in sighted children (Thompson, 1941). Evidence such as this lends credence to the view that phylogenetic traits are largely acquired through maturation.

Studies on *premature practice* demonstrate the phenomenon of maturation by showing that practices that are ineffective at one stage of development become more effective at a later stage despite an absence of practice during the intervening period. One study showed that youngsters taught to read by traditional methods at age five appeared to fare adequately in reading during first grade, but, when they entered second grade, they had forgotten so much that teachers had to practically start all over (Keister, 1941). Thus, it is questionable whether all the effort expended by teachers and pupils at age five was worthwhile using *regular teaching methods.*

In studies on *delayed practice,* children who would ordinarily be considered ready for a given activity are not allowed to practice it until a later age when increased readiness presumably attributable to maturation is present. The relative superiority of postponed practice has been demonstrated in a number of studies involving motor activities (buttoning, stair climbing, cutting with scissors, and ring tossing) as well as tasks of a more cognitive nature (learning vocabulary, arithmetic, and memorizing digits) (Gates and Taylor, 1925; Hilgard, 1933).

Prior Learning

The idea of sequence learning and prerequisite courses is based on the assumption that basic skills are necessary before more advanced and complex tasks can be profitably taught. Many "spontaneous" concepts can be developed through incidental experience and thereby increase the student's readiness for meaningful learning at a higher level. For example, the child, through his own actions and mental efforts, acquires a variety of concepts about reality (e.g., car, horse, blue). The development of spontaneous concepts, which are particularly noticeable during the preschool years, lays the foundation for the later acquisition of "nonspontaneous" concepts, which are usually acquired in school as a result of direct instruction. Nonspontaneous concepts also differ from spontaneous concepts in that they are characterized by conscious and deliberate control over the act of thought.

There are at least two fundamental reasons why specific school instruction is necessary for the acquisition of nonspontaneous scientific concepts. (1) Although spontaneous concepts provide a springboard for the acquisition of scientific concepts and for their down-to-earth exemplars and everyday referents, they also can interfere with later learning because of the child's idiosyncratic and intuitive understanding of many concepts. Consider the explanations of natural phenomena offered by children in the four to seven range. These are often characterized by analogies to human behavior, reference to salient visual characteristics of the situation, causal linking of events only accidentally associated, and confusion of one's own actions with the event or simple statement of fact. Youngsters in this age range might say that the wind blows when we or the trees move, that boats float because they were made that way or because they are alive, or that the sun follows us. While the child may correct many of these faulty notions of reality without the benefit of formal instruction, he may also remain unaware of the inconsistencies in his thinking or unconcerned about them. A child's experience with lightning and electric motors is hardly sufficient for the average student to develop a mature understanding of electricity. Indeed, many abstract concepts, such as photosynthesis or ionization, can only be acquired through direct instruction, since they are not available through direct experience. If left to his own direction, it is questionable that a child would develop many scientific concepts. (2) Much valuable readiness time would be wasted if we waited for the child to develop scientific thoughts through his own undirected and spontaneous interactions with his daily environment when these very concepts could be easily learnable much earlier through instruction.

Teaching Methods and Materials

The readiness age for any given task is always relative in part to the method used. It is not absolute. Several investigators have, for example, been able to advance appreciably the typical age of reading and writing by utilizing the preschool child's curiosity and urge to explore by placing extensive reliance on actual manipulative activity and by programming stimulation at appropriate rates and in suitable forms (Pines, 1963; Fowler, 1962; Rambusch, 1962). O. K. Moore taught three-year olds to read, spell, and type by the touch method — all through the use of a special typewriter. The keys on the typewriter are painted different colors and the child's fingernails are painted similar colors, each nail being painted to match the color of the keys to be struck by that finger. The youngster starts with only a few keys. The teacher might say "d" and have the child punch the "d" key, then "o," and "g." Then this would be done in sequence — "dog." Next, letters are shown on cards and vocalized at the same time until the child can type the word "dog" from just hearing the word. Using this procedure, Moore (Pines, 1963) claims effective results.

The acquisition of intellectual skills other than reading, writing, and typing has also been accelerated by providing radically different but suitable contrived instructional approaches. We know that it is possible to teach elementary school students many ideas in science and mathematics once thought too difficult for youngsters that age (Bruner, 1960; Brownell, 1960; Dienes, 1964). For instance, Suppes (1966) has taught geometrical constructions in first grade and introductory college logic to fifth graders and even bright first graders. A point worth remembering is that many ideas are hard to learn simply because we do not know how to teach them well.

School Adjustment of Boys: An Example of Interactional Complexity[1]

It is difficult to disentangle the effects on readiness of maturational, experiential, and instructional influences as they occur in the classroom setting. The complex interaction among these factors is well illustrated by the higher incidence of school maladjustment among boys than girls. Various explanations have been advanced to account for the fact that boys have greater difficulty in adjusting to school than girls. (Factors relating to affective readiness are included in the following example in an effort to portray more realistically the intricate nature of educational readiness.)

MATURATIONAL FACTORS

The first broad set of explanations has to do with the genetic, constitutional, or maturational factors. Hypotheses of this type are based on such facts as the males' higher infant

---

[1] The topic of discrimination against females is discussed in Chapter 12 in conjunction with the topic of "the hidden curriculum."

mortality rate, their greater susceptibility to infections, their higher morbidity rates for many diseases, and the greater longevity of females. Although specific empirical support is still lacking to verify the exact role that chromosomal mechanisms may play in sex differences, it does appear that males show greater biological vulnerability in many ways (Glidewell and Swallow, 1968). In brief, the male may simply be an inferior biological organism and this inferiority may reflect itself in the classroom.

Maturational differences have also been invoked as an explanation of the more rapid rate of physical development among girls. While it is common knowledge that girls mature faster physically than boys, few probably fully appreciate the magnitude of these differences. By age six, for instance, boys are 12 months behind girls developmentally and by age nine, this difference has increased to some 18 months (Bentzen, 1963). Males unquestionably mature much more slowly, reaching puberty from 1½ to 2½ years later. Maccoby (1966) opines that sex differences in intellectual development parallel physiological development in that "girls get off to a faster start in language and in some other aspects of cognitive performance." Other investigators also report that males reach full physiological and mental maturity in their midtwenties—approximately 3 to 5 years later than females (Garai and Scheinfeld, 1968). Such differences suggest that teachers may often be asking boys to achieve beyond their present developmental level—a condition that frequently leads to misbehavior and school maladjustment.

INFLUENCE OF PRIOR LEARNING

The second broad set of explanations centers around psychological or cultural factors. Boys in many respects are probably subject to more conflicting demands by society than girls are. Consider the trait of aggression.

Cross-cultural studies reveal that boys are trained for self-reliance and earning a living, while girls are trained for obedience and responsibility. Accordingly, boys are permitted more open expression of aggression by the society at large. School expectations regarding the expression of aggression differ, however. Here the boy is expected to conform and be passive (and yet be competitive and assertive). It is little wonder that boys challenge teachers' authority and that teachers, in turn, behave more dominantly toward boys and subject them to greater criticism and disapproval. Girls, by contrast, receive higher grades in school, partly because they are culturally conditioned to release tensions through psychological escape mechanisms such as withdrawal and repression, while displaying outward compliance and passivity. Thus, girls are apt to hide their concerns and resentments behind a facade of politeness and obedience, while boys are inclined to act out their problems. The girl's mode of adjustment makes the teacher's job easier, but the boy's activity orientation is at odds with school standards, which stress conformity and modesty. This sex prejudice or discrimination is reflected in the finding that boys receive more disapproval and lower grades even when the sexes are equated on school achievement as measured by standardized tests. The preponderance of female teachers at the elementary level probably works to the detriment of boys, especially socially maladjusted boys. As expected, boys generally see school as a feminine institution.

Another cultural factor also places greater pressure on boys. The male, since he is eventually expected to assume the role of primary breadwinner, is more extrinsically valued; his worth as a person is judged largely on his accomplishments. Thus the male is expected to achieve at a high level even though he is less ready for school from a physiological standpoint.

INSTRUCTIONAL METHODS AND MATERIALS

How well boys perform in school also seems related to educational practices and policies within a school. There is evidence to suggest, for example, that the use of programmed reading materials results in improved reading performance for males. Many teachers have also reported the benefits accruing from the use of reading materials holding masculine appeal, such as adventure stories. Recent studies on single-sex classes indicate the need for a reexamination of traditional views with regard to the effectiveness of coeducation. Single-sex classes may be a way of affording equal educational opportunities for both sexes. Research findings suggest that in certain subject-matter areas, males learn better in all-male classes. This seems to be especially true of slow-learning boys learning to read in first grade (Garai and Scheinfeld, 1968). Future research might discover that other conditions of learning that can be manipulated by the teacher affect performance of the sexes differentially.

By now, it should be apparent to the reader that it is extremely difficult to tell why boys are less ready to learn than girls and, more generally, *which* particular component of readiness contributed *what* amount to *what* behavior in *which* children.

NATURAL VERSUS ACCELERATED COGNITIVE READINESS

There is little disagreement about the general determinants of readiness or about the fact that cognitive readiness influences one's efficiency in school learning. Although most theorists view development as the product of maturation and learning, there is considerable controversy concerning the relative influence that the various readiness factors exert.

Arguments in Favor of Produced Readiness

Many psychologists and educators feel that we *can* and *should* teach readiness rather than wait for it. Here are some examples of what certain well-respected psychologists are saying about benefits of providing enriched environments.

Hunt writes that: "With a sound scientific psychology of early experience, it might be feasible to raise the average level of intelligence as now measured, by a substantial degree. In order to be explicit, it is conceivable that this 'substantial degree' might be of the order of 30 points of I.Q." (1961, p. 267)

Similarly, David Page asserts: "In teaching from kindergarten to graduate school, I have been amazed at the intellectual similarity of human beings at all ages, although children are perhaps more spontaneous, creative, energetic than adults. As far as I am concerned, young children can learn almost anything faster than adults do if it can be given to them in terms they can understand." (Quoted in Bruner, 1960, pp. 39-40)

Although he has modified his views regarding revisions needed in the schools, noted psychologist Jerome Bruner continues to defend his earlier assertion that "any subject can be taught effectively in some intellectually honest form to any child at any stage of development" (1960, p. 33). "I have a lot of scars from controversies over that dictum. But there has not been one single shred of evidence that goes counter to it." (Bruner, quoted in Hall, 1970)

Burton White of Harvard states: "Within 30 to 50 years—the kind of child who is rated outstanding today will be considered merely normal as a result of more skillful child-rearing." (Pines, 1969)

John Goodlad, the innovative dean of the graduate school of education at UCLA, contends that first grade should be abolished and replaced with an "easy primary" unit for youngsters aged four to seven.

Moore (Newsweek, 1972) states, "It is madness for Piaget to say that children cannot handle certain kinds of logical relationships until later on. Nobody in his right mind would suggest postponing learning to speak until age 5, saying, 'Oh he'll pick it up.' The same thing is true of reading and writing, learning to express oneself in another medium besides speech. It's also true, in a sense, of the domain of numbers."

Siegfried and Therese Engelmann have authored a book entitled *Give Your Child a Superior Mind*. Parents were offered a money-back guarantee that their child could, by the age of five, read approximately 150 words a minute, add columns of figures, tell time, subtract, multiply, and divide, understand concepts, and among other intellectual feats, score high on their first IQ test.

We can summarize the arguments in favor of the "teaching readiness" approach as follows.

1. Most of the quotations cited above imply the existence of a critical period for intellectual development—a time when children allegedly have an optimal degree of readiness for the acquisition of intellectual skills. Burton White states, "At the age of nine months all hell is breaking loose. First, the kid begins to be capable of understanding language. Second, there is the development of the attachment between mother and child." So critical is this period, White believes, that "if you do a lousy job of nourishing the child's intellectual curiosity, you have essentially wiped him out." (Newsweek, 1972)

2. Earlier acquisition of specific intellectual skills cannot help but benefit the student. The student who learns to read at age four and to reason about various subject matters will inevitably have an advantage over the child who started these processes some 2 or 3

years later. If critical skills are taught early, the child is bound to increase the total amount of learning by the time he graduates from high school or college. In other words, an earlier yield will eventually produce a larger yield.

3. Having accumulated the fundamental skills from earlier learning experiences, the child has a foundation that facilitates later assimilation of more abstract, general, and precise presentations of the same or similar subject-matter content. Because the young child can grasp many scientific concepts on an intuitive level, failure to provide suitable training opportunities not only wastes available readiness, but also wastes valuable time in junior and senior high school that could be used for advanced instruction. Produced readiness, then, makes maximal use of readiness during the early years and frees the individual to concentrate on more valuable activities later on.

4. Early instruction also insures against the acquisition of misconceptions. Young children acquire subjective and animistic conceptions that persist and compete with more mature understandings, especially when they are not corrected by instruction.

5. Given early and satisfactory instruction, the student tends to develop favorable attitudes toward various subject matters, thereby preventing the formation of early negative attitudes toward schooling. What is tedious and monotonous for the older child may be fun to the younger child. As Kohlberg (1968) notes, "Many preschool children and kindergarten children have considerable desire for learning 'big-kid' or adult skills such as reading and find school a much more interesting place if there is opportunity for such learning." Thus, regardless of the effects on later abilities, the interest principle suggests that there is something of value in a suitable program of early instruction: the formation of desirable motives and interests. The finding of joy or satisfaction in learning can go far in developing a will to learn and positive attitudes toward the school.

6. Likewise, various investigators have found that suitable early instruction results in increased self-confidence and more mature personalities. Stress emanating from an appropriate challenge can stimulate growth and maturity.

7. Many present-day preschoolers are ready for reading and other kinds of early instruction because of their enriched experiential backgrounds. Children of today have larger vocabularies, have been exposed to the stimulation of television, have traveled more, and have been exposed to more books in the home as well as a higher standard of living than children of earlier generations. Proponents of early education stress the need for more flexible and stimulating preschool and kindergarten programs so that today's more enriched pupils will not be subjected to a boring, holding-back experience. Games, coloring, storytelling, singing, and rhythms, it is argued, will not provide adequate intellectual stimulation.

8. Intellectual training should not be delayed merely on the theory that an older student can invariably learn anything more efficiently than his younger counterpart. Instruction in reading might be more successful at age eight or nine, but this alone is insufficient reason to postpone the activity for 3 or 4 years. If a child has *adequate* readiness, instruction can be profitably undertaken, and waiting beyond this point means that many specific learnings that could have been acquired during the interim fail to occur (Ausubel and Robinson, 1969).

9. Certain skills that could be more easily mastered later (for example, reading) are needed earlier in the daily activities of the average or above-average student.

Arguments in Favor of Natural Readiness

Those who emphasize built-in maturational forces subscribe to the concept of *natural readiness*. According to this viewpoint, the child should be allowed to become ready for school at his own pace. Hymes, a well-known child psychologist, has aptly expressed the "letting development appear" approach: "All the evidence says: Readiness comes as a healthy child grows and matures. Time is the answer—not special drills or special practice." (1958, p. 10) In a similar vein, Dr. Zike states that, "Only about 25% of the children in kindergarten have reached the neurological maturity to cope with the symbolization necessary for reading. The eye may be ready to receive the visual image, but for more than 75% of the children, the neurological system has not reached the maturity needed to make connections between what they see and what they understand. There is nothing that can be done to speed up this readiness—only time can do this."

The "wait and see" approach to readiness formulated by the early maturationalists has had its creditability enhanced as a result of Piaget's work. Although Piaget's followers allow for the interactive effects of learning and maturation, they note that their approach does not generate great optimism as to the possibility of acceleration of cognitive development. For all practical purposes, the Piagetian approach agrees with the maturationalists that specific early training of cognitive functions is often useless as far as the development of "spontaneous" concepts (life, death, sex role, conservation) is concerned. Even with respect to "scientific" concepts, which clearly fall in the domain of the school, the Piagetians argue that it is by no means clear that preschool children are capable of developing a meaningful understanding of them. Although direct instruction in preschool science may contribute specific information, they contend that it is unlikely to contribute much in the way of "scientific" conceptualization. The Piagetians readily grant that specific early learnings (for example, naming and discriminating unfamiliar animals) can be achieved, but they argue that these learnings are unlikely to have long-range, generalized effects on cognitive development.

Let us now review the major arguments advanced by modern-day maturationalists to support the resurgence of interest in the natural approach to the development of readiness.

1. Formal learning is best delayed until about the age of six or seven when most children can learn rules. It is facility in rule learning—and not in rote learning—that is crucial in formal instruction (Elkind, 1971). Higher scores on arithmetic tests can be achieved by rote knowledge of addition and subtraction, but scores so attained reflect little genuine capacity to order quantitative relations.

2. Instruction is more effective when given to older children as compared to younger children (Baer, 1958; Hall, 1963; Tyler, 1964). Students learn more quickly when instruction is postponed until they are more ready. Early learning offers no real advantage, since those who started later soon catch up.

3. There is a growing body of research suggesting that language development, which is so important for success in at least traditional forms of schooling, follows essentially the same sequence despite what might be marked cultural (environmental) differences (Lennenberg, 1967). No culture exists in which children have not mastered the essentials of their native tongue by age four (McNeill, 1970). The development of the basic features of language seems very similar all over the world, and these language universals develop naturally through maturation and everyday exposure to the languages of others. The linguistic

competence of the young child exceeds what would be expected on the basis of his experience. Some built-in mechanisms for generating sentences must be posited.

Modern maturationalists cite the following reasons in their opposition to the *produced readiness* approach.

4. One set of arguments advanced against produced readiness involves the undesirable side effects associated with the overemphasis on cognitive development. Among the possible unhealthy outcomes are:

a. Excessive pressure to enter college.

b. Exploitation of the child as a status symbol by "good parents" who "only want the best for their child."

c. Parental pressure for increased homework.

d. Projection of frustrated parental ambitions onto the child, that is, the child is to achieve the upward mobility that parents themselves never accomplished.

e. Jeopardizing the child's healthy image of himself.

f. A feeling by the child that he is valued more for academic accomplishment than for himself as a member of the family and society.

g. An emphasis on early reading, which is harmful because it interferes with the child's serious intellectual work, his exploration of the world and the exercise of thought (Furth, 1970).

h. Experiencing frustration and failure so repetitiously that the student loses interest in school and regards learning as incapable of providing him with satisfaction, much less real excitement.

5. Another argument against the teaching of readiness approach has to do with "the environmental mystique." Although no one denies the influence of environment on cognitive development, we actually know very little about changing the intellect of the child.

We have only hypotheses and preliminary findings. The pearls of experience, if they exist, are yet to be discovered. It is much too early to speak in terms of certain specific events producing intelligence (Zigler, 1970). We do not know whether it is better to present preschoolers with an academically geared program, to stress the importance of play and curiosity, or to provide a wide variety of massive stimulation.

6. The majority of the evidence to date indicates that specific training cannot speed up the Piagetian stages of intellectual development. Even formal schooling appears to have no influence on Piagetian tasks (Kohlberg, 1968).

7. In addition to a considerable body of earlier evidence that enrichment of an already adequate environment has little impact on a child's intelligence (NSSE Yearbook, 1940), recent preliminary studies on Head Start youngsters (Westinghouse and Ohio University, 1969; Goldberg, 1970) suggest that the school has thus far failed in its efforts to help educationally retarded students to catch up.

8. Despite the popularity of the critical period hypothesis, it should be noted that the evidence for it derives primarily from the study of perceptual, motor, and social characteristics among animals. Whether it is safe to generalize from lower-level animals to man and from perceptual, motor, and social traits to intellectual ones is debatable. Moreover, it has never been empirically shown that *optimal* readiness occurs at a given age period for particular kinds of subject matter learning, and that permanent deficits occur unless adequate conditions for development are present during those periods (Ausubel, 1968). More credible explanations of irreparable cognitive deficits state that these conditions result from prolonged intellectual deprivation and from the gradual loss of flexibility to respond to environmental stimulation as intelligence, interests, and personality become increasingly crystallized.

9. Perhaps one of the most serious practical objections leveled against accelerated readiness is the increased costs that it would entail. In experiments frequently cited as evidence for accelerated readiness, either tutoring or very-small-group techniques were used as the basic teaching method. The per-pupil expenditures in experimental programs have been several times those normally allotted in the public schools. In general, it appears that the more money spent, the more successful the program.

The Issue Reexamined

The basic issue might be recapped by asking whether readiness is an absolute phenomenon determined by the student's own rate of development or whether readiness is a matter of how clever we have been in devising techniques to capitalize on whatever abilities the student has at the time. Readiness is a term that merely expresses our ignorance regarding the methods of effectively programming instruction; and, once the appropriate programs are available, students are "ready" to accomplish academic tasks before the typical age. Seen in this perspective, readiness becomes an unnecessary concept, because it is seen as something always present—the "any subject can be taught effectively in some intellectually honest form to any child at any stage of development" philosophy. Translation of the environment into terms the child can understand produces readiness.

While the "natural approach" to readiness might accurately be labeled "a mischievous half-truth" (Bruner, 1966), the same charge might also be realistically leveled at the "produced readiness" approach. Advocates of this latter philosophy have been overzealous about the prospects for change and over-confident about the benefits of intervention. Moreover, they are often selective in marshalling evidence (Elkind, 1969). Consider the classic study by Skeels (1966), who arranged for 13 mentally retarded orphans (the experimental group) to be transferred from the orphanage to an institution in which they were to be cared for and loved by mentally retarded girls, whose mental ages ranged from five to nine. Another group of orphans remained in the original orphanage to serve as a contrast group. A follow-up study at adulthood revealed striking differences. All 13 individuals in the experimental group were self-supporting or married and functioning as housewives. In the contrast group, four were still institutionalized and unemployed. The others who had been released from the institution were characterized as "hewers of wood and drawers of water." There were also drastic differences regarding educational level. The experimental group completed a median of the twelfth grade, whereas the contrast group completed a median of less than third grade.

This study illustrates the importance of early *intellectual* stimulation as a means of producing mental development. An equally plausible interpretation — particularly in light of Skeel's own stress on the loving care given — would be that affectional ties (a commonly acknowledged objective of the natural approach to readiness) provided the emotional bases necessary for spontaneous intellectual development. Keeping in mind the mental ages of the mother substitutes, it seems odd to argue that greater cognitive readiness was produced as a consequence of *intellectual* stimulation. Thus, while this study is often cited as evidence of our ability to produce readiness through cognitively oriented intervention programs, it could just as easily be cited as supporting the natural approach to cognitive development.

While proponents of the "readiness to be taught" viewpoint do have some favorable preliminary findings, intriguing hypotheses, and speculations, they have as yet to prove their point. A multidimensional concept of readiness (as opposed to a unidimensional concept) that takes maturational factors, prior learning, and teaching strategies into account seems better suited to explain the complexities associated with the concept of readiness, because school achievement is most accurately attributed to both the individual's growth pattern and situational determinants. Although the contention that we should teach readiness instead of wait for it does have considerable merit, differences in the individual's growth pattern cannot be neglected.

Zigler's comments are apropos:

"The formal intellect of the child is not as plastic as supporters of the environmental mystique would have us believe. The notion that we will produce a homogeneous race of geniuses through the programming of experiences is a daydream, a daydream I find to be contrary to a very basic biological law; namely, the law of human variability. We are not going to repeal that law. The very nature of the gene pool of our population will always guarantee variability in cognitive development." (1970, p. 406)

On the other hand, there is the opposite danger of assuming that readiness is a fixed attribute of the child. In the past, the concept of maturation was practically synonomous with the concept of readiness in the minds of most educators. The result was a waste of much valuable readiness time. Even today it is not uncommon to hear teachers state that a failing student will be ready to profit from instruction once he is a year older. It is as though there is a magical biological timetable that is expected to unfold automatically, independent of formal learning and teaching methodology. Readiness does not depend simply on the passage of time, nor is it an unalterable reality. Just as many of today's educational innovations designed to teach readiness are characterized by a strong, perhaps excessive, environmentalistic bent, today's proponents of individual growth patterns also place undue reliance on internal, biological factors.

The approach to readiness should not be an either-or matter. To do our best in improving learning and teaching we will require a certain openness instead of a commitment to either rigid tradition or innovative but unproven ideas. We need programs that capitalize on an awareness of the environment's impact on the student, and the student's impact on his environment. The televison show "Sesame Street" represents an interesting and seemingly realistic compromise in that it bor-

rows from a number of sources. Certain basic concepts included in "Sesame Street" are based on Piaget's insights. For example, with respect to cognitive processes, "Sesame Street" sought to help children to deal with objects and events in terms of concepts such as ordering, classification, and relationship. To illustrate further, we cite their objectives relative to the development of classification skills.

1. Given at least two objects that define the basis of grouping, the child can select an additional object that "goes with them" on the basis of size (height, length), form (circular, square, triangular), function (to ride in, to eat, etc.) or class (animals, vehicles, etc.).

2. Given four objects, three of which have an

"It was one of those gratifying days that make teaching worthwhile. I finally taught them something they hadn't already learned on 'Sesame Street.'"
(Drawing by Tony Saltzman, from Phi Delta Kappan, *June 1973)*

attribute in common, the child can sort out the inappropriate object on the basis of size, form, function, and class.

3. The child can verbalize the basis for grouping and sorting.

Although they used Piaget's work as a guide, the developers of "Sesame Street" did not limit their statement of instructional goals to those emanating from a developmental approach. Instead, more diverse goals were sought to give children what they could use "in order to cope with and improve their own environments." (Lesser, 1972) Thus, for instance, we find that the viewers were also given instruction in letters and numbers, goals that Piagetians feel contribute little to one's long-range cognitive development.

The instructional strategies as well as the goals of "Sesame Street" are also truly interdisciplinary. For example, in keeping with Piaget's theory, children are confronted with surprises and incongruities. The use of modeling techniques, borrowed from learning theorists with a strong environmental orientation, constitutes the primary means for achieving objectives pertaining to social attitudes. From the world of commercial television comes the use of music and sound effects, animation, and numerous visual gimmicks known to attract, direct, and hold children's attention. From research on human-information processing came the caution that messages fed simultaneously through two modalities (e.g., vision and hearing) might interfere with each other.

Thus, instead of relying on commitment to a particular theory in developing goals and techniques, the producers of "Sesame Street" chose selectively in an effort to develop what they considered the best readiness program possible. Children can learn a great deal from a well thought out, yet relaxed and entertaining educational program that takes advantage of optimal readiness.

PIAGETIAN THEORY: BASIC CONCEPTS

Jean Piaget has been busily engaged in the study of children for approximately 50 years. His contributions to psychological literature fall into three areas: intellectual, moral, and perceptual development. Our concern will be with his notions of intellectual development. Although criticized by some for his casual research methods, he may have contributed more to our understanding of cognitive development than any other psychologist. The vast majority of curriculum revision projects of recent years have drawn heavily on his thinking, and many educators hope to discover in his views a workable theory of instruction.

The following questions illustrate those that we explore in our review of Piaget's contributions.

1. Do children of varying ages actually have a different method of thinking?

2. What is their method?

3. Do all children use the same method?

4. Does a child's style of thinking follow a definite sequence of development until it reaches the stage of abstract thinking used by adults?

5. Does each child reach this point only as he matures or can this process be influenced, that is, accelerated or slowed down, by outside factors?

Answers to these questions might well give us some insight into

Children's reactions to daily life situations.

Unexpected emotional responses in children (e.g., crying when the head of a chocolate Easter bunny is broken off because he thought it was alive).

Methods of daily communication with the young child.

The child's approach to academic learning.

Ways in which to predict learning ability.

Ways in which to support learning ability.

Timing of teaching.

Methods of teaching.

Choice of subject matter in teaching.

Other aspects of teacher training.

Other aspects of parent education (Roeper and Sigel, 1968).

For Piaget, intelligence is seen as a special instance of adaptation. Intellectual adaptation is always the result of an interaction between the processes of assimilation and accommodation. Assimilation refers to the fact that the child relates what he perceives to his existing knowledge and understanding. Moreover, in assimilation, the child tries to keep his present comprehension of the world intact, even if new perceptions of the world must be distorted to fit comfortably into his existing view of the world. The child molds information from his environment to suit his own needs. One child, for example, who conceives of a particular youngster as aggressive, might well interpret his innocent play as hostility.

Accommodation is the opposite of assimilation. In accommodation, the student adjusts his conceptual understandings to fit his new perceptions. It is, in short, adaptive change to outer circumstances with the student being changed in some way by his interactions with the outside world. A young child, for example, might conceive of "boat" as a toy to sail in the bathtub. As a consequence of later exposure to first-hand experiences with boats and books about boats, his conception of boat becomes broadened. The child "accommodates" his notion of boat to his new experiences.

Intellectual development proceeds as the child continues to interpret new experiences in light of old experiences (assimilation) and changes his ideas to fit his new experiences (accommodation). The term adaptation simply refers to this simultaneous and continual assimilation-accommodation process.

What are the determinants of intellectual growth? According to Piaget, they are fourfold and include *maturation* or biologically regulated growth, *social transmission* or the passing of information from one person to another through language and education, *experience*, and *equilibration*. Piaget heavily emphasizes the last factor. Fundamentally, Piagetian theory is a balance theory—a balance between previous conceptions and incoming information. If the two correspond, there is a balance. When the child receives new information that does not fit with what he already knows, his mind is thrown into a state of disequilibrium. According to Piagetian theory, the student's equilibrium must be disturbed if mental development is to occur. Imbalance produces a state of cognitive conflict that is uncomfortable to the student. In an effort to reduce the conflict, the student is propelled to a higher level of equilibrium until a "grand equilibrium" is finally reached.

Let us return to our example of the concept "boat." The young child who conceives "boat" as a bathtub toy is thrown into a state of disequilibrium when he initially finds out that boats have different shapes and different purposes (e.g., aircraft carriers). At first, he is puzzled (cognitive conflict) by this new knowledge. Motivated by this bewilderment, he gradually assimilates this new knowledge to the old and accommodates the old to the new. As a consequence, he arrives at a more mature notion of boat, thereby restoring his intellectual equilibrium. Continuous adaptation through assimilation and accommodation leads to higher levels of equilibrium and results in a series of qualitatively different stages. Intellectual structures associated with the earlier stages of development are more readily thrown into a state of disequilibrium as a result of incoming information than in the later stages of development. Once adolescence is reached, the intellectual structures become increasingly stable and undergo little fundamental modification during the rest of one's life. It is to the topic of stages that we now turn our attention.

Stages of Intellectual Development

"Stage" implies the existence of an orderly progression of identifiable phases of development that are qualitatively different from one another and generally characteristic of youngsters of a given age range. Piaget has delineated four sequential phases, each marked by characteristic and identifiable ways of thinking.

1. The *sensorimotor* stage—from birth to eighteen months.

2. The *preoperational* stage—from approximately two to seven years of age. This stage is, in turn, divided into two substages.

a. The preconceptual stage—from two to four years of age.

b. The intuitive stage—from four to seven years of age.

3. The *concrete operations*—from roughly seven to eleven years of age.

4. The *formal operations*—from eleven or twelve years of age on.

There is nothing absolute about the ages at which a child enters a given stage, although the majority of students in a given age range will display the kinds of thinking characteristic of a given stage. What the stage theorist regards as absolute is the sequencing or ordering of stages. Stage one must come before

stage two, stage two before stage three, and so on.

Although many of us have worked with youngsters at different levels of development, few, if any of us, have insight into what thought is like for the preschool child, the elementary school pupil, and the junior-senior high school student. Herein lies one of Piaget's main educational contributions. Let us now examine what thought is like: first for the preschool child, then for the elementary school pupil, and finally for the junior-senior high school student. Although the origins of intelligence date back to infancy, we will not discuss this early period because educators have not yet developed formal programs for those so young.

THE PRESCHOOL CHILD (INTUITIVE STAGE—AGES FOUR TO SEVEN)

Piaget uses the term "intuitive" in its everyday usage or meaning, as something is grasped by the mind immediately without the intervention of any deliberate, rational thought process. Whereas logical thought is characterized by internal consistency, completeness, and correctness, the preschool child's judgments are fragmentary and inconsistent. Three characteristics of thought at this stage are responsible for this state of affairs: (1) The child's understanding of concepts is based largely on what he sees, that is, his thought is perceptually dominated or stimulus bound. He relies on surface appearances and on what strikes him first and most vividly in his approach to problem solving. The child cannot free himself from basing conclusions on what he sees. The difficulty, of course, arises from the fact that appearances can be deceiving. (2) Typically, the child's comprehension of a situation, event, or object is based on a *single* perceptual aspect of the stimulus. The dimension focused on tends to be the one that is most noticeable from a perceptual standpoint. It is difficult for the child to coordinate or process more than one relationship at a time. (3) Thought is irreversible at this time, that is, the child cannot return to the starting point of a mental sequence without having altered his conception of the problem. Imagining the original problem situation seems extremely difficult.

The following example should make the foregoing clear. Suppose that two rows of pennies are lined up parallel to one another with 10 pennies in each row. The young child who can count to 10 will tell you that both rows have the same number of pennies. Then, while the child is watching, the teacher spreads one row out, making it twice as long as the other row. Now when queried, a preschooler will typically tell you that the longer row contains more pennies than the shorter row. Why? Because he is fooled by appearances (perceptual dominance), because he focuses only on the length of the row (single dimension) and because he cannot mentally picture the starting point of the problem (irreversible thought). What must the average first grader think when he is shown a relatively small globe of the world and a large map of the United States, only to be told that the former is larger than the latter? To better understand the child's thinking at this stage, the reader might try explaining to a typical preschooler that one thin dime is the equivalent of two larger nickels.

THE ELEMENTARY SCHOOL CHILD (CONCRETE OPERATIONS — AGES SEVEN TO ELEVEN)

With the advent of the elementary school years, three qualitatively new capacities emerge and thought becomes more similar to that of the adult: (1) *Reversibility of thought* now appears. Reversible thought assists the child's problem-solving ability in subject-matter areas such as arithmetic (2 + 3 = 5, 5 − 3 = 2), science (transforming water into various forms and back to its original state), and social studies (tracing cause and effect). There can be no logical intelligence without reversible thought. (2) *Conservation* in the physical science sense also occurs. That is, the child now realizes that certain attributes of the world (amount of liquid, weight of an object, etc.) remain stable despite superficial modifications in appearance (change in the shape, color, or weight of a container). The conservation of number problem cited earlier is now handled successfully by the child. The ability to conserve enables the student to recognize certain fundamental constancies about his world; this knowledge facilitates his problem-solving efforts. (3) *Part-whole concepts* and *serial-ordering* abilities develop. Previously the child had difficulty thinking about the part (subordinate class) and the whole (superordinate class) simultaneously. The child, until the elementary school years, had difficulty in grasping the fact that he was a resident of a given street, a given neighborhood, a given city, a given state, and a given country — all at the same time. The ability to deal with class-inclusion problems, that is, to group data into classes, is basic to school success, since every subject-matter area involves subclasses and supraclasses.

Serial ordering refers to the ability to arrange objects according to some quantified dimension such as size or weight, that is, to order items sequentially from the one containing the least amount of some variable to the one containing the greatest amount. The seven-year old thus knows that 10 cents is more than 5 cents, and that 5 cents is more than 1 cent, and therefore 10 cents is more than 1 cent. Acquisition of the concepts of "greater than" and "lesser than" gives the elementary school student another edge over his preschool counterpart.

How does thought at this stage differ from adult thought? The answer lies primarily in its concreteness. Thus, while the child can reason logically about the relationships and things with which he has had direct personal experience, he encounters difficulty as soon as he has to deal with hypothetical situations or contrary-to-fact assertions. The elementary school child, for example, can apply the notion of greater than and lesser than to pennies, but he cannot handle the more general rule that if A is greater than B, and B is greater than C, then A is greater than C. In other words, he cannot generalize his knowledge about familiar coins to objects or situations that are unfamiliar or have no particular content. He reasons best about concrete objects and events. Herein lies the significant weakness of thought during these years.

THE JUNIOR-SENIOR HIGH SCHOOL YEARS (FORMAL OPERATIONS — AGE ELEVEN OR TWELVE ON)

Other qualitative changes in thought emerge when the youngster enters the junior high school period. The adolescent's greater cognitive sophistication stems from an increased capacity for abstraction, his ability to test hypotheses, and his ability to deal systematically with possibilities.

While the data operated on by the mind during the elementary school years were concrete objects and materials, the data processed by the adolescent are verbal assertions. In other words, verbal propositions or statements (which contain the concrete materials and objects symbolically) constitute the raw materials on which the mind operates. As an abstract thinker, the adolescent no longer needs the concrete empirical props or crutches except in unfamiliar or difficult subject-matter areas. His thought has now become more divorced from immediate experience. The adolescent also displays a far greater capacity to generate hypotheses and to test them in a systematic fashion. He now employs a kind of logical process at a level of

abstraction approaching that of scientific reasoning. He can use, at a relatively high level, "if-then" type statements much like a scientist might. Since his thought is no longer tied to the present and the concrete, he can develop hypotheses and make certain deductions, all in advance of his data and observations. Moreover, he can delineate at the outset all of the possibilities. He no longer confines his thinking to what he observes or what *is*. He can now go from the possible to the real in an exhaustive, logical fashion. For example, if he is simply told that factors A, B, C, D, and E are associated with the occurrence of a given phenomenon, he can consider all the possible combinations that could produce the phenomenon in question. Unlike his elementary school counterpart, he can combine several rules to deal in a systematic way with problems containing several elements. He need not necessarily know what the factors are, for he can deal with the form of the argument. Hence, the name "formal operations."

The adolescent can now evaluate the logic and quality of his own thought. This kind of activity represents one of the highest forms of abstraction. He can think about his own thinking! He can now consider his own thought as an object and reason about it. Equipped with his new powers, he becomes introspective and self-critical. As many educators know, not all of these newly found thought processes are turned inward. Now that the adolescent is capable of seeing many new possibilities, he critically analyzes the older generation's values and behaviors.

PIAGETIAN THEORY: EDUCATIONAL IMPLICATIONS

Piaget's theory will have an impact on three aspects of the teaching-learning process: assessment of the child's readiness, placement of curriculum content, and teaching strategies. Although it is impossible to separate these three aspects in everyday practice, we will do so for convenience of presentation.

Readiness of the Child

ASSESSING INTELLECTUAL DEVELOPMENT

The assessment of developmental readiness, a problem that administrators and teachers face constantly, is a matter of assessing the child's readiness to profit from a given program of instruction. Developmental readiness pertains to the student's general cognitive maturity or predominant mode of intellectual functioning. The teacher might ask, for example, if the student is functioning at the level of concrete operations or formal operations? Through careful observation of student performance or by means of Piagetian tests, the teacher can make such a determination, provided that he is aware of the attributes characteristic of thought at various stages. Having made such a diagnosis, the teacher is in a much better position with respect to knowing, in a general way, appropriate teaching strategies and the difficulty level of the curriculum most suitable for students. Thus, with educationally deprived students at the elementary school level, who typically have difficulty in shifting intellectual gears from intuitive thinking to "concrete operations," the teacher may shy away from teaching methods and curricula that require reversible thought, classification skills, and conservation abilities. However, teachers should not avoid striving toward the gradual development of these skills. This proposition simply states that such procedures would not match or correspond with the child's general level of thinking at this time. It is axiomatic to say that we must always start where the child is.

If Piaget's stages do form a reliable scale of progressively more complex mental activity, then the basis for an alternative method of mental testing is available. This new kind of intelligence test emphasizes the *quality* of children's reasoning instead of tabulating right and wrong answers. Whereas conventional intelligence tests chart the symptoms of intelligence, the Piagetian tests now in the making at the University of Montreal's Institute of Psychology analyze the central mental processes by which a child arrives at an answer to a question. Conventional tests also tend to overlook the diagnostic value of wrong answers. The new Piagetian approach recognizes that wrong answers can often tell more about a child's thinking than right ones "because they fall into easily recognizable types that seem to be tied to distinct stages of mental development." (Pinard and Sharp, 1972, p. 65) To illustrate, consider the child who says a nail sinks to the bottom of a tank of water "because it's tired" and the child who says it sank "because it's made of iron." While both explanations are wrong, it is apparent that these two children are at two different stages of mental development. Equating the two youngsters because they both failed the item overlooks a potential source of valuable information. Finally, Piagetian tests involve the use of problems that identify genuine stages of intellectual development instead of using test items tied to chronological age on the assumption that each 6- to 12-month period marks a significant step in mental development.

The New York City Board of Education in conjunction with Educational Testing Service (Loretan, 1966) has already incorporated Piaget's views in efforts to find alternatives to traditional intelligence testing for evaluating school readiness. The Piagetian procedures used in this project, known as *Let's Look at First Graders*, focus on the transition from prelogical to logical concrete thinking—a transition normally occurring at the first-grade level. The *Teacher's Guide* provides descriptions of six major areas of intellectual development, together with behaviors illustrating each. The six areas and the developmental concepts subsumed under each area are:

1. Basic Language Skills: Auditory discrimination and attention, listening comprehension, learning to communicate, language for thinking.

2. Concepts of Space and Time: Learning shapes and forms, spatial perspective, the notion of time.

3. Beginning Logical Concepts: Logical classification, concepts of relationship.

4. Beginning Mathematical Concepts: Conservation of quantity, one-to-one correspondence, number relations.

5. Growth of Reasoning Skills: Understanding cause and effect, reasoning by association, reasoning by inference.

6. General Signs of Development: Growing awareness and responsiveness, directed activity, general knowledge, developing imagination.

In contrast to standardized measures of intelligence or readiness, *Let's Look at First Graders* provides no quantitative scores or norms. Instead, it is designed to yield only qualitative descriptions of the child's current developmental level in basic intellectual skills. Furthermore, assessment has much less of a testlike atmosphere because it is made in the natural classroom setting in which diagnosis and instruction are combined.

Piaget's work not only provides us with an overall index of logical ability, but it offers the added advantage of allowing us to assess development with respect to particular areas of major concern to educational planners—con-

cepts of numbers, space, time, causality, and matter. Many students and also adults, who generally function at an abstract, verbal level, might well function at a more concrete level in certain disciplines that are basically new, unfamiliar, or foreign to them. Many of us, despite our brilliance, might need instruction of a very concrete nature in physics and biochemistry simply because we are not versed in these areas. Such unevenness is not unexpected when we are dealing with phenomena that are determined by multiple and variable factors. We do not, however, need 4 years of concrete experience, as the elementary school child does, before advancing to the use of higher-order thought processes in these disciplines, because we can draw on our general ability to function abstractly in other areas. Nevertheless, when beginning a new topic, learning should often be based on new concrete experiences or the adolescent's past experiences.

Piaget has not developed tests of logical intelligence for every subject-matter area, but some of his work on the development of specific concepts might be useful. His work in the area of number concepts, for example, might provide a new kind of readiness test that assesses the student's understanding of the components of number, classes, and asymmetrical relations and his readiness for more formal kinds of mathematical problems.

Although Piagetian tests are not yet available from the major test publishing companies and few school districts have devised Piagetian-based readiness tests, teachers can acquire skill in assessing the student's readiness by reading about Piaget's "experiments" or interviews with children. The pedagogical potency of such interviewing experiences is reflected by Millie Almy (1966, p. 135):

"The teacher who has mastered Piaget's method has immediately at his fingertips a powerful tool for appraising the child's progress. We do not see it as a tool replacing the more traditional methods of assessment. Standardized intelligence and achievement tests serve purposes for which Piaget's techniques are not suitable. But a well-constructed Piaget interview provides the teacher with something more than he customarily gets from standardized test results. This is a picture of the ways the child organizes (or fails to organize) information. His errors and his misconceptions are revealed *as they occur.* From this direct observation of his functioning in a problem-solving situation, the teacher can derive many clues as to either his readiness for more complex learning or the kinds of experience he may need before he can move ahead. Although many of Piaget's experiments are obviously most relevant to a particular area of the curriculum, the information to be gained from using a given experiment to interview a child is seldom limited to that one experiment but carries implications for the child's performance in other similar tasks.''

ACCELERATING DEVELOPMENT

An issue of considerable import to educators and psychologists alike concerns the extent to which readiness can be accelerated. Discussion of this question serves nicely to illustrate the interrelatedness of the three broad areas for which Piagetian theory has educational relevance. As noted earlier, there have been significant changes in the concept of readiness since 1950. Is it possible, as Jerome Bruner, the noted Harvard psychologist, contends, that "Any subject matter can be taught effectively in some intellectually honest form to any child at any stage of development"? With respect to particularized subject matter areas, experimental projects have demonstrated the feasibility of teaching preschool children to read by altering the nature of reading instruction. Various projects have shown that many scientific and mathematical

ideas can be grasped by elementary school students provided that concrete aids are utilized. The child can develop, for instance, a basic grasp of probabilistic reasoning through the use of games of chance such as roulette or those in which lots are drawn. Readiness, approached in this fashion, demands that the school be ready for the child — not that the child be ready for the school, as in previous years. Many concepts can be taught earlier if they are translated into terms that the youngster can understand at his level of cognitive maturity. Many things are undoubtedly difficult for students to learn simply because we do not know how to teach them very well. For example, as teaching strategies for translating abstract concepts into concrete terms improve, we can expect greater accomplishments with regard to this kind of acceleration. There are, however, probably some limitations to acceleration of this type. Ausubel, who suggests that Bruner probably intended to overdramatize the extent to which early learning is possible, notes that it might prove difficult to teach the notion of an imaginary number or Einstein's concept of relativity to a three-year-old (1968). Other limitations associated with accelerating the curriculum content of a given discipline include (a) the additional time and effort required to present concepts in ways that younger students can comprehend and (b) the emotional risks associated with early learning. Later learning might not only be more efficient than early learning, but it might offer less threat to emotional well-being.

How about acceleration of the Piagetian stages? Must instruction in any subject matter area wait for the appearance of a given stage of development or can the stages be speeded up? Can we, for instance, take a group of students who function at the level of concrete operations and raise them to the level of formal operations by giving them specific instruction? Evidence *thus far* indicates that possibilities of such acceleration are limited. This is to be expected if the notion of stage is valid. Piaget refers to this as the "American Question." He is not only skeptical of our ability to speed up the child's timetable of thought, but he cannot understand why we would want to do so.

Before a final verdict, however, it should be noted that most experiments have been of the short-term variety, involving only a limited number of learning trials. It may be that intensive long-term studies might yield more favorable results. Although rigorous in experimental design, the rationale underlying American studies has been naive in assuming that a few trials would produce a higher-order mental operation. Moreover, a final decision on the merits of acceleration would be premature before a greater variety of teaching methodologies have been attempted.

Placement of Curriculum Content

Educators and psychologists have long felt the need for a rational basis for determining the age or grade placement of curriculum content. In the past, because of the absence of any master plan, we have had to rely on tradition, experience, and intuition. It could be quite helpful to know the average age at which a given cognitive stage occurs in a given society and the limitations and capabilities characteristic of each stage relative to specific subject-matter areas. Equipped with this kind of knowledge, we would have at our disposal a timing device that would enable us to predict the minimal ages or grades at which specific content items could be taught. Piaget's stage theory might have merit for this kind of curriculum-pacing strategy.

As Ausubel notes, there are three steps or phases to developing such a master plan.

1. Ascertain the essential attributes of each cognitive stage. That is, spell out the kind of cognitive tasks characteristic of a given stage but not of earlier stages. For example, the ability to deal with part-whole relationships would not ordinarily occur prior to the coming of concrete operations.

2. Determine the extent to which these "psychological landmarks" can be accelerated.

3. Finally, relate specific content items to these "landmarks." For instance, having ascertained that the ability to deal with part-whole problems emerges at the stage of concrete operations and that an understanding of fractions depends on the child's having reached this stage, one would conclude that age seven might constitute the earliest point at which fractions could be meaningfully taught (Ausubel, 1969).

Just as Piaget's developmental findings might serve to determine the optimal time for introducing certain basic concepts, they would also enable us to guard against the student's developing erroneous or unclear understandings because of premature exposure. If certain concepts are introduced too early, the student may be using intuitive thought to grasp the ideas and therefore gain an inferior understanding of them. If existing programs were examined using Piaget's findings as a criterion, we might find that many concepts are now taught too early. For instance, one well-known science program has the following behavioral objectives relative to classification skills at the first-grade level: (1) identify variations in objects and organisms that may have many features in common, then state these differences and (2) describe features common to each member of the group. Lessons designed to enable students to discover differences among various objects *simultaneously* require concrete operational thought—something that most first graders do not possess. Pupils characterized by intuitive thought typically handle these problems by searching out one difference, then reporting it and then looking for another difference, reporting it, and so on. It is simply too difficult for them to process several dimensions simultaneously and to discover features common to all members of the group.

Piaget's system has merit not only for the evaluation of the grade placement of content in traditional areas of instruction, but also for generating some interesting experimentation. Ideas deserving further experimentation include the following:

1. Youngsters seemingly understand the meaning of number when they have mastered classes and asymmetrical relations. Therefore, they might profit from the experience of grouping objects on the basis of similarities and differences *before* they experience exercises in counting.

2. The order of instruction in geometry might proceed from topological concepts through projective to Euclidean concepts. Although formal geometry could probably not be taught in its most complex forms, one could begin at a very concrete level to introduce some of the underlying concepts that could eventually lead to a truly formal understanding.

3. In the science field, there appears to be a natural development in terms of conservation of mass, weight, and volume. The first occurs around age seven, the second around age nine or ten, and the third at eleven or twelve.

4. In social studies it may prove difficult to teach cause-effect relationships about prejudice before the child is capable of reversible thought. Furthermore, it may be unreasonable to expect students below the age of ten or eleven to be capable of mentally putting themselves in another position. Because of their egocentricity, young children are not even aware that other persons see things from a different viewpoint, to say nothing of empathizing with others.

5. With respect to geography, students who have not yet developed class inclusion abilities will not be able to understand that Chicago is a part of Cook County, that Cook County is a part of Illinois, that Illinois is a part of the United States, and so on.

6. Formal scientific experimentation appears best postponed until high school. Nevertheless, younger students might benefit from practical experience with proportions, probabilities, introductory logic problems, and so on.

While Piagetian theory might offer us some general guidelines for determining the placement of curriculum content, we need studies demonstrating that certain kinds and levels of subject matter demand certain specific prerequisite skills to guarantee student success. That is, we must know that learning in a given subject-matter area is more efficient if preceded by particular experiences. As Ausubel and Sullivan (1970) note, until the principle of readiness is particularized in each subject matter area with respect to various subareas, levels of difficulty, and instructional strategies, the principle will not have realized its fullest pedagogical utility. It would be extremely helpful, for instance, if we could say that a given student might not be ready for reading but is ready for arithmetic, and that within arithmetic he might be ready for multiplication, but not for division, and that he might be ready for multiplication by one teaching method and not by another. Fortunately, there now seems to be greater research interest in this type of particularized approach to readiness than in the past.

Bruner, borrowing heavily from Piagetian theory, advocates a spiral curriculum in which certain fundamental concepts are re-visited at each stage of cognitive development. In other words, the subject matter is revisited from time to time as students pass through a series of stages paralleling the stages of cognitive maturity. Each reintroduction of a topic or principle builds on earlier learnings and leads to a more mature understanding of the ideas in question. There is much to be said in favor of such a procedure. For one thing, early introduction of concepts helps guard against the formation of erroneous conceptions that children often develop about the physical and biological universe. Second, early instruction of a satisfying nature helps to produce positive attitudes toward school subjects. Third, such training lays the foundation on which to build later learnings in junior and senior high school. The task of translation is not always an easy one, however. Careful attention must be devoted not only to the selection of concepts to be taught with respect to their ease of translation, but also to their potential for facilitating the acquisition of concepts to be presented later. Unfortunately, there is currently a dearth of specific guidelines for the selection of such concepts in various subject-matter areas. Additional information and experience arising from new curriculum projects should help fill this void.

Teaching Strategies — Instructional Techniques

LEARNING BY DOING

One of the most clearcut implications for teaching strategies centers around learning by doing. Although by no means a new suggestion for educational practice, Piaget's research has reinforced this idea. For intellectual development to proceed, the student must have an active exchange with his sur-

roundings. Prior to the junior high school period, it is especially important that the pupil be given concrete aids and materials to manipulate in order to promote clear and stable understanding of the world. Children must be given the opportunity to be active in the classroom, to explore, to touch, to test, to find out, and to manipulate, because this sort of concrete learning is, according to Piagetian theory, a prerequisite for more verbal, abstract understanding. The child must operate on the data to which he is exposed, because thought grows out of the internalization of concrete motor activity. An example of the use of concrete experience with respect to teaching the geometrical notions of perspective and projection is provided by Bruner, who states:

". . . There is much that can be done by the use of experiments and demonstrations that rest on the child's operational capacity to analyze concrete experience. We have watched children work with an apparatus in which rings of different diameter are placed at different positions between a candle and a screen with a fixed distance between them so that the rings cast shadows of varying sizes on the screen. The child learns how the cast shadow changes size as a function of the distance of the ring from the light source. By bringing to the child such concrete experience of light in revealing situations, we teach him maneuvers that in the end permit him to understand the general ideas underlying projective geometry." (1960, p. 44)

Similarly, to understand classification the child must have had experience in grouping objects together on some dimension; to analyze, he should have pulled them apart; to understand the ordinal properties of number and series, he must have arranged objects in some order (Adler, 1965). Piaget's greatest contribution might be his demonstration that the child is the principal agent of his own education and mental development. Gradually, these actions become carried out in the mind (internalized), and the child's need for concrete aids decreases. At this time the student becomes a more abstract learner and greater use can be made of verbal presentations. Until this time, however, a Piagetian-derived program would emphasize transactional experiences in which the child physically operates on his environment.

DISTURBING EQUILIBRIUM

Another technique relates to the notion of equilibration. As you will recall, the student's intellectual equilibrium must be upset in order to develop a more mature concept; if we are content with our inaccurate or incomplete knowledge, our search for a solution in a problem-solving situation may end prematurely. As Ginsburg and Opper (1969) note, "One way of putting the matter is to say that interest and learning are facilitated if the experience presented to the child bears some relevance to what he already knows but at the same time is sufficiently novel to present incongruities and conflicts." Therefore, teachers must set the stage for concept acquisition by disturbing the pupil's cognitive harmony. Remember that motivation may stem from the internal push of cognitive inconsistency and perturbation. Teachers can challenge students by pointing out disonant elements in a given problem, by confronting them with contrasting viewpoints (e.g., democracy and communism), by confronting them with contradictions, and by providing moderately novel or surprising experiences. The social studies teacher might, in a discussion of human behavior, point out that people are basically alike. We all have needs for belongingness, for safety, for a sense of recognition, and so on. Having concretized this generalization through numerous exemplars, the teacher might then ask the students if they are not

also basically different from everybody else. The apparent incompatibility between the two assertions initially baffles or puzzles the student, causing him to think over these notions and to arrive at a fuller appreciation of basic needs and individual differences. Such strategies cause intellectual discomfort—a state of personal dissatisfaction that the child tries to reduce. Few of us like to experience a discrepancy between our perceptions and external reality. In the process of conflict reduction, the child achieves a higher level of balance. As you will see in later chapters, Bruner favors a discovery approach to resolve disequilibrium, whereas Ausubel contends that verbal presentation of subject-matter combined with concrete aids in the form of demonstrations and exercises can accomplish this objective more efficiently. For efficiency, the presentation of concepts and generalizations should be at the highest level of abstraction of which the individual student is capable (Ausubel and Robinson, 1969).

FACILITATING LOGICAL THINKING

Teachers can also help by giving an assist to the child's transition from a concrete to an abstract level of thought. They can help to develop such skills as reversibility by tracing cause and effect situations backward and forward. Teaching addition and subtraction in juxtaposition is one such approach. This would also be possible with multiplication and division. For example, start with the number six, square it to get thirty-six; reverse the process by taking the square root of thirty-six, and we are back at the number six, where we started.

Teachers can also help promote classification abilities. In one preschool program for the disadvantaged, lessons with a real collection of fruit were developed. Once the child learned the names of various fruit, he was asked to give the teacher an apple, an orange, a cherry, or whatever was requested. Then, the child was asked, "Do I have any cherries?", "Do I have any fruit?", and "Do I have more cherries than fruit?" Exercises such as these help to enforce the fact that subclasses can be combined into a supraclass, that the supraclass is larger, that all members of the subclass are combined in the supraclass while only some members of the supraclass are members of the subclasses. It is also important that students be given practice in multiple classification. An orange, for instance, can be classified as a fruit, as a color, as an object to be thrown, and so on.

USING GROUP WORK

Finally, Piaget places great stress on group work as a means of socializing intelligence. One of the prime deterrents to an objective view of the world is the child's egocentric thought. He is incapable of viewing objects or events objectively, because he can only view them as related to himself. Piaget feels that socializing experiences assist the student in becoming emancipated from his own egocentrism. By pitting his thoughts against those of others, he gains a perspective of other's views and positions. By talking with others, he realizes that they do not always share his perceptions of reality. Such interaction leads to conflict and argument, that is, to a state of disequilibrium. In the process of "proving" his point, the child is forced to reevaluate his beliefs and to clarify his thinking. Consequently, he arrives at a more objective perception of the issue in question. It would seem that many topics, for example, the desirability and feasibility of racially integrated schools as a means of producing educational equality, discussed in buzz groups or by panels, would facilitate the socialization of intelligence. Thus, we see (1) that there is an important cognitive benefit accruing from social interaction (the discrimination between perceived

reality and actual reality) and (2) that physical manipulation and concrete manipulation are not the only means of learning (Ginsburg and Opper, 1969).

How effective the group process is in socializing intelligence probably depends on several factors—the nature of the group, the skill of the teacher as a group leader, beliefs of the community, the topic at hand, and so on. Nevertheless, too little attention is devoted to the socialization of intellect. Teachers and administrators commonly discourage discussion between students because the noise is disruptive. Although noise may interfere with student learning, the exchange of student opinion, whether planned or spontaneous, should have a definite place in the educational setting. Society cannot afford to neglect the socialization of intelligence through debate and argumentation.

Administrative Policy

1. Since the development of pedagogical skills stemming from Piaget's discoveries seldom receive emphasis in university teacher-training programs, in-service programs might serve this end. One activity might center around developing skills in individual interviewing to sharpen insights into student thought processes. Having given Piaget-like interviews to their students, teachers might discuss the strategies used in questioning as well as the insights thereby gained relative to instruction. Another activity might involve the logical analysis of subject matter. Teachers might, for example, discuss the sequencing of certain concepts with respect to an area of interest or specialization.

2. Piaget's discoveries suggest that young children need to manipulate things in order to learn. This observation means that teachers should provide numerous opportunities to learn by physically acting on the environment. Implementing this principle of active learning requires, however, a reorientation concerning what is considered desirable classroom conduct. Many teachers, we find, hesitate to allow greater physical freedom for fear that the principal will view them as deficient in classroom disciplinary skills. The realization that students must first perform on a physical level before becoming able to manipulate on a mental level should encourage administrators to support teachers who run active classrooms. An enriched, benign educational program that takes its cues from the child's developmental level can go far in promoting self-actualization in its students.

3. Although rarely viewed by administrators in a positive light, student arguments and debate can have desirable intellectual and personal outcomes. Dialogue forces one to reevaluate his beliefs and develop skills in group interaction. The desirability of this kind of social interaction suggests that administrators should accept and encourage some noisy classroom practices. Vows of silence may be appropriate for certain religious orders, but they can make classrooms authoritarian and boring.

4. Principals should encourage teachers to have at least some experience in experimental programs designed to accelerate the acquisition of advanced subject-matter content. The teacher might want to try this on a limited scale, initially at least, with just a few students. Their findings could increase insights into children's thinking processes, as well as contribute to the body of knowledge on curriculum placement.

5. Piaget's findings also have relevance to the grouping of students. Because youngsters often learn a good deal through social interaction with their peers, an ungraded plan covering a wider age span might provide increased intellectual stimulation. Moreover, individual differences among the ages at which a student enters and leaves the stage of concrete operations suggest that benefits might accrue from an ungraded plan.

Summary

1. Readiness refers to the student's ability to profit from instruction given a reasonable amount of effort and practice.

2. The concept of readiness has changed in many respects during the past 20 years. Foremost among the changes was an increased belief in the plasticity of intellect accompanied by additional effort to accelerate the rate and ultimate level of mental development. More recently there has also been a renewed interest in the personal and social aspects of self-actualization.

3. Cognitive development always proceeds in two ways concomitantly—general and specific—and it is necessary to consider both facets of readiness in appraising a student's cognitive readiness.

4. Maturational forces, prior learning, and instructional strategies all interact in complex ways. Because of the multidimensional nature of readiness, it is very difficult to state with much certainty *which* particular component contributed *what* amount to *what* behavior in *which* children.

5. There is considerable controversy over the "natural" versus the "produced" approaches to readiness. Readiness programs need not be an either-or matter; instead they should reflect an openness to capitalize on our knowledge regarding man's innate self-regulatory capacities, the impact of cultural and environmental forces, and advances in teaching methodology.

6. Piaget believes that intellect develops in response to four stimulants: maturation; social transmission through education and language; richness of environmental experience; and, most important, equilibration achieved through the student's own actual influence or transformation of objects and events in his surroundings. The first three factors play a part in the development of logical intelligence, but are not sufficient.

7. The child struggles to assimilate new information to old information and to accommodate the old to the new, and having succeeded, returns to equilibrium but at a higher level than before.

8. According to Piaget, the development of logical intelligence can occur only when the youngster's equilibrium is disturbed, only when he is discomforted by a state of cognitive conflict. Intellectual structures associated with the earlier stages of mental development are characterized by a less stable equilibrium in that they are relatively modifiable through new encounters.

9. Piaget describes four major stages of thought: the sensorimotor stage from birth to 18 months; the preoperational stage from two to seven years of age; the concrete operational stage from roughly seven to eleven years of age; and the formal operational stage from eleven or twelve years on. Each stage is characterized by a different way of thinking and a different capacity for thinking.

10. Piaget's work offers us a framework for assessing a student's overall logical intelligence as well as development of specific concepts. Any serious attempt to diagnose readiness must address itself to both of these aspects.

11. The speeding up of specific learnings (e.g., age of reading), although more easily achieved than the speeding up of Piaget's stages of intellectual development, is unlikely to have long-range developmental effects. In contrast, the acceleration of change in cognitive structure is extremely difficult to achieve but apt to have long-range general effects, because an advance in one step of Piaget's invariant sequence may lead to an advance in the next step.

CHAPTER 4
Personality Factors and School Readiness

"May I please be excused? I have a tension headache." *(Drawing by Weber; © 1972. The New Yorker Magazine, Inc.)*

The Development of Dependency
Character Development
The Development of Anxiety and Insecurity
Aggression

Successful students are secure, assertive, self-confident, reasonably independent and self-directing, consistent in meeting the expectations of others, and highly motivated to learn. Furthermore, they model their lives after an inspiring model, enjoy competing with others, show social and task responsibility, and achieve a happy balance between freedom of self-expression and the normal restrictions of school life. These personality characteristics are important for success at all levels from kindergarten through college. In fact, they are personality characteristics of the successful person even in the postschool years.

Students who fail in school are often characterized by no forward thrust and aspiration, intense fears, limited frustration tolerance, an inability to accept social behavior limits, little or no task orientation, and an avoidance of situations that might involve failure (Brenner, 1967). Briefly, students lacking in affective prerequisites experience difficulty in school with respect to its social demands and with regard to achieving traditional academic objectives.

This chapter will aid educators in developing a fuller appreciation of the ways in which personality factors can facilitate or impair school readiness.[1] For each personality factor discussed, we will describe the behaviors indicative of the trait, antecedents of these behaviors, adaptive and maladaptive outcomes, and most important, management implications for teachers.

[1] The topic of achievement motivation will be discussed in Chapter 7, Motivation and Attitudes Toward Learning.

<table>
<tr><td>

OBJECTIVES FOR
CHAPTER 4

</td><td>

1. List some of the personality factors important to success in school.
2. Identify the behaviors generally associated with the common adjustment problems in school.
3. List the adjustment outcomes associated with faulty and adequate resolutions of common social and emotional problems experienced by students.
4. Discuss the causes of favorable and unfavorable adjustment outcomes.
5. Describe the educational implications for each of the personality factors presented.
6. Give examples of the application of instructional and management strategies to the solution of actual cases involving personality factors.

</td></tr>
</table>

THE DEVELOPMENT OF DEPENDENCY

Perhaps the most dramatic and important change that occurs during the first year of life is the advance in interpersonal relationships. It is usually assumed that the first social tie that develops—the bond between mother and infant—serves as a prototype for all later interpersonal relations. For our purposes we will use the term "attachment" or "dependency" to refer to this core relationship. The intense affect associated with the strong interdependence of the mother-child relationship is believed by many authorities to be the basis for most, if not all, socialization. The young child who develops a sense of trust emerges from infancy with a sense of security and is better able to deal with personal anxieties. A close relationship with the mother also facilitates moral development and proper expression of one's aggressions. In a sense, then, attachment or dependency constitutes a kind of social glue, cementing in the cornerstone of socialization processes. As Ferguson (1970) notes, "The fact that children . . . value the presence, attention, and approval of significant others, and fear their loss, has been considered a most powerful motive for conformity to the expectations of these others, for imitation and identification, for the acquisition of values, for the internalization of behavioral controls, for academic achievement, and for many other aspects of socialization."

Signs of Dependency

How does dependency manifest itself? Persistent display of the following signs is regarded as indicative of dependency. The first sign is *seeking help*. Instead of taking the initiative, the dependent child goes to the adult for help not only when he encounters some obstacle in attempting to perform an assignment, but even when the task is of a routine nature. Seeking assistance also shows up when the student is asked to make even small decisions by himself. He would rather lean on others than be self-sufficient. Another sign of dependency is *attention-getting* behavior. The dependent child habitually wants the adult to watch him or talk with him or look at something he has produced, such as a drawing. Attention-getting behavior may also show up in the form of whining. *Seeking physical contact* is another behavior suggestive of dependency. The child may want to sit on the parent's lap or cling to his mother tenaciously. *Physical proximity* or the desire to be close to an adult is a fourth sign of dependency. *Passivity* is another characteristic commonly observed in the dependent youngster. He may prefer to sit by himself and do nothing instead of joining classmates in a game. Finally, dependency can also be manifested in the *seeking of approval or reassurance*. The dependent individual is very sensitive to what others think of him.

Some authors believe that seeking attention and wanting approval represent more mature forms of behavior than seeking physical contact or proximity do, since the former are characteristic of older children while the latter are more characteristic of younger children. Not only does the nature of the dependent response change with age, but the object of the dependency also shifts with age. As the child matures, emotional dependence on peers increases while emotional dependence on adults decreases (Heathers, 1955). A partial explanation of this shift might be attributed to the fact that older children are more socially rewarding to one another than younger, nursery school children are (Charlesworth and Hartup, 1967).

Most workers agree that there are two varieties of dependency—instrumental or task-oriented and emotional or person-oriented. In instrumental dependency, the child seeks help in reaching a given goal. The student, for example, might depend on his teacher for completion of a given arithmetic assignment. He seeks help in *doing things*. In emotional dependency, the child seeks the *social responses of others*, for example, approval as a goal, per se. Chronologically, instrumental dependency (the seeking of another as a means of securing assistance) apparently precedes emotional dependency (essentially

affiliation or attachment). The sexes probably do not differ appreciably in terms of overall dependency. Some workers believe, however, that because of cultural forces, the former has been typical of boys and the latter typical of girls. Traditional sex roles might be changing, and it will be interesting to see whether task-oriented dependency remains characteristic of males as a group and person-oriented dependency remains characteristic of females as a group.

While parents are initially very accepting of the child's total reliance on them, it is not long, particularly in our society, before the child is expected to relinquish some of his dependency and strive toward becoming a more self-reliant individual. Both sexes, although to varying degrees, are expected to become increasingly self-sufficient—to forgo some of their instrumental dependency. Yet both sexes, again perhaps to varying degrees, are expected to remain emotionally attached or dependent on parents and friends. In light of these cultural expectations, it is hardly surprising that we learn to simultaneously depend on others and to be independent of others. We learn new ways to be helped and to help ourselves.

Roots and Consequences of Dependency

SEQUENCE OF DEVELOPMENT

While we cannot plot the developmental course of dependency behaviors as we can that of physical development, recent research has alerted us to a number of steps involved in the process. First, the infant develops the capacity to distinguish between himself and his external surroundings—a sense of separateness from the environment. Later in this phase, the baby may cry when held by someone other than the mother or primary caretaker. Next, the infant develops specific expectations toward the mother and shows by his behavior that he expects certain responses to his signals. Finally, a confidence relationship—a higher-level relationship involving trust—is established. He can now leave his mother and explore strange surroundings, secure in his knowledge that the mother will be there to comfort him if necessary (Yarrow and Pederson, 1972).

We can describe the developmental course of dependency with reasonable accuracy, but theorists vary appreciably in their identification of factors responsible for healthy and unhealthy outcomes of dependency socialization. We will restrict our discussion to theories regarding outcomes that require attention from the classroom teacher.

TOO MUCH DEPENDENCY

Let us first examine the pattern of strong dependency or "overdependency," for which there are two proposed theories, both of which focus on parent attitudes. One theory, proposed by Levy (1943), suggests that *maternal overprotection* may lead to overly dependent behavior in children. In his study of 15 cases of overprotective mothers, he found their children to be passive, dependent, and submissive. Heathers (1953) likewise concluded that dependent behavior may stem from maternal overprotection. The mothers in Heathers' study not only permitted dependent behavior but also reinforced it.

Another prevalent theory views dependent behavior in children as a result of *maternal rejection*. The notion that maternal rejection results in dependent behavior in children receives considerable support from empirical research, as evidenced in Hartup's (1963) review of the literature. According to this view, the child's dependency needs are frustrated, with the result that the child, lacking sufficient support and nurturance, is unable to progress successfully through the experi-

ences culminating in independence. Frustration of the child's requests for assistance and emotional support is quite apt to occur in our culture because of the societal emphasis on early independence training. Many parents and teachers, in their eagerness to develop independence in children, fail to recognize that dependency is a prerequisite for independence. Paradoxically, the child can become independent only after he has learned that he can depend on his parents' acceptance, approval, and support.

What becomes of the dependent child? Will he always remain dependent? The only longitudinal study on dependency underscores the importance of cultural influences on the developmental stability of this drive (Kagan and Moss, 1960). The results suggest that passive dependent behavior remains stable over time for the dependent female, but not for the dependent male. The results are interpreted in light of societal pressures for the male to become self-reliant and autonomous and for the female to be passive.

TOO LITTLE DEPENDENCY

Not all youngsters are given the opportunity to learn dependency. As noted above, the social-learning theorist views dependency as a consequence of the mother's or caretaker's satisfying the infant's needs; that is, the mother's presence is associated with a state of comfort and well-being, while her absence is associated with anxiety. When children are deprived of a continuing relationship with a caretaker, it is difficult for the kind of learning process described above to occur. Furthermore, there is a tendency in our society for parents and teachers to overlook the importance of originally learned dependency. Youngsters who have failed to learn dependency are frequently difficult to socialize since they have not learned to desire approval from others. People interested in day care centers are particularly concerned about the child's having a close relationship with a single caretaker.

We do not want to leave the reader with the impression that adverse effects *inevitably* follow as a consequence of maternal separation. Whether negative consequences occur following maternal separation depends on a number of factors, such as the age of the child, the stress involved in separation, the length of the separation period, the kind of care given during the separation period, and the amount of subsequent trauma in the child's life. If the infant is separated while forming a close attachment, if separation is accompanied by other stresses such as illness, if this is followed by a prolonged stay in an impersonal, unchallenging environment, and if the child has a later history of repeated traumatic experiences, such as unsuccessful placement in a number of foster homes, he is apt to suffer severe emotional and intellectual damage. On the other hand, the negative consequences can be lessened by separating the infant before attachment develops, by reducing stress at the time of separation, by making the new surrounding warm and stimulating, and by returning the child to his mother or by finding an adequate mother substitute (Wenar, 1971). Some authorities assert more strongly that *quality* day care programs (one form of maternal separation) can promote healthy development.

Educational Implications

The following guidelines are relevant to the instruction and management of the overly dependent student.

1. Select a goal that will help him become more self-directing and less dependent on teacher support. The dependent student will frequently need guidance in acquiring such important behaviors as making decisions more independently, exploring the classroom environment, defending his own judgments and opinions, working on his own, playing alone, and leaving the teacher or parent.

2. Proceed toward your goal in a *gradual* manner. Guard against the natural tendency to make him self-reliant overnight. The following case study illustrates how one teacher helped a girl student to become more independent without frustrating her dependency needs.

"Mrs. Brown observed that when she gave Marcia arithmetic assignments requiring no more than 15 minutes to complete and stayed near her, she completed the assignments quickly with few errors. But when Marcia was given assignments requiring more than 15 minutes to complete and consisting of problems equivalent in difficulty to those contained in shorter assignments, she worked only while Mrs. Brown was near her. Since Mrs. Brown did not stay near Marcia throughout the time she worked on longer assignments, she seldom completed these and made many errors on those which she did not finish."

"It appears that physical proximity of the teacher is reinforcing to Marcia. In this instance, Mrs. Brown paired her presence with verbal praise: 'Keep up the good work Marcia.' She began by giving arithmetic assignments to Marcia that could be completed within 10 minutes. Gradually assignments were made that required increasingly more time to complete. During arithmetic seatwork, Mrs. Brown systematically scheduled her presence near Marcia on a variable schedule of reinforcement (that is, in a way unpredictable to Marcia) and praised her for her efforts. Praise was also issued from afar in order to encourage Marcia to complete assignments. Because Mr. Brown was observant, she is able to use those conditions that contribute to Marcia's desirable work habits." (Stephens, 1970)

Note that the teacher did not simply leave the student on her own. Instead, she provided emotional support while helping Marcia to be increasingly independent of her presence. Mrs. Brown did not strengthen Marcia's dependent ways through overgratification nor did she thwart Marcia's reliance on the teacher's presence.

3. The dependent student is likely to change his behavior on the basis of whether others approve of it or not. Because of this susceptibility to social influence, teachers can make effective use of social rewards (praise, recognition, and approval) in motivating the dependent youngster to become more mature. Doing things for himself must become more rewarding than having others do them for him if behavioral change is to occur.

4. Be sure that other students are not doing the dependent youngster's assignments for him and depriving him of valuable learning experiences.

5. Be sure that you are not reinforcing dependent behavior by your nearness, attention, and affection.

6. Be consistent in your process of systematic weaning.

CHARACTER DEVELOPMENT

Overview

Following the early work of Hartshorne and May (1928 to 1930) and the work of Piaget (1932), there was little activity and interest in the development of moral character. Psychologists generally avoided the topic of moral development in children, because psychological matters pertaining to moral character were thought to be unverifiable and inappropriate topics for psychology as a science. In so doing, psychologists neglected one of the most significant components of personality makeup. It was not until the late 1950s that there was a renewed interest in the study of moral development in children. Today psychologists from various schools of thought recognize that development of moral character is essential if the child is to become socialized in the ways of his particular culture. In the course of development children must learn to channel aggressive and hedonistic impulses, to establish internal controls for behavior, and to comply to a reasonable extent with societal expectations. If they fail to do so, they and/or society will most likely suffer.

What is conscience? We define it as the internalization of *standards* and *prohibitions* that govern one's activity. The preschool child certainly feels bad when he has transgressed, but primarily because he fears external parental disapproval. Later, around age four or five, the locus of anxiety or fear comes from within, and the child experiences guilt when he has transgressed. With the onset of an internal censor, the child is no longer as dependent on external sources to regulate his behavior. Research has concentrated more on the negative side of conscience (guilt and resistance to temptation) than on the positive side. We have been more concerned, perhaps regrettably so, with the "thou shalt not's" (prohibitions) than with the "thou shalt's" (standards).

Roots of Character Development

The child is not born with a conscience. How does he eventually acquire internal standards that regulate the expression of his basic urges and determine the goals he sets for himself? The specifics of conscience formation are not fully known, but three basic factors play a central role in the development of moral character: the child's cognitive level, cultural factors, and child-rearing practices.

COGNITIVE FACTORS

Let us look first at cognitive development. Since moral behavior and knowledge both have a cognitive component, it is not surprising that they are influenced to some extent by the child's level of intellectual maturity. The use of reasoning is associated with high conscience development, but it assumes only limited relevance to the very young child because of his limited intellectual powers. Once language comprehension develops, it is easier to explain the expected standards to him, and labels ("good," "bad") can be attached to specific behaviors. Anxiety thus becomes attached to certain misdeeds, and the discrimination between what is desirable and what is undesirable is facilitated. Moreover, once the child has developed greater linguistic facility, he can be taught to substitute words and ideas for the physical expression of certain impulses. For example, the parent can encourage the angry child who possesses language to tell mommy what he's angry about, so that he feels less of a need to express his anger through physical means. Or the teacher might ask a child to write about an anger-inducing incident in lieu of fighting. With more years of experience, the older child not only understands more fully the expectations set for him but also the rationale underlying them. He has both a deeper understanding and appreciation of certain moral concepts and a more highly developed facility for self-evaluation and self-criticism.

Kohlberg, a cognitively oriented psychologist who has written much about moral development, offers a new approach—one that rejects the two common interpretations that moral behavior is purely a matter of immediate situational forces and rewards and that moral character is a matter of deep emotions fixed early in childhood (Wright, 1971). For Kohlberg, the predisposition toward proper conduct is related to the youngster's slowly developing capacity for judgment and to certain ego strength factors (formerly referred to as willpower), such as the ability to predict consequences, delay gratification, and focus attention.

Kohlberg's developmental scheme closely relates to Piaget's work on moral judgment, but it is also a major advance both in conceptual refinement and empirical anchorage. There are six developmental stages that fall into three fundamentally different levels of moral orientation. Movement from one stage to the next is regarded by Kohlberg largely as an outgrowth of the child's cognitive development. Moral thought is seen as behaving like all other kinds of thought, with progression through the stages characterized by increasing differentiation and integration. The basic themes and primary attributes of the levels and stages follow.

Preconventional Level. Control of conduct is external, both in the sense that the standards conformed to consist of pressures or commands emanating from sources outside of the individual and in that the motive is to avoid external punishment, to secure rewards, or to have favors returned.

Stage 1. The moral orientation is founded on punishment and its avoidance. There is an unquestioning deference to those who have the power to punish, but there is no true moral obligation and no concept of the rights of others. "Might is right."

Stage 2. Stage two is a hedonistic morality. Acts that satisfy one's needs are defined as right. One conforms to rules for the purpose of gaining favors and rewards from others. "You scratch my back and I'll scratch yours."

The Conventional Level. Morality is measured in terms of performing good acts and maintaining the conventional social order or the expectation of others. Control of the individual's conduct is still external in that the rules adhered to are still those of others, but now the motivation to comply with these expectations is internal.

Stage 3. The good boy–good girl orientation is predominant. Moral behavior is that which pleases or helps others and is approved by them. The individual seeks approval for being nice. In judging another's actions, the child now considers the other's intentions, for example, did he really mean to break my bat? In short, right action is defined by general consensus and the motive behind the right action is the desire to remain accepted by others.

Stage 4. The moral orientation is toward authority, fixed rules, and keeping social order. This might be called the "law and order" stage. Right behavior involves doing one's duty and showing respect for authority. Moral obligation is equated with duty to social and religious authority, and the motive underlying moral action is the desire to avoid letting authority down and incurring its censure.

The Postconventional Level. At the third level of moral maturity, control of conduct is now internal; the standards conformed to come from within the individual and the decision to act is based on an inner process of thought and judgment concerning moral matters. There is a thrust toward autonomous moral principles, which have a valid basis and application apart from the authority of the groups or individuals who espouse them and apart from the individual's personal identification with these groups or persons.

Stage 5. A social-contract orientation is now dominant. Norms of right and wrong are defined in terms of laws or institutionalized rules that are rooted in a rational consideration of social utility. The relativism of personal values and opinions are clearly recognized as well as the corresponding need for procedural rules in reaching a consensus. Laws are not frozen, as in the "law and order"

stage, but can be changed when they no longer express the will of the majority, maximize social welfare, or promote institutional functioning. Fundamental to this stage is the recognition that all individuals have rights irrespective of their race, sex, or social status.

Stage 6. Finally, morality is oriented toward individual principles of conscience (as well as existing social rules and standards). Conduct is governed by internalized ideals regardless of others' reactions. Although the importance of law and social contract are acknowledged, moral conflict is generally resolved in light of broader moral principles, such as the Golden Rule, the greatest good for the greatest number, or the categorical imperative. The universal principles of justice, the reciprocity and equality of human rights, and respect for the dignity of mankind as individual persons form the basis of conscience. The Stage 6 individual uses words such as "duty" or "morally right," but in a way that implies universality, ideals, and impersonality. Expressions such as "regardless of who it is" or "I would do it in spite of punishment" are in evidence.

The age differences obtained in research studies thus far lend credence to the assumption that these stages occur in the expected developmental order, although the findings are convincing only with respect to the kind of social structure found in Western cultures. The major contribution of Kohlberg's theory lies in the fact that it sensitizes us to the cognitive dimensions and prerequisites of a mature moral orientation (Hoffman, 1970).

CULTURAL FACTORS

Cultural factors are also known to influence moral development. They largely determine the *contents* of conscience, that is, the standards and prohibitions the child will learn. Lower-class parents tend to place great emphasis on conformity to external cues or to authority, while middle-class parents emphasize internal regulation of behavior. Consistent with this differential emphasis is the finding that lower-class boys behave more aggressively and experience less guilt in the process than do middle-class boys (Mussen, Conger, and Kagan, 1969). In the lower classes, the child's parents and peer group provide models or behaviors to be imitated that differ from those of the middle class. The delinquent, for instance, who is a daily witness to aggression and norm violation in his neighborhood, is provided with a value system that is at odds with the value structure of the school.

CHILD-REARING FACTORS

A third factor in conscience development has to do with child-rearing practices. The study by Sears and his associates (1957) found that love-oriented techniques, such as the use of praise, warmth, reasoning, and the withdrawal of love, were more effective than materialistic techniques that employ physical punishment and deprivation of privileges. The effectiveness of love-oriented practices probably stems from four aspects of parental behavior.

1. Warmth makes the child dependent on adult approval and lessens his need for deviant behavior to secure attention. It is interesting to note that parents of delinquents are typically less accepting, solicitous, and affectionate than parents of nondelinquents (Glueck and Glueck, 1950).

2. The presentation of a model of self-restraint results in the imitation of socially acceptable behaviors.

3. The use of reasoning increases the child's understanding of the expectations set for him and gives him additional training in making moral judgments.

4. Certain aspects relating to the timing of punishment are also important. For example, punishment administered upon the initiation of the transgression makes for the development of more effective controls, while punishment administered after the misbehavior is related to the development of guilt (Becker, 1964).

Outcomes of Character Development

DANGERS ASSOCIATED WITH SEVERITY

There are two dangers associated with the development of internal controls. Conscience may be too strict or conscience may be too lenient. Both extremes can pose hardships for the individual and for society. Expecting too much and expecting too little of the child can have equally undesirable consequences. If conscience is too strong, it may inhibit behaviors that are not in need of censorship. Such unnecessary restrictions reduce the child's sense of excitement and ability to enjoy life. In the extreme, a restrictive conscience can create conflicts and produce feelings of guilt, self-dissatisfaction, depression, and inhibition—symptoms commonly associated with neurosis.

Since conscience consists of attainment ideals as well as prohibitions, there is a possibility that a student with a demanding conscience will strive for standards that are difficult if not impossible to attain, thus resulting in excessive anxiety and frustration on his part. The reader is perhaps familiar with the student who focuses not on the 19 problems he had correct but on the 1 problem he had wrong, or the student who is upset because his straight "A" average was ruined by a "B" grade. Such youngsters are unduly harsh and severe with themselves, and consequently enjoy life less. A certain amount of striving, ambition, and self-dissatisfaction is desirable, but too little self-satisfaction can become a definite handicap.

DANGERS ASSOCIATED WITH LENIENCY

At the other extreme is the child whose conscience is too lenient. This deficiency may manifest itself in norm-violating behaviors such as cheating, lying, truancy, or delinquency. This youngster often behaves as though rules did not apply to him. In the more severe cases of antisocial behavior, the child may not experience appropriate guilt feelings for his misbehavior. Two major investigations dealing with delinquent youth reported that both middle-class and lower-class delinquents are deficient in self-critical guilt reactions (Bandura and Walters, 1959; McCord and McCord, 1956). Similarly, Kohlberg (1964), in his study of lower-class delinquents, noticed that his subjects were functioning at an early stage of premoral judgment. He concluded that "simple developmental arrest" characterized the majority of his subjects. Lacking the ability to control their own behavior, these youngsters require constant external surveillance. However, external supervision is not a feasible means of handling this problem, because one cannot oversee all of the child's activity.

OPTIMAL SELF-DIRECTION

Ideally, the child should have an optimal amount of self-control. On the prohibitive side, he should be able to experience realistic guilt when he has committed a serious transgression. On the self-realization side, moral development should assist in the development of an integrated personality that can seek and achieve culturally congruent goals. Unfortunately, it is difficult to achieve a mature conscience in our society, since cultural pressures often discourage one from thinking through matters of a moral nature for himself. One is taught not to question moral authority, but to accept it with humility.

Educational Implications

Discussion of the educational implications of moral development can be conveniently divided into three parts: the cognitive, behavioral, and affective aspects of morality. The cognitive implications pertain to the moral judgments the child makes about the correctness of choices in various situations involving moral conflict. The behavioral aspect deals with the student's ability to resist temptation or to perform altruistic acts. The affective implications involve the emotional reactions (e.g., self-disgust) following violations of conscience.

MORAL JUDGMENT

One of the major educational implications has to do with the stimulation of moral judgment. The development of character requires more than preaching or conventional moralizing by teachers. Indeed, preaching and exhortation are probably the least effective methods. "To be more than 'Mickey Mouse,' a teacher's moralizings must be cognitively novel and challenging to the child, and they must be related to matters of obvious, real importance and seriousness." (Kohlberg, 1969) This does not mean that the moral matters discussed must always be immediate and real life issues. Any issue can be of potential value as long as the conflict situations are challenging and capable of generating serious, lengthy debate. The pat little stories in school readers depicting the inevitable triumph of virtue or showing everyone as really nice will not advance moral development. Only the discussion of interesting and difficult moral conflicts can disturb the student's equilibrium and stimulate moral judgment (e.g., discussion of drugs, abortion, bussing). Too often teachers dwell on trivial classroom rules that have no moral meaning outside of the classroom.

In order to disturb the student's equilibrium, careful consideration must be given to the match between the teacher's level of moral explanation and the youngster's stage of moral development. Conventional moral training has not had much impact on student's moral judgments, because it has disregarded this problem of developmental match. It has usually involved a set of adult moral clichés that are meaningless to the child, either because they are too abstract or too patronizing, talking down to the student. Explanations that are too abstract or beneath his level are apt to be meaningless to the student. A series of studies (Turiel, 1969) suggests that the communicating of moral messages should be aimed at a level one stage above the student's current stage and secondarily at the child's own level. If the level of explanation too far exceeds the child's level of understanding—that is, by two or more stages—he will be unable to show any appreciable understanding of the moralizing. While children can comprehend moral communications beneath their level of understanding, they do not seem to accept it as readily as if it is slightly in advance of their level, but still comprehensible. It is perhaps worse to err by being at too low a level, because the child loses respect for the message (Kohlberg, 1969). Nobody enjoys being talked down to. The teacher must begin by listening to the student's level of moral judgment and then involving him in dialogue at the next stage of moral development. Furthermore, the teacher must become concerned with the child's moral judgments as well as the child's conformity to the teacher's behavior or judgments.

MORAL CONDUCT

It is also essential that school authorities exemplify the kinds of moral behavior they want to develop in their students. Teachers must practice what they preach or run the risk that their practices will counteract their moral verbalizations. Because a teacher's authority often protects him from social feedback from his students, a teacher can slip into the habit of exemplifying bad manners, bullying, or even mild sadism without realizing it. To teach justice requires just schools. To teach altruistic behavior requires observation of charitable acts. The potency of an altruistic model is demonstrated, for instance, in one study showing that elementary school pupils were more likely to donate highly valued gift certificates to children of a fictitious orphanage if they had seen an adult do so (Rosenhan and White, 1967). Remember that we teach by example and that a teacher must be fully aware of the example he is setting. "The first step for anyone who has to take responsibility for the moral education of children should be to examine the morality of his own actions toward them." (Wright, 1971)

In addition to the use of suitable models, the schools can foster moral conduct through consistent use of punishments and rewards. Various studies suggest, for example, that the ability to resist temptation is related to the timing, frequency, consistency, intensity, and rationality associated with the use of punishment. More will be said about the role played by reward, punishment, and modeling as means of modifying behavior in the chapter on classroom discipline. It is sufficient at this point to note that care must be taken to see that rewards and punishments are associated with the moral behaviors that we wish to strengthen or weaken, respectively. It is possible for a school to encourage excessive compliance, lying, snobbery, and expediency and to discourage truthfulness, altruism and integrity without the staff intending to do so.

MORAL AFFECT

The perfectionistic child who has been taught to require unusually high standards of himself must be helped to achieve with less effort and concern. There are various ways to reduce tension. When assigning a theme, the teacher can specify that spelling must be correct, but that punctuation will not be graded on that particular task. The use of speed tests should be curtailed. Shorter assignments should be given so that the perfectionistic student can succeed without extraordinary effort. If several quizzes or exams are given, the practice of dropping the two lowest scores in arriving at a grade is a special comfort to the perfectionistic student. Parents should also be helped to see that overconcern hinders, not helps performance (Verville, 1967).

The following case illustrates how one teacher worked with a student with excessively high standards. Jim, a nine-year-old fourth grader, was a "model student." He was responsive to teacher demands and extremely meticulous in carrying out assignments. His perfectionistic tendencies were readily evident. If he completed a math assignment with 95% accuracy, he focused on the 5% that he got wrong. If a theme did not turn out the way he wanted it, he would tear it up in disgust, become angry, and be on the verge of tears. In short, Jim became very self-punitive when he felt that there were shortcomings in his performance.

After discussing Jim with the school psychologist, the teacher launched a multi-pronged attack on the problem. Jim's comment that his teacher never made mistakes and that he should not, either, led her to believe that she had been providing Jim with a perfectionistic model to live up to. She realized that she had also been inadvertently rewarding Jim's perfectionistic tendencies by praising him when he got "100" and by withholding praise when his paper was less than perfect. She knew he could be a good student and she expected him to be just that. Now she had to change her tactics somewhat. She still wanted him to be a competent student, but he had to learn that the world does not always fall apart because of human errors.

One of the first things she did was to stop rewarding his flawless performances and to begin rewarding him for just good performance, for example, she would write on his paper, "Jim, that was a tough assignment and you did a good job on it." In brief, she tried to ignore "undesirable" or perfectionistic behavior, and to strengthen "desirable" behavior, that is, "good performances."

She also discussed some historically well-known people, carefully pointing out their strong points, but also noting that all of them failed at something in their lives. For instance, even the brilliant Einstein admitted confirming only 1 in 1000 of his ideas. Later, she asked the students to think about an incident that in some ways might be comparable with those discussed earlier. Jim was a little bit shaken after hearing how many people had events in their lives that did not go as planned. Then the teacher pointed out how she had "goofed" in her first year of teaching, but how the occurrence of such errors had actually made her a better teacher and person today.

Another technique involved playing "stump the teacher." This game was used as a reward on Fridays when the class had worked hard. Students were free to ask any question on any subject. Jim's teacher, although competent, could not, of course, answer all the questions addressed to her. Jim and the rest of the class would laugh when she did not know the answer and she would laugh with them, thereby showing that she could be less than perfect and yet self-accepting. The message implicit in these modeling incidents was that "I don't know everything, but yet I am an adequate and worthwhile person both in my own eyes and the eyes of others."[2]

The teacher also taught Jim the difference between "good mistakes" and "poor mistakes." The former entails the use of the correct process, even though execution of the process leaves something to be desired. Through this technique, Jim was able to become more accepting of certain types of mistakes. Once he had learned to be more accepting of "good mistakes," he was encouraged to become more accepting of the poor mistakes, too.

The parents were also well aware of the stress and strain associated with their son's perfectionistic ways and were eager to do whatever they could. In a conference with the parents, the teacher explained some of the strategies that she had used in school and encouraged them to carry these over to the home. The father, a journalist, could point out, for instance, that he had to rewrite almost every article he published despite his years of experience and training, yet he was still respected as a person of talent. Such experiences were to be related in a casual, nonobvious way, so that Jim would not get the impression that others were just trying to make him feel good following a "failure" experience. By the end of the school year, Jim no longer tore up papers in disgust. Although he still set high standards for himself, he seemed more self-accepting and reported that he could live with himself more easily now.

We have discussed the overly conscientious student. How about the student who has the opposite problem? For the student with

too little guilt, the school must provide a well-controlled, highly structured classroom environment that will permit the management and realignment of unacceptable conduct. Since internal controls are not well developed in this child, greater reliance has to be placed on external controls or supervision. The learning experience should be structured so that it consistently strengthens the behavior that the school is trying to promote and weakens the behavior that the school hopes to extinguish. This student needs a "reality rub" in which the teacher unapologetically lets him know what the standards are and what he will get for compliance with them. He must come to know in a very personal way that there are rewarding alternatives to his way of coping with the world.

THE DEVELOPMENT OF ANXIETY AND INSECURITY

Overview

Teachers, while rightfully concerned with the acting-out student, are also confronted with and often perplexed by the anxious, insecure child. Although less disruptive to classroom order than his aggressive counterpart, the anxious youngster can leave teachers feeling helpless in their efforts to assist him in becoming more responsive to the classroom setting. For example, the teacher cannot get Jimmy to talk in front of the group, or Sally to associate with her classmates, or Joe to overcome his fear of algebra, or Don to conquer his anxiety about tests, or Clarence to become more assertive and to defend his rights, or Audrey to stop worrying about making occasional mistakes on assignments. Behaviors such as these probably do not interfere with the performance of the class as a whole, but they do keep the individual so

[2] Ideally, in a good classroom, questions for which the teacher would not know the answer would often be raised.

afflicted from realizing his educational and social potential. The plight of anxious-withdrawn children has been aptly described by Morse and Wingo (1969, p. 395).

"All teachers will have in their classrooms children who are models of conformity yet whose behavior should be considered a problem. There are the unhappy children who have not organized themselves for productive work, the ones who feel grossly inadequate and unimportant, the quiet and withdrawn children, and the shy or fearful ones who often file quietly in and out of school and receive no more than passing consideration. Yet these children are discipline problems as much as the aggressive, noisy youngster, for they too have not yet learned the mature self-direction that will make their behavior both satisfying to themselves and acceptable to others."

Anxiety is most likely a universal phenomenon in children and is clearly exhibited by age three (Temple and Amen, 1944). Major sources of anxiety in children center around the possibility of physical harm, the loss of parental love, feelings of guilt, cultural deviation, and feelings of inadequacy as reflected in an inability to master the environment, for example, one's school work (Mussen, Conger, and Kagan, 1969). In adolescence, the search for ego identity is added to this list of anxiety sources as a teenager attempts to discover where he is going in life, what his assets and weaknesses are, and how he fits into his newly found roles.

How Does Anxiety Manifest Itself?

EFFECTS ON INTELLECTUAL PERFORMANCE

In its more extreme forms, anxiety may result in school phobia, a condition in which the student is so fearful that he is unable to leave home and come to school. In its less extreme forms, the individual is apprehensive, ill at ease, and feels that some impending danger is imminent, for example, "I just know something is going to go wrong." Overcompliance to authority, nervous habits, overreaction to criticism, preference for adult company or that of younger children, withdrawal into fantasy as a means of coping with or escape from stressful situations, fear of change in one's daily routines or surroundings, and an inability to face up to stressful conditions are also common manifestations of anxiety.

Current research on anxiety reveals that, when intense, it can have undesirable effects on both intellectual and personality functioning. In terms of intellectual operations, highly anxious students tend to score lower on:

1. Intelligence tests given at both the elementary and secondary school levels.
2. Achievement tests given at both the elementary and secondary school levels.
3. Creativity tests.

In brief, high anxiety appears to affect adversely complex intellectual tasks such as those typically required in the classroom. Available evidence suggests that the effects of anxiety become increasingly detrimental to school achievement as the child advances through the elementary school years.[3] Reading achievement is more adversely affected in highly anxious students than arithmetic achievement, perhaps because of the greater

[3] Whereas high anxiety is related to inferior school performance among elementary school students, this does not appear to be the case among college students. At the college levels, performance on complex tasks is not impaired as long as the students do not perceive their performance as a threat to their feelings of adequacy. Fortunately, by the time a student reaches college, academic tasks have lost much of their threat value.

emphasis placed on reading in our culture and because reading is a more complex skill than arithmetic at the early grade levels (Hill and Sarason, 1966). The evidence further suggests that very anxious children might perform best in a nonthreatening, secure classroom. Classroom observations, for example, showed that highly anxious boys are less task oriented than low-anxiety boys are. Greater insecurity is also evident in their relationships to the teacher. Curiously, anxiety seems to effect girls differently; highly anxious girls, in contrast to those low in anxiety, evidence less distractibility and stronger achievement motivation.

EFFECTS ON PERSONALITY

Turning to the influence of high anxiety on personality and social functioning, Ruebush (1963) has noted the following.

1. High-anxiety pupils, when compared to those low in anxiety, are not as popular with their peers.

2. High-anxiety children are more susceptible to propaganda.

3. High-anxiety children have more negative self-concepts and are more self-disparaging. Body image also seems impaired.

4. Dependency is also characteristic of high-anxiety children, although more so for boys than for girls.

5. Anxiety decreases the probability of open expression of aggression toward others, but increases the probability of their having feelings of anxiety about aggressive impulses or feelings they experience.

6. Inhibitions and anxiety tend to go hand in hand, as manifested behaviorally by indecisiveness, cautiousness, and rigidity.

Three particular points should be remembered about the anxious, inhibited individual.

First, fears are formed very easily in anxious students, that is, fear responses are more rapidly acquired in the highly anxious person than in his nonanxious counterpart. Second, fears are not only readily established in anxiety-provoking situations, but they also have a strong tendency to spread to similar situations. Anxiety facilitates generalization. For example, a fear of a particular teacher might spread to the fear and avoidance of other teachers. A fear learned through association with one exam might make one apprehensive about other exams. A fear of fractions might carry over to other kinds of arithmetic problems yet to be mastered. As Quay (1963) notes, "All of this means that unpleasant and fear-producing experiences are apt to have results quite beyond the immediate setting and such experience should be minimized for this type of child whenever possible."

Finally, once formed, these fear reactions become difficult to eliminate. These avoidance patterns are not learned through reasoning. Thus, in a similar or identical situation, fear more than reason dictates how a person will react. A major factor involved in the durability of avoidance behaviors hinges around the fact that the phobic individual does not test his fears against reality. The person who is afraid of dogs simply stays away from them. He knows that they bite! He does not need to prove that again. Consequently, he never learns that most dogs do not bite under ordinary circumstances. In other words, the intense anxiety prevents the student from discovering how unrealistic his fears actually are. Seen in this light, it is not surprising that fears are resistant to extinction and the student fails to develop new ways of behaving.

POSITIVE EFFECTS

While anxiety does sometimes become a crippling force, we should not regard it as necessarily undesirable and therefore try to shelter youngsters from it; mild to moderate anxiety can facilitate the student's social adjustment and encourage problem solving and inventiveness. It is extremely difficult to improve a student's behavior when he himself is unconcerned about it. Anxiety-producing experiences should not be avoided, but instead should be used to develop immunity to stress. By anticipating normal crises (e.g., entrance into school), the teacher can help students to cope more adequately with stressful encounters. Few would quarrel with the notion that mastery of stress is a growth-inducing experience. In fact, there is a growing body of evidence suggesting the value of some noxious stimulation during the early years of life. Obviously, youngsters should not be exposed to needless anxiety-producing experiences; however, it is equally undesirable to eliminate anxiety or to reduce it to an absolute minimum, since adequate socialization requires some feelings of anxiety on the child's part. Moreover, youngsters of this generation will probably have to learn to live with more anxiety as adults than we live with now. Somewhere between the extremes, there is an optimal level of anxiety. If anxiety deviates markedly from this level in either direction, the socialization process is hindered.

How Does Anxiety Arise?

Very little empirical research has been conducted on the antecedents of anxiety. Sarason (1960) reports that mothers of high-anxiety children are quite defensive in interviews. Such evasiveness and guardedness, although in themselves clues to the personality makeup of these mothers and their manner of interacting with their children, have nonetheless hampered research on the relationship between child-rearing practices and the development of anxiety. Even though research evidence concerning parental role in the production of childhood anxiety is sparse, clinical experience with anxious children and their parents has offered some insights into its development. Cameron (1963) has discussed the following ways in which children can be given training in anxiety.

1. By having a model who is anxious, the children may become habitually apprehensive simply as a result of incidental associations with parents and teachers.

2. Some children are taught to search out every conceivable danger in their everyday lives. We recall the case of a divorcee who was obsessed by the idea that her ex-husband would come and take her only son, as the man had once threatened. The mother alerted the son to this ever-present danger, and taught him to lock all doors at home, to keep the shades drawn, to stay indoors as much as possible, and to be especially careful on his way to and from school. She also alerted her son's teachers and principal about the possibility of kidnapping so that they, too, might convey this concern to him. It is little wonder that this youngster became terribly tense and apprehensive.

3. Some children are used as confidants by their parents. In this role, they are exposed prematurely to difficulties of adult adjustments, such as financial burdens and marital problems. Lacking the necessary maturity to understand fully such problems as well as the ability and experience to cope with them, the children become overwhelmed and disillusioned by the uncertainties of life. Consider the boy whose mother continually tells him how bad his father is, how he does not pay the bills, how unfair he is to her, how she could have married a better man, and so on. The child's parental loyalties thus become divided, and a fundamental source of his personal security is thereby undermined. Such a child is obviously vulnerable to strong feelings of personal anxiety.

Parents are not the only sources of premature exposure to life's problems. Mass media can also produce uncertainty in children by providing vicarious experiences for which they are not psychologically ready (for example, the soap operas on television).

4. Perfectionism can also make children anxious. The parent or teacher who is never satisfied with the child's performance, who habitually tells him that he could do better and who sets standards above the child's ability level produces a self-dissatisfied child who is open to feelings of anxiety over his failure to live up to expectations.

5. Overpermissive parents or teachers are also likely to have highly anxious children, because children need definite limits set for them to feel secure. Without such limits, the child is not sure of the boundaries of his behavioral freedom. Consequently, environmental predictability is lessened and uncertainty is heightened.

6. Frequent or intense punishment is commonly associated with anxiety in children. Anxiety based on punishment may be reflected in a concern over bodily harm or through concern over rejection by others. Such reactions may be particularly acute for the anxious child who has learned that not measuring up to expectations is associated with punishment of some kind (i.e., corporal punishment, ridicule, dirty looks).

7. The curriculum should be flexible enough to maximize the student's chances of success and minimize his chances of failure. When students are asked to perform assignments that are grossly inconsistent with their abilities, needs, or cultural backgrounds, they are apt to experience anxiety and fear out of self-doubt and out of an inability to please the teacher. Other policies regarding curricular practices such as grading, promotion, and grouping, if not handled intelligently, can also cause considerable anxiety among students.

8. Demands for increased academic competence have also probably placed students under greater pressure. Since educational achievement is seen as a means of maintaining international status and superiority as well as personal prestige and gain, students (especially the males) are valued largely on how they can achieve and excel in school. Youth can respond constructively to challenge, but we must guard against their being caught up in an unremitting pressure to excel, with an extreme emphasis on speed and grades (McNassor, 1967).

What Can the Teacher Do to Overcome Student Anxieties?

1. Identify Anxious Students. Teachers must be on the alert because the student experiencing strong anxiety particularly the bright but anxious student — is not as easily spotted by teachers as one might suspect. With respect to identification, it should also be noted that boys are less apt to voice their anxieties than girls.

2. Set Appropriate Goals. Teachers and parents must set realistic goals for the anxious child. Constant reminders of the disparity between the child's level of performance and the standards set for him can produce considerable anxiety. Ironically, lowering expectations to a level more commensurate with the child's development can improve the child's schoolwork by decreasing the child's anxiety.

3. Minimize Threat. The teacher can optimize the anxious child's learnings by keeping the number of evaluative situations to a minimum, by providing easy tasks in which failure and criticism are unlikely, by providing personal support, and by removing time limits from tests so that there is no penalty for the often slow and cautious problem-solving approach of the anxious youngster. Allowing the anxious student a second chance on exams can also reduce his sense of threat. For example, he might be allowed to earn half credit for correcting each item he missed on an exam or project. Report cards using letter grades should be delayed as long as possible during the elementary school years, particularly in the case of anxious students.

4. Respect Student Worth. It is imperative that the teacher's response to inadequate performance does not convey the attitude that failure and being personally liked by the teacher are in any way related.

5. Assist Student in Accepting Rewards. Recognize that teacher praise is often not a reward for the shy child, at least not initially. Such youngsters commonly have unfavorable self-concepts, and the praise given by the teacher is at odds with what others have communicated to them and with what they believe about themselves. Consequently, the teacher's use of praise generates dissonance and makes the child feel uncomfortable. Where verbal approval produces unfavorable classroom behaviors such as discomfort, defensiveness, unrealistic aspirations, and incredibility (they suspect such nice words), the teacher should consider the use of tangible or activity rewards. For instance, one elementary school student with a low self-estimate but high standards would typically tear up and discard art or written assignments whenever the teacher praised her in front of the class. This student could, however, accept points to be spent on activity rewards selected from a reward menu and nonverbal praise in the form of written comments on her assignments. ("Not bad! That was a tough assignment.") The teacher must be alert to the possibility that praise might sometimes assume partly aversive qualities. This type of ambivalent reaction should not

deter the use of rewards, however. In fact, do not let this child divert you from using rewarding behavior. (Shy, withdrawn children are adept at getting others to leave them alone.)

6. Help Desensitize Student. The use of desensitization procedures is particularly effective in overcoming intense fears and anxieties. The logic underlying these procedures is simple and straightforward. Identify the events that evoke marked emotional discomfort, arrange the fear producing events into a graded list proceeding from the least to the most disturbing, and associate the unpleasant events with something that elicits intense pleasure. Through repeated association with something pleasant, the feared situation eventually loses its unpleasant connotations. When the individual can relax in the face of what was once an upsetting situation, he has been desensitized.

The use of desensitization procedures is well illustrated in the case of a girl who was afraid to speak in front of a group. Mickey was a bright sixth-grade girl who was referred to the school counselor because she became acutely anxious when asked to read aloud, give a report, or perform in any way before her peers. Although she would participate in class discussions and had warm relationships with others, she had always been unable to speak before a group, despite her desire to do so. A conference was held and it was explained that "learning a behavior a little at a time in a relaxed manner" can often help people perform behaviors that previously caused appreciable anxiety. Mickey met with her school counselor once a week for 6 weeks. During these sessions, she role-played behaviors involved in giving an oral report. Initially, she role-played getting out of her seat and coming to the front of the room. Practice in oral reading was also undertaken, but this was done initially when Mickey was still in her seat. The variety and length of activities were increased weekly. Liberal reinforcement was given for gains made, for example, "Hey, that's great!", and progress was constantly called to her attention. She was encouraged to rehearse these behaviors, but only if she felt comfortable in doing so.

A plan of action was designed to gradually increase her oral participation in front of her classmates. Mickey was included in a social studies committee that gave weekly reports on various countries that they were studying. She did not have to participate beyond the point that made her anxious, however. Her first role consisted in standing by a large map at the front of the classroom and pointing out regions that were being discussed by other members of the committee. Later, members of the committee, at the prompting of the teacher, increased Mickey's role by asking questions that, on intellectual grounds alone, she could readily handle. Mickey was thanked by other members for her active role and she was told that she had done a fine job. The committee sat in a semicircle while giving the report, and Mickey's seat was situated so that she did not have to face the audience directly. Mickey gradually became more relaxed while giving reports in front of the class. By the end of the school year, Mickey had reached the point that she volunteered to give an oral report on class accomplishments in social studies (Hosford, 1969).

This case illustrates the combined use of gradual exposure to threatening situations, the pairing of unpleasant tasks (talking in front of the class) with something pleasant (peer and teacher approval served as the anxiety-neutralizing features), and the use of role playing or rehearsal (overlearning). School personnel were careful not to overwhelm the student by forcing her into situations in which the anxiety was unbearable, yet they were also careful to give her opportunities to confront the feared situation. Intrinsic rewards were also probably operative in that she was happy to master her difficulty.

7. Enlist Peer Group Aid. Consider the use of the peer group in drawing out the anxious, shy child. Direct attention from an omniscient and omnipotent teacher often makes the anxious withdrawn child feel more self-conscious and insecure, with the result that withdrawal tendencies become even more pronounced. Select a student with whom the shy child feels somewhat comfortable and have him assist the retiring individual in becoming more outgoing and assertive. For example, the teacher might say, "Jim, I think Jerry (the withdrawn child) might like to play this game with you. Why don't you ask him."

8. Provide For Overlearning. Give the anxious student opportunities to overlearn the skill(s) to bolster his confidence. We can all remember how helpful it was to prepare for anxiety-producing events (our first date, first exam in college, first job interview). Preparation can take such forms as self-rehearsal, role playing, or watching others. Guided participation in which the teacher or a peer actually takes the anxious youngster through the feared situation is a very useful technique in overcoming fears.

9. Provide a Predictable Classroom. Anxious students respond well to definite, dependable, and consistent classroom routine. This student needs a predictable classroom environment. Many aggressive, acting-out students are novelty seekers and thrive on frequent change in daily routines, but this is not the case with anxious-withdrawn individuals. Novelty for them is threatening, because in learning new concepts or in adjusting to new situations, they are not sure what is going to happen next, and this is upsetting. Teachers should be alert to the fact that these students require extra attention when new concepts or skills are being introduced; this involves change, which means that uncertainty and anxiety will intensify and perhaps interfere with the assimilation of these new ideas. For example, even shifting from division by one digit to division by two digits may make the anxious student nervous. A little extra instructional attention and personal support at these transition points will be worth the time invested by the teacher. Remember that a structured experience with a given kind of problem or situation reduces the anxiety associated with novel learnings. Gradually, the anxious student can be exposed to less structured tasks.

10. Programmed Learning. Programmed instruction also seems to hold considerable promise as a teaching technique for the frightened student. While anxiety typically interferes with the learning of complex intellectual tasks, it tends to facilitate the learning of less difficult kinds of assignments. Our task then becomes one of devising ways in which the student's anxiety enhances instead of inhibits the use of his intellectual abilities. Programmed instruction is one approach to accomplishing just this (Quay, 1963). By breaking down complex tasks into simpler sequences, we have transformed what was once a deterrent force into a facilitating one. What was once the student's disability has now become a source of strength. Programmed instruction also minimizes anxiety by insuring a high rate of success or correct answers. This helps him to develop greater self-assurance and thereby increases the probability of a more assertive approach to life. In addition to the use of programmed instruction, a greater emphasis on rote learning, which requires persistence instead of improvisation, might also be indicated because anxiety facilitates learning of a routine nature.

11. Other guidelines. Treatment of the anxious, avoidant student include the following:

a. Instruct these youngsters individually or in groups of six or less.
b. Reinforce *all* emerging social behavior.

c. Ignore occasional antisocial behavior on their part. Do not punish them for aggressive behavior unless it becomes too intense or frequent (Spaulding, 1967).

AGGRESSION

Whether intended to obtain some material advantage or to hurt another individual, aggressive behavior is very common in children. Sears and his associates (1957) reported that almost all mothers had to handle instances of intense aggression directed against them by a preschool child. Moreover, teachers frequently find aggressive students difficult to manage, especially male students, who tend to express their aggressiveness in direct, physical and nonconforming ways. Childhood aggression is so common that it is thought to be almost universal. Yet if the child is to become a socialized adult, he must relinquish a certain amount of his aggression or learn new modes of expressing it. Again, there are dangers involved in the socialization process. Socialization of aggressive behavior must not be so harsh that it severely inhibits those aspects of its expression that are necessary for a successful adjustment both in childhood and in later life. Without assertiveness, competitiveness, and self-confidence, the child is placed at a distinct disadvantage in coping with the demands of life, because it is not the meek or submissive who inherit the earth in our success-oriented culture. Instead, in our society as in many others, training in and encouragement of assertiveness, exploitiveness, and achievement-striving represent particularly important aspects of the socialization process. Training in aggression is necessary not only for fulfillment of one's economic role, but also for other aspects of psychosocial functioning. Unless children are responsive to socialization pressures in this area, societal punishment of either an

"I'm not a problem child. The way I handle other kids I *create* problem children!" *(Drawing by Joe E. Buresch. From* Today's Education, NEA Journal, *1972)*

overt or a covert nature is likely to be their fate.

A certain amount of aggression is a sign of a robust and well-balanced personality. We consider it both normal and desirable for the child to defend his rights and to fight back if the situation warrants it. The child should not be made to feel guilty or fearful in exercising his right to justified anger. On the other hand, aggressive impulses cannot be allowed a free rein, because such freedom can also have equally undesirable socialization consequences. The aggressive child is not at peace with himself or with his peer group. Since aggressive attacks elicit aggressive responses, it is not surprising to find that the hostile, acting-out child is unpopular (Winder and Rau, 1962).

Theories of Aggression

Theories of aggression vary in the degree to which they stress biological factors compared to psychological factors, such as learning and experience. Early psychoanalytic theorists such as Freud assumed that the child is born with an aggressive drive, but the ways in which it is expressed are learned. Later, ethologists such as Lorenz favored a modified instinct view in which aggressive responses are seen as innate responses to particular stimulus patterns. We will examine a different modification of the instinct position, in the form of the "frustration-aggression" hypothesis, as well as theoretical positions that emphasize learning experiences as determinants of aggressive behavior.

Probably the most widely known explanation of aggressive behavior is the *frustration-aggression hypothesis*. According to this view, aggression is a highly probable response to a frustrating situation. Where one encounters aggressive behavior, one can assume that it has been initiated by frustration. There is some evidence to support this assumption. One study found that aggressive male pupils had fathers who severely punished aggression in the home (Eron et al., 1961). In comparing a group of delinquents with nondelinquents, Glueck and Glueck (1950) reported a higher use of physical punishment and lower usage of reasoning among parents of delinquents. We feel that these findings support the position that aggressive behavior is learned as a consequence of early childhood interactions within the family setting. It has become increasingly evident, however, that the frustration-aggression hypothesis is inadequate to account for all aggressive behavior. This theory probably applies best to particular types of individuals as well as to particular types of frustrating experiences. Recent evidence leads us to a second theory, which centers around the concepts of modeling and reinforcement.

Various authorities have emphasized the role of *imitation and reinforcement* in the acquisition and maintenance of aggressive behavior in children. According to a social-learning-theory viewpoint, exposure to aggressive models should lead to aggressive behavior on the part of the child. This view is reasonably well substantiated by several experimental studies that show that even though the subject may not have been frustrated, increases in aggression follow exposure to aggressive models. In keeping with this theory, lower-class children manifest more overt physical aggression than middle-class children do, presumably because the lower-class model is typically more overtly aggressive. McCord, McCord, and Zola (1959) noted that boys who had deviant parental models were more apt to engage in antisocial activities. In brief, both laboratory and real-life field studies generally buttress the notion that imitation plays an important role in the genesis and maintenance of aggressive behavior.

Authorities, who are aware of this modeling influence, have again become concerned about the effects of viewing violence on mass media (Liebert and Naele, 1972).

Adjustment Outcomes

ANXIETY OVER AGGRESSION

Undue concern over one's own aggressive impulses is related to repeatedly harsh punishment of aggressive behavior. The youngster characterized by this concern typically feels uncomfortable and ill at ease in situations that arouse aggressive impulses in himself or others. He usually responds with feelings of guilt, fear, self-deprecation, or embarrassment. Yet, because punishment itself is a frustration and pain, the anger the youngster experiences does not decrease, but increases, leaving him in an ambivalent and conflict-laden status. In brief, severe punishment increases feelings of aggressiveness, and this can serve to intensify his anxiety, since he has no suitable means of expression. A vicious circle is thereby established and the child — because of his psychological makeup — is denied the right to even justified anger.

UNCONTROLLED AGGRESSION

Whereas the combination of parental restrictiveness and hostility often produces neuroticlike problems in children, such as the one described above, the combination of parental permissiveness and hostility is commonly found in cases of maximal aggression and delinquency (Becker, 1964). In other words, the highest level of aggressive behavior occurs when the child is persistently subjected to conditions that promote feelings of hostility in him and at the same time fail to impose limits on his acting-out behavior when he expresses his hostility.

Although still widely accepted, the catharsis theory of reducing overt aggression, which emphasizes the tension-releasing features of emotional release, has received surprisingly little empirical support. According to this view, the release of aggressive behavior should produce a diminution of such behavior, that is, aggressive behavior should extinguish itself if allowed unrestricted expression. Actually, it appears that a permissive approach to the treatment of acting-out behavior in children achieves the opposite effect. In a permissive atmosphere, the child is less fearful of punishment and his inhibitions decrease. Cathartic release may be appropriate for withdrawn youngsters, but its use with excessively aggressive children certainly seems contraindicated. Despite the negative evidence to date, however, the catharsis theory continues to receive wide acceptance among professionals in the field.

PASSIVE AGGRESSION

Another undesirable outcome occurs in the case of the student who develops a preference for passive-aggressive modes of coping with hostility toward authority figures, such as teachers and parents. The passive-aggressive child commonly sees teachers and parents as unjust and tyrannical and himself as being badly used by those in control. Because of harsh, repressive tactics on the part of parents in early life, this child comes to fear retaliation for any direct expression of negative feelings toward authority figures. Thus, in contrast to the child who engages in open aggression through such behaviors as hitting, grabbing, pulling, and destroying, the passive-aggressive individual learns to release his anger through more veiled maneuvers. Angry outbursts give way to stubbornness, sullenness, and pouting; productive accomplishment valued by authority figures gives way to dawdling, procrastination, inefficiency, and obstructionism in the classroom. Poor academic performance together with conformity to the letter of the law but not the spirit of the law serve as aggressive acts against those who try to dominate him. This student resists teacher authority by *habitually* bringing the wrong book to class, forgetting assignments at home, losing his place when reciting, needlessly sharpening pencils when he should be working, or interrupting his work to go to the bathroom. Such children want freedom and resent being told what to do or having demands made of them. Yet they cling to

dependency. To teachers, they seem lazy, unsociable, irresponsible, and critical of others, while being overly sensitive to others' criticism of them.

Educational Implications

How should aggressive behavior in a child be handled? Very permissive handling of outbursts leads to increased aggressive activity on the child's part. If the teacher is both permissive and punitive, the child is apt to become even more highly aggressive, and perhaps even delinquent. And if the teacher is restrictive and punitive, the child will probably become socially withdrawn and intrapunitive. So neither overly strict nor overly permissive treatment seems to be the desirable way of coping with this kind of behavior. The following guidelines are offered.

1. The teacher must let the disorderly student know that his overly aggressive behavior will not be tolerated. The student must know that this behavior is out of bounds.

2. Firm, narrow, and clear-cut limits must be set. A no-nonsense, "I mean business" approach must be adopted and a specific routine should be followed.

3. To the extent that it is possible, do not leave this student unsupervised. Because of his poor internal controls, external surveillance is necessary.

4. Try to instruct him in small groups of six or less, or assign him to a work station in the classroom where he can work alone.

5. Hostile behavior must be stopped, but use techniques other than physical force if at all possible. The generation of additional frustration and anger must be avoided or minimized in the management process. Punitiveness and firmness are not the same.

6. Unacceptable aggressive behavior should result in the student's being socially isolated immediately.

7. The teacher can help promote better control in the student by setting an example of self-control. The teacher who explodes when things go wrong hardly provides a model worthy of emulation. But the teacher who remains calm and rational when frustrated does teach self-control through his example.

8. The reasons underlying the rules prohibiting certain forms of aggressive acts should be explained to the troublesome student. If the explanations are geared to the student's level of understanding, the standards for conduct become more meaningful and less arbitrary or authoritarian.

9. A teacher-student relationship characterized by warmth and personal interest also reduces the likelihood of deviant behavior. Students are less apt to offend someone they care about.

10. The acting-out student must be taught that such behavior is inappropriate under certain circumstances, but acceptable at other times and places. Pushing and shouting is unacceptable in the classroom and lunch line, but appropriate in football games and tug-of-war matches. Remember that the objective of socialization is not to squelch aggressiveness, but to direct its expression along acceptable lines.

11. In the care of the passive aggressive student, the teacher should: (a) set broad limits, (b) give the student a voice in terms of assignments and the rate at which they are to be accomplished, (c) not supervise closely but be watchful enough to reward cooperative and productive behavior, (d) ignore delay and resistance and (e) avoid direct commands and confrontations (Spaulding, 1967). The use of educational contracts is helpful in implementing the steps outlined above (see Chapter 7).

Summary

1. The school must consider personality factors in the student's makeup if it is to assist youth in realizing their intellectual, social, and personal potentials.

2. Socialization techniques that are either too severe or too lax are apt to interfere with adequate resolution of common developmental problems. Proper socialization practices, on the other hand, lead to feelings of self-worth and self-realization.

3. Excessive dependency manifests itself in behaviors such as seeking physical contact, seeking to be near others, seeking attention, seeking praise and approval, and resisting separation.

4. Instrumental dependence refers to seeking help in doing things. Emotional dependence refers to seeking personal attachment or nurturant attention from other people.

5. Dependent behavior is more likely to remain stable over the years for females than for males. This pattern of stability may change, however, as sex roles continue to change.

6. Desirable outcomes of the socialization of dependence needs in-

clude the development of a sense of trust as well as responsiveness to various forms of social approval. In this sense, dependency is a prerequisite for most future socialization. Undesirable outcomes include submissiveness, passivity, a sense of inadequacy, whineiness, and standoffishness.

7. Teachers must encourage independent behavior without frustrating or overindulging the student's dependency needs.

8. Conscience refers to the internalization of "do's and don'ts" that regulate moral judgment, conduct, and emotion.

9. The specifics of moral development are far from being fully understood, but it is clear that cognitive, child-rearing, and cultural factors play an important role in character development.

10. The student with an overly strict conscience is prone to feelings of guilt and low self-esteem. Because this student sets excessively high standards for himself, school can become drudgery as he tries to live up to his expectations.

11. The student with too lax a conscience might well encounter difficulty because of unacceptable, rule-breaking antics.

12. An optimal level of character development allows for self-realization both at the societal and personal levels.

13. A sound program of character education will address itself to the cognitive, behavioral, and affective aspects of moral development.

14. Nervous habits as well as feelings of inadequacy are commonly associated with anxiety.

15. A moderate amount of anxiety is healthy in that it promotes social and intellectual performance.

16. Anxiety that is either too high or too low appears to impair both intellectual and social performance.

17. For the highly anxious students, fears form easily, spread readily, and are difficult to extinguish.

18. The use of desensitization procedures, programmed instruction, overlearning, and a structured classroom are among the strategies beneficial to the management and instruction of the anxious, insecure student. Remember that the effects of anxiety on performance depend partly on factors under the teacher's control, such as task difficulty, type of instruction, and evaluation procedures.

19. A reasonable amount of aggression is a sign of a healthy individual.

20. The combination of frustration, hostile models, and a permissive atmosphere is most conducive to the development of aggressive individuals.

21. In coping with the acting-out student, the teachers must set firm and clear-cut limits, avoid being punitive, provide a structured classroom setting, offer an example of self-control, and explain the reasons for classroom regulations.

CHAPTER 5
Education of the Disadvantaged Child

"Due to factors beyond my control—having to do with the combined influences of heredity and environment—I was bad today and had to stay after school."
(Drawing by Saltzman, 1974)

Scope of the Problem
Scholastic Performance of Minority Groups
Explanations of Poor School Performance
Educational Interventions

Chapters 3 and 4 dealt with readiness as it pertains to children in general. This chapter focuses on one of the most ambitious undertakings in the entire range of human behavior, the development of persons who are regarded as having adjustment problems because their style of life runs counter to what might be designated as the mainstream of American life. The problem of the disadvantaged child has existed for as long as societies have advanced to a point where there are layers of organization, customarily referred to as "classes" or "subcultures." The problem is new only for those who have recently come on the scene. While the poor have always been with us, the current situation is differentiated from the past as a result of three major social and economic changes (Goldberg, 1970). (1) As the affluence of our society has spread, the poor have become a more readily identifiable minority. (2) Although, in absolute numbers, the number of jobs has increased, the nature of currently available work calls for "brains," not "hands." There is less and less employment available for the unskilled and semiskilled in our increasingly technological society. By 1985, only one fourth of the working population is expected to be engaged in goods production, and the demand for educated personnel is expected to show the greatest increase. (3) Whereas poverty was formerly widespread among several ethnic and racial groups, it has today become identified with a few such groups—the Indians, blacks, Mexican-Americans, Puerto Ricans, and poor whites from isolated rural areas. This situation has resulted in the articulation of demands by minority groups for a more equitable share in the good life.

OBJECTIVES FOR
CHAPTER 5

> **1.** Describe the various populations referred to as "educationally disadvantaged."
> **2.** Evaluate the three indices of school achievement used to measure the educational performance of minority group students.
> **3.** State the explanations advanced to account for the school performance of minority group youth.
> **4.** Describe the various educational programs designed for the educationally disadvantaged.
> **5.** Evaluate the outcomes of compensatory educational programs.

SCOPE OF THE PROBLEM

Many terms have variously been used to refer to those groups living under substandard economical conditions, such as "culturally deprived," "culturally disadvantaged," "underprivileged," "educationally disadvantaged," the "poor," and members of the "culture of poverty." Such euphemisms have been attacked as being theoretically inadequate, lacking in explanatory accuracy, and engaging in negative stereotyping (Friedman, 1967). Aside from identification in terms of socioeconomic and minority group status, there is no clear-cut conceptual or operational definition of this population. In our present state of ignorance, it is practically impossible to distinguish between those individuals who do poorly in school because of impoverished backgrounds and those who function in a similar fashion because of an inherent lack of ability to learn (Telford and Sawrey, 1967). Regardless of the term one prefers, it is important to remember that the disadvantaged are not a homogeneous group, as the common label might imply. While having poverty in common, members of the disadvantaged come from a variety of backgrounds and geographical locations.

Because definitions of the disadvantaged differ, it is difficult to obtain an accurate esti-mate of how large this population is. In America's big cities, the estimates of the proportion of persons who are disadvantaged run about 1 in 3. Granting that nobody knows for sure how many disadvantaged youth there really are, we will tentatively accept the 25% incidence figure provided by the Report of the Joint Commission (1970). Bear in mind, however, that ethnic, racial, and geographical differences are of such a magnitude that the percentage may vary from 1 or 2 in some schools to nearly 100 in others (Barbe, 1967).

Another useful way to describe the disadvantaged is to indicate their race, ethnic origin, and place of residence (Havighurst and Moorefield, 1967). In order of size, the disadvantaged may be grouped and described as follows.

1. Urban whites. These are children of Caucasian parents, some of whom are recent immigrants from Europe or rural areas while others are second and third generation urban dwellers. For example, many third and even fourth generation Italian Americans still think of themselves as Italian and perpetuate many old-country attitudes, values, and behaviors that impair their school performance.

The population of urban whites might quite appropriately be called the "invisible poor," since they are not readily identifiable on the basis of color, nor are they as geographically concentrated as certain disadvantaged groups are. Furthermore, the poor whites are far less aware of their limitations, are less organized, less militant, and less aware of the opportunities that might be made available to them. The *percentage* of underprivileged Anglos is relatively small (approximately 10 to 20%) in comparison to the percentage of poor in minority groups (about 75%), but in terms of *actual numbers,* disadvantaged urban whites constitute the largest such group.

2. Urban blacks. These are the ghetto dwellers, most of whom are children of rural migrants to the big cities. The rat-infested flats of Chicago's West Side or New York's Harlem are infamous illustrations of the plight and disillusionment experienced by the black city dweller.

3. Rural blacks. Most rural blacks live in the southern states. The shacks of the cotton hands in Mississippi reflect the poverty and disadvantage of this group.

4. Rural whites. In terms of residence, this population is about equally divided between the southern states and rural northern areas. People in the hills and hollows of Appalachia constitute the most publicized group of poor rural whites. The severity of their cultural circumstances is reflected in the fact that the average adult has a sixth-grade education and that only one in four completes high school (Frost and Hawkes, 1970).

5. Mexican-Americans. There are approximately 3½ million Mexican-Americans, most of whom are found in the Southwest. They constitute the largest ethnic group in Texas, New Mexico, Colorado, Arizona, and California. According to 1960 census data, 51% had an income less than $3000. Many have migrated to the North in search for a better life.

6. Urban Puerto Ricans. Many of these are concentrated in a few urban centers. Their economic and social mobility has been greater than that of blacks, although they constitute a sizeable group of the ethnically disadvantaged.

7. American-Indians. About 400,000 of the total 550,000 Indians live on approximately 200 reservations scattered throughout 26 states (Farb, 1968). In many respects, "the vanishing Americans" seem to be the most disadvantaged group. For example, approximately 90% live in tin-roofed shacks, leaky adobe huts, brush shelters, or even abandoned cars. Unemployment ranges between 40 and 75% and the average Indian family lives on $30 a week. The average age at death is 43 years—25 years less than for the white man. The average red man completes about 5 years of schooling, the worst record of any minority group.

SCHOLASTIC PERFORMANCE OF MINORITY GROUPS

In tests of scholastic achievement, blacks score significantly below the average for whites and Orientals. The American Indian, Puerto Rican, and Mexican-American score below whites but above blacks on tests of school achievement. The achievement gap remains fairly constant throughout the elementary and secondary school periods (Coleman et al., 1966). During the 10-month school year, low-income students as a group generally progress 7 months in reading (Report of the Joint Commission, 1970). By eighth grade, lower class youth are typically 2 to 3 years behind grade level.

The limited educational attainments of minority groups are also reflected in dropout rates, which are particularly high among some groups. For example, 60% of Indian children drop out of school between eighth and twelfth grades (Ablon et al., 1967). The dropout rate for Puerto Ricans in New York City is 70%. In the metropolitan North and West, black students are three times as likely as white students to drop out of school by the age of sixteen or seventeen. Comparative data on white and nonwhite youth show that the dropout rate among youth 16 to 21 years of age was 42% for white boys, 29% for white girls, 61% for nonwhite boys, and 44% for nonwhite girls (Federal Programs Assisting Children and Youth, 1968). As expected, those who drop out usually have a history of school failure that began early in elementary school. Leaving school might be called a "search for an alternate identity." Unfortunately, most drop out before they are exposed to occupational and vocational information and skills that could aid them in their search for a new identity. It is hardly surprising that the nonwhite high school dropout is at the bottom of today's job market.

Finally, the educational disadvantage of the poor shows up in the fact that they have the smallest percentage going on to higher education. Only about 5% of low-income students go on to college compared to a national average of 40 to 50%. While the average educational attainment levels of the poor are increasing, the percentage of both whites and nonwhites with college educations has remained remarkably stable over the past decade. More disturbing is the finding that among black sons of white-collar workers, more than 7 out of 10 went into manual occupations, whereas less than 1 in 4 of their white counterparts did so (Miller et al., 1967). The percentage of disadvantaged youth in higher education may rise appreciably in light of open admissions policies and the strong demand for but short supply of black college graduates. Whether those admitted will graduate from college will depend partly on the nature and amount of support given them.

EXPLANATIONS OF POOR SCHOOL PERFORMANCE

Various explanations have been advanced to explain the plight of the disadvantaged. These run the gamut from child-rearing practices to genetic selection. Many authorities write as though they know the basic cause(s), but too little is known to permit definitive conclusions at this time. As you will see, each of the following theories has its merits, but also its limitations. Some of the explanations presented are contradictory, while others simply supplement each other. All writers agree substantially on the facts (e.g., the high incidence of health problems among the poor), but there has been widespread disagreement and often heated debate as to the interpretation of the facts. Since the various theoretical stances have influenced the development of action programs designed to ameliorate this condition, examining their rationales can prove instructive.

Genetic Selection

The tendency for black youth to obtain below average IQ scores has been reported for more than 50 years, and the literature on this topic is vast. One recent text, for example, reported a total of 382 studies on this subject (Shuey, 1966). The data are quite consistent; on the average, blacks score about 15 IQ points below the average of the white population in IQ. Only 15% of blacks exceed the white average. These findings hold fairly true across the 81 different tests of intelligence reported by Shuey. When socioeconomic level is controlled, the average difference drops to about 11 IQ points. According to the classification system accepted by the American Association of Mental Deficiency, the average black child would be classified as a slow learner.

Blacks have fared no better on the so-called "culture-fair" tests. In fact, they tend to score lower on tests of this type than they do on the more conventional tests of mental ability. No one seems to question the finding showing that blacks score lower on traditional tests of intelligence. There is considerable debate, however, as to the causes of their lower average score.

The notion of ethnic or racial superiority or inferiority is not a new one. Even Aristotle has been quoted on this topic (Gossett, 1963, p. 6). In the United States, this controversy has centered largely around the issue of black inferiority because blacks constitute the largest *racial* minority in our country. Since the 1920s, the opinions of social scientists in the United States have undergone a dramatic reversal from general acceptance to general rejection of the hypothesis of inherent racial inferiority of blacks (Cartwright and Burtis, 1970). Today, it appears that the majority of leading American social scientists believe that there have been no scientifically demonstrated relationships between race and intellectual capacity. As expected, social scientists favor cultural explanations when accounting for racial differences in measured intelligence. Here are the conclusions reached by such professional groups as psychology, sociology, and anthropology.

"There are differences in intelligence test scores when one compares a random sample of whites and Negroes. What is equally clear is that no evidence exists that leads to the conclusion that such differences are innate. Quite to the contrary, the evidence points overwhelmingly to the fact that when one compares Negroes and whites of comparable cultural and educational background, differences in intelligence diminish markedly; the more comparable the background, the less the difference. There is no direct evidence that supports the view that there is an innate difference between members of different racial groups . . . We regret that Professor Garrett feels that his colleagues are foisting an 'equalitarian dogma' on the public. There is no question of dogma involved. Evidence speaks for itself and it casts serious doubt on the conclusion that there is any innate inequity in intelligence in different racial groups. . . ." (The Society for the Psychological Study of Social Issues, a division of the American Psychological Association, 1961)

The above quotation is not intended to convey the impression that all social scientists endorse the views of this professional organization. An increasing number of psychologists have been impressed with recent scientific writings suggesting a genetic basis for racial differences. Foremost among the new hereditarians has been Arthur Jensen, the nation's most controversial educational psychologist, whose published papers, "Social Class, Race and Genetics" (1968), and "How Much Can We Boost IQ and Scholastic Achievement?" (1969), have caused more public debate among educators and psychologists than any other two articles in recent history. It is difficult to discuss the views that he presents in these papers, especially in any telescoped way, without being misunderstood. Certainly one does not want to be misunderstood on such an important and emotional issue. Yet since the American public has been made aware of the debate through popular periodicals (*Life, Newsweek, Saturday Review,* and *Time*), it seems that prospective teachers should have some awareness and understanding of this significant issue.

In commenting on his papers before the House Subcommittee on Education, Jensen (1970) has this to say regarding the following topics.

INHERITANCE OF INTELLIGENCE

"Much of my paper was a review of the methods and evidence that leads me to the conclusion that individual differences in intelligence, this is, IQ, are predominantly attributable to genetic differences, with environmental factors contributing a minor portion of the variance among individuals. The heritability of the IQ—that is, the percentage of individual differences variance attributable to genetic factors—comes out to about 80 percent, the average value obtained from all relevant studies now reported. These estimates of heritability are based on tests administered to European and North American populations and cannot be generalized to other populations. I believe we need similar heritability studies in minority populations if we are to increase our understanding of what our tests measure in these populations and how these abilities can be most effectively used in the educational process."

SOCIAL CLASS DIFFERENCES

"Although the full range of IQ and other abilities is found among children in every socioeconomic stratum in our population, it is well established that IQ differs on the average among children from different social class backgrounds. The evidence, some of which I referred to in my article, indicates to me that some of this IQ difference is attributable to environmental differences and some of it is attributable to genetic differences between social classes—largely as a result of differential selection of the parent generations for different patterns of ability. I have not yet met or read a modern geneticist who disputes this interpretation of the evidence."

RACE DIFFERENCES

"The fact that different racial groups in this country have widely separated geographic origins and have had quite different histories which have subjected them to different selective social and economic pressures make it highly likely that their gene pools differ for some genetically conditioned behavioral characteristics, including intelligence, or abstract reasoning ability. Nearly every anatomical, physiological and biochemical system investigated shows racial differences. Why should the brain be any exception?"

THE IMPLICATIONS OF RACE DIFFERENCES IN EDUCATION

"Since educators have at least officially assumed that race and social class differences in scholastic performance are not associated with any genetic differences in growth rates or patterns of mental abilities but are due entirely to discrimination, prejudice, inequality of educational opportunity, and factors in the child's home environment and peer culture, we have collectively given little if any serious thought to whether we would do anything differently if we knew in fact that all educational differences were not due solely to these environmental factors."

Even if one accepts Jensen's basic position as to the relative contribution of genetic and environmental influences on intelligence there are certain cautions (noted by Jensen and others) that the reader should bear in mind.

1. Evidence for the heritability of intelligence is impressive, but it is less discouraging than it appears at first glance. For example, Cronbach (1969), a noted authority in the area of tests and measurement, points out that persons having the same genes are distributed over an IQ range of more than 25 points.

2. IQ or abstract reasoning ability is just one of man's mental abilities. Despite the importance attached to the IQ in our society, it is obviously not the only educationally or occupationally relevant ability. A broader assessment of the spectrum of abilities and potentials constitutes an essential aspect of improving the education of disadvantaged youth.

3. Heritability has no meaning with reference to an individual. There is no way in which the hereditary and environmental components of a given individual's IQ can be partitioned. Heritability estimates permit only a probablistic inference as to the average amount of difference between an individual's obtained IQ and the genotypic value. Group averages are of little practical value to the professional educator when it comes to planning for a specific student.

4. The primary purpose of intervention programs is not to raise IQ but to promote valuable school achievements. Fortunately, scholastic achievement appears to be much more subject to environmental influences than intelligence is. Support for this assertion comes from a study in which the relationship between IQ scores and academic-achievement scores were examined for children of varying degrees of kinship. The results in Table 5-1

indicate that environmental differences affect school achievement to a much greater degree than intelligence (Burt, 1958). Note that varying the environment of identical twins lowers the IQ correlation by only 10 points, but it lowers the achievement correlation by 22 points. Moreover, unrelated children reared together are much more alike in school performance than in intelligence. Although the heritability estimates for school accomplishment increase with grade level and are somewhat lower for relatively simple forms of learning (e.g., arithmetic computation) than for more abstract learning (e.g., arithmetic reasoning), large-sample twin data from the National Merit Scholarship Corporation indicate that 60% of the variability in high school students' rank in the graduating class is accounted for by *between families* environmental components. Jensen (1969) concludes that individual differences in school performance are determined only about half as much by heredity as differences in intelligence are. The role played by noncognitive factors (values, attitudes, habits, and motivation), which are largely environmentally determined, will be discussed shortly.

Table 5-1
Environmental Influences On IQ And Achievement

	IQ	Academic Achievement
Identical twins reared together	$r = .93$	.90
Identical twins reared apart	$r = .83$	.68
Fraternal twins reared together	$r = .59$	.83
Siblings reared apart	$r = .47$	.53
Unrelated children reared together	$r = .27$	.52

The studies reported up to this point have relied primarily on a unidimensional concept of intelligence that is quite inadequate as a basis for understanding ethnic and social class differences in ability. One landmark study of differential abilities among various ethnic and social groups is significant because of its methodological design and substantive findings (Lesser, Fifer, and Clark, 1964). In this investigation four mental abilities—verbal ability, reasoning, number facility, and spatial conceptualization—were examined in 320 first-grade children from four ethnic groups—Chinese, Puerto Rican, black, and Jewish—with each ethnic group divided into a middle and lower class. The major findings were that both ethnic membership and social class exert strong but different effects on the four different abilities tested. Whereas social class affects the *level* of performance, ethnicity affects the *patterning* of abilities (see Figure 5-1). In each ethnic group, the middle-class subjects exceed the lower-class subjects on all four mental abilities. The differences between social levels varies, however, from one ethnic group to another, with social class status having the greatest impact on blacks and the least impact on the Chinese. The rankings on the four measures of mental abilities were as follows.

Verbal ability—Jews, blacks, Chinese, and Puerto Ricans.
Reasoning—Chinese, Jews, blacks, and Puerto Ricans.
Numerical ability—Jews, Chinese, Puerto Ricans, and blacks.
Spatial ability—Chinese, Jews, Puerto Ricans, and blacks.

This study has attracted widespread attention because of its concern with the qualitative as well as the quantitative aspects of intellectual functioning. The identification of differential deficits and strengths in the functioning of disadvantaged populations constitutes a more constructive approach to the study of ethnic group differences in intelligence than the reporting of a single, quantitive score.

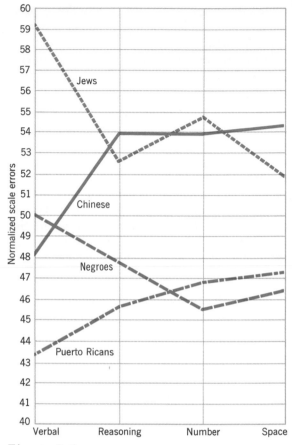

Figure 5-1.
Patterns of normalized mental ability scores for different ethnic groups. *(From Lesser, Fifer, and Clark, Mental Abilities of Children from Different Social-Development, 1965, 30, Ser. No. 102. Copyright © 1965 by The Society for Research in Child Development, Inc. Used by permission)*

Prenatal and Postnatal Medical Care

Inadequacies of prenatal and postnatal care are highly related to the incidence of prematurity, birth defects, mental retardation, infant mortality, and other disabilities. For example, inspection of the medical histories of children with adjustment problems revealed more complications of pregnancy and a greater incidence of prematurity than existed in a group of matched subjects (Pasamanick and Knobloch, 1966). Such complications, particularly evident among hyperactive, confused, and disorganized youngsters, also occurred more frequently in children having hearing defects, strabismus, delinquent symptoms, and school accidents.

The total impact of prenatal damage is admittedly difficult to determine, but most authorities agree that it is greater than it should be, especially among the very poor. Data from several large cities indicate that between 20 and 50% of women who delivered in municipal hospitals have had no prenatal care or have received it too late. The majority of these women came from low-income groups (A Look at Problems in Prenatal Service Programs, 1966). Chronic untreated illnesses and malnutrition were not uncommon. Health matters remain unchanged following birth. For example, one third of Indian infants die between the first month and first year of life, largely from preventable diseases. Moreover, most of the 600,000 preschoolers who attended Head Start in 1965 had never been to a physician or dentist and had not received immunizations (Report of the Joint Commission, 1970). Approximately 80% of health problems found among Head Start youth were newly discovered during attendance at these developmental centers and about 75% of these were thought to require further care (North, 1969). Even more shocking is the finding that 70% of the 16 to 20-year-old youths enrolled in Job Corps programs had never been to a physician (U.S. House of Representatives, 1965). While this country as a whole enjoys the highest standard of living in the world, the nation is far from achieving the best record with respect to health care. Obviously, promoting greater use of public-health services should help to reduce the amount of organically based factors that contribute to the marginality of potential that seems to typify members of the lower class.

Malnutrition

A great deal of publicity has been recently devoted to hunger and malnutrition among poverty groups in the United States, particularly because inadequate diets can conceivably produce damage to the nervous system and impair school performance. The existence of "hunger counties" was documented in a controversial report entitled "Hunger, U.S.A." Some of the more important findings were:

1. One fifth of United States households have "poor" diets.

2. In households of low-income levels, 36% subsist on "poor diets."

3. There are 256 counties of the United States that should be declared hunger areas.

4. The worst possible health conditions exist among migrant farm workers and on certain Indian reservations.

5. Existing federal food programs are terribly insufficient (Citizen's Board of Inquiry, 1968).

According to this report, there are some 10 million malnourished Americans. However, the Committee on Agriculture (1968) claims, on the basis of reports from health officers in these hunger areas, that there are very few hungry people in these counties. As is so often the case in research on emotionally laden issues, investigators on both sides draw conclusions and then proceed to prove them. This may well have happened to some extent in this instance.

Investigation of the relationship between malnutrition and learning ability has been hampered by a number of factors. Foremost among these are:

1. *The lack of a precise scientific definition of malnutrition.* It is not easy to identify the point on a continuum at which the human being can be considered malnourished (Frost and Payne, 1970). Identification is a relatively easy matter in the case of severe malnutrition, but a difficult judgment in the case of milder malnutrition, which is more common in our country. Certainly, everyone who craves food cannot be labeled malnourished, nor can all thin people automatically be regarded as suffering from malnutrition.

Malnutrition covers a variety of nutritive deficiencies and we must discover which, if any, of these are most closely related to the development of intellectual growth. What, for example, is the role played by various vitamin deficiencies, protein deficiencies, or limited caloric intake? No methods exist to identify and quantify the biochemical abnormalities of mild, moderate, and severe malnutrition (Eichenwald and Fry, 1969).

2. *Generalization from studies on rats and other cultures.* Most of the evidence showing a relationship between inadequate diets and retarded development has been based on animal experiments and on people from developing countries. The rat may well not represent a suitable model for the study of human development, nor do the experimental conditions resemble those typically encountered

by malnourished infants. The inadequacy of diets in developing countries is thought by most experts to be greater than that found among our poor. Whether mild or moderate malnutrition has effects similar to those associated with severe malnutrition remains unanswered.

3. *An inability to separate clearly the effects of malnutrition, infection, and social environment.* In field studies on humans, it is difficult to disentangle the effects of such intimately related factors as inadequate diet, infection, and social-emotional deprivation, all of which can produce similar physical conditions. It is known, for instance, that severe sensory and social-emotional deprivation can lead to a physical wasting away. Unfortunately, the factors listed above are commonly associated with one another, so that it is difficult to isolate the effects of malnutrition (Read, 1972).

In conclusion, grossly inadequate prenatal and infant nutrition can affect development of the brain, which attains more than two thirds of its adult weight during the first year of life. The extent and severity of malnutrition as well as its relationship to intellectual development deserves high priority in future research studies. While there is no question that malnutrition should be considered as a contributing factor to the disadvantaged child's adjustment, experts in related scientific fields caution us against overly simplistic one-factor explanations, emphasizing that enriched diets, by themselves, are unlikely to produce the dramatic improvements that are now being claimed in some quarters (Report of the Joint Commission, 1970). The "good breakfast" philosophy, although an essential part of a total intervention program, will not, in and of itself, put an end to the problems of the disadvantaged child.

Differences in Class Values

Another cluster of explanations is advanced by those who view the adjustment difficulties of disadvantaged students as resulting from value conflicts between lower-class youth and middle-class educators. Research on noncognitive factors (values, attitudes, and achievement motivation) has consistently found significant effects related to social class and ethnic group (Rosen, 1956, 1959; Miller and Swanson, 1960; McCandless, 1967). Major differences in the values of lower-class and middle-class persons in the United States are summarized in Table 5-2.

This list does not apply to all lower-class persons. A classic exception, for instance, is the lower-class Jew who, if anything, has a higher achievement motivation than his middle- and upper-class counterparts. These values are simply more common in certain social classes.

The core of middle-class culture is achievement. All resources are organized for production. Participants in the system receive an abundance of material gains—houses, cars, refrigerators, dishwashers, and hi-fi sets. The niceties of such affluence are comforting, but the actual cost of these gains is seldom objectively reckoned. Things are always going to be better, greater gains are to be expected. All the person has to do is work and keep on working. If he is not getting the benefits of material rewards, it is because he is not working hard enough. The middle-class person has his eye on the future. He is concerned with developing abstract intellectual skills for thinking and planning. He must live a carefully planned life pattern with calculated moves toward anticipated "improvement." Immediate rewards available today are inconsequential and are to be forestalled in exchange for a glorious tomorrow. To stay on his narrow, achievement-oriented path, he

Table 5-2
A Comparison Between Lower-Lower Class and Middle-Class Values

Lower Class	Middle Class
Present time orientation	Future time orientation
Preference for concrete and tangible	Preference for abstract
Adventurousness and spontaneity	Responsibleness and control
Acceptance of "fate" without worry	Use of intellect to plan and think
Immediacy or gratification	Delay of gratification
Emphasis on physical activity and the sensual, with tolerance for violence	Violence a last resort
Indulgence and low aspiration	Criticalness and high aspiration

Table 5-3

Child Rearing and Family Life-Styles More Prevalent Among the Very Poor Compared with Patterns Associated with Effective Adaptation to the Demands of Today's Society[a]

Patterns Reported To Be More Prevalent among the Very Poor	Patterns Conducive to Adaptation to Today's Society
1. Inconsistent, harsh physical punishment.	1. Mild, firm, consistent discipline.
2. Fatalistic, personalistic attitudes, magical thinking.	2. Rational, evidence-oriented, objective attitudes.
3. Orientation in the present.	3. Future orientation, goal commitment.
4. Authoritarian, rigid family structure; strict definition of male and female roles.	4. Democratic, equalitarian, flexible family structure.
5. "Keep out of trouble," alienated, distrustful approach to society outside family; constricted experiences.	5. Self-confident, positive, trustful approach to new experiences; wealth of experiences.
6. Limited verbal communication; relative absence of subtlety and abstract concepts; a physical action style.	6. Extensive verbal communication; values placed on complexity, abstractions.
7. Human behavior seen as unpredictable and judged in terms of its immediate impact.	7. Human behavior seen as having many causes and being developmental in nature.
8. Low self-esteem, little belief in one's own coping capacity; passive attitude.	8. High self-esteem, belief in one's own coping capacity; an active attitude.

must know where he has been, and more important, where he is going. Priding himself on being responsible, he is intolerant of those who do not have a shoulder to the wheel of "progress." Although many may go into debt, money is regarded as something to be cautiously spent, and one loses face if his debts are overdue.

By contrast, members of the lower-class culture place greater emphasis on "being" instead of "becoming." Believing that no one person or group can really beat the system (so why fight it?), the lower-class person's orientation is current and directed to the here and now. It makes no difference how much or how hard you might work; events are largely prearranged. This transitory orientation accounts for many significant personality fea-

Table 5-3 (cont'd)

Patterns Reported To Be More Prevalent among the Very Poor	Patterns Conducive to Adaptation to Today's Society
9. Distrust of opposite sex, exploitive attitude; ignorance of physiology of reproductive system and of contraceptives.	9. Acceptance of sex; positive sexual expression within marriage by both husband and wife valued as part of total marital relationship; understanding of physiology of reproductive system; effective use of contraceptives.
10. Tendency not to differentiate clearly one child from another.	10. Each child seen as a separate individual and valued accordingly.
11. Lack of consistent nurturance with abrupt and early granting of independence.	11. Consistent nurturant support with gradual training for independence.
12. Rates of marital conflict high; high rates of family breakdown.	12. Harmonious marriage; both husband and wife present.
13. Parents have low levels of educational achievement.	13. Parents have achieved educational and occupational success.

^a This table, because it is so condensed, may be misleading, since several topical fields have been merged (i.e., mental health, educational achievement, social acceptability, conscience formation, and family stability). For data differentiating these fields, see Catherine Chilman, *Growing Up Poor*, U.S. Dept. of Health, Education, and Welfare, Washington, D.C.: Government Printing Office, 1966.

tures of the lower-class person, who is more spontaneous and impulsive in loving and in fighting. His belief in a kind of magic makes him adventuresome and ever ready to "travel on," where he may find new friends or greater fortunes. He mistrusts anyone who approaches him to do something today for a reward promised 2 weeks or 1 month from now.

The disadvantaged child will encounter adjustment difficulties if he is expected to adapt a set of values, beliefs, and mores different from what he has acquired. When eval-uated according to the standards of his particular cultural group, he is very well adjusted. Teachers trained to work with the middle-class child may be puzzled by behaviors that only reflect differences between the values of the lower-class culture and those of the middle-class culture. It is difficult for the middle-class teacher to empathize and to communicate with youngsters whose style of life is so different from theirs. This usually operates to the child's disadvantage. As Deutsch (1960) notes, "School . . . represents society's demands that they (lower-class children) bridge social class orientations for a few hours a day, five days a week. No catalyst is provided for this transition, and few plans have been made to facilitate the child's daily journey across the chasm.''

Family Life Patterns

Like all youngsters, children in the very low socioeconomic groups are strongly influenced by the cultural patterns of the people in their environment, particularly by the life-styles of their families. Studies on family life patterns focus on unemployment, parental educational level, broken homes, overcrowding, out-of-wedlock children, and child-rearing practices. Findings from various studies (e.g., Moynihan, 1965) have concluded that families who live in long-term poverty are often disorganized and unstable. An overview of related studies strongly suggests that very poor families often fail to adopt life-styles that are conducive to successful adaptation to various aspects of today's society (see Table 5-3).

The patterns listed on the left side of Table 5-3 are not limited to very poor families, nor are they found universally among the very poor. Moreover, these patterns are not presented as an indictment of low-income parents or as an attempt to demean a whole population. Instead, these patterns are best viewed as adaptations to the poverty situation and the social structure that fosters life-styles that are hostile to favorable adjustment.

Language Differences

Many authorities feel that language differences are central to the disadvantaged child's problems, since they limit progress in school. Earlier findings in the area of language suggested that social differences in a child's cognitive functioning resulted from social class differences in the nature of parent-child relationships and modes of communication. Bernstein (1964), for example, postulated two linguistic codes—the "restricted," "public," or "limited" code and the "elaborated" or "formal"—which, although not necessarily class linked, will arise in most closed subcultures or closed communities.

Restricted codes are characterized by simple short and often incomplete sentences. The use of subordinate clauses is rare and there is less use of qualifying adjectives, adverbs, or conjunctives. Distinctions are blurred and transactions with the environment are sorted into a few simple categories. Slang and clichés, on the other hand, are quite common. Accordingly, the language of the disadvantaged student, which is "restricted," is more concrete and less precise than that of the middle-class student. It makes little difference whether a student says "What's your destination?" or "Where are you going?", because the differences in these illustrations have more sociological than intellectual significance. The more complex and precise explanation advanced by the physician—"streptococcal infection of the pharynx"—can, however, communicate finer differences in meaning than the layman's term—"sore throat." The earthiness, simplicity, picturesqueness, seeming originality, vividness, and liberal use of slang make the language of the disadvantaged student seem richer than it actually is. The freer use of language obscures its impoverishment (Telford and Sawrey, 1967).

The "elaborated" or "formal code," which is more commonly developed among middle-class children, seeks to express a wider and more complex range of thought and to make its nuances precise. In contrast to the more concrete, informal, and expressive orientation of the "restricted" code, the "elaborated" code promotes the abstract, relational, and categorical aspects of language.

More recent research indicates that Bernstein's notions of a "restricted" and "elaborated" code do not fit with the facts. Indeed, linguists are now challenging the concept of primitive language on the part of the black child. The "deficit" hypothesis might well be replaced by a "difference" hypothesis. Research by Labov (1968) on blacks in Harlem shows that the syntactic structures of Negro speech and standard English are basically the same. Cross-cultural studies also indicate that social groups do not differ much in the fundamentals of language.

If the difference hypothesis is correct, what implications might this have? It might suggest that compensatory education programs are based on the faulty assumption that poor children need remedial training in language (Ginsburg, 1972). The teacher must come to view educational difficulties as a difference, not as a disability. There is no need to create new skills. Instead, the teacher must get the child to transfer skills he already has to the task at hand (Cole and Bruner, 1972). Finally, assessment of poor children's linguistic competence requires the study of the nonschool style of language (e.g., verbal insults), which may reveal the richness of middle-class youth (Houston, 1970).

Inadequacies of the Schools

SCHOOL FACILITIES

Without denying the experiential deficits in the early childhood of the disadvantaged youngster, some authorities place the blame for the academic retardation existing in depressed areas directly on our educational institutions. A leading spokesman for this viewpoint is Kenneth B. Clark, who emphasizes the school's role in producing equality of scholastic accomplishment. According to this theory, there would be minimal, if any, differences among middle- and lower-class students if we had better teachers and expanded educational resources. Inferior academic performance is not explained by any deficits the student has when he enters school. It is a result of poor teaching by a rejecting staff. It is the educational system and not the learner that must be overhauled. Clark (1965) charges that contemporary theories of social deprivation have (1) merely substituted notions of environmental immutability and fatalism for earlier notions of biologically determined educational unmodifiability, and (2) obscured the real reasons for the educational retardation of lower-status children. As Clark (1965, p. 131) states: ". . . these children, by and large, do not learn because those who are charged with the responsibility of teaching them do not believe they can learn, do not expect that they can learn, and do not act toward them in ways which help them to learn." Criticisms of the schools have generally centered around the need for curriculum change (e.g., multiethnic urban-oriented reading series), decentralization of school control, desegregation of educational facilities, modification of teacher attitudes (from rejection and fatalistic negation to a belief in the educability and dignity of disadvantaged youth), and for change in teacher preparation programs.

The above position certainly seems tenable, but research studies do not always substantiate the plausibility of this viewpoint. The research on school desegregation, for example, reveals rather inconclusive evidence of a relationship between ethnic integration and achievement (St. John, 1970). Some studies do suggest that black students perform better in nonsegregated schools. Other studies, however, indicate that racial integration *per se* is not significantly related to school achievement. Research studies to date have not been adequately designed to permit a firm conclusion. The following questions are illustrative of those unanswered by current studies. Were the integrated students a superior group to start with? (This question could be answered by randomly assigning bussed students to integrated and segregated schools, but politics and parental preferences have not permitted this.) How long lasting is the stimulation or embarrassment associated with "guinea pig effect" or being a newcomer in a group? (This issue could be resolved through longitudinal studies that follow up the adjustment made by students, but no such study has been done to date.) Is it segregation-nonsegregation that is most important or the *quality* of education, regardless of the racial composition of the class? (This is a particularly thorny problem because of the difficulty involved in equating schools on quality.) Conclusive answers to issues such as these must await adequate real-life tests conducted on large-scale, long-run studies of top quality schooling in segregated and desegregated schools. The hypothesis that the academic performance of minority group children will be higher in integrated than in equivalent segregated schools provided that they are supported by the staff and accepted by the peers is certainly plausible, but it remains a hypothesis at this time (St. John, 1970; Armor, 1972).

Evidence from the Coleman Report (1966), a $1¼ million nationwide survey conducted by James S. Coleman, a sociologist with long-standing ties with the field of educational research, even challenges the notion that school facilities for minority children are inferior to those for the majority. This landmark project, which included more than 645,000 students and 60,000 teachers in 4000 public schools, prompted the conclusion that on the basis of such indicators of school quality as teacher-pupil ratio, number of volumes per student in the library, laboratory facilities,

and teacher qualifications, school facilities for minority and white students are remarkably alike. No consistent advantage was found for any particular group, and differences in the quality of education available to the various racial and ethnic groups were small when compared with differences between the geographical regions (Northeast, Midwest, South, Southwest, and West). In terms of these indicators of school quality, the educationally disadvantaged in our country are not the racial or ethnic minorities, but youth—regardless of race—living in the South and in the rural North. Variation in school facilities and curriculum, as defined in the Coleman Report, is not as closely related to pupil achievement as we might believe.

In summary, some authorities believe that we in the United States have come closer to realizing the goal of equality of educational opportunity than most people realize (Mosteller and Moynihan, 1972). Others vehemently disagree. Still others contend that quality education will not reduce socioeconomic inequality, since schools are not well suited to solve the poverty problem (Jencks, 1972). The idea that schools can be a tool of social change is hotly debated today.

TEACHER EXPECTATIONS

There is some evidence to indicate that teachers do hold different attitudes toward advantaged and disadvantaged students. Yee (1968) in his study of 50 schools in the San Francisco and central Texas areas found that on the whole, the teachers of disadvantaged children held more negative attitudes toward teaching and toward their students than teachers of advantaged children. Teachers of the disadvantaged showed "traditionalistic and inflexibly negative attitudes toward child control," while teachers of the advantaged showed "a more permissive, positive and flexible attitude" (p. 278). As the school year progressed, classroom interactions with disadvantaged youth become more and more teacher dominated, students become more conforming, the classroom atmosphere grew colder, and school became less appealing. The teacher's attitudes of warmth and permissiveness have a greater impact on the attitudes of lower-class children than on middle-class children. It is interesting to note that seasoned teachers (9 years or more experience) were more negative than inexperienced teachers. This study emphasizes the need for teachers to pay closer attention to the affective needs of poor youth.

One aspect of teacher attitudes—teacher expectations as it influences student achievement—has generated considerable controversy. The best-known study in this regard was conducted by Rosenthal and Jacobsen (1968), who reported that a teacher's expectations of a student's intellectual abilities, through unknown but presumably subtle ways, are communicated in a way that elicits the expected performance. Because of the severe criticism of this study (Thorndike, 1968; Snow, 1969), more carefully conducted research must be carried out before a definitive resolution of this issue can be achieved. Even more damaging to the self-fulfilling prophecy theory is Barber's (1969) report that five attempts to replicate the Rosenthal and Jacobsen finding failed to uncover any evidence substantiating the debilitating effects of teacher expectations. The above studies certainly do not preclude the need for and the possibility that future overhaulings of the educational system will foster the educational progress of disadvantaged students. Many authorities do recognize, however, that we must overhaul the students as well as the educational system if we are to advance the scholastic achievements of lower-class youth. A one-pronged approach will not do the job.

Conclusion

Like other complex and multifaceted problems confronting behavioral scientists, the plight of the disadvantaged can be approached on different levels. We can, for instance, attack this problem from a psychological, sociological, or biological vantage point. Because it is virtually impossible from a practical standpoint to investigate all aspects of the problem simultaneously, various professional specialties have approached the problem, with each stressing certain determinants.

Given our current fund of information, social class differences in behavior leave open a broad spectrum of possible interpretations. At one end of the continuum, there is the genetic school of thought whose views, although speculative, probably merit more attention than they have received. Research in this area has been neither encouraged nor welcomed because of our social and political values as social scientists. Edward Zigler, who was the first director of the Office of Child Development, put it this way:

"The continuing neglect of genetic considerations now that psychology has matured is probably related to the American ethos. The egalitarian tradition of the United States has unquestionably contributed to the absence of research on possible genetic influence on social class differences and to the near-absence even of discussion that might lead to it." (Zigler, 1970, p. 100)

At the other extreme, there are those who view social class differences in behavior as the sole consequence of variations in the social environment. The sociological-ecological position emphasizes a variety of environmental determinants. According to this view, the complex of factors that cause and perpetuate the woes of the disadvantaged are mostly beyond the control of poverty-stricken individuals, who might be viewed as a kind of fallout resulting from rapid technological advances in our country. Inherent in this approach is a concern over such community phenomena as prejudice, poverty, unemployment, poor medical services, inadequate educational programs, variations in value systems, the plight of cities, social organization, and family instability. The major treatment thrust takes the form of massive, federally financed programs designed to correct the major deficits in the social system.

A third view—the psychological approach —also involves environmental explanations. This approach differs from the sociological-ecological approach, however; it focuses more on the individual's problem than on community shortcomings. Psychological explanations also differ from sociogenic explanations. They seek specific and internal (personal) causes, while the latter offers broad causes external to the individual. Among the factors seen as influencing the disadvantaged child's adjustment are undesirable child-rearing practices, poor self-concept, feelings of alienation and despair, a need for escapism, and undeveloped intellectual-linguistic capabilities. The child's psychological makeup is such that he encounters difficulty in trying to meet his needs for security, acceptance, and status. Because the disadvantaged child's condition is viewed as a psychological disability, correction of the problem is generally sought through (1) efforts to change child-rearing practices that affect linguistic, cognitive, and personality development and (2) individual counseling, which is designed to overcome the personal problems that prevent an adequate adjustment to society.

Somewhere between the extreme genetic and the social-psychological interpretations lies an interpretation that stresses the interaction among a variety of forces. A child's development is not solely or primarily the result of his genetic makeup, his class member-ship, or specific child-rearing practices. Instead, development is the product of long-term, continuous interaction of a multiplicity of forces within the individual, his family, and community. We might like to believe that relatively simple, one-factor, short-term, inexpensive solutions will remedy the problems of the disadvantaged student, but such a view overlooks the fact that human development cannot be enhanced unless all of its aspects are recognized and treated simultaneously in a coordinated way, especially during the early years of life (Report of the Joint Commission, 1970).

EDUCATIONAL INTERVENTIONS

The problems of the disadvantaged cannot be reduced or prevented unless there is a coordinated, simultaneous attack on all the factors involved. A total program would mean that: free, high-quality education from preschool through vocational and university training must be available to all youth; the poverty environment must be radically altered through adequate housing, recreation, and other community services; adequate job opportunities and wages in both the public and private sectors must be forthcoming for the unemployed and the underemployed; public assistance must be sufficient to provide a decent living and administered in a way consistent with human dignity; free, high-quality, physical and mental health and social services must be offered for those who cannot afford them; and the disadvantaged must be accorded equal voice in the planning and development of these and other community services (Report of the Joint Commission, 1970).

While acknowledging that all of these services are essential in dealing with the problem, our discussion will be delimited to the programs that, if not educational in the traditional sense, have had very close association with the schools. We will examine various approaches employed by the schools in honoring their responsibilities to children of poverty.

Most attempts at educational intervention for remedying the problems of the disadvantaged have been directed to the correction of deficits in language, motor, or general experiential areas. Educational procedures are based on the premise that such disabilities can be compensated for by providing an enriched or an adjusted environment. For discussion purposes, programs are divided into those at the preschool level and those geared to older youth.

Preschool Programs

The downward extension of educational programs to the preschool poor has received encouragement and support from many sources. Included among these are political decisions, organizations dedicated to preschool education, current social commentaries, and a strong belief in environmental determinants of ability. Among psychologists, it was Bloom's analysis of longitudinal studies of the development of intelligence that constituted the fundamental rationale of Head Start and other preschool programs for intellectual stimulation of the disadvantaged. On the basis of his review, Bloom (1964) concluded that the preschool period is a time of extremely rapid mental development and that environmental influence will have its maximum impact on intellectual development during its period of most rapid growth. As a child matures, Bloom believes that more intensive intervention efforts are needed to produce a given amount of change in a child's intellectual performance—if it can be produced at all later—and that the emotional risks are likely to increase. Cognitive stimulation can, how-

ever, to an appreciable degree, overcome deprivation up until the period of stabilization around age six or seven. Bloom estimates that the difference between an impoverished and an enriched environment is conservatively 20 IQ points. A difference of this magnitude could easily mean the difference between special class or regular class placement as a child and between a semiskilled or a professional job as an adult. It is easy to see why Bloom's views have had a tremendous impact on the development of preschool education.

Although interest in preschool programs has been increasing markedly, there is a considerable divergence of thought among psychologists upon whose models preschool practices are based. This is to be expected, since early childhood education is still a fairly new field.

HEAD START PROGRAMS

It is impossible to discuss preschool education without focusing on Project Head Start, which was initiated in the summer of 1965 and patterned after the most common model available at that time—the traditional preschool program. More than ½ million children were enrolled and a staff of more than 100,000 paid and volunteer workers were involved. In the fall of 1965, these services were extended to full-year programs in certain centers. By 1967, more than 2 million youngsters had taken part in over 13,000 centers at a cost of $220 per child enrolled in summer programs and $1050 per child in the full-year programs. These centers have been distributed evenly over rural and urban areas, but the urban centers have tended to be larger, accounting for 60% of Head Start youngsters. Over 40% of these children are black, 20% are white, 10% Puerto Rican, and the remaining 20% are spread out over Mexican Americans, American Indians, Orientals, and

Eskimos. Head Start programs vary from center to center, but their common goal is the enhancement of the child's intellectual performance, his social attitudes, and his self-esteem. Consistent with these objectives, the educational programs included medical, nutritional, dental, psychological, and social service components.

Class enrollments in Head Start programs cannot exceed 15 children. Generally, there is one teacher, one paid aide, and at least one volunteer per class, so that there is at least one adult for every five students. Classes operate 3 to 4 hours per day except for full-day programs that operate a minimum of 15 hours per week as required by federal guidelines. The typical day consists of such activities as breakfast, dramatic play, blockbuilding, creative experience with unstructured activities (e.g., painting), informal experiences in language, music, and literature, outdoor work and play, cleanup, and lunch. This program is similar to the routines followed in conventional nursery schools.

The Head Start programs also sought to capitalize on the influence of the parent as a source of attitudes about school and to train the parent to become an effective teacher in the home. Training with the parent was carried out through observation of and participation in the preschool classes, through regular home visits made by visiting teachers, through small-group classes, which mothers may be paid to attend, or through some combination of these methods. Instruction given the mothers ranged from pointing out the advantages of regular school attendance to specific ways of improving work-habit skills of children. The concern of Head Start was with the child's total environment. There have been failures as well as successes, and the programs have drawn both criticism and praise. The most general criticism has been that many of the gains achieved through compensatory preschool programs have washed

out by the time the child completes kindergarten or first grade. Much of the benefit is apparently lost when children enter the regular grades. This indicates the need for follow-through programs that extend beyond the preschool programs.

By far the most extensive evaluation of Head Start was carried out for the Office of Economic Opportunity by Westinghouse Learning Corporation and Ohio University. The basic question posed by the study was: To what extent are the children now in the first, second, and third grades who attended Head Start programs different intellectually and socially from comparable children who did not attend? To answer this question, a sample of children from each of 104 Head Start centers who were now in first, second, and third grades was matched with a control group who had not attended Head Start. The battery of tests given consisted of three cognitive measures (school readiness, academic achievement, and language development) and three affective measures (self-concept, desire for achievement, and attitudes toward school, home, peers, and society). The major findings were that: (1) Summer programs seemed to be ineffective in producing any gains in intellectual and personal-social development that persist into the early elementary grades. (2) Full-year programs appeared to be ineffective in promoting personal-social advances, but were marginally effective in producing gains in cognitive development, which persisted at least in grades one to three. The programs appeared to have a greater impact on certain subgroups of centers, notably in predominately black centers, in scattered programs in core cities, and in southeastern centers. Although the magnitude of most of these differences were small, they were statistically significant and indicated that the programs evidently had some limited effect on youngsters who had attended full-year centers. (3) Head Start youngsters, whether from summer or full-year programs, still scored considerably below national norms on standardized measures of language development and academic achievement, although school readiness at grade one approached the national norm. By the end of third grade, their academic achievements on the average fell almost 1 year below the national average. (4) Parents of Head Start enrollees voiced strong approval of the program and its impact on their youngsters. Parents also reported substantial involvement on their part in the centers' activities (Westinghouse and Ohio University, 1969).

Aside from the limitations inherent in the study, it should be noted that the Westinghouse study constituted only a partial evaluation in that it did not attempt to assess the effects of Head Start on medical or nutritional status, family life, on the total community, on the schools, or on the morale of the children. Among the broader benefits of Head Start are a forced attention to the instructional problems of poor youth, the development of new teaching materials, the identification of children whose problems of physical and psychological health might have otherwise gone unnoticed, the establishment of new techniques and broader concepts of evaluation, the creation of new careers for professionals and paraprofessionals, and increased enthusiasm and support from those parents who had been alienated from the schools (Evans, 1971).

There is still much to be learned about viable preschool programs, but the evidence regarding full-year programs suggests that we might be on the right track. Implementation of the following recommendations should lead us closer to the development of effective programs:

1. Convert summer Head Start programs into full-year or extended programs.

2. Full-year programs should

a. Be extended downward toward infancy and upward into the primary grades.

b. Vary teaching strategies with the characteristics of the students.

c. Concentrate on the remediation of specific deficiencies identified through diagnostic study.

d. Train parents to become more effective teachers of their children.

3. Develop experimental programs to assess the adequacy of new approaches. Innovations that prove successful could then be instituted on a larger scale.

4. The agency conducting the dual research and teaching missions should be granted the organizational autonomy and identity necessary for such experimental programs (Westinghouse and Ohio University, 1969).

A PIAGETIAN-DERIVED PRESCHOOL

The Piagetian preschool program to be described is similar to other innovative programs in its focus on the attainment of specific cognitive objectives, but it differs dramatically in that (1) many traditional nursery school materials and activities are used to accomplish its goals, (2) a broader range of activities (play, aesthetic pursuits, construction projects, and social exchanges, as well as strictly cognitive pursuits) are relied on, (3) placement of logically sequenced activities is guided by a theoretical framework, (4) self-directed exploratory learning and manipulation of classroom materials are preferable to direct, didactic instruction strategies, and (5) a greater emphasis is placed on social interaction within the peer group as a means of enhancing qualitative aspects of intellectual development. What follows is an account of one exploratory preschool curriculum based on Piaget's developmental stages (Sonquist et al., 1970).

The basic rationale of this Piagetian-derived program is that compensatory preschool programs can best build a solid foundation for intellectual development by ensuring that the potential of early stages are fully realized. Viewed in this manner, the function of the preschool centers around the facilitation of the transition from peroperational intelligence to concrete operational thought.

For Piaget there are three areas of knowledge, each based on a different source of feedback. There is (1) physical knowledge — the child's understanding of the external world — which is based on feedback from the results of actions on objects; (2) logical knowledge, which is based on the internal consistency of the child's thought, and (3) social knowledge, which is derived from associations with people. Although discussed separately, all three areas must be integrated in the actual classroom. With this caution in mind, let us illustrate how these three kinds of knowledge might apply to preschool education.

Physical knowledge at this stage of development means learning about the properties of objects by discovering how they react when acted on in different ways. How do young children learn about the nature of matter? Through a variety of actions (crushing, dropping, folding, pushing, blowing, kicking, smelling, opening, stretching, cutting, floating, squeezing, pouring, hitting, breaking) on various objects. As a consequence of such actions and observation of the results, the young child gradually comes to know much about his physical world, particularly its regularity. The young child can handle questions involving predictions (What will happen if . . .?), but questions involving explanation (Why did this happen?) are beyond his comprehension (Kamii and Radin, 1970). Although preschools can benefit from observing the changes that result from direct action on objects, the teacher should also avoid transformations that are too difficult for young children (e.g., the changing of water into steam).

Piaget distinguishes between two kinds of logical constructions — logical-mathematical relationships and spatio-temporal relations. It is not the function of preschool education to teach concrete operations, but to lay the foundation for their eventual development. The following outline provides a convenient overview of the two types of logical knowledge and their subcategories.

1. Logical-mathematical reasoning.
a. Classification (uniting, disuniting, reuniting).
b. Seriation (comparing and ordering).
c. Numbers (arranging, disarranging, rearranging).
2. Spatio-temporal reasoning.
a. Spatial relationships.
b. Temporal relationships.

We will attempt to convey the flavor of a Piagetian-derived approach by examples of methods used to teach the prerequisites for logical-mathematical reasoning.

Classification. The ability to classify is fundamental to intellectual development and success in school from the very first day at clean-up time on through high school biology. There are a variety of ways in which preschools can provide classification experiences. Children can group objects by the situation to which they belong because of physical proximity (e.g., chalk and blackboards). This is the first principle of unification and the easiest type of grouping. Classification can also be based on what the child does with the objects. A third type of classification entails the abstraction of the objects' characteristics (e.g., sorting blocks by color or by shape). The objects used for sorting purposes should be those already familiar to the children.

Seriation. Seriation skills can also be developed. The simplest seriation task involves the ordering of sizes (the big, the bigger, and the biggest doll). To begin with, the child must be given experience in making comparisons between objects of two grossly different sizes (big steps and little steps, big trucks and little trucks). When the ordering of two sizes has been mastered, the child is given objects of three or more sizes to order. The use of dramatic play can make the seriation tasks interesting. Using the same basic approach, comparisons can be taught regarding the ordering of other qualities, such as hardness and loudness. A wide variety of materials and activities should be used in teaching the prerequisites for seriation.

Numbers. One of the basic difficulties that the preschool child must overcome is his tendency to quantify a set of objects by the amount of space they occupy. Establishing one-to-one correspondence is the first strategy used. Linear ordering is one helpful activity in this regard. Using two identical sets of heterogeneous objects, the teacher arranges one set in a line and asks the child to make a copy with the other set. Linear ordering forces the child to focus on each object separately and decreases the likelihood that he will base his numerical judgments on the size of the space occupied.

Once numerical equivalence has been established by one-to-one correspondence, games involving the addition and subtraction of objects are introduced. To lay the foundations for reversible thought, the teacher can arrange objects in one configuration (e.g., a straight line), disarrange them (e.g., a pile), and then rearrange them. Note that during the preschool years, stress is placed on the importance of the child's own actions on the objects instead of on language development.

Piaget's rich descriptive data, which depict the general stages of intellectual growth as well as the development of certain specific fundamental concepts (e.g., matter), have provided a framework for sequencing preschool activities geared to promote cognition. Seen in this perspective, the broad goal of the compensatory preschool is to facilitate the transition from sensorimotor acts to concrete thought, which the child will need once he enters the primary grades. How successfully the Piagetian-based preschool lays the foundation for concrete reasoning is not yet known, but this approach is receiving enthusiastic support as a generally superior framework for early childhood education.

Programs for Older Youth

Preschool programs are essential if young disadvantaged children are to realize their educational potential. At the same time, we clearly need to modify existing programs beyond the preschool period to reach the even larger body of older disadvantaged students.

Alterations in existing educational programs for older youth have stressed one or more of the following innovations:

1. Project Follow Through was implemented in 1967 in an effort to sustain the modest gains made in preschool programs for the disadvantaged. In support of a philosophy designed to promote educational alternatives, 19 "program models," each reflecting somewhat different intervention orientations, have been subsidized. These "planned programs," although not totally different from one another, differ along dimensions such as structure, parental involvement, and cognitive orientations. Early anecdotal reports have been optimistic, but only time and objective evaluation of this ambitious plan will determine its real effectiveness (Evans, 1971).

2. Curriculum enrichment is becoming a popular provision for the disadvantaged whether or not the students have had prior preschool experience. Three general types are evident in the curriculum of the various programs (Barbe and Frierson, 1967). *Cultural enrichment* emphasizes activities such as field trips and often an expansion of offerings in music, art, and drama. The *enrichment of communication skills* is a second stated objective of most programs. It concentrates on the development of all or some combination of skills involving speaking, reading, listening, understanding, and feeling. *Enrichment of academic skills* such as reading, arithmetic, and writing is also found in numerous programs throughout the nation. The objective is to modify the materials and present them in a way that will make students with limited backgrounds more receptive to classroom offerings. The use of multiethnic, urban-oriented reading series is one example of this kind of modification.

As is evident from the above description, developing curricula for the disadvantaged need not call for a repudiation of the traditional bases of curriculum planning. A new emphasis, not a new course, is needed (Crosby, 1967).

3. Many schools now attempt to hire teachers who are better prepared in teaching procedures appropriate to the disadvantaged learner. Special teacher training programs such as the Elementary Internship Program at Michigan State University can provide extended internship experiences (the junior and senior years) in inner-city schools.

4. Parental and community involvement is also characteristic of many programs. Home visits by staff members, individual parent counseling, parental visits to schools, field trips with parents, informal group meetings, discussion panels, Big Brother Movements, and the hiring of community-school directors are among the most prominent techniques used in promoting closer ties between the community and the school.

5. Work-study programs have thrived at the high school level. Although these programs vary considerably in terms of specifics—the type and extent of supervision, kind of job, amount of pay—the objectives are remarkably similar: (1) to provide for a better articulation between classroom learnings and work experiences; (2) to establish desirable work habits; (3) to enhance self-esteem; (4) to sustain youth on their way to graduation; (5) to offer adequate work models (parent images) for those who often have none; and (6) to provide economic assistance (Spiegler, 1967). While we must await evaluation of work-experience programs, it does appear that they provide a second chance for alienated youth to enter the achievement-oriented, competence-based mainstream of American life.

6. A diverse staff is another way of providing for the educational needs of disadvantaged youth. In addition to administrators and regular teachers, ancillary personnel include nonprofessionals, remedial teachers, librarians, psychologists, counselors, social workers, and volunteer workers.

7. In recent years there has been an urgent concern expressed on behalf of disadvantaged college youth. To facilitate the adjustment of these students, colleges and universities have reexamined admissions policies, supplemented present academic skills through subfreshman, noncredit, or remedial classes, established special centers (e.g., Equal Opportunity Programs), provided additional financial aids, offered tutorial assistance, added courses on various phases of black culture, and provided professional counseling of an educational, vocational, and personal nature. The idea of special help for "high-risk" students at the university level is far from new, but the focus on the disadvantaged is of recent vintage.

8. Adult education programs are becoming more available for those who cannot achieve the American Dream through graduation from college. The basic purpose of adult education is to help people better prepare themselves for their present positions and for new occupations (Campbell, 1967). Many of the classes are held in college buildings; this helps to give adult students a sense of dignity. Much remains to be done to persuade the disadvantaged to avail themselves of adult education programs, even though enrollment in these programs is increasing daily.

How effective are educational programs for older minority group students? It is too early to reach a conclusion regarding the results of work-study programs and those at the college level, but the evidence regarding programs at the elementary and secondary levels has not been highly encouraging. For example, none of the special programs in New York City have been able to demonstrate consistent gains (Goldberg, 1970). The widely hailed Higher Horizons project failed to produce significant effects on academic achievement (Terte, 1965). Similarly, the value of the New York City More Effective Schools program emphasizing smaller classes, ancillary staff, different instructional materials, and the like has been questioned following objective evaluation (Fox, 1967). Perhaps it is unreasonable to expect consistently favorable outcomes from programs that were so often put together on enthusiasm and humanitarianism rather than on technical know-how; based on training periods that were too brief; presented too late in the developmental period; influenced by political pressures; and characterized by lack of any consistent approach. In many instances, a school's efforts have been held back by public opinion, by the prevailing influence of the family, and by attitudes and practices in the community. Once public acceptance of the need for change is forthcoming, the school should be better able to produce change.

Just as it is well to be benignly skeptical of overly optimistic findings, it is probably best to avoid being overly pessimistic about current research findings. The study of cognitive processes is, after all, still a relatively new field, one very much in its formative stages. As our knowledge about cognitive development advances, we will hopefully be in a better position to offer programs that can have a significant impact on the lives of minority group children. To discredit compensatory programs at this time would be illogical and unwarranted.

Future Trends

What does the future hold in the way of compensatory education programs for the disadvantaged? This is a difficult question to answer with any degree of certitude, but it looks as though innovations will center around parent education programs, the development of day-care centers, a greater emphasis on noncognitive factors in adjustment, and pluralism in the curricula.

PARENT EDUCATION

A number of recent projects suggest that parents are able to develop skills that contribute to the education of their young children. Merle Karnes (in press) reports impressive results in an infant tutorial program at the University of Illinois in which parents from impoverished homes were trained to enhance the educational development of their children. The Mothers' Training Program began in 1967 with 20 mothers and their children ranging in age from 1 to 3 years. The mothers, who generally spent 2 years in the program, met on a regular basis as a group and learned the skills necessary to teach their children at home. At home, the parents set aside a regular time for daily training sessions with the child. Staff members made home visits at least once a month to check on progress of the mother and child and to help with any problems. The results were impressive, with significant gains reported in IQ and linguistic performance.

The Florida Parent Education Program (Gordon, 1969) is based on the following assumptions: (1) language develops best from observing adult models and by exposure to such models in the home; (2) attitudes toward learning are acquired primarily at home; (3) the parents' self-esteem, attitudes toward school, and expectations for success influence the child's performance, attitudes, and self-esteem; (4) children learn best when home and school share in the educational experience. It is interesting to note that children who watched Sesame Street the most and learned the most were those whose mothers watched with them and discussed the program with them; (5) parents themselves gain in self-esteem and feelings of competence when they see they are capable of teaching others; and (6) parents will continue to promote the child's growth after the formal program ends.

Although the preliminary findings on parent involvement have been encouraging, there is another force on the horizon that may well go in the opposite direction of parent involvement and teaching. This is day care.

THE DAY-CARE BOOM

Because of the importance attached to the early years of life, some preponderantly negative evaluations of Head Start programs, the pressure from women's liberation groups, black militancy, and the push from the federal government for people on welfare to be-

come economically independent, we expect intervention programs to be introduced at an earlier age and extended over a three-year age span (ages three to six). Few authorities in the field doubt that the day-care business is in for a mighty boom. As Zigler notes, "It is coming to America in giant strides." (Newsweek, 1970) Many believe that the federal government will eventually finance the general expansion of the day-care network. Since day care means different things to different people, the types of programs may well run the gamut from glorified baby sitting in somebody's home to a franchised center where the curriculum is defined by educational experts and the books audited by profit-minded businessmen (Newsweek, 1970). Concern has been voiced over the quality of day care because of the rapid and unregulated growth envisioned. While most experts would concede that children could prosper in a well-planned and lovingly staffed center, they also recognize that it will be difficult to insure quality day-care programs. However, the several propelling forces noted above will most likely lead to the establishment of an unprecedented number of day-care centers in the United States.

NONINTELLECTIVE FACTORS

Cognitive objectives will continue to have a high priority in compensatory programs, but increased attention will be directed to nonintellective factors that influence adjustment. Zigler, who accounts for changes in the quality of intellectual function on the basis of change in the child's motivation, believes that affective processes are more malleable than cognitive processes. The latter may lose much of their plasticity after the third year of life. According to this view, changes in motivation, together with a concerted attention to skill development, can produce at least limited shifts in cognitive achievement. It is not

"Good-morning, pre-head starters . . ." *(Drawing by Henry Martin. From* Phi Delta Kappan *Magazine, 1969)*

that the character of the basic cognitive processes is actually changed, but that other changes, such as motivation, enable a child to use his potential more effectively.

Increased attention must also be devoted to changes in a student's attitudes. Most people lose their jobs or otherwise encounter difficulty because of attitudinal deficits, not because they lack technical skills. Arguing with the boss, coming to work late or leaving early, fighting with co-workers, an inability to delay gratification, and the like all detract from an individual's ability to adapt successfully in a middle-class culture. Even if schools were able to increase the average disadvantaged student's intellectual and educational attainments to a point where they were on a par with the average middle-class student, the minority-group student would still be apt to encounter adjustment difficulties because of nonintellective differences between himself and his middle-class counterpart. Future innovations will probably include more emphasis on affective changes, starting in the preschool and continuing throughout the student's educational program.

PLURALISM IN THE SCHOOL CURRICULUM

Although it is probably necessary to expose the minority-group student to certain middle-class values (e.g., motivation to achieve) if he is to be more fully accepted, there is at the same time a need for a pluralistic educational philosophy that will enable him to develop his own unique characteristics and values in order to develop a sense of pride in his own identity (Goldberg, 1970). Many voices are decrying the total imposition of a middle-class value system on the disadvantaged. They say this approach is an attempt to rob the ghetto child of his identity. There appears to be considerable merit to a pluralistic philosophy, but there is also the danger that too strong an emphasis on the minority member's unique characteristics and values could result in increasing his isolation, thereby decreasing the number of options open to him in his future (Goldberg, 1970). Some balance between the current common curriculum and a curriculum more specifically designed to foster a sense of uniqueness, a sense of identity, and a sense of power and control seems a realistic and desirable approach to a difficult and delicate problem.

As Mathias et al., note (1970), let us hope that when the historians of the next century examine the crises occurring in education during the latter half of this century, they will not speak to our inability to provide the kinds of mass education that we have come to expect by tradition as part of heritage.

Summary

1. The problems of minority groups have received increasing attention as a consequence of three major social and economic changes in our country—the spread of wealth which made the poor a more readily identifiable minority, an increased demand for trained personnel who could assume responsible positions in a technological society, and the articulation of demands by minority groups for more equitable treatment.

2. Because definitions of the disadvantaged vary, it is difficult to agree on the extent of the problem. An estimated incidence of 25% is probably realistic.

3. Poor urban whites constitute the largest single group of disadvantaged, while the American Indian appears to be the most impoverished group.

4. In addition to language differences, perceptual deficiencies, physical and concrete forms of expression, and a low self-image, the disadvantaged as a group are further characterized by lower scores on IQ and achievement tests.

5. Attempts to explain the problems encountered by the minority child in school run the gamut from genetic formulations to inadequacies in the schools. Like other complex and multifaceted problems

confronting the behavioral sciences, social class differences in school performance can be attacked in various ways. Professional specialists often account for the problem in terms of their particular competencies and biases when, in fact, social-psychological difficulties of this magnitude rarely have a single cause.

6. One explanation that has stirred heated debate centers around the inheritance of intelligence. There seems little question but that inheritance does play a significant role in intellectual development among people who have been raised in reasonably stimulating environments. It is not clear, however, as to the relative contribution that genetic influences make for individuals reared under adverse environmental circumstances. Furthermore, school achievement, in contrast to intelligence, seems more subject to environmental than genetic influence.

7. Social class differences in values, particularly those relating to school achievement, determine to a large extent whether a student will be successful in his formal educational encounters.

8. Child-rearing practices and family life-styles among lower-class families are often not conducive to successful adaptation to the demands of today's society.

9. Because of the importance attached to verbal facility in standard English in our schools, differences in language patterns have come to be viewed by many authorities as central to the disadvantaged student's academic retardation.

10. Research on such factors as school desegregation, teacher expectancies, and the quality of school facilities has failed to show a clear-cut relationship between these factors and student achievement. There is evidence indicating that teachers do hold different attitudes toward disadvantaged youth, but cause-effect relationships between teacher expectations and scholastic attainment are not well understood at this time. These findings, of course, do not preclude the possibility that future investigations will more clearly delineate relationships between suspected shortcomings in the schools and academic accomplishment.

11. We know that health problems are more common among the lower classes, but we do not know in any precise way what impact these problems may have on school adjustment.

12. Any serious efforts to alleviate the problems associated with poverty will undoubtedly require a coordinated program of services.

13. Although programs of educational intervention now exist on all educational levels, national attention has been focused primarily on preschool programs.

14. Head Start programs, as a group, apparently have not lived up to their original promise, but they have given an impetus to preprimary education. The year-long programs, as well as those that are highly

structured and cognitively oriented, have yielded the best results. Even though the results have not been altogether glowing, we should not be unduly disheartened, for these were our first efforts and some of them were hastily conceived and implemented. It should also be remembered that the amount of time that children spend in summer Head Start programs constitutes less than 2% of their waking hours from birth to age six.

15. The Piagetian-based programs emphasize intellectual attainments.

16. Future innovations could well center around parent involvement and teaching, the expansion of day-care centers, increased stress on noncognitive factors in adjustment, and pluralism in our curricula.

PART III
LEARNING AND INSTRUCTION

CHAPTER 6
Learning:
Process and Theories

"It wouldn't be so bad if you had to learn something you already knew once in a while." *(Drawing by Reg Hider from* Today's Education, NEA *Journal, 1973)*

The Learning Process
Two Theoretical Traditions
Functionalism, Dimensional Analysis, and Models

Everyone spends much of his lifetime learning, in the ordinary experiences of life or in school. There is much to learn, and it is doubtful if anyone learns as well as he should or as much as he could. Perhaps the major concern of teachers is how learning, especially school learning, can be made as effective and efficient as possible.

Teachers study children's efforts to learn knowledge and skills to help them to do better. Psychologists have also studied learning under more carefully controlled conditions to better understand learning and how it may be improved. This chapter is the first of several about the ideas and findings of psychologists that teachers can use to help students learn.

OBJECTIVES FOR CHAPTER 6

1. Define learning and distinguish it from performance and behavior.
2. Define the stimulus and response elements of learning and describe the role of these elements in examples of learning.
3. Describe the phases of the learning sequence and give examples of the methods teachers sometimes use to help learners during each phase.
4. State the necessary conditions and describe the sequence of events in (a) classical conditioning and (b) instrumental conditioning. Give examples of each from (a) the laboratory and (b) real life.
5. Suggest several methods of (a) encouraging insight and (b)

OBJECTIVES
Continued

discouraging fixation. Illustrate these from your experience.

6. Use the concepts of "life-space" to describe the way you have been influenced at some time by your experience.

7. Describe the differences in the teacher's activities when arranging for: (a) the formation of associations, (b) the strengthening of a desired response, (c) the occurrence of insight, and (d) the cognitive restructuring of an area of experience.

8. Identify the learning theories that might be credited with recognizing the importance of such factors as learner activity, reinforcement, repetition, knowledge of results, understanding, the specification of objectives, the organization of course content, goal setting, and the learner's perception of himself.

9. Explain the difference between a theoretical and a functional approach to the study of learning.

10. Differentiate between models and theories and state two reasons models are more widely accepted and less controversial.

THE LEARNING PROCESS

This section describes characteristics of the learning process that are not dependent on what is learned. Three approaches are used that define learning, identify common elements of learning, and explain the sequence of events in the process.

A Definition of Learning

Everyone has some understanding of learning, but a more formal definition of learning is needed to separate examples of learning from other behavioral events.

Learning is the process by which one's capability or disposition is changed as a result of experience.

Several concepts of this definition require further clarification. We describe learning as a *process* of change rather than a product. The products of learning include facts, concepts and principles, skills, attitudes and values, and behavior of various kinds. As a process, however, learning has some common features that may be studied regardless of what is being learned. This is our concern now.

The distinction that we suggest between process and product is not always made, even by writers of professional texts. Different learning outcomes may be referred to as different varieties of learning (Gagné, 1970). This approach appears similar to our common tendency to speak as if the products or the subject matter, for example, English, mathematics, and foreign language, were the learning.

Our definition of learning indicates that the products of learning include both what one is capable of and what one is predisposed to do (after Gagné 1970, p. 3). Again, other authors may refer only to changes in behavior (Garry and Kingsley, 1970, p. 10; Hilgard and Bower, 1966, p. 2). Demonstrating that one does something now that he did not do previously is, in fact, the only way learning can be proved objectively. Nevertheless, we also know that one does not always perform just because he has learned and is capable. In some instances one's attitude or predisposition restrains performance. Not everyone who can use algebraic notation for the solution of time and distance problems will do so. Sometimes the opportunity to behave in ways that demonstrate a learned capability does not arise immediately. For example, you may learn some new concepts from this book today. This change may not be exhibited in changed behavior until you are quizzed on the material, or perhaps not until you are in a teaching situation. Learning is central, within the individual and not always observed in behavior.

Finally, not every change in capability or disposition qualifies as learning, not even every change that is the result of some type of experience. Changes in the individual that come about as a result of his growing older, larger, or stronger do not qualify as learning. Many such changes are the product of the interaction of heredity and learning.

Changes in capability that are related to experience in a sense but are not considered learning include those that result from exercise, fatigue, exposure, deprivation, overindulgence, and the use of drugs. Because of these possibilities, some psychologists prefer a definition of learning that specifies changes that result from training or practice (Garry and Kingsley, 1970, p. 10) or "reinforced practice." (DeCecco, 1968, p. 243) Reinforced practice may be read here as practice with satisfying consequences. The clearest examples of learning are surely associated with deliberate practice or instruction. Restricting our definition of learning to such examples would have the disadvantage, however, of appearing to commit us prematurely to particular theoretical explanations of learning that emphasize repetition and reinforcement

as necessary conditions for learning. It may also exclude some examples of informal learning that we wish to consider.

Elements of Learning

Examples of learning differ yet each has three basic elements (Gagné, 1970, pp. 4-7): (1) the learner, (2) the stimulus or stimulus situation, and (3) the response. The investigation or management of learning is concerned with the variables, that is, features of these elements that may be changed. In this section, the elements of learning are briefly defined to clarify the terms we will be using in this chapter and those that follow.

A *stimulus* is an object or event in the learner's environment that affects the sense organs of the learner. More than one stimulus, that is, stimuli, occurring at about the same time, are referred to collectively as the stimulus situation. The sense organs of the learners transmit nerve impulses to the central nervous system. There the impulses are interpreted and translated into nervous or muscular responses. Of course, the internal portions of this process are not observable. We are describing the way the learner is presumed to react to the stimulus in responding.

The *response* is simply the nervous, including mental or muscular, activity of the learner that results from stimulation. Because the precise nature of nervous and muscular activity is often difficult to observe and describe, we frequently refer instead to the effects of this activity, which we call a performance. Learning is commonly inferred from the observation of a performance following exposure to a stimulus situation. The precise movements of the organs of speech that result in the pronunciation of a new word are not easily seen or described, for example, but the effect or performance, that is, the sound of the word, is. Now we will consider the relationships of stimulus, learner, and response in several phases of learning that have important implications for instruction.

Phases of Learning

There is a sequence of events in learning. Any example of learning may be viewed in terms of five phases or stages: (1) attention, (2) perception, (3) acquisition, (4) retention, and (5) transfer. The interaction of the learner with stimuli of the environment at each stage is somewhat different; and differences among theoretical explanations of learning have arisen partly because particular theorists concentrated their study on some phases of the process to the relative neglect of other phases. A broader view is useful in the management of instruction. An awareness of implications of the importance of each stage also helps one maintain perspective with respect to the contributions of psychologists with differing theoretical orientations.

ATTENTION

As an initial phase of learning, attention may be considered a necessary preparatory *set*, a readiness for some stimuli rather than others (Travers, 1967, p. 417), which may sometimes be checked by observing what a learner looks at or listens to. A young boy watches a baseball game through the window and does not hear the question about geography. A young lady appears to be concentrating on others' clothes, hair styles, or makeup; she does not see the fascinating (to the teacher) solution to a problem in geometry. Neither has begun the process of learning as expected because of an inappropriate attention set. On the other hand, the reader of this text has (we hope) been looking at new terms, information, and ideas, instead than, for example, scanning the page for errors in spelling or punctuation, as a publisher's proofreader would be set to do. Attention prepares students for the perceptual phase of learning.

PERCEPTION

In this phase of learning the input to the senses is registered and meaning is added. The result, that is, what is perceived, depends partly on prior learning and partly on what stimuli or parts of stimulus situations one attends to. The student who has learned to identify the parts of a flower, for example, still perceives a flower differently at different times. He may perceive petals, sepals, pistils, and stamens in his botany class because his attention is directed to them; in his art class, he may attend to the same flower as a beautiful whole.

Perception is not just a matter of differentiating and registering the information in one's environment. It often involves a complex interrelating of information from the environment and information retained from prior learning. A small amount of new information from the environment may be combined with what one already knows and believes to form a view of situations and events. This accounts for why several witnesses may give quite different accounts of the same incident. Even if all observed the same thing, each would use different internal information to complete a perception in which the observed and inserted elements would be almost impossible to separate.

The student's perception of a situation has affective components also. Thus, a spelling bee may be an enjoyable game to one child, a threatening ordeal to another. In managing the perceptual phase of learning teachers attempt to see the learning situation through the eyes of the student. They may ask questions such as: Can he make the necessary discriminations? Is he attending to the right things? Will the significant features of the situation be evident to him? Does he find it attractive, uninteresting, or threatening?

ACQUISITION

This is the phase of learning in which one acquires a new capability or disposition. Before he could not (or was not disposed to) make some response to a perceived stimulus; now he can (or will tend to).

Although the place of the acquisition phase in learning is conceptually quite clear, it is difficult to separate from the perceptual phase that precedes it. Some psychologists suggest that perception includes seeing the way to achieve one's goals. With this "insight," learning is said to be essentially complete. One has new knowledge of ways of responding to a situation. In our efforts to organize information and theory for use by teachers, we will use the suggestions of theorists who share this view, but also those of stimulus-response or S-R theorists, who tend to believe that a response is essential to learning. In the S-R view, the consequences of one's responses is the critical factor in determining what he acquires (learns).

RETENTION

Something learned cannot be demonstrated or used unless it is retained for at least a brief time. A change in the learner's capability or disposition of no duration would be trivial, if it could exist, and unworthy of further consideration. The products of learning of concern to psychologists and educators can be recalled or reinstated for use for at least a brief time.

There is evidence for two types of retention: short-term and long-term retention (Adams, 1967; Travers, 1970, pp. 144-163). Short-term retention is demonstrated when we hold information just long enough for im-

mediate use. We recall, for example, a telephone number, an address, directions for assembling a toy, or similar information just long enough to use it. Short-term memory functions in perception when we hold information about the stimulus situation in mind until we complete our inspection of it.

When the products of learning persist beyond an immediate occasion for their use, from a few minutes to a lifetime, long-term retention is observed. Long-term retention is clearly intended in education, although we sometimes differentiate between what needs to be retained only long enough to expedite further learning and what needs to be retained permanently.

Little is known about the physiology of retention, but there is reliable evidence that our efforts to improve retention should give attention to what is learned initially and how this learning is organized, to the distribution and type of practice or review, and to what is learned before and later.

TRANSFER

All educational efforts aim for a carry-over from one performance, topic, course, or level to another or from school to life. When learning in one situation helps (or hinders) us in mastering another and different situation, transfer has occurred.

Logically, transfer cannot occur unless there is some permanency to the effects of initial learning; hence, transfer and retention are closely related phenomena. In theoretical questions concerning the permanency of learning, retention refers to later reproduction of learning products in situations exactly like that in which the original learning occurred, whereas transfer refers to the effects of learning in different situations. In reality, however, no two situations are exactly alike, so any demonstration of retention must involve transfer to some degree.

In questions concerning the retention and transfer of school learning, there is an important distinction to be made between merely reproducing something previously learned and using the products of learning. Retention, but little transfer, is required when a learner is asked to recall information in the following manner. Give the formula for the acceleration due to gravity. List the names of the astronauts who have walked on the moon. Outline the steps we learned for preparing a slide for the microscope. Run through the scale you practiced yesterday. Show me the preliminary adjustments to be made in this audiometer before using it for a hearing test.

In contrast both retention and important and significant transfer must occur when learners apply previously learned knowledge and skills in new tasks. A child just developing a concept of dilemma may use it to classify a situation in which he wants to work for better marks, but knows his friends will taunt him if he does. A Scout who has learned that combustion requires a supply of oxygen arranges his paper and sticks to create a draft for his campfire.

In a more complex example, that of finding approximately how long it will take a heavy object to reach the ground if it is dropped from an airplane at 31,000 feet when the airplane had a downward velocity of 128 feet per second, the student might recall the formula for distance in terms of velocity and time ($d = Vt$), that for the space traveled by a freely falling object ($s = \frac{1}{2}gt^2$) and the value of 32 for g. Then he might conclude that d and s should total 31,000, substitute values into an equation combining the formulas for d and s, transfer terms, and perform other operations in conformance with principles that have been learned for the solution of equations.

A distinction is sometimes made between lateral and vertical transfer (Gagné, 1970, pp. 335-338). Lateral transfer is observed when a student is better able to perform other somewhat similar but novel tasks of about the same level of complexity. For example, the student who learns that a triangle with sides of 3, 4, and 5 is a right triangle can use this knowledge to check the squareness of a box he is building, a post, or the baseball diamond. When he learns the word pregame, he may be able without further instruction to give the meaning of preview, preschool, preset, presoak, preamble, and many other new words.

Vertical transfer occurs when the products of earlier learning are used to learn more complex or advanced things. One uses addition, subtraction, and multiplication in learning the more advanced skills, such as long division. Many learning tasks involve a hierarchy of concepts, principles, and skills. The simpler or more fundamental ones lay the basis for easier learning of others.

Transfer is not always helpful, of course; it has a negative as well as a positive side. Negative transfer occurs when old learning interferes with new and makes it more difficult. Learning new acts in old situations often leads to such problems, for example, when a driver changes from an automatic to a stick shift, or when a boy discovers teachers prefer "he doesn't" to "he don't," or when a science student uses the wrong formula in the solution of a problem.

The conditions that improve acquisition and retention generally lead to superior transfer also. Recommendations relating to transfer in later chapters relate to topics such as (1) learning products that have the greatest potential for transfer, (2) set or intention to transfer, (3) practice in situations similar to those to which transfer is desired, (4) avoidance of interference, and (5) sequential or cumulative learning.

The process of learning begins with attention by the learner, proceeds with his perception of the stimulus situation and acquisition of new knowledge or response, and leads finally to retention and transfer. All of these phases appear to be involved in any learning, although the prominence and duration of each varies. For some learners attention, perception, and acquisition appear to be appropriate and immediate; others hesitate, linger over these phases of the process, and need help with them. Retention may last for a few minutes or a lifetime, and transfer does not occur until the occasion for it arises.

TWO THEORETICAL TRADITIONS

Theories are the result of man's seemingly insatiable desire to organize his world in a meaningful way. Essentially, a theory of learning is a systematic interpretation of observations about learning. In other words, it is an attempt to explain the "how" and "why" of learning. Typically, a theorist proposes a general description of the course of learning and an organized set of laws or principles relating the variables of learning situations.

Two theoretical traditions in psychology have guided most attempts to find principles of learning of wide applicability. *S-R associa- tion theories* have been the most popular in America. Theorists with this orientation examine the way the learner reacts to changes in his external environment. They present learning as a matter of establishing or changing an association between the learner's responses and the stimuli that prompt or reinforce him. "Conditioning" and "behaviorism" are other terms frequently applied to association approaches, although each of these terms has another, somewhat more restricted meaning.

The second general class of theories will be called *cognitive theories*, although the terms "goal-insight," or "field" theory are used

somewhat similarly. These theories focus attention on events inside the learner as well as on those of his environment. Each learner is assumed to have a different mental organization of knowledge built up from past experience. Learning involves an internal reorganization of knowledge that integrates new material or experiences with material previously learned. It is described as a change in the learner's knowledge, understanding, or "cognitive structure," not in how or when he responds.

The usefulness of either S-R of cognitive theories lies in their making clear the conditions that lead to the prediction and control of learning. For the teacher this means the achievement of educational objectives. The "truth" of each type of theory may be considered a function of its usefulness. No theory is completely true, but in a given context the one that summarizes, predicts, explains, and allows for the control of learning better than its competitors is "truer" for that situation.

The major evidence for theories of learning comes from the laboratory, and many factors of importance in school learning have not been taken into account. Consequently, whenever we attempt to apply theories in the classroom, there is the risk of error. Nevertheless, it may be argued (by those who have to make decisions in practical learning situations) that theories that have support in some situations are worth consideration in others. They may at least suggest how to start "experimenting."

A second argument for the teacher's knowing and using psychological theories is that he has the same urge to simplify and generalize as the psychologist. If a teacher is not guided by the psychologist's views, he will probably form a "theory" of his own that has far less to recommend it. All too frequently it will be based on folklore, intuition, trial and error, or uncritical imitation.

We believe, too, that teachers must know

something about theories in order to understand professional literature and to evaluate the frequently heard charge that this or that practice is based on an outmoded or discredited theory, or equally insistent claims that proposed changes are in line with the "new psychology." Actually, few educational practices can be so sharply separated in terms of psychological theory, but in each instance, the teacher will want to satisfy himself that this is the case.

S-R Association Theories

Association is one of the oldest concepts in psychology. It can be traced to the Greek philosopher Aristotle, who lived in the fourth century before Christ, and it was popular with a distinguished group of British philosopher-psychologists of the eighteenth and nineteenth centuries. These early associationists did *not* focus on stimuli and responses, however. They were concerned about how ideas are associated in the mind. That is why their views are considered "unscientific" or "primitive" by modern associationists. They asked questions such as, "Why is it that one thought leads to another?" or "Why do we tend to associate 'eggs' with 'Easter,' for example, or perhaps with 'ham' instead?"

Although they were not S-R theorists in the usual sense, the early associationists did suggest several principles that were later incorporated into S-R theory. They agreed on the importance of contiguity, for example. Ideas or events that occur together in experience tend to be associated so that the later one suggests the other. There was general acceptance also of the principle that a single simultaneous occurrence would not establish a permanent association. In instruction one should plan to have ideas that are to be associated occur together again and again. As we have seen, repetition is recognized today as an important factor in learning.

German associationist Hermann Ebbinghaus (1913) helped to give associationism an experimental base. He amassed an enormous amount of data on the time that it took him to learn and relearn series of nonsense syllables, such as ROP, FIM, JIX, and so on. He provided the first curves of retention to show how the amount of learning retained decreases with time, and investigated the factors influencing the learning and retention of verbal associations.

About the same time that Ebbinghaus was making associationism more experimental, physiological studies of the nervous system showed that some nerves transmitted information about the environment from the sense organs to the brain, and others transmitted information from the brain to the muscles that responded. This insight led psychologists to begin to think of learning as the formation of associations between stimuli and responses: modern S-R associationism was born.

When association psychologists study the way stimuli in the environment affect observable behavior, they can be considered *behaviorists*. Associationists of the 1920s, such as J. B. Watson (1930), insisted that the psychologist should concern himself only with behavior that could be directly observed. His approach to the study of thought, for example, was through subvocal movements of the speech organs. Present-day associationists have generally moved away from such extreme behaviorism, and they admit the presence of *intervening variables* or variables within the learner that affect the relationship between the observed stimuli and responses. They continue to believe that investigators should study behavior that can be seen and measured in some way, however, and that any worthwhile psychology of learning must depend on such observations. In this respect they are behaviorists.

CLASSICAL CONDITIONING (STIMULUS SHIFTING)

A puff of air will make the eyelid blink. Now, if a musical tone is sounded each time air is about to be directed into the eye, the tone alone will come to cause the blink. The simplest type of S-R associationism, *classical conditioning*, has been demonstrated. The association of the response (the blink) has moved or shifted from one stimulus (the puff of air) to another (the musical tone). In the process, a new association (tone-blink) is formed. The earlier association (puff-blink) is not destroyed, of course.

The stimulus that elicits the response before conditioning (the puff) is called the *unconditioned stimulus* (US); that which becomes effective after conditioning is called the *conditioned stimulus* (CS). Before conditioning the response is said to be *unconditioned* (UR); after conditioning, when it follows the tone, it is said to be *conditioned* (CR). The use of this terminology and the sequence of events in conditioning is shown in Figure 6-1.

Pavlov and Watson. A Russian physiologist, Ivan P. Pavlov (1849-1936) and an American psychologist, J. B. Watson (1878-1958) were pioneers in the study of this type of S-R associationism. In one of his best-known demonstrations, Pavlov (1927) used a simple signal, a buzzer, just before giving a hungry dog food (US). After several such pairings, the sound occurring just before the food each time, the dog salivated (CR) at the sound (CS) alone. The response of salivation was then stimulated by the previously neutral signal.

Watson's most famous demonstration (1930) taught Albert, a child about 1 year old, to fear a white rat, which attracted him initially. Watson frightened the child by clanging a metal bar when presenting the rat. After he did this several times, the sight of the rat alone produced the response of fear. Watson's demonstration is often cited in attempts to show how some of our apparently irrational emotional reactions may be established.

Classical conditioning may be viewed as one means of arranging contiguity, or the near simultaneous occurrence of a stimulus and response. An unconditioned stimulus, such as the puff of air, is used to prompt an unconditioned response, such as the blink, in the presence of a neutral stimulus, such as the musical tone. After some repetition the response is associated with the new stimulus.

Mowrer's Emotional Conditioning. O. H. Mowrer (1960) has restudied the data of classical conditioning and concluded that only emotional responses are conditioned. Furthermore, the emotions are always one of

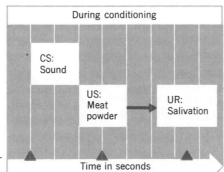
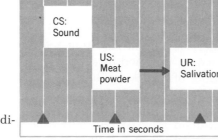

Figure 6-1.
Events in classical conditioning.

two general types: fear or "feeling bad" and hope or "feeling good." When Pavlov's dog salivated, he did so, according to Mowrer, because he was conditioned to feel hopeful; the saliva was merely an accompaniment of the feeling. Similarly, Watson's Albert was conditioned to feel fearful at the sight of the rat, and his avoidance responses were the result of that fear. Mowrer distinguishes between the conditioned emotions and the approach or avoidance responses that accompany them.

A simple example of the way Mowrer believes hope and fear may control responses is given by Bugelski (1964). A boy practicing shots with a basketball adopts a position, sets his legs, sights, flexes his arms, and releases the ball. Stimuli produced by these movements, called "kinaesthetic" or "proprioceptive" stimuli, flow into his nervous system and are present to serve as CS at the time the sight of the ball going through the basket or missing it (US) makes the boy feel good or bad (UR). If he is successful, stimuli from the previous set of muscle movements are associated with feeling good. The next time he starts to throw the ball the same way the movement-induced internal stimuli (CS) begin to occur, he will again feel good (CR) and continue to adjust his muscles to make them more like those previously successful. The more similar they become, the better he feels. If, on the other hand, the new stimuli from his muscles are not like those that have previously been successful, he will begin to feel bad. This is inhibiting. He immediately changes his movements and only feels good again when they become more like the previously successful ones. A similar analysis may be applied to any other performance.

In Mowrer's interesting interpretation of emotional conditioning, feeling good and feeling bad become associated with the subject matter or tasks of the school (conditioned stimuli) as a result of being paired with liked or disliked instructors (unconditioned stimuli). Later the student will recall and seek out subject matter or tasks that make him feel good and forget and avoid those that make him feel bad or fearful. The teacher's job, in this view, is to make students feel good about his subject. The teacher's success may be judged by what his students like to do later.

INSTRUMENTAL CONDITIONING (THE REINFORCEMENT PRINCIPLE)

About the time that Pavlov was investigating classical conditioning, E. L. Thorndike (1874-1949) undertook a series of experiments (1898) that placed less emphasis on a definite stimulus and more on the selection of responses by reinforcing them with satisfying consequences. This was the beginning of a second important theoretical tradition in S-R psychology. It was to become known as *instrumental* or *operant conditioning*.

Thorndike's Connectionism. Thorndike's research with animals and humans (1898, 1913, 1932) convinced him of the central importance of reinforcement in learning. In a typical experiment he put a young, hungry cat in a slatted box with food outside. The cat thrashed about wildly until by chance he hit a latch that won his release. If the animal was placed in the box a second time, the latch-hitting response that led to food occurred sooner. Other responses, such as clawing, biting, and scratching at other parts of the box, became less frequent. In repeated trials in this situation the successful responses tended to occur more immediately, whereas the unsuccessful ones became rare. The general rule that "S-R connections are strengthened by satisfying consequences" was Thorndike's "law of effect." As we have seen, the same essential principle is now called reinforcement.

As initially stated, Thorndike's law of effect suggested that "annoyers" weakened connections just as "satisfiers" strengthened them. Later, however, he modified this principle to place major emphasis on satisfiers and minimize the role of annoyers.

Thorndike's recognition of the role of reinforcement in response selection was probably his most important contribution, but he is also given credit for emphasizing two important preliminary steps: (1) identifying the specific response that will be reinforced in advance, and (2) keeping the learner active and attentive until that response occurs.

Skinner's Descriptive Behaviorism. B. F. Skinner (b. 1904) is the most influential of currently active reinforcement theorists. He is considered a major theorist, although he has frequently spoken out against conventional theories, including S-R approaches that make use of logically inferred intervening or internal variables. He is an avowed behaviorist, and admits to being a theorist only in the sense of attempting to interpret observed data and familiar facts in the light of scientific analysis (1969).

Skinner refers to stimulated responses as "respondent behavior" and classical conditioning, in which responses are *elicited* by obvious stimuli, as "respondent conditioning." He himself is interested, as was Thorndike, in the control of responses that seem to be *emitted* by a learner. Because the function of emitted behavior seems to be operational in or on the environment, he has termed these "operants" or "operant responses." He has written (1938, p. 2): "A respondent is a behavior affected by stimuli preceding it. An operant is a behavior affected by stimuli following it." He refers to the process of increasing the strength of operants by reinforcement as "operant conditioning." Others know the same process by the title of this section, that is, *instrumental conditioning.*

Consider a typical experimental demonstration of instrumental or operant condition-

ing. A hungry rat is placed in a small box containing a lever that releases a pellet of food each time it is pressed (Figure 6-2). The box is Skinner's own invention, designed to simplify Thorndike's box by eliminating the need for the animal to escape. First, the rat is trained to go to a tray for food. This is done by introducing a click or some other signal that is immediately followed by food. Soon the rat goes to the tray each time he hears the click. In the next stage of training, the click sounds and a pellet of food is given only when the rat pushes the lever. Before long the rat will push the lever regularly whenever he is in the box.

Stimulus Discrimination. Now suppose two distinctive stimuli, a bright light and a dim light, are alternately turned on in the box, and the rat is reinforced for bar pressing only when the bright light is on. The bright light soon becomes a cue for bar pressing, that is, it marks the occasion for reinforcement. The dim light, on the other hand, provides the cue for not responding, and the bar pressing in its presence gradually disappears; this is referred to as "extinction." The situation we

Figure 6-2.

One version of Skinner box.

have been describing is an example of "stimulus discrimination."

Skinner's brand of conditioning attempts to account for all behavior — pigeons pecking a disk, humans solving a problem, social behavior, and private awareness, as well as rats pressing a bar — by a simple stimulus-response formula. Responses (R) are made to discriminative stimuli (S^d) as a function of "contingencies of reinforcement" (S^{rein}). In our example, the bright light is the S^d that signals the appropriate time for a bar press response, because the S^{rein} of food depends on its presence. S^{rein} does not occur when the bright light is out. The term "contingencies" refers to the conditions on which reinforcement depends, such as: (1) what the response is, (2) when it occurs, and (3) the type of reinforcement given.

Response Differentiation or Shaping. The preceding example of the bar-pressing rat focuses on stimulus discrimination, or the learner's selection of the significant *stimulus*. Skinner's success with selecting *responses* is even more striking. He has called this the "differentiation of response," although it is somewhat analogous to discrimination of stimuli. The average force of the rat's press on the bar might be determined, for example, then only presses of above-average force rewarded. Soon somewhat more forceful presses would occur regularly. If, after a new average press force has become established, an experimenter were to restrict reinforcement to still more forceful presses, the rats will learn to press harder still. This process can be continued and the rat will press harder and harder until some limit, determined by the rat's size and strength, is reached.

In more dramatic demonstrations, rats have been taught such unrodentlike behavior as shooting baskets. This is done by systematically reinforcing closer and closer approximations to the desired behavior, a procedure called "shaping." After a rat has learned to press the bar of a Skinner box regularly, food would be given only when he approached the ball after pressing the lever. When this pattern is well established, the procedure would be changed so he would be fed only after touching the ball. Still later, food supply would depend on his picking up the ball. Later still, he would be fed only when he moved toward the basket; then only when he put the ball into the basket; and eventually only when he tossed it into the basket. Obviously, success with such a process requires patience and a considerable degree of skill. At each stage the new response to be reinforced must be chosen so that it is nearer the terminal behavior desired than the response that is typical at that stage of training, but still enough like what has already been learned so that it occurs often enough to permit fairly regular reinforcement. Chapter 14 describes the use of shaping to change the behavior of a student who was a discipline problem.

Reinforcement Schedules. When a response pattern is being established or shaped, *continuous* reinforcement, that is, the reinforcement of every correct response, is desirable. Then, some type of *intermittent* reinforcement may give better results. An intermittent schedule may make reinforcement contingent on some number of desired responses. This is a *ratio* schedule. An experimenter may, for example, give a rat a pellet of food after every third bar press, or a teacher may comment favorably each time a shy child has given several answers in class. Another schedule would call for reinforcement after a given interval of time has elapsed, regardless of the number of desired responses that occur in the interval. This is *interval* reinforcement. The interval may be *fixed* at every 10 minutes, every day, every Monday, and so forth, or it may be *variable*. From the human learner's point of view, he is on a fixed interval schedule of reinforcement if he can predict when

Card-playing carp has been taught to discriminate between cards and almost always selects a winning poker hand for herself. Her trainer accomplished this with reward-based conditioning. *(By Carolyn J. Strickler from "Teaching Animals—With Electronic Language,"* Popular Mechanics, *Copyright © 1970 by The Hearst Corporation)*

reinforcement will occur. If reinforcement occurs several times a day or week on an unpredictable schedule, it is variable rather than fixed reinforcement.

The fixed and variable schedules differ in the predictability of the reinforcement; the ratio and interval schedules differ in the criteria on which reinforcement is based, that is, number of reinforcements or elapsed time.

Of the several types of schedules investigated, variable interval reinforcement has proved the best from the standpoint of a high rate of responding and resistance to extinction. Either animals or students on a fixed interval of reinforcement tend to wait until the interval of nonreinforcement has nearly elapsed before responding. Students who expect a weekly quiz, for example, are on something like a fixed interval schedule. They often wait until the night before to study. When the time for reinforcement cannot be predicted, on the other hand, learners are encouraged to respond continually in order to receive the reinforcement whenever it comes. Instructors who use unannounced "pop" quizzes place students on a variable interval schedule. If the teachers using regular quizzes and the teachers using pop quizzes were to both stop giving quizzes altogether, whose students would be likely to continue studying for the longest period of time? Probably the students who had been given the unannounced quizzes would continue to prepare because they could never be sure that their quizzes had been permanently discontinued.

Types of Reinforcers. Like other S-R psychologists, Skinner distinguishes between "positive" reinforcers that present pleasure and "negative" reinforcers that remove pain. Examples of positive reinforcement that tend to increase the behavior they follow are praise, food, money, honors, applause, attention, and special privileges. In general, punishing or unpleasant circumstances are negative reinforcers, because their removal increases the behavior that precedes the removal. For example, suppose a teacher is scolding a student, the student apologizes, and the scolding stops. Because an end to scolding tends to increase apologizing behavior for this student, it is a negative reinforcer. Scolding and other forms of punishment are not always effective, however. In order for punishment to "work," the response that ends it must be a desirable one. If pun-

ishment or the threat of punishment leads to studying, fine; however, it may lead to truancy, daydreaming, or other forms of avoidance. Strong negative reinforcers, in particular, can reinforce individual avoidance behavior that is almost impossible to extinguish because each successive avoidance further strengthens the avoidance response whether or not the negative reinforcer would actually have been forthcoming. Avoiding the threat is enough. This is the reason that extinction of undesirable responses by neutral stimuli, for example, by ignoring them, is often wiser.

Applications. Skinner and his disciples have shown an intense interest in applying their knowledge of learning to practical affairs. Skinner has played an influential role in the development of programmed learning and teaching machines, which he sees as devices for the shaping of human behavior (Skinner, 1954). In addition, he has applied his principles to the problem of getting psychotic patients to respond to social stimuli (Skinner, 1957); he has written a fantasy of a utopian community (*Walden,* 1948); and, more recently, he has proposed the use of his methods to shape society in a controversial book, *Beyond Freedom and Dignity* (1971).

Skinner has been a strong advocate of a technology of teaching (1968) that emphasizes programmatic presentation and learning as a consequence of doing. Whether we use programmed texts, teaching machines, or conventional classroom procedures, our plan should be to lead students toward desired terminal behaviors by means of carefully prepared sequences of intermediate steps. The teacher, like an experimenter, must have both the desired terminal behaviors and the intermediate steps clearly in mind. An actual response by the learner at each step is necessary, because responses must occur before they can be "shaped" by reinforcement.

Cognitive Theories

The views of the theorists who will now be considered differ from those of the stimulus-response associationists in several important ways: (1) they view learning as a change in knowledge, not a change in response; (2) they more freely infer mental processes such as purpose, insight, and understanding; and (3) they believe a successful performance to be more closely related to understanding of relationships in the present situation than to past experiences.

Although the cognitive- versus stimulus-response cleavage among theories is an obvious one, you should know that it is not the only division possible. Two of the theories presented in this section, those of Lewin and Tolman, are sometimes described under "purposivism," a view of learning and behavior that emphasizes the importance of the motives or purposes of the learner. Gestalt views, and those of Lewin and Tolman also, may be classed as "perceptual field" or "phenomenological" theories because of the attention given to the way people interact with and organize the stimuli of their environment.

GESTALT PSYCHOLOGY

American psychology of the late 1920s and early 1930s was dominated by S-R behaviorism. The views of a group of German psychologists burst on this scene, as one observer put it (Hilgard, 1964, p. 54) "like a breath of fresh air." Max Wertheimer (1880-1943) and his colleagues, Kurt Koffka (1886-1941) and Wolfgang Köhler (1887-1967), believed that man's inner processes was a proper study of psychologists, and they scorned attempts to explain thought or behavior in terms of an "atomic structure" of associations.

These Germans, who all emigrated to America eventually, believed we react to our perception of patterns. When confronted with a problem, we learn, not by associating stimuli and responses, but by seeing new patterns in situations. In German, "gestalt" suggests pattern, shape, or configuration. Hence, this new view became known as "gestalt psychology."

Insight. The Gestaltists introduced the concept of "insight." This has been described as getting the point, grasping the idea, or catching on. With insight the learner grasps the essential relationships in a situation. He knows what leads to what and how to reach his goal. It often appears to occur suddenly with a feeling of discovery or understanding. Köhler (1925) reported insight in the problem solving of apes, and Wertheimer (1959) described its occurrence in the problem solving of children.

Köhler carried out many of his investigations while on Tenerife in the Canary Islands during World War I. In one experiment a banana was placed outside the cage of a hungry chimpanzee who had two sticks, each too short to reach the food. The food could be reached, however, if the sticks were joined like the sections of a fishing rod. No amount of trial and error seemed to provide a solution for the animal. When the solution did come, it often occurred suddenly, like a "bright idea." This was intelligent behavior, Köhler said, based on a perception of what was required to solve the problem. It seemed to fit the description of insight.

One of the problems Wertheimer used in his study of insight and understanding in children required them to find the area of a parallelogram. If the child really understands how to get the area of a rectangle by dividing it up into squares and multiplying the number of squares in a row times the number of rows, and he thinks about his new problem,

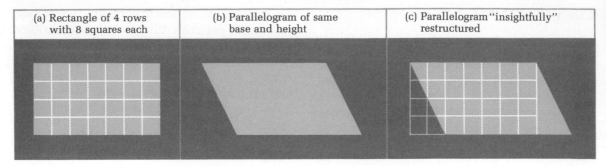

(a) Rectangle of 4 rows with 8 squares each	(b) Parallelogram of same base and height	(c) Parallelogram "insightfully" restructured

Figure 6-3.

Wertheimer's parallelogram problem. (*a*) Rectangle of four rows with eight squares each. (*b*) Parallelogram of same base and height. (*c*) Parallelogram "insightfully" structured. Parallelogram *b* is equal in area to a rectangle of the same base and altitude because the "projection" of one end may be used to "fill out" the other end.

Wertheimer said, he will be struck by the fact that a parallelogram would look like a rectangle if it were "restructured" by filling out one slanted end with a piece from the other end (Figure 6-3). When children realize this,

Figure 6-4.

The Goblet and Faces: Which is the figure and which is the ground?" (After Rubin, E., *Synsoplevede Figurer.* Copenhagen, Gyldenalska, 1917.)

they discover that the formula for the area of the parallelogram (base times height) is the same as it is for a rectangle.

Hilgard (1964, pp. 61-62) sees the insight point of view as essentially that learning proceeds better when the components of a problem are so laid out that their relations are evident and a sensible solution is possible. He finds this equivalent to learning with understanding. He points out that this gestalt emphasis has been adopted, after some transformation, by most psychologists, including those sympathetic to S-R views.

Gestalt psychologists found evidence for a number of factors that influence how we perceive a situation and whether or not we gain insight. We invariably try to impose some structure of our own that is simple, regular, and complete with no loose ends. This is the "law" or principle of "pragnanz." Regularly spaced dots, for example, are seen as a line (. . .), a triangle (. ˙ .), or a square (: :); they are seldom seen as only dots. Any perception also has a "figure" that stands out and an undifferentiated background or "ground." As long as you are interested, the print of this book is figure, but it fades into the ground as your attention wanders (Figure 6-4).

Other principles of perceptual organization were advanced by the gestaltists to help explain why some insights occur and some do not. The "law of similarity" suggested that similar words or other symbols are easier to associate and recall than dissimilar ones. The "law of proximity" suggested why Köhler's apes found it easier to join two sticks to reach a banana when the sticks and banana were placed nearer each other.

Fixation. Insight, Wertheimer and his associates found, is often delayed or thwarted by the learner's fixation on some features of the situation to the exclusion of others. Thus, the chimpanzee may never notice the stick, and we may cling misguidedly to a false premise or assumption concerning a problem we face. This is simply illustrated in the dot problem of Figure 6-5 and many other familiar "brain teasers." The problem is to connect the dots by drawing four continuous straight lines without lifting the pencil from the paper. Most people assume incorrectly that they may not extend the lines beyond the dots. If insight is the essential element in intelligent problem solving, fixation is its archenemy. How to prevent and overcome fixation is a major instructional problem to which we will return in a later chapter.

The influence of the gestalt psychologists in contemporary psychology and education is great. Their views have been transformed and absorbed into other systems, rather than neglected. We may close this section as we began it, with a reference to Hilgard (1964, p. 77), who states that the influence of gestalt psychology must be recognized whenever there are references to wholes as different from their parts, and to cognitive processes (insight and understanding) as deserving prominence in any discussion of learning.

LEWIN'S FIELD PSYCHOLOGY

Kurt Lewin (1890-1947) and his students developed a view of individual and group behavior that was a derivation of gestalt theory but more concerned with issues of motivation, the self, and personality. Like gestalt theory, field theory was a way of viewing and thinking about the way an individual may perceive the situation and himself at any particular time.

At any given time, Lewin believed, each person is steered by internal tensions that cause him to seek certain goals, objects, or conditions in the environment. Some of these tensions correspond to primary or physiological drives; others correspond to secondary or learned ones.

When a person has a goal, he often has some belief about the means by which he can attain it, about what leads to what, or which actions lead to which effects (Heider, 1960, p. 157). A person's conception of these relationships was said to be part of his "life space" or psychological "field."

Life Space. The "life space" was not described in "objective" or "physical" terms; it was said to consist of one's own perception of what is real about himself and his environment. Thus, an object or condition that does not influence a person is not part of his life space. On the other hand, something that he

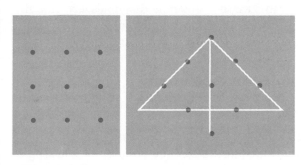

Figure 6-5.

Dot problem: Connect the nine dots by four continuous straight lines without lifting the pencil from the paper. Solution (rotated 45°) is shown in the figure on the right.

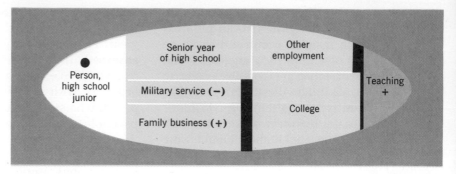

Figure 6-6.

Topological diagram of a high school junior's life space. At present the student is in high school. His goal is to become a teacher. Now he sees three regions open to him: (1) the last year of high school, (2) military service, which he sees as undesirable anyway, or (3) employment in the family business, which he thinks he might like. From his last year in high school, he could enter college or other employment, but the barrier between military service or the family business and college appears inpenetrable. He foresees some difficulty, too, in qualifying for teaching through college, although this appears to be the only route that offers any hope of reaching his goal. Note that in this geometry the sizes and shapes of the region could be greatly changed without altering the meaning of the diagram.

reacts to as if it were there is, even though it is physically absent. If you feel you are obsessed by demons, they are part of your life space. What you *think* is not seen as the key fact here; how you *feel and act* are the primary factors. If you *act as if* you fear the boss, that fear is an element of your life space, whether you realize it or not. Thus, a person's life space includes himself and everything that influences him.

A person's life space is continually changing. One minute he may be oblivious to elements of his environment that may dominate him the next. A suitor may be indifferent to a potential rival, for example, until that rival's intentions and chances are revealed.

Lewin saw behavior as the result of an interplay among the forces and other elements of the life space, including the goals one is seeking, the situations he is trying to avoid, and barriers that restrict his movements (psycho-

logically, not actually). The relationships among these elements was suggested by diagrams similar to Figure 6-6. Lewin's system is sometimes called "topological," because he also made use of a form of mathematics used in the preparation of maps.

In Lewin's diagram distances are not important, only the relationship of the regions and the difficulties of passing from one region to another. These determine what paths one may follow, and the barriers and the positive or negative nature of the region suggest the paths one is most likely to follow.

Learning Processes. Field theory shares with gestalt psychology the concept of learning as reorganization or restructuring. The structure of one's life space as he himself perceives it is a cognitive structure, and learning or insight occurs as a result of changes in this structure. Such changes take several forms.

"Differentiation" is a process of structuring or "mapping" some region of our psychological world in more detail. This is roughly equivalent to acquiring more knowledge about it. Lewin (1942, pp. 224-227) uses the example of a man who arrives at the railroad station in a strange city and does not know how to get to an apartment he has rented. This area of his life space is almost completely unstructured. As the man seeks and obtains help in finding transportation, some differentiation takes place. The apartment and the station are connected by the street car that he rides. Gradually, he finds his way about the city, to and from a new job, stores, the houses of friends, and so on. Finally, he knows how to get from one place to another in any part of the city. A previously unstructured area is now cognitively structured or differentiated. Lewin believed much of learning is a process of finding our way about some part of our life space.

Cognitive structure changes also when new elements are introduced. Suppose our man in a new city buys a car. Some old routes suddenly become more feasible for him and thus acquire new meanings. More changes occur because he thinks of going new places and doing things that he never thought of before.

Still another way in which cognitive structures change is a result of changes in our needs. The common examples involve satiation or development. We tire of most activities if they are repeated too often in much the same form. This is one reason for variety in educational activities. Our newcomer to the city soon tires of a restaurant that always offers the same fare. Likes and dislikes also change with age and physiological development. Our hero with the new car is a young man who now drives long distances to visit girls whom he ignored or avoided a few years before. Any change in the attractiveness of an activity or thing may change its meaning for us, hence, our cognitive structure.

Field psychology also introduced the "self concept" as the part of the life space that deals with one's knowledge and beliefs about himself. Lewin's student Hoppe (1931) developed the related concept of "level of aspiration," that is, the degree of success that one expects to achieve on a given task. Still other studies related to motivation suggested that people have better memories for incompleted than completed tasks (Zeigarnik, 1927) and that people voluntarily resume interrupted activities more often than complete activities (Ovsiankina, 1928). Some of the implications of Lewin's motivational contributions will be discussed in later chapters.

Practical Implications. Lewin would have the teacher begin with the learner's motives instead of with his stock of rewards and attempt to channel these motives into the available educational activities. Then the goal would be to widen and perfect the learner's life space. The psychological world to be learned is somewhat unique for each individual. His motives and perceptions are not exactly like those of anyone else. In contrast the associationists tend to posit the existence of objective reality and truth that determines "correct" behavioral goals for all learners.

TOLMAN'S COGNITIVE BEHAVIORISM

The psychological system of Edward C. Tolman (1886-1959) was cognitive and purposive. It was also a type of behaviorism. He was attracted by the problems of gestalt and field theory, but he also admired the methods of Watson. He succeeded as well as anyone in combining the advantages of the cognitive and S-R approaches.

Tolman's theory was *purposive* in that he believed that it was the search for goals that gave meaning to most behavior. He found conventional S-R accounts satisfactory for some simple, almost mechanical forms of behavior, but the rest "always seems to have the character of getting-to or getting-from a specific goal-object or goal-situation" (Tolman, 1932, p. 10). His approach was *cognitive* in that he saw learning as a method of getting to know *what leads to what*. If associations are what is learned, he reasoned that these must be associations between internal representations of situations and internal representations of actions that might be taken. In short, learning is the forming of ideas that have the nature of expectations.

Tolman was a *behaviorist,* because he believed that observable behavior and the conditions that produce it are "all that there is to be studied." (Tolman, 1932, p. 41) He firmly rejected introspection or examining the contents of one's mind as a source of data. But if he believed this, how could he write about purposes and cognitions? He did not think of these as independent variables to be observed and manipulated, but as intervening variables. He is credited with inventing a formula used by many S-R psychologists: (1) stimuli initiate behavior; (2) internal processes intervene; and (3) behavior emerges (Hilgard and Bower, 1966, p. 193).

Molar Behavior. The behavior Tolman studied was *molar* behavior, acts or performances that start from a given situation and end by changing that situation, such as when you tip your hat, bat a ball, or read a book. He was not concerned with the host of physiological changes or "muscle twitches," which he called *molecular* behavior. Molar behavior has these commonsense characteristics. (1) It is goal-directed. The individual is going somewhere or getting something done. (2) It takes place in the world of things — paths, tools, and obstacles — and it deals with these things. (3) If there is a choice, it selects shorter or easier ways of reaching goals. (4) It is changeable and teachable.

Cognitive Maps. We have said that Tolman saw learning as the acquisition of expecta-

tions that may be acquired by association. An array or network of related expectations was thought to make a "cognitive map" or "cognitive structure"; more informally, we may think of it as "knowledge of the situation." Learning occurs when one's cognitive structure changes as a result of new insights.

A motivated learner uses his cognitive maps to choose a behavior route that he expects will lead to what he desires. From this point of view the signs of Thorndike's puzzle box led his cats to expect that clawing the latch would lead to escape. Insight might be ideational "running back and forth" until a behavior route leading to the desired expectation is perceived. One's "cognitive map" of a situation may indicate a choice of behavior routes to a given objective. Each such alternative may be considered provisional, however, a hypothesis that the results of experience will confirm or deny. Practice or repeated experience strengthens expectations, not responses. Notice that "confirmation," as it is used here, suggests informative feedback instead of mechanical reinforcement of responses, and that punishment may be as informative as reward.

Evaluation. Evaluations of Tolman by psychologists and educators differ. Psychologists generally credit him with views of great promise and then lament his lack of success in providing more systematic laws and/or a more comprehensive experimental program. He has disappointed the sophisticated theorists, but this has not prevented them from incorporating many of his ideas into their own systems (Hilgard, 1964). He seems to have shamed other theorists into devising intervening variables, which are similar to expectations in their service to the learner. Several reviewers of more recent S-R developments find many of them sounding more and more like Tolman (e.g., Hill, 1964).

Several leading contemporary theorists

have continued to elaborate Tolman's view that learning is the restructuring of knowledge that takes place when we achieve insight into new materials or situations. The contributions of two of these theorists, Jerome Bruner and David Ausubel, are referred to frequently in later chapters on learning and problem solving.

Educators, including many educational psychologists, find Tolman's conclusions about learning relevant to education. His views, like those of other cognitive theorists, suggest that teachers should start with the goal of the learner and then structure their materials and methods to make it easier for the learner to understand how this goal may be achieved. In addition, we suggest the following implications of his theory. (1) Learners should be informed of the significance of different actions, but reward is *not* essential. (2) Students learn by being shown or told as well as by doing. (3) The degree of students' learning will not be evident until they are motivated to perform; hence, evaluation will not be possible in the absence of incentives.

FUNCTIONALISM, DIMENSIONAL ANALYSIS, AND MODELS

Relatively few contemporary psychologists embrace either cognitive or associative theories wholeheartedly. The theoretically "silent majority" willingly accepts the research findings of both schools, but not the explanations. The primary concern of these psychologists is not theory, but experimental relationships that show how response variables are a "function" of (dependent on) situational variables. The research findings of differing theoretical schools are accepted without the interpretations.

Some functionalists, beginning with John Dewey (1858-1952) in the early twentieth century, have been known for the stress they place on the "utility" of learning to the learner. Utility is another meaning of function. Behavior is described by this group as an adjustment to a situation. The individual varies his responses to a problem until something he does solves it. Thereafter, the solution will be quicker and more direct. Seen in this way, learning seems to be a matter of acquiring new or more useful behavior. This notion of a dynamic adaptive learner helped to popularize the concept of the "whole child" who reacts "in toto," not just with mind or body or with this or that ability.

DIMENSION ANALYSIS

One of the identifying characteristics of psychologists with functionalist leanings is a preference for "operational" definitions of terms, that is, definitions in terms of the operations of measurement. An operational definition of learning, for example, would be stated as "a measured change in performance which occurs under the conditions of practice" (McGeoch and Irion, 1952, p. 5). When we use such definitions, we neatly sidestep problems of theoretical interpretation.

Operational definitions of the variables in learning situations have aided functionalist efforts to describe learning situations in terms of their "dimensions," a term that is nearly equivalent to "factors." Examples of factors or dimensions include task complexity, meaningfulness of material, distribution of practice, and the measured abilities of learners.

The dimensional approach is data oriented, not theoretical. Established experimental relationships are highly prized, and presentations for teachers are based on explanations of how these have a bearing on the practical understanding and control of learning. A preference for dimensional analyses and exploration of relationships is evident in the work of educational researchers who investigate problems of curriculum and methods, and the authors of most comprehensive texts, such as this one, share this orientation to a degree.

The search for dimensions without theory has a weakness, however. As research goes on, a very large number and variety of relationships may be found. In the absence of overarching interpretations, how do we establish priorities among the principles on our "generally accepted" list? When learners falter, how is our attack on their problems to be organized? What do we try first? We may have masses of data and innumerable principles relating some outcomes to some inputs, but no unifying "gestalt." We may come to know much more about the trees than the forest. This is the risk of being "data crazy and theory shy."

MINIATURE THEORIES AND MODELS

Today's psychologist with a distaste for traditional theory, who nevertheless sees the need for a conceptual framework to organize his data, turns to "miniature theories" or "models." A miniature theory is intended to be useful for only a limited set of learning situations or tasks; there is no attempt to explain learning "in general." Underwood (1964) for example, has a theory specifically for rote verbal memorization of nonsense syllables. Other psychologists have developed theories of social learning by imitation (Bandura, 1969), learning subject matter presented by books and teachers (Ausubel, 1963), concept identification (Trabasso and Bower, 1968), and curiosity (Berlyne, 1954, 1966). These are only a few examples.

When psychologists wish to emphasize the tentative and speculative nature of their thinking, they often refer to a "model" rather than a theory. The term "theory" suggests a structure of known facts and principles. A "model" need be nothing but a representation of a system that is useful in understanding or studying it. Models may be physical replicas (a globe representing the world), descriptions (the account of the phases of learning in this chapter), or symbolic (a table of organization or a set of equations). They provide an "as if" picture of interactions among the elements and dimensions of events or situations without implying a truthful explanation. Models appeal to the functionalist bias because any number may be used so that we may get on with the exploration of basic relations affecting learning of different types without a commitment to any systematic theory.

Models of the processing of information as it enters and passes through the nervous system have become especially popular since about 1955 when Newell, Shaw, and Simon (1958) and Newell and Simon (1963) began work on a computer program that proved theorems in symbolic logic. Most IP (information-processing) models use computers to simulate (reproduce) human performance on particular tasks (Halworth, 1969). Many also use complex mathematics. Like miniature theories, each applies only to some very specific and limited examples of behavior. A simple model of human memory is shown schematically in Figure 6-7.

Two models of the teaching-learning process were described in Chapter 1. In comparison with psychological models of learning or information processing, teaching-learning models are simpler, more general, and less fully developed. In summary form they often present little more than a description of tasks believed critical for effective teaching and give the order in which these tasks are to be performed.

How are teaching-learning models related to theories and models of learning? It would be misleading to suggest that they are the result of orderly programs of research and developmental activities designed to translate basic theory and research into practice. The typical approach to instructional design is

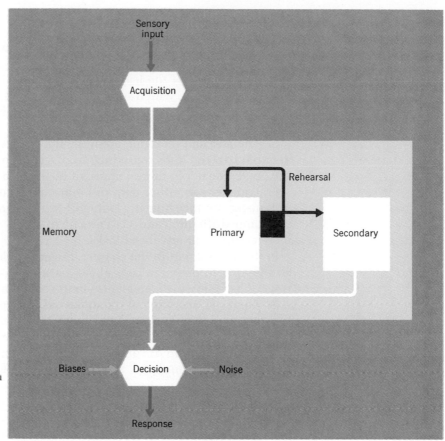

Figure 6-7.
"A Model of Human Memory." Reprinted from Norman, Donald A., *Memory and Attention.* New York: Wiley, 1969, p. 152.

more like the way automotive engineers develop a new car. Engineers do not begin with a research program to test physical and chemical principles in applied settings. Instead, they use their ideas, knowledge, and skill to build a car and try it out. An evaluation leads to changes and an improved version. Successive tryouts are used to perfect the model. Similarly, teaching models that are suggested by the developers' knowledge and beliefs about learning are tried out, revised, and perfected in educational practice.

Summary

The first section of this chapter provided an overview of the process of learning, which may be summarized as follows.

1. Learning is a *process* by which one's capability or predisposition is changed as a result of experience.

2. Three *elements* interact in any example of learning: (1) the

stimulus, objectives or events of the environment that affect the learner; (2) the *learner* himself; and (3) the learner's *response.*

3. Learning is usually inferred from performance or the effects of a response on the environment.

4. Five *phases* of the learning process are (1) *attention* to the stimulus; (2) *perception,* which adds meaning to the stimulus; (3) *acquisition* of new capabilities or predispositions in relation to the stimulus; (4) *retention;* and (5) *transfer.*

5. Transfer and retention are intimately related, but retention is predominant in the later reproduction of verbal or verbalizable information, and transfer is more important in the application of learning.

6. Transfer can either help or hinder us in later learning. Two types of transfer are recognized: (1) *lateral transfer* to similar tasks of about the same difficulty, and (2) *vertical transfer,* which prepares us for more complex or advanced tasks.

In the second part of the chapter, theories of learning were presented as attempts to organize facts about learning in meaningful and useful ways. The following statements summarize the points made.

7. There is insufficient evidence of the practical usefulness of theories, but they suggest hypotheses that merit tryout in the classroom, and they should be known if one is to be professionally literate.

8. *S-R association* or *conditioning* theorists have examined the ways responses are stimulated and changed by changes in the external environment.

9. In *classical conditioning* the near simultaneous occurrence or *contiguity* of stimulus and response is all important.

10. Classical conditioning theories have been called "stimulus substitution" theories, because an initially neutral stimulus is substituted for (acquires the response eliciting power of) an effective one.

11. Among classical conditioning theorists, Pavlov studied simple reflexes and Mowrer tried to show that conditioning of the emotions of hope and fear may control all behavior.

12. The *instrumental* or *operant* conditioning theorists have shown how responses that appear to be emitted instead of stimulated may be selected, controlled, and modified by reinforcement.

13. Among instrumental conditioning theorists, Thorndike emphasized the selection of responses in trial and error situations and Skinner contributed most to our knowledge of how the "contingencies of reinforcement" are used to "shape" behavior.

14. *Cognitive* theorists, in contrast to the S-R associationists, have found knowledge of internal processes crucial to the understanding and control of learning.

15. Among cognitive theorists:

    a. *Gestaltists* studied the factors influencing the learner's perception of situations.

b. *Lewin* emphasized motives and one's conception of relations in his "life space."

c. *Tolman* saw learning as the acquisition of expectations about situations and the probable results of alternative actions. Expectations form patterns and may be used, somewhat like maps, to plan the attainment of goals.

16. Differences among theories are related to the type of learning studied:

a. Stimulus-response views emerged from studies of the memorization of arbitrary associations in which the stimuli and responses were simple, definite and obvious, or puzzlelike situations in which a correct response was usually accidental.

b. The first cognitive psychologists selected relatively complex problem situations with "built-in" relationships or structures, which when known, permitted quick and easy solutions. Then they paid particular attention to factors influencing the learners' perception and use of these relationships.

17. We are indebted to S-R theories for recognition of the importance of (a) learner activity, (b) repetition, (c) reinforcement, and (d) the encouragement of novel behavior through "shaping."

18. Cognitive theorists have stressed the importance of (a) presentation of the perceptual and structural elements of problems, (b) the organization of knowledge, (c) learning with understanding, (d) feedback or knowledge of results, and (e) goal setting by the learner.

19. *Functionalism* is a theoretically neutral position held by psychologists who are more interested in investigating the variables affecting learner performance on a specific set of tasks than in attempting to explain all learning.

20. Functionalists define the variables they study operationally, that is, in terms of how each variable is to be measured.

21. Models are an "as if" representation of the elements and variables of a particular learning situation or set of problems. They are not intended to describe learning in general, and they do not explain it in the sense of why it occurs.

CHAPTER 7
Motivation and Attitudes Toward Learning

"Your Drive Doesn't Seem To Match Your Goals, Hudson!" *(Drawing by Phil Frank from John D. Shingleton and Phil Frank, Which Niche? 1969)*

Characteristics of Motivation
Psychological Explanations
Developing Motivation for Learning Tasks
Developing Attitudes and Interests for the Future

Motivation is a very general term for conditions that cause one to begin an activity and pursue it with vigor and persistence. In everyday terms motivation refers to the "why" of behavior, just as ability means the "can." When we question one's motivation, we assume he *can* but ask, "*Why* does he?" or "*Why* doesn't he?" Although this is the only chapter with the word motivation in its title, related material may be found throughout this book. Motivation must be considered in any discussion of behavior, but it is a major topic of Chapters 12 and 14.

A contemporary issue explored in Chapter 12 is students' freedom to choose what they will learn. The major argument for permitting students to learn only what interests them is that in theory such an approach should minimize motivational problems. The counterargument is that students do not always make the choices that will be best for them and society. Colleges and employers require specific competencies, and there would seem to be advantages in acquiring these in an efficient, organized way. A desirable balance between freedom and control must be sought. We will refer to this problem again, but this chapter will help teachers arouse and maintain student interest in a structured curriculum with limited options, while minimizing conditions that will cause students to resent or dislike learning.

OBJECTIVES FOR CHAPTER 7

1. Describe several general characteristics of motivation that are essential to an understanding of its meaning and effects.
2. State the characteristics of programs designed to increase students' "achievement motivation."
3. Discuss three theoretical explanations of motivation.

OBJECTIVES
Continued

4. Describe four elements of a general program for developing motivation for school learning and recommend instructional practices related to each.
5. Tell how competition and cooperation may be used effectively.
6. Outline a strategy for analyzing especially difficult or perplexing problems in student motivation.
   Recommend principles and procedures for developing attitudes and interests to motivate students to continue learning independently.

CHARACTERISTICS OF MOTIVATION

We have stated that motivation refers to the "whys" of behavior. The following is a small sample of motivational questions.

Why does a baby creep?

Why does a child run fast?

Why does Johnny try to learn science?

Why doesn't Johnny use better English?

Why do students demonstrate?

Why do teachers strike?

Why do men land on the moon?

We can learn several things about the meaning of motivation by examining such questions closely. (1) Motivation is inferred from observations of behavior. (2) Motivation gives direction to behavior. (3) Motivation energizes behavior. These assertions will be explained, and then we will examine several other characteristics of motivation that are not so immediately evident.

Motivation Is Inferred

Motivation and ability are the two most widely used explanations of behavior. They are alike in that neither can be observed di-

rectly. How do we know whether the Johnny mentioned in our list of questions was motivated or not? We only see his performance. The answer is that if Johnny performs as expected, we *infer* that he had both ability and motivation. If he does not, we infer that either motivation or ability was lacking. If we have reason to believe he has the ability, then we conclude he lacks motivation.

The concepts of ability and motivation were related historically in the efforts of Binet and Henri that led to the development of the first IQ test. Their problem was to separate those students who failed to learn in school because they *could not* from those who failed because they *could but would not*. Their solution was the development of a test of school-like tasks. Those who performed well on this task were said to have school ability; those who did not were said to have low mental ability compared to their age or grade mates. A natural assumption in this work was that those who demonstrated adequate mental ability on the test, but did not perform in school, did not want to perform well, that is, they were not motivated.

Motivation Directs Behavior

The study of human behavior in relation to any activity, including each of those mentioned in our list of questions, suggests clearly that some persons move toward it and participate in it while others tend to move away. We infer, therefore, that our motivation directs us toward some activities and away from others.

In school some students move toward the challenge of new ideas while others do not, preferring the security of the familiar. Some seek good grades and adult approval; others find their rewards in a youthful "counterculture." Adults seek or avoid work, sports, concerts, parties, and any of countless other activities, each according to his motives.

Motivation Energizes Behavior

Motivation implies action and effort, not merely approach or withdrawal. From the standpoint of the teacher, motivational questions include those about how to increase the vigor or effort of learning activities, not merely how to get students to participate. Thus, motivation is seen as a matter of degree. It may be weak, moderate or strong, and this degree will affect the enthusiasm and energy that students bring to learning.

Motivation Is Intrinsic and Extrinsic

Activity that leads to learning may be its own reward. In other words, it may continue for no reason other than its own occurrence. When the reason for acting is in the action, motivation for it is said to be *intrinsic,* in contrast to *extrinsic* motivation, which depends on other rewards external to the action itself.

Support for the reality and importance of intrinsic or self-motivating activities comes from the psychological laboratory and our own experience. Psychologists have observed laboratory animals explore, solve puzzles, or manipulate equipment for no obvious reward other than the activity itself. Children's play

also often appears self-sustaining or self-motivating, and our experience suggests that intrinsic motivation plays an even more prominent role in sustaining behavior of higher quality in terms of cognitive development. This may be what keeps the artist in his garret and the scientist in his laboratory.

Some educators suggest that all educational activities should be intrinsically motivating. They may argue that if learning activities are properly chosen and presented, no social or artificial rewards external to the activities will be necessary.

In the real educational world, however, students perform learning tasks whose desirability is determined by adults. It is too much to expect that every student will find every learning activity intrinsically motivating. It is necessary to hold forth the promise of additional rewards external to the actual task. In other words, there must be the promise that learning will get the learner something else he wants. This is a type of contract (Homme, 1969) that simply may be expressed as, "If you do what I want, you will get something you want."

Any realistic approach to educational motivation must recognize the reality and importance of both intrinsic and extrinsic motivation, as we do in this chapter. Intrinsically motivating situations and activities will be suggested to arouse students and to focus their attention on learning tasks. Sometimes these tasks may be so selected and presented that students' intrinsic motivation will be sufficient to achieve the instructional objectives. When it is, we may know it by the learners' spontaneity and exuberance, and there will be no need for exhortation or cajoling.

Extrinsic motivation is also of central importance in our approach to classroom motivation. One reason for this is some things must be taught whether or not students are intrinsically motivated. Then, too, some activities that are not attractive initially become so once we gain some initial competency or skill. To put it crudely, it may be desirable to "bait the trap" with something else the learner likes.

In reality, the motivation of students is seldom all one thing or another, all intrinsic or extrinsic. If a student has some intrinsic motivation for a task, additional extrinsic motivation may make the task even more interesting and increase the effort he puts into it. We might also argue that if external rewards must be used to motivate some students, and this will probably be the case more often than not, it is not practical or desirable to withhold the bonus of external rewards from those students whose seemingly spontaneous motivation makes your job easier and more enjoyable.

Motivation May Be Too Intense

We should not conclude that more motivation is always better. Although learning may increase with motivation up to a point, most of the evidence suggests a decrease in the quality of learning with too much motivation (Weiner, 1969). How much is too much depends on the complexity of the task and the tolerance of the individual learner for emotional stress. Strong motivation, especially that associated with fear or anxiety, tends to be better for relatively easy or routine tasks, but not for difficult or complex problems. Both difficulty and tolerance for stress are highly individual matters that depend on the capability of the learner and his personality characteristics.

As a general rule, moderate levels of motivation will result in the greatest efficiency in learning, especially if problem solving is required. Increase motivation gradually, and be prepared to stop if there are signs of disturbance or disruption such as overexcite-

ment, aggression, freezing, or an inability to give more than stereotyped "unthinking" responses. The next section suggests the need to be especially alert for such signs with students with certain types of personality.

Achievement Motivation and Other Personality Factors

A desire to excel or do things well is a personal characteristic of persons with high "achievement motivation." (Atkinson, 1965; McClelland, 1965) Individual differences in this characteristic exist at every age and grade, and may be relatively stable from childhood to young adulthood (Moss and Kagan, 1961).

Parental influences are believed to be the crucial determinant in the development of this characteristic in the young child. As Singer and Singer (1969, p. 242) comment:

"The parents of boys with a high need to achieve are themselves models of people who frequently engage in achievement behaviors. They set goals of excellence for their children and reward them for progress toward those goals and punish them for failure to make progress. They allow a choice of routes to excellence but do not reward lack of effort, and certainly punish failure. How to accomplish a task may be up to the boy, but he must accomplish it somehow. It is not surprising, therefore, that, for the sons of such parents, reaching standards of excellence acquires emotional value which helps to motivate them to succeed."

We cannot do much about changing the parents of our students, and psychologists disagree about the probable success of efforts to increase an individual's need for achievement by direct training. Atkinson (1965) sees greater promise in increasing one's expectancy of success as another factor in motivation, which we discuss in a later section of this chapter. Another psychologist, McClelland, (1965, 1972) recommends training programs to increase achievement drive. Such programs were first used to increase the competitive efforts of businessmen, but their use with children has been on the increase recently.

An appropriate program for the development of achievement-motivation, according to McClelland (1965), should have these characteristics.

1. It must teach participants about the concept of achievement motivation and its importance in becoming successful.

2. It must create strong positive expectations that the student can, will, and should become more achievement oriented.

3. It must demonstrate that the change sought is consistent with the demands of reality, the individual's own makeup, and cultural values.

4. It must get the student to commit himself to accomplish realistic, practical, and specific goals as a consequence of his new motive to achieve.

5. It must have the student record his progress toward the goals to which he is committed.

6. It must provide an atmosphere in which the individual feels honestly accepted and respected as a person capable of directing his future.

Programs such as those McClelland has described are designed to produce persons with a new understanding of achievement motivation that will lead them to take moderate risks, to face the challenge of moderately difficult tasks, to set realistic goals, to have confidence in their ability to handle specific problems, to

seek feedback on performance, and to defer gratification. In brief, they are expected to learn to have a high need for achievement and behave as high achievers do.

Dozens of achievement motivation courses have been given hundreds of pupils. A full description of these and a manual for teachers has been provided by Alschuler, Tabor, and McIntyre (1970). What are the results? McClelland's review (1972) describes some quite dramatic gains in the achievement of students in grades eight and ten, as measured by tests and grades. More out-of-school, achievement-related activities, such as earning money, career planning, and competing in games, are also reported after achievement training. Another interesting finding is that similar changes in students have been observed following training in achievement-motivation techniques for teachers. Although experimentation with achievement-motivation programs has been reported at all grade levels, the present training programs appear best suited to the junior high school years and above.

When interpreting the results of training designed to improve achievement motivation, McClelland (1972, p. 145) cautions that what has been demonstrated is improved *learning* and effective *instruction*. While a change in achievement motivation may be *inferred* from performance, it is not proved. The results might, in fact, be attributed to a change in one's expectation of success, instead of an increase in any basic need for success.

Although the advantages of achievement motivation in achieving school success are evident, too much achievement motivation may create problems for a student. We sounded a note of caution with respect to the intensity of motivation in the immediately preceding section. Achievement motivation that is too intense could cause one to overreact to additional "pressure" for achievement in ways that disrupt both achievement and social relations.

One's response to external pressure is affected by other aspects of his personality, also. Introverts, for example, tend to be more "inner motivated" than extraverts; hence, they are more easily overstimulated by external pressures, such as that associated with threats or competition. The same is true for persons who are characteristically apprehensive or anxious. Introverts and "high-anxious" students tend to respond well to moderate motivation, reassurance, a calm demeanor, and considerable freedom. Extraverts and "low-anxious" students, on the other hand, may need external rewards, exhortation, rivalry, or other forms of pressure. Furneau (1962) found that extraverts tended to fail examinations in a permissive, nonstructured university setting and perform better in a more highly structured school situation. The introverts in his study appeared to have the opposite tendency. They performed better in the permissive situation and appeared to "go to pieces" more easily under pressure.

A special word of caution is needed with respect to emotionally unstable and slow children. The tolerance of the emotionally disturbed child for strong external motivation may be lower than that of the normal child. At the same time, the disturbed child is less capable than most children of performing well under stress. The child who is severely limited in what he can do is easily threatened and, hence, is also easily disturbed by strong motivation. Moderate levels of motivation are especially recommended for both the disturbed child and the slow learner.

PSYCHOLOGICAL EXPLANATIONS

Probably the most popular explanation of motivation in psychology is that everyone is continually striving to either achieve pleasure or to avoid pain. The roots of this view, sometimes called "hedonism," extend far back in history. It clearly dominated the thinking of psychologists in the eighteenth and nineteenth centuries.

Early in this century Freud (1953) introduced an important elaboration of the pleasure-pain principle by accepting unconscious as well as conscious motives. In his view one's actions might be dictated by sources of pleasure or pain of which he is no longer aware, such as a traumatic experience of early childhood.

Drive Reduction

More recently explanations of motivation closely related to the pleasure-pain principle have used terms such as "needs" and "drives." A need is said to exist within the individual that gives rise to a drive that compels him to act. He learns to pursue actively some goals instead of others when their attainment reduces his drive and satisfies the related need. Thus, the need for food leads to a hunger drive that is reduced by a hearty meal.

Food and other needs related to survival, such as water, warmth, oxygen, and shelter, are "primary" needs. An important step in the development of the drive-reduction theory was the concept of learned or "secondary" needs (Miller and Dollard, 1941). The idea is that objects and activities that are not strictly essential for survival can acquire drive-producing properties when they are associated with primary need reduction in the experience of the individual.

It is suggested, for example, that a need for social approval begins to develop when an infant associates his mother's smiling face and pleasant words with feeding. Once acquired, the need for social approval may serve as the basis for further acquired needs, such as the need to achieve in school (Mussen, Conger, and Kagan, 1963) or even the need to get a good grade. Given such elaborations of the origins of motivation, we realize that individuals differ greatly in what they choose and strive for simply because of differences in their past experiences and associations. This is why one man's pleasure may be another's poison.

Anxiety is an acquired drive with which we are all familiar. It is related to fear and associated with rapid heart rate, pulse beat, perspiration, and the like. It is often called the universal acquired drive, because it is aroused by such a wide variety of threatening situations. Anxiety reduction is reinforcing, and we learn to do things that make us less anxious. The anxiety principle might suggest that you should generate anxiety in your students and then arrange for them to reduce their anxiety by performing school tasks. This cannot be recommended as a general procedure, however, the effects of anxiety and the threats that produce it are often unpredictable and undesirable.

Although drive-reduction explanations of motivation are widely held among psychologists today, there are other popular views. An important array of theorists, of which White (1959) and Fowler (1965) are good examples, as well as a large number of practitioners, believe some activity is its own reward. Curiosity, exploration, and manipulatory activities appear to occur in the absence of opportunities to reduce any obvious drives. In fact, these activities appear to be more characteristic of apparently well-fed and satisfied individuals than of those who are hungry or otherwise in need (Harlow, 1953). The uses of surprise and incongruity in classroom motivation are described at a later point in the chapter. Such observations have led to other explanations of motivation. The next few paragraphs present a brief overview of one popular position.

Self-Actualization

A point of view that we will call "self-actualization" is frequently presented in opposition to drive reduction. The theorists we refer to here see motivation as being at the very heart of human behavior, but find the drive-reduction account too narrow and mechanistic to account for all behavior. Maslow (1954) postulates a hierarchy of needs that included at the lower levels physiological and psychological deficits, such as food, safety, and approval. He believes, however, that the self-actualizing person has had these needs satisfied and is free to strive toward fulfilling his potential as an individual. Rogers (1963, 1969) sees the individual as striving toward the enhancement of himself, and Combs and Snyyg (1959) find the overriding human motivation to be the achievement of personal adequacy. They believe each individual is striving to enhance the adequacy of his self in his own eyes. Allport (1955) writes about "creative becoming," the highly individual and personal nature of motivation, and its independence of physiological needs.

A basic assumption of these authors is that self-actualization, that is, the maximum development of one's potential as an individual human being, may and should become one's dominant motive. Then, individual behavior is unpredictable in terms of drive systems common to all men. Another key concept is that the best source of information about an individual and his motivation is the individual himself. We must find out why a person does what he does from his own point of view. As Combs and Snygg (1959, p. 11) state:

"People do not behave solely because of the external forces to which they are exposed. People behave as they do in consequence of how things seem to them. We run very hard from the danger we *think* is there and ignore the danger we do not know exists. Behavior in this frame of reference is seen as a problem of human perception."

The conclusions of self-actualization theorists are appealing for a variety of reasons. They are optimistic; individuals can be trusted to do what is right for them. They tend to confirm our everyday observations of the highly individualistic and unpredictable nature of human behavior and the dangers of assuming that what we find attractive or unattractive appears the same to others.

Unfortunately, both the theories and the observations they suggest appear to us to be inadequate when we try to assess the individual's perception of self and reality in order to predict his behavior. To date the yield of such attempts has been low (Clark, 1970).

The Information-Processing Model

Recently, a number of psychologists have found it useful to view the student as a "super computer" (e.g., Newell, Shaw, and Simon, 1958; Miller, Galenter, and Pribram, 1960; Biggs and Lyman, 1971). J. B. Biggs has developed the implications of this approach for education. He emphasizes (Biggs and Lyman, 1971, p. 10), however, that he is "not *identifying* men with machines." He states that "it is useful for the purpose of predicting behavior to pretend that men behave *as if* they were machines, which is quite a different thing."

A computer "program" refers to the detailed instructions that determine what it does with information given it. Biggs describes two programs that appear to be built into human "computers," which may account for what is commonly called motivation. First, there is the "complexity program," which controls the rate or speed with which information is processed. It is responsible for what

could be described as a drive for information. When the complexity program is operating, people feel restless, curious, and ready for new experiences.

The second major program of which Biggs writes is the "economy program." Because there is a limit on the amount of information that man can deal with at one time, there must be a program for compressing or combining items of incoming information so that it can be interpreted, stored, and/or acted on. Although the brain appears to have unlimited capacity for storing information, we can only give our attention to a small number of *independent* items at one time. This number is estimated to be about seven, and Miller (1956) has written of this in an article entitled "The Magical Number Seven, Plus or Minus Two." It is important to note, however, the stress on the word "independent." If a number of different facts can be grouped together into one class, we can deal with all of them as one item. Thus, we might group all odd numbers into one class and all even numbers into another, and deal with all numbers as two items of information to be considered in a problem. Another example is what we do when we memorize a poem. With practice, a phrase, a whole line, or a stanza becomes a single unit.

The process of transforming information into more manageable forms by the economy program is called "coding." Information is stored in the memory in coded or organized form. When new information is received, the economy program first attempts to apply the existing, previously formed codes. When necessary, it expands or revises these codes to facilitate the accommodation of the new information. Then we may say that we have learned more than information, we have learned a new and more generally applicable code.

The complexity and economy programs together can account for much of what has been called motivated behavior, that is, they explain why one acts as he does. When the information one is receiving from the environment does not quite "fit" his existing codes, his complexity program is activated and he seeks more information. At the same time, his economy or coding program functions to direct his attention in ways likely to get the additional information needed to permit coding. Thus, the complexity program provides the "engine" for information-seeking behavior, and the economy program directs it until coding occurs. When coding is accomplished, the communication may signal the need for other acts.

There are two types of situations in which incoming information does *not* activate the complexity or "go" program. First, if existing codes are entirely adequate to deal with incoming information, quite routinely, no additional information is sought. One example of such a situation is that of the driver who adjusts to traffic and road conditions habitually with little or no conscious attention. Coding is routine and the indicated responses are automatic.

The second type of situation in which the complexity program is not active occurs when existing codes are completely irrelevant to the incoming information. Then the information is meaningless. Coding is impossible and more information does not appear useful. If the information is to be processed at all, it must be in the way we learn meaningless material, that is, by rote. In such a situation a student will usually do nothing, unless further information is received that is coded as meaning that memorizing will bring external rewards and failure to memorize will bring punishment.

What do teachers do about differing psychological approaches to motivation? Some, consciously or unconsciously, tend to give priority to one or another regularly as difficulties arise in their work. Some, probably the majority, seek to apply impartially the insights of each view that appear to have implications for school learning, and to temper and extend the whole by the addition of facts and judgments that bear no obvious relation to any systematic position. This is our preference and the task to which we now turn.

DEVELOPING MOTIVATION FOR LEARNING TASKS

The practical management of motivation is a complex and delicate task. It remains something of an art. Theoretical principles have provided no simple formulas that tell us just how to get the most from each student in each situation. We believe the practices described in this section to be consistent with theory, however, and the practices of good teachers. We recommend efforts to increase achievement motivation directly with special programs that incorporate McClelland's recommendations. But we emphasize that instructional planning should also include *constant* attention to at least four elements: (1) attention, (2) positive expectancies, (3) incentive contingencies, and (4) feedback and consequences.

Gaining Attention (and Controlling Distractions)

Attention has been described as the initial phase of learning (Chapter 6). Attention is not an all or nothing, either-or matter, but students must give some attention to a learning activity if they are to learn from it. Moreover, we expect them to learn more or better, up to a point at least, when attention improves.

Every human is continuously bombarded by stimuli, but most of this stimulation is not in his awareness. He has a limited capacity for attention and that attention is easily diverted from the learning task by stimuli related to other needs, interests, and events. How can you get a student's attention and hold it?

SURPRISE AND INCONGRUITY

Much of the art of getting attention involves the use of surprise and incongruity. The TV show "Sesame Street" for young children and "Laugh In" for the older set held attention by capitalizing on the unexpected in timing (we had to follow the action closely to avoid missing something); in loudness or in rhythm; and, of course, by the dramatic, unusual, or zany incident. You may use similar techniques to get attention. Occasionally use dramatic and humorous examples; make intentional errors and pretend to be chagrined when you are caught; challenge children and pretend surprise when you cannot stump them; and surround students with unfamiliar objects to introduce a new topic of study. An expectation of the unexpected holds attention. You will also find that personal references, a technique not available to TV producers, will almost always get attention.

As we pointed out earlier in the chapter, psychologists who think of humans as information processors believe that the central nervous system constantly monitors the flow of information from the senses (Raulerson, 1971). Only when exceptional situations arise, when information is received that is a little unusual in that it does not fit in with previous experiences, is the individual alerted. Then his attention is switched to observation, the processing of information, or memory search. This is one explanation of the attention-generating effect of the unexpected that we have been describing. It may also help to explain the fact that when what we see and hear is repetitive or merely what we expect, the attention wanders.

A great many experiments with laboratory animals support the suggested positive effects of novelty and opportunities to explore or manipulate on the attention of many species of animals other than man (Fowler, 1965). Animals and man appear to share the tendency to seek new perceptual inputs, which we commonly refer to as curiosity.

An interesting further observation that may have practical implications is that curiosity and exploration appear to be heightened after an interval in which normal stimulation is lacking. Travers (1970, p. 123) suggests that there may be times in an educational program when a dull and boring task might be used to prepare students to attend. If this is true, the typical student in the typical school is probably all too well prepared to respond to the attention-getting devices we are suggesting.

ATTENTION SIGNALS

So far we have been writing about the events and situations that almost always attract attention. We may also teach children to give us their attention on signal—when we close the classroom door, snap our fingers, clear our throat, or say "Class, listen now." To be effective such signals must stand out in relation to the background noises and activities of the classroom.

Attention signals will tend to be learned and remain effective if they are usually accompanied by interesting motivational events of the type we have been discussing or by extrinsic rewards. An example we have adapted from Becker, Engelmann, and Thomas (1971) shows how association with a previously effective attention-getting device (waving the arm) and extrinsic rewards (praise and a picture) may be combined to teach an attention response to a verbal signal. The suggested routine would probably have to be repeated a number of times if students were to learn to respond promptly and automatically to the pay attention signal.

1. "Everybody pay attention and I'll show

you an interesting picture."

2. Pause.

3. "Pay attention."

4. At the same time a hand signal such as a wave is used to get attention.

5. Children are praised for paying attention.

6. The picture is shown.

DISTRACTIONS

The teacher must also control distraction, that is, attention to things other than those related to the intended learning. The same factors that attract students to learning may attract them away from it. When students are supposed to be attending to learning activities, unrelated stimuli that are new, novel, unexpected, or of special significance to them will distract them. Street noises are more distracting to the country visitor than the city dweller and the spoken word is more distracting than quiet music, especially if the words are about us, and unless we are musicians. Because distractions can never be eliminated, Seagoe (1970, p. 118) recommends helping students become accustomed to normal adult distractions. This would include, for example, noise in a shop, movement, but not laughter or singing, in a library, and almost complete quiet in a discussion or lecture, unless one has the floor.

Developing Positive Expectancies

The vigor and persistence of learning efforts are influenced by one's knowledge or beliefs about what he will achieve. The learner's expectation of achievement or accomplishment is our concern in this section. The promise of rewarding external objects or events is discussed in the next. The expectation of achievement is considered separately from expectation of other rewards because of our belief in the central importance of achievement in motivating school learning. In a sense, all or nearly all other rewards are supplementary and temporary, at least from the standpoint of our objectives.

Expectancy is obviously influenced by past experience with what leads to what. A student's choice among courses, dates, or restaurants clearly depends on what he has previously learned about the alternatives. His experiences today just as certainly affect his motivation for future activities. For this reason motivation is both a goal of learning and a factor in its effectiveness.

OBJECTIVES

More directly and immediately, teachers may influence the expectations of students, and thereby their motivation, by describing (or showing) the intended outcomes of learning activity and how these may be gained. Bryan and Locke (1967), who worked with college students, reported, for example, that students with initially low motivation responded better when specific goals were established. Kennedy (1968) found that younger subjects, third and fourth graders in a low socioeconomic area, did better in arithmetic when goals were set, either by the teacher or themselves, than when they were simply encouraged to do their best.

A learner is able to anticipate the results of his activities and regulate his behavior more efficiently when objectives are made clear to him (Popham, 1968). The clearest objectives tell him what he will learn to do. "You will be able to type 40-50 words a minute without error" and "You will be able to read a French newspaper" are examples of course objectives. "You will learn how to add numbers such as 135.65 and 13.341" and "You will be able to state the major factors contributing to the depression of 1929" illustrate objectives of daily activities.

More specific objectives do not *guarantee* more learning in every situation, however. For one thing, students may not use specific objectives to best advantage unless they are taught to do so. On the other hand, some students have probably learned how to use general objectives well and are skillful in translating these into more specific terms on their own.

Jenkins and Deno (1971) used general objectives with one group of college sophomores and more specific objectives with a comparable group. They found that the two groups achieved equally well on a test over the same social studies unit. Although the authors suggest that the teachers and students of their study may not have known how to use the specific objectives, a comparison of their "general" and "specific" objectives suggests that it is likely that for these learners one type of objective had almost the same meaning as the other. Examples of each follow.

General Objectives	*Specific Objectives*
"Learn what common pitfalls in social science data collection procedures must be avoided."	"Given the name of one of the data collection procedures listed below, the student should be able to select from alternatives the major advantage or limitation of the technique: Observations Interviews Questionnaires etc."
"Know the prominent social scientists and their contributions."	"Given a description of the key contribution of a social scientist, the student should be able to identify this social scientist from sets of four alternatives which include: Thomas Carlyle Auguste Comte Sigmund Freud Herodotus etc."

The meaning of objectives to students is undoubtedly more important than any particular format. There should be a promise of new capabilities for students in our objectives. When clearly perceived by students, this promise tends to motivate them, whether they seek achievement for its own sake or for the approval of others. Of course, not every new capability will be equally attractive to all. Nevertheless, the importance of objectives as a basic approach to increasing student motivation should be accepted.

REAL-WORLD RELATIONSHIPS

Students may know exactly what they will be able to do as a result of learning, but fail to see why they need or want this new capability. In terms of the discussion of Chapter 2, the *ultimate* objectives are not clear. Students may lack the knowledge or information that they need to link school to other situations. You may help them translate expectations in the academic setting into expectations in the real world. This is what teachers are doing when they present spelling as an aid in writing letters to friends who have moved away, arithmetic as a requirement for serving as class treasurer, or shop skills as a means of earning money for a class trip.

Student's long-term hopes and ambitions for a home, family, and career represent remote expectations to which the achievement of school tasks may also be related. The experience of many teachers suggests greater success when school work is tied to short or intermediate concerns as well as to long-term life interests. Attempts to see into the remote future are not always wise or convincing. You will be well advised to give heed to the relationship of school tasks to more immediate problems, characteristic of those faced by the age group with whom you are working. One teacher, for example, reported accelerated interest and achievement in the study of measurement when eighth-grade students were encouraged to chart and interpret their own physiological changes. A concern for bodily changes is one of the characteristics of this age group. The desire for acceptance and recognition by one's peers is almost universal. Any related topic or method is likely to generate interest.

OPTIONS AND INTERESTS

A student's expectations may be heightened if you recognize his special interests and arrange learning activities that appeal to him. There are many possibilities. Skills, such as reading, writing, experimenting, and reporting, can be initiated and practiced with topics and materials that he helps select. He may gain knowledge and develop concepts with a variety of methods and sources, such as books, interviews, audiovisual aids, and field trips, and there are usually several options for demonstrating achievement including tests, oral and written reports, demonstrations or exhibits, role playing, and group problem

"Why should I think of the future? It hasn't done anything for me." (*Drawing by Reg Hider. From Today's Education,* NEA Journal, *1972*)

solving. The more options the student has, the greater the likelihood that you can find ways to make what he does important to him.

In a unit on communication, for example, some children will wish to build a telephone or radio; some will wish to work on quite different means of communication, or do research on historical research, or report the problems of communicating with space ships, or draw sketches, plans, or illustrations, or prepare articles for the school newspaper or scripts for class plays.

Although descriptions of teaching often recommend using student interests to motivate learning and build interests in the topics studied, little related research has been reported. An exploratory study by Craig and Holsbach (1964) warrants attention here because of the paucity of other investigations.

In this study the interests of eighth-grade general science students were inventoried with respect to (1) science content areas (living things, the human body, the earth, the universe, and matter-energy) and (2) specific ways of learning (hearing about, taking apart, going to see, explaining, solving problems, etc.). Then, each student who revealed a *disliked area* was given supplementary learning experience in that area by means of *liked activities*. Student interests were surveyed again immediately after study of each area and at the end of the school year. The results for all areas showed consistently that when liked activities were provided, interests in the content areas increased. No such changes were noted for students who did not engage in liked activities.

Other results of the study showed that when students with initially high interests in an area were given further experience in that area by means of typical school activities they said they disliked initially, these activities become less disagreeable. All of the following were chosen as "liked" at least twice as frequently after the study as before: explain, work on class projects, answer questions, and give reports.

The results of this study suggest several promising hypotheses. They suggest that school experiences can develop student interests. They encourage the use of existing interests in particular ways of learning to develop interests in science areas, and, conversely, the use of existing content interests to develop interests in other ways of learning.

Although students respond most readily to activities when they already have an interest in it, we do not counsel abandoning objectives if learning cannot be based on the immediate interests of students. Many student interests are probably casually learned and quite transitory. New interests are rather easily developed by experience in situations where learning is pleasant or when learners see that the tasks have value for them.

LEVELS OF EXPECTANCY

We have been discussing learner expectancies for the outcome of his activities as if there were no question about his success. We have been writing of the importance of the learner knowing what is to be accomplished or gained. Now we turn to his beliefs about what he can and cannot do and how these beliefs influence what he tries to do.

Much of the evidence about how people set their expectations comes from studies of "levels of aspiration." This is the level of performance that one expects to reach on a familiar task. It could just as well be termed his "level of expectancy." One's level of aspiration is related to his achievement motivation and to his "self-concept," that is, his beliefs about himself and his competencies (Hamachek, 1968).

The German psychologist Hoppe (1930) first described how achievement-motivated individuals set their aspirations. Atkinson (1965) is a current student of how students' aspiration may be used to improve achievement. A desire to do as well as they can tends to force their expectations up, while a desire to avoid failure tends to pull them down. Their actual expectations are a compromise between these two opposing tendencies. After success, achievement-motivated persons tend to raise their expectations if the task is perceived as easy. If they did not, continued success would come too easily and there would be no feeling of accomplishment. After failure, these achievement-oriented individuals persist in their attempts to succeed unless the task is seen as too difficult. When this happens they may lower their expectations to protect themselves against continued failure.

What about the student with low achievement motivation? Success on an easy task appears to encourage this individual to choose additional tasks of about the same difficulty. Failure on an easy task discourages him, and he may not persist without encouragement. Sometimes he chooses a much more difficult task, perhaps because failure to achieve an impossible goal is not seen as a threat to his self-esteem.

A classic experimental study of success and failure in student expectations is that of Pauline Sears (1940). She worked with three groups of upper elementary school children: (1) a "success" group accustomed to high grades in school; (2) a "failure" group with a history of low grades; and (3) a "differential" group that had been successful in reading but unsuccessful in arithmetic. All were given a series of 20 speed tests in arithmetic and reading. After each test each child was asked to estimate the amount of time it would take him to do the next task. The effects of previous experience with success and failure were apparent in that the success group realistically increased both their expectancy and their achievement from test to test, whereas the failure group did not. These students lowered their expectations, left them the same, or set them so high they were certain to fail again. The third group was like the success group in reading, the area in which they had been successful previously, but like the failure group in arithmetic.

In a second phase of the Sears' experiment half of those in each group were praised frequently for their performances after taking a test, while the other half were severely criticized. The students who were praised to make them feel successful now tended to set realistically higher goals for each succeeding test, even those with a previous history of failure. On the other hand, the students who were criticized to make them feel they had failed were much more variable in their expectation.

Some tended to lower their goals; others set them unrealistically high. Students with a previous history of success were better able to cope with apparent failure on the tests than were students with a previous history of failure. For most students an expectation of and motivation for realistically improving performance appears to depend on success experiences.

Success is a highly individual matter, of course, and related to one's achievement motivation. The student who wanted an "A" is disappointed with a "C," while the student who wanted a "D" or "F" is happy to get it. What each student considers success is defined by what he hoped for and expected. You should help students set goals so that success comes to all with reasonable frequency. The evidence suggests that this will not be difficult with achievement-motivated students who have a history of academic success. Such students generally set their own standards and work toward them. To feel success they must feel challenged. Tasks for these students should not be too easy.

Students with a record of past failures may need more help in setting goals. The highly motivated but unsuccessful students may have expectations (hopes) that are so high they are doomed to fail again and again. The unmotivated unsuccessful students may set their standards unrealistically low. For students with a record of past failures, the "successful" level of achievement for tomorrow should usually be set just a little above the performance of today. Small steps are the surest when we attempt to build self-confidence. Tasks can be broken into subtasks, and extra help provided so that success is definitely within the reach of each student.

The individualization of expectations, which we are describing, is a way of encouraging a student to compete against his own previous record instead of against those of other students. The uses of self- and other-competition are considered further at another point in the chapter.

ESTABLISHING INCENTIVE CONTINGENCIES

"Incentive" and "contingency" are popular terms in current psychological literature. A consequence of an act is called an incentive if the anticipation of it is attractive or repelling. The consequences that follow an act are contingent on it. Positive incentives contingent on an act promise a reward for acting; negative incentive contingencies promise punishment. Hence, when there are positive "incentive contingencies," our tendency is to "do it"; when there are negative "incentive contingencies," our tendency is "do not do it."

You will probably require little convincing of the influence of incentive contingencies on behavior; they are obvious factors in decisions affecting your own behavior. You know also that teachers use incentive contingencies to intensify learning activity. Positive incentives include the promise of approval, prizes, privileges, and high marks. Examples of negative incentives are the threat of disapproval, loss of privileges, and low marks. Both positive and negative incentives have their uses, but the effects of positive incentives or rewards are more predictable than the effects of negative ones. Punishment may weaken the response it follows, or it may suppress it temporarily or only in the presence of the punisher. In addition, punishment may lead to undesirable anxiety, negative attitudes, and open hostility. Therefore, learning generally proceeds better when positive incentives receive the greater emphasis.

THE USES OF PUNISHMENT

The uses of incentives for academic and disciplinary purposes have much in common. The same kinds of incentives are available, whether the problem relates to educational behavior or social behavior. The same principles should govern their use. Consequently,

"If you spell these 10 words correctly, you get an all expense paid trip to Disneyland!" *(W. James Popham and Eva L. Baker, ESTABLISHING INSTRUCTIONAL GOALS, © 1970. By permission of Prentice-Hall, Inc., Englewood Cliffs, New Jersey and Vimcet Associates)*

we have deferred a full discussion of the various types of incentives and their use to a later chapter on discipline (Chapter 14). Chapter 14 also describes in detail the constructive use of punishment. At this point it is enough to note that despite what we have said about the generally greater effectiveness of positive incentives, the following generalizations hold true.

1. Some use of negative or aversive incentives in education is natural and inevitable.

2. Correcting errors and the withholding of privileges or rewards serve better in schools than harsher forms of punishment.

3. Negative incentives should come early rather than late in order to redirect the student when he first begins to err or misbehave.

4. Punishment after undesirable behavior should be followed immediately by an opportunity to gain rewards by correct behavior.

5. Punishment, when used, should be systematic, impartial, and without moral or emotional overtones.

An example of the classroom application of the above principles with three tenth graders in a French class has been provided by Hall and others (1971). The students, two boys and a girl, had been receiving D and F grades on quizzes about homework and classwork. The teacher then established a "baseline" for the performance of each student by carefully scoring and recording quiz grades for at least 10 days. Letter grades were coded as follows: A = 4, B = 3, C = 2, D = 1, and F = 0. During the period of baseline operations, the students' average quiz scores were 0.35, 0.40, and 0.74, all below a D.

Following the tenth session one student was told that he should stay after school for special help with the material covered whenever he received a D or F. Similar contingencies were established for a second student

after 15 days and for a third student after 20 days. None of the three students received any Ds or Fs after the contingency was set for them. Their averages increased to 3.6, 2.8, and 2.2, out of a possible 4.0.

The same authors report several other classroom studies involving entire class groups and pupils ranging from the primary age level to seniors in high school. They interpret the results as implying ". . . the general application of systematic punishment procedures which do not result in strong emotional behavior related to classroom problems."

INCENTIVES AND REINFORCEMENT

You will have already noted that we tend to use incentives, rewards and punishments, and reinforcement interchangeably. Evidence of the role of incentive contingencies in directing and energizing behavior comes from the numerous studies of reward and punishment and often are discussed under the topic of "reinforcement." If there is a difference between the role of consequences as incentives in motivation and their role as reinforcers in learning, it is a subtle one. Glaser's review (1969) calls attention to a growing doubt that reinforcement can be separated from motivation and suggests that the terms may eventually become indistinguishable. Reinforcement psychologists believe that reinforcement is the crucial factor in learning, that is, they believe a response must be followed by reinforcement if it is to be learned. Once a response is learned, whether or not it is used may be said to depend on the incentive value of the promised rewards.

The influence of incentives on the use of previously learned responses is especially clear when we abruptly stop doing something we are quite capable of doing simply because the incentive is no longer there. For example, a frequently expressed concern of teachers is that even the best students will stop using the knowledge and skill that they have acquired in school when they are no longer promised grades or other forms of recognition.

From this point of view, the effects of incentive contingencies on learning are indirect rather than direct, that is, incentives lead the learner to participate in learning activities so that he has more opportunity to learn. Participation may be the real requirement (Ausubel and Robinson, 1969, p. 373). If it were feasible to lead an algebra student to respond mechanically, much as we teach a dog to shake hands by lifting his paw, the student would probably learn algebra, although not very efficiently. Our aim in motivation is to encourage more voluntary and vigorous participation. Of course, when an incentive that leads one to act is received, the effect may be that described as reinforcement, that is, the learner may perform the act even more frequently and promptly in the future.

CONTINGENCY CONTRACTING

Several authors have described programs for the systematic application of research findings in the management of learning. The approach recommended by Homme and others (1969) in a manual entitled "How to Use Contingency Contracting in the Classroom" is an example that will illustrate the meaning of such programs for teachers. A contingency "contract" offers the student something he wants when he does something you want him to. In other words, the incentive (Homme says "the reward") is contingent on the performance of an act or the completion of a task.

The incentives favored by Homme are privileges or the opportunity to do something, that is, a student is promised an opportunity to do something he wants to do. This is an application of a principle set forth by Premack (1965). Although the Premack principle, as it is called, may be stated more formally, the practical meaning is that any activity that students choose to do when given the opportunity may be used to motivate them to engage in other activity.

A contract of the type we are discussing may be stated informally or written. Teacher and student may work it out together. Lovitt and Curtiss (1969) found that when rewards to be received were specified by the student himself, they were generally higher, but the student's work was more satisfactory, even in those instances when the rewards were not higher.

In the introduction to Homme's book, Wesley C. Becker tells how Homme first tried the Premack principle out of desperation when attempting to control the behavior of three-year olds. He found that children who were running and screaming kept right on running and screaming when he asked them to "come and sit down." Because he saw that they liked to run and scream, push chairs, and work puzzles, he decided to make these activities contingent on sitting down and listening, watching the blackboard, and being quiet for a short time. He told them that if they would sit and listen or watch for a few minutes they could run and scream a while. Gradually, he was able to extend the work time required to earn a given amount of playtime.

Homme is quoted as reporting, "This kind of contingency management put us in immediate control of the situation. We were in control to the extent that we were able to teach everything in about one month that we could discover was ordinarily taught in first grade." (Homme et al., 1969, p. viii)

Although it is possible to contract with groups of students for certain accomplishments, the method works best with individualized instruction, which is less difficult than might be supposed. The preparatory steps (Homme et al., 1969) are:

Card 1.	Read pages 27-32 of your test.
	Take the progress test.
	If passed, take 5 minutes for reward time.
	If not passed, see the teacher.

Card 2.	Do the 20 problems corresponding to text pages 27-32.
	Take the progress test.
	If passed, you may take 7 minutes for reward time and choose an item from the menu.
	If not passed, see the teacher.

Figure 7-1.
Examples of Task Cards.

1. Divide the objectives of the course into daily tasks.

2. Collect materials and assign to tasks and subtasks.

3. Prepare diagnostic tests for use in (a) assigning subtasks to each student according to his needs and (b) checking the accomplishment of assignments.

4. Prepare a separate card for each subtask (Figure 7-1).

5. Prepare a "menu" or list of incentives from which students may choose a reward. (See Chapter 14 for examples of different types of readily available rewards.)

On a typical day we may suppose the teacher would have sorted the task cards and used the results of previous testing to assign tasks to students ahead of time. As the period begins, each student is given a task card and allowed to choose the reward he wants from the list or menu. When a student finishes his task by passing the progress tests, he goes to a special part of the room, the reward area, to pursue the activity he has chosen. When his reward time is up, he returns to the task area to receive another assignment.

The following rules are prominent in Homme's elaboration of his approach.

1. State the terms of the contract clearly. The student must know exactly what is expected and exactly what he will get.

2. Payoff after the performance, never before. This is called "Grandma's rule" of first work, then play.

3. Payoff immediately.

4. Use frequent small rewards instead of a few large ones. This is particularly true initially, as rule 5 suggests.

5. Begin by contracting for a "small, simple to perform approximation of the final performance desired." It is no use asking for something students cannot do. They are more likely to be able to do one problem correctly, initially, than all the problems at the end of the chapter.

6. Make contracts fair on both sides. This simply means that the incentive must be seen as worth the task. You should not ask students to work a day for 2 minutes of play, and you should not promise them the day off for 2 minutes of work.

7. State the contract positively. It should be in terms of what you get for something you do, not in terms of what you get if you do not do something or what you do not get unless you do.

8. Contract for achievement rather than obedience. Students who merely do what you tell them to remain dependent on you.

9. Use contracts systematically and continuously. One should ask "what is the incentive for the student" for almost every expected performance.

10. Finally, begin to shift to self-contracting, that is, have the student set his own tasks and incentives.

Homme has reported that those who use these rules in the management of motivation are rewarded by finding children happy, unspoiled, and eager to perform (1969, p. 21).

SELF-MANAGEMENT

Homme's last rule suggests gradually transferring responsibility to the learner himself. This is a particularly attractive aspect of contingency management programs. After some experience with contingencies set by others, training in self-contracting may begin. At first teacher and students work together on choosing tasks and incentives. Gradually, there is a shift so that incentives are contingent on not only the student's performance, but on his setting of goals and evaluating that performance as well. After the student can evaluate his own performance, he is also asked to reward himself. Now he sets the contingencies, performs, evaluates his performance, and reinforces himself accordingly. It becomes possible to contract with students to make and complete their own subcontracts for a day, a week, or an even longer period.

While self-management is being encouraged, external rewards are gradually replaced by more symbolic and internal rewards, perhaps just the recognition by the learner that he has met his goal or behaved responsibly. The ultimate goal is the individual's control of his own behavior with a minimum of external supports.

Some success has been reported for merely counseling college students to contract with themselves for study behavior (Fox, 1962). Students were advised to set a specific time each day for study and always to follow study time with a fun activity. Any area of study is likely to require some monotonous, tedious work. Anyone is certainly more likely to do this work well if he spaces it out and follows each work session by more interesting activities.

Feedback and Consequences

When one attempts to achieve an objective, his expectation of continued progress is stimulated by knowledge of progress so far and of how he might do better still. His tendency to continue or change what he has been doing is also affected by his satisfaction or dissatisfaction. Another term for consequences that inform the learner of the results of his action is "feedback." We will first consider feedback and then discuss other events that are more clearly associated with pleasant or unpleasant feelings, satisfaction or dissatisfaction than with information or knowledge useful in guiding performance.

FEEDBACK INFORMATION

There is considerable evidence of the importance of feedback and the variables in its use. A marked improvement in student performance may be expected with systematic provisions for giving feedback. For best results we suggest that the information be detailed and specific. Although we do not find as much evidence on this point as we would wish, it is apparently better to put encouraging comments on student papers (Page, 1958; Sweet, 1966) or to supply the correct answers (Bourne and Pendleton, 1958; Chansky, 1960) than merely to tell students "right" or "wrong." It is probably better still if they can be told why they are right or wrong and what should be changed (Bryan and Rigney, 1956). Finally, Sassenrath and Gaverick (1965) found that discussion of midsemester examinations had a beneficial effect on final examination scores.

Immediate as opposed to delayed knowledge of results is recommended. Although exceptions have been reported, most investigations have found immediate feedback to be the more effective (Mayer, 1960; Sax, 1960). In any ongoing sequence of behavior where one act prepares us for another, information about our success at each step is obviously required immediately if it is to guide our next move. Finding out about one's errors later in a "postmortem" evaluation is unlikely to help in this way.

Feedback about specific acts is sometimes quite simple and direct. It may be generated by the task itself. In programmed instruction, for example, the student chooses among the options given and then checks his choice against the answers provided. More often than not, however, students will need help in evaluating their performance.

There is still another type of feedback in which the teacher plays a central role. This is information that relates the learner's present acts to other objectives. Overall progress is rarely readily apparent to learners, and you should plan to provide your students with information about the relevance of their efforts to other more general goals in and out of school.

Finally, the available evidence suggests that the frequency of feedback is important. Several investigators have reported that continuous feedback is superior to intermittent feedback during concept learning (Bourne and Haygood, 1960; Chansky, 1960). When the opportunity for peeking or looking ahead to the answers is impossible, better results have been obtained with continuous feedback in programmed instruction, also (Anderson, Kulhavy, and Andre, 1971). Of course, when students do look ahead, as they have been able to do in some studies, they may provide some of their own feedback. Our conclusion is that teachers should assume that it is important to provide continuous as well as immediate and complete knowledge of results.

The obstacles in the way of more continuous knowledge of results in classroom situations are not insurmountable if we have students check their own work and each other's. You might, for example, check one spelling, arithmetic, or handwriting paper for each child each week, at unannounced times. The rest of the time the children can be given model answers so they can do their own checking or rating. Students may exchange papers for checking, but this is no better in terms of feedback of results, and it may cause arguments and undesirable comparisons. Whether checking is by the student, the teacher, or the student and teacher together, supplying the right answers is better than merely checking wrong ones.

Similar principles apply in providing feedback for more complex tasks, such as composition, crafts, or laboratory work, but procedures vary. Model answers or performances are of value, and it is helpful to have products discussed in class. Class evaluation should, according to Seagoe (1970, p. 53) consist of three parts: (1) a favorable or reassuring comment; (2) an analysis of inadequacies or problems; and (3) a specific and positive suggestion for improvement. While learning to do a specific task better, students also learn how to criticize constructively.

You may use individual progress charts to strengthen the feeling of achievement and the expectation of further gains. Again, a private record may be less embarrassing to individuals than a public display—unless, of course, the record is of group achievement. Report cards, even when modified to tell more than the conventional letter grades, are considered a means of reporting achievement over longer periods of time. They provide little motivation or guidance to learners in the achievement of specific tasks or objectives, simply because the information they provide is too little and too late.

CONTINGENT AND NONCONTINGENT CONSEQUENCES

The principal events to which we refer in this section are those consequences offered the learner as contingent incentives in the manner described in previous sections. In other words, they fulfill an agreement based on incentives. They represent the fruit of the student's labor, and they are reinforcing because they encourage the type of behavior they follow. If you fail to honor such contracts with the promised consequences, your effectiveness quickly declines. You are also dishonest.

Unexpected and unanticipated reinforcers that are built into the teaching presentation help to keep student motivation at a high level en route to the promised consequences. Either content or style of presentation can be made reinforcing by continuing to build in novelty, suspense, drama, and surprise, as we recommended for gaining students attention initially.

There is some evidence that massive doses of approval, even when it is undeserved and directed at no particular accomplishment, may be effective in improving performance. Cormier (1970) conducted an experiment with disadvantaged eighth graders to test the effects of praise that was contingent on specific accomplishments. To his surprise he found that liberal praise was effective even when it was *not* contingent on accomplishments. The teachers he worked with were drilled to see the good side of students. During the "noncontingent praise" phase of the study, the teachers gave unearned praise to the class as a group at least 10 times during a class period, regardless of what was happening. Any inappropriate behavior was ignored.

Cormier's findings are tentative, and at this point we do not know if similar results will be found with students of different ages or students who are accustomed to being praised for school achievement. Another investigator (McAllister et al., 1969) coupled direct disapproval of individual students who talked in class with praise to the whole class for being quiet, whether they were or not. She found this combination very effective in reducing inappropriate talking in a senior high school English course.

A teacher who acts as if learning were exciting and interesting and as if he finds the experience rewarding tends to have students who react in the same way. Our suggestion that students tend to behave as they observe another behave is supported by the extensive research of Albert Bandura (1969). Modeling, or learning by imitation, is an important method of developing general attitudes toward learning, which will be discussed under that topic.

MATERIAL REWARDS

The question of "How much?" is usually asked with respect to material consequences. Food, trinkets, toys, and many other prizes have been used experimentally, primarily with children (see Chapter 14). Because it is often inconvenient to award prizes immediately, tokens may be given. These are accumulated and used as money to purchase things later.

The results of experiments with material rewards are inconclusive. They are "worth a try" if students will not respond to other appeals, but a recent review of studies with young children (Lipe and Jung, 1971) suggests that material rewards are generally no more effective than praise statements.

We agree with Hewett (1968, p. 254), who comments on the success of his system for dealing with emotionally handicapped children. He states that it is not *what* you give a child, or *how much* (value) you give him that is most important. "The 'big idea' is that the child's accomplishments are being acknowledged in a systematic fashion and that he comes to recognize that his behavior controls certain consequences. . . . There is no magic in giving tangible rewards. . . . It is the system with which such rewards are associated that will guarantee their success."

The advantages of tokens and prizes, when found, probably occur because teachers use them more systematically than they do praise. Like many teachers, you may find it difficult to praise students, especially for seemingly small accomplishments. This attitude will interfere with your effectiveness, and you should work to overcome it.

Competition and Cooperation

Competition among individuals and groups for opportunities, honors, and material gain is a characteristic of our society. John W. Gardner (1961) in his book, *Excellence*, subtitled "Can We Be Equal and Excellent Too" points out that ". . . ours is one of the few societies in the history of the world in which performance is a primary determinant of status."

Despite the advantages of our society, it is obvious that in competition some people (the winners) achieve their status at the expense of others (the losers). Cooperation, on the other hand, is a group activity in which individuals work together toward a common goal. Many activities are a blend of cooperative and competitive efforts. Groups of cooperating individuals often compete. This is what

we mean by a "team effort." In these groups competition among the individuals to make the team often precedes their cooperation for group goals. The relative value that we place on cooperation and competition is not very clear when team members are selected for their ability to cooperate, that is, by competition in cooperation.

Any external analysis of the cooperative and competitive elements of school situations is likely to be inadequate, moreover, because the reactions of individuals are so different. Some children are competitive under cooperative conditions, others are cooperative under competitive conditions, and still others ignore both cooperation and competition in their preoccupation with tasks (Ausubel and Robinson, 1969, p. 420).

Competition may have both desirable and undesirable effects on personality development. A comparison of the positive and negative contingencies associated with it helps account for the both. Winning will be ego enhancing, at the least, and prestige, popularity, and prizes may also be promised. At the same time, losers, or even those who do not choose to compete, may be threatened by a loss of self-esteem, social status, and prestige.

On the credit side of competition, there is evidence that average achievement is greater under competitive conditions than when children work anonymously (Ausubel, 1951) or for group prizes (Maller, 1929). It may make routine activities more interesting and can help build group morale (Fiedler, 1969). On the debit side of the ledger appear the inhibiting and disturbing effects of competition that is too intense. It may foster feelings of inadequacy among the less able and lead to generally negative reactions such as aggression, resentment, and dishonesty. "Winning at all costs" may be either the result of misplaced values or a strategy of desperation.

Extreme reactions to the potential dangers

of competition have sometimes resulted in an overemphasis on group work on the supposition that this teaches cooperation and principles of democratic living. The efforts of a group, it has been reasoned, must be invariably superior to those of individuals, since "two heads are better than one."

In practice these results are not always forthcoming. Group members may antagonize each other. A working group may never come to grips with the task. You know the modern adage that states, "The surest way to kill a project is to give it to a committee." If the committee does succeed, the work may be that of only one or two individuals. Finally, the evidence does not support the claim that a group solution to a problem is invariably better than that of the ablest individuals in the group (Marquardt, 1955).

Efforts to eliminate competition are futile and ill advised. The productive approach is to use the competitive impulses of students constructively and in ways that reduce the probability of harmful effects. The following recommendations appear to be justified.

1. *Arrange for all competitors to have a fairly equal chance of winning.* The two principal methods are: (a) have students compete with others of approximately the same ability, and (b) give recognition for a wide variety of non-academic achievements, such as neatness, punctuality, and dependability, and for interest and skill in arts and crafts, music, or special hobbies.

2. *Have students compete against their own record or against accepted standards.* Each student can experience progress if he works to improve his own spelling score or his understanding of arithmetic. Individual progress charts are useful and should be confidential.

Bloom (1968) has won new friends for the old practice of having students compete against accepted standards instead of against the performance of other students. Bloom, and other advocates of what is termed "mastery learning," begin with a careful definition of standards for the performance of the learning task. Then each student is motivated toward this performance. The progress of each student is monitored, and help is provided as needed. Some students will take much longer than others to achieve "mastery," that is, to achieve the standard, but in some situations at least eventual success appears to be within the reach of all.

It may be argued that Bloom's approach merely shifts the basis of competition so that students now compete in terms of the time they require to reach the standard. It is possible, however, that the differences in the amount of time students take to master a skill are less threatening to ego or prestige than traditional scores and grades. The achievement of "mastery," at whatever cost in time, may be a positive incentive for further efforts, but we cannot be certain of this.

3. *Play down the importance of winning.* In team competition, winning at all costs must not overshadow all other considerations, including courtesy, honesty and fair play. Favor spontaneous games that minimize the value of long and arduous preparation. Keep the rewards and penalties short lived and of small value, more an occasion for humor and fellowship than for prideful comparisons. Rotate players among teams to avoid the development of too much team spirit and the continual domination of some groups over others. These suggestions are meant to apply to physical as well as mental competition. Interscholastic competition will not have all these characteristics, but even there some precautions are necessary to avoid open hostility and the resemblance to gang warfare.

Analyzing Special Problems

There are always some students who fail to respond to normally effective procedures. They do not participate in learning activities or complete learning tasks as expected. Why? Do these problem students lack skill, opportunity, or motivation?

Some students may not be *able* to perform as expected because of physical deficiencies or lack of prerequisite knowledge or skill. Check this possibility out by working with individuals. See how each performs when you set goals that you know he can achieve if he tries.

Inquire about obstacles that get in the way of task completion. Be sure that each one knows the objectives and has ready access to information about what is to be done when. Are the needed time, equipment, and materials available? Are the conditions under which the task is attempted uncomfortable or too distracting? Are there hearing, vision, or health problems?

Assume that you have concluded that a student's problem is motivational; he has the ability and opportunity to perform, but he will not. What may be done to pinpoint the difficulty? The general remedy for motivational troubles is greater, more insightful use of the elements described in preceding sections, that is, attention, expectancies, incentives, and consequences. Do not fail to recognize, however, that some students may fail to respond because their expectations are not what we thought them to be and they do not see the incentives and consequences as we supposed they would.

TAKING THE STUDENT'S VIEW

When a motivational problem persists you should carefully reexamine your procedures from the point of view of the students you are failing to reach. For greater success with a particular student give particular attention to *his* expectancies and the incentives and consequences *as he sees them.* You can get some clues to his perceptions by observing him closely and talking to him and to those who know him best.

Mager and Pipe (1970) suggest taking the point of view of the student who can perform but does not as you ask three questions.

1. *Is performance punishing?* The student who is given extra problems when he completes his algebra assignment promptly and accurately may think so. The student who suggests a novel solution to a school social problem and wins both the work and the jeers of fellow classmates may think so. Would privileges instead of extra duty do more to encourage these students? Might they then be envied, not pitied?

The slower student whose efforts always lead to failure and rebukes may also find performance punishing. Can tasks be adjusted to his level of competence and praise be given even for small achievement?

Cormier (1970) and his research team at the University of Tennessee found that students react well to praise given for such things as working independently, responding to questions (even if wrong), paying attention to directions, and following through. He suggests being spontaneous, smiling, and keeping at it, even if you feel a bit foolish at first.

2. *Is nonperformance or other performance rewarding?* Does a student get more of what he seeks when he fails to perform than when he does? Suppose you overheard two teachers talking about a child who does not do his homework. The conversation goes like this.

"In spite of all I do Tim won't do his homework assignments."

"What do you do about it when he doesn't turn in an assignment?"

"Everything I can. I make an extra effort to spend a little time with him and tell him how good a student he could be if he would only try. I help him, and I give him extra time. Everything."

"What do you do when he turns in an assignment promptly?"

"He hasn't yet. I suppose I'd hand it back to him and ask him to correct the errors."

This teacher's relationship with Tim is similar to that of the diner and waitress described by Mager and Pipe (1970, p. 65). The customer says, "Y'know everytime she gives me bad service, I tip her a little extra. . . . But it doesn't seem to work. She *still* gives me bad service."

How about the students who find that daydreaming about last night's date or tomorrow's game is more enjoyable than listening to poorly prepared and confusing examples and explanations? Then there is the student who has found that when grades are assigned, time spent memorizing the summaries at the end of each chapter pays better than class participation or even class attendance. These are only a few examples of situations in which changing motivation calls for altering the balance of benefits associated with performance and nonperformance of educational activities.

3. *Does performing really matter?* Sometimes it seems to the student that performance of learning activities does not change anything. From his point of view nothing will happen if he does; nothing happens if he does not. If he sees things this way, we have not succeeded in building positive expectancies. The approaches we have recommended have not been tried or they have not worked with him. Furthermore, he apparently does not find that any important incentives or consequences are contingent on performance.

Would you believe the following comments by students? "The teacher doesn't read our book reports, so why bother with them?" "I don't get anything out of class discussion so why stay awake?" "I'm going to be a coach. Why do I need to study literature?" "Everyone gets a good grade for just coming to class. Why do anything else?" You will have no difficulty adding to this list of observations. Each one calls for changes — either in student perceptions or classroom realities.

Teaching in the Absence of Motivation

The motivation of students, let us remind you again, is a complex and uncertain task. You will not always do it well; sometimes the results of your efforts will seem negligible. When this happens, the best advice (and the provisions of your contract with the school system) suggests that you continue teaching your subject. Ausubel and Robinson (1969, p. 385) point to evidence that shows that students learn something, almost in spite of themselves, even when effort and intentions appear to be lacking.

Teaching in the absence of motivation is a procedure of last resort. We would not expect the short-term results to be gratifying. But small successes, some pleasant associations, and greater familiarity with the content and activities of a subject area may eventually bring about a change in students' attitudes toward it. We discuss developing positive attitudes in the next section.

DEVELOPING ATTITUDES AND INTERESTS FOR THE FUTURE

A cherished goal of teachers is to send students forth wanting to use what they have learned and eager to learn more. Teachers want students to have favorable attitudes toward school subjects and an interest in related activities. In the preceding sections we implied that the goal was motivating students to achieve educational objectives related to knowledge and skill. Here motivation itself, as expressed in the attitudes and interests of students, is the objective. An art teacher, for example, is successful in meeting this objective if students who have had his course seek out further experiences with art, want to learn more about it, and appreciate and enjoy it throughout their lives. In other words, if they come to find art intrinsically motivating.

School-related attitudes and interests are a natural consequence of a motivational program for daily activities and an index of the success of this program. If provisions for gaining attention, developing positive expectancies, establishing incentives and providing desirable consequences are a regular part of your course, students will have many pleasant associations with the materials and methods of the course. Such associations generate positive attitudes. When they are present, the attitude of your students toward your subject area near the end of the course will be at least as positive, if not more so, than at the beginning. On the other hand, if the course has been boring, if day-to-day motivation has been lacking, you may expect this to be reflected in worsening student attitudes.

We make three assumptions in this section. (1) Positive attitudes and interests can be identified. (2) Positive attitudes and interests can be developed and strengthened by regular exposure to positively motivating conditions. (3) Attitudes and interests are predictive of future behavior.

Attitudes toward learning and school subjects are used as examples here, but we fully expect similar considerations to be useful in the development of a wide range of social and cultural attitudes. Some of these are given specific attention in Chapters 4, 5, 12, and 14.

Assessing Attitudes and Interests

Attitudes and interests are outcomes of learning. Interest is a term used to refer to a desire for activities. Attitude refers to how one acts and feels toward objects, persons, institutions, and events. The distinction between a positive attitude and an interest does not seem necessary here, so we will use the term positive attitudes to include interests. Positive or favorable attitudes (and interests) are associated with approach tendencies and feelings of pleasure, whereas negative attitudes are associated with avoidance, withdrawal, and dissatisfaction.

Attitudes may be recognized in the approach and avoidance tendencies evident in what persons *say* and *do*. What persons *say* or *say they do* may be surveyed by attitude and interest "tests" or questionnaires. What persons *do* may be observed and summarized on rating scales, checklists, or anecdotal records. These instruments and procedures are described in Chapter 17.

As measurement, these informal approaches are crude. It is important to begin somewhere, however, and there are several reasons why we may not be as concerned about some of the limitations of these procedures for present purposes as we would in other applications. First, the results are used to grade our efforts, not the students'. Hence, information from questionnaires and observations is collected for the class as a whole; individual responses may be kept anonymous. Second, we are not concerned at this stage of our sophistication with matters of fine degree, but simply with classifying attitudes as positive or negative and behavior as approach or avoidance. Finally, our use of a variety of evidence instead of reliance on a single type of report or observation, provides some safeguards against errors in judgment.

What evidence should we look for? Mager

suggests doing three things (1968, p. 29). (1) Ask yourself what your friends do or say that reveals their likes or dislikes. (2) When others comment on the likes and dislikes of their acquaintances, ask what these persons do or say that leads to this conclusion. (3) Jot down the events that lead you to believe a student is either favorably or unfavorably disposed toward a subject.

You should have no difficulty in reaching some conclusions about the attitudes of the two students for whom the following notes were made:

Student A	*Student B*
"Turned in every assignment promptly and did more than was expected."	"Failed to turn in three of four assignments on time."
"Asked to see the teacher outside of class for suggestions on further reading."	"Asked to be excused from class to participate in pep rally."
"Library records reveal additional reading of books by authors introduced in class."	"Reported inability to find any material on assigned topics."
"Seldom late or tardy. Always asks about work missed."	"Absent from class at least once a week; frequently tardy."
"In class discussion asked about points not covered in text. Volunteered information about his own related activities."	"Yawns, looks out window during class discussions. Seldom comments."
"Asked about future related courses and possibilities for independent study during interviews."	"Asked why this subject is required and if he'll have to take any more of it in college."

A useful statement of an objective is as essential to success in the development of desirable attitudes as to the achievement of any other educational goal. Although our concern is for how a student acts after he leaves your influence, you probably will not be able to check this. You can periodically check a student's approach and avoidance behavior while he is in your class, however.

A practical approach is to state your objective in terms of an expected increase in the number and percentage of approach responses recorded for students from the time you begin working with them to the time they leave you. At the very least you would wish to leave them with attitudes as positive (or no more negative) than when you first met them. Both questionnaire responses (what students say they do) and observations of student behavior (what you see them do) should be used for evidence.

Determinants of Attitudes

CONDITIONS AND CONSEQUENCES

Conditioning accounts of learning (Chapter 6) have called attention to the importance of the conditions associated with learning. Emotional responses (feeling good or feeling bad) and approach or avoidance tendencies may become attached to the subject matter or tasks of the school as a result of being paired with pleasant or unpleasant events.

One function of the teacher is to arrange for students to feel good in the presence of content and activities that he wants the student to learn to like and seek in the future. The teacher may expect, moreover, that a student will learn to avoid subject matter or tasks that have repeatedly occurred with stimuli that made him fearful, or uncomfortable, or bored him. Well-liked teachers are themselves a source of favorable associations with the subjects they teach. Which teachers will be liked? Which ones are not?

Student preferences in teachers have apparently not changed much in 30 years. Surveys completed in 1934 (Hart), 1947 (Witty), 1960 (Ryans), and 1964 (Solomon et al.) show that students like teachers who are warm and considerate, cheerful and friendly; for that matter, so do principals, supervisors, and other teachers. Furthermore, there is some evidence to link such teacher characteristics with the amount of work performed by students (Cogan, 1958), their productiveness (Ryans, 1961), their creativity (Sears, 1963), and their interest in the subject matter (Reed, 1961).

What are some of the sources of unpleasant associations? Among events that may cause physical or mental discomfort are those associated with punishment or the threat of punishment. Physical pain may attend physical punishment. More common but equally distressing are the times students are made to feel unworthy by ridicule, sarcasm, unfavorable comparisons, or the spotlighting of their failures.

Probably no less important in the establishment of negative attitudes are conditions that lead to boredom and frustration. Students become bored when tasks are monotonous, repetitive, and without personal meaning — in short, the very opposite of the conditions recommended to capture and hold student attention.

A student is frustrated by obstacles to his successful performance — unclear assignments, inadequate materials, insufficient time, and problems of hearing and vision.

Neither should we ignore physical discomfort and distractions — excessive noise, extreme temperatures, uncomfortable seating, and unnecessary restrictions, such as sitting passively for long periods of time.

It should not be necessary to point out the inappropriateness of using subject matter or learning activities as punishment. The point is not one of the appropriateness of punishment, but only the certainty that one dislikes what he is made to do as punishment. You well know how a student will feel about arithmetic when you tell him, "Just for that you can do twice as many problems for tomorrow." What will be the effect of, "I was going to assign one book report, but if you're going to take that attitude you can do three."?

THE INFLUENCE OF MODELS

Desirable models, like conditions and consequences, were recommended as a regular part of the ongoing motivational program. Repeated exposure to models who display appropriate behavior will further the development of desired attitudes.

Not all models have the same influence. The effect on student attitudes is greater if the model has prestige in the student's eyes or if he finds the model similar to himself. The football coach is a more prestigious and effective model for boys than the spinster Latin teacher. Other students are often effective models also. This is one reason for shifting part of the responsibility for classroom management, including motivation, to the students whenever possible.

There can be no guarantee that a student will imitate a given model. Whether he does or not is largely determined by (1) characteristics of the model, (2) characteristics of the observer, and (3) the consequences (pleasant and unpleasant) associated with the behavior of the model or with imitating that behavior.

The first set of factors, relating to *characteristics of the model*, include such things as the model's perceived expertise or competence, status or prestige, firmness, personal warmth, age, sex, ethnic status, and organizational affiliations. Thus, for example, students readily identify with a warm accepting teacher, with school celebrities, and with older students.

Characteristics of the observer that influence imitative behavior include such factors as the student's sex, race, socioeconomic level, and personality characteristics (dependency needs, achievement motivation, hostility level, cooperativeness, etc.). Thus, we find that boys imitate aggressive behavior more readily than girls; dependent youngsters and those with a cooperative set (as opposed to a competitive orientation) are more apt to imitate others, and angry and authoritarian students respond readily to aggressive models (Flanders, 1968).

The *consequences* that students expect if they model their behavior after that of another person is probably more important than the characteristics of either the model or the observer (Bandura, 1969). If a model is reinforced for his behavior, the tendency of the student to imitate that behavior is increased. On the other hand, if the model is punished, the student will tend not to imitate him. A promise of attractive consequences can be introduced in other ways. For example, a teacher having only average social power and status in the eyes of his students may be able to promote imitative behavior simply by telling them that they will be handsomely rewarded for it. A final consideration in relation to consequences is that a student is more

likely to imitate the behavior of models if he has been rewarded for doing so in the past. In other words, students learn to imitate a model's behavior when the conditions and consequences of doing so are gratifying.

The potential of both live or filmed models for changing attitudes has been demonstrated in numerous experiments (Bandura, 1969, 1971; Bronfenbrenner, 1972; Bryan and Schwartz, 1971). Children have been taught to share and to donate to charity, for example, and adults have lost their fear of snakes and been influenced to come to the aid of a "lady in distress." We have chosen, however, to describe a nonexperimental example of modeling from an English literature classroom (Clarizio, 1971).

The teacher of this English course recognized that reading may be a dull and boring task for many junior and senior high school students, so he usually arranged to have his students find him reading an interesting but worthwhile book as they filtered in for class. While reading, the teacher would occasionally chuckle, frown intensely, smile delightedly, or look deep in thought. Often, a student would ask about the book or make a comment such as, "It must be funny to make you laugh." Then, the teacher would tell the class the general plot of the story, but not the outcome. If asked about the outcome, he would say enthusiastically, "I haven't quite got that far yet." Sometimes, he would read an interesting or humorous part of the book aloud to whet students' appetites further. Still another tactic capitalized on a student model. If he knew a student had been reading an interesting book on auto racing, he might say, for example, "George, weren't you reading a book about cars?" If George responded with enthusiasm, the teacher would follow up with, "What was so interesting about it?" or "What was the name of the book again?" In this example, both models, the teacher and George, would be seen by students as "rewarded" for reading activity because of their keen enjoyment of it. The effects would be judged by evidence of increased reading and greater enjoyment of reading by the members of the class.

THE EFFECT OF PERSUASION

Experiments designed to compare the influence of models and persuasion on information suggest that there is little reason to expect that information alone has much effect on changing attitudes or related behavior. Persuasive arguments appear to hold little promise unless the promised results are forthcoming (Bandura, 1969, p. 601). You may persuade someone to believe he will enjoy Shakespeare if he will only try it; however, his belief will be shortlived if he fails to find the promised pleasure. He may give Shakespeare a fairer trial if you tell him in advance that he may not like Shakespeare at first but, if he sticks with it, he will change his mind (McGuire, 1964). This approach may prolong your influence, but your listener's attitudes will revert to what they were originally sooner or later, if the rewards are long delayed.

Authors of television commercials have learned that information and persuasion alone are not as effective as portraying the good things that happen to an admired model. They *show* you that when an actor-model uses "Essence E," it proves his masculinity and independence, enhances his social prestige, and leads to amorous advances by beautiful ladies.

COGNITIVE DISSONANCE

Social psychologists have experimentally evaluated the hypothesis that attitude changes occur after exposure to events that appear incompatible with previously held beliefs. There are two major methods used to create a state of intellectual inconsistency or "cog-

nitive dissonance." (1) Induce one to behave in a manner inconsistent with his attitudes. (2) Inform him that the attitudes of prestigious other persons are incompatible with his own. Rokeach (1971) has used a third method, that of calling attention to inconsistencies that exist in one's own thinking.

In a typical dissonance experiment, subjects' attitudes are first assessed through self-reports; they are then persuaded or bribed in one way or another to do things that contradict their personal views. Students who dislike mathematics might be asked, for example, to write an article for publication in the school paper urging every student to take more science. The more public the exposure of the contradiction, the better. Several studies (Festinger, 1957; Cohen, 1964) suggest that students' attitudes toward mathematics might be more favorable following this experience.

Some theorists suggest a greater change when the pressure to engage in the inconsistent behavior is less. If the personal rewards or the coercion is too great, the person may find ample excuse for behaving inconsistently. On the other hand, if he can be led to behave in an inconsistent manner voluntarily, he will be obliged to justify his behavior by finding unexpected attractions in the new point of view.

An interesting application of dissonance for changing student attitudes is mentioned by Bandura (1969, p. 620). A student's attitude may be changed, if you lead him, little by little, to take over some of the teaching chores. Increased privileges and rewards may be offered as incentives. Because a teaching role will be opposite to the student's previous attitudes about school activities, the conditions for dissonance and attitude change exist. The promise of this approach will be no surprise to experienced teachers who have observed that putting a problem student "in charge" may bring about a marked improvement in his behavior. When peer group members can be used in this way, they not only change their own attitudes, but they may become excellent models for changing the attitudes of others.

The second major approach, informing persons how other important persons act and feel, is sufficiently similar to modeling to require no additional comment. At least a temporary adjustment of attitudes might be expected.

Rokeach (1971) has used his approach to produce rather enduring changes in the importance university students give to the values of equality and freedom. His method was to have students rank 18 values, including freedom and equality. They also wrote a statement about their position toward civil rights demonstrations. He then showed them data to indicate that Michigan State students rank freedom first and equality eleventh. He told them these data meant that "Michigan State University students, in general, are much more interested in their own freedom than they are in the freedom of other people." Data that suggested further inconsistencies in students' attitudes toward civil rights demonstrations were also presented.

In the next phase of the experiment Rokeach asked the subjects to rate how satisfied or dissatisfied they were with (1) what they found out about their values and attitudes and (2) their ranking of each of the 18 values. These ratings of self-satisfaction-dissatisfaction were found to predict value changes.

Significant increases in the values students assigned to equality and freedom were found to persist 3 to 5 months and 15 to 17 months later. More direct evidence of the effect of the treatment was obtained by arranging a mail solicitation to membership by the NAACP, a civil rights organization. After two solicitations, one at 3 to 5 months, another at 15 to 17 months, 197 subjects receiving the attitude change treatment responded to the appeal in some way, as compared to 169 control subjects who did not receive the treatment.

Rokeach's approach has not, to our knowledge, been used to influence students' attitudes toward learning or subject areas of instruction. However, the relatively enduring results that he reports as a result of a rather brief treatment may have implications for efforts to change these attitudes, as well as others that you accept as educational objectives. More will be said about attitude change in relation to prejudice in Chapter 12.

Summary

1. Motivation for a school activity may come from an *intrinsic* interest in an activity itself or from the promise of *extrinsic* or external reward or punishment.

2. A desire to achieve is a personality characteristic related to parental influences, but courses that emphasize the importance of "achievement motivation" and provide for the achievement of reasonable goals may effect desirable changes in school-age children.

3. A learner's tolerance for strong motivation is affected by his personality and ability. Extroverts need and tolerate external pressure better than introverts. Special care must be taken with emotionally disturbed and less able children.

Psychological Explanations

4. *Drive-reduction* theories explain motivation as a drive generated by internal needs related to pain or pleasure. Although drive is originally undirected, we learn to seek objects or conditions that will reduce our drive and satisfy our need.

5. Curiosity, exploration, and other "positive" motives appear to occur in the absence of need and are not adequately explained by drive reduction theories.

6. *Self-actualization* views hold that we are motivated to act in ways that we believe will lead to greater self esteem and personal adequacy.

7. *Information-processing* models account for actions by supposing that we function as if we were computers.

Developing Motivation for School Learning

8. *To gain attention* (and control distraction):
   a. Use natural attention getters such as novelty, surprise, drama, and challenge.
   b. Teach students to give attention on signal by associating signals with natural attention getters and rewards.
   c. Help students to become accustomed to the distractions normally present in different work situations.
9. *To develop positive expectancies:*
   a. Describe or show the intended outcomes (objectives) of learning.
   b. Help students to relate these outcomes to their interests and to the world outside the classroom.
   c. Develop realistically higher levels of expectancy. Students with low achievement motivation or a history of failure require special attention. Set goals well within reach, use praise liberally, and minimize the penalties of failure.
10. *To establish incentive contingencies:*
    a. Emphasize positive incentives (privileges, approval, reward) instead of negative incentives (blame and punishment), because the effects of the latter are less predictable.
    b. When negative incentives are necessary: (1) use loss of privileges rather than harsher forms; (2) redirect behavior; (3) follow with opportunities to gain rewards; and (4) be systematic, impartial, and unemotional.
    c. Use "contingency contracting" to offer students the opportunity to do something they want to do for first doing something you want them to do.
11. *To provide feedback and consequences:* make feedback or

knowledge of results during school tasks frequent, immediate, specific, complete, and related to general as well as specific objectives.

12. *Manage competition so that:*
    a. All competitors have an approximately equal chance of winning.
    b. Students compete against their own records or accepted standards, as in "mastery" learning.
    c. The importance of winning is played down and overemphasis on team spirit avoided.
13. *When analyzing special problems* of motivation, try to see the problem from the point of view of the learner and change conditions if:
    a. Performance is punishing.
    b. Nonperformance or other performance is rewarding.
    c. Performing does not really make a difference.

Developing Attitudes and Interests

14. Use observations and questionnaires to assess approach and avoidance behaviors related to attitudes and interests.
15. State an objective in terms of increasing the number and percent of approach responses (and decreasing avoidance responses) during the course of instruction.
16. Encourage positive associations with your teaching area by getting students to like you and to feel good during activities related to your teaching areas. Minimize negative associations by combatting boredom, frustration, fatigue, and failure. Never use school work as punishment.
17. Provide models (admired persons or persons like the learner) who demonstrate desirable attitudes and related behaviors.
18. Experiment with "dissonance" to stimulate change:
    a. Induce students to act in ways that are incompatible with the attitudes you wish to change.
    b. Inform students of the attitudes of admired and respected persons that differ from their own.
    c. Point out inconsistencies in their own beliefs.
19. Limit persuasion to those situations where promised incentive contingencies actually follow related behaviors.

CHAPTER 8
Knowledge, Learning, and Retention

"I just don't understand how someone who has memorized the words to 300 Rock and Roll records can't remember a few historical dates." *(Drawing by Glen Dines from* Today's Education NEA Journal, 1973)

Knowledge Objectives
Psychological Approaches to Knowledge Learning
Learning and Remembering
Recommendations for Instruction

A number of authors who have attempted to classify and characterize educational objectives have given specific attention to knowledge. Bloom et al. (1956, p. 28) identifies 12 classes of knowledge objectives. They define knowledge as "Little more than the remembering of the idea or phenomenon in a form very close to that in which it was originally encountered." But they also acknowledge the importance of knowledge when they write, "Knowledge is quite frequently regarded as basic to all the other ends or purposes of education. Productive thinking cannot be carried out in a vacuum but must be based on the knowledge of some of the realities." (1956, p. 33)

Psychologists have other terms for knowledge learning. Jensen (1969) refers to "associative learning." Gagné (1970) describes "verbal association" and "multiple discrimination." Tennyson and Merrill (1971) call attention to the similarity in the use of these terms and what we ordinarily refer to as "memorization." Briggs (1968) calls this "reproductive" learning.

Some psychologists see knowledge as much more than memorized associations, however. Those with a cognitive orientation prefer terms that suggest that knowledge has meaning for the individual, such as "identification" or "representation." These psychologists do not deny the existence of rote learning, but they believe that knowledge learning is more often a matter of relating new knowledge to what we already know (Ausubel, 1968). It is this relationship that gives meaning to new knowledge.

| OBJECTIVES FOR CHAPTER 8 | 1. Write knowledge objectives at different levels of generality to illustrate the range of knowledge outcomes. |
| | 2. Distinguish between cognitive and S-R approaches to knowledge learning by giving examples of the concepts and procedures emphasized by each. |

**OBJECTIVES
Continued**

3. Know which types of knowledge items studied in school tend to be retained well and poorly.
4. Explain how the methods used to measure retention affect conclusions about how well students retain what they learn.
5. Describe three types or stages of memory that psychologists have postulated and tell how each stage functions with respect to other stages.
6. Give examples that illustrate the possible effects of each of the following processes on memory: proactive interference, retroactive interference, obliterative subsumption, reconstruction, and repression.
7. Give examples of good and poor teaching practices with respect to (a) organizing informational material for learning and (b) providing reinforcement and feedback after students try to learn.
8. Select a learning task in which interference with a similar task that might be undertaken at about the same time is probable. Describe the steps you might take to reduce interference in this situation.
9. Present a plan for review of a segment of knowledge acquired in one of your own courses that illustrates our recommendations with respect to the distribution of review and the type of study or practice during review.

KNOWLEDGE OBJECTIVES

Knowledge is the simplest outcome of cognitive learning. It is valued for itself and as a prerequisite for more complex learning. Every course of instruction includes knowledge objectives. An overview of the number and varieties of cognitive objectives has been provided by Metfessel, Michael, and Kirsner (1969), and the parts of their table of objectives that deal most directly with knowledge are shown in Table 8-1.

A typical objective has at least three parts: (1) a noun, such as "ability," or an adjective, such as "able"; (2) a verb, such as "state" or "define," or an infinitive such as "to state" or "to define"; and (3) and object, for example, "terms" or "principles."

Table 8-1 provides concrete illustrations of typical knowledge objectives. It is also an aid in preparing statements of objectives for different types of knowledge. The left column of the table lists the main classes of knowledge (Bloom et al., 1956). To state an objective for any class, simply select an infinitive from the second column and an objective from the last column. Thus, for the first classification, "Knowledge of terminology," you might select "To recall" from the second column and "Names" from the third column. The objective would be "ability to recall names." Similarly, an objective related to another classification, "Knowledge of principles and generalizations," might be "ability to recognize laws."

A glance at other entries in the third column will suggest the number and variety of things that students must learn to "know."

Chapter 2 reported a difference of opinion among educators and educational psychologists regarding the degree to which objectives should spell out the behavior expected of students. Table 8-1 suggests objectives that have some of the characteristics of objectives stated in terms of desired student behaviors. The infinitives favored refer to activities instead of unobservables such as "to know," "to understand," or "to appreciate." Statements based directly on the table represent an intermediate level of specificity, however. Ability to recall "names," for example, does not say which names, which class of names, or even the subject area from which the names would be drawn. Such objectives do not have other characteristics of the most specific behavioral objectives illustrated in Chapter 2 in that they do not give (1) the situation or "context" in which the names will be recalled or (2) the standard or "criterion" of performance expected.

Although objectives such as those of Table 8-1 are not "behavioral" in the strictest sense of that term, they are relatively easily made more behavioral if a more specific (and longer) list of outcomes is desired. Some examples for several types will be presented.

1.10 *Knowledge of Specifics*

    1.11 Knowledge of Terminology
Example from table: "Ability to define terms."
More specific example: "Is able to define the term 'compound.'"
Still more specific example: "When asked to respond orally in class (context) is able to define 'compound' in the exact words of the text (criterion)."

    1.12 Knowledge of Specific Facts
Example from table: "Ability to recall factual information."
More specific example: "Ability to state the regions where air masses originate and the direction of movement in summer and winter."
Still more specific example:
"Given a map of the Northern Hemisphere (context), marks the regions where at least three (criterion) air masses originate and correctly indicates the direction of movement in summer and winter for each of the three (criterion)."

1.20 *Knowledge of Ways and Means of Dealing with Specifics*

    1.21 Knowledge of Conventions
Example from table: "To identify symbols."
More specific example: "Ability to state the meaning of proofreader's marks."
Still more specific example: "Given a page of edited manuscript with proofreader's marks, states orally or in writing the meaning of at least 9 out of 10 marks."

    1.22 Knowledge of Trends and Sequences
Example from table: "To recognize sequences."
More specific example: "Ability to state the stages in the life cycles of insects."
Still more specific example: "When the names of the four stages in the life cycle of a housefly are written on the chalkboard, the student is able to number these in the exact order in which they occur."

1.30 *Knowledge of the Universals and Abstractions in a Field*
Example from table: "To identify laws."
More specific example: "Ability to identify a correct statement of the general gas laws."
Still more specific example: "Given a list of correct and incorrect statements of the relationships among the temperature, pressure, and volume of a gas, checks all correct statements of the general gas law."

Table 8-1

Instrumentation of the Taxonomy of Educational Objectives: Cognitive Domain for Knowledge (Metfessel, Michael, and Kirsner, 1969. By permission of the Clinical Psychology Publishing Company, Inc.)

Taxonomy Classification	Key Words	
	Examples of Infinitives	Examples of Direct Objects
1.00 Knowledge		
1.10 Knowledge of specifics		
1.11 Knowledge of terminology	To define, to distinguish To acquire, to identify, To recall, to recognize	Vocabulary, terms, terminology, meaning(s), definitions, referents, elements
1.12 Knowledge of specific facts	To recall, to recognize, To acquire, to identify	Facts, factual information, (sources), (names), (dates), (events), (persons), (places), (time periods), properties, examples, phenomena
1.20 Knowledge of ways and means of dealing with specifics		
1.21 Knowledge of conventions	To recall, to identify, To recognize, to acquire	Form(s), conventions, uses, usage, rules, ways, devices, symbols, representations, style(s), format(s)
1.22 Knowledge of trends, sequences	To recall, to recognize, To acquire, to identify	Action(s), processes, movement(s), continuity, development(s), trend(s), sequence(s), causes, relationship(s), forces, influences

You should practice writing other objectives, such as those from the table, and the more specific examples, as well. An examination of these examples show that the more general objectives, which are nevertheless in terms of behavior, will require only an infinitive to show the action expected and a word or phrase to name the type of thing acted on. More specific objectives require more specific identification of both the action and the object and a statement of both "context" and "criterion" as follows:

1. A verb or infinitive naming an observable action.

2. The specific object of the action.

3. The "givens" of the situation in which the action is to be observed.

4. The standard of performance expected.

Table 8-1 (cont'd)

Taxonomy Classification	Key Words	
	Examples of Infinitives	Examples of Direct Objects
1.23 Knowledge of classifications and categories	To recall, to recognize, To acquire, to identify	Area(s), type(s), feature(s), class(es), set(s), division(s), arrangement(s), classification(s), category/categories
1.24 Knowledge of criteria	To recall, to recognize, To acquire, to identify	Criteria, basics, elements
1.25 Knowledge of methodology	To recall, to recognize, To acquire, to identify	Methods, techniques, approaches, uses, procedures, treatments
1.30 Knowledge of the universals and abstractions in a field		
1.31 Knowledge of principles, generalizations	To recall, to recognize, To acquire, to identify	Principle(s), generalization(s), proposition(s), fundamentals, laws, principal elements, implication(s)
1.32 Knowledge of theories and structures	To recall, to recognize, To acquire, to identify	Theories, bases, interrelations, structure(s), organization(s), formulation(s)

PSYCHOLOGICAL APPROACHES TO KNOWLEDGE LEARNING

Teacher education programs have traditionally focused attention on the teacher's organization and presentation of learning material *before* the learner responds. This emphasis is consistent with the theoretical tradition in psychology, which we have called the cognitive approach. Students are seen as capable of organizing and thinking. Teachers try to help students carry out these activities efficiently.

A somewhat different emphasis was suggested for the competing theoretical tradition of behaviorism or S-R psychology. This tradition suggests principles of learning related to the control of the performance of the learner by conditions of practice and reinforcement *after* a response by the learner.

Cognitive Emphases

Cognitive psychologists, you will recall from Chapter 6, think of a student with purposes and a store of knowledge. In learning or reaching decisions, they believe he seeks information to relate to his needs and prior knowledge. His search for knowledge is selective. He tends to see what he looks for and to overlook or be unaware of details that do not relate to his need or "fit in" with his beliefs. If he lacks transportation, for example, he sees an approaching automobile as the cab he needs; not as a Checker, Plymouth, or Ford; not as a 1972 or a 1974 model, with or without wheelcovers. His previous knowledge of cabs makes him "see" a cab as having much the same size and characteristics regardless of how near or fat it is or the angle at which he sees it.

From the cognitive point of view observations and facts have "meaning" when they are categorized, coded, or otherwise related to need or knowledge. Rote learning or verbatim memorization is considered rare, although it would be the only choice if a learner is completely unprepared, in the sense of having a related store of knowledge. Nonsense syllables may approach meaninglessness, but any name has some meaning for all but the youngest child. Most learners will know that objects have names, and they may have a mental image of the object to associate with a name he hears or sees. Similarly, the names or words for concepts, principles, and even more complex products of learning may be related to information or ideas about reality that one already has.

The conditions of efficient learning accepted by cognitive psychologists are suggested by their view of the learner. These conditions relate to the interaction of the learner with his environment and the ways in which new information may be presented to aid his perception of useful relationships. Every learner is encouraged to think about what is being taught and to seek to organize and relate new material to what he now knows.

Repetition with feedback of results may be recommended to insure the correctness of perception, but the gradual strengthening of responses by practice is thought unnecessary. Instead the teacher can often produce the desired behavior at once by giving the student insight into the demands of a new situation.

ORGANIZATION OF KNOWLEDGE (CODING)

Many of the cognitive psychologist's recommendations for improving learning and retention are based on the simple principle that *organization facilitates learning.* The organization of material to be learned may enable us to overcome our limited ability to attend to more than about seven items at once. By organizing the material into larger units or "chunks," a process that some call "coding," we can deal with larger "information-rich" units instead of "information-poor" units (Miller, 1956, 1968).

The advantage and the generality of this process is emphasized in George Miller's statement:

"It is conceivable that all complex, symbolic learning proceeds in this way. The material is first organized into parts which, once they cohere, can be replaced by other symbols—abbreviations, initial letters, schematic images, names, or what have you—and eventually the whole scope of the argument is translated into a few symbols which can all be grasped at one time." (1956, p. 45)

Miller (1956, p. 43) provides an illustration of the advantages of coding by computer operators who learn to "read" a string of lights, each of which may be on or off, almost instantly. No more than a few lights can be remembered individually; but, when they are coded into sets of two, three, four or more, the task is well within the capacity of an operator. A three-to-one coding is illustrated in Figure 8-1. Once the operator learns the

Lights to be remembered	○○○	○○○	○○○	○○○	○○○	○○○
Coded equivalents	3	0	5	1	7	4

Code:

●●● = 0   ○●● = 4
●●○ = 1   ○●○ = 5
●○● = 2   ○○● = 6
●○○ = 3   ○○○ = 7

Example of coding three elements into one for learning and recall.

new code, he can handle three times as much information as he could previously. This may be seen as a simple trick, but somewhat analogous methods may serve us well in more complex situations.

One situation where coding is applied to great advantage is in language. Sounds are grouped as words, words as phrases, phrases as sentences, and sentences as narratives—each of the larger units contains much more useful information (for our purposes read information as ideas) than the same number of component parts—yet we receive, learn, recall, and work with larger units readily, apparently quite unaware of the coding we do.

The result of coding or chunking is often a hierarchial arrangement or organization. Such an arrangement may be a universal tendency in human information handling. We see it in the way libraries classify books, scientists group plants and animals, and students are taught to outline papers. Such examples lend weight to Ausubel's recommended use of "advance organizers."

ADVANCE ORGANIZERS

Ausubel (1968) is a leading contemporary cognitive theorist. He advocates the use of verbal propositions that help learners relate new knowledge to what is previously known. According to his view, the most general statements or ideas are to be presented and learned first, those of somewhat lesser gen-

erality next, and specific details last. This ordering principle is called "progressive differentiation."

The sequence of instruction suggested by Ausubel is the opposite of that suggested by S-R psychologists, whose views will be considered next. Figure 8-2 contrasts the cognitive and S-R beliefs about sequence in learning facts, concepts, and principles. The cognitive view suggests proceeding from the top down, learning more general principles, then concepts, then facts and other details. S-R approaches suggest starting from the bottom and working up.

RECEPTION VERSUS DISCOVERY

Jerome Bruner (1966), another leading contemporary cognitive psychologist, agrees with Ausubel that the desirable course of

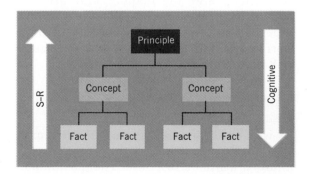

Figure 8-2.
Cognitive and S-R views of sequence in learning.

learning is from the general to the particular, but he is a proponent of relatively independent problem solving in which one learns by the "discovery" of useful relationships. Ausubel provides a model for meaningful "reception learning" and advocates direct teaching or guidance in relating facts to the more general ideas previously learned. Bruner, on the other hand, would confront learners with a general problem. Needed facts and data, he believes, are learned best when they are found independently and related to solutions in the course of problem solving.

THE TEACHER'S ROLE

The ability to organize information for learning may be a characteristic of all persons, but it does not follow that this ability is always used or used well. Our own experience and evidence from continuing research shows that information may not be processed at all if learners are not motivated to do so (Anderson, 1970). The efficient use of organization in processing information depends also on both the learner's previous knowledge background (Kumar, 1971) and the direction he receives (Kumar, 1971; Rohwer, 1972). We conclude that the teacher's responsibility as a manager of instruction will include (1) motivating the learner to try to organize his learning, (2) providing him with background knowledge, and (3) helping him use this knowledge in the organization of new knowledge. These are ways a teacher may help the learner respond effectively when he faces a task that requires knowledge learning.

Stimulus-Response Emphases

As we have stated, S-R approaches give most attention to the conditions that accompany or follow a learner's response. The most important of these are reinforcement and practice. In a typical procedure the teacher tells or shows the exact content to be learned. Then he has students practice responding with knowledge of results. When he can, he supplements knowledge of correct results with additional reinforcements, such as words or smiles.

To learn a procedure a student practices it with a checklist. As he practices, his correct responses are confirmed and his errors ignored or corrected. To learn the names of chemical symbols, he is given a list of names and symbols for study. Then he is asked to give the names of symbols shown alone. He is prompted at first; with more practice prompts become unnecessary.

SHAPING AND FADING

An important aspect of the association strategy is the method of forming complex responses. "Shaping" is a procedure of initially reinforcing approximations to the desired responses, then gradually raising the standards for correctness to the desired final level. If the task is to learn the names of unfamiliar figures, including that of a parallelogram, a student might say "paragram" or "parallel figure." If such a response were to be given on the first practice trial or so, reinforcement would not be withheld; later it would be, unless the name of the figure were given exactly.

"Fading" is illustrated by the gradual withdrawing of prompts until the student is able to respond independently. Initially, prompts are used liberally. Gradually they are withdrawn, a few at a time, until the student can respond correctly on his own. Meanwhile shaping also occurs. If a prompted response is an approximation to the desired independent response, it is reinforced initially. Later a student must respond with fewer and fewer prompts, that is, more and more perfectly, to earn a reward. Finally, reward is given only for a correct response without prompts. Thus, fading and shaping go hand in hand.

CHAINING

Gagné (1970, p. 131) reminds us that learning a name may be more than a simple S-R link between a stimulus object and a naming response. He describes naming as the formation of a stimulus-response "chain." He offers the following account.

"When a child is shown a parallelogram and told its name and conditions are right, he will connect the appearance of the object (S_1) with the response of observing its characteristics (R_1). This response is in turn a stimulus (S_2) for naming the object (R_2). Saying the word parallelogram in the presence of the object appears to weld the parallelogram-observing S_1-R_1 link to the seeing-naming S_2-R_2 link so that we have:

$$S_1 \quad \rightarrow \quad R_1\text{-}S_2 \quad \rightarrow \quad R_2$$
$$\text{Object} \qquad \text{Observing-} \qquad \text{Naming}$$
$$\text{Seeing}$$

VERBAL STATEMENTS

Gagné suggests that acts or other knowledge items may be learned like names, and verbal statements of all types (definitions, rules, principles, etc.) may be learned as longer chains of S-R associations in which each response becomes the stimulus for the next response of the sequence. If the individual words in a sentence, for example, have been learned previously, use instructions or an example to get students to give the words in the proper order. Then reinforce them for this performance. Finally, arrange for repetition or practice with continuing reinforcement for correct performances.

One of the functions of practice in this situation is to eliminate mistakes that may occur because of incorrect associations. The first word in a sentence, for example, not only tends to prompt the second word but also the third and fourth words, and other parts, also. As a result, words may occur in the wrong order. Repetition provides the conditions for overcoming such tendencies by rewarding the correct order and ignoring or correcting wrong ones.

DISCRIMINATION LEARNING

Another type of knowledge learning described in S-R accounts is called "multiple discrimination" (Gagné, 1970) or "discrete element memorization" (Merrill, 1971). The task is learning a set of associations so that the learner responds differently to each of a number of different but somewhat similar stimuli. Examples include discriminating among different amounts, colors, shapes, symbols, acquaintances, foreign words, makes of car, and many other objects or events. This type of learning might be preceded by the learning of a name for each of the objects or events to be discriminated. The task, then, is largely one of eliminating interference among responses to the different members of the set, that is, weakening tendencies to give the name of one member of the set to another, such as calling yellow "orange" or indicating a "6" as a "9." If individual names of the objects or symbols to be discriminated have been learned, they may be presented together, perhaps by presenting collections of objects or presenting pictures or symbols on the chalkboard. Then students are asked to match stimuli (symbols or objects) with responses (names); correct responses are confirmed or reinforced, while incorrect ones are not. This practice, perhaps with variations to heighten interest, would be repeated as many times as necessary to eliminate errors.

Especially long verbal sequences or especially large sets of items to be discriminated may be broken into parts for learning, although there are no reliable guides to just how large each part should be.

PROGRAMMED LEARNING

S-R emphases on practice and reinforcement is evident in the "programmed" or self-

| 5 | The basic idea of programed learning is that the most efficent, pleasant, and permanent learning takes place when the student proceeds through a course by a large number of small, easy—to—take steps. |
| | If each step the student takes is small, he (is/is not) likely to make errors. |

| is not | PRINTED IN THE U.S.A. |

6	A <u>program</u>, then, is made up of a large number of small, easy—to—take steps.
	A <u>student</u> can proceed from knowing very little about a subject to mastery of the subject by going through a _____ .
	If the program is carefully prepared, he shoud make (many/few) errors along the way.

| program   few | |

7	Programed learning has many features which are different from conventional methods of learning.
	You have already learned one of these principles.
	This principle is that a student learns best if he proceeds by small _____ .

| steps | |

8	The features of programed learning are applications of <u>learning principles</u> discovered in psychological laboratories.
	You have learned the first of these principles.
	You can guess that we call it the Principle of Small _____ .

| Steps | |

Figure 8-3.   Example of a Linear Program (From *The Principles of Programmed Learning,* Copyright © 1961 by Teaching Machines Incorporated.)

9 The principles on which programed learning are based were discovered in (psychological/astrological) laboratories.

The first of these principles is the Principle of Small Steps.

psychological

10 The first principle of programed learning is

The Principle of ___ _____ __ _____ _____ .

Small Steps

PRINTED IN THE U.S.A.

11 What is the first Principle of Programed Learning?

_____ ___ _____ _____ _____ _____

The Principle of Small Steps.

instructional materials that this theory has helped to popularize. The materials developed are similar to those shown in Figure 8-3. Because all students work through the items in the same straight "path" or sequence, this type of program is called a "linear" program.

During learning, a student sees only one small item or "frame," such as one of those shown in Figure 8-3, at a time. Others are covered. He makes his response, then he is allowed to see the answer as a reinforcement. Hundreds of such items are used to lead the student by many small steps to the per-

formance desired. At each step he is given enough clues so that an error is unlikely and reinforcement is likely. The items are arranged or "programmed" to provide many repetitions.

As learning proceeds, the hints or prompts are faded (dropped out) until the learner is responding with the degree of independence that the authors of the program desire. Active responding, reinforcement, and repetition are evident in learning from programmed materials. The principle of shaping by successive approximations is represented by the movement from an almost completely prompted response, which is acceptable initially, to a completely independent one, required eventually.

In the sample program of Figure 8-3, for example, he is given the "principle of small steps" in frames 5 and 6, in frames 7 to 10 the principle is repeated in various ways and the learner is asked to give more and more of the answer himself. Finally, in line 11, he states the principle himself. Later frames provide systematic review of this and other programming principles.

S-R AND COGNITIVE PROGRAMS COMPARED

The contrast between the S-R and cognitive approaches to knowledge learning may be illustrated by a comparison of their styles in the preparation of self-instructional materials. "Teaching machines" are devices for presenting programmed materials to the learner. A brief sample of a cognitive program about teaching machines appears in Figure 8-4. Because different students follow somewhat different "paths" in completing such a program, it is called a "branching" program.

In the program of Figure 8-4 a substantial amount of information is presented, and the student is asked to use that information in answering a question. On the basis of his answers he is directed to new information that either confirms his response or attempts to correct a misconception it reveals, perhaps by presenting the information again in a different way or simpler way.

There are several important differences in this sample of programming and that presented for the S-R approach in Figure 8-3. Each item or frame of the cognitively planned program is organized to teach. Another look at the S-R example or any S-R instructional program reveals that their conceptual organization is much less apparent. The S-R approach does not emphasize exposition, inter-pretation, or explanation of information because it is "response centered."

S-R principles suggest asking for the recall of information, because this is what is to be practiced. Cognitive programmers, on the other hand, are satisfied with recognition responses that reveal understanding or the lack of it. They are not concerned with practicing particular responses.

Another difference in the two types of programs is in the treatment of errors. The S-R program is designed to provide frequent reinforcement for correct responses, and the program is planned so that almost every response is correct. The cognitive programmer, on the other hand, cares little for reinforcement. He does not seek to eliminate errors. In fact, he may find they serve a useful purpose in clarifying the learner's perception of correct and incorrect relationships in the material. It may be important for the learner to experience typical errors, so that he may more clearly see how to avoid them.

Laboratory Studies of Verbal Associations

For 20 years Hermann Ebbinghaus (1913) learned, relearned, and memorized lists of nonsense syllables or three-letter combinations, such as SYN, XAD, and NOF. He chose these syllables because they were "meaningless," that is, they had not been previously learned and associated with each other as words would have been.

Ebbinghaus was the pioneer in the study of verbal associations, a popular psychological topic. His work was even more remarkable because he was both the experimenter and the only subject. His method was to write each syllable on a slip of paper, shuffle a large number of slips (over 2000), draw out a dozen or more, learn them, reshuffle, and draw out another set to learn. Today, the syllables are

Page 6

In 1924, Dr. Sidney L. Pressey invented a small machine that would score a multiple-choice examination automatically at the time the answer-button was pushed.

Although he designed it as a testing machine he perceived that by a simple expedient he could use the machine as a teaching device. All he had to do was to design it so that, for each question, the correct answer-button had to be pushed before a subsequent question would appear in the window.

From this simple beginning, the concept of "teaching machines" has grown until now the educator is faced with many types and styles, from the simplest cardboard device costing pennies to incredibly complex electronic wonders costing thousands of dollars.

But don't despair. All "teaching machines" have three characteristics in common:

1. They present information and require frequent responses by the student.
2. They provide immediate feedback to the student, informing him whether his response is appropriate or not.
3. They allow the student to work individually and to adjust his own rate of progress to his own needs and capabilities.

•   •   •

Now, based on the three criteria listed above, is the educational motion picture, as it is normally used, a "teaching machine"?

 * Page 6   Yes
** Page 4   No

---

 * The student who answers "Yes" is referred to page 6.
** The student who answers "No" is referred to page 4.

The educational motion picture, as it is normally used, *does* present factual information but does *not* satisfy any of the other conditions set down for a "teaching machine"; no response is called for, no feedback is given, and the student has no control over his rate of progress.

The standard educational motion picture, then, is similar to a well-prepared lecture, but is not a "teaching machine."

Please read the conditions on page 8 again and then select the other alternative.

Page 4

Right! The educational motion picture, as it is normally used, is not a "teaching machine."

1. Although the motion picture presents information, it does not require periodic responses from the student in the form of answers, selections, or motor responses.
2. Since it does not ask for responses, it does not indicate whether the responses are appropriate or not.
3. It does not allow the individual class member to adjust his rate of progress to his own needs and capabilities.

•   •   •

Imagine, however, an educational motion picture which requires that the students answer questions periodically on a printed answer form. Would this then constitute a "teaching machine"?

Page 2   Yes
Page 12   No

Figure 8-4.
Sample pages from a branching program. *(From Cram D., 1961, Copyright © Fearon Publishers.)*

often mounted on a cylinder or drum. As the drum turns, it exposes one syllable at a time and the learner's task is to anticipate the next item on the list. The amount of time the learner sees each syllable is generally about 2 seconds.

There are many variations of presentation procedures, of course. In the "paired associates" method, pairs of syllables are presented. After the first time through the list, the memory drum presents the first member of each pair for a given time before the second member appears. The subject's task is to name the second member of the pair when the first appears.

Investigations of this type of verbal learning have related the rate of learning, as measured by the number of presentations or the time required to learn a list, to the length of the list, the meaningfulness of the listed items, the spacing of presentations, the distribution of practice, and many other variables. Retention of material learned has been studied in relation to the time between learning and testing, the nature of the learner's activity in this interval, the rate of initial learning, and the degree of learning. The degree of learning and "overlearning" is measured by the number of trials or repetitions following the first perfect recitation.

The nature of the errors in learning and remembering lists has revealed a great deal about the course of such learning, also. A "serial position effect" has been observed, for example. The syllables or words near the beginning and end of a list are learned first and best; those just past the middle of the list are the most difficult to learn. Serial position effects occur when learning spelling words, vocabulary lists, mathematical or chemical symbols, and English sentences, as well as nonsense syllables.

Although the learning of verbal associations is closely related to an S-R or an association tradition in psychology, recently the role of mental images as links between items to be associated has been extensively investigated. Rohwer (1970) reviewed a series of experiments by himself and others and offered some recommendations for the instruction of school age children. The first of these concerned the manner in which information can best be presented to children to take advantage of the most efficient learning strategies.

1. Stimulus or cue words to which children are to respond should be of the type likely to prompt images of reality in the children's mind.

2. Pictured stimuli are likely to be more effective than word stimuli.

3. Items to be associated should be presented along with some meaningful verbal statement, such as "the cow jumped over the moon."

4. For older children (grade 6) it is better to show items to be associated in some type of interaction (the cow jumping the moon) or in spatial relation (the cow over the moon) rather than just together (the cow and the moon).

Rohwer's second set of recommendations suggested teaching children two types of learning strategies to increase their learning power.

5. Verbal elaboration techniques, such as using two words that are to be associated, perhaps cow and moon, in a sentence.

6. Visual imagery, for example, imagining that they see the cow jump over the moon.

The prominence of nonsense syllables and word lists in the world of the psychology of verbal learning has probably been a factor in the tendency of more than a few educators to too readily doubt the significance of psychological studies for the practice of teaching. This is unfortunate, we believe, and we hope the preceding sections have shown it to be an uninformed and inaccurate assessment of the value of the findings. For one thing, similar considerations are important for learning and retaining the alphabet, mathematical and chemical symbols, color codes in electronics, and other lists and tables. Then, too, some of the variables found to affect prose learning were suggested by verbal learning studies. The study of imagery provides an example. Anderson (Anderson and Hidde, 1971; Anderson and Kulkavy, 1972) has extended the laboratory studies of imagery to the learning of meaningful prose. He reports that imagery instructions, that is, asking students to create mental images of the things and events described in sentences and longer prose passages, will help students learn those things and events.

LEARNING AND REMEMBERING

The words "learning" and "remembering" are often used in much the same way. Teachers do not routinely separate objectives for learning and remembering. Saying that one has learned to recite a poem means that he remembers it. The two words are not always interchangeable, however. You would not say that you *learn* that you had fish prepared this way the last time you had lunch in the school cafeteria, and you would not use *remember* to report acquiring the skill of constructing a poi for a poi-poi dance, or the knowledge that an "Angstrom" is a unit of length equal to one hundred-millionth of a centimeter.

Learning suggests a change in knowledge, capability, or behavior; remembering suggests retrieving stored information or repeating behavior. However, one must learn something to remember it, and learning cannot be demonstrated unless one remembers at least until he is tested. Thus, we recognize a difference between learning and remembering, but

we expect that the distinction will seldom be clear cut.

Measuring Retention

How well and how long will school learning be retained? An answer must depend on what is learned and how we measure retention. The three most commonly used methods for measuring retention of knowledge are (1) recall, (2) recognition, and (3) relearning or "savings."

RECALL

A recall test of retention requires a learner to independently state or otherwise supply the expected answers. The corresponding objective test form for recall for names, dates, places, and the like is the "fill in," "completion," or "short answer" item. Examples are: "The three major parts of the insect's body are: _____, _____, and _____." "Who were the authors of *Pygmalion in the Classroom?*"

One's ability to recall organized information on an object or event is tested when we use "essay" or "free response" items, such as, "What steps did labor take to protect its own interests in the three decades after the Civil War?" or "Name the private and public organizations that are most active in efforts to prevent and control communicable diseases in the State of Michigan and describe the programs and methods of each."

RECOGNITION

Recognition is demonstrated by one's ability to select a correct response from among other incorrect alternatives. The familiar multiple-choice test is a test of recognition. Retention, in the form of recognition, is often remarkably good, and learners frequently score much higher on tests of this type than they would on tests requiring that they supply the correct answer. The difference between performance of students in recognition and recall tests may be that recognition requires less complete retention than recall. You may not be able to recall an entire name, face, or statement, but you may remember something about it that corresponds to some characteristics of the correct option in a recognition test. Experiments have been conducted that show that when correct and incorrect items on a recognition test differ only slightly so that partial recognition on the basis of previous knowledge is difficult or impossible, recognition is not superior to recall (McNulty, 1965, 1966). When persons are given partial cues to items to be recalled, which might help them in much the same way as their recognition of parts of the correct response in a recognition test, recall is improved also (Howe, 1969).

RELEARNING

The last measurement technique we will discuss is the relearning method. When this method is used, the time or number of trials persons require to reach a learning objective is recorded. After an interval in which forgetting occurs, subjects reach the same objective and the number of trials or the amount of time required for relearning is compared with the number or amount required the first time. The difference or "savings" represents the effects of retention. Although this method of measuring retention is less common and probably less generally useful than recall or recognition, it is probably the most sensitive of the three. Burtt (1941) demonstrated, for example, that reading Greek to a fifteen-month-old boy had a pronounced effect on the boy's relearning of the same passages years later. Burtt repeated the same 20 lines of Greek for the boy each day for 90 days; then he read 20 other lines to him each day for 90 days; then, a third set of lines for 90 days, and so on until the boy was three years old, when

all contact with Greek ceased. Five years later when the boy was eight, the boy relearned the passages he had heard in 30% less time than it took him to learn other Greek passages he had never heard before.

Later, at fourteen years of age, the boy's Greek "savings" had dropped to 8%. Finally, when the boy was eighteen, no savings attributed to the early learning of Greek was detected. After the many observations of dramatic losses in the ability of students to recall items learned only recently, this evidence of the persistence of some effects of learning for many years is welcome.

Another indication of the persistence of memory beyond the point of recall is reported by Hart (1965). He found that even when persons cannot supply answers to questions, they are sometimes sure they know them. On a recognition test over such items his subjects answered 73% of the questions that they could not answer for a recall test. They did not do as well on a recognition test on items that they said they did not know; they recognized the answers to only 43% of these items. Thus, it appears that we not only remember a good deal even when we are unable to recall it at a particular time, but that we are often, but not always, aware that we remember things we can't recall.

PERCENT RETAINED

At any time after learning the amount retained appears greatest if measured by savings or relearning, somewhat less by measures of recognition, and less still by measures of recall. The results of many different investigators are summarized by the curves in Figure 8-5.

Conclusions about the actual percentage retained at specific intervals after learning—an hour, a day, a month, and so on—are difficult because results are different for different learning tasks. Ebbinghaus' data for forgetting of nonsense syllables indicated retention of

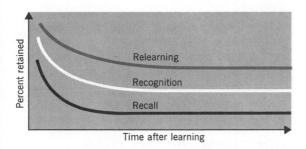

Figure 8-5.

Retention and methods of measurement.

after learning. This loss means it would take 80% as much time to learn the same list again as it took initially.

Although these results have been widely quoted, sometimes to disparage the value of learning knowledge, what happens with nonsense syllables is probably *not* too characteristic of school learning. Data from Tyler (1934) for different test exercises and different learning tasks are given in Table 8-2. These recall and recognition results are not comparable to the savings data from Ebbinghaus. What they do show is much less loss in the ability to recognize terms than to recall them, and much less loss for the recall of factual information than names and terms. The most complex learning products, characteristic of those considered in Chapter 9, showed gains over time rather than losses. The suggested explanation is that these learn-

less than 50% after 1 hour—even when measured by the most favorable method, that of savings. Forgetting nonsense syllables continues at a somewhat reduced rate reaching 25 to 30% savings (70 to 75% loss) in a day or so, then the loss levels off and the savings is still at 20 to 25% (75 to 80% loss) a month

Table 8-2

Retention of School Learning One Year Later (From Tyler, R. W., Science Education, *1934. By permission)*

Learning Task	Average (Mean) Scores			Percent of Gain Retained
	Beginning of Course	End of Course	One Year Later	
Naming structures of animals in diagrams	22	62	31	23
Identifying technical terms	19	83	66	74
Recognizing (relating) the functions and structures	13	39	34	79
Applying Principles to unfamiliar situations	35	65	65	100
Interpreting results of unfamiliar experiments	30	57	64	125

ing products were recognized and used in other situations after they were first learned.

Three Stages of Memory

Psychologists who study the way learners process information often assume two or more types of storage or memory. Recent evidence (Kumar, 1971) supports the existence of three levels: (1) "sensory" memory or SM; (2) a short-term memory or STM, where we hold information while we are working with it; and (3) a long-term memory storage or LTM, containing relatively permanent information. Evidence of *memories*, rather than a single all-purpose memory, comes from both neurophysiological and psychological investigations.

Milner (1959) reported that surgical removal of part of the brain did not destroy short-term memory, but information could no longer be transferred to longer-term memory. Psychological studies have demonstrated that only a few items of information can be held in short-term memory, and these only for a very brief time without rehearsal, whereas there is no apparent limit to the amount of information in our long-term storage.

THE SENSORY MEMORY (SM)

Some current views hold that sensory impressions (images, tastes, touch, etc.) briefly persist (a fraction of a second) in the first level or SM stage of memory. Then they are either transferred to the other levels of memory, replaced by new information from the senses (Neisser, 1967) or simply fade away. We appear to possess a mechanism for scanning the centers of our sensory inputs. This is a very selective process and only information that we recognize and consider important is passed on to other stages of memory, often with information from long-term memory. What is passed on depends, then, on our pre-

vious knowledge, and our attention or set (Atkinson and Shiffrin, 1968). When we are looking up a friend's telephone number, many different names and numbers are scanned, but we only attend to and retain the digits of the number opposite the name we are interested in.

SHORT-TERM MEMORY (STM)

This is called the "working memory," because here is where one is said to hold information that occupies his attention while it is being processed. Unless the information in the short-term memory is being processed or rehearsed, it vanishes in a few seconds. Holding a telephone number in mind while we dial it is a typical use of STM.

The capacity of STM is estimated to be about seven separate individual items, but information coming from the SM may be grouped or coded in larger units as it is received to greatly expand its effective capacity. We have referred to accounts of this process earlier in the chapter, describing how stored and new information interact in coding. In a simple example of coding all odd numbers might be grouped in one class and all even numbers in another for some types of problems. Our capacity would still be limited to about seven units, but each of these units would contain information about many numbers, not just one.

LONG-TERM MEMORY (LTM)

Transfer of information from STM to LTM requires either repetition or encoding (Atkinson and Shiffrin, 1968). Of the two processes, repetition appears much less efficient for longer-term storage, but it is useful if a code is unavailable, because the learner lacks the knowledge or ability to find or construct one.

Information can be stored in LTM and retrieved in a variety of forms, including words, sounds, or images, but little is known about the actual mechanism of storage. We have already described Ausubel's views on the hierarchial arrangement of knowledge in memory and we have noted that human tendencies in cataloging and communicating information suggest a mental organization somewhat like the one he postulates. Beyond this, we can only speculate.

Explanations of Forgetting

You may have taken it for granted, as many persons do, that what we learn just fades away after a time unless it is rehearsed or used. But the evidence suggests that this is improbable. We do not forget while we are asleep (Jenkins and Dallenbach, 1924; Newman, 1939), and experiences long forgotten often return with remarkable clarity, spontaneously or as a result of probing by psychoanalysts or surgeons.

Psychologists favor other explanations of forgetting. They do not believe that knowledge gradually fades away like an old photograph in the sun. Their explanations of forgetting are related to their beliefs about learning. If learning is the formation of S-R associations, forgetting may occur because of interference among these associations. But if learning is a matter of change in cognitive structure, forgetting may be the result of a failure in that structure. Another possibility, offered by those concerned with the learner's purpose in learning, is that forgetting is motivated; we may remember what we intend or wish to remember and forget the unpleasant or useless. These possibilities are examined in this section.

INTERFERENCE

Evidence for the theory that forgetting is the result of interference among learned associations comes from studies of verbal learning.

In a typical demonstration (Underwood, 1967), a subject is asked to memorize a list of paired items, such as DAX-neutral, VOH-pretty, PEL-hybrid, QVS-auto, and so on. If he studies this list until he is first able to give the correct response word to each stimulus syllable—"neutral" for DAX, "pretty" for VOH, and so on—he will recall about 80% of the items correctly 24 hours later. To assess the effect of interference, the demonstration is varied. After the subject has learned the first list of items (List 1), he is asked to learn a different list of word responses (List 2) to the stimulus syllables of the first list; DAX-yellow, VOH-agile, PEL-flashy, QUS-unclean, and so on. Now, when his recall is tested 24 hours later, he can give the correct responses to only 40% of the items of either List 1 or 2. Forgetting has been increased by 40%. You should not be surprised at this finding. Learning a new response word to an old stimulus is like trying to learn a friend's new telephone number or married name. In the laboratory the conclusion that interference is the cause of the forgetting is supported by the fact that in trying to recall the response to the original list, responses from the second list are often given, and vice versa.

An important factor affecting interference, hence forgetting, is the degree of similarity among the items learned. It is much more difficult to learn and remember a list of similar syllables or words than a list of dissimilar ones. Underwood (1967) said that many college students are unable to learn a list of syllables in which the same letters appear in different items, such as XQV, KHQ, VHX, VKQ, HUK, after an hour of studying. A list composed of different letters, such as VHN, KXT, CGQ, MWS, and BJP is much easier to learn. Again, interference and confusion among the associations is suggested.

In the example just described, learning List 2 interfered with memory of List 1. It also works the other way. Having learned List 2 before List 1 can also interfere with memory of List 1. The later-to-earlier learning type of interference is called "retroactive" to distinguish it from the earlier-to-later learning interference, which is called "proactive."

Proactive and retroactive interference effects in learning may be studied by using them with comparable groups, as illustrated in Figure 8-6. Groups A and B learn the tasks in a different order. Group C is provided as a control group. For this group memory for the initial task should be subject to little interference from later activity, because later associations are quite different or dissimilar. If subjects of Group C were to sleep during the List 1 to test interval, interference would be expected to be at a minimum.

Both proactive and retroactive interference have been demonstrated with a variety of learning materials in addition to words and syllables. These effects have been found with memory for sentences and for concepts (Underwood, 1967). Although the majority of studies have required word-for-word recall, Cunningham's review (1972) lends support to the assumption that recall of the meaning of prose and discourse is similarly affected.

Interference is expected in school situations, therefore, and our experience indicates that it does occur. A student comes to any topic of study with previous responses or knowledge that make new learning more difficult. This is a proactive effect. When incompletely learned tasks or material are followed by the introduction of new but similar material or tasks, retroactive interference is observed. What can be done about these problems?

Theory and investigations suggest three general approaches to reducing interference that can be useful in school situations. These, which we will expand on later, are:

1. Improve the original learning.

2. Distribute practice and review.

3. Inform learners of potential sources of interference.

COGNITIVE RESTRUCTURING

Many contemporary theorists assume an organized store of knowledge to be a human characteristic. New knowledge that becomes part of an organized network of retained facts, concepts, and generalizations is "meaningful" and likely to be retained. Conversely, as Bruner states, "Knowledge one has associated without supporting structure to tie it together, is likely to be forgotten." (Bruner, 1960, p. 31)

SUBSUMPTION

Suppose a student who knows about parallelograms learns that a new figure, a rhombus, is a special case of a parallelogram, that is, one with four equal sides. In the learner's

Group	Initial Task	Interpolated Task	Retention Task
A. Proactive:	Learn 2 $\longrightarrow$	Learn 1 $\longrightarrow$	Test for 1
B. Retroactive:	Learn 1 $\longrightarrow$	Learn 2 $\longrightarrow$	Test for 1
C. Neutral or Control:	Learn 1 $\longrightarrow$	Unrelated $\longrightarrow$ activity	Test for 1

Figure 8-6.
Experimental design for measuring interference in learning.

knowledge of geometric figures the new definition for rhombus may be considered "anchored" to the previous one for parallelograms and probably to related definitions of square, rectangle, and other figures as well. Initially, a learner can remember the definitions of both a parallelogram and a rhombus. Although they are similar, they can be separated. They can be dissociated. As time passes, however, the learner may lose his ability to distinguish the two. The new definition of rhombus may be "assimilated" or reduced to the more general definition of parallelogram, so that it can no longer be separately stated. Definitions for both the rhombus and the parallelogram may lose their identity in the still more basic idea of any four-sided figure, that is, a quadrilateral. This example is cited by Ausubel and Robinson (1969) in support of a general human tendency to reduce all knowledge to more basic general ideas in memory. They explain forgetting as the inability to separate specific information and less inclusive ideas from more general ones. This process is called "obliterative subsumption." We fight against it by improving initial learning and meaningful practice.

Subsumption is not all bad. It also serves a useful purpose by helping us avoid information "overload." It would be extremely uneconomical, for example, to remember every specific example of objects with rectangular dimensions, such as a stamp, a book, a box, or a brick. The reduction of all these specific examples to the general idea of rectangles helps us to avoid mental confusion. From this point of view it is the proper balance between differentiation and subsumption, which is hard to judge and arrange. In any particular situation the question is, "Do we need to remember the forest, the trees, or both?"

RECONSTRUCTION

Quite a few cognitive psychologists find evidence that remembering is not mere reproduction of the past, but an active process of reconstructing what a new situation demands from the contents of memory (Kumar, 1971). When we are asked to remember and cannot, we invent an answer that seems reasonable and familiar in the present circumstances. Differences between what we previously learned and what we now "know" may be attributed in part to invention and logic as well as retention *per se*. The process we are describing also has some of the characteristics of hypothesis testing and may be viewed as an example of the transfer of knowledge to new problem situations, a topic of the next chapter.

Bartlett (1932), one of the early students of reconstruction, had subjects study a story, a paragraph, or a drawing. When they were later asked to reproduce the original material, he found the material quite distorted. Often only isolated and striking details that happened to fit the learner's expectations were recalled.

Cognitive psychologists of the Gestalt school introduced the terms "leveling" and "sharpening" to describe some of the most common changes in the learner's reconstruction of previously learned material. In leveling, irregular or unusual forms, facts or figures are reduced to more regular or familiar ones. A distorted circle is remembered as perfectly round, or an incomplete circle is recalled as complete, or an ambiguous inkblot is recalled as a familiar figure.

In sharpening, some element of a recalled figure or fact is accentuated. An acquaintance's small eccentricity may be magnified until it dominates our description of his personality, or his slightly irregular nose may become an enormous beak. As you see, leveling and sharpening are somewhat opposite tendencies. It is not always clear why leveling occurs instead of sharpening or vice versa, but factors such as familiarity or other relationships in cognitive structure may be operating.

The influence of a learner's prior knowledge on his memory for new information has been suggested in these paragraphs, as it was in our description of subsumption. Other evidence for such influences comes from an experiment in which two groups of learners were given different names for the same set of stimulus figures. Figure 8-7 shows how these names affected learners' attempts to reproduce the figures (Carmichael, Hogan, and Walter, 1932). Similar individual differences in reproduced figures occur when learners supply their own labels (Herman, Lawless, and Marshall, 1957). In this situation a learner's choice of labels for figures and therefore his memory for them will be influenced by his knowledge and set.

INFORMATION RETRIEVAL

A computer is incapable of forgetting information stored in its memory banks. The information in a computer's memory banks is there for use, if we can just find it and relate it to our present needs. For theorists who use the computer as their model of the learner, failure in recall is a failure in information retrieval; the information is there but unavailable in usable form.

Figure 8-7.

Effects of labels on later reproductions of figures. (*From L. Carmichael, H. P. Hogan and A. A. Walter, Journal of Experimental Psychology, Vol. 15: 73-80, 1932)*

An important practical implication of this information-processing emphasis is that practice in retrieval of information in the form needed should be much more effective than simple repetition or rehearsal. Spending a relatively larger amount of available study time in formulating questions and composing answers related to assigned reading, for example, is a more effective study procedure than simply rereading the assignment. The information theorist calls this "rehearsing the appropriate retrieval process." There is no doubt about the advantages of this study procedure. It is a standard recommendation of "how to study" manuals. Those of a different theoretical bent might say, however, that the advantage lies in practicing the response required on the test. Still others would say it is in the feedback you receive about gaps or errors in knowledge that need more attention.

MOTIVATED FORGETTING

Both conscious and unconscious motivation have been suggested as causes of forgetting. Conscious efforts to forget (or remember) are usually referred to as "intentions"; forgetting due to the functioning of needs and drives of which we are unaware to make us forget is called "repression."

Intention. A learner who intends to remember may be expected to learn more than one who does not. He will have more to remember, for one thing. This does not tell us, however, if he has the ability to control the memory process itself. An early investigation by Ausubel, Schpoont, and Cukier (1957) casts doubt on the effect of instructions to remember *after* learning had already taken place. A group of undergraduate students instructed to remember a historical passage immediately after an initial test on it remembered no more after 2 weeks than a second group that was not instructed to remember.

Since then, several studies by Weiner with nonsense syllables for learning material showed that instructions to remember (1966) or forget (1968) may make a difference. There has been speculation that the learner's rehearsal of the items he is instructed to remember may be responsible for improved performance in later tests, but Weiner and Reed (1969) instructed subjects to forget nonsense syllables at several different intervals after learning. Instructions to forget given right after learning to discourage rehearsal, or later, after some rehearsal might have occurred, reduced retention almost equally. This finding suggests that rehearsal is not the complete explanation.

We judge that instructions to remember, and the learner's intention to do so, will have the greatest effect before learning, but that similar instructions after learning will affect his retention to some degree also.

A person's greater recall of unfinished tasks, as compared to his memory for completed ones, has sometimes been cited as evidence of the effects of intentions. This is the "Zeigarnik effect" named for the investigator who reported it some years ago. Other investigators (Rosenzweig, 1943; Atkinson 1953) have reported results that they say show that the Zeigarnik effect is valid only when the learner's concern is with the task instead of with his own competence. Learners who believe failure to complete a task reflects unfavorably on their ability may tend to *forget* uncompleted tasks, not remember them. This finding is best explained in relation to unconscious suppression of an unpleasant event or "repression."

Repression. Sigmund Freud and other psychoanalysts postulated that materials and events that are unpleasant or that produce anxiety are usually dropped from memory. This is assumed to be an automatic process of which the individual is frequently unaware. It is termed "repression." There is some evidence that such effects occur. For example, Stagner (1931) demonstrated that individuals recall more pleasant than un-pleasant associations, and Edwards (1941) and Levine and Murphy (1943) reported that persons remember more arguments consistent with their views than against them.

Investigators have not always succeeded in separating motivational from cognitive effects, however. Learners may recall more of the pleasant and favored ideas and experiences because they have a better knowledge background related to these when they encounter them. So they learn them better.

Zeller (1950) has probably presented the most persuasive evidence of the operation of repression. He arranged a personal failure experience for one group of students and success for another group, shortly after each group had mastered a list of nonsense syllables. Next he showed that the students experiencing failure did not do as well on a later test of recall than those experiencing success. Then (and this was the particular contribution of his study) he arranged for the students who had previously experienced failure on an experimental task to become successful at it. Finally he demonstrated that students showed improved recall of the non-sense syllables after their failure (which had presumably led to repression) changed to success. The suggestion is that repression occurs, but it is not always permanent, and it may be removed when the negative affect associated with the material to be recalled is removed.

RECOMMENDATIONS FOR INSTRUCTION

In this section we use the theory and research reported earlier in the chapter to make several recommendations for teaching. Although the findings and explanations of scholars differ, the practical implications of their contributions are more often complimentary than contradictory. What we learn from cognitive psychologists about organizing learning material should not blind us to the value of S-R findings about practice, and our attempts to establish a predisposition or set for meaningful learning should not lessen our efforts to reinforce achievements.

In other words, it is not necessary to choose theoretical sides. Although our recommendations have different theoretical origins, all are useful in the classroom. This does not mean that the usefulness of different suggestions will not vary with the instructional task. If you follow our recommendations, your approach will be nearer a cognitive model, emphasizing organization and learner orientation, when you teach organized or organizable material. On the other hand, you will find your practice closer to a conditioning model, with an emphasis on conditions of reinforcement and practice, when you teach associations that are more difficult to organize and make meaningful.

Organize Knowledge Learning Tasks

Three aspects of the organization of knowledge content that affect your work as a teacher will be considered here. First, because your course objectives will include more than can be learned during a single class period or lesson, these objectives must be partitioned or divided into smaller sets and the sequence of these sets must be planned. A second consideration is the organization of one set of knowledge items that are to be presented or acquired at about the same time, for example, in an activity that lasts from about 5 minutes to 1 hour. A third aspect of organization for knowledge instruction is that of providing a meaningful context for new knowledge learning. Here you will be concerned with relationships between to-be-acquired knowledge and prior knowledge, that is, between the new and the old, the unfamiliar and the familiar. Our suggestions with respect to each of these aspects or phases of an instructional program begin with a general recommendation.

1. *Carefully sequence knowledge objectives with respect to objectives for other outcomes.* In any subject area or course of study one element of learning may facilitate another to some degree. In some subject fields, such as mathematics and science, it is apparent that some objectives must be achieved before others, and curricula have been designed in which prerequisite lessons are carefully identified for each new lesson (*Science — A Process Approach*, 1967). In other subject fields, such as history, the optimum order is not as apparent, but we seldom expect all orders to be equally effective.

The knowledges or skills a student brings to any given task as a result of previous learning determine his "readiness," and organizing an instructional sequence is an exercise in planning the continual readiness of the learner. By analyzing the task of the learner as he faces each new objective, we seek to identify what must come first if he is to succeed.

Our logical analysis of learning tasks and our study of student difficulties are the guides in planning the sequence of instruction. Some examples of task analysis for this purpose are provided in Chapter 9. In general, the rule is that if a student needs knowledges A, B, and C and skills L, M, and N to learn to solve problems X, Y, and Z, learning to solve these problems will be easier and better if we teach A, B, and C and L, M, and N first. Of course, if a student comes to a problem-solving situation without the prerequisite knowledge, we may be able to make up for his lack (our failure) in the way we present the new situation. The best plan, however, is surely to attempt to plan our courses so that the learner comes to each new objective fully prepared by reason of past achievement.

For cognitive objectives, such as concept and principle learning, that are higher than knowledge in Bloom's taxonomy, we always ask what knowledge is prerequisite. We should not expect students to acquire a concept of a trapezoid without first knowing specific examples, or to generalize about the effects of air masses on the weather without knowledge of the characteristics of air masses, or to complete the chemical equation $2H^+ + (SO_4)^- \rightarrow (\ \ )$ before learning that S stands for sulfur, O for oxygen, and so on (Gagné, 1968).

The examples in the preceding paragraphs in which concepts, principles, and problem solving appear to follow the learning of other knowledge and skills should not get us in the rut of asking only the question, "What knowledge should come before these new concepts and principles?" It is just as important to ask, "What concepts and principles will facilitate acquisition of this new knowledge?" Remember that almost any information presented in words will be meaningless unless students have the concepts for which the words stand, and knowledge of the central concepts and generalizations of a field of knowledge is a major factor in the ease of acquiring and retaining further information in that field.

The authors find that the best strategy is to work back and forth between objectives for knowledge and other types of cognitive outcomes, keeping in mind that (1) some knowledge is always prerequisite to other learning and problem-solving behavior, but (2) once acquired, concepts, principles, and problem solving are major tools in the acquisition of further knowledge.

2. *Help the student find structure and relationships in each learning situation.* Take a minute to study the following array of numbers. Then try to reproduce it from memory.

4	9	2
3	5	7
8	1	6

"I remember things best if she makes a singing commercial out of them." *(Drawing by Reg Hider from* Today's Education, *NEA Journal, 1971)*

What was your strategy? You probably did not depend on mere repetition, but searched for relationships that would link the numbers with each other or with your prior knowledge. Hunter (1964) has given this simple task to hundreds of students, and reports that almost all looked for relationships that would aid learning and retention. Among the strategies used (O'Connor, 1971) are: (1) relationships with personal information, for example, a birthdate or a house number; (2) relation-

ships with previously learned associations, for example, Columbus—1492; (3) noting sequences of numbers, for example, 4, 5, 6 (diagonal) and 3, 5, 7 (middle row); (4) forming rules, for example, each row, column, and diagonal adds to 15.

This is a simple demonstration of the human learner's preference for organization in learning. By replacing an original set of observations with a smaller number of more informative items, the learning task and the memory load become more manageable. The entire array of numbers can be replaced by two abstractions: (1) the position of the sequence 3, 4, and 5 and (2) each line (column, row, or diagonal) totals 15. The gain in economy and efficiency of learning by those who take advantage of the possibilities for organizing the task content is evident.

It follows that if there is a natural order in the material to be learned, the teacher should work with students to expose it. A familiar example is the "nines table." Learning these multiplication facts has sometimes been regarded as a rote memory task, but with the table on the chalkboard ($9 \times 1 = 9$, $9 \times 2 = 18$, $9 \times 3 = 27$, etc.) you can show (1) how to find the left digit of each product (it's always one less than the multiplier) and (2) how to find the right digit of each product (subtract the left digit from 9). Thus, in $9 \times 7 = 63$, the left digit of the product or 6 is one less than the multiplier 7, and the right digit of the product, that is 3, is 9 minus 6.

Not all factual material has the same degree of natural structure, of course. Mathematics tends to be more highly structured, in this sense, than history. Order and sequence can usually be introduced, however, by the "organizer" technique. Each lesson can be preceded by one or more general propositions to which the new material can be related.

Any introductory material at a higher level of generality and inclusiveness than the learning material itself may serve as an advance organizer (Ausubel, 1963, p. 29). A statement or proposition may be used as an organizer. Learning the social principle that technological progress leads to major changes in culture and society could, for example, be an organizer for the study of many different historical periods or places, and the concept of balance or form could be used for some topics in a number of disciplines, including art, literature, mathematics, and government. A given organizer may be used with more than one segment of content, and there is no one *best* organizer for any given segment of content. Material on the public schools might be preceded by organizers that establish a perspective relating to government, economics, psychology, sociology, or architecture. The choice will depend on the objectives.

Organizers need not be statements, of course. An outline, a diagram, a demonstration, or a film can serve the purpose. The form of an organizer is less important than that it be clearly understood and capable of providing an overall framework for the organization of more specific information or subordinate ideas that follow.

Some associations are so completely arbitrary that any relationships introduced to facilitate learning and retention will be arbitrary also. Nevertheless, even in these situations, mnemonic devices such as "*i* before *e* except after *c*" and "thirty days hath September, April, June, and so on" should be used to introduce some order in learning.

Rohwer's (1972) continuing research on the learning of word pairs, such as "bat-cup" and "arrow-glass" has implications for the use of relationships to link arbitrary associations. He finds the use of order or relationships, which he calls "elaboration" among learners over a wide range of ages, from at least age four on. It is significant for the work of the teacher, however, that not all learners use the process spontaneously, even though they are capable of doing so. Learners of different ages,

for example, characteristically require different degrees of prompting in the use of the elaboration process. At the earliest ages (three to five) maximum prompting, such as actually describing an event that connects the words to be associated, appears essential to optimum learning by all individuals. By about age seven, however, words or picture prompts will suffice. From ages nine to twelve Rohwer finds that merely directing the subject to think of an event that links the pair of words is enough. Rohwer reported that between twelve and eighteen years-of-age students from high socioeconomic groups characteristically use organization techniques without any prompting, if they are given the task of associating word pairs. An important difference was found for students from lower socioeconomic groups; they continued to require some prompting in the use of organization.

Rohwer's conclusion regarding imagery in association learning is that if we vary our level of prompting for groups of different age levels and background, we can insure the learning ease and efficiency of nearly all students. We interpret this as supporting the importance of a planned program of helping individuals to organize knowledge learning.

In this section we have made three main points. (1) Organized learning is a general human tendency. (2) Organization is the basis for more efficient knowledge learning. (3) Students require help in organizing learning situations.

3. *Present new information in a familiar context.* This recommendation and the preceding one are intimately related and almost inseparable. We have stated that organization and relationships should be used to establish a meaningful context. The relationships of most use to a learner for this purpose will be those that are most familiar, that is, most closely related to his prior knowledge. When relevant relationships to prior knowl-

edge exist and become evident, the new material is already partly learned.

One way of systematically relating new material to previous knowledge is the use of "comparative" organizers. An example is provided by Ausubel and Youssef (1963). They gave students a preliminary paragraph that pointed out the similarities and differences between Christianity and Buddhism before the study of details about the Buddhist doctrine. Their data showed that the retention of facts about Buddhism was related to both (1) the student's knowledge about Christianity, and (2) the use of the Christian-Buddhist organizers.

The choice of Christianity as a source of comparative organizers in Ausubel and Youssef's experiment was the result, of course, of the fact that their subjects were Christians. Therefore, the use of Christian-Buddhist organizers helped them relate the new to the more familiar. The more these Christians knew of their own religion, the more effective this proved to be. Comparing Buddhism to Zen Buddhism would not have been as initially effective, simply because Zen Buddhism would not have provided as familiar a context, even though the relationships between Buddhism and Zen Buddhism may be closer than between Buddhism and Christianity.

The recommendation that we look to a student's prior knowledge for relationships useful in new learning suggests that the most effective relationships, codes, or organizers vary from individual to individual. This is true, and an instructor-supplied relationship may not be optimal for some learners. As others have noted (Newsom, Eischens, and Looft, 1972), the teacher can only make an "educated guess" as to which organizer will be most effective. A more individually oriented method might be to let the students supply the organization. You might, for example, ask each student to give you a summary of the instructional material, and use

these summaries for ideas about relationships to stress to the entire class, to smaller groups of students, or to particular individuals. It should be noted, however, that teachers do have considerable control of students' prior knowledge through their sequencing of instruction, and an effective longer-term strategy is to have each lesson provide context and organizers for those that follow. Ausubel and Youssef, in the experiment already cited, did find that after subjects had learned about Buddhism with the aid of Christian-Buddhism organizers, their new knowledge of Buddhism could then be used to provide organizers for the study of another unfamiliar religion, Zen Buddhism.

Establish Appropriate Sets and Intentions

Our treatment of motivation in Chapter 7 emphasized the importance of students knowing what they are to learn and why that learning is important. Our recommendations there should be reviewed in relation to knowledge learning—keeping in mind that the more arbitrary, unfamiliar, and divorced from daily activities new information is, the greater the need for teachers to help students understand why they should try to learn it.

Trying to learn is important but so is *how* one tries to learn. We have emphasized the advantages of organized, strategic learning. Now how do we cultivate an intent to use this approach in preference to rote memorization? Three general approaches have promise.

1. *Use instructions.* The first and most direct way to establish a set to organize learning is through instructions. This approach was illustrated in the context of word association tasks by Rohwer's study. You may recall, he found that after about age nine children would look for relationships linking words, if they were told to do so. In prose learning

tasks Frase (1970) found that telling high school students about the organization of paragraphs to be learned resulted in superior recall, presumably because they then used the organization of the paragraphs to advantage.

2. *Ask questions.* The student's attention can be directed to particular aspects of textual materials by preceding questions. General investigations have shown that such questions result in readers learning more about the topics and ideas questioned and less about other things (Frase, 1970). This type of attention control might be used to direct attention to organizing reading material in efficient ways. Questions might be used in similar ways in lectures or discussions.

Our suggestions for the use of instructions and questions are approaches to establishing short-term sets for learning material to be presented almost immediately. There is little evidence relating to the permanence of sets for organized learning. Rohwer (1972) did find, however, that older learners from upper socioeconomic groups used relational strategies automatically in memorizing word pairs. We do not know that this was a result of their being encouraged to use similar strategies over a long period of time, but that might be the explanation. We recommend planning instructions as if it were, profiting from short-term gains in learning efficiency, hoping for lasting changes in learning behavior.

3. *Reward efficient learning strategies.* We stated that there are two general approaches to establishing learning sets. The second method is by the management of consequences, a procedure we recommended in Chapter 7. This approach makes a "successful" performance in learning tasks contingent on the use or efficient procedures, frequently and over an extended period of time.

You can make it clear to students that *how* they learn is as important as *what* they learn,

and reward them accordingly. For many learners an escape from the drudgery of inefficient methods will be reward enough.

Provide Knowledge of Results

Organization and set may enable students to acquire knowledge more efficiently. It is equally important that they be given information about results. Student's responses—to our questions, in the performance of tasks, or during discussions—are occasions for giving them information that may enable them to check, then confirm or correct their knowledge.

Although there will be great individual differences in learner response to knowledge of results—younger and more able students profit most—several generalizations are possible.

1. *Make knowledge of results specific and detailed.* Knowledge of results will usually improve achievement, but to be most effective this knowledge must be specific, not general. Although some variation in a student's response may be acceptable when he demonstrates his knowledge, the emphasis should be on his ability to accurately repeat or reproduce what was previously presented for learning. Therefore, he needs to find out exactly what he does and does not remember accurately.

The premium that is placed on accuracy in learner tasks used as "tests" for knowledge learning is evident in these typical examples. "State the French equivalents to the listed English words." "Write the chemical symbols for the following list of elements and compounds." "Recite the 'Gettysburg Address' from memory." "Give the formula for the area of a circle." "Moving the decimal point in a number three places to the right _____ the number by _____?" or "List in order the steps that should be taken in adjusting the timing of an internal combustion engine." Most of these recall examples have their counterparts in multiple choice or recognition tests, of course; and the actual performance of procedures by students may sometimes be substituted for oral or written reports. If we know a student can use the tools as required, we can ask him to adjust the timing of an engine to check his knowledge of the required steps.

When a student is asked to demonstrate his knowledge in situations such as those in the preceding paragraph, he will benefit most if he is given information that helps him to make specific corrections in his knowledge and related responses. Your objective should be to prompt an entirely correct performance, although you hope to give him general encouragement as well. Your role is somewhat like that of someone with a script, ready to prompt an actor who may stumble over his lines. If he needs help, you whisper the exact words he needs, not merely, "A little

sharper on the recall in the second act, please." You should be similarly specific with the information a learner needs to improve his knowledge.

2. *Give knowledge of results promptly.* Prompt knowledge of results is superior to delayed information. When a student is correct, it helps him to find out immediately; if he is in error, the sooner he corrects the error the better. This point has been made previously in our chapter on motivation. Report cards with their As, Bs, and Cs are examples of evaluations that are so long delayed (and so general) that they are notoriously inefficient in improving specific performances.

There are some obvious practical difficulties in providing immediate feedback to students in the typical school situation, however. Recognition and concern for these difficulties have been factors in the development of methods of individualizing instruction (Chapter 11). These methods rely heavily on programmed self-instructive materials to

(From W. James Popham and Eva L. Baker, Planning on Instructional Sequence, © 1970. By permission of Prentice-Hall, Inc. and Vimcet Associates)

provide immediate knowledge of results. Carefully worked out programs for knowledge instruction, which do not require expensive or elaborate equipment for presentation, are now available to teachers in many areas of the curriculum.

Programmed instructional materials may be regarded as a means of enabling learners to check their own work. The use of self-checking as an approach to providing immediate and individualized knowledge of results will be described in the last recommendation of this section, relating to encouraging learner independence in evaluation.

3. *Emphasize the positive and the correct.* It is more informative to tell a student he is right than to tell him he is wrong. When a right answer is given, wrong answers tend to drop out. On the other hand, when errors are stressed, they tend to be remembered. When a student makes a mistake the best procedure is to prompt or provide a correct answer in its place. Our point here is related to an earlier one of the need to be specific when giving knowledge of results.

The recognition of accomplishments instead of failures has motivational as well as informational value. In other words, knowledge of success is reinforcing; knowledge of failure is not (Chapter 7). For this reason, also, knowledge acquisition, like other types of learning, proceeds better when attention is directed to the positive instead of to the negative aspects of a learner's performance.

Combat Interference Among Similar Tasks and Materials

Interference among learning tasks and materials most frequently stems from their similarity. "To" and "too" are often confused, but we have no problem with "to" and "very." You may not recognize differences in "ei" and "ie" in words such as "believe" and "receive," but neither of these is confused with "it" or "or" and seldom with "ee." You have no problem remembering order of occurrence of the major wars of the United States, because the circumstances surrounding each are so different, but it would be difficult for most people to correctly order the campaigns of the Civil War.

To combat interference of new learning tasks or materials with previously learned tasks (retroactive interference) or what is usually a more serious problem, interference of previous learning with new learning (proactive interference), potential forms of confusion must be identified. Look for similarity between the old and new, in the stimulus to which the learner responds or in the expected responses. An analysis of learner errors will reveal additional points of confusion that may be overlooked in a preliminary task analysis.

Once the probable sources of interference have been singled out for special attention, their effect can be lessened by (1) systematically introducing dissimilarity and (2) providing additional practice on troublesome points. Distributed instead of massed practice is also recommended, but its effect is seen in retention, not in initial learning.

1. *Make similar tasks less similar.* In planning to make similar materials or tasks dissimilar, we should keep in mind the total context for learning. Different colors, symbols, or drawings may be used to introduce contrast into otherwise similar materials. Sometimes simply practicing similar but different tasks in different rooms results in less interference.

2. *Provide additional practice.* Probably the most generally efficient approach to reducing interference between tasks or similar materials is simply that of "overlearning" each one. Therefore, potentially interfering tasks should receive additional practice.

Simply instructing learners with respect to where confusion is apt to occur may be helpful, perhaps because it makes them more alert for the differences that do exist or leads them to rehearse on their own.

Provide for Appropriate Review

Knowledge does not automatically become permanent and readily available for use at any time in the future. Although the most important factor in retention is the adequacy of initial learning, it is often necessary to provide reviews to insure retention.

1. *Distribute practice and review.* The optimum distribution of review after learning varies with our purpose. As a general rule, short review periods, scheduled frequently at first and then at increasingly longer intervals are best. Review periods may be considerably longer for meaningful material than for that which is learned by rote, however. As every student knows, even "cramming" or the massing of practice and review just before a test may be effective for immediate recall of meaningful material. Nevertheless, there is abundant evidence that for continued or delayed retention spaced review is more effective. If learning must be compressed into a relative short period of time, say a day or two, it will still be better to alternate intensive study periods with more relaxing activities (Gibson, 1941).

The advantages of special practice have been dramatically demonstrated in the laboratory. Underwood (1967) describes an experiment by Keppel in which subjects were tested under two different schedules of learning for different sets of word responses to the same set of stimulus words. Subjects who learned the fourth set over a period of 4 days (two tests a day) demonstrated 34% retention of it after a month, whereas those who learned all four sets in 1 day had forgotten

the fourth set almost completely after a week. The suggestion is that distribution of learning trials reduced interference among the several lists.

2. *Choose the form of review that fits the learner's need.* Increasing the amount of time spent in self-recitation or efforts to recall independently during review and decreasing the time spent in mere repetition or rereading is generally good practice in meeting the learner's needs for retention. If verbatim recall will not be required, the restatement of content in one's own words is also recommended to make it more meaningful. Review can also be tailored to judgments of the learner's need. If free recall will be needed, it should be practiced; if recognition is a sufficient objective, practice may be organized around recognition exercises. Similarly, if the learner only needs to be able to find and/or relearn material fairly quickly when he needs it, this may be practiced.

Encourage Independence in Learning

A principal role of the teacher is to help learners to independence in learning. Because we cannot always be there to organize material for learning, provide knowledge of results and so on, students must be equipped to do it themselves. We have already referred to instructions and the encouragement of sets for organizing knowledge learning. Students can easily be taught to check their own work also. A variety of standard resources — dictionaries, encyclopedias, atlases, and texts — as well as other knowledgeable persons and specially prepared keys, samples and specimens can be made available for their use in self-evaluation. As students assume more and more of the responsibility for obtaining their own knowledge or results, make your own evaluations less frequently, at irregular times, and without announcement.

Instruction and class discussion can be planned to focus attention on the procedures for gaining, checking, and retaining knowledge, as well as on knowledge itself. Then, opportunities should be provided for these procedures to be practiced with feedback and reinforcement for doing well. In other words, seek to apply the recommendations of this text to teach both the process and the products of knowledge learning.

Summary

1. The *objectives* of knowledge learning were described as learning to remember information, ideas, or phenomena "in a form very close to that in which it was originally encountered."

2. New knowledge is considered *meaningful* instead of arbitrary when it is organized and related to prior knowledge. Terms that suggest meaningful knowledge learning are "identification" and "representation."

3. Knowledge objectives may be stated at different levels of generality, depending on our purpose. The more general statements require only:

    a. An action word or phrase (e.g., to recognize, to state or to describe).

    b. A word or phrase to show the thing acted on (terms, facts, statements of principes, etc.).

More specific statements of objectives that may serve as the basis for checking performance also describe:

    c. The "givens" of the situation in which knowledge is checked (e.g., "given a page of manuscript containing punctuation errors").

    d. The standard of performance expected (e.g., "recognizes 90% of the punctuation errors").

Psychological Approaches

4. *Cognitive approaches* assume a learner with purposes and prior knowledge. Attention is focused on organizing and presenting learning materials so that the learner finds order and familiar elements in it.

    a. "Coding" is a form of organization in which information items are grouped into larger chunks for easier processing.

    b. "Advance organizers" are general statements or ideas presented first and learned as a framework to which less general ideas and details are related.

5. *Stimulus-response approaches* focus on the conditions that follow learner responses.

    a. Associations are formed when reinforcement follows a response to a stimulus.

b. Verbal statements may be learned as "chains" of S-R associations in which a response to a stimulus is itself a stimulus for another response that, in turn, is the stimulus for a third response, and so on.

c. In "discrimination learning" sets of stimuli (objects, pictures, symbols) are presented together, and correct responses (identifications) are reinforced, while incorrect ones are not.

d. A learner's behavior is "shaped" by reinforcing an approximation to the response desired initially, then gradually requiring closer and closer approximations to it as a condition for continued reinforcement.

e. "Fading" of prompts is illustrated when the learner's response is fully prompted at first; but then he is required to respond with fewer and fewer prompts, until he is responding independently with no prompting.

6. Self-instructional programs illustrating *cognitive* principles present a substantial amount of material organized to teach, use diagnostic questions to reveal errors, and direct learners to supplementary information to correct errors. S-R programs are composed of small items or frames, presented to all learners in the same sequence. Learners respond to each item and are given immediate knowledge of results.

7. Laboratory studies of memorizing lists of nonsense syllables have found that the learning and retention of syllables are related to many characteristics of the list and the distribution of practice.

Learning and Remembering

8. At any time after learning the percentage retained is greatest when measured by relearning, less when measured by recognition, and least when measured by recall.

9. The degree of retention is affected by what is to be retained. The recall of nonsense syllables drops to less than 50% in 1 hour. In tests of the retention of school outcomes after 1 year, memory was poorest for recall of terms; much better for recognition of terms, functions and structures; and an actual increase in the ability to apply principles and interpret results was noted.

10. Three *stages of memory* have been postulated: (a) a "sensory" memory or SM, which receives inputs from the senses; (b) a short-term, small capacity "working" memory or STM; and (c) a long-term memory of apparently unlimited capacity or LTM.

11. Coding or the "chunking" of information into larger units is used to increase the capacity of the STM to examine data that it received from the SM or retrieved from the LTM.

12. Psychological explanations of forgetting include:
    a. *Interference* of previous learning with later learning ("proactive" interference), or later learning with previous learning ("retroactive" interference).
    b. *Cognitive restructuring,* when a learner can no longer separate related ideas in memory, or when he reconstructs the knowledge of the past, partly from recall and partly by invention.
    c. *Motivated forgetting,* either by conscious intention or the unconscious repression of unwanted or unpleasant associations.

Recommendations for Knowledge Instruction

13. *Sequence knowledge objectives with respect to objectives for other outcomes.*

14. *Help the student find structure and relationships in each learning situation.* Emphasize the natural structure of content; teach coding, advance organizers and mnemonic devices; and encourage mental imagery.

15. *Present new information in a familiar context.* The most useful relationships, codes, or organizers for new learning are those based on prior knowledge.

16. *Establish appropriate sets and intentions.* These relate not only to what is to be learned and why but also to *how.* Instructions and the management of consequences are advocated to develop a predisposition to use strategic learning in preference to rote memorization.

17. *Make knowledge of results specific, prompt, and positive.* Knowledge of the correct answer is more informative than knowledge of wrong ones and more encouraging.

18. *Combat interference among similar tasks and materials.* Identify potential sources of interference, find ways to introduce contrast, and provide additional practice on the troublesome or easily confused points or items.

19. *Distribute practice and review.* In general short review periods are best, scheduled frequently at first and then at increasingly longer intervals. Review periods may be considerably longer for meaningful material than for that learned by rote.

20. *Choose the form of review that fits the learner's need.* Although it is usually more profitable to spend more time in self-recitation or efforts to recall than in rereading, consideration should be given to practicing the specific form of retention that will probably be required of the learner.

21. *Encourage learner independence.* Attention should be given to longer-term sets for organizing learning and to skills for using references for self-checking of results. Teach both the process and the products of knowledge learning.

CHAPTER 9
Cognitive Skills I:
Concepts and Principles

"A rose is a . . . sort of like I mean a . . . you know . . . rose . . . is . . . like . . . you know, . . . a rose . . . right?" *(Drawing by Booth; © 1972 The New Yorker Magazine, Inc.)*

The Nature of Concepts and Principles
Objectives for Concept and Principle Learning
Psychological Studies and Issues
Recommendation for Instruction

Knowledge is basic to all learning, but it is not the prized goal. Teachers are often urged to look beyond the "memory" level of learning to objectives that will enable students to use their knowledge, understand new situations, and solve problems. The transition desired is from knowledge to concepts, principles, and problem-solving abilities. This change is characterized by a shift, for the learner, from dependence on repetition of past learning to greater independence in achievement.

If the goal of knowledge learning is retention, that of cognitive skills and abilities is *transfer*. The essential nature of these skills is that they are transferable, that is, useful in new and different situations. A term that is often used in about the same way as transferable is "generalizable." These types of learning outcomes have also been called "productive" to contrast them with "reproductive" knowledge learning (Briggs, 1970).

Two classes of skills — concepts and principles — are paramount in intellectual functions. They are the subjects of this chapter. Problem solving requires skills of independence and creativity. They are considered in Chapter 10.

OBJECTIVES FOR CHAPTER 9

1. Classify representative examples of learning outcomes as knowledge, observable concepts, or principles.
2. Describe the interrelationships of different types of cognitive skills in the intellectual life of the individual.
3. Write representative objectives for concept and principle learning.

OBJECTIVES
Continued

4. Compare and contrast S-R, mediated S-R, and cognitive descriptions of the conditions for concept learning.
5. Describe "teacher guidance" and "learner discovery" and summarize the results of research and the importance of each in principle learning.
6. Describe a typical laboratory study of concept formation and discuss the differences between such studies and concept learning in the classroom.
7. Choose a principle in an area in which you are knowledgeable and construct a learning hierarchy to show how prerequisite concepts and principles are combined in the attainment of the target principle.
8. Develop a systematic plan for teaching a simple concept, such as "orange," "A," "4," or "higher than" that illustrates good and poor practice in presenting instances to aid the discrimination of (a) critical properties and (b) irrelevant characteristics.
9. Describe several different methods of teaching a definition and compare their effectiveness with each other and with a combination of methods.

THE NATURE OF CONCEPTS AND PRINCIPLES

Concepts are revealed when learners respond to things or events as members of a class instead of to their individual characteristics. We have, for example, some of the same reactions to any dog because of our concept of dog, although a Chihuahua would never be mistaken for a Great Dane. Similarly a friend is a friend because of our concept of "friend." Charlie, an old school chum, may be a lazy, sloppy, untrustworthy rascal who has little in common with the bustling little lady across the street who has been the neighborhood conscience and crutch since anyone can remember, except that both are friends.

The importance of concepts and principles in all intellectual life is generally accepted by psychologists and educators. By enabling us to transfer our learning from one situation to another, they free us of the need to know and remember every separate item of our experience, but we do not find similar agreement when we ask, "What is a concept?" The differing theoretical backgrounds and experiences of authors have led them to describe concepts in somewhat different ways.

Different Concepts of "Concepts"

Concepts have been defined as (1) learned responses, (2) mental constructs, (3) properties of objects of events, and (4) the "big ideas" of a course of study.

Perhaps the most popular view is that concepts are a characteristic of the learner. Thus, we have referred to a concept as a common response or reaction to members of a class of objects or events. Concepts may also be presented as less observable characteristics of the learner, as products of the mind, constructed by processing information from many specific experiences. Information about animals, for example, is gained by observing different animals; this information is processed mentally to form a concept or "image" of them. Then, our behavior toward animals is influenced or "mediated" by this internal construct.

Other authors describe concepts in terms of the external characteristics of the things or events of a class, and do not refer directly to either the internal or external characteristics of the learner. De Cecco (1968, p. 388) defines a concept simply as "a class of stimuli which have common characteristics." Thus, animals have some characteristics not shared by non-animals. So do books, although individually they may be as different as *Little Women* and the *Oxford Standard Dictionary*.

The definitions that refer to characteristics of objects or events and those in terms of learner responses (physical or mental) may not be as far apart as they seem, however. If a stimulus is a stimulus because it produces a response in the learner, a common stimulus characteristic is common because it leads to similar responses by the learner. For many purposes it may make little difference whether we refer to one or the other in our definitions and descriptions.

Finally, educators writing about what is to be taught in an area of study, such as science or social studies, often call fundamental processes, ideas, or relationships "concepts." An example from science is "When units of matter interact, energy may be exchanged, but the sum of the energy remains constant." (Novak, 1966, p. 249) An author in the field of communications has suggested, "Grammar (syntax), vocabulary, and pronunciation are the three aspects of language, which differentiate one dialect from another." (Swenson, Hesse, and Hansen, 1971, p. 2) These "con-

cepts" are obviously far more complex than those usually studied experimentally by psychologists.

The complex concepts of curriculum makers are still based on classification, but what is being classified are *relationships*. When the science example of the preceding paragraph is learned, descriptions of relationships among events can be classified as conforming to the requirements of the conservation of energy or as incorrect and in need of reinterpretation. When one has the communication concept about dialects, he can use the relationship to identify dialects. In the next section we will explain that these relational concepts are frequently called principles or generalizations, and are usually learned by definition instead of by simple observation.

Defined Concepts (Principles)

The simplest concepts about objects (including living ones) and some of their properties (size, shape, color, etc.) are typically learned by direct observation of examples or instances. These have a single critical characteristic (e.g., red) or a combination of characteristics, all of which must be present (e.g., a square must have equal sides *and* right angles). Other concepts are more abstract or complex, however, and are much more difficult to learn by observation of examples. Instead, we acquire them when they are defined in relation to other concepts we already know. You are learning concepts of educational psychology this way.

Relationships among concepts (classes) that define new concepts are also called principles (Gagné, 1966, p. 89). Many are extremely useful in governing our behavior, and we find them expressed in forms that focus attention on the learner's behavior or what he

1. Concepts about *objects:*	Living things, man-made things, cars, fish, plants, and so forth.
2. Concepts about *object properties:*	Mass, heat, state, structure, parts, shape, size, surface properties, and color, for example.
3. Concepts about *object relationships in space:*	Order, location, direction, relative position, relative size, number, family relationships, arbitrary relationships, and so on.
4. Concepts about *events in time and space:*	Conservation of mass, movement, change in energy, changes in group composition (such as addition), and changes in government, for example.
5. Concepts about *relationships among events in time and space* (cause and effect):	"For every action there is an equal and opposite reaction"; "Responses followed by reinforcement are strengthened."

Figure 9-1.
Classification of concept types. *(From Teaching: A Course in Applied Psychology* by Wesley C. Becker, Siegfried Engelmann, and Don R. Thomas. Copyright © 1971, Science Research Associates, Inc. Reprinted by permission of the publisher, p. 1971)

is able to do as a result of learning a principle. For example, the principle "Heat will melt solid objects" may be stated as "Melts objects by adding heat." Other principles in this form are: "Represents forces and their direction as parts of triangles"; "Doubles pints to get quarts"; "Doubles the final consonant when words end in 'ing'"; and "Strengthens responses by reinforcement." You will notice that in this "behavioral form," a principle is stated in exactly the same way you might state the objective if you wished students to learn to use a principle.

The prevalence and importance of defined concepts in school learning is evident in the classification of concepts in Figure 9-1. You will recognize that concepts of the first type and some of those of types two and three are learned by direct observation, usually very early in life, but that the majority of other types are usually taught by definition and example. You will also see that the concepts of the curriculum builder, which we referred to in the preceding section, are concepts about object relationships, events in time and space in relationships among events in time and space. Terms such as generalizations, ideas, hypotheses, or conclusions are also frequently used, somewhat loosely, for such "principle concepts."

Public and Private Meanings

Many if not all concepts have both a private and public aspect, that is, the members of the concept class have characteristics that nearly all of us can agree on, but they also have a special meaning for each individual because of his unique experiences. The commonly recognized characteristics of a dog lead to its dictionary definition as "an animal, a mammal, a quadruped, a carnivore, etc." This is termed the "denotative" meaning of the concept "dog." My personal associations with dogs may also lead me to think of them as "terrible nuisances" or "man's best friends" or "men whom I think of as dogs because they are despicable fellows I don't want anything to do with." These extra "personal" meanings are called "connotative."

OBJECTIVES FOR CONCEPT AND PRINCIPLE LEARNING

In research studies concept attainment is most often measured by a sorting task, such as sorting squares and nonsquares into different groups. The objective for the learner might be "Correctly sorts a variety of squares and nonsquares." Things are not so simple and straightforward in the classroom, however. Although one's ability to identify instances and noninstances provides irrefutable evidence about some simple concepts, classroom objectives reflect a greater emphasis on more complex concepts and on students' ability to use concepts for a variety of purposes in addition to the classification of examples.

Classroom concepts also tend to call for words from the student rather than physical acts, because language increases the efficiency of communication. A student might be asked, for example, to state the properties that distinguish related concepts, such as plants and animals, or to describe a possible solution to a pollution problem using concepts that have been studied in class. It is not always feasible to call for actual demonstrations by the student.

Table 9-1 identifies several types of objectives that teachers often have for concept and principle learning. The format of Table 9-1 is similar to that of Table 8-1 for knowledge objectives, but the terms used in Table 9-1 are not Bloom's (1956), as they were in Table 8-1, because his taxonomy has no divisions for concept learning specifically. It is easier to focus on the objectives of concept learning apart from those for other outcomes when we modify Bloom's terminology. The several types of application objectives were suggested by categories used by Davis, Alexander, and Yelon (1974).

Objectives of the first type listed in Table 9-1, that is, classifying, are best for simple concepts, such as those that young students learn by observing or sorting examples. Objectives of types 2.00 and 3.00 call for words, and, unless we take special precautions, the words students use may be merely memorized and inadequate as evidence of concept attainment. We recognize that this may happen when we say a person "uses the words but doesn't understand them." One may be able to repeat the definition of a classificatory concept, for example, without being able to use it.

Our objectives for defined concepts include much more than simple classification, of course, and this is evident in objectives 2.00 to 4.00. In one sense, objectives 2.00 through 4.00 aim for higher, more complex concept mastery than objective 1.00. There is far more to the mastery of the concept "light," for example, than being able to classify occurrences as "light" or "not light." But in interpreting the results of tests of objectives 2.00 to 4.00, we must keep in mind that students who fail may do so either because (1) they lack some of the other concepts used to define this one, or (2) they have not succeeded in combining previously known concepts to define the new one. Either might cause failure. This will be apparent in the examples that follow.

The pattern of the examples of objectives for concept and principle learning is based on Table 9-1, just as those for knowledge

Table 9-1

Instrumentation of Objectives for Concept and Principle Learning (Metfessel, Michael, and Kirsner, 1969). (By Permission of the Clinical Psychology Publishing Company, Inc.)

Objective Classification	Examples of Infinitives	Examples of Direct Objects
1.00 *Classifying*		
1.10 Physical (i.e., sorting)	To classify, to sort, to point to, to choose, to group, to select	Positive and negative instances, examples and nonexamples, objects or events that belong
1.20 Verbal (i.e., naming)	To name, to label, to match, to identify, to choose	Same as 1.10
2.00 *Defining*		
2.10 Concepts	To define, to state, to give, to write	Concepts, classes, definitions
2.20 Properties	To state, to give, to list, to describe, to write, to select, to choose	Properties, characteristics, common elements, (or names of properties, characteristics, etc.)
3.00 *Relating*		
3.10 Concepts	To compare, to contrast, to relate, to combine, to differentiate	Concepts, classes, principles, objects, events
3.20 Properties	Same as 3.10	Same as 2.20
4.00 *Applying*		
4.10 Prediction	To predict, to estimate, to extend, to hypothesize	Consequences, results, outcomes, changes
4.20 Control	To control, to conduct, to arrange, to manage, to establish	Situations, behavior, events, factors, conditions
4.30 Explanation	To explain, to interpret, to account for	Events, outcomes, results, changes, phenomena
4.40 Inference	To infer, to conclude, to deduce, to determine	Causes, factors, conditions
4.50 Problem solving	To solve, to resolve, to provide, to produce, to devise, to find	Problems, difficulties, solutions

The student will be able to identify . . . *at least five* unknown substances. *(From W. James Popham and Eva L. Baker, Planning on Instructional Sequence, © 1970. By permission of Prentice-Hall, Inc. and Vimcet Associates)*

learning in Chapter 8 were based on Table 8-1. You should recognize the verb-infinitive-object pattern from the table; with the more specific examples, you should be able to identify conditions, the performance, and the criterion.

1.00 *Classifying* (best for observed concepts)

Example from table: "Ability to classify examples and nonexamples of concepts."

More specific example: "Is able to classify examples and nonexamples of iambic pentameter."

Still more specific example: "Given a printed collection of English verses, checks those that are examples of iambic pentameter." Criterion: 100% accuracy.

2.00 *Defining*

2.10 Concepts

Example from table: "Ability to define concepts."

More specific example: "Ability to define 'propaganda.'"

Still more specific example: "When asked to write a definition of propaganda in his own words, the student writes a statement judged by the teacher to be equivalent in meaning to that given in the text."

2.20 Properties

Example from table: "Ability to describe the properties of given concepts."

More specific example: "Can describe the critical or common properties of 'vectors.'"

Still more specific example: "When asked to state the properties of a vector, states that it is (1) a quantity, with (2) direction and (3) magnitude, which is (4) usually indicated by an arrow." Criterion: All four properties must be given without teacher prompts.

3.00 *Relating*

Example from table: "Ability to compare this concept and related ones."

More specific example: "Can describe the differences in socialism and communism."

Still more specific example: "Given the task of describing the differences in a student's life in a communist country, such as China, and the United States, includes at least three of the points discussed in the assigned readings."

4.00 *Applying*

4.10 Prediction

Example from table: "Is able to predict consequences."

More specific example: "Ability to predict the effect of temperature changes on the humidity of the air."

Still more specific example: "Given the temperature and relative humidity of a body of air, correctly states the effect on the relative humidity if the air is cooled without adding moisture."

4.20 Control

Example from table: "Is able to control conditions."

More specific example: "Conducts an interview in accordance with psychological principles."

Still more specific example: "Given a simulated patient, the student will conduct an interview lasting for 15 to 30 minutes and react 'correctly' to 90% of the emotional disturbances expressed by the patient." A correct response is one that in the judgment of the instructor applies the principles of psychological interaction presented in the textbook, "The Dynamics of Interviewing." (from Davis, Alexander, and Yelon, 1974, p. III.5)

4.30 Explanation

Example from table: "Is able to explain observed phenomena."

More specific example: "Is able to explain characteristic behavior of the Japanese in terms of parental practices."

Still more specific example: "Given descriptions of typical behavior for Japanese adults and descriptions of Japanese childrearing practices is able to select the practices that best explain each behavior and state the related principle." Criterion: Agreement with *Teacher's Manual* for course text.

4.40 Inference (similar to explanation except that conclusions are not given but are to be inferred).

Example from table: "Is able to infer causal factors."

More specific example: "Ability to use principles of air movement to infer the probable causes of heating problems."

Still more specific example: "Given a scale drawing of an unevenly heated room and data on the temperature of numerous locations throughout the room, the student relates the temperature differences to the location of the warm and cold air registers and marks the location of each on the drawing." Criterion: Each register is placed within 5 feet of its actual location.

4.50 Problem Solving

Example from table: "Is able to solve problems."

More specific example: "Is able to use the rule for finding the average of a set of numbers."

Still more specific example: "Given any set of whole numbers and the task of finding the mean, uses standard statistical formula correctly."

PSYCHOLOGICAL STUDIES AND ISSUES

Psychologists have generally chosen one of two approaches in their attempts to account for concept learning. You will recognize these as logical extensions of the S-R and cognitive approaches described for knowledge learning in Chapter 8. Therefore, we need to comment only briefly on these two views before turning to the findings of investigations.

S-R Associations versus Cognition

In the S-R view a concept is a learned association between a class of stimuli with a common element or elements and a common response by the learner. It is acquired under the now familiar S-R conditions of contiguity (occurring together) of the stimulus and the response, reinforcement and repetition. The contrasting cognitive view emphasizes the active role of the learner in processing information, formulating hypotheses, and testing these by tryout and feedback. Initial hypotheses are modified if necessary, and tried again. With "insight" the learner gets the point, grasps the idea, or catches on. He now knows the basis for the concept class or understands the rule.

There is, of course, no single S-R or cognitive approach. Instead, there is a collection of related views by different theorists that have a general set of characteristics, which we have called "S-R" or "cognitive." An important variation or extension of the basic S-R approach is found in "mediation theory." In the mediation approach one does not learn to identify objects or events with a class response because of direct associations (as in (a) below) but because of an "in between" or mediating verbal or physical response to them (as in (b) below). This is an S-R "chain." The objects are stimuli for a mediating response that becomes a stimulus for the concept response.

(a) *S-R Association*

apple
hot dog   R
                   (concept
cake   of food)
steak

(b) *Mediated S-R Association*

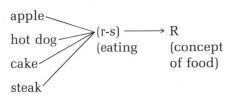

This extra mediational step in the learning process enables S-R theorists to explain more examples of concept learning. Why, for example, do such a wide variety of food objects elicit a common or concept response pattern? Certainly it is not because of similar appearance. However, they can be grouped together or recognized as "alike" from the point of view of our response to them. We eat them all, and the eating response, or the thought of eating, can be associated with the word "food," and other reactions that are part of our concept of "food."

Many mediating responses that are the basis of our classifying objects and events together appear to be internal or unobservable. Language or word mediators are especially common. After the initial associations of eating different foods, the word food or the image of eating may come to mind when we see them again and act as a mediating response. In another example we might learn the label "green" for each of a collection of green objects. Later, whenever we see a member of green objects "family," the word "green" is suggested. This silent language response can be a link that ties various "greens" together to form a general concept of green.

Because many mediating responses are said to be internal and unseen or "in the mind," S-R mediational explanations of concept formation seem much closer to cognitive explanations than simpler S-R approaches that have emphasized observable behavior. An essential difference remains, however. The cognitive or hypothesis-testing models of concept formation assume the learner to be in control as he attempts to make sense out of his experience. S-R theories, no matter how complex, still suggest that the control rests in the conditions of the environment.

Other theoretical differences that were noted in Chapter 8 for knowledge learning are also true for concept learning. In comparison with S-R theorists, the cognitivists give first attention to the organization of the stimulus situation (to encourage insight). S-R theorists, on the other hand, call attention to the conditions that follow the learner's response (to strengthen associations). Those who seek to strengthen associations expect them, and concept formation, to be a gradual process. On the other hand, a sudden or "all at once" achievement of concepts is said to be characteristic of cognitive insight. In this chapter, as in Chapter 8, we consider the emphases of both theoretical approaches, together with the findings of nonpartisan researchers, to generate a more comprehensive set of recommendations for school learning situations.

Research on Learning Concepts by Observation

The contributions and the limitations of psychological research on concept learning will be more fully understood if we examine the approaches and findings. We will consider typical laboratory studies of concept learning by the observation or manipulation of objects and the research on defined concepts or principles separately.

LABORATORY STUDIES OF CONCEPT LEARNING

Concept studies use a characteristic vocabulary. The stimulus objects (or pictures or words) that the learner is to classify or sort are called "positive instances" or "negative instances," depending on whether they are or are not examples of the concept. Each instance has several "dimensions" (the characteristics we have been calling properties or attributes). Dimensions are "critical" or "noncritical," depending on whether they determine membership in the class or not. Thus, shape is a critical dimension of a circle, but size or color are not.

Dimensions may have different "values." Instances of a square may have the dimensions of size, among others, and size may have different values, such as small, medium, and large.

Figure 9-2 from Ellis (1972) was constructed to show positive and negative instances of the concepts "green" and "square" and the dimensions (attributes) of size, color, and shape. One dimension is critical for each concept: color for "green," shape for "square." One attribute (size) is noncritical for both con-

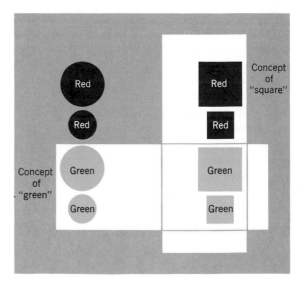

Figure 9-2.

Schematic diagram showing positive and negative instances for the concepts "square" and "green." *(From H. C. Ellis FUNDAMENTALS OF HUMAN LEARNING AND COGNITION, © 1972 by Wm C. Brown & Company, Publishers)*

cepts. Each dimension has two values. Size is large or small. Color is red or green. Shape is round or square. Positive instances are within the labeled dashed lines; negative instances are outside the lines.

THE EXPERIMENTAL PROCEDURE

A series of experiments by Bruner, Goodnow, and Austin (1956) are among the best-known laboratory investigations of concept formation. They are similar to many earlier and more recent laboratory investigations. In a typical experiment subjects would be shown a board with a number of objects. They are told that the objects can be divided into two groups, according to their attributes. One member of a group is identified by the experimenter; then the subject selects additional objects and is told the group to which each belongs. This continues until the subject recognizes the concept. The procedure just described is a "selection" procedure in which subjects choose the object on which they wish information. A second procedure is a "reception" procedure, in which objects are presented in an order determined by the experimenter, and the subject is asked to classify each as it is presented. After each response, the subject is told whether or not he is correct.

Psychologists have gained considerable knowledge of concept learning by such experiments, and a rather lengthy list of their findings has been compiled by Clark (1971). There is convincing evidence, for example, that the teacher or experimenter should present several (about four) positive or negative instances at the same time, instead of presenting and then withdrawing one at a time. It is evident, also, that the smaller the number of critical attributes needed to define a concept, the easier it is to learn, and that learners should be given feedback for both correct and incorrect responses on each trial. These and other findings about learning concepts by observation of instances will be incorporated in our recommendations for teaching concepts in a later section. Our purpose here is to characterize the research on this type of concept learning and call attention to its limitations.

LIMITATIONS OF LABORATORY STUDIES

The most important limitation of the laboratory research on concept learning is that very few school tasks are of the nonverbal, inductive type that have been most often studied. With few exceptions only young children are expected to learn this way in school. One exception is for some visual forms, such as the patterns of an electrocardiogram or the "graceful movements" of dancing, because these are too intricate to describe adequately in words. By far the greater number of school concept-learning tasks are verbal, however, and call for learning definitions.

There are additional limitations of the research evidence that make us temper our use of the findings with the lessons of experience, even for nonverbal observational learning. Those enumerated by Carroll (1964), Glaser (1968), Clark (1971), and Martorella (1972) include the following.

1. In the laboratory, concept dimensions (attributes) are obvious and easy for learners; in the classroom, the dimensions themselves may be difficult concepts.

2. In the laboratory, the critical dimensions of concepts have only one or two values (such as present or absent, large or small); in school, the range of values that dimensions can have is extremely wide.

3. In school learning, neither all the concept instances nor all their dimensions can be completely observed or even listed.

4. In school, remembering many words and concepts is an important problem that has been almost entirely ignored in the laboratory.

5. Most of the research on concept learning has been done with young adolescents instead of with the wide range of ages encountered in the classroom.

Research on Learning Defined Concepts (Principles)

Research on the learning of concepts that must be defined or explained has centered around several questions. Findings with respect to three of these questions are discussed here. (1) How should concepts be organized or sequenced for learning? (2) How much guidance or direction should learners be given? (3) How do the results of different teaching methods compare? A fourth question about developmental trends in concept learning or the qualitative changes that occur in conceptual learning as children mature is discussed in Chapter 3 under the heading of cognitive development.

LEARNING HIERARCHIES

Most of our knowledge about the sequencing of learning comes from studies of "learning hierarchies." The definition of a concept or the statement of a principle expresses a relationship among other, often simpler or less inclusive, concepts and principles. Thus, the concept of living things may be defined in terms of plants and animals. Animals, in turn, are defined in terms of the attributes of voluntary movement, sensory and nervous organs, and so on, that are also concepts that may need further definition. We are reminded of those fleas with lesser fleas who had "still lesser fleas to bite 'em and so *ad infinitum.*"

The sequential and hierarchical nature of another set of principles, expressed in the form of the learner's behavior, is shown in Figure 9-3. As in other hierarchies, the lowest level identifies concepts that must be known at the start. The learning at higher levels requires the concepts from lower levels.

We assume that any defined concept is part of a hierarchy, somewhat like those of our examples, and that the ease of learning that concept by definition depends on having previously learned the simpler concepts that enter into the definition.

We can also look at a learning hierarchy in terms of the potential for transfer from one level to another. When we have mastered a given set of concepts, we expect positive transfer to related "higher-order" concepts, because they depend on what has been already learned; that is, learning a set of concepts at one level makes the task of learning others at higher levels easier. This is "vertical" transfer, which we have distinguished (Chapter 6) from "horizontal" transfer, of the type that occurs when a principle we have learned for the solution of a problem enables us to solve other similar problems on the same conceptual level.

Gagné and his co-workers (1968, 1971, 1973) have been most active in the demonstration and investigation of hierarchies. Although Gagné's concept of hierarchies does not limit them to defined concepts or principles, he finds that hierarchies relating to educational topics are often composed largely of principles, which he now prefers to call "rules" (1970).

Figure 9-3 was reproduced from Gagné and Bassler (1963), and was used also in Gagné (1970) to describe the hierarchial or pyramid-like nature of the learning of rules for a topic in mathematics. When interpreting hierarchies, two points are important. (1) It is not assumed that the sequence described is the only one possible; others might be developed that would have the same final outcomes.

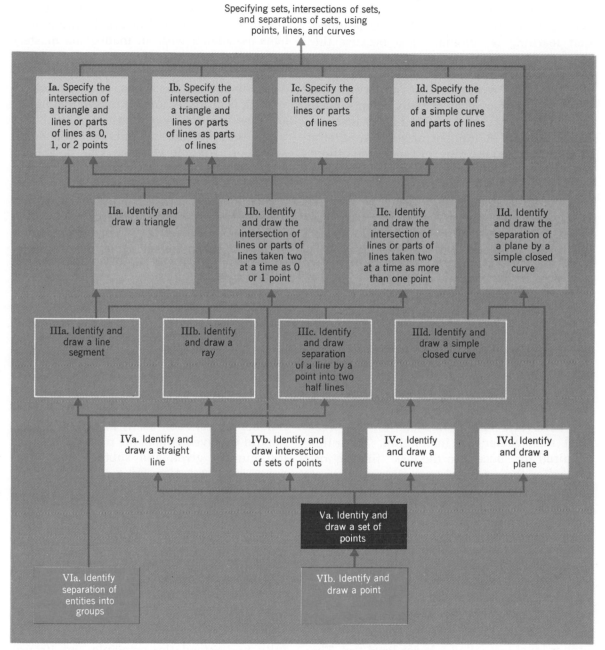

Figure 9-3.

Hierarchy of principles to be acquired in a topic of elementary nonmetric geometry. The topic to be learned is shown in the topmost box. *(From R. M. Gagne, and O. C. Bassler,* Journal of Educational Psychology, *54: 123-131. Copyright © 1963 by the American Psychological Association. Reprinted by permission)*

(2) All conditions for learning of rules at each level are not portrayed; it cannot be assumed that learning is automatic just because the identified prerequisite concepts have been mastered. Instruction will still be necessary.

What is the evidence that mastery of the concepts at one level actually affects mastery of concepts at the next higher level as hypothesized? A number of studies, chiefly of mathematical learning, by Gagné and others have shown that the suggested relationship does, indeed, hold.

Gagné and others (1965) developed an instructional program to teach sixth graders the rules of Figure 9-3 in the exact order shown. The results showed that the learning at each level was, as predicted, highly dependent on learning at lower levels. For example, only 1 out of 72 students who performed correctly on a test of rule IIa had not performed well first on rule IIIa, and none of the students who did not succeed on rule IIa had succeeded on rule IIIa. Other comparisons yielded similar results.

An earlier study by Gagné (1962) is a straightforward test of a hierarchy of rules. We believe it has implications for the practical management of instruction. The rules required for success in the task "finding formulas for the set of 'n' terms in a number of series" were arranged in a sequence similar to others we have described. Then a group of ninth-grade boys was tested on the final rule. If any boy failed, he was given a test for the next highest rule of the hierarchy, and so on, working down until he passed. Then, Gagné designed instruction to teach the boys the tasks they had failed and tested them again. Initially, the results showed that there were no instances in which a boy who passed a higher level test failed a lower level test. The performance of the boys on previously failed tasks after instruction also supported (1) the hierarchial nature of the learning material

and (2) the effectiveness of instruction that is designed to overcome specific learning problems associated with an inadequate mastery of prerequisite concepts.

The structure of mathematics is more evident, of course, than that of other subject areas. It is probably for this reason that nearly all investigators have chosen mathematics when they sought to study the sequential nature of principle learning. One of the few exceptions is a study by Okey and Gagné (1970). They found that a chemistry topic was better taught when the instructional procedures were based on learning hierarchies. As this field of investigation matures, we may expect to find an increasing number of studies from fields other than mathematics.

GUIDANCE AND DISCOVERY

When the objective is the learning, application, and retention of principles, should learners be given these principles or required to discover them more or less independently? A fairly typical experimental task is designed to teach learners rules for finding the sums of number series, such as, 1, 2, 4, 8, 16, ___ ___. Should we give learners the rule: "Double the last number given and subtract one" [e.g., $1 + 2 + 4 + 8 + 16 = (16 \times 2) - 1 = 31$]? Or should we encourage them to find the rule for themselves by working with this and other sample problems? Giving learners the rule is a form of "guidance." Encouraging them to find it without help is often referred to as a "discovery" method. Guidance is seldom complete in the sense that the learner has to do nothing. Even with the guidance provided by the statement of the principle, you probably had to work out a few examples before you fully understood the principle and its use. Other forms of guidance that require more of the learner consist of hints, clues, or cues that do not give the learner the principle, but make it easier for him to find it. For example, we might say "Perhaps we should compare the last number in the series with the sum of the series for several examples and see if that tells us anything." Or, "Let's see: when the last number is 4 the sum is almost 7 or about 2×4; when the last number is 8, the sum is 15 or almost 2×8, and when the last number is 16, the sum lacks but one of being 2×16."

Research studies employing a variety of methods and materials have addressed this question of the effects of guidance or direction by the experimenter when subjects are to learn a principle. In spite of the differences and deficiencies of these studies, a review of the results leads to the conclusion that giving the learner rules and examples of their use is more effective than expecting them to find the rules independently (Craig, 1969). Also, when a general method or strategy for finding rules (rules for finding rules) is the objective, explaining that strategy (Roughead and Scandura, 1968) or guidance in finding it (Gagné and Brown, 1961) is more effective than examples only or the opportunity to discover.

Other findings for principle learning indicate that best results are obtained when the rules or other information given learners apply only to the problems for which the learners are later responsible. Principles that hold for an unnecessarily wide variety of problem situations give the learner less specific information about what to do in particular situations. Hence, he makes more mistakes. On the other hand, if the principles are so specific that they work with only some of the problems given later, learners err in trying to use rules when they do not apply (Wittrock, Keislar, and Stern, 1964).

You must make a careful distinction between the objective of learning a given principle or principles, the situation we have been discussing, and the objective of learning to discover new principles independently. In the first case we are concerned with teaching particular principles, and we can conclude that much guidance is desirable; in the second, we aim to develop independence in problem solving. When we consider this objective in the next chapter, our conclusion about the uses of guidance will be different.

A major limitation of research on discovery, like that on learning concepts by sorting objects, is that they are of short duration and require learning only a few items. Worthen (1968) was concerned with this and other differences between experimental and classroom learning situations. Regular teachers used his textlike materials in mathematics with fifth- and sixth-grade children every day for 6 weeks. After 5 and 11 weeks, tests showed that a discovery group did better than a group taught by teacher expositions. This finding seems to contradict our previous conclusions about being generous with guidance when teaching principles. However, we see the situation studied by Worthen as more like the one in which students learn to *discover* principles than one in which they learn specific principles.

When Worthen's students were asked about a large number of concepts and principles, weeks after they learned them, they may not have been able to recall them right away. They may have had to work them out again, a task that is much like discovery (or rediscovery). The learners who had previously practiced discovery, the "discovery group," would be expected to discover better than the learners who had no practice in discovery, that is, "the teacher exposition" group.

Because the situation studied by Worthen appears typical of many school situations, his results underline the importance of attention to teaching independence in finding principles, in addition to teaching them particular principles. (This is our concern in Chapter 10.)

TEACHING METHODS

Five methods of teaching defined concepts were compared by Johnson and Stratton (1966) in an experiment with college students. The methods, which you will recognize as typical of those used by teachers, were defined by the materials studied by the students. The methods were:

1. *Definitions*. Students studied definitions of concepts and then wrote their own. An example is:

"When two or more people express different opinions, get excited and contradict each other, the event is called an *altercation*. Thus an *altercation* is a social interaction characterized by heated exchange of opposing arguments. Now write a definition of *altercation* in your own words." (Johnson and Stratton, 1966, p. 50)

2. *Sentences*. A short story was read by students in which each of the concept names appeared twice. Instructions were to read the story and learn the words. Then students were asked to complete sentences using the words.

3. *Classification*. Students classified short descriptions of objects and events as instances or noninstances of the concept. Five instances were presented at each of six trials and correct answers were supplied after each trial.

4. *Synonyms*. Students were told to learn the meanings of the concepts and short statements were presented, such as: "Alacrity means eagerness" and *"Altercation* means squabble." Then students matched other synonyms to the concept names of four trials and were given answers after each trial.

5. *Mixed Program*. Abridged definitions, two synonyms and one example of each concept, were given students. Then they were asked to do one synonym matching exercise and one example classification exercise with correct answers provided.

The group of students taught by the mixed program received higher scores on tests over learned concepts nine days after learning, regardless of whether the tests called for definitions, classification, synonyms, or use in sentences. There were no differences among other methods. The researchers concluded that concepts of the type studied can be taught to students equally well by a variety of methods, but that a combination of methods typical of those commonly used by teachers and textbook writers, is the best practice.

In their experiment, Anderson and Kulhavy (1972) showed that college students can easily learn concepts from statements of definition providing they have the other concepts referred to in the definition. When their subjects used concept words in sentences, their learning was better than when they simply read the definition. They regard this as evidence that requiring subjects to process the information they receive enhances their learning. These results suggest that procedures that actually require learners to work with definitions, rules, or principles will improve learning, just as similar procedures were reported as effective for association or knowledge learning (Chapter 8).

RECOMMENDATIONS FOR INSTRUCTION

Children acquire their first concepts by observing objects and events without the aid of language. The difference between this learning and learning by definition is clear. But by the time the child is old enough to attend school, he has some language facility. Language begins to play an important role in teacher's efforts to aid his learning from examples. When teachers say something like, "See how we can tell this is a 'whatsit' and that one isn't," and point to the features of an object that make it a member of a concept class, the line between learning by observation and by definition is fading fast. The fact is that there are relatively few instances of "pure" concept learning by observation in the schools. There is certainly a difference, however, in the way we teach when we depend on words alone and when we give students a chance to observe and classify concept instances "first hand."

Teaching Observable Concepts

Once you have identified a concept or concepts that you believe will be best taught by the observation of examples, there is a rather orderly sequence of steps to be followed in preparation, teaching, and evaluation, and some rules to guide the performance of each step. Our recommendations have been derived from the theory and research previously discussed and from Clark's (1971) comprehensive review of experimental research. Together these recommendations form what might be called a model for teaching observable concepts. Although it cannot be followed slavishly, as a general guide it should do much to make the teaching task easier and more effective. This model will be described and illustrated in this section. But first a brief review of our terminology.

"*Critical properties or attributes are those characteristics that distinguish members of a concept class (positive instances of a concept) from nonmembers of the class (negative instances).* Critical properties may be said to "define" a concept. Even though no formal definition is attempted, these properties make the difference between members of the

class and nonmembers. Thus, equal sides, right angles, and straight sides are critical attributes of squares; they are the characteristics used to separate squares from nonsquares.

Noncritical properties or attributes are irrelevant to the distinction between members of the class and nonmembers. They do not enter into the crucial differences. For example, size, position, and color are not important when distinguishing squares and nonsquares.

Each critical attribute has some range of values that is acceptable in members of a concept class, others that are unacceptable. Sometimes there are only two values of a critical property, present or absent. The acceptable value is simply "present" and the unacceptable one, "absent." Such a property is "fixed." Other critical attributes are "variable," that is, they have a range of acceptable values. The values for degrees of an "acute angle," for example, may vary from almost closed (∠) or zero degrees, to almost "square" (∟) or 90 degrees. The unacceptable range of degrees for an acute angle would include those from 90 degrees (∟) to 180 degrees (—).

Noncritical or irrelevant attributes may have different values or the same value in positive and negative instances of a concept. For example, size is not a critical attribute of "squareness." Instances of squares and nonsquares may be of the same size or quite different.

You should now be ready to proceed to our recommendations for the teaching of observable concepts.

CONCEPT ANALYSIS

The first step in teaching a concept is to seek the answers to several important questions about it.

1. On what critical properties should we focus attention?

2. What range of values for critical properties is acceptable in members of the concept class?

3. What are the most frequently observed noncritical properties that students should learn to ignore?

4. Are there particular examples (instances) of nonconcept members that will be especially difficult to distinguish from concept members and therefore need special attention?

A close examination of instances and noninstances of the concepts will suggest the answers to these questions.

For the concepts "square" and "m" we can list:

		Square	"m"
1.	Critical attributes	Equal sides Right angles Straight sides	Three "legs" Position
2.	Frequently observed noncritical characteristics	Size Position Color	Size Color Style of writing or printing
3.	Other concepts sharing some critical characteristics	Rectangles Equilateral Triangles and parallelograms	"n" "w" "E"

The results of such a concept analysis will identify the properties (they are merely simpler concepts) that will be taught. It also shows irrelevant concepts that will be varied in the examples observed to show that they have no bearing in the distinction between concept instances and noninstances. Finally, the presentation will be planned to eliminate confusion with members of other concept classes that share some of the critical properties of members of the concept class being taught. We will want to be sure to compare a square with a rectangle, for example, to show that four right angles are insufficient to separate a square from other common figures.

When we seek to teach more complex concepts by observation, a supplementary analysis may be completed specifically for comparisons that will probably cause problems.

If we were teaching the concept "dog," for example, we would readily identify "wolf" as difficult to distinguish from dog, and, if we wished our concept of dog to be complete or precise, we would have to plan to include specific comparisons between dogs (as positive instances) and (wolves) as negative instances. What should the comparison emphasize? An analysis following more general analysis and focusing on "dog" versus "wolf" would help us tell.

	Dog	*Wolf*
1. Critical attributes	Bark	No bark
	Smaller	Larger
	Duller teeth	Sharper teeth
2. Irrelevant characteristics	Position	
	Situation observed	
	Canine shape	
	Color	

PREINSTRUCTIONAL ASSESSMENT

Tactics for preinstructional assessment with concept instruction will not be described at this point; they differ little from the procedures used quite generally. Here we will emphasize what it is we need to assess before teaching. Once we identify the knowledge or concept we wish to measure, we would, of course, design situations or materials that require students to demonstrate that knowledge or concept. A further discussion of approaches to assessing concepts will be given under "*postassessment*." Parallel procedures are used to check prerequisite concepts before instruction.

Do students already know the concept we plan to teach? We should find out. It is possible that they do, and we may conclude that it is unnecessary to teach the concept again. It is more likely, of course, that some students will know the concept and some will not. This would call for some individualization of instruction, perhaps with those students with the concept helping others to learn it.

If teaching the concept is indicated by our preinstruction evaluation, it will be important to find out if students have the prerequisites for learning the new concept. Teaching and learning a concept will be easier and more effective if students have already learned:

1. The concept name.

2. Associations of the concept name with a few specific examples of the concept.

3. Names for the critical properties of the new concept.

If the prerequisites to concept learning have not been learned previously, they must be taught now, whether the teaching of prerequisites is considered part of concept teaching or a prerequisite to concept teaching. It is fairly often necessary to teach children to call several specific examples of the concept by the concept name. This is knowledge teaching, not concept teaching, because the associations are specific ones, not generalized to other members of the concept class. For example, we might teach "angle" as a specific response to "V" written on the chalkboard, the points of a particular star, and the corner of a desk before moving into instruction on the general concept of angle.

One reason for classifying the items we have listed as prerequisites is because it is extremely helpful to be able to refer to the names and critical properties of concept instances verbally. When teaching a square, we will wish to call attention to the "equal sides." If students have the concepts of "equal" and "sides," including the concept names, our task and theirs is greatly simplified. There is a hierarchy of concepts, which we have discussed previously, and simpler, more basic concepts should be learned before "higher-order" concepts related to them and in a sense defined by them.

DEMONSTRATION AND PRACTICE ON CRITICAL PROPERTIES

Recognition of the critical properties that determine whether or not an item is an example of a concept is the central task in learning a concept. A fuller statement of the topic to be discussed now would be "demonstration and practice to develop the ability to recognize the range of values of a critical property that are acceptable in a member of a concept class."

We have explained that there are two types of concept properties: (1) *fixed*, with only one acceptable value (present) and one unacceptable one (absent) and (2) *variable*, having several different acceptable values and/or several different unacceptable ones. The basic tactic for teaching each one is somewhat different.

1. *To teach a fixed critical property, present pairs of one positive and one negative instance.*

2. *To teach a variable critical property, present a series of instances, all positive or all negative, which demonstrate the range of values, while keeping other properties constant.*

Let us use our familiar example of the equal sides of a square to illustrate the first teaching rule. If we use figures cut out of paper, we might present the pairs of figures shown at the left in the following example. Those at the right would be less effective because too many characteristics other than the one we are attending to are also changing, that is, size, color, and position, in addition to the equality of the sides.

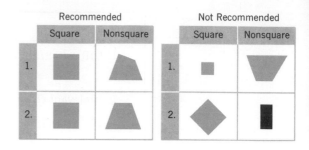

It is important to note that this set of examples would not teach *all* the critical characteristics of squares, only one. Another series based on the critical principle of "equal angles" or "square corners" would also be needed. It might be useful to you to prepare the examples you might use to teach this critical property.

The teaching strategy for a *variable* critical property does not begin with pairs of positive and negative instances. Instead several positive instances are presented (or several negative), each with a different value for the critical property. The object is to demonstrate the range of acceptable and unacceptable values. Again other properties are held constant. Note that in the following example for angle, an attempt is made to demonstrate or show the limits or "boundary conditions" of the range of values. The lower limit for the degrees of an acute angle is near zero; the upper limit is almost 90 degrees, or a right angle.

Series of Positive Instances for Degrees of an Acute Angle		Series of Negative Instances for Degrees of an Acute Angle	
Recommended	Not recommended	Recommended	Not recommended
1.		1.	
2.		2.	
3.		3.	
4.		4.	

Again, only one critical characteristic is shown in any one series. Sometimes a series used for a variable characteristic will be followed by positive-negative sets of pairs for a fixed characteristic. When teaching the concept of an acute angle, we might use pairs such as ($\llcorner$ $\diagup$) and ($\measuredangle$ $\wedge$) to show that the lines defining the angles are to be closed at the "point."

Instances are grouped the same way for both *demonstration* and initial *practice*. A fairly typical approach would be to begin with a demonstration. The teacher points to instances and says, "This is a square," or "This is not a square." He also uses words and other cues to direct students' attention to the critical attribute and how it may change from instance to instance. Then additional examples are presented, and students are asked to make the identifications and explanations while the teacher provides feedback.

DEMONSTRATING AND PRACTICING WITH NONCRITICAL PROPERTIES

A fuller statement of the purpose of this type of instruction would be "to teach students to ignore changes in irrelevant characteristics while concentrating on the characteristics that really determine whether an observed instance is a member of the concept task." The basic tactic is to present a series of positive instances in which the critical characteristics do not change while the most commonly observed irrelevant characteristics do. The following is an example of such a sequence for the concept "square."

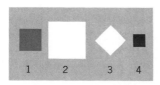

Again, series of this type are recommended for both presentation and related practice.

ADVANCED PRACTICE

In advanced practice mixed series of positive and negative instances are presented with variation in both critical and noncritical characteristics. A variety of materials such as drawings, pictures, paper cutouts, and available objects are used. Students either sort or mark instances as positive or negative, examples or nonexamples. No prompts (hints, clues, or helpful directions) are given before students respond, but feedback and confirmation are given after they respond.

The instances used should differ from those previously practiced, and generally, they are more complex. The critical properties are not as obvious. Initial teaching examples of the concept "mammal" would make the differences between mammals and nonmammals obvious, perhaps with closeups that show hair and breasts. Flies, grubs, and fish might be contrasted with cows and humans. In advanced practice there would be instances in which the critical differences are far less obvious—a duck-billed platypus might be shown with a duck and a whale with a large fish. As these examples suggest, practice on pairs of instances and noninstances will be useful in helping to insure that particularly difficult distinctions are made, but the order of positive and negative instances (mammals and nonmammals) should be random.

SEQUENCING TEACHING-LEARNING ACTIVITIES

We have described the teaching of both a critical property and the range of irrelevant properties, but how are these two types of teaching activities to be combined? The order must be systematic, but no one order of activities will be best for all concepts or all learners. We can suggest an order for activities that will be quite generally useful, but we emphasize that some modification of the order we suggest may be more efficient or effective in a

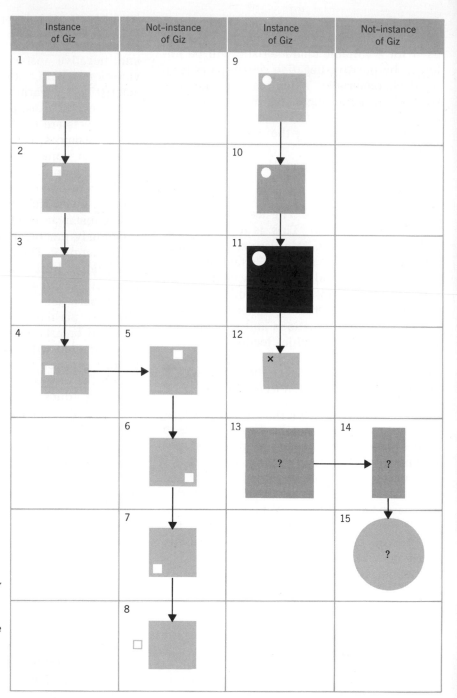

Figure 9-4.

What is a Giz? A sequence of instances designed to teach an artificial concept. *(From TEACHING: A COURSE IN APPLIED PSYCHOLOGY by Wesley C. Becker, Siegfried Engelmann, and Don R. Thomas. © 1971, Science Research Associates, Inc. Reprinted by permission of the publisher)* particular situation with particular learners.

Our generally recommended approach is as follows.

Phase 1. Tell and show students what they will learn to do, for example, point to several "m's" among other letters and say "you will learn to tell which letters are "m.""

Phase 2. Teach the most obvious critical property.

2.1 For *fixed* properties present positive-negative pairs.

2.2 For *variable* properties present positive series followed by negative series.

Phase 3. Teach the variety of values for the most frequently observed irrelevant or non-critical properties.

Phase 4. Repeat Phase 2 for each additional critical characteristic.

Phase 5. Provide advanced practice with feedback.

Note: When the results of practice reveal a lack of mastery, repeat the preceding phase(s).

Becker, Engelmann, and Thomas (1971) provide some examples of artificial concepts, which we use as illustrations here because you will not already know the concepts.

Two possible sequences for "made-up" concepts are presented in Figures 9-4 and 9-5. If the sequencing is effective, you should have little difficulty learning the concepts before continuing with our explanation, even without a teacher's help. Stop and try it!

Were you able to learn the concept of Figure 9-4? A "Giz" has to be a square with a smaller figure in the upper left corner or quadrant. The shape of the smaller figure and the size, location, or surface pattern of the outside figure are unimportant.

If you remembered the tactics we suggested for designing a teaching sequence, you probably found the task easier, because you

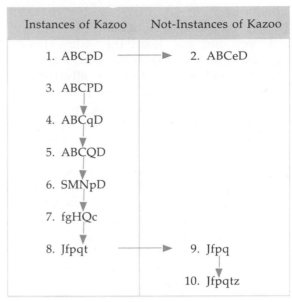

Instances of Kazoo	Not-Instances of Kazoo
1. ABCpD ⟶	2. ABCeD
3. ABCPD	
4. ABCqD	
5. ABCQD	
6. SMNpD	
7. fgHQc	
8. Jfpqt ⟶	9. Jfpq
	10. Jfpqtz

Figure 9-5.

What is a "Kazoo"? Sequence of instances designed to teach an artificial concept. *(From Becker, Engelmann, and Thomas, 1971, p. 277.)*

could guess the function of the several different series of instances. The first series of positive instances (1 to 4) show the range of acceptable values for a critical characteristic, as we recommended. The only thing that changes in this series is the location of the smaller object, a critical property. The next series of not-instances shows the range of unacceptable values for this same property, that is, where the small figure cannot be. Then the series of positive items from 9 to 13 show the irrelevant or noncritical properties, things that do not matter. They rule out the shape of the smaller object, the size of the square, the location of the square, and the surface pattern. The arrangement of instances 13, 14, and 15 permits two pair-wise comparisons, 13 versus 14 and 13 versus 15. They show that the shape of the outside figure must be a square. This is a critical property with only two values (present or absent) for which comparison of positive-negative instance pairs is an effective tactic.

If you did not learn the "Giz" concept readily from the sequence of instances and are inclined to question its effectiveness, remember that we also recommend a teacher who will suggest "what to look for" and provide other forms of fairly direct guidance. You were on your own in what was essentially a "discovery" situation.

Sometimes, depending on the sophistication of the learner and the premium placed on efficiency, it is possible to combine Phases 1 and 2 of our suggested sequence in the same series of instances. This is illustrated in Figure 9-5 where instances 3 to 8 for the concept "Kazoo" are used to show that p and q are acceptable for the letter in the fourth position (critical property). This same series shows that whether the letters are small or capital is irrelevant. Note, however, that the full range of values acceptable for the critical property has not been demonstrated. We do not know the boundary conditions. Unless we have learned to trust those who present concept instances to demonstrate the full range of acceptable values, some question remains. Would "l" or "m" be acceptable? We can guess. This ambiguity is not the result of combining Phases 1 and 2; it is the result of the failure to include a series of negative instances to show the range of unacceptable letters in the fourth position, specifically whether or not "l" and "m" are to be included. Experienced concept learners may not need to have unacceptable as well as acceptable values demonstrated; inexperienced ones do.

By the way, a "Kazoo" is a five-letter combination with a "p" or "q" in the fourth position. The paired comparisons 8 and 9 and 8 and 10 establish that the characteristic of word length has only one acceptable value, five letters.

POSTASSESSMENT

Data gathered during advanced practice may be adequate to judge the achievement of objectives for teaching a concept. If more formal assessment is desired, an appropriate test would present a wide variety of positive and negative instances to be physically sorted or marked "concept" or "nonconcept." When possible, the exam items should be somewhat different from those previously used for practice.

Tests can serve a diagnostic purpose, also, if they are planned to provide clues to the specific difficulties of students who fail to learn the concept. Do students know the required component concepts? Do they have a faulty concept of the relationship among components? If so, what is their error?

Your objectives for students' concept learning may go beyond classification, although this is fundamental to concept learning, and include their ability to state definitions, identify critical properties, and so on. If so, you will want to construct test items that also measure these behaviors. You will want to ask students to recognize or to give definitions and have them point to, describe, or choose correct descriptions for critical properties.

ADDITIONAL TACTICS THAT ARE GENERALLY EFFECTIVE

The tactics listed here supplement our previous suggestions. A few are repetitious. Unless otherwise indicated, each is advisable in every phase of concept teaching.

1. Teach one concept at a time.

2. For initial presentations and practice make critical properties obvious.

3. If students have previously learned to call some items by the concept name, try to include these items in your introductory instances.

4. Teach each critical attribute of a concept separately.

5. For initial teaching present about four instances simultaneously and allow them to remain in full view of the learners.

6. For variable characteristics present a positive series of instances before the negative instances.

7. Use language and other cues liberally to direct students' attention to the critical properties. For example, use a cardboard "ruler" to show that the sides of a square are all the same.

8. Whenever possible, allow students to manipulate instances physically.

9. Provide immediate and complete feedback (including explanations of "why") during practice.

10. Individualize practice as much as possible.

TEACHING DEFINED CONCEPTS AND PRINCIPLES

As the language facility of the child develops, we come to depend more and more on words to teach him concepts. Finally, when children have words for the many concepts they have acquired by observation and they are able to understand our directions, we tell them the relationship they are to learn, and use words to describe examples of it. We use definitions to teach concepts and we ask students to define concepts to show that they have learned.

The overall outline of the steps we describe for teaching concepts through definition is similar to that used to describe the teaching of concepts through the observation of instances.

PREINSTRUCTIONAL ANALYSIS AND ASSESSMENT

Our preinstructional analysis of a defined concept or principle is directed toward the lower-order concepts or principles that the student is to learn to relate. These may be relatively easy to identify, as with the principle "round things roll" or it may require the construction or use of a hierarchy of related principles similar to that of Figure 9-3. In either case the approach is to ask ourselves, "What does the student need to know or be able to do before he can be instructed in this principle?" We have described this process in Chapter 8 in relation to sequencing knowledge instruction, and Gagné's research on this topic was considered in the present chapter.

Whether or not a simple or an elaborate hierarchial analysis is necessary, effective instructional planning requires that we attempt to identify concepts prerequisite to the one we will teach. This principle is clear, but we will, of course, make mistakes in applying it. Considerable trial and error are often necessary before we can be even reasonably sure of an effective ordering of learning outcomes. The concepts and principles that we believe to be prerequisites are assessed, and, when necessary, taught in preparation for undertaking the new learning.

PRESENTATION

The functions of a presentation by a teacher or text are (1) to describe the expected outcome, (2) to help the learner recall prior concepts or principles that will be needed, (3) to tell or to show the new concept or principle, and (4) to demonstrate the concept or principle. The teacher's actions that relate to these functions will be stated as prescriptions.

State the Expected Outcome. Here, as in the corresponding step for teaching an observable concept, you tell or show or both tell and show what students will be able to do after learning the principle. For example, you may say, "You will be able to tell if an animal is a mammal" or, in another instance, "You will be able to compute the amount of work done from the force it takes to move an object a given distance." This step helps to keep students' attention focused on what it is they are to achieve.

Stimulate Student Recall of Prerequisite Learning. Although this step is often omitted in practice and may not be essential to some students' learning, it helps to insure that more students will be ready to profit from the presentation of the new concept or principle. The tactic may be either one of telling and showing or one of questioning, which prompts student recall. Examination of the definition or rule "Work is the product of the force acting upon a body and the distance through which the body moves" suggests that the student should recall the concepts "product," "force," "distance," "equals," and "multiplies."

The teacher may proceed by saying, "You will recall what we mean by force. . . . Force means. . . . An example of force is . . . , etc." Or he might well say, "Who remembers what we mean by force? Give me an example."

The teacher may add a demonstration: "When I attach this spring to a block, like this, and pull the block across the table, the spring scale tells me I'm using a force of 10 pounds." Alternatively, he can say, "John, use this scale to show me a force and how it might be measured."

Some combination of telling, questioning, and showing would then be used to stimulate students to bring to mind the other concepts needed, that is, "distance," "product," and so on.

Tell and Show the Concept of Principle. There are several equally effective ways of presenting a definition or principle. Johnson and Stratton's research, which we have described in this chapter, demonstrated equivalent results when students did any of the following: (1) studied definitions, (2) read situations demonstrating the use of the concept, (3) classified short descriptions of the concept, and (4) studied synonyms for the concept. Johnson and Stratton's methods did not permit the separation of the concept presentation from students' practice with it. Also, their college student subjects were sophisticated learners. Their results suggest, however, the effectiveness of a "mixed method" that combines several types of presentation.

The teacher should use both a statement of the concept or principle and examples or demonstrations. Thus, if we were teaching "altercation" (one of Johnson's concepts), we might first offer a definition and then an example. "An *altercation* is a social interaction characterized by a heated exchange of opposing arguments." For example, when two or more people express different opinions, get excited, and contradict each other, the event is called an *altercation*." (Johnson and Stratton, 1966, p. 50.) We might continue with, "Another example of an altercation would be. . . ." A film clip of an altercation might also be shown as an example, or an altercation might be staged.

If the definition were one of work in terms of force times distance, we could simply write the statement on the board, so it could remain in full view, then demonstrate the principle by pulling a block or other weight a given distance with a spring balance that would measure the force. As the measures of weight and distance were identified, they would be matched with the terms in the definition on the chalkboard and the value of the work computed in foot-pounds. This might be described as "providing a model of performance." Additional examples taken from areas of students' experience would be described verbally.

In the preceding illustrations of telling and showing we gave the rule first, then the examples. We might well give one example first, however, to arouse interest, then the rule, and then explained examples. An introductory example is useful when it puzzles or intrigues the students or is seen by them as an interesting problem.

Seeing the instructor jump up on a chair and announce he had just done 300 foot-pounds of work is an example that might motivate students to want to learn more about the principle defining work, especially if he asks how much more work this is for him than it would be for them. One of the objectives of a social studies class was, "Humans exert influence on groups of people." (Briggs, 1970, p. 131) In this situation interest in further study might be sparked by an anecdote of an individual who got into trouble following another's advice, a short film of the unexpected consequences that followed the passage of a law, a recording of a stirring speech on a controversial issue, or a brief experiment that shows how a person's beliefs can shift when they are told what others believe. Statements of the principle and further examples in the context of social studies content would follow the discussion of these examples.

STUDENT PERFORMANCE

Following the presentation of the concept or principle and demonstrations of its use, students are asked to state the principle and demonstrate it. Their ability to state and demonstrate the principle is the evidence of their learning.

Students State the Definition (Principle). An expression of the required relationship in the student's own words should be requested instead of a formal definition. If necessary, use verbal prompts, such as "How are force and distance related in the definition of work?"

Should the student attempt a statement of the principle before or after he demonstrates it? If he can state it before, with prompting, it will serve as a self-prompt or self-guidance for his performance. After he demonstrates knowledge of the principle by performance, a verbal statement is a useful summary of what he has done. This may facilitate retention. Gagné describes a final verbalization as "Optional, but useful for later instruction." (1970, p. 203) We believe it useful to ask the student (1) to attempt a statement of the desired relationship, (2) to describe or show "how it works," and (3) to reexamine and perhaps revise his initial statement.

Students Demonstrate the Principle. Now, we say to the student of "work," verbally or in writing, "Show how you would calculate the work done in lifting your 200-pound teacher 4 feet off the ground." Or, if we have taught the rule for finding the sum of a series of consecutive odd numbers beginning with one, an example we used earlier in the chapter, we might say, "Find the sum of the first 29 odd numbers, the first 54, and the first 36." In still another situation we would say "Form the plural of these nouns." In all these situations the "show me" nature of our expectation for the student is evident.

Additional Practice for Retention and Transfer. There is evidence that many principles can be learned without repetitive practice, providing the prerequisite concepts and principles are known (Gagné, 1970, p. 202). Principles are often retained well over long periods of time without such practice (Chapter 8).

Principles should be reinstated and demonstrated, of course, when they are used in the formation of still more complex relationships, that is, concepts and principles at still higher levels of hierarchies, such as that of Figure

9-3. To provide for this is simply to follow the preceding recommendations for new principle learning.

Providing opportunities for students to use a principle with a wider variety of situations than those encountered in initial learning is a form of practice often recommended for improved transfer. It is argued that principles should be taught as keys to a large class of problem situations, not just those studied in class, and that the way to do this is to apply the principle to widely varied examples. "When a student finds the diameter of a circle by dividing the circumference by the value of pi (3.14) he can also be learning to find the diameter of trees and tanks and even the earth." (Craig, 1966, p. 19)

Some psychologists counter this argument by suggesting that if the student has an adequate concept of "circle," "circumference," "diameter," and so on, the hoped for transfer will be automatic. If he has not mastered these component concepts, it is seen as a problem in teaching these concepts, not in teaching the principle. Even though, it is a long established principle that the degree of transfer from one learning situation to another depends on their similarity for the learner (McConnell, 1942), we conclude that it is advisable to make sure that a learner recognizes the full range of situations in which a principle is applicable. One way to do this is to give him practice beyond the point of initial learning in applying the principle in a variety of contexts representative of those to which transfer is expected.

It is also known that similar definitions and principles, if acquired at about the same time, will tend to interfere with each other. Entwistle and Huggins (1964) found, for example, that learning several principles of electric circuits made the retention of each principle more difficult. When interference among different principles is suspected, additional practice on each one is advised.

POSTASSESSMENT

Student achievement of defined concepts and principles will be quite evident when it is possible to monitor their performance as closely as our preceding recommendations have suggested. When this is not the case, however, as when learning is from textbooks or other prepared materials, a test of achievement is constructed of "state" and "show me" situations of the type described in the section on student performance. Of course, "select a statement" or "choose the example" situations may be used, also. A review of the typical objectives that were presented earlier, particularly the more specific statements of those objectives, will suggest other test forms that may be used to assess the outcomes of definition and principle learning.

SUMMARY OF TACTICS FOR TEACHING DEFINED CONCEPTS AND PRINCIPLES

The following statements summarize and supplement our preceding suggestions for teaching defined concepts and principles.

1. Assess component concepts and principles.

2. State the expected student outcomes clearly.

3. Prompt recall of prerequisite learning.

4. Use a variety of approaches (mixed method) for both presentation and student performance.

5. State the relationship and describe or demonstrate its application before requiring performance by students.

6. Ask students to state the principle and demonstrate its use.

7. Use guidance liberally in the early stages of student performance, then gradually withdraw it.

8. Provide immediate and complete feedback during student performance.

9. Provide additional practice to combat suspected interference.

10. Provide for use in widely varied contexts, representative of those to which transfer is expected.

11. Individualize student performance as much as possible.

Summary

1. Cognitive abilities or skills are related and interdependent products of learning that we can transfer to previously unencountered situations.

2. When a person learns a *concept*, he learns something about a class of objects or events (e.g., "green," "light," "go") or their attributes ("small," "red," "high"), and he can extend what he learns to new members of the concept class.

3. The relationships among different concepts define new concepts that may be called principles (e.g., "Green lights mean go").

4. When one learns a *principle*, he can respond appropriately in situations never learned specifically.

5. Concepts may be learned by observation or definition.

6. Definitions summarize the public aspects of a concept, that is, what it should mean to everybody. Almost everyone has some unique experiences with examples of a concept that also give it a personal or private meaning.

7. Objectives for concept and principle learning include: (1) classifying, (2) defining, (3) relating, and (4) applying.

a. The classification of examples is particularly appropriate for concepts learned by observation.

b. Defining and relating require words and admit the possibility of pupils "merely memorizing."

c. Applications—including prediction, control, explanation, inference, and problem solving—call for demonstrating the use of the principle.

8. Theoretically, concept learning may be viewed as an association between a class of stimuli and a common response controlled by external events (S-R) or as an "insight" from problem solving under the learner's control (cognitive).

9. An important variation in the basic S-R explanation suggests that different concept instances are first associated with a common act (e.g., eating). Through this common "mediating" act they are associated with the concept and its name (e.g., "food").

10. Research on learning concepts by sorting objects into classes has few parallels in classroom learning.

11. Research on the learning of principles establishes the importance of learning hierarchies, guidance of the learner, and a "mixed" method of instruction.

a. Hierarchies schematically show how a principle depends on the prior learning of prerequisite concepts and principles, which in turn may depend on learning other concepts and principles still earlier, and so on down to the most basic abilities.

b. Guidance may be given by a verbal statement of a principle, a demonstration, or with other prompts. When the objective is the learning and retention of a principle, not learning how to discover principles, the evidence suggests "be generous."

c. When teaching defined concepts or principles, a combination of methods of instruction may be more effective than any single method.

12. Recommendations for teaching concepts through student observation of concept instances and noninstances include:

a. In general, follow this sequence. (1) State the objective. (2) Teach the most obvious critical attribute. (3) Teach the commonly observed irrelevant attributes. (4) Repeat step 2 for other critical attributes. (5) Provide advanced practice on mixed positive and negative instances.

b. If an attribute has a *fixed* range, show pairs of concept and nonconcept instances; if an attribute has a *variable* range, present a series of instances to demonstrate the range of acceptable values while holding irrelevant attributes constant.

c. Teach students to ignore attributes that are irrelevant by presenting a series of positive instances in which the irrelevant attributes change, but the critical ones do not.

13. A concise list of suggestions for teaching defined concepts was given at the end of the "recommendation" section immediately preceding this summary.

CHAPTER 10
Cognitive Skills II:
Problem Solving and Creativity

"Actually, I wish the Winthrop boy weren't *quite* so creative. That was supposed to be a potholder." *(Drawing by Tony Saltzman)*

"I'll say one thing for Tommy Hendershot. When he sets out to find a solution for a problem, he explores every possibility." *(Drawing by Tony Saltzman)*

Independence in Problem Solving
Heuristics and Strategies of Independent Problem Solving
Creativity and Problem Solving
Objectives for Independent Problem Solving
Psychological Analyses and Investigations
Instructional Developments
Recommendations for Instruction

Whenever one has a goal that is not easily attainable, he has a problem. Problems are solved by principles or rules, and problem solving is one of the important objectives in teaching concepts and principles.

Each of us encounters problems, however, for which no solution rules have been learned. If one is to solve such problems he must do so by discovering or inventing solutions on his own, or independently. In so doing previously learned concepts and principles may be combined in new ways to form new and often more complex principles.

OBJECTIVES FOR CHAPTER 10

1. State representative instructional objectives for independent problem solving.
2. Describe S-R and cognitive approaches to the study of problem-solving behavior and compare their conclusions about it.
3. List the general steps in John Dewey's strategy for problem solving and state several heuristics for the achievement of each step.
4. Demonstrate by example the tactics used in several experimental approaches to the improvement of inquiry skills.
5. State the similarities and differences between the methods recommended for teaching content principles in a subject such as mathematics and teaching general rules for problem solving.
6. Choose a course or subject area and describe a plan for combining the following: (1) direct teaching of concepts and principles, (2) the problem-solving method, and (3) developing general inquiry skills. Show how your plan takes into account the advantages and disadvantages of each approach or emphasis.
7. Compare and contrast the direct teaching of principles, the problem-solving method of teaching principles, and teaching

OBJECTIVES CONTINUED

general rules for problem solving with respect to (1) objectives, (2) efficiency, (3) dependability of results, and (4) other possible advantages and disadvantages.

8. Describe and illustrate the importance of creativity in problem solving.
9. Identify the factors that contribute to "rigid" thinking and give an example of how this may blind a learner to an apparently obvious solution to his problem.
10. Demonstrate several strategies that have been recommended for "freeing the imagination" to solve problems more creatively.
11. Summarize the methods, the findings, and the conclusions of those who have sought to define the relationships among creative abilities, IQ, school achievement, and personality.
12. Devise a reinforcement strategy to "shape" students' use of a general heuristic for problem solving when you monitor their problem-solving attempts.

INDEPENDENCE IN PROBLEM SOLVING

We may use a number series task as an example for independent problem solving. You probably would have no trouble finding the sum of this series of odd numbers: 1, 3, 5, 7, 9 = ___. You can readily use addition rules you already know. But suppose you are asked to find a *quick* way to find the sum of any series of the same type *without adding,* and are given other examples such as these:

1. The sum of the first 3 odd numbers, 1, 3, 5 _ _ = 9.
2. The sum of the first 5 odd numbers, 1, 3, 5, 7, 9 = 25.
3. The sum of the first 9 odd numbers, _ _ _ _ _ _ _ = ___.
4. The sum of the first 10 odd numbers, _ _ _ _ _ _ _ = ___.
5. The sum of the first 20 odd numbers, _ _ _ _ _ _ _ = ___.
6. The sum of the first 29 odd numbers, _ _ _ _ _ _ _ = ___.
7. The sum of the first N odd numbers, _ _ _ _ _ _ _ = ___.

If you persisted, you may have solved our number series problem and found that the sum of this type of series is the number of terms (odd numbers) in the series multiplied by itself or squared. In other words the sum of the first 20 odd numbers is 20×20 or 400, and the sum of the first N odd numbers is $N \times N$ or N^2, where N stands for your count of the numbers in any series. If you solved this problem, you not only obtained the answers to the examples listed, but you also learned something new about solving problems (unless, of course, you happened to know it already). That something is the new principle or rule.

Why, you may ask, should anyone be asked to learn a principle in this way? Would it not be simpler, quicker, and surer if he were simply told the principle with a few examples to clarify its use? When the objective is a particular principle, direct teaching is often more efficient, as stated earlier in the section on guidance and discovery. Nevertheless, we must be concerned with problem solving and efforts to improve students' ability to solve problems independently, because obviously everyone has problems to solve when teachers and texts are not available.

HEURISTICS AND STRATEGIES OF INDEPENDENT PROBLEM SOLVING

Although we can illustrate independent problem solving and arrange situations to encourage some independence in problem solving, we cannot anticipate the nature of all the problem situations our students will have to face in the future. Therefore, teachers have sought to teach rules and procedures for problem solving that will be useful to students in many different problem situations. General "rules of thumb" for problem solving, such as the usefulness of a period of incubation for ideas (when you are temporarily "stumped" it often pays to leave a problem and come back to it later), are often referred to as "heuristics." What we refer to as "strategies" are somewhat more formal sets of rules or procedures.

John Dewey's description of a general strategy for problem solving, which he first presented in a book entitled *How We Think* (1910), has had a tremendous impact on education and teaching methods. His strategy has been idolized right down to the present as "the scientific method," "rules for critical thinking," "the method of disciplined inquiry," and "the steps of problem solving." Every teacher and student has used this strategy in some form. As summarized by R. L. Thorndike (1950, p. 196) the phases of Dewey's approach are:

1. *Becoming aware of a problem.* The route to some objective is blocked, routine behavior is not directly successful, and the individual realizes a problem exists.

2. *Clarifying the problem.* The problem, sensed at first only in general terms, is made more sharp and specific in terms of just what end is to be achieved and just what is known or what resources are available.

3. *Proposing hypotheses for solution of the problem.* Specific proposals are suggested and elaborated for dealing with the problem situation.

4. *Reasoning out implications of hypotheses.* Bringing together the hypothesis and the relevant facts which are known to him, the individual reasons out what follows from the hypothesis which he is considering.

5. *Testing the hypothesis against experience.* The conclusions which follow from the hypothesis are tested against known facts or by experiment and the gathering of new facts, to see if the conclusions are valid and the hypotheses supported.

Actual problem-solving behavior is not this logical and orderly; it is usually confused, illogical, and disorderly. When struggling with a problem, one typically jumps from one phase to another, back and forth between hypothesizing, clarifying the problem some more, testing, and so on, in no particular order.

Dewey's description is of an ideal pattern of problem solving that may be employed to advantage in reminding us of gaps in our reasoning or in our more formal efforts to organize a report of what has been achieved; it is seldom, if ever, a description of what any particular problem solver is doing.

General strategies for problem solving may be supplemented by a large number of more specific heuristics. The following list, which has been compiled from a variety of sources, is representative, not exhaustive.

Clarifying the Problem

1. Prepare a full and accurate statement of:
a. The known facts and conditions
b. The unknown facts and conditions

2. Specify the requirements of a solution and classify them as essential or desirable.

3. Identify and eliminate all restrictions *not* required.

4. Carefully define the "gap" between what is given and what is required.

Proposing Hypotheses

5. Review the given and required elements.

6. Attempt to restructure the situation by placing or thinking of the given and required elements in new relationships.

7. Reflect on your past experience with problems that are similar in some way.

8. Study the history of the problem. What have others done about it?

9. What do others think about the problem? Get their ideas.

10. Look for circumstances under which the problem disappears or does not occur. Does this suggest a cause?

11. Never assume something cannot be done or that it must be until you have checked it out.

12. Back up and/or look back occasionally to be sure nothing has been overlooked.

13. Use techniques such as "brainstorming," "part changing," and "checkerboard" to "free the imagination." (These techniques are described later in the chapter.)

14. Leave the problem for a while and come back for a fresh look later.

15. Look for more than one possible solution.

Reasoning Out Implications of Hypotheses

16. Use "if-then" logic to identify what should be true if the hypothesis is correct. Check the facts.

17. Use "if-then" logic to deduce the consequences of implementing a proposed solution. Check against solution requirements.

18. Check each step of a proposed solution to see if it is logically correct. Try to prove that it is correct.

Test the Hypotheses

19. Test each hypothesis with a sample of conditions and situations. Check the results with solution requirements.

20. Check each step of the solution to see that it was completed correctly.

21. Check alternative solutions for adequacy, efficiency, economy, and so on, before accepting any one method.

22. Generalize. Find other problems that might be solved in the same and similar ways.

23. Check for desirable and undesirable "side effects" and "spin-offs."

General

24. Be precise, systematic, and thorough.

25. Be objective and open-minded.

26. Do not be impatient.

27. Do keep accurate records.

Because problem solving leads to new principles, we may think of heuristics and strategies for problem solving as "rules for discovering rules." This phrase may help us to realize that problem solving is not an entirely new idea. The principles for problem solving are a special set of principles, but they may be taught or discovered by learners, just as other principles are.

CREATIVITY AND PROBLEM SOLVING

Independent problem solving requires the learner to put together the products of previous learning in new ways. This is what Bloom et al. (1956) refer to as "synthesis"; it may also be called "creativity" or "divergent" thinking (Bloom, Hastings, and Madaus, 1971, p. 193). An imaginative or unique solution is often

"Mary! Mary!" *(Drawing by C. Barsotti; © 1972 The New Yorker Magazine, Inc.)*

expected, in contrast to situations requiring "convergent" thinking or the production of an answer that may be known in advance. Independence in the achievement of creative or divergent solutions to problems is a most important educational outcome, because with it we look forward, not backward, and seek to prepare students for a future in which they may make plans and products that are uniquely their own.

What of the "truly creative" individuals such as Michaelangelo, Shakespeare, Edison, or Einstein? The achievements of these great men may be considered problem solving, just as our successes in achieving lesser goals are. The results of their creative problem solving were most extraordinary and significant in their effects on the lives and thinking of others, but there is no reason to believe they were the result of mysterious powers beyond learning or learning of an entirely different nature that is unrelated to the heuristics and strategies that enable students to solve prob-

lems more creatively. No one knows who will be truly creative or how he becomes so.

OBJECTIVES FOR INDEPENDENT PROBLEM SOLVING

As we have stated, we will have objectives for known and teachable general rules for problem solving. These would be stated in the manner previously illustrated for principles, whether our teaching method is exposition and example or learner discovery. Discovery objectives would call for the learner to acquire the principal under different conditions, but the desired terminal behavior would not change.

There are several types of objectives, however, that are somewhat different from those previously illustrated in that they call for independence and divergent or creative behavior in the production of unique communi-

Table 10-1
Implementation of Objectives for Divergent Productions.
(After Bloom, 1956; Metfessel, Michael, and Kirsner, 1969.)

Objective Class	Key Words	
	Examples of Infinitives	Examples of Objects
1.00 Production of a unique communication	To write, to compose, to produce, to document	Original, creative or unique; compositions, descriptions, articles, essays, verses, music
2.00 Production of a plan or proposed set of specifications	To develop, to design, to devise, to plan, to specify, to propose	Plans, ways, means, solutions, specifications, diagrams, experiments
3.00 Derivation of principles, rules, or relations	To derive, to develop, to create, to synthesize, to invent, to formulate, to discover, to hypothesize	Concepts, principles, relationships, hypotheses, theories, generalizations, models

cations, products, or principles. Several types of objectives, typical of this type, are suggested in Table 10-1 and then illustrated.

1.00 Production of a Unique Communication
Example from table: "Is able to write an original essay."
More specific example: "Is able to develop and express his own views on national policy."
Still more specific example: "Given statements by leading policy planners of America, Britain, and Russia, each of whom claims to describe the conditions necessary for a lasting peace between the East and West (conditions),

writes his own views of the necessary conditions for such a peace, including a line of policy that the United States might follow (terminal behavior)." Criterion: The teacher judges the essay to be informed, coherent, thoughtful, and different from the views expressed by the authors of the given statements.

2.00 Production of a Plan or Proposed Set of Specifications
Example from table: "Is able to design experiments."
More specific example: "Is able to design original experiments to test the usefulness of the principle of reinforcement in the typical classroom."

Still more specific example: "Given a set of observations from laboratory experiments on conditions in human learning and alternative hypotheses, which are both possibly correct and capable of experimental test, describes an original experiment or experiment that could be conducted to decide between the hypotheses. Criteria: The proposed experimental procedures must be (1) original, (2) possible with the equipment and facilities available, (3) capable of deciding between the given hypotheses, and (4) in agreement with the principles of good experimental design as described in manuals on experimentation with human subjects.

3.00   *Derivation of Principles. Rules or Relations*

Example from table: "Is able to formulate hypotheses."

More specific example: "Is able to propose hypotheses to account for factual information on physiological functioning."

Still more specific example: Given the following hypothetical information: (1) preliminary observations of a physiologist on the digestion and absorption of fat; (2) the hypothesis he first proposed to explain the functions of body organs in this process; and (3) further observations that have led the physiologist to reject his first hypothesis as inadequate. Terminal behavior: The student derives and states a refined and expanded hypothesis or hypotheses. Criteria: The proposed hypothesis must be (1) consistent with *all* the given observations, (2) consistent with generally accepted physiological principles, and (3) capable of an experimental test.

PSYCHOLOGICAL ANALYSES AND INVESTIGATIONS

Psychological theorists have approached the study of problem solving with the same basic assumptions evident in their treatment of other varieties of learning. These approaches, which will be familiar to you by now, are briefly reviewed in this section. Then we turn to a consideration of the findings from research on problem solving and creativity that have influenced our recommendations for instruction.

Learning Theory Approaches

For the S-R theorist, problem solving is a trial-and-error process in which successful responses are reinforced by their consequences while unsuccessful ones are not. The history of this explanation of problem-solving behavior goes back to E. L. Thorndike's (1898) descriptions of cats escaping from puzzle boxes, which we introduced in Chapter 6. On a succession of trials in the box the specific response that enabled a cat to escape was observed to occur more and more frequently, while his ineffective clawing, scratching, and biting became less frequent. The suggestion of S-R theorists is that humans solve problems in a somewhat similar fashion, except that their trial-and-error behavior is more often unobservable or "covert," that is, "in their heads."

The contrasting cognitive views, emphasizing the learner's perceptual reorganization of the problem in an effort to achieve insight into the solution, also have a long history. The early experiments of Köhler (1925) with chimpanzees attempting to reach bananas by joining sticks and Wertheimer's (1959) observations of children's imaginative solutions to the problem of finding the area of a parallelogram were also described in Chapter 6. The essence of the cognitive psychologist's advice for the encouragement of problem solution is to lay out the components of the problem situation so that the relations are evident and a sensible hypothesis regarding its solution is possible.

The use of computers to simulate human thinking and problem-solving processes is a relatively recent development (Simon and Newell, 1964; Reitman, 1965). Psychologists attempt to identify some of the rules and procedures people use to solve problems, perhaps by having them "think aloud," and then program a computer to process information similarly.

If the computer is successful, the machine processes are described as a type of "as if" explanation of problem solving. These explanations are lengthy and complex, even for a limited variety of simple problem situations, which does not begin to characterize the variety and flexibility of those solved by humans.

The research literature on problem solving is large but not very systematic. Several "nuclei" or centers of interest in the investigation of problem solving have been identified, however, and these will be used to organize our presentation of some of the findings that have implications for teaching.

Learning Sets and Rigidity

"Sets" or predispositions to view a problem or react to it in a certain way (Chapter 6) have been shown to influence success in problem solving. A student or experimental subject may try to solve a problem in a particular way because he has been instructed to do so or because he has become accustomed to one approach. If this method works, it helps him. He does better than he probably would without his set. We can call this positive transfer.

On the other hand, if the method does not work, he may persist unreasonably and be blinded to other possibilities for solving his problem. We then say he is "rigid." Interference or negative transfer because of set is also referred to by psychologists as "fixation" or "functional fixedness."

Cognitive psychologists, particularly those of the Gestalt school, have given much attention to the problem of the fixation of persons on inappropriate solutions. Rigidity as a result of habit or previous success with an approach was beautifully illustrated years ago by Abraham Luchins (1942). He used the water jug problems shown in Figure 10-1, which we adapted from Sheerer (1971), a recent investigator of similar problems.

With each problem the task is to measure out the quantity of water listed in the last column using only three pitchers of the sizes given in columns a, b, and c. The typical subject soon discovers this pattern: fill b; fill a from b; fill c from b twice; then the desired amount is left in b. This is not the best way to solve problems 6 and 7, and it does not work at all for problem 8; nevertheless, most subjects continue to use the method because it worked before. In 6 they might simply fill a and pour off enough water to fill c; in 7 they could fill a and c and pour the contents into b; and in 8 they must use the easier method suggested for problem 6.

Birch and Rabinowitz (1951) provided another example that brings home both the difficulty and the importance of breaking an interfering set if new approaches are to be considered. The subjects of one of their groups were taught to use an electric relay to close a circuit; those of another group were taught to use a switch to do the same thing. Then all of the subjects were given a problem in which it was necessary to use either the switch or the relay as a weight to form a pendulum. Fixedness was revealed when none of the subjects who had previously used

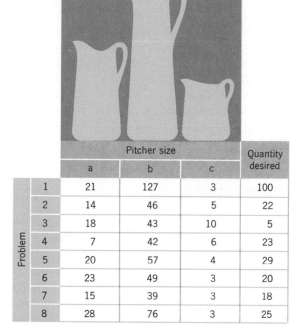

Problem	Pitcher size			Quantity desired
	a	b	c	
1	21	127	3	100
2	14	46	5	22
3	18	43	10	5
4	7	42	6	23
5	20	57	4	29
6	23	49	3	20
7	15	39	3	18
8	28	76	3	25

Figure 10-1.

Problem series to illustrate fixation because of habit. Measure out the quantity of water specified in the final column using only the three pitchers of the size specified under a, b, and c. The procedure that works for problems 1-5 can be used for problems 6 and 7, but there is an easier method. Problem 8 requires a different procedure. *(Adapted from Scheerer, 1971.)*

the relay in a circuit now used it as a weight; they all used the switch instead. Similarly those who had previously used the switch in an electric circuit chose the relay for a pendulum weight. Apparently these subjects persisted in thinking of these pieces of equipment in the way they had originally used them. In contrast, a control group of subjects who had no electrical experience with either the switch or the relay used them about equally often in pendulum problems.

Sets are not always harmful! As Crovitz notes (1970, p. 94); "It is lovely to do things in a routine way, without having each time to decide how to do it. Very general methods are especially good, for their field of application is so very wide." Harlow's (1959) studies illustrate how sets may serve a very useful function in problem solving.

In one investigation Harlow taught subjects of low mental ability to make simple discriminations, for example, choosing the larger of stimulus objects, regardless of some changes in the way they were presented, such as which was on the left and which was on the right. These subjects learned this discrimination slowly; only after many trials could they perform without error. Eventually, however, they learned to make each discrimination quickly and correctly when it was first presented. Then it appeared that solutions occurred suddenly, as in descriptions of insight.

Harlow's explanation for the change in the ability of his subjects was that they had acquired a set for this type of problem in previous trials. More important, from his point of view, was the belief that he had helped to explain why it is that some learning appears to proceed through trial and error, as the S-R theorist suggests, and other learning appears to be characterized by insight, as the cognitive theorist expects. His suggestion is that whether or not we find a gradual strengthening of the correct response or a sudden errorless solution depends on how much previous experience learners have had with problems of the same class, whether or not they have "learned how to learn" problems of the given type.

Discovery and Inquiry Training

Two general hypotheses receive support from recent research on discovery (Craig, 1969, p. 501).

1. Guiding learning—that is, stating or showing the content, principles, or methods which are to be learned—gives better results if the objectives are learning, retention, and application of what is learned.

2. Discovery techniques—that is, allowing the student to discover what is to be learned—are more effective if the objective is the inference and use of new principles or methods.

Evidence for the first of these hypotheses was presented in a previous section on principle learning. Our concern here is with the second hypothesis, because independent problem solving involves the discovery of new principles.

Of the two hypotheses, that relating to discovery has the lesser research support, but available evidence favors discovery techniques over giving guidance in the preparation of learners for problem solving. When Guthrie (1967) gave college students experience deciphering codes without any rules, he found they were superior to a group given the rules when tested on later problems based on different rules. Gagné and Brown (1961) also found discovery groups better than a rule-given group at finding untaught formulas for the sums of number series, similar to the problems in our earlier example of a discovery situation. We have previously described Worthen's investigation of discovery approaches and interpreted his results as favoring a discovery hypothesis in a fairly typical classroom situation.

We conclude that when later discovery is expected, that is what students should practice. When learners are successful in finding independent solutions, this behavior is encouraged. In addition, they may learn something about heuristics or strategies of discovery that will help them with some types of problems later. From a somewhat different view, they may acquire a set or predisposition for independent discovery efforts.

Faith in discovery methods has probably been more influential than any evidence from research for the widespread interest among educators in the development of procedures for discovery or inquiry training. These procedures and the enthusiasm of their advocates have prompted several well-known curriculum reform projects. Two of these developments are described at a later point in the chapter under "Instructional Developments."

Group Problem Solving and Brainstorming

How does the creativity and problem-solving success of a group compare with that of individuals? With few exceptions researchers have found that the average performance of small groups is superior to that of the average individual in every phase of problem solving—clarifying the problem, collecting information, suggesting solutions, and verifying solutions (Klausmeier, Harris, and Wiersma, 1964). Duncan (1959) found, however, that the best individuals do better than the average group, and there is some evidence that solving problems individually is sometimes better preparation for individual problem solving, if this is to be expected later, than working with a group (M. Goldman, 1965; Klausmeier, Harris, and Wiersma, 1964). In a group some individuals avoid active participation in the problem-solving process, and, as a result, may be poorly prepared to solve similar problems independently.

The most widely studied group strategy for problem solving is "brainstorming." In this technique, originated by Osborne (1957), a problem is posed and group members are encouraged to generate as many ideas about possible approaches and solutions as possible. Criticism of the quality of the ideas is to be suspended while this is done. The object is to overcome rigidity or the tendency to think only of conventional approaches.

Research results on the value of group brainstorming are contradictory. Some find it an effective means of encouraging more good ideas (Parnes and Meadow, 1963), but others report that individuals working alone under similar instructions do as well or better than when they work together (Taylor et al., 1958; Dunette, et al., 1963). Regardless of how the overall quality and quantity of ideas compare for group and individual brainstorming, a group experience may be useful as a teaching or training technique. It has been used to advantage as a warm-up for individual efforts (Lindgren and Lindgren, 1965; Lindgren, 1967), and the positive effects of taking a course in brainstorming may persist for some time (Parnes and Meadow, 1963).

The value of instructing students to produce a quantity of ideas without regard to quality has been criticized by researchers. Torrance (1961) used the brainstorming approach with pupils in the primary grades. Both he and Guilford (1962) found that instructions to produce clever and unusual ideas increased the number of high-quality ideas, although the number of low-quality ideas did decrease. Guilford suggested that evaluative instructions may be either desirable or undesirable, depending on whether or not group members are afraid to be unconventional.

A reasonable interpretation of the evidence on group work in problem solving is that when a group effort results in the pooling of individual talents, it increases the likelihood of a superior solution. Often there will be one or more individuals in the group who could do as well individually, but there will also be those who could not. Participation in group problem solving, especially the production of a larger number of diverse alternative hypotheses, may improve the individual's ability to solve problems later, but only if he participates actively in the earlier group

efforts. Therefore, smaller groups are preferred because it increases the probability of individual participation. There is no advantage in encouraging persons to produce ideas without regard to quality, unless they are reluctant to try to be original or clever.

The Correlates of Creativity

Considerable research has been conducted on the relationships between creativity and other cognitive and personality characteristics. Two methods of investigation are (1) administering tests of a variety of characteristics to the same individuals and studying the correlations among test results, and (2) identifying individuals whose achievements in some area are recognized to be exceptionally creative and contrasting their characteristics with those of people in general.

Numerous studies have shown only a moderate relationship between measures of intelligence and divergent or creative production of the type identified in Guilford's (1966) comprehensive analysis of human abilities. Correlations of .25 to .50 are typical (Getzels and Jackson, 1962; Crockenberg, 1972), and these have been interpreted as showing that different abilities are being measured. Unfortunately the different tests designed to measure different aspects of creativity, for example, listing many different uses for common objects (semantic spontaneous flexibility) and writing clever titles for short stories (originality), vary so much among themselves that results for two tests of creativity are little more related than a measure of creativity and one of intelligence (Thorndike, 1963). Wallach and Kogan (1965) claim to have developed tests of creativity that are more homogeneous and independent of general ability than previous measures, but the issue remains unsettled.

One conclusion is warranted, and that is

that neither tests of intelligence nor tests of a particular aspect of creativity will be useful in identifying students who are high in creativity. Students who are high in IQ will vary widely with respect to each of a number of measures of creativity, and students who are high on one measure of creativity will vary widely with respect to another measure of creativity.

The research on the relationship between scores on creativity tests and academic achievement is also difficult to interpret. Some investigators find little relationship between the two (Flescher, 1963; Edwards and Tyler, 1965; Wallach and Kogan, 1965), but others find that measures of creativity have as high a relationship with academic achievement as intelligence test scores do (Getzels and Jackson 1962; Torrance, 1962; Yamamota, 1964). Again, the differences among tests of creativity may be the reason for such apparently contradictory evidence. Some may be related to achievement, some not be.

Edwards and Tyler (1965) suggest that when intelligence is equal, there should be a negative relationship between creativity and achievement, because convergent thinking or getting the conventional answer is more often rewarded by high grades than original or nonconforming contributions. This is what they found in their study of ninth-grade students. Students in the upper third of their class in creativity, as well as intelligence, did not receive grades that were as high as students who were in the upper third of their class on intelligence only.

We get a somewhat but not entirely different picture of the relationship between intelligence and creativity from studies of the characteristics of individuals who have made notable and original contributions to art, literature, and science. Evidence of this type invariably shows the creative individuals to be more intelligent than noncreative individuals working in the same field (Terman and Oden, 1959; Hitt and Stock, 1965). But it is not a case of the more intelligent, the more creative. Instead, it appears that a level of intelligence somewhat above average is needed for a truly outstanding creative contribution, but above that level, still higher intelligence does not seem to be a factor (Terman and Oden, 1959; MacKinnon, 1962).

There have been numerous studies of the personalities of persons judged to be creative in a wide variety of fields of endeavor. A comprehensive review is provided by Getzels (1969). Adjectives such as open-minded, tolerant, insightful, original, independent, skeptical, and verbally fluent have been used to describe the creators. They are also said to be venturesome, self-sufficient, mature, determined, industrious, enthusiastic, and self-confident, and blessed with a sense of humor. These are positive traits, but a few social characteristics are often mentioned that some might consider less desirable. Various investigators have reported that creative individuals are more interested in ideas than other people or other people's opinions, and they show greater than average tendencies to be rebellious, disorderly, egotistical, and exhibitionistic.

INSTRUCTIONAL DEVELOPMENTS

In this section we describe three efforts to improve the problem-solving ability of students. The major emphasis in each is on the improvement of inquiry (discovery) skills. The inquiry model of J. Richard Suchman has been used experimentally with elementary school children. The high school biology curriculum development by the Biological Sciences Curriculum Study Committee of the National Sciences Foundation has been used by many schools throughout the country. The approaches to stimulating creative problem solving, which have been developed by E. Paul Torrance and other authors, are incorporated into materials made available to teachers, and they have formed the basis of experimental school programs.

These programs are believed to be representative of current efforts to apply psychological ideas to the curriculum for the improvement of students' problem-solving skills. We regard them as promising. Publications by the users of these approaches are often supportive and sometimes enthusiastically so; but the expected results have been less often verified. Reliable experimental evaluations of the effects of a general program upon student achievement are difficult to arrange—because of the practical problems of taking all the necessary factors into account. No general evaluation of this type is available for the BSCS or for other curricular innovations that have been widely adopted.

Inquiry in Elementary Science

J. Richard Suchman (1962) developed a model for training in scientific inquiry while at the University of Illinois. His method was to analyze the process and procedures of creative research personnel. More recently he has developed and published curriculum materials for elementary school science (Suchman, 1966).

As represented in his curriculum materials, Suchman's model has three general phases. In Phase I students are presented with a puzzling situation. In Phase II they collect data and generate hypotheses. The students may be asked to answer a series of leading questions or they may be encouraged to ask the teacher yes or no questions, somewhat like the television game "Twenty Questions." They may perform experiments or collect data in still other ways. As data is collected students try to propose ideas or hypotheses about the problem solution or explanation, the reasons "why."

In Phase III students and teachers work together to analyze their strategies, understand the consequences of particular approaches, and identify the most effective methods of attack.

One of Suchman's early demonstration films showed a bimetallic strip made of two thin strips, one of steel and one of brass, fused together (Suchman, 1962). This is held in a flame, and it begins to bend downward. Then, when the strip is dipped into cool water, it straightens out again. The problem question is, "Why does the strip bend and then straighten out again?"

First, children ask questions to verify the facts about what happened, the initial conditions, and the changes that occurred. Then they shift to "test" questions. They ask questions about what would happen "if." For example, a student may ask, "If the temperature of the strip had not been raised, would it still have bent as it did?" The teacher would answer, "No." This should tell the inquirer that temperature is a factor in the explanation. Someone may follow up this lead and verify the role of temperature by a question such as, "Would the bending have been greater, if the temperature change was greater?" The answer is, "Yes."

In the next stage of inquiry the children may attempt to discover the physical principles that produced the changes by analyzing the information they have. They suggest hypotheses and test them to see if they are tenable. They might, for example, hypothesize about the relationship between the temperature and the volume of different metals.

The entire inquiry session may be tape-recorded. The tape is played back to the group and the teacher helps the children to evaluate their use of inquiry strategies. This technique is useful in focusing attention on the heuristics and strategies of problem solving, which Suchman finds that children tend to ignore. The critique makes them aware of the process of inquiry, which is Suchman's main interest. By comparison, the specific content or subject matter is unimportant.

Inquiry in High School Biology

The inquiry model of the Biological Sciences Curriculum Study Committee was developed in the 1960s under the auspices of the National Science Foundation. The goal of this approach was to teach high school students to solve problems in ways similar to those of the research biologist. In broad outline the teaching method was to introduce the student to an area of biological investigation, help him to identify a problem encountered in that investigation, and lead him to find ways to overcome the problem. Finally, the student was encouraged to design investigations that eliminate the difficulty as a source of possible error in the interpretation of research findings.

The inquiry model can be best understood perhaps by looking at an example taken from materials called "Invitation to Enquiry 3." (BSCS, 1965, pp. 57-58) This "Invitation" describes an investigation in which seeds are germinated in two glass containers. Both have moisture, but one is placed in the light and the other is kept in the dark. The student is asked to interpret the finding that all the seeds in both containers germinated (sprouted).

The students are expected to propose hypotheses that are not based on the data; one example would be that moisture is necessary. This would provide the teacher with the opportunity to point out that there is no data to support this conclusion, because we did not try it without moisture. Further questioning directs the students' attention to what was *different* in the two conditions. They are then led to state as clearly as possible the

problem that this experiment was designed to investigate.

Once students state that the problem was to investigate the light factor, they are asked to interpret the results again; this introduces them to a problem in data interpretation. We cannot say that this investigation only shows that light is not a factor in the germination of *all* seeds, just those tested. Now they are to begin to find out how to deal with problems such as this.

The BSCS instructions for the teacher explain the objective at each step of the inquiry and offer suggestions that may be used to be sure students benefit as expected. If questions or hypotheses by students are forthcoming as expected, the teacher is advised to introduce them in a way that will encourage students to participate similarly. In this particular lesson, the teacher's attention is focused on the importance of a clear statement of the problem and the students' understanding of how this affects both the design of an experiment and the interpretation of the findings.

As a result of lessons such as the one we have described, students are expected to learn ways of seeking knowledge and develop both a respect for scientific knowledge and an awareness of its limitations.

Although it is clear that the BSCS approach emphasizes the process of inquiry in science, there is some doubt about how much it uses inquiry as a teaching method. Herron (1971) analyzed the laboratory manuals prepared for this program and reported that 45 out of 60 of the laboratory exercises completely eliminated independent discovery by specifying for the learner the problem, the ways and means of its solution, and the answers. The remaining 17 exercises supplied the problem and the ways and means, but not the answers; hence, some requirement of learner discovery remained. Finally, investigations of teacher activities in the classroom (Balzer, 1969, 1970) have found that very little of BSCS teachers' classroom activities (about 6%) have anything to do with teaching scientific process behavior.

Creative Problem Solving in the Classroom

E. Paul Torrance is a pioneer in efforts to put ideas about creativity into practice. He has written and spoken on the subject for over 20 years, and has published experimental teaching materials for use in elementary and junior high schools (Cunnington and Torrance, 1965; Myers and Torrance, 1965). He reports (1970) that he is also formulating a hierarchy of creative reading skills for a series of reading books for use with disadvantaged children.

Torrance regards creativity as a special type of problem solving in which the results or products have novelty and value, at least to the problem solver and perhaps also to others.

This type of problem solving frequently requires the modification of or rejection of old or conventional ideas.

Activities to encourage creative problem solving have three fundamental characteristics according to Torrance (1970). (1) They have "incompleteness or openness." (2) A product is produced and used. (3) Children's questions and ideas are respected and used. Each of these characteristics will be described and illustrated.

INCOMPLETENESS AND OPENNESS

Tasks and activities with this characteristic are said to be intriguing and especially powerful motivators. To illustrate their attractiveness he asks people to choose one of the two tasks in Figure 10-2. Most persons (over 80%) choose the incomplete task.

There are many strategies for creating in-

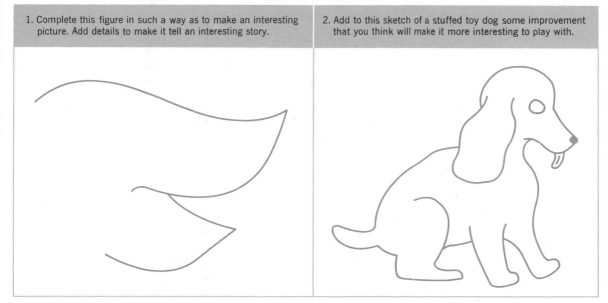

Figure 10-2.

Two tasks to illustrate the attractiveness of "incompleteness." (Reproduced from E. Paul Torrance, ENCOURAGING CREATIVITY IN THE CLASSROOM, p. 111. Copyright © 1970 by Wm. C. Brown & Company. By permission.)

Table 10-2

Examples of Strategies to Create or Maintain
Incompleteness or Openness in Learning Activities.

(Reproduced from E. Paul Torrance, ENCOURAGING CREATIVITY IN THE CLASS-ROOM. Copyright © 1970 by Wm C. Brown & Company. By permission.)

Prior to a Lesson, Activity, or Assignment

1. Confrontation with ambiguities and uncertainties.
2. Heightened anticipation and expectation.
3. The familiar made strange or the strange made familiar by analogy.
4. Looking at the same thing from several different psychological, sociological, physical, and emotional viewpoints.
5. Provocative questions requiring the learner to examine information in new ways.
6. Predictions from limited information required.
7. Tasks structured only enough to give clues and direction.
8. Encouragement to take the next step beyond what is known.

During a Lesson, Activity, or Assignment

1. Continued heightening of anticipation and expectation.
2. Encouragement of the creative and constructive rather than cynical acceptance of limitations.
3. Exploration of missing elements and possibilities made systematic and deliberate.
4. Juxtaposition of apparently irrelevant or unrelated elements.
5. Mysteries and puzzles explored and examined.
6. Open-endedness preserved.
7. Ongoing predictions from limited information as new facts are acquired.
8. Surprises heightened and deliberately used.
9. Visualization of events, places, and so on, encouraged.

Following a Lesson, Activity, or Assignment

1. Ambiguities and uncertainties played with.
2. Constructive response called for (a better way, a more beautiful effect, etc.).
3. Digging deeper, going beyond the obvious, encouraged.
4. Elaborating some element through drawings, dramatics, imaginative stories, and the like.
5. Search for elegant solutions encouraged (i.e., the solution that takes into account the largest number of variables).
6. Experimentation and testing of ideas encouraged.
7. Future projections encouraged and improbabilities entertained.
8. Multiple hypotheses encouraged.
9. Reorganization and reconceptualization of information required.
10. Syntheses of diverse and apparently irrelevant elements required.
11. Transforming or rearranging information or other elements.
12. Taking the next step beyond what is known.

completeness or taking advantage of it to motivate creative thinking. Torrance suggests the list reproduced here as Table 10-2.

PRODUCTS

A creative activity for children often begins with their producing something imaginative —a drawing, a story, a song, a drama, a game, or some object. Then they may use the initial product as the basis for other activities, such as writing or telling a story, putting on a play, inventing a dance, painting, or experimenting. In the following excerpt from Torrance (1970) he describes a situation where the initial product was a drama about life in a pool.

"In one of these exercises, the children were shown an attractive original drawing of a pond with frogs, lily pads, and insects. The children were asked just to imagine that they could enter into the life of the pond and become anything in the pond that they wanted to be. Each child was then asked to choose what he wanted to be in the life of the pond. As a result, we had frogs, alligators, a crocodile, fish, mosquitoes, water, sticks, tree roots at the bottom of the pond, and even the fog that rises over the pond some mornings. Then we created the drama of life in the pond. The frogs jumped, croaked, and sang their song. The alligator entered the pond and the jumping and croaking stopped; we paused to wonder why. The fog came over the pond, and we wondered how this made the frogs, fish and other living things feel. The crocodile mistakenly attacked the foot of the tree at the bottom of the pond, and we paused to wonder why he made this mistake.

"Immediately after this dramatic creation by a group of twenty-four children, they were asked to draw some event that might occur if they could enter into the life of the pond." (Torrance, 1970, p. 6)

Later this drama about the pool was used as the source of ideas for stories for reading instruction, number situations for arithmetic (How many frogs on the bank, how many in the pond, how many altogether?), and themes for paintings.

PUPIL QUESTIONS AND IDEAS

Respect for children's questions and ideas is almost synonymous with respect for their creative needs. Such respect rewards and encourages their creative efforts. Several simple rules have been built into the material Torrance has prepared for teachers. His rules are (Torrance, 1970, p. 22):

1. Respect the questions children ask.

2. Respect the ideas they present.

3. Show them their ideas have value.

4. Encourage opportunities for practice and experimentation without evaluation.

5. Encourage and give credit for self-initiated learning and thinking.

Although these rules for encouraging creativity may appear self-evident, Torrance does not find teachers acting as if they know them. A major problem, he suggests, is that they do not know how to respect questions and ideas. He asks teachers to really reflect on what it means to be respectful of the questions and ideas of others and to train themselves to be respectful.

A useful technique for this purpose is to have teachers prepare descriptions of incidents in which they tried to be respectful of questions and ideas. Then they are asked to study and discuss these incidents with others to help decide how well they succeeded. The following list of questions is given to guide the preparation of the descriptions (Torrance, 1970, p. 23).

1. What was the question (idea)? Who asked

(expressed) it? What were the general conditions under which it was asked (proposed)?

2. What was your own immediate reaction?

3. What was the immediate reaction of the class?

4. In what way was respect shown for the question (idea)?

5. What, if any, were (would be) the observable effects (immediate and/or long range)?

Table 10-3 presents the records of two incidents that show how the questions are used to prepare materials for discussion. You might wish to discuss the incidents in Table 10-3 and speculate about the effects of a less respectful teacher response.

Table 10-3
Incidents Showing Respect for Children's Questions and Ideas.

(Reproduced from E. Paul Torrance, ENCOURAGING CREATIVITY IN THE CLASSROOM. Copyright © 1970 by Wm C. Brown & Company. By permission.)

Question Incident: Would You Turn Communist? (Grade 6)	Occasion: During social studies period, while discussing living conditions of the Russian people, one boy asked "Mr. _____, would you turn Communist if the Russians captured America?"
	Immediate Teacher Reaction: Does he feel we eventually will be attacked by the Russians? Why?
	Immediate Reaction of Class: General reaction—What would happen if America were attacked and captured?
	Way Respect Shown for Question: The children really, seriously considered or thought about the question.
	Effects: Your prediction?
Idea Incident: More Mature Behavior by "Pretending?" (Grade 1)	Occasion: As we were discussing rules and manners for first graders, one six-year-old boy said, "I am going to act like a doctor going to school all day."
	Immediate Teacher Reaction: If you act like a doctor today, we'll have a perfect classroom.
	Immediate Class Reaction: Others suggested that they all pretend to be a grown-up person.
	Way Respect Shown: There was no ridicule, and all the children were encouraged to pretend to be someone special.
	Effects: Your prediction?

TRAINING THE IMAGINATION

You will find another set of suggestions for teaching creativity useful also. A general sequence for problem solving and several intriguing ways of stimulating creative ideas have been described in a guide developed by Davis and Houtman (1968), entitled *Thinking Creatively: A Guide to Training Imagination*. Their sequence for creative problem solving has four major steps (Davis and Houtman, 1968, p. 126).

1. *State the problem clearly*, for example, get money.

2. *List the main types of solutions*, for example, earn, borrow, sell, or rent.

3. *List specific ideas for each main solution*, for example, earn by mowing lawns, babysitting, finding a regular job, and so on. Borrow from parents, bank, or friend Gregg. Sell car.

4. *Rate the "goodness" of each specific idea* (after considering "pros" and "cons"), for example, mowing lawns is "doubtful," borrowing from the bank is "poor." Finding a job is "best." Selling car is "no good."

The methods Davis and Houtman recommend for stimulating ideas are:

1. *Part-Changing*. "If you want to change something, just list the main parts and then think of different ways to change each part" (p. 24). This procedure resembles the third step of their general sequence.

2. *Checkerboard*. Make a blank checkerboard and list one set of properties at the top, another at the side. To invent a game, list the materials and equipment that you have along the top and things players can do at the side. Then examine the intersection of each row and column to see if the combination of the materials at the top (e.g., net) and the activity

at the side (e.g., crawling) suggests something new.

3. *Checklist*. Use their suggestive list to generate ideas about any object. Change color? Change size? Change shape? Use new or different materials? Add or subtract something? Rearrange things? Identify a new design? [A similar list was suggested earlier by Torrance (1961)].

4. *Find Something Similar*. Whenever you have a problem think of the way others (animals, plants, and people in different situations) handle a somewhat similar situation. The authors suggest that you could tackle a problem with the school parking lot by thinking of how bees, squirrels, ants, shoe stores, and clothing stores arrange the things they store (p. 96).

RECOMMENDATIONS FOR INSTRUCTION

The "miracle" of the human intellect is most evident in problem solving. We speak of miracles because we are amazed, but also when we do not fully understand what we see. There is much that we do not know about human problem solving, but there is no need to build a mystique around the process or to fold our hands in helpless wonder because we lack complete knowledge of it. We do know some important things about problem solving and how to teach it.

First of all, teaching problem solving cannot be separated from teaching knowledge, concepts, and principles. As we have seen, concepts are formed from specific knowledge, principles are formed from concepts, and problems are solved with principles. *Independent* problem solving goes one step further; it is the discovery of new principles to solve new problems. We conclude that prior learning is undoubtedly the single most important factor in independent problem solving and that teaching of clear organized bodies of facts, concepts, and principles is the best preparation for problem solving.

How teachers may help students improve their ability to use their knowledge in the solution of new problems is the topic of this section. Two possibilities are described. First, problem solving may be used as a method for teaching principles. This method gives students more practice in independent discovery of principles than teacher-dominated methods, which emphasize the telling or showing of principles. Second, there are general rules for teaching problems that may be taught and practiced. These are the heuristics and strategies of problem solving. Then we consider ways in which these approaches and teaching for other objectives may be combined in educational settings. Finally, we again present a summary list of teaching tactics. Use of the special set of strategies whose objective is that of stimulating students to break with conventional patterns of thought and generate more and better hypotheses for problem solving will not be given separate attention in this section, but teachers are urged to try the techniques suggested by Torrance (Table 10-2) and the devices recommended by Davis and Houtman.

Problem Solving as a Method for Teaching Principles

The problem-solving methods that we consider in this subsection are, first and foremost, methods of teaching principles. The context of the subject comes first; improvement of problem solving comes second. They differ from the method of teaching principles described previously because the principles to be learned are not given to students; students are required to discover them without spe-

cific help. The guidance of the teacher or textbook writer is there, but it is indirect. The general procedure can be called "guided practice in independent problem solving."

When this approach is chosen over others, the choice is dictated by a desire to improve students' ability to discover relationships and solve problems independently. The assumption is that practice in discovering relationships with guidance will have this effect.

A full statement of a typical problem-solving method would include the same general steps we previously described for principle learning. We build on the previously learned capabilities that are to be related in the new principle. A clear objective for student achievement is stated. Pre- and post-instructional assessment procedures continue to be important. The differences, as we have suggested, are in the presentation and performance procedures. In the problem-solving method the teacher presents a problem, but no solution rules; student performance is emphasized.

The general steps of this procedure have been summarized by Craig (1968, p. 181).

1. Have students state a clear goal.

2. Prompt them to recall related concepts and principles.

3. Use thought-provoking questions or suggestions to help them find order in the situation. Do not tell them the answers or the principles determining the solution, however!

4. When they solve the problem, ask them to state the principles of solution and/or to use it to solve other problems.

Craig also offers the following example of how the steps might be followed if the problem was that of finding the area of a parallelogram.

Suppose students know how to find the area of a rectangle, which the teacher has drawn on the board; but are puzzled when he draws another parallelogram that does not have right angles. The several phases of instruction are as follows:

1. The goal is stated as, "A way to find the area of *any* parallelogram."

2. The teacher's prompting of related principles goes something like this: "You recall how we found the area of a rectangle? . . . (Student answers 'yes') . . . Show me on the board . . . (Student multiplies the length of the rectangle, 4 inches, by the width, 2 inches, and says, 'Eight square inches') . . . Right."

3. The instructions to guide interpretation are: ("How can you make this other parallelogram into a rectangle? . . . (Student volunteers, 'Cut out this end with a piece from the other end') . . . Right! . . . So what's the area if the parallel sides are four inches each and the distance between them is two inches . . . (Response is, 'Same as for the other rectangle, eight square inches')."

4. The attempt to test knowledge of the principle and diagnose errors proceeds as follows: "Who can give us a rule? . . . (Student responds with, 'Cut it up and make a rectangle') . . . Is it necessary to cut it, or can you just use the values given? . . . (Another student says, 'Multiply the length of one of the parallel sides by the distance between them') . . . Try this new problem to see if your rule works . . . etc." (Craig, 1968, p. 181).

In practice, a variety of tactics has been used to encourage students and lead them in promising directions during problem solving. Suchman's techniques and those of the BSCS curriculum materials have been described at an earlier point in the chapter.

Problem-solving methods have been called "guided practice." We may add that it is usually guided practice in using a more or less general problem-solving strategy. The strategy inherent in the list of steps we have quoted is apparent if we compare them, restated slightly, with one of the most generally used problem-solving strategies, that recommended by John Dewey:

Problem-Solving Method	*Dewey's Strategy*
1. Puzzling situation.	1. Becoming aware of problem.
2. State a goal.	2. Clarifying problem.
3. Recall related ideas.	3. Proposing hypotheses.
4. Search for solution method.	4. Reasoning out of implications of hypotheses.
5. Test the solution rule.	5. Testing out the hypothesis.

Thus, it appears that with problem-solving methods students are practicing a set of rules for problem solving, that is, a strategy. If this strategy is learned, it can function to guide a learner's further problem-solving efforts, whether or not this strategy is expressed in words.

Probably the strategy should be described in words. Probably students should be made aware that they are practicing a strategy for learning principles while they learn principles. As we have noted, direct attention to making students aware of the strategies they have used in problem solving is a feature of

Suchman's inquiry teaching and of the BSCS curriculum materials. We recommend teaching students the logic of the steps they follow in discovering principles as a method of making that practice more effective.

Teaching Problem-Solving Rules as Principles

We have discussed methods of teaching content that may also improve problem-solving skills. Now we consider the direct teaching of problem-solving rules and make them the primary objectives of instruction. With this change of emphasis content becomes a vehicle for practicing rules; its specific nature is almost irrelevant.

General rules of the type listed in the section entitled "Heuristics and Strategies" are not true principles because they have not been proved and may not even be provable. We have confidence in them in many situations, however, because they are based on thoughtful analyses of the behavior of successful problem solvers and they have survived "the test of time."

Like principles, the general rules for problem solving are relationships among other concepts or principles. Unlike most principles, however, they are not limited to a particular class of problems in one content area. They are useful for finding principles needed to solve many types of problems in quite different areas, perhaps as different as mathematics, national policy, and repairing the family car.

Are these generally useful "rules of thumb" to be taught like principles? Can they be presented by the teacher, then demonstrated and applied by students? Or will a different approach be necessary?

Before we attempt to answer, consider what it means to say that problem-solving rules are "very general." This actually means that these rules apply in a general way to a wide variety of problems, but they provide specific solutions for none. In other words, a statement of a "rule of thumb" is only a generally useful guideline. It does not communicate with any degree of precision or completeness what one must do to solve any particular problem. Any demonstration of the use of the rule is similarly limited; the demonstrated use of the rule is probably representative of appropriate behavior in only a small sample of the situations in which the rule is to be used.

The point of our argument thus far is that the information a teacher is able to communicate verbally or by demonstration is insufficient to tell a student much about what he must do to use the rule. The conclusion we reach is that the student must try using the rule under the supervision of the teacher. This may be considered a discovery situation for him, and telling him the rule is little more than a broad hint that may aid his discovery.

We would list the same procedural phases for the learning of both problem-solving rules and content principles—that is, pre- and postinstructional assessment, presentation, performance, and advanced practice—but here we place much greater emphasis on the need for students to have advanced or continual practice in using problem-solving rules. Teacher statements and demonstrations should be used when teaching a problem-solving rule, but this will not be sufficient to change student behavior significantly. Continued practice in the use of the rule over an extended period of time is necessary.

SHAPING PROBLEM-SOLVING BEHAVIORS

There are many abilities that cannot be easily communicated to students in any direct way. How, for example, do you tell students to shoot basketballs accurately, draw artistically, or use poetic expressions? We are suggesting that problem-solving behaviors, for example, stating a problem clearly, using relevant information effectively, and avoiding premature or precipitate judgments, should be added to the list of such abilities.

With behaviors of this type, the teacher's presentation is characteristically brief. Then a trial performance by the student or students is arranged, and the teacher's behavior shifts from that of teacher to judge. He observes students' performance, prompts occasionally, corrects when necessary, and reinforces responses in the direction suggested by the rules governing a "proper" performance.

The S-R term "shaping" is a reasonably apt expression for what teachers may do to change student performance in the desired directions. You will recall shaping as a procedure of reinforcing any response of a student that is better than his typical response. When an improvement results, however slight, this becomes the expectation, and the teacher reserves his approval for responses that are better still. In this manner, the student is encouraged to respond in ways more and more like the instructor's concept of an "ideal" response.

When selective reinforcement is used with students, we recommend that teachers not be content with a simple "good" or "right" for reinforcement. They should also attempt to make it clear to the student why a particular performance is better or more nearly in accordance with what is expected.

For an example in the context of problem solving, assume that a teacher is trying to teach students to avoid precipitate judgments or delay their choice of a hypothesis until all alternatives have been checked by logic and the obtainable facts. A teacher has told his students about this rule. He has tried to explain it to them and show them how it would affect one's behavior in several problem situations. Now he wishes to have them use it.

For a practice problem, he may pose a question such as, "What would Lincoln decide regarding a continued U.S. military presence in Southeast Asia, if he were alive and President today?" Craig (1966) has described how a teacher might proceed in such a situation.

"The teacher plans a free discussion, for he does not know exactly what more he can do or say in this particular situation to help students learn to hold back and be less precipitous in their decisions. Although he knows student suggestions and actions relative to the objectives he has chosen will vary in quality, he cannot specify in advance the particular response that should be reinforced. If he stopped to reflect on the matter, he might be encouraged or amused by the fact that psychologists who shape the behavior of rats might also have difficulty in describing exactly what movement their 'pupil' should make at any given point in training. This teacher is confident, however, of his ability to recognize the right kind of response, and he will be ready to reinforce it when it occurs. (We can be sure he would, for example, reinforce any suggestion that the class collect and organize pertinent facts about Lincoln and how he decided the crucial issues of his time.) He knows the reactions of students as individuals and will try to choose words and actions that will work best for each. He expects that several students will help him by recognizing and approving several types of appropriate behavior.

"He will try to reinforce any improvement— that is, any act or suggestion that is better than that typical for individuals of this group up to this time. Of course, today's improvement may be ignored or noted as a step backward next week. His judgment is sometimes faulty also, so that under his tutelage there is some retracing of steps, some learning that must be forgotten later. Even an especially skillful administration of reinforcement does not produce dramatic changes in a single discussion; but to be optimistic, he hopes that after today there will be an increase in probability, if not a detectable difference, in some students' willingness to look for more facts, to consider different alternatives, and so on, before urging that they 'get started on something.'" (Craig, 1966, pp. 77-78)

DIRECT TEACHING

Fortunately, some rules for problem solving are easier to teach. Some rules, particularly those for a limited set of special problems, are less general and may be learned readily by the procedures recommended for principles of science and mathematics. Rules for troubleshooting particular types of equipment are often of this type. When learning to diagnose malfunctions in a television receiver, for example, students learn such principles as, "When the picture is weak but the sound good, the problem must be in units carrying only the visual signal." For a person with some knowledge of TV circuits, this rule limits the malfunction to one of four components, and these can be eliminated one at a time. Other heuristics in the same area are (1) make the easiest or most economical check first and (2) if checks are equally easy and economical, begin with the last first (in our example this would be the picture tube), and work back. In other situations where a much larger number of units must be checked, the so-called "half-split" method is taught. In this method the middle of the signal path is checked first to eliminate all units on one side or the other of this point. The next check is planned to halve the remaining possibilities, and so on. Rules of this type are for use with a well-defined and limited set of problems. It should be obvious that they are more specific and more easily communicated (in terms of exactly what should be done) than

the more general problem-solving strategies are.

Synthesis of Teaching Methods for School Settings

Three instructional strategies for achieving objectives related to principles and problem solving have been described: (1) teaching principles directly, (2) using problem solving to teach principles, and (3) teaching general rules for problem solving. The contributions and some of the advantages and disadvantages of these methods are compared in Table 10-4.

As a method of teaching principles, problem solving is less efficient and more time consuming than direct teaching. It does, however, provide an opportunity for students to practice solving problems within a limited content area. Teaching general rules of problem solving has the potential, we believe, to contribute to an even more general improvement of problem-solving skills. But this is also a time-consuming approach. Its results are somewhat uncertain, and it does not teach content in any organized way.

How are we to balance the contributions, definite and potential, and the limitations of these approaches in a school program? There are no pat answers, but some assumptions appear reasonable; and if they are, some tentative conclusions (speculations) follow. Obviously, however, this is an area in which we are unsure of our knowledge. Better, more comprehensive research with large numbers of students and substantial segments of the school program is sorely needed.

First, we assume that school programs will continue to be organized around content areas. A thorough grounding in content is of first importance, even when independent problem solving is the ultimate objective. We

Table 10-4.
Summary Comparison of Objectives, Advantages and Applicability for Methods of Teaching Principles and Problem Solving.

Teaching Method	Objectives		Relative Advantages		Range of Applicability
	Primary	Other	Efficiency	Dependability	
Direct teaching	Content principles	—	Most	Most	Content area only
Problem-solving method	Content principles	Problem-solving skill	Intermediate	Intermediate	Related content areas
Teaching rules for problem-solving	General problem-solving skill	—	Least	Least	Many content areas

expect few courses to be constructed around problem-solving strategies independent of content.

The most efficient method of teaching content principles is by direct teaching, and we expect and support the decision to give this method the most emphasis. Problem-solving skills should not be neglected, however. Therefore, some principles of each subject area should be taught by problem-solving methods. When some aspects of a course are more fundamental and more thoroughly agreed on and substantiated than others, we suggest direct teaching. Problem solving can be used in areas that are more controversial and exploratory. The potentially greater motivational value of problem solving, especially for students accustomed to other methods, can be used to advantage periodically to "recharge" students or renew their interest. Then we may take advantage of this interest to teach more content directly. When interest

begins to lag again, more problem solving might be scheduled, and so on.

More general problem-solving strategies are important also, although we can be less confident about the results of our efforts to teach them. We are sufficiently optimistic, however, to urge that one or more units of each course be devoted to teaching the heuristics of problem solving, beginning with problems based on the specific content of the course. Then, a continuing consideration of problem-solving methods and their importance to further progress in the area of study should be planned. Some attention would be given to the implications of these methods for behavior in areas of experience outside the course or subject area, but this would probably not be a major effort in terms of the proportion of student or teacher time.

To summarize, we recommend some use of each method at every educational level and in every subject: (1) the most time would be in teaching content principles directly; (2) the problem-solving method for teaching principles would be used periodically to practice problem solving in the content area but also to stimulate interest; and (3) at least one unit and continuing reference to general problem-solving rules would be planned for every course. Our suggestions amount to an endorsement of a "mixed" method, reminiscent of our conclusions about the best way to teach defined concepts and principles.

Summary of Tactics for Teaching Independent Problem Solving

The following nine statements summarize and supplement our earlier recommendations for instruction, which are designed to help students learn to solve problems on their own.

1. Give priority to the teaching of knowledge, concepts, and principles as a foundation for later problem solving.

2. When teaching principles, depend primarily on the direct method (Chapter 9), but plan to teach some of the principles in each course by the problem-solving method.

3. Use direct teaching of principles with more fundamental and substantiated content and problem solving to explore new and controversial areas.

4. Use problem solving as a method to provide practice in problem solving and to arouse students' interest.

5. To teach principles by the problem-solving method (1) have students state a clear goal, (2) prompt them to recall relevant concepts and principles, (3) use thought-provoking questions to guide thinking, (4) when students have a solution, ask them to state the principle, (5) have them use the principle to solve other problems, and (6) direct attention to the problem-solving strategies they are practicing.

6. Plan some direct teaching of general rules for problem solving. Use the approach recommended for teaching content principles with the additional provisions given in points 8 and 9.

7. When teaching general rules of problem solving, provide for students to use these rules with a wide variety of problems over an extended period of time.

8. Use selective reinforcement and feedback during student use of a general rule of problem solving in attempts to guide (shape) student behavior in the directions indicated by the rule.

9. Use the suggestions and techniques of Torrance, Davis, and Houtman and others to "free students' imagination and stimulate them to propose more creative hypotheses for problem solving."

Summary

1. General rules for problem solving (heuristics and strategies) include clarifying the problem, proposing hypotheses, reasoning out the implications, and testing hypotheses (Dewey). Many general and specific rules supplement this overall strategy.

2. Creative problem solving results in imaginative or unique (divergent) hypotheses and solutions.

3. Objectives for problem solving require the production of unique communications, plans, or products.

4. Theoretical explanations of problem solving have contrasted trial-and-error (S-R) with perceptual organization, hypothesizing, and "insight" (cognitive).

5. Recently psychologists have used computers to attempt to simulate the problem-solving processes of humans.

6. Sets or predispositions to solve problems in a certain way improve one's ability to solve other problems of the same type, but they may also make him "rigid" and blind him to new approaches when they are needed.

7. Research suggests giving students practice in discovering problem solutions when the objective is to improve students' ability to discover new solutions and principles independently.

8. Participation in group problem solving has been shown to improve the participants' ability to solve problems independently.

9. Brainstorming with a group has been shown to increase individuals' production of ideas later. The quality of ideas need not be deemphasized unless the participants are afraid to be unconventional.

10. Creativity is moderately highly related to intelligence, but neither IQ tests nor achievement are adequate to select creative individuals.

11. Psychologists' ideas about the process of problem solving have led to experimental teaching and major revisions of the curriculum, but a systematic evaluation of curricular efforts to teach general inquiry and problem-solving skills is not available at this time.

12. A variety of activities and techniques to "free the imagination" of students and encourage the production of novel hypotheses and problem solutions has been proposed and used experimentally.

13. A concise but comprehensive summary of tactics for teaching independent problem solving appears at the end of the "recommendations" section immediately preceding this summary.

CHAPTER 11
Educational Provisions for Individual Differences

"That's the trouble with independent learning, it's over-regimented." *(Drawing by Short and Weaver Cartoons)*

Definition, Types, and Extent of Individual Differences
The Value of Individual Differences
Intellectual Differences
Intraindividual Differences
Educational Provisions for Individual Differences
Individual Differences in Teachers

The previous chapters have concentrated on some general characteristics of students and some general principles of psychology that apply to all individuals. Knowledge of these general characteristics and principles is vital for successful teaching. We hope, however, that you have not been lulled into thinking that for educational purposes all individuals are alike. This chapter will focus on the differences among and within individuals and the meaning of these differences for the educator.

OBJECTIVES FOR CHAPTER 11

1. Know the definition, types, and extent of individual differences.
2. Describe and defend the values you hold concerning individual differences.
3. Know some various definitions of intelligence.
4. Recognize the general conclusions and implications regarding the stability of intelligence.
5. Know of, choose, and apply various educational provisions for individual differences.
6. Be alert to the individual differences of teachers and the educational implications of such differences.

DEFINITION, TYPES, AND EXTENT OF INDIVIDUAL DIFFERENCES

"We hold these truths to be self evident . . . that all men are created equal." Stirring words. But what do they mean? Do they deny the existence of inborn individuality? Of course not. What the writers had in mind was the phrase expressed in the Virginia Bill of Rights written 3 weeks earlier. "All men are by nature equally free and independent."

If equal means identical there is simply no doubt that people are born unequal. Individuality is as inescapable as the fact that we are humans, and can never be obliterated (Williams, 1967, p. 5). Children are not only created unequal, but they also become more different as they grow older. By the time they enter school the inequalities among them have greatly increased. Indeed, the most persistent, discouraging problems faced by teachers are related to the fact that pupils differ from each other in so many ways (Thomas and Thomas, 1965, p. v). If teachers are to deal effectively with individual differences among pupils it is essential that they understand the kinds and extent of individual differences that exist.

Definition and Types of Individual Differences

The term *individual differences* refers to the dissimilarities among the various members of a group in *any* characteristic that can be identified. These differences may be physical characteristics, such as height, weight, and visual and auditory acuity or psychological characteristics, such as emotional stability, motivation, aggression, dependency, interests, or persistence. All social, personal, intellectual, and academic characteristics are a part of individual differences.

Extent of Individual Differences

Although differences exist in many characteristics, for illustrative purposes we will discuss only some physical and cognitive differences. Others may be equally important, but since our measures of such variables are not as refined, the differences are a bit harder to document.

PHYSICAL DIFFERENCES

Perhaps one of the more apparent physical differences among individuals is height. As people grow older, the variability increases. By the age of puberty some youngsters are nearly twice as tall as others of the same age and sex.

One point that is particularly important when discussing the differences on any characteristic is that there exists considerable variability even at what one might call the extremes of the distribution. This variability, while sometimes relatively unimportant, can be quite important in certain circumstances. Variability in height illustrates this. The middle 10% of the North American adult male population is clustered around 5 feet 7½ inches to 5 feet 8½ inches. But the height of the tallest 10% of the population ranges from 5 feet 11 inches to over 7 feet. And this variability is quite important in college or professional basketball! The same concept applies to other differences. A person whose motivation, creativity, or intellectual capabilities barely place him in the top 5% of the population differs considerably from the person who exceeds 9999 out of every 10,000.

Although the magnitudes of observable external differences in the structure of the body are enormous, the internal parts of the body are even more variable. Williams (1946, 1953, 1956, and 1967), a noted biochemist, has been one of the most prolific writers on the extent and importance of biochemical individuality. In his book, *You Are Extraordinary* (1967), Williams describes and gives illustrations of many of these differences. For example:

1. We each have natural perfume distinctive enough so that a bloodhound can trail and identify us.

2. The gastric juices of about 5000 people who had no known stomach ailment varied a *thousandfold* in their pepsin content. As Williams points out: "If normal facial features varied as much as gastric juices do, some of our noses would be about the size of navy beans while others would be the size of twenty-pound watermelons." (p. 13)

3. Sex glands in "normal" males vary from 10 to 45 grams. Undersexed males may have glands weighing only ½ gram. Kinsey, in surveying the frequency with which semen is ejaculated, found one "healthy" man for whom this occurred only once in 30 years. At the other extreme was an attorney who estimated a frequency of 45,000 times in a 30-year period!

4. Some individuals completely lack pain receptors. The density (frequency) of pain receptors among other individuals varies considerably.

The last example given above relates to differences in the receptor nerves. As Williams points out, individuals are highly distinctive with respect to the number and distribution of nerve endings. Since these nerve endings are the only source of information, these differences are extremely important. Individuals also start life with brains that differ enormously in number, size, and arrangement of neurons. These physiological differences in the nervous system lead us quite naturally into a consideration of some cognitive differences.

COGNITIVE DIFFERENCES

While external physical differences may be the most obvious, the psychological differences that exist in children may be of even greater educational significance. (Certainly some of these psychological differences are related to physical differences.) It is somewhat more difficult to document differences in such variables as motivation, perseverance, or creativity, because psychologists have not developed very refined measures of these variables. Nevertheless, any observant teacher realizes that students differ enormously on these variables. Psychologists do have some fairly well-established procedures for measuring aptitude and achievement, and we will discuss these differences. Keep in mind that the variability of many other characteristics in individuals is likely to be as great as the variability in aptitude. These other characteristics as well as aptitude will affect achievement levels.

APTITUDE DIFFERENCES

One way to illustrate the variability of aptitude is to use the concept of mental age. While most modern-day aptitude tests do not report a mental age, some measures do, and we can use those results for illustration. A person who received the same score on a test as an average eight-year old would be given a mental age of eight; if a person received a score equal to an average ten-year old, he would be assigned a mental age of ten, and so on. As in the case for height, mental age variability increases as chronological age increases. By age twelve some students are intellectually like the average nine-year old while others are operating intellectually like the average sixteen-year old. (An increase in the variability of a characteristic is *not*, as some have seemed to think, a sufficient argument for the importance of environmental effects. If one person is developing at a slower *rate* than another, differences will increase with an increase in age regardless of the reason, genetic or environmental, for the slower rate of development.)

Perhaps a more impressive way to illustrate the extreme differences in intellectual functioning is to discuss some of the accomplishments of a few very gifted individuals. Terman (1917) reports on some of the early accomplishments of Sir Francis Galton, a well-known psychologist in the late 19th century.

Before his fifth birthday Francis wrote the following letter to his sister.

My dear Adele,

I am 4 years old and I can read any English book. I can say all the Latin Substantives and Adjectives and active verbs besides 52 lines of Latin poetry. I can cast up any sum in addition and can multiply by 2, 3, 4, 5, 6, 7, 8, 9, 10, 11.

I can also say the pence table. I read French a little and I know the clock.

Francis Galton
Febuary 15, 1827

College sophomores struggling with Homer are usually impressed with the following anecdote about Galton.

"By six, . . . he had become thoroughly conversant with the Iliad and the Odyssey. At this age, a visitor at the Galton home made Francis weary by cross-questioning him about points in Homer. Finally the boy replied, 'Pray, Mr. Horner, look at the last line in the twelfth book of the Odyssey' and then ran off. The line in question reads, 'But why rehearse all this tale, for even yesterday I told it to thee and to thy noble wife in thy house; and it liketh me not twice to tell a plain-told tale.'" (quoted from Terman, 1917)

A second example of a very gifted student is Mike Grost. Mike began his college career at Michigan State University at the age of ten. He was awarded a bachelor's degree at fifteen, and a master's degree at sixteen. At the time of this writing he has entered Yale and hopes to obtain his doctoral degree in mathematics before his nineteenth birthday. When Mike was in kindergarten his teacher asked what kinds of flowers are found in Michigan. Mike answered, "In botanical terminology, the word 'flower' refers only to the blossom of a plant. They refer to the blossom, leaves, root, and stem as a flowering plant. However, a gardener may refer to the entire plant as a flower. In our geographical area we are likely to find a large variety of woodland and prairie flowers, plus, of course, species of the imported or . . . ." (Grost, 1970, pp. 42-43) At this point the teacher interrupted Mike!

To give examples at the opposite extreme, there are people who never learn to talk, do not become toilet trained, and are completely unable to take care of themselves.

Even though admitting that such extremes do exist, the skeptical teacher may think he is unlikely to encounter such differences in the classroom. To be sure, you are extremely unlikely to encounter a child in your classroom who cannot talk at all. And we grant that the probability of a Galton or a Grost in your class is small. Yet children such as Mike Grost *do exist* in the elementary school. And, of course, even small variations in mental ability can and do have a significant impact on school achievement.

ACHIEVEMENT DIFFERENCES

What kinds and degree of achievement differences can we expect in the public schools? Considerable, and variability in achievement increases as chronological age increases. Some people interpret this as evidence for schools' failures. They suggest, however, that the increase in variability in height is "how nature works." This difference in interpretation of very similar data is hard to support.

A useful rule of thumb for expected ranges of achievement is as follows. Excluding the 2% at each extreme of the distribution, the range of achievement is about two thirds of the chronological age of the usual student at the grade level under consideration (Cook and Clymer, 1962). Thus, in fourth grade, where the usual age is nine, we would expect to find a six-year spread ($2/3 \times 9$) in achievement. In the seventh grade, where the average age is twelve, we would expect to find an eight-year spread ($2/3 \times 12$) in achievement. As Cook (1941, p. 29) has summarized: "In any grade above the fourth a teacher may expect that almost the complete range of elementary-school achievement will be represented." Project Talent data (Flanagan et al., 1964) clearly illustrate that in high school a considerable number of ninth graders score higher than the twelfth-grade average in every subject matter area.

Hopefully we have convinced you. Individual differences do exist, and for every conceivable characteristic. What should, and what can, the schools do about this phenomenon?

THE VALUE OF INDIVIDUAL DIFFERENCES

Is it true, as Whitehead asserted, that Americans care more for equality than they do for liberty? How equal do we want to be? How equal can we be? Can we be equal and excellent, too? What are the difficulties a democracy encounters in pursuing excellence? These, and others like them, are some of the challenging questions facing our country. John Gardner (1961) discusses these questions admirably in a book entitled *Excellence: Can We Be Equal and Excellent Too?*

Three Approaches to Society

Gardner discusses three contesting philosophies: *hereditary stratification, equalitarianism,* and *competitive performance.* The principle of hereditary stratification, obtaining our place in society by virtue of the royalty of birth, is practiced somewhat, but has never really been considered an acceptable principle in our society. However, when this principle is not followed, society has to decide what to do with the dramatic individual differences in ability and performance that emerge. "One way is to limit or work against such individual differences, protecting the slow runners and curbing the swift. This is the path of equalitarianism. The other way is simply to 'let the best man win.'" (Gardner, 1961, p. 5)

Gardner classifies the three principles as follows.

1. Emphasis on individual competitive performance.
2. Restraints on individual performance.
a. Hereditary stratification.
b. Equalitarianism.

Although stratification is aristocratic and equalitarianism is antiaristocratic, both impose restraints on individual performance and aspirations. Gardner recognizes that either equalitarianism or competitive performance can be carried to extremes, but he seems to favor the latter.

"In its moderate form, emphasis on individual achievement allows a healthy play to individual gifts, holds out an invitation to excel but does not necessarily sanction the ruthless subordination of those who are less able, less vigorous or less aggressive." (1961, p. 20)

Free competition, however, is not always desired by the public. The freedom to excel also places a burden of responsibility and pressure on a person. A person born to low status in a rigidly stratified society has a better self-image than a person who loses out in free competition, because in the latter case, "the loser knows that the true reason for his lowly status is that he is not capable of better. That is a bitter pill for any man." (Gardner, 1961, pp. 71, 72) These losers in a free society will desire to diminish emphasis on performance as a determinant of status.

Gardner believes we should strive to produce excellence without arousing hostility on the part of those unable to attain it. He poses the problem as follows.

"How can we provide opportunities and rewards for individuals of every degree of ability so that individuals at every level will realize their full potentialities, perform at their best and harbor no resentment toward any other level." (1961, p. 115)

Equal Opportunity

One reason we do not know the answer to the above question is because our society has never, in practice, provided equal opportunity for all. (For example, some blacks, American Indians, Chicanos, and poor whites have gone to schools of poor quality, and women, as well as the minority groups already mentioned, have not always been given an equal chance for admission into professional schools.) In fact, society is not even clear on what the phrase equal opportunity means. Some argue that equal opportunity means identical treatment. However, this view is held by only a minority. Most realize that, given what we know about individual differences, identical treatment of individuals is almost bound to lead to unequal opportunity. Some define equal opportunity as an equal expenditure of funds per pupil. Others argue that to provide equal opportunity we must spend more on those students coming from disadvantaged homes (Wise, 1969). Coleman (1966) defines equality of opportunity as equality of outcome and suggests that input measures are spurious considerations. This philosophy seems somewhat counter to the proposition expressed in the Rockefeller report on education. They state, "The great advantage of the conception of equality of opportunity is that it candidly recognizes differences in endowment and motivation and accepts the certainty of differences in achievement." (1958, p. 16) Robinson (1965, p. 157) takes the position that "The closer we come to attaining equality of educational opportunity the greater become the inequalities of education, as the capable come closer to reaching their potential and widen the gap between themselves and the less competent."

Diversity or Conformity

We do not believe our goal should be to make everyone alike in skills, knowledges, attitudes, and interests. Even if such a goal were advisable, it would be impossible to attain. Even if all individuals had equal ability in general, their patterns of ability would differ. Although we wish to mention *intra*individual differences (differences within an individual) later, it seems appropriate to quote Dolbear (1908) regarding the diversity-conformity issue.

"In Antediluvian times, while the animal kingdom was being differentiated into swimmers, climbers, runners, and fliers, there was a school for the development of the animal.

"The theory of the school was that the best animals should be able to do one thing as well as another.

"If an animal had short legs and good wings, attention should be devoted to running so as to even up the qualities as far as possible.

"So the duck was kept waddling instead of swimming. The pelican was kept wagging his short wings in the attempt to fly. The eagle was made to run and allowed to fly only for recreation.

"All this in the name of education. Nature was not to be trusted, for individuals should be symmetrically developed and similar for their own welfare as well as for the welfare of the community. The animals that would not submit to such training, but persisted in developing the best gifts they had, were dishonored and humiliated in many ways. They were stigmatized as being narrow-minded specialists, and special difficulties were placed in their way when they attempted to ignore the theory of education recognized in the school.

"No one was allowed to graduate from the school unless he could climb, swim, run, and fly at certain prescribed rates; so it happened that the time wasted by the duck in the attempt to run had so hindered him from swimming that his swimming muscles had atrophied, and so he was hardly able to swim at all; and in addition he had been scolded, punished, and ill-treated in many ways so as to make his life a burden. He left school humiliated, and the ornithorhynchus could beat him both running and swimming. Indeed, the latter was awarded a prize in two departments.

"The eagle could make no headway in climbing to the top of a tree, and although he showed he could get there just the same, the performance was counted a demerit since it had not been done in the prescribed way.

"An abnormal eel with large pectoral fins proved he could run, fly, climb trees, and swim a little. He was made valedictorian."

In general, one can expect more growth from time spent in developing his greater talents than from attempting to develop his weaker powers. Dael Wolfle (1960), the executive director of the American Association for the Advancement of Science and at one time the director of the Commission on Human Resources and Advanced Training suggests that:

"From the standpoint of society, the best way to distribute talent is to take maximum advantage of differences in aptitude, interest, and motivation by having each individual concentrate on the thing he can do best. . . . Have one man become the best he can possibly become in one line and another the best he can possibly become in another." (1960, p. 542)

In general we should develop individuals who are strong in some fields and weak in others instead of individuals who are mediocre in all. Anything can, of course, be carried to an extreme. Our society, in order to maintain some stability, must insist on conformity in many matters. And it is the schools' responsibility to educate, so that society's members will conform when necessary or desirable. Yet we must also insist on diversity. Tyler and Brownell (1962) stated it nicely.

"The task of the schools is, therefore, twofold: It must foster conformity without sacrificing diversity; and it must encourage diversity without preventing conformity. . . . Human variability is real, inevitable, ineradicable, desirable, and indeed essential. . . . Human diversity is a key to social progress and a challenge to better education. . . . In our schools we must foster both conformity and diversity, neither at the expense of the other." (1962, pp. 326-327)

Your Values as a Teacher

Regardless of the stated opinions of others regarding the value of diversity versus conformity, the teacher should consciously examine his own beliefs and actions. Is assigning the same homework to everyone in class indicative of a belief in conformity? Is giving different assignments an indication of a belief in diversity? As Thomas and Thomas (1965, p. 35) point out: (1) teachers are often not consciously aware of their own value systems; (2) *stated* values do not always seem to guide decisions; (3) some values a teacher holds seem to conflict with other values; and (4) certain values may be impossible to bring to realization, because they are inconsistent with the facts of life.

There is no easy way to help a teacher (or prospective teacher) examine the values he holds concerning individual differences. Yet such an examination would surely be worthwhile. One approach would be for each teacher to take a value inventory. Thomas and Thomas (1965, pp. 46-49) have developed a 30-item inventory that could be quite useful.[1] One is to agree to disagree with statements such as the following:

"In planning his methods of instruction, the teacher should emphasize those activities which will suit the needs of the majority of the class, even though this may mean neglecting the needs of one or two of the less able pupils."

"Since the students with the greatest ability will ultimately contribute the most to society, the teacher should give more time and

thought to meeting their needs than to meeting the needs of the average or below-average pupils."

"Since the average and above-average students can work on their own rather well, the teacher should spend a major portion of his time aiding the least able students because they are the ones in greatest need of help."

"Separating students into different classes according to their abilities (so the most capable are in one room and the least capable in another) is undemocratic. It violates the ideal of equal educational opportunities for all."

"A good way to give each pupil a fair opportunity to learn is to group him with others of like ability. Thus he competes with his intellectual peers and is not bored or overwhelmed by material too easy or too difficult for him. This ability grouping is democratic because it provides for each one according to his needs."

Spending more time discussing statements such as these would greatly benefit an individual in developing and understanding his own values. Consider another proposition; suppose two individuals with the *same genetic capacity* enter first grade with different levels of achievement. Is it the school's role to close the gap? Would that be providing equal or unequal opportunity? Or assume, as most everyone would, that within a group of first graders there is some positive relationship between genetic capacity and knowledge. Now, in general, should the differences in performance within this group increase or decrease with subsequent schooling? Teachers must consider these kinds of questions. Reading some of the literature referenced so far in this chapter should assist in that consideration.

Because educators are primarily concerned with those cognitive individual differences that affect school achievement, we will turn to a consideration of a construct popularly termed intelligence.

[1] For another technique related to value clarification see Simon, et al. (1972).

INTELLECTUAL DIFFERENCES

One of the major problems encountered in talking about intellectual differences is a precise definition of what intelligence means. We can certainly agree that Galton and Grost, who were discussed earlier, are more intelligent than average. But what is intelligence really, and how can we measure it?

Definitions and Theories of Intelligence

The definitions of intelligence generally fall into one or more of three categories: the capacity to (1) think abstractly, (2) learn, or (3) integrate new experiences and adapt to new situations. Some of the more common definitions of intelligence are as follows:

Binet: ". . . the capacity to judge well, to reason well, and to comprehend well." (1916)

Stoddard: ". . . the ability to undertake activities that are characterized by difficulty, complexity, abstractness, economy, adaptiveness to a goal, social value, emergence of originals, and to maintain such activities under conditions that demand a concentration of energy and a resistance to emotional forces." (1943)

Terman: ". . . the ability to think in terms of abstract ideas." (1916)

As you can see, psychologists do not all mean the same thing by intelligence. Some, such as Binet and Simon (1916) or McNemar (1964), conceptualize intelligence as a global characteristic and have designed tests of intelligence that report a single score. Others, following the lead of Thurstone (1933), believe in a theory of multiple factors. The *Primary Mental Abilities* test developed by Thurstone provided scores on five factors: verbal meaning, number facility, reasoning,

perceptual speed, and spatial relations. Guilford (1967, 1969), one of the more recent and prolific writers on intelligence, postulates many factors of intelligence. In his structure of intellect model he categorizes these factors under three broad dimensions according to (1) the process or operation performed, (2) the kind of product involved, and (3) the kind of material or content involved. He then subclassifies under each of these dimensions five operations, six types of products, and four types of content. Looking at the three main headings as faces of a cube, he ends up with 120 ($4 \times 6 \times 5$) cells within the cube, each representing a different aspect of intelligence (see Figure 11-1).

Thus a person could conceivably be capable of divergent thinking on symbolic content when the product is an implication and not be so capable when the product is a transformation. Guilford claims to have demonstrated empirically that 82 of the 120 different structure-of-intellect factors exist (1967). He argues that each factor should be tested separately and that tests giving a global score are somewhat misleading.

From the preceding discussion it should be readily evident that there are many different theories concerning the structure of intelligence. Some theorists feel that intelligence is a general attribute; others feel that there are many different aspects to intelligence. However disconcerting it may be, one must realize that psychologists cannot agree as to the real nature of intelligence. While theoretical psychologists generally adopt the view that there are specific factors of intellect, most also believe there is a general factor. Practical psychologists are still very inclined to use tests of general intelligence, because these tend to be well developed, easier to use, and equally predictive.

Because of this lack of agreement, there are a wide variety of tests that are often subsumed under the phrase *intelligence tests.*

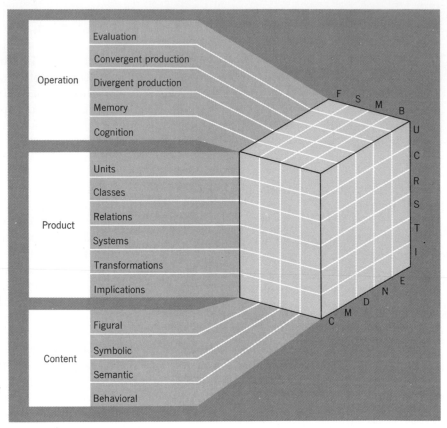

Figure 11-1.
Guilford's "three faces of
intellect." *(Reproduced
by permission of the
author and McGraw-Hill
Book Company from J. P.
Guilford's* The Nature of
Human Intelligence, *New
York, McGraw-Hill Book
Company, 1967.)*

They do not all measure the same thing. They are not even designed to do so. A rather important implication is that, when discussing differences in intelligence, one must be completely aware of how these differences have been measured. We should resist the temptation to generalize about all intellectual differences from a single test.

Stability of Intelligence

Because intelligence is now generally considered to be influenced by both heredity and environment (see Chapter 3), it logically follows that, as a person's environment changes, so might his intelligence or so at least might his score on an intelligence test, which is an operational definition of intelligence.

The extent to which intelligence is a stable or variable construct is very important. If there were no stability to intelligence test scores, then the test would be a useless instrument. On the other hand, if intelligence test scores were completely stable, then we might adopt fatalistic attitudes concerning a student's prognosis.

The research findings (Bloom, 1964) suggest that intelligence test scores are very unstable during the early years of a person's life. Bayley (1949), for example, found no relationship between intelligence measured at age one and age seventeen. Certainly the tested intelligence of children under five years old is fairly unstable. Although it is hard to know whether this instability is primarily caused by imprecise measuring instruments or trait instability, it nevertheless implies that important, irreversible decisions should not be based on early intelligence test performance.

With increased age, the stability of intelligence test performance increases rapidly. In general, longitudinal studies have suggested that intelligence is a fairly stable characteristic after age five. Bayley (1949) found the correlations between intelligence test scores at ages six and seventeen to be +.78 and at ages eleven and seventeen to be +.92. (This is considered a very high degree of relationship. See Chapter 15 for a discussion of correlation.) However, Bayley's data were based on individually administered intelligence tests. Hopkins and Bibelheimer (1971) have recently conducted a five-year study on the stability of intelligence using a popular group intelligence test. They found that the stability was somewhat less than what one would expect to find on individually administered intelligence tests.

In spite of the reasonably high stability for groups of children, individuals can show considerable growth or decline in intelligence test scores. Honzik, Macfarlane, and Allen (1948) reported a study where, over the period of ages six to eighteen, 59% of the children changed by 15 or more IQ points. Studies such as this should impress on us the fact that although scores on intelligence tests are reasonably stable and therefore useful as *guides* in both short-term and long-term decision making, scores can and do fluctuate, and permanent decisions (or labeling) should not be done *solely* on the basis of a single intelligence test.

Recently there have been several books (see, for example, Engelmann and Engelmann, 1968) and a few research studies (see Pines, 1969) suggesting that through proper intensive early stimulation, one can succeed in raising the intelligence of children. An article (Pines, 1969) on Head Start programs reported that J. McV. Hunt had mothers of disadvantaged children watch the administration of intelligence tests and afterward coach their children on the test items. This results in an average gain of 30 IQ points! One must be very careful about drawing any conclusions from such data. It may be misleading both to theoreticians and to practitioners. Biehler (1971, p. 447) offers the following analogy to help clarify the point.

"Assume . . . that a particular child has extremely poor vision. If you helped this child memorize the materials used in testing his vision, would you be improving his sight? With training he could pass the test with a perfect score, but would he see any better? What might happen if on the basis of the test the child was placed in a situation in which he had to have perfect vision? Would he be able to perform satisfactorily? Or would it make more sense to get an *accurate* estimate of his sight and assist him to make the most of the actual vision he possessed?"

Ignoring the research where there is fairly direct teaching for the test, there is some evidence to suggest that a considerable change in environmental conditions is needed to affect a test score greatly after the first 5 formative years. This is one reason why there has been so much emphasis on such programs as Project Head Start.

INTRAINDIVIDUAL DIFFERENCES

The earlier section on diversity versus conformity indicated that individuals differ within themselves. This difference is referred to as within trait or intraindividual variability. We wish to emphasize the inaccuracies of two occasionally held myths. If one writes about extreme cases of intraindividual differences to illustrate the degree of within trait variability that can exist, some people conclude that superior talents must be associated with inferior abilities in other respects (like the false idea that a girl cannot be good looking, rich, intelligent, and passionate, or that geniuses are sickly). This is simply not the case. Compensatory talents are not the general rule. In fact, there *tends* to be a positive relationship between different traits. More intelligent people tend to be healthier, better athletes, and have better personalities than less intelligent people. Yet we wish to make sure that you do not become a victim of the myth at the opposite extreme. There are intraindividual differences. A person good in English need not necessarily be good in mathematics. An extremely able mechanic may be relatively inarticulate. We should also mention that intraindividual variability increases throughout the school years.

Idiot Savants

Idiot savants (or wise idiots) are individuals who have superior capabilities in one (or possibly a few) area(s), but are so intellectually deficient that they can not even take care of themselves. There is some general feeling that idiot savants are severely emotionally disturbed. But we do not bring the subject up to discuss either etiology or prognosis. We do not expect a teacher to have an idiot savant in his classroom. We bring up the subject because idiot savants have bizarre enough characteristics that a description of one is likely to be remembered. And a teacher who remembers that idiot savants exist in the world will never forget that his students also have intraindividual differences.

What is a description of an idiot savant? Rife and Snyder (1931) describe a twenty-seven-year-old man as follows.

"As a small child he would scribble figures on the bathroom tiles or other places whenever he could get hold of a pencil. He never learned to talk, and even now cannot perform such simple requests as pointing to his eyes or ears. In school he could do absolutely nothing, so was sent home, and at sixteen was admitted to the Institution. His hearing is normal. . . . Although he is incapable of carrying on a conversation, or of understanding spoken requests, one may make one's desires along mathematical lines known with a pencil. When a pencil and paper were taken, and the figures 2, 4, and 8 written in a vertical column, the patient immediately continued the series 16, 32, 64, etc. When the series 2, 4, 16 was started, he immediately continued this one, the sixth number being 4,294,967,296. Then $9-3$ was written, in the attempt to indicate square root. Under this, several numbers such as 625, 729, and 900 were written. The square root of each was immediately and correctly written. Any problem of multiplication of several digits by several digits was done immediately, only the answer being written." (1931, pp. 553-554)

Typical Variability

Idiot savants are interesting but, of course, quite unusual. How much, and in what ways, does the average student vary? Interindividual variability across *traits* is generally about 75 to 80% as large as the variability of a group of people on a single trait.

The intraindividual variability in *cognitive* differences is not as great as that across all traits. Scores on tests of different aptitudes correlate higher than scores of different traits in general. Nevertheless, even within the cognitive area variability does exist. A person who scores high on the verbal subtest of a dif-

"I'm a rapid reader but a slow understander." (Drawing by Reg Hider from Today's Education/ NEA Journal, 1963)

ferential aptitude test may be quite low in numerical aptitude or abstract thinking. A person scoring high on an achievement test in English may be below average in history, science, or art.

This concept of intraindividual differences is important to educators. For example, if we were to group students into homogeneous classes according to their scores on intelligence tests, the students would still be very heterogeneous with respect to other characteristics. This is not an argument against grouping; it merely points to a limitation of such grouping. We will discuss this more fully in the next section.

EDUCATIONAL PROVISIONS FOR INDIVIDUAL DIFFERENCES

Because pupils differ from each other in so many ways, there is a real challenge for education. How can schools be run to provide for the needs of all individuals? In general, education has been set up and planned for groups, not individuals. This is partly because the extent and implications of individual differences have not always been recognized by educators, partly because educators have realized that there is a great deal that all individuals should learn in common, partly because it is more economical to teach a group of people at once instead of teaching each one separately, and partly because educators just do not know enough about *how* to provide for individual differences.

Educators, in general, do believe that more attention should be paid to the individual needs of pupils, and within the economic and technical limitations imposed on them they have tried several approaches. There are various ways we could classify educational provisions for individual differences. We will first present a general conceptual scheme used by Cronbach (1967). After that we will discuss some more specific procedures.

Adaptations: A General Schema

Cronbach (1967) discusses adapting education to individual differences in terms of the patterns shown in Table 11-1. Under procedures 1a. and 1b., both educational goals and educational instruction are fixed. Where the duration of schooling is altered by sequential selection, as in 1a., one is operating under the assumption that every child should go as far in school as his abilities warrant. Thus, some people would drop out of school early (maybe after eighth grade), while others would continue through postdoctoral study.

Training to criterion (1b.), is based on the opposite assumption, that there are some common learnings that everybody should attain, so we should keep instructing a person on those topics until learned—regardless of how long it takes. Failing (retaining) a person who does unacceptable work is an example of one specific procedure following this general scheme. A programmed instruction procedure that allows rate of learning to vary but keeps the criterion constant is another. Any approach that fixes the criterion and has the student "work to mastery" follows this general scheme. As Cronbach (1967, p. 25) points out, if such a procedure were followed in its pure form it would extend the education of some youngsters until they are oldsters. Obviously, it is based on the premise that the individual differences that exist are primarily due to the rate of learning. This is probably not true. Even if it were, such a process would lead to a cumulative deficit—something strongly deplored by many educators.

Adaptation by matching the goals to the in-

Table 11-1
Patterns of Educational Adaptation to Individual Differences. (Taken from Robert M. Gagné, Learning and Individual Differences, *Columbus, Ohio: Charles E. Merrill Books, 1967, p. 24.)*

Educational Goals	Instructional Treatment	Possible Modifications to Meet Individual Needs
Fixed	Fixed	1a. Alter duration of schooling by sequential selection. 1b. Train to criterion on any skill or topic, hence alter duration of instruction.
Options	Fixed within an option	2a. Determine for each student his prospective adult role and provide a curriculum preparing for that role.
Fixed within a course or program	Alternatives provided	3a. Provide remedial adjuncts to fixed "main track" instruction. 3b. Teach different pupils by different methods.

dividual is the policy suggested in 2a. Teaching some students algebra while we teach others general math, teaching some physics and others shop, some creative writing and others shorthand, are examples of this plan. Adaptation by changing goals is making a decision not only about education, but about the eventual role the individual should play in society. While this differentiating of goals takes place eventually (e.g., at the college major level), most educators feel that it would be a grave mistake to use such an approach in the elementary grades.

The remedial approach suggested in 3a. attempts to minimize individual differences, so that at the end of remediation the students can be taught by the same procedures used by those who did not need the remediation. Although Cronbach calls this hole patching and suggests its uses may be limited, Carroll (1967) points out that this approach can be fruitful when the need for remediation is due to some basic characteristic such as a fundamentally wrong attitude about school, a fundamental subject matter misconception, or a specific perceptual disability that affects a pupil's learning. While the remedial approach is likely to be useful in some instances, the evidence regarding the relative stability of individual differences in such things as learning rates, ability patterns, and styles of learning suggest that this approach will often be inefficient if indeed not doomed to failure.

The approach suggested in 3b. of altering instructional *methods* for different pupils is the one most favored by educators in general. Yet educators have only recently begun seriously researching the individual differences by instructional method (aptitude-treatment) interaction. For example, maybe one should encourage independence in some students by not providing assistance and minimize frustrations in others by helping them. Some students learn by discovery, others need more guidance in their learnings. At this stage of

our knowledge we are really asking teachers to function as clinicians when they follow this type of process.

The teacher forms an impression of the best way to help a student, and this impression may or may not be correct. Until further research tells us more about aptitude-treatment interactions, it may be wise to provide our teachers with some clinical skills. Teachers must at least be aware of individual differences and know that these differences call for differential treatments. Teachers must be aware of children as *individuals*, not as just members of a group.

The patterns shown in Table 11-1 are, of course, not mutually exclusive and all can be adapted within a single school system. At times fixed goals are appropriate, but we certainly do wish to educate diversely. At times we should fix the treatment and alter the time duration; at other times we should do the opposite. And, of course, at some level of schooling selection procedures are quite appropriate.

Schools have used many different specific procedures in an attempt to provide for individual differences. We will discuss some of these methods under the headings (1) administrative provisions, (2) classroom provisions, and (3) individualized instruction. These three categories are, of course, closely interrelated and discussing them separately is for the sake of convenience.

Administrative Provisions

Any school system is obviously organized into subunits. Teachers and students are assigned to groups, and many decisions must be made about who goes into what group, and how often the grouping should be changed. In organizing schools, we can set up procedures that partially provide for individual differences. We will discuss some of these under the headings of homogeneous grouping, non-graded schools, and acceleration and retention procedures. Knowing what we do about individual differences we should not be surprised that educators do not all agree on the "goodness" of these various methods. However, they do all seem to agree on one point. No scheme of school *organization*, however elaborately worked out, can provide for all the types and ranges of learner variability. Teachers must also be alert to and provide for individual differences within the groups of students they are assigned. As Wolfson (1967, p. 354) points out: "School organization in itself does not bring about any change in the essentials of teaching. . . . in fact, teachers may move from one form of organization to another without modifying their behavior one iota." If administrative provisions are to be effective in improving student learning, teachers will have to learn how best to make use of them.

HOMOGENEOUS GROUPING

Discussing the issue of grouping typically produces more heat than light. Often when an educator is asked if he is for grouping, he will respond with a strong affirmative or negative without even asking what basis of grouping is being advocated. Given the present teacher-pupil ratio, it is obvious that students must be grouped. The only meaningful question is, "On what basis?" Historically, it has been common practice in America to group only on the basis of chronological age. However, during the past half-century educators have begun wondering whether other bases should not also be considered.

As Vernon (1958) suggests, there must be some restrictions on group heterogeneity. One should not attempt to teach 15 mongoloid six-year olds and 15 university students in the same group. In reducing heterogeneity Vernon suggests that any grouping should be based on some stable and enduring characteristic; that it can be accurately assessed; that it has a major influence on educational progress; and that it is acceptable to society. Age meets these criteria, but many psychologists feel that ability and achievement are other characteristics that partially meet the criteria. Of course, neither ability nor achievement is completely stable, neither can be assessed with complete accuracy, and neither is acceptable to all of society as a characteristic to be used in grouping. Both do seem to have a major influence on educational progress, however, and are probably, after chronological age, the most often used bases for grouping. We will divide the remainder of this section into three subsections. First we will talk about ability and achievement grouping for those students who fall in the middle 80% of the population. Then we will briefly consider special classes for the slow learner and for the gifted.

Other criteria for grouping are discussed elsewhere in the book. Later in this chapter we discuss briefly the concept of classroom grouping for teachability. In Chapter 12 we will discuss various types of classroom atmospheres. Because of personality variables, some students work better in one type of classroom, others work better in other types. Thus, grouping on personality variables can also be beneficial.

Ability and Achievement Grouping for the Nonexceptional Child. Opponents of ability grouping often state that it is based on the false assumption that homogeneous grouping on ability will result in a class so homogeneous that teachers will not have to concern themselves with individual differences. That statement is false. Students grouped on any single characteristic will differ on many other important variables. However, this is probably an unfair argument against the proponents of ability grouping, since it is doubtful if many (or indeed any) of them base their position on such an obvious falsehood. What the proponents of ability grouping argue is that heterogeneity on one important variable will be reduced, and this reduction will make the teacher's task of providing suitable instruction somewhat easier.

The amount of research on the efficacy of ability grouping is both prodigious and inconclusive. Several people have summarized the research at various times in the past. (See, for example, Ekstrom, 1959; Passow, 1962; Borg, 1964; and Findley and Bryan, 1971). All of these reviews of the literature come up with essentially the same general conclusion: empirical research is inconclusive and conflicting. If it were our intent to sway a novice in the field in one direction or another on this controversy, we could do so by a careful selection of which research we cite. We will refrain from such indoctrination. The research data neither proves the superiority or inferiority of ability grouping. The administrative device of grouping on any basis, in and of itself, does not guarantee greater learning.

Many educators debate the issue of ability grouping on the basis of values. Some argue that ability grouping is not democratic (see Urevick, 1965), while others argue that it is (Hall, 1965). There is at least some legal precedent that suggests ability grouping is undemocratic (Bickel, 1967). It is probably true, however, that courts generally have not fully grasped the educator's distinction between equal opportunity and equal treatment. Most educators feel that, given individual differences, equal treatment results in unequal opportunities.

There is general consensus that students should be exposed to other students who are heterogeneous with respect to values. The cogency of this statement as an argument against ability grouping, however, is diminished somewhat when one realizes that often

those who use this argument have also stated, quite correctly, that grouping on the basis of ability leaves one with a heterogeneous group on other variables. Nevertheless, ability grouping can result in some stratification on the basis of race or socioeconomic status, and this is probably something one should avoid. Conant (1959) suggests that in high school homerooms and courses where opinion, attitude, and values are important (such as social studies) should be heterogeneous. On the other hand, he believes that in courses where the primary purpose is the acquisition of skill or knowledge (such as geometry), students should be grouped by ability or achievement.

Some reasonable summary statements regarding ability grouping follow. Most of these statements are relatively noncontroversial, but some educators would quarrel with each of them.

1. The evidence regarding how ability grouping affects both achievement and personality variables is equivocal.

2. Ability grouping will reduce, but certainly not eliminate, individual differences.

3. Ability grouping, in and of itself, is not a solution to anything. If ability grouping is to work, teachers must behave differently.

4. Most teachers prefer to work with homogeneous groups (Albrecht, 1960; Ream, 1968).

5. The majority of parents with children in ability-grouped schools are in favor of grouping (Otto, 1954, p. 202).

6. Ability grouping, if done at all, should be done differently for different subjects.

7. Ability grouping is more common and is more worthwhile after seventh grade than it is prior to that.

8. Ability grouping is impractical in small schools.

9. Ability grouping must be flexible. (One of the major complaints against ability grouping is that it is too rigid; students become "typed" and are not permitted to move into more able groups.)

10. Grouping should never be done on the basis of a single score (such as an intelligence test score). Achievement tests, aptitude tests, *and* teacher judgments should all serve as criteria for any grouping procedure.

One approach that involves grouping on ability is called stratified heterogeneous grouping (Findley and Bryan, 1971). Assume that one has a school building with 90 third graders being taught in three self-contained classrooms. If one wanted to reduce the heterogeneity of the students in a class and at the same time avoid the stigma of putting students in a high, average, or low class, one could proceed as follows. First, rank the 90 students on some combination of variables, such as aptitude and achievement tests and teacher recommendations. Second, divide the 90 students into 9 groups of 10 each, putting the top 10 students in group 1, the 10 next best students in group 2, and so on. Third, assign teacher A groups 1, 4, and 7, teacher B groups 2, 5, and 8, and teacher C groups 3, 6, and 9. Under this procedure there would be no top or bottom class, but each class would have a narrower range than that expected under a completely random assignment. Teacher A would not have any of the bottom $2/9$ of the students, teacher C would not have any of the top $2/9$, and teacher B would have none of the top $1/9$ or bottom $1/9$ of the pupils. This approach may well offer enough of the advantages of homogeneous grouping without some of the disadvantages to become the most favored grouping procedure.

Special Classes for the Mentally Retarded. Historically a variety of terms, and definitions of these terms, have been used when discussing youngsters whose cognitive (or intellectual) abilities are considerably below their peers. The term "mental retardation" is most frequently used, and has been defined by Kidd (1964) as follows.

"Mental retardation refers to significantly sub-average intellectual functioning which manifests itself during the developmental period and is characterized by inadequacy in adaptive behavior."

There are, of course, degrees of retardation. Approximately 0.5% of the population (or 1 person out of every 200) is so retarded that they are referred to as the "trainable" (or if very retarded, as the custodial) mentally retarded. These types of people are typically unable to become literate and are not usually found in the public schools. We will not consider them further. There is another group comprising approximately 10 to 15% of the students (depending on whose definitions one follows), who are referred to as "educable mentally retarded." They can typically acquire the basic skills taught in the first four or five grades of school. The more intelligent of this group are occasionally referred to as mildly retarded or slow learners. How should the school provide for these children? The most frequent administrative arrangement for educating mentally retarded pupils has been to place them in special classes (Reynolds, 1969). The supposed advantages of special classes are as follows. (1) The classwork can focus on the special learning problems of these children. For example, they need concrete, abstract training; they need special help in reading and computing; and their attention span is short so activities need to be changed more frequently. (2) A teacher who has had special training in the education of the retarded can be assigned to the class. (3) The learner will feel less confused, inadequate, and overwhelmed in a class composed of his intellectual peers instead of in a heterogeneous class.

Much research seems to indicate, however, that retardates in regular classes achieve better than those placed in special classes (Johnson, 1962; Reynolds, 1969). Johnson states that:

"It is indeed paradoxical that mentally handicapped children having teachers especially trained, having more money (per capita) spent on their education, and being enrolled in classes with fewer children and a program designed to provide for their unique needs, should be accomplishing the objectives of their education at the same or at a lower level than similar mentally handicapped children who have not had these advantages and have been forced to remain in the regular grades." (Johnson, 1962)

Nevertheless Johnson still argues for special classes (1962, 1967). For one thing, research studies show that personality adjustment is superior in the special classes. The retarded child is often isolated and rejected in a regular classroom (see, for example, Johnson, 1950; Johnson and Kirk, 1950). Also, Johnson feels that he can explain, and find a remedy, for the paradoxical research findings.

In the past the orientation of teacher preparation programs for the mentally handicapped has placed too much emphasis on disability instead of ability. Johnson feels realistic stress should be placed on students in special classes and that teachers must approach the education of these children with a positive instead of a negative attitude.

Dunn (1968), who for years promoted special classes, has recently suggested that special education for the *mildly* retarded is not justified. He is concerned that the label of "mentally retarded" is both inaccurate and harmful for many of the socioculturally deprived children with mild learning problems. He suggests that these children would be much better off in regular classes. Dunn, however, still believes that we need special classes for the moderately and severely retarded children. He does not suggest where the division between mild and moderate retardation is, but he would obviously suggest moving many of the kinds of children who in the 1950s and 1960s have been placed in special classes back into the regular classroom.

Kolstoe (1972) replies to the critics of programs for the mildly retarded. He reexamines much of the data on which criticisms have been based and suggests that much of the criticism is unfounded. Furthermore, he specifies that one of the *major* functions of programs for the retarded is to teach skills of employability and self-management. He cites several research studies and concludes that work-oriented special programs are superior to regular classes in terms of employment success after leaving school.

At any rate, many people now argue that too many children have inappropriately been placed in special classes (and perhaps actually given the label of mentally retarded). This is especially true of low socioeconomic minority group students (Mercer, 1971, 1972).

The recent trend is to provide special education services within the framework of a regular class. When special classes are provided, great care must go into determining who should be placed in these classes. The grouping must be flexible and continuous assessment should take place to determine whether some children can be moved out of the special class into a regular class (see Cormany, 1970). Also, if a school does provide special classes, it should make every effort to provide some integrative activities. Recess, lunch, gym, and music are examples of activities that could be integrated. A work preparatory sequence of experience should be provided to help bridge the gap between school and community living.

Special Provisions for the Gifted. There are many different ways to provide for the gifted.

Acceleration and individualized instruction, both to be discussed in subsequent sections, are possibilities. Providing special classes may be one aspect of acceleration. However, acceleration can be accomplished without special classes, and special classes need not necessarily lead to accelerations. Therefore it is appropriate to consider them separately.

Definition and Characteristics of the Gifted. Historically the definition and identification of the gifted, like that of the mentally retarded, has leaned heavily on intelligence as defined by general intelligence tests. Those individuals who score in the top 16% of the general population on intelligence tests (IQ above 116) are often referred to as "academically talented"; those in the top 2 to 3% (IQ above 130) are referred to as "gifted." Using the ratio IQ concept, a ten-year old who had an IQ of 130 would have a mental age similar to that of the average thirteen-year old. An eight-year old with an IQ of 138 would have a mental age of eleven.

There are, however, some severe limitations of using only measures of general intelligence to define (or identify) the gifted, and the concept of giftedness has been expanded. Actually the definition given by Witty (1951) more than two decades ago, while never used extensively in identifying the gifted, illustrates this broader concept. Witty said that a gifted person is one who shows consistent and extraordinary ability in any area of potentially valuable activity. Educators are increasingly emphasizing the importance of concepts such as creativity when discussing giftedness (Frierson, 1969).

Regardless of the specific definition one uses, it is generally agreed that the gifted will, as a group, tend to:

1. Learn rapidly and easily.

2. Retain what they learn.

3. Show curiosity.

4. Have good vocabularies, read well, and enjoy it.

5. Reason well, generalize, see relationships, and think logically.

6. Be healthier and more well adjusted than the average person.

7. Seek older companions.

Concern for the Gifted. Interest in providing for the gifted has not been as consistent as interest in providing for the mentally retarded. Immediately after the launching of Sputnik teacher training institutions showed considerable interest in programs for the gifted, but the enthusiasm never did pervade the public schools. And, because of the social and political developments of the 1960s and 1970s, the training institutions have themselves shifted to an interest in educating the disadvantaged. A recent comprehensive study by the U.S. Office of Education reported that only four states had adequate programs for the gifted. In a report to Congress the widespread neglect of the gifted was described as a universal increasing problem and a tragic waste of human resources (Washington Report, 1972). As Durr (1964, p. 3) points out, the general indifference that we feel toward the loser in the tortoise-hare race is similar to the indifference we have toward those students with the greatest potential for intellectual races.

Part of this indifference is due to a general feeling that the gifted do not need any special attention. The attitude that "cream will rise to the top" is a prevalent one. Actually, many gifted do excel, compared to their more average peers, without receiving instruction appropriate to their needs. But if they were challenged to the same extent as their peers, they would do much better. After the gifted get so far head in the intellectual race, they become unchallenged. Tremendous talent is often wasted. One possibility for meeting the educational needs of the gifted is through special classes.

Homogeneous Grouping. The trend among college education professors appears to be against grouping. There is considerable sentiment in favor of providing for needs of even the gifted children in the regular classroom. However, specialists in educating the gifted seem in favor of grouping, unlike specialists in educating the retarded, for example, Dunn. Even when teachers in regular heterogeneous classrooms provide challenging assignments for the gifted, "they rarely have the time to guide these efforts because of the demands of the less able students." (French, 1964, p. 183)

Much research on grouping the gifted shows it to be worthwhile. Achievement is generally improved for the gifted when they are grouped in homogeneous classes. (See, for example, Gallagher, 1960.) These achievement benefits seem to persist (Dunlap, 1955; Brumbaugh, 1955); social adjustment and attitudes often improve and snobbishness decreases (Drews, 1961), and students and parents approve (Drews, 1961; Wagner, 1960).

ACCELERATION AND RETENTION

Two other administrative procedures that attempt to help accommodate the varying needs of pupils are acceleration and retention. Nongraded schools, which may result in either acceleration or retention but are not primarily designed for such procedures, will be discussed in the next section.

Acceleration. Acceleration is any procedure that allows an individual to proceed through his formal schooling at a faster rate than usual. For gifted youngsters this is both possible and valuable. There are many reasons why this may be a valuable accomplishment. There is an increasing demand for talented and trained individuals in our society. Human time is irrecoverable. Worcester estimated that if 3% of our school children were

each accelerated 1 year "our country would have gained for its use more than 1,000,000 years of its best brains in a single generation" (1956, p. 34). Our training periods for top jobs have increased considerably. More and more individuals are attending college and graduate school. This increased training period means that a person does not become productive as early in life. Yet Lehman (1953, 1954) has shown quite conclusively that outstanding contributions come from individuals when they are still quite young. Thus it seems important that gifted people enter productive work as soon in life as possible. Acceleration is not only valuable for society, it is of value to the individual. A gifted person, if accelerated, will be less bored, will develop better work habits, and will become financially self-supporting closer to the age he reaches his physiological and psychological maturity.

There are many methods whereby an individual can be accelerated. Early school entrance, grade skipping, going to summer school, carrying a heavy load, early admission to college, and advanced placement programs are among the more popular. Acceleration by any of these methods seems, on the basis of fairly solid research evidence, to be beneficial. Yet too few schools take advantage of such procedures.

"Perhaps what is needed is some social psychologist to explore why this procedure is generally ignored in the face of such overwhelmingly favorable results." (Gallagher, 1969)

Retention. Retention, often termed nonpromotion or failure, has in the past been practiced to a considerable degree. While the policy of retention has more recently been viewed in a negative fashion and many educators have suggested it be abandoned, Glover's (1965) data suggest that the retention rate has not changed as much over the years as one might hope. The basic rationale for a retention policy is that much learning is sequential and that children must master the early material before going on to the more advanced. This is generally true. We do not want to underemphasize the importance of the learning principle discussed earlier that to teach effectively we must consider the readiness (or entry behavior) of the learner. However, to teach a child at a level appropriate to him does not mean that retention is needed. There is no necessary reason why certain materials must be taught in certain grades.

The research on nonpromotion suggests quite clearly that the effects of retention are more negative than positive. A person who repeats a grade is more likely to achieve poorer than better the second year (see, for example, Otto, 1954 and Ellinger, 1965). Not only is learning not improved, but the persons attitude toward both himself and school suffer (Gilmore, 1968). Repeaters are more apt to eventually drop out of school (Thomas and Knudsen, 1965) and exhibit poor behavior patterns while in school.

Based on such research, educators are more and more advocating a social promotion policy that requires almost automatic promotion of a child each year. This can be overdone, of course. Social promotion, regardless of achievement, is certainly not appropriate in professional schools. Nevertheless, if we are concerned about doing what is best for the child, research evidence shows quite conclusively that few children should be retained in any elementary school. (It may be beneficial to repeat a certain *course* in high school before proceeding to the next course in the sequence.)

However, for those youngsters who are younger than their classmates, or who are socially and emotionally quite immature, retention may be beneficial (Boesel, 1960; Ilg and Ames, 1965). In those few cases where retention is advisable, it should be done in kindergarten or first grade. Retention should never occur without first talking to the parents (and perhaps the child) about their attitudes toward such a procedure.

In conclusion, retention is certainly one of the least effective ways to accommodate individual differences. It should never be used unless we have reason to believe that for some reason the student will do better the next time around.

NONGRADED PLANS

Ability grouping, acceleration, and retention have been suggested as administrative procedures that may result in more effective provisions for individual differences. Another, presently more popular plan is to use nongraded classes. Nongraded classes can result in either acceleration or retention, but that is not their primary purpose.

In 1955, Goodlad published an article in the *NEA Journal* entitled "Ungrading the Elementary Grades." Since the 1955 article, and especially following the publication of a book by Goodlad and Anderson (1960), much has been written about the nongraded school. More and more lower elementary schools have set up nongraded systems. Some high schools have also implemented the idea (Brown, 1963).

Basically the nongraded plan is an attempt to (1) do away with grade designations and (2) provide learning activities at an appropriate level of difficulty for each individual. Rollins points out that "truly nongraded schools seek ultimately to abolish any kind of grouping at all." (1968, p. 25) Thus, ungraded classrooms as a concept approaches individualized instruction.

Ungraded classes are found most frequently in the early elementary years. Instead of having "grades" K through 3, a school has units of work through which a child proceeds. When a child has learned what is typically covered by the end of third grade, he is placed into fourth grade. Most children would go through this ungraded primary sequence in the traditional 4 years, a few would make it in 3 years, others in 5 years. Not having to accomplish a certain amount each year allows a child to pace himself.

An advantage of the nongraded school is that it supposedly removes the stigma of failure that exists when a child spends 2 years in the same grade. However, this argument is largely vacuous. First there should be very little "repeating of grades" in the traditional graded schools. Second, if a child in an ungraded primary must spend 5 years in this ungraded program before being placed in fourth grade while all the students he started school with only need to spend 4 years in the program, it will be difficult to convince either the student or his parents that he has not been subjected to the stigma of failure.

Research on the benefits of the ungraded schools, like the research on ability grouping, is inconclusive. McLoughlin (1968), in a review of 33 studies on nongraded schools, concluded that ". . . the academic development of children probably does not suffer from attending a non-graded school. . . ." (See Webb, 1965 and Heathers, 1966 for other reviews.) The research on the emotional effects of nongraded is also equivocal.

In general, the lack of superior results in nongraded schools is interpreted not as a failure of the theory, but as a failure of the teachers in such programs to adapt their instructional methods to the plan (McLoughlin, 1972).

While the research evidence is about the same for nongraded and ability grouping, current educational writers are much more favorable to the former plan. This may be because it moves us philosophically, if not in practice, closer to the goal of individualized instruction. It is probably more consistent with our political and social values.

The popularity of an ungraded program is illustrated by the fact that Hawaii expects to have a statewide ungraded program replacing grades K to 3 by 1974. It is their hope that the program *will* permit more individualized instruction.

Classroom Provisions

None of the administrative provisions discussed can, by themselves, provide for individual differences. It is the teacher in the classroom who must meet this challenge. Teachers have to be aware of individual needs, dedicated enough to attempt to cope with them, and ingenious and energetic enough to organize their classes so that they can.

"I'm in the nongraded third grade." *(Drawing by Short & Weaver Cartoons from* Phi Delta Kappan, *1972)*

GENERAL CONSIDERATIONS

Teachers must remember several general factors when dealing with individual differences. The most important is the necessity to plan. It is not easy to meet the different needs of 30 individuals in a class. Planning must take place each day, and plans must remain flexible. The best type of classroom organization involves a combination of many procedures. Sometimes it is best to work with the whole class; at times the class should be divided into subgroups; individual tutoring is sometimes necessary. Sometimes a teacher should differentiate assignments, and class or small group projects may be appropriate.

A second important consideration is the need to know the students. If a teacher is to form subgroups on any basis (such as achievement level, common interests, or friendships), it is essential that he know the students well enough to group correctly. If differential assignments are to be made, the teacher must know who can handle which assignments. Knowledge of entry behavior, or readiness, is essential. It is not easy to know students well enough to provide for their unique needs, but it is important. In Chapter 17 we discuss several methods or techniques of evaluating that are helpful in getting to know the students.

A third point is that teachers will need to accept more noise and (apparent) confusion in a class that provides for individual differences. A classroom in which all students are doing the same thing in the same way is usually more orderly than a classroom where a variety of activities are being carried out. Teachers occasionally feel embarrassed when visitors find their classrooms in disarray, and probably too often administrators judge teaching effectiveness on the basis of neat, orderly classrooms. Neither teachers nor administrators should be concerned about noise in the classroom if that noise arises from purposeful activity. However, classrooms should not be chaotic. Students must be working toward well-defined goals, and teachers must maintain control. It is sometimes a bit more difficult to maintain control over students who are doing a variety of things. We discuss classroom discipline in Chapter 14 and, at that point, present some techniques helpful in maintaining the proper amount of control.

A fourth point is that if teachers do not work with all children at once by treating them all alike, they must promote independence in their students. Some students have trouble working without constant supervision. But if a third-grade teacher is to divide his class into four reading groups and help one group at a time, the remaining students must be able to carry on constructive work by themselves. There are two major hurdles that must be cleared for effective independent study. First, the assignments must be made sufficiently clear, and second, the students must have the prerequisite skills to work on the assignments. The first hurdle is simply a matter of effective communication. The teacher must make sure that each child knows what he is to be working on. The second hurdle is related to knowing the students (point two above). Certain skills may need to be taught to the students before they can work independently. What these skills are will vary by subject and grade level. In science it may be how to use the laboratory equipment. In history it may be how to use the library. In shop it may be how to use an arc welder. It is the teacher's responsibility to determine whether or not a student has the necessary background to proceed independently before giving him this freedom.

DIFFERENTIATING ASSIGNMENTS AND OBJECTIVES

We have discussed earlier the necessity for both conformity and diversity in education.

Most teachers have a minimal set of objectives that they hope all their students will reach. By the end of third grade, perhaps, a teacher may hope that all students can do cursive writing, that they can add and subtract two-digit numbers, that they can read at some minimal level, and so on. Students should continue working toward these goals until they reach them. But what does one do with the students who reach these goals early in the year? Basically there are two avenues open: acceleration or enrichment.

When accelerated a pupil moves further and further ahead of his class, but learns the same subject matter that they will be covering later. Classroom acceleration is based on the same principle as administrative acceleration, discussed earlier. This procedure is effective if teachers in all the grades in a school practice it. Students can then eventually be far enough ahead to skip a grade, but will not have to skip any of the subject matter. Successful classroom acceleration depends on each teacher knowing the curriculum of the grades above the one he is teaching; teachers generally do not have this knowledge.

In enrichment procedures the faster learners do not just proceed in the same direction that the slower learners will travel later. Instead new activities that broaden the pupil's education are provided. There are two general types of enrichment: "same area" enrichment and "other area" enrichment. In "same area" enrichment the added assignments or activities come from the same subject matter area, for example, doing an in-depth study on the economic conditions of the South during the Civil War when the rest of the students simply learn about some of the military battles. In "other area" enrichment the added activity does not have to be related to the regular school program. For example, a student who already has learned what the teacher expects him to know about the Civil War may be allowed to do library research on any topic that interests him. With either enrichment procedure the teacher should attempt to make sure that the assignment is of interest to the pupil and that it challenges his imagination and ingenuity.

Most educators seem to prefer classroom enrichment to classroom acceleration (Thomas and Thomas, 1965). Success is not as dependent on cooperation among teachers across grade levels. In choosing appropriate activities as enrichment the teacher must keep in mind what objectives or goals are to be met and whether the activity is really enrichment or whether it will be in the child's curriculum at a higher grade.

WITHIN-CLASS GROUPING

A common procedure for dealing with individual differences is *within*-class grouping. Many of you are probably familiar with the groups of robins, bluebirds, and so on, that elementary teachers devise. Unlike grouping into homogeneous classes, there is little professional criticism of within-class grouping. Students generally are aware of the levels of the various groups, but the degree of isolation by levels is considerably less than what occurs in homogeneous classroom grouping. (There is nothing wrong with calling the top group of readers "robins" if one wishes. But the name does not obscure the level. Students soon figure out the level of each group of birds!)

The *major* advantage of within-class grouping over homogeneous classroom grouping is that the within-class groups can be very flexible. The groups should vary depending on the purpose of instruction, the interests of the children, and so forth. Thus, the groups should likely be of somewhat different composition for reading, science, mathematics, social studies, art, and music. Furthermore, depending on the topic, the groups may be formulated on quite different bases from week to week. This flexibility allows for almost complete heterogeneity in the good sense that a student is likely, at some time or another, to be grouped with every other student. The flexibility also assures some homogeneity on a particular dimension relevant to a particular instructional strategy or goal. Thus, within-class grouping is generally effective. A disadvantage is that like all methods of classroom provisions for individual differences, it demands planning and hard work for the teacher.

		Objectives	
		School determined	Learner selected
Media or method	School determined	Type A Individually diagnosed and prescribed	Type C Personalized
	Learner selected	Type B Self-directed	Type D Independent study

Figure 11-2.
Types of individualized instruction.

Individualized Instruction

The ultimate in providing for individual differences is to provide completely *individualized instruction*. Under more traditional approaches, such as those covered in the previous section, this goal is almost impossible to obtain. Advocates of newer procedures, such as programmed instruction, maintain that such programs show great promise in individualizing instruction. Perhaps we should look at just what individualized instruction really means. *Individualized instruction consists of planning the curriculum and conducting the instructional techniques to meet the unique needs of each student.* Individualized instruction does not mean that one must teach students individually, that students must study in isolation, or that the study will be without supervision. Instead, it means that curriculum and instructional techniques will be student oriented and individually tailored to meet the unique needs of each student. [Shane (1970) prefers the term *personalized* curriculum as being a more descriptive term.]

One cannot refer to individualized instruction as a single uniform procedure. Although contemporary programs do have many aspects in common, they also differ considerably from each other. Edling speaks of four general types of individualized instruction as illustrated in Figure 11-2. The two basic issues are who determines the instructional objectives and how they should be taught. In Type A the school determines the objectives for each student and the manner in which he is to attain them. In Type B the objectives are set by the school, but the learner can choose his own method of study. In Type C the learner selects his own objectives, but the school determines the method of study. In Type D the learner selects both the objectives and the manner in which he is to attain them. Of course, even for a single subject matter area at a given grade level, some combination of all four of these types might exist. Types A and B are most often found in required subjects, while Types C and D more often occur in elective courses. The most frequent type of program probably is Type A where both the objectives and media are determined by the school. Often the objectives and media—although school determined—will differ for different children. At other times the objectives will be constant for all learners (e.g., in the basic skill areas in early elementary school), but the means of reaching the objectives will vary. Many existing programs actually use the same media for all students. But, to be considered an individualized program, *at least* the material must be *individually paced* so that each child is working at his own speed.

Regardless of the particular type of individualized instruction program, a teacher's job ideally involves doing (or assisting the pupil in doing) several basic tasks (Heathers, 1971).

1. Deciding on and specifying in behavioral terminology the desired objectives.

2. Assessing the extent to which the student already has mastered the objectives.

3. Assessing the student's learning characteristics (or learning styles) to determine the best media for achieving the objectives.

4. Using the assessment data mentioned in points 2 and 3 above to develop a specific plan with the student.

5. Monitoring the pupil's progress, assessing his mastery of the tasks, and determining whether the student is ready for further tasks.

As can be seen, an individualized program demands considerable diagnostic and evaluative skills on the part of a teacher. Determining and specifying objectives, measuring present student inputs (including both level of achievement on the objectives and data on learning styles), and continually monitoring each of 25 to 40 pupils' progress in order to guide the subsequent learning tasks is a demanding job. The fact that diagnosis and evaluation are so necessary and yet so demanding for a truly individualized instruction program accounts for the attention given to them in many recently developed programs.

Although most individualized instruction programs are still at a developmental stage, and although there are more students being taught in groups than by truly individualized approaches, we would like to discuss several programs for individualized instruction.

PROGRAMMED INSTRUCTION

Using programmed materials and the principles of programmed instruction is one of the newer and more publicized ways of providing for individual differences. Actually "programmed" is really a very general term for many different approaches to individualizing instruction. The programmed materials may be presented by texts or by machines, including computers. Chapter 8 presented some examples and explanations of programs.

Lindvall and Bolvin (1967) and Thomas and Thomas (1965) have listed some ways that programs have been used in schools. They can be effectively used as (1) basic texts, (2) enrichment work, (3) remedial work, and (4) outside assignments. In all of these uses the programmed materials do help in individualizing instruction. Unfortunately their primary use has probably been as basic texts, and often the only individualization has been in terms of *rate*. Students all work at the same time, all start at the beginning of the same program regardless of past achievements, all use the same media, and all proceed to master the same objectives.

If different programs are used for different students, as would be done in the enrichment, remedial, and outside assignment uses, more individualization is possible.

Lindvall and Bolvin (1967) conclude that the reason programmed instruction has failed to make its potential impact on the schools is because the schools have tended to adopt programmed materials instead of the *principles* of programmed instruction. If separate programs are not incorporated into the on-going instructional sequence, much of their total effectiveness will be lost. For example, if one student can complete a program in 10 hours and it takes another student 40 hours, one must know what to do with the first student while the slowest finishes the program. Thus, it would be preferable to program the *entire school curriculum*. We will discuss a program that attempts to do that, but first we will discuss the general idea of mastery learning.

MASTERY LEARNING

Mastery learning is being strongly advocated as "one of the most powerful ideas beginning to shape educational views and practices." (Block, 1971, p. iii) The idea of mastery learning is certainly not new (see Washburne, 1922; Morrison, 1926), but it has been recently revitalized following the publication of a paper by Carroll (1963) entitled "A Model of School Learning." Essentially the model suggests that the degree of learning is a function of the time the student spends on the material divided by the time needed. More precisely Carroll suggested that degree of learning is some function of the time allowed and the perseverance of the student divided by the student's aptitude for the task, his ability to understand the instruction, and the quality of instruction.

Bloom (1968) agrees with the basics of the model and suggests that the degree of learning required should be fixed at some "mastery" level and that the instructional variables should be manipulated so that all (or almost all) students achieve mastery. Bloom states that "Most students (perhaps over 90 percent) can master what we have to teach them." (1968, p. 1) If the model is correct and if people should all persevere until they have "mastered" the material, then the mastery learning model of instruction should be employed—and mastery testing must be used to determine whether mastery has occurred.

Tentative evidence (Block, 1971) suggests that in many subject matter areas students can all achieve some (often arbitrarily) defined level of mastery. Carroll (1971, p. 31), however, points out that if the task is very difficult, or if it depends on special aptitudes, there may be a number of students who never make it. Becoming a 4-minute miler and a concert pianist are examples.

Excluding the extreme 5% of the students the time ratio between slower and faster students is about 6 to 1, although Bloom et al. (1971, p. 51) suggest this may be reduced to about 3 to 1. Glaser (1968, p. 28) reported that after 3 years of individually prescribed instruction (see the next section) in mathematics, one student had covered 73 units while another had covered only 13 units. Whether or not it is educationally worthwhile to have a student persist for 3 to 6 days, weeks, or years on a task others can complete in 1 day, week, or year is debatable. He probably should for those few basic skills that are essential for survival and that must be achieved before further hierarchical skills can be acquired. For other things we attempt to teach in school—such as understanding of modern literature—it is unlikely that a mastery model should be employed. There is even some doubt if it would work for such a subject. As both Block (1971, p. 66) and Bloom (1971, p. 33) point out, mastery learning strategies are most effective for closed subjects (those whose content has not changed for some time) and those that emphasize convergent instead of divergent thinking. The implications for education of this admission by mastery advocates are not always fully appreciated. However, Cronbach (1971, p. 52), in a reaction to one of Bloom's mastery learning papers, brings the issue into sharp focus.

"I find the concept of mastery severely limiting, and in trying to find out where my distress lies, I finally focused on one word in the Bloom paper: he states that mastery learning is *closed*. Training is closed. In education the problems are open."

• • •

"I see educational development as continuous and open-ended. 'Mastery' seems to imply that at some point we get to the end of what is to be taught." (Cronbach, 1971, pp. 52-53)

Mastery Learning and Grades. Bloom begins his 1968 paper with the statement that "Each teacher begins a new term with the expectation that about a third of his students will adequately learn what he has to teach." As his paper proceeds it is apparent that he bases this statement on the fact that if a teacher graded on a normal curve (which many do not), about 33% would receive As or Bs. He suggests that "we proceed in our teaching as though only the minority of our students should be able to learn what we have to teach." What Bloom is doing, of course, is to attach his own absolute standards of interpretation to a normative reporting system. If a teacher gave a student a C because he (the teacher) was using a normative system and because the student was average (i.e., in comparison to others, he was close to the middle), the grade of C in no way indicates inadequate performance. The symbols A to F can obviously take on any meaning a person assigns them. But if a teacher assigns them on a relative basis, it is hardly appropriate for someone else to interpret them on an absolute basis. We do not doubt that if those who score below a normative based A were to continue studying the course material most of them could, in time, achieve as well as the A students did originally. But we wonder why average performance should be interpreted as inadequate by a student, teacher, or educational psychologist, or why mastery should, as Bloom suggests, be considered identical to an A grade. One may well want students to

"master" a certain amount of material before being allowed to advance to a higher unit or course. Whether one labels this mastery as an A or a D is irrelevant as long as the meaning is made clear. We will talk more about this point in the section on grading (Chapter 16).

Mastery Learning and Self-Concept. With regard to self-concept and mental health Bloom et al. (1971, p. 56) feel that "Mastery learning can be one of the more powerful sources of mental health. We are convinced that many of the neurotic symptoms displayed by high school and college students are exacerbated by painful and frustrating experiences in school learning. If 90 percent of the students are given positive indications of adequacy in learning, one might expect them to need less and less in the way of emotional therapy and psychological help. Contrarily, frequent indications of failure and learning inadequacy are bound to be accompanied by increased self-doubt in the student."

Leaving off the first sentence of the above quotation we are inclined to agree (although no good evidence exists). The question remains, however, whether the mastery learning approach will decrease a student's painful and frustrating experiences in school learning or increase the positive indications of adequacy in learning. We think that the student who is forced to spend 10 weeks on a unit that another student finished in 2 weeks will perceive that experience to be more painful and that he will have experienced more indications of failure and inadequacy than if we had assigned him a grade of "C" or "D" after the first 2 weeks. There is some tentative evidence that the mastery approach *lowers* self-concepts (Newsnotes, 1972, p. 140).

These last few paragraphs have not been written to denigrate the mastery learning approach. The mastery learning-testing model is very useful for some situations. But it is probably not such an all-pervasive good that some of its proselytizers would suggest.

THE INDIVIDUALLY PRESCRIBED INSTRUCTION PROGRAM: A MASTERY LEARNING APPROACH

In 1964, the Learning Research and Development Center at the University of Pittsburgh and the Baldwin-Whitehall School District initiated a program for individualized instruction in the elementary school. This program has been given the name Individually Prescribed Instruction (IPI). IPI is conducted in grades K through 6 in reading, arithmetic, science, handwriting, and spelling. The basic principles of programmed instruction were used in developing the IPI curriculum. Objectives were written in terms of desired pupil behaviors, organized into areas and levels, and sequenced for effective pupil progress; materials were such that pupils could work independently, without constant teacher supervision; students begin at an appropriate level and progress at their own rate, and immediate feedback is provided. The pupil evaluation involves four types of instruments: placement tests, pretests, curriculum-embedded tests, and posttests.

A flow chart of the steps in the cycle for evaluating and monitoring pupil progress in the IPI program is shown in Figure 11-3.

Placement tests are administered at the beginning of the school year and provide a general profile of pupil performance over many units of work. These placement tests have been constructed for each level of the curriculum and would be similar to standardized achievement tests, only they are suited to the particular objectives of the IPI curriculum. A pupil is considered to have achieved proficiency on any unit in which he scores 80% or better. This criterion level is admittedly arbitrary (Lindvall and Cox, 1970, p. 17) and serves only as a guideline for a teacher's decision.

As a result of placement testing, intra-individual differences will appear. Within a placement test for a given level a student may master some areas and not others. In order to further place an individual, certain sections of the next higher or lower level placement tests will be administered. Table 11-2 shows some hypothetical results of a mathematics placement test. A fourth-grade pupil was administered level C and was found to be proficient in the first four areas, but lacked complete proficiency in the other areas. Thus the teacher decided to give the sections on areas 1 to 6 in the level D test (areas 5 and 6 had no sections in the level C placement test). The student showed proficiency in areas 3 and 4 of the level D placement test, so he was given the level E placement test on these two sections. Since he did not show proficiency at this level, the placement testing was completed. Now the teacher should administer the pretests for level C for areas 7 to 12, level D pretests for areas 1, 2, 5, and 6, and level E pretests for areas 3 and 4.

The *pretests* are an extension of the placement tests for each specific unit in the curriculum. The items on a unit pretest measure achievement on each of the skills in that unit. There are more items per skill on the pretests than on the placement tests, and therefore can be more *diagnostic* in determining pupil strengths and weaknesses. If the pupil achieves proficiency (85% or above) in *every skill* on the pretest, he is given the pretest for the next unit. If not, he is assigned work in those skills where he scored below 85%. Thus a student may only be asked to study 1 or 2 skills within a unit.

These pretests only indicate where a pupil is deficient, not which instructional procedures would be best. Ideally, other data, such as measures of general scholastic apti-

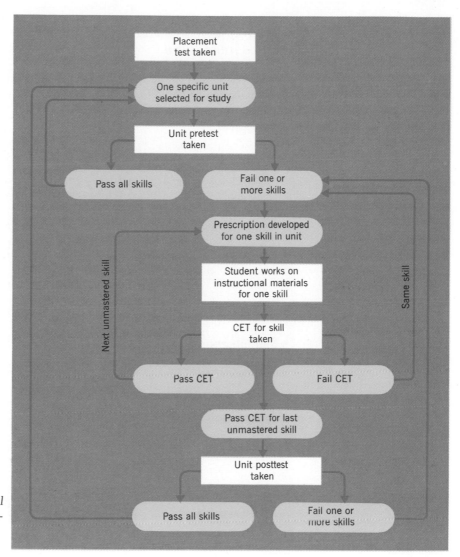

Figure 11-3.
(Reprinted from Lindvall
and Cox, 1969, with per-
mission of the authors
and publishers.)

tude, reading level, interests, and learning styles, would help determine which method would be utilized in the instructional process. The IPI program has not yet developed very far along these lines.

A *curriculum-embedded test* (CET) is composed of two parts. The first is a short test used in monitoring the pupil's progress toward a particular objective. The second part of the CET measures the student's performance on the very next objective. In a sense, it is a very short pretest designed to help assess the transfer and generalizability of skill from one objective to another. These CET's are a part of the instructional materials and appear as a summary of a specific task.

Unit *posttests* are also given to monitor pupil progress. These posttests are usually

Table 11-2
An Example of IPI Mathematics Placement Test Scores for a Fourth-Grade Pupil.

(Adapted from C. M. Lindvall and Richard C. Cox, THE IPI EVALUATION PROGRAM, AERA Monograph Series on Curriculum Evaluation, No. 5, © 1970 by Rand McNally and Company, Chicago, p. 18. Reprinted by permission of Rand McNally College Publishing Company.)

Area	Level C		Level D		Level E	
	% Score	Teacher Decision	% Score	Teacher Decision	% Score	Teacher Decision
1. Numeration	100	Proficiency	60	Give pretest		
2. Place value	80	Proficiency	40	Give pretest		
3. Addition	100	Proficiency	100	Proficiency	60	Give pretest
4. Subtraction	80	Proficiency	80	Proficiency	40	Give pretest
5. Multiplication			40	Give pretest		
6. Division			40	Give pretest		
7. Combination of processes	60	Give pretest				
8. Fractions	60	Give pretest				
9. Money	60	Give pretest				
10. Time	33	Give pretest				
11. Systems of measurement	60	Give pretest				
12. Geometry	60	Give pretest				

alternate forms of the pretests and help to determine whether the student is ready for the next unit of work. The criterion for proficiency is the same as on the pretests—85% or better on each skill.

IPI has expanded far beyond the single school district using it in 1964. In the 1969-1970 school year 164 schools had adopted IPI and more than 1000 school districts had applied for the program (NewsFront, 1969). Recently the mathematics portion of the program has become commercially available.

The popularity of IPI is probably deserved. It is based on sound principles of learning. The major weakness is, as mentioned previously, that we simply do not know enough about how individual differences and instructional procedures interact to enable us to construct really effective differential programs. Consequently students are all asked to learn the same objectives (usually by the same technique), only varying in rate of learning. A second problem related to IPI-type procedures is that a heavy demand is placed on accurate and continuous evaluative procedures. One of the frequently mentioned advantages is that IPI eliminates the stigma of failure. We are doubtful that this is true. A student who is on Level III materials when his age peers are on Level VI materials will probably be a more conspicuous "failure" than if he were socially promoted in a graded system. IPI, like other such programs, uses the computer to help in the storage and reporting of information on pupil progress. Two other similar programs are Comprehensive Achievement Monitoring (CAM) (IPI Working Paper 20, 1971; IPI Working Paper 21, 1971) and the Program for Learning in Accordance with Needs (PLAN) (Flanagan, 1971).

CONCLUDING STATEMENT

Individualized instruction is increasing in American education. While there are many methods of individualizing instruction the most prevalent type of program is where both the objectives and media are determined by the school (Type A in Figure 11-2). While there can be considerable variation in these programs, they all demand that increased attention be paid to the diagnosis and evaluation of student progress. All programs should require extensive pretesting to determine the entry behavior of an individual both with respect to subject matter achievement and

styles of learning. Various procedures should be established to help the teacher-student team choose appropriate objectives and learning strategies. There should be frequent testing or monitoring of a pupil's progress while in a program, and a posttest to determine final achievement. Most programs place great emphasis on detailed objectives and frequent feedback to students regarding their progress. Computer facilities are often used to assist in collecting, analyzing, storing, and disseminating information. Usually decision rules are established to assist in using the test data. The tasks of the teacher are much harder in individualized instruction and many, at least initially, are opposed to the programs. Some, in fact, are almost incapable—either because of psychological variables or lack of training—of handling such programs. One more important aspect of individual differences is too little discussed and too often ignored: the individual differences of teachers. We will now turn to a brief discussion of that topic.

INDIVIDUAL DIFFERENCES IN TEACHERS

The previous sections of this chapter have emphasized the individual differences of students. We hoped to make you sensitive to these differences. We have referenced numerous articles and books that deal with this topic. Almost every basic text in educational psychology devotes considerable space to the topic of individual differences among students. Unfortunately very few deal with the topic of individual differences among teachers. As Jackson (1962, p. 76) points out:

"Given this interest in the individuality of children and its meaning for education, it is somewhat surprising to find the lack of a corresponding concern for the individuality of teachers. If we have advanced in our educational thought to a position where we view children as individuals, each calling for slightly different educational action, we continue, nonetheless, to think of teachers as teachers, each the intellectual and psychological equivalent of the other. Worse than this, in our search for the method of teaching or the method of handling individual differences, we imply that the personal characteristics of teachers are largely irrelevant to the educational decisions that determine how children should be taught."

It is, of course, nonsensical to ignore the individual differences among teachers. They exist, and we should recognize them. Some teachers, for example, can just snap their fingers or shake their head and maintain good control in the classroom. Others may shout, cajole, and/or threaten, and still not have any control. Some can hold a class spellbound during the exposition of new material but be quite maladroit in the handling of intimate discussion groups. Others have the opposite types of skills. Educators have probably long been aware of such differences, and certainly recognize the truth when it is pointed out to them. Yet little has been done about taking these differences into account when assigning teachers either *tasks* or *students*. Some teachers and some tasks just do not mix. Likewise, some teachers and some students do not mix.

But we do not wish to leave you with the impression that absolutely nothing has been done in adapting to teacher differences. In team teaching, for example, attempts are made to utilize the special talents of each teacher by giving them differential assignments on the team, thus matching tasks and teachers to some extent. Teachers are also matched to some extent with pupils. Teachers of the gifted should (and typically do) have different types of training, skills, and temperament than teachers of the retarded. Those who teach in the affluent suburbs are most likely different from those who teach in the rural areas or the inner cities.

Thelen (1967) has been exploring the concept of classroom grouping for teachability. All teachers find some students more "teachable" than others. However, they do not all agree on which particular students are most teachable. Each teacher has his own way of teaching, and he will be most successful if his classes are composed of students who conform to his definition of teachability. As Thelen points out, "Certain combinations of student and teacher are simply destructive, with each playing on the other's anxieties or weaknesses . . . ." (1967, p. 34) While this should be obvious, schools have not done much with teachability grouping. Some of the obstacles have been pointed out by Thelen. The first is profound hypocrisy. There is almost an "official belief" that all teachers should be effective with all students. A second obstacle is that many educators seem to believe that there is only *one* right way to teach. Some other obstacles are practical. For example, there is no point in talking about matching students and teachers in small schools where there is only one teacher of some subjects.

You, as a prospective teacher, may someday find it necessary to point out to your principal that individual differences exist in teachers as well as in pupils, and that this can be used to advantage in a school instead of being considered an unfortunate fact of life. You can best provide for the individual differences (both inter- and intra-) of the pupils in your school building if you are aware of your own strengths and weaknesses (intraindividual differences) and how these compliment the talents of other teachers in the building (interindividual differences).

Summary

1. Individuals are born with biological differences.

2. The variability among individuals increase as they grow older.

3. Excluding the 2% at each extreme of the distribution, the range of achievement is about two thirds of the chronological age of the usual student at the grade level under consideration.

4. The position an individual teacher takes with respect to differing social philosophies will dictate, in part, whether that teacher will primarily value diversity or conformity.

5. Definitions of intelligence generally fall into one or more of three categories: the capacity to (1) think abstractly, (2) learn, or (3) integrate new experiences and adapt to new situations.

6. Most psychologists adopt the position that while there are specific factors of intellect, there is also a general factor.

7. Intelligence test scores are reasonably stable after age five, but individuals can and do change, and decisions about individuals should not be based on the results of a single test.

8. Intraindividual differences exist and are important to keep in mind when considering such educational procedures as grouping.

9. One can adapt education to individual differences by modifying the educational goals or the instructional treatment.

10. No type of school organization can provide for all the types and ranges of learner variability. Within any method of organization teachers must also work with individual learners.

11. The empirical research on the efficacy of homogeneous ability grouping is inconclusive and conflicting.

12. A recent trend is to reduce the number of children placed in special classes for the retarded.

13. Most research on grouping the gifted shows that it is worthwhile.

14. Acceleration is any procedure that allows an individual to proceed through his formal schooling at a faster rate than usual.

15. Research evidence suggests that judicious acceleration procedures are worthwhile. Too few schools take advantage of such procedures.

16. Research suggests that the effects of retention are generally more negative than positive.

17. Ungraded classes do away with grade designations and attempt to provide learning activities at an appropriate level of difficulty for each individual.

18. Research on the benefits of the ungraded schools, like the research on ability grouping, is inconclusive.

19. In providing for individual differences in the classroom, teachers must keep in mind the need to (1) plan, (2) know the students, (3) accept more noise, and (4) promote independence.

20. There are two general types of enrichment: "same area" and "other area." Both can be used effectively.

21. The ultimate in providing for individual differences is to provide completely individualized instruction.

22. Programmed instruction can assist in the individualization of instruction.

23. The mastery learning model suggests that degree of learning is a function of the time spent on the task. The mastery learning model is useful for some types of learning, but probably not for others.

24. Various programs designed for the individualization of instruction are being developed.

25. The individual differences in teachers should be considered when assigning teachers either tasks or students.

26. Team teaching is one example of an effort to match teachers to tasks.

27. Classroom grouping for teachability is an example of matching teachers with pupils.

PART IV
CLASSROOM DYNAMICS

CHAPTER 12
Social-Psychological Aspects of Education

"Don't be such an induvidualist, Cosgrave. If you look different from the rest of us, no one will know you're a nonconformist." *(Drawing by Tony Saltzman)*

Characteristics of School Life: The Hidden Curriculum
Classroom Climate and Leadership Style
Peer Relations and the School
Prejudice and Education
Changing the Schools

In our society most youngsters between the ages of five and eighteen spend a large portion of their waking hours in the role of "student" in a place provided by society called a "school" where they are expected to become educated under the guidance of "teachers" directed by "administrators." (Getzels, 1965) The student's response to the school is the result of the interaction between his own individual personality patterns and his assigned role as student in a complex organizational structure. In Chapter 4 we examined how individual differences in student personality can influence school adjustment. In this chapter we will take a closer look at selected aspects of educational institutions. Particular attention will be paid to the hidden curriculum, the authority structure, peer group influences, racial prejudice, and school change.

OBJECTIVES FOR CHAPTER 12

1. Give examples illustrating how "the hidden curriculum" relates to the student's adjustment to school.
2. Discuss the significance of authoritarian, democratic, and laissez-faire climates for classroom achievement and morale.
3. Compare the philosophies and practices of Summerhillian free schools, parent cooperatives, and progressive public schools, and evaluate the outcomes associated with attendance at each.
4. Identify the problems still confronting free schools.
5. Describe the major characteristics of peer relationships during the preschool years, middle childhood, and the adolescent

period, and explain the educational significance of peer group relations as they pertain to school size, peer group norms, cross-age programs, and teacher power.

6. Identify three origins of prejudice and the effects of prejudice on minority and majority youth.
7. Evaluate the two main ways in which schools attempt to change racial attitudes.
8. Identify the major problems encountered and ways used in efforts to change schools.

CHARACTERISTICS OF SCHOOL LIFE: THE HIDDEN CURRICULUM

Much of the material in this section can be summarized by stating that every school has two curriculums that the student must cope with and master. The one that educators have most often studied might be designated the "official" curriculum. Its content consists of the 3 R's and all of the other courses for which study guides, workbooks, and teaching materials are produced. Most curriculum reform has centered about this clearly visible official academic curriculum.

The other curriculum is often referred to as the "hidden" or "unstudied" curriculum because it has received scant attention from educators. This hidden or organizational curriculum also has its 3 R's, but its content consists of rules, regulations, and routines that students must learn if they are to make a successful adaptation to the social institution called the school.[1]

Students are rewarded for their performance in both curriculums. Judging from the way in which rewards and punishments are dispensed, one sometimes gets the impression that good behavior is more important than good work. As long as one is a "model" student, he will get by. If one tries hard and keeps his nose to the grindstone, he will be promoted at the end of the year, even though his academic accomplishments might be minimal. Neatness, punctuality, effort, and courtesy pay off for students, as do other forms of institutional conformity. Failure to comply with institutional expectations (for example, making too much noise or pushing in line) are apt to draw the teacher's displeasure. Regrettably, the personal qualities that play an essential role in intellectual mastery (probing, exploring, challenging) are not of the same order as those that characterize institutional conformity (passivity, docility, submission). Although the attributes underlying individual expression and compliance with the wishes of others seem incompatible at face value, some students are apparently able to strike a reasonable balance between them. How often this occurs and under what circumstances, no one seems to know. Let us turn at this point to a discussion of various features of the hidden curriculum that the student must master if he is to make his way in school.

Crowded Conditions

Classrooms are congested places. Typically, 30 students occupy a classroom that takes up less space than that of an average family.

[1] The reader who is interested in reading further about the hidden curriculum is referred to Phil Jackson's *Life In The Classroom* (1968), which provides the basis for much of the material presented in this section.

Teachers and materials are few in relation to the number of students who want them. Because of these ecological conditions in the classroom, sharing teacher attention and materials becomes an essential activity. Furthermore, some students demand more of the teacher's time and attention, leaving less for other students. Student interruptions and environmental limitations (e.g., not being able to check out a library book because the card is missing) are also common, petty annoyances of the school day. Because of the heavy social traffic, the teacher must direct a great deal of her energy to managing the flow of classroom activity instead of to instruction.

Although most boys adjust to school expectations, it is the boys, not girls, who bear the brunt of the teachers' control messages. Boys are designed by the larger culture to be independent, but classrooms are not well designed for exploration of private interests and active pursuits. As a consequence, boys arc ill prepared for the demands of communal school life. Individual desires, because of the crowded conditions, are frequently thwarted. Individuality, under these congested arrangements, is apt to be given a relatively low priority. In one traditional nursery school, the number of episodes interfering with the natural pursuit of the students' desires was estimated to be 64,000 per 97 students over the course of a full year (Jackson and Wolfson, 1968)! Just as childhood is a time of many skinned knees, Jackson and Wolfson note, it is also a time of many skinned psyches. Whether or not they leave scars, they are a significant part of the "stuff" that makes a young student's life what it is. Silberman (1971) makes the interesting observation that classrooms provide less freedom of movement, less personalized facilities, and more distraction than do most adult work settings. Learning to share is a valuable experience, but psychological privacy leading to individual growth is also desirable, and perhaps

even more difficult to achieve in a surrounding with too many people.

Delay, Denial, and Interruption

Three of the most noticeable features of classroom life are delay, denial, and interruption—all of which stem in part from the crowded conditions in the classroom. Life in the classroom is much like life in the military in the sense that much of one's time is spent waiting. Students often wait in line for recess, for lunch, and for dismissal. They also wait to have their papers inspected. Bright students often have to wait for the slow students. Teacher permission must be awaited before talking, reciting, getting a book, and the like. Students are forced to prepare for a future that is several years away. No one knows for sure how much of the student's time is spent in neutral. Learning to wait is one of the adjustments one must make upon entry into school.

Denial is also commonplace in school. It is impossible for everyone's request to be met or voice to be heard. Students are asked to leave an activity because the next activity has to begin on time. Foregoing their desires is something youngsters have to become accustomed to at school.

Interruptions come at many times during the school day. Students disturb other students. Teachers interrupt students. Time and time again the student must redirect his attention to his studies following petty interruptions. Perhaps this is an inevitable price one has to pay in crowded classrooms.

Patience, Resignation, and Masquerade

What is the significance of delay, denial, and interruption? Examining the strategies needed to cope with these mundane features of institutional life is helpful in answering this question. One common strategy is that of developing patience. The development of patience can facilitate one's adjustment to school and other aspects of life.

If carried too far, however, it can lead to a state of resignation that is tantamount to psychological surrender—an abandonment of one's own desires and plans. To react calmly to daily frustrations can be healthy, but to disengage one's feelings from his school work is not consistent with the development of intellectual curiosity.

The use of masquerade is also a widespread reaction to the institutional constraints of delay, denial, and interruption. Deciding whether a student is patient or resigned can sometimes be difficult, since students are adept at the business of faking involvement. Students quickly learn to nod their heads in agreement at the proper times, to disguise their ignorance, and to verbalize concepts on the fringes of their knowledge. Sizing up teachers and conning them can become more important than genuine intellectual mastery.

Evaluation

Evaluation is another feature of institutional life to which the student must become accustomed. Prior to school entrance, the youngster is customarily granted acceptance simply because he is a member of the family. Once he enters school, however, he is judged to a much greater degree on the basis of his academic accomplishments, and he must learn to cope with a constant spirit of evaluation. Few other settings evaluate an individual during the course of his life as often as the school does. Although the child is evaluated at home, in the community, and on the playground, his taking of tests is confined primarily to the school setting and his progress

becomes a semipublic record.

The student is evaluated not only by his teacher and his peers; he learns to evaluate himself. Some of the judgments about him, he learns, are made openly, while other judgments are made privately or are rarely given him (for example, his IQ score). Evaluation is not confined to scholastic gains, but spills over to include appraisal of one's adjustment to institutional expectancies and personal qualities—two seemingly peripheral aspects of the student's progress.

How does the student adjust to evaluation? Several strategies are noteworthy. The first is to behave in a fashion that enhances the likelihood of reward and reduces the probability of punishment. The second involves the publicizing of favorable evaluations and the concealing of unfavorable ones. Saving face can become more important than actual mastery. The third consists of trying to win acceptance and approbation from peers and teachers at the same time. In other words, one has to learn to be a good student and a good guy, too. Still another way of coping with evaluations entails devaluing appraisals. The uninvolved student "plays it cool" by becoming neither upset by failure nor elated over success. Getting by instead of getting ahead becomes the goal.

Power Relationships

Another aspect of classroom life to which the students must become habituated lies in the difference in power between himself and teachers. Students are to be passive, compliant, and pleasant. They are told where to sit and how to walk, talk, and dress. They are told how much homework to do and when it is to be completed. The teacher is the only person in the classroom who is given the responsibility and power to order students. Indeed, the organizational life of most public schools is dominated by a concern with controlling students (Johnson, 1971). Regrettably, rules often serve the purpose of managerial efficiency instead of student needs.

The hypothesis that many students view themselves as helpless recipients of meaningless and arbitrary orders is given support in a study involving almost 7000 high school students in the greater New York and Philadelphia areas (DeCecco, 1972). The statements of two thirds of the students indicated very clearly that they viewed themselves as victims of high-handed orders, autocratically enforced, and that their situation would improve only with their involvement in rule making. Matters of school governance and individual rights accounted for more than 50% of incidents involving institutional conflicts. These students were far more concerned with the lack of choices in their daily school experiences than they were concerned about racial and political issues. Moreover, in less than one fifth of the incidents cited did the students report having had any voice in the resolution of the problem. More than 90% of students believed that tensions escalated because of the way school authorities attempted to terminate conflict in the schools. When educators arranged for students to negotiate from positions of equality, however, tensions were reduced.

The above study raises a number of interesting points. First, and perhaps most obvious, school authorities must recognize that the *official* powerlessness of students has become an important source of institutional conflict. While students do have influence, they are not legitimately invested with power. Second, it is apparent that school authorities have few skills in coping with student activism. The strategies often employed—glossing over the issues, distorting issues, bringing in police—seldom lead to a constructive use of conflict that could promote both personal and organizational growth and development. Training in how to cope effectively and constructively with student-school conflicts is desperately needed. Third, students also need help in developing their negotiating skills. At the negotiating table, they often take extreme positions, present conflicting demands, refuse to compromise, and are duped by token concessions (Johnson, 1971). While students have learned how to escalate situations, they have failed to use conflict constructively. Finally, it must be realized that giving students a say in the decision-making process will not undermine the school as an institution. To the contrary, the school cannot improve or maintain itself as a viable organization without the students' commitment to the educational program. There is a growing body of evidence suggesting that commitment to the school program will result from participation and involvement in the planning and carrying out of the program. As Johnson (1971) comments, "People enjoy, affirm, and are committed to activities they make for themselves; they resist activities imposed upon them by others. While sharing decision-making power with students may increase the short-term complexities of planning a viable educational program, in the long run it should improve the school's functioning."

Sexual Discrimination

Students very quickly learn that different behaviors are expected from boys than from girls, and that each sex is entitled to a different set of rewards and punishments. For the male, one of his unhappy incidental learnings is that he and the school do not get along very well. He discovers that he must function in a way that is opposed to his lifestyle. The school with its emphasis on neatness, good manners, and docility clearly places the boy at a disadvantage. Boys quickly learn that they are naughtier than girls and that they have trouble competing with girls for good grades. Boys constitute two thirds of all grade repeaters in the elementary school years. In part, the less adequate adjustment of boys to school might well stem from the fact that school life during the elementary school years is too much a woman's world.

Although girls fare better during the elementary school years they, too, suffer from sex typing (Sadker and Sadker, 1972). Schools reinforce neatness, conformity, and docility while they discourage active curiosity, analytical problem solving, and a competitive achievement orientation. Reading books portray girls as helping with the housework, baking cookies, and babysitting for their brothers. The message of female inferiority also manifests itself in texts of America's history. There is much to read about male heroes such as George Washington, Ben Franklin, and Paul Revere. But aside from Betsy Ross, there is little about female characters that might fill most youngsters with respect and admiration. Recorded history is replete with material about our founding fathers, but says almost nothing about our founding mothers. Female subservience is again modeled for girls as they watch the female teachers take orders from principals, about 80% of whom are males.

Elementary school teaches girls about keeping their place. Fortunately, there is now considerable concern about sexist practices and about equality of opportunity. Hopefully, the day will soon arrive when females will no longer have to feel guilty or fear social rejection over their achievement oriented behavior. Society cannot afford the loss of female talent. Even more important, females should not be robbed of their initiative and self-respect.

Concluding Statement

What then, is life like in the school? "It would seem to be a life of contradictory demands and competing tendencies, a life in which discovery and disappointment go hand in hand, where the unpredictable and the routine are combined daily. These monotonous settings of desks and blackboards and books provide a stage for the cyclic enactment of a full drama, a play that is at once boring and exciting. . . . School is a puzzling place, and the puzzles are not all intellectual ones." (Jackson, 1966)

CLASSROOM CLIMATE AND LEADERSHIP STYLE

It is difficult for anyone who has been a student or an observer of classrooms not to recognize the differences that exist in classroom climates. Indeed, one of the most salient characteristics in a classroom operation is the extent to which the teacher shares his leadership role with students. At one end of the continuum is the teacher who is directive, structured, and controlling. At the other end is the teacher who is nondirective, unstructured, and permissive. While certain educators and parents feel that students have been given too great a voice in the decision-making process, others feel that the schools have been too restrictive toward students. Some contend that student unrest stems from authoritarian schools. On the other hand, some feel that student unrest stems from permissive schools.

Many labels have been applied to this issue of leadership style in educational settings. For the most part, investigators have dichotomized the leadership dimension referring to classroom climates as teacher centered-learner centered, dominative-integrative, traditional-progressive, directive-nondirective, or authoritarian-democratic. Different terms may be used but the question is basically the same: Who makes most of the decisions?

Authoritarian-Democratic-Laissez-Faire Atmospheres

The classic study in this area was performed by Lewin, Lippitt, and White (1939) who observed the reactions of ten-year-old boys in a club situation to authoritarian, democratic, and laissez-faire leadership styles. In the authoritarian setting, productivity (as measured by the number of masks made) was highest; however, the boys showed little interest in their work and exhibited 40 times more overt hostility toward each other than boys in the democratic group did. There was a moderate amount of aggression in the democratic groups, but most of it was friendly. The boys offered constructive advice to one another, had satisfying social relations, showed a high degree of interest in their work, assumed individual responsibility, and were capable of sustained work in the absence of the leader. The laissez-faire group, where complete freedom reigned, showed low morale, low productivity, much aggression, and a great deal of confusion.

Later research has not, however, consistently confirmed the above findings. In one summary of research on classroom atmosphere, it was found that 11 studies reported greater learning for learner-centered groups, 8 found teacher-centered methods to be superior, and 13 showed no difference (Anderson, 1959). One consistent finding is that democratic leadership in most situations is associated with higher morale, a fact worth noting in its own right. Even this conclusion must be viewed tentatively, because authoritarian leaders have been given unduly punitive and impersonal roles to play by researchers. Morale might prove to be equally high in authoritarian settings wherein the leader assumed a friendly and personal stance. With respect to educational settings, morale does seem to be higher under learner-centered conditions, provided that there is not an undue emphasis on grades. It is certainly reasonable in a democratic society to grant the student a greater voice in the decision-making process as he grows older, particularly at and beyond adolescence. If a student is to eventually assume a responsible role in a democratic society, he must be given opportunities for self-direction.

The Free Schools

As noted above, the issue of classroom climate has been surrounded by controversy for some time. If anything, in recent years the debate has soared to new levels. Fashionable new labels such as the "open classroom," the "free school," or the "school without walls" have been frequently used.

THE TEACHER'S ROLE

In the open school there is a sharing of power. The teacher exercises control by structuring an environment responsive to the students' abilities, interests, and styles of learning. Contrary to the opinion of many, teacher authority is not to be abandoned. Instead, an environment hospitable to learning is created in which "there is what might be called a natural, legitimate basis for the authority of an adult working with children." (Featherstone, 1971b) Actually, adults become more important in a proper informal setting, affording more, not less guidance.

Proponents of the free school movement readily recognize that removal of adult authority from a given group of students does not necessarily free them. Instead, the abandonment of adult authority sentences youth to the tyranny of their peers. Liberalizing the repressive atmosphere of our schools—a desirable end in its own right—will not automatically promote intellectual development. We need more humane schools, but we also must be concerned with intellectual development. As Featherstone, a respected proponent of the free school movement (1971b, p. 19) notes, "Informality is pointless unless it leads to intellectual stimulation." Jonathan Kozol (1972) also addresses himself to the free school's needs to teach the hard skills, noting that "Harlem does not need a new generation of basketweavers. It does need radical, strong, . . . obstetricians, pediatricians, lab technicians and defense attorneys" (p. 33).

The open school will become as grim and joyless as the traditional school if students realize that they are not accomplishing very much. The hypothesis that schools can do without many of its formal structures will stand or fall by whether students and teachers have important, useful things to do with their freedom (Featherstone, 1971b). The teacher must assume responsibility for creating a stimulating learning environment in which he serves a subtle but decisive role as stage manager, catalyst, and pace setter for group and individual pursuits. The atmosphere in the open school may be termed one of "structured permissiveness."

THE STUDENT'S ROLE

The child is free in the sense that he controls the direction and rate of his learning. Skills and interest in reading are developed, for instance, in many different ways. Some children may spend extended periods of time doing workbook exercises. Others may listen as the teacher reads to them. Still others may go off by themselves and read books on widely varying topics. Then again, some may not do any reading for a long stretch of time. Writing is often a major activity; students keep diaries, write stories or poems, or prepare reports on scientific experiments. In mathematics the choice of activities can run the gamut from conventional workbooks, to use of the Cuisenaire rods, to the construction of a model bridge. Students do meet periodically, however, with the teacher to discuss their choices, goals, and commitments.

The students are free in other ways, too. They can talk without permission, come and go when they wish, work out in the corridor alone or interact noisily with others in small groups, and have more casual relationships with teachers. Children are freed from letter grades and age-grade distinctions so that students from kindergarten age through the upper grades can mix with one another. Although the classroom is the usual work place, its work does extend into the community and the community into it. In short, the informality of the school affords flexible scheduling and a more natural environment.

While this movement is akin to a cult with its liturgy written by the romantic critics, there is no educational gospel as such. There is no fixed set of practices. Because of its desire to relate education to the student's needs, interests, and abilities, the open school may take many forms. An activity that worked well one year might be replaced the next year because of its unsuitability for the needs of the new group. The open school is continually working. It is not a final solution.

Open schools emphasize the notion of freedom and agree in their opposition to large classes, teachers with absolute power to administer a state-directed curriculum to rigidly defined age groups, the emphasis on obedience and adult discipline, frequent student evaluation, motivation based on competition, ability tracking, and so forth. There are, however, important differences among the types of free schools. We will distinguish between the Summerhillian free school, the parent cooperatives, and the very progressive elementary schools.

"The teacher said we could do whatever we wanted to do today—so I came home!" *(Drawing by Mal Gordon from* Phi Delta Kappan, *1971)*

Types of Free Schools

THE SUMMERHILLIAN MOVEMENT

Before the current wave of free schools, almost all of the open schools in the United States were Summerhillian in nature. The Summerhillian schools, or the "classical" free schools, tend to be quite small. When they are boarding schools, they are also very expensive. In contrast to other types of free schools, the Summerhillian movement has emphasized the emotional and expressive aspects of personality instead of a formal, academic curriculum or job preparation. Development replaces achievement as the basic objective.

Neill's Summerhill is probably the best known open school, as well as the most un-compromising alternative to conventional instruction. It is a small school. Typically, there are about 25 boys and 20 girls in attendance with ages ranging from five to sixteen. The main idea is "to make the school fit the child." (Neill, 1960) Lessons are optional, there is no deference to teacher as teacher, exams are anathema, and learning in itself is not as important as personality and character. It is predicated on a faith in the goodness of the child who is regarded as innately wise and realistic. Neill feels that it is possibly the happiest school in the world. There are no truants, homesickness is rare, there is seldom a fight between students, and there is no fear of the staff. The child lives his own life. "In the disciplined home, the children have *no* rights. In the spoiled home, they have *all* the rights. The proper home is one in which children and adults have equal rights. And the same applies to the school." (Neill, 1960, p. 107)

PARENT COOPERATIVES

Parent cooperatives are typically formed by young, white, liberal, middle-class parents who do not want their children subjected to the compulsory and authoritarian features of public schools. Parents call other parents. They organize a meeting and decide to start a free school. They hire sympathetic teachers who are willing to sacrifice financial reward for the intrinsic satisfactions of the job. Often one or more parents will teach full-time in the school. A parent board is invested with official power over school affairs, but most of the day-to-day operation is left to the staff. Despite adjusted tuition rates, these schools do not really appeal to poor minority-group parents who are more interested in freeing the school from centralized control than in freeing the child from coercive and regimented approaches to learning. The middle-class parents are emphasizing pedagogical freedom while lower-class parents are emphasizing political freedom in the form of community control (Graubard, 1972).

PROGRESSIVE PUBLIC SCHOOLS

Although the phenomenon of free schools is very limited in terms of the number of schools and participants involved, the impact on public school reform might well be relatively great. In fact, there are many very progressive elementary schools on the fringe of the free school development. Like older progressive schools of the 1930s, the newer ones are well-organized, well-equipped, fairly expensive, and rather professional about staffing. In contrast, the parent cooperatives tend to have looser organization, less equipment, and fewer certified teachers. Furthermore, parents and students have a much greater part in all

aspects of education in parent cooperatives than they do in the progressive schools administered by professional staffs.

Research on Free Schools

SUMMERHILL

While Neill contends that his self-demand style of education at Summerhill is highly successful, and he selectively chooses instances to support his contention, more objective evidence is less flattering. Bernstein (1968), who interviewed 50 graduates of Summerhill, found vastly disparate personal reactions to the school. Of the 50 graduates, 10 graduates had high praise for the school, stating that it "had given them confidence, maturity, and had enabled them to find a fulfilling way of life." (p. 38) By contrast, 7 of the 50 saw their experiences at Summerhill as harmful to their development, contending that the school experiences had "led them to find more difficulty in life than they might have otherwise experienced." (p. 40)

One point of interest had to do with the length of attendance. Those who enrolled at Summerhill for the fewest number of years tended to believe that they benefitted the most, whereas those who attended the longest seemed to have difficult and persistent adjustment problems. The major complaint voiced by the majority of graduates pertained to "the lack of academic opportunity and inspiration, coupled with a dearth of inspired teachers." (Bernstein, p. 41) The classrooms there are apparently as dull, dreary, and traditional as many classes elsewhere. To quote Neill, "We have no new methods of teaching, because we do not consider that teaching in itself matters much." (p. 4, 1960)

Graduates who later had children of their own rarely sent them to school at Summerhill. And those without children at the time of interview indicated they would want their children to attend Summerhill for no more than a year or two and then only when they were below the age of ten.

The social emphasis at Neill's school may have had a therapeutically beneficial effect on *some* of his students and a deleterious effect on others. In no instance did the educational program afford the kind of academic discipline that the graduates later wished they had received.

STUDIES ON OTHER FREE SCHOOLS

In what might represent the most extensive and careful work yet done on traditional versus modern education, Minuchin and associates (1969) studied the effects of two progressive and two traditional public schools on the cognitive and social functioning and the self-views of fourth graders attending the schools. The traditional schools saw their basic task as fostering the students' mastery of an established body of knowledge and skills. Accordingly, "teaching was directed to a body of knowledge, as organized in textbooks and curriculum syllabi, to be mastered at a level that would make it available to recall and replication in its original form and meanings." (p. 36ff) The modern schools viewed their task as that of promoting the children's curiosity, exploration, spontaneity, and self-direction and had in common a preference for instructional methods involving discovery, discussion, experimentation, and activity. The basic findings were:

1. There is little evidence that modern schools make for superior or even for systematically different cognitive functioning in comparison to traditional schools. The students of the two types of schools were much alike with regard to problem-solving processes and imaginativeness in nonproblem solving settings. Qualitative reports did suggest that modern school pupils were more unified and effective in a group problem-solving task in comparison with traditional school students. This finding may be due to the smaller class sizes in the modern schools, however.

2. With respect to social attitudes, children from modern schools tended to be more clearly identified with their schools than children from traditional schools. That is, peer group affiliation is fostered somewhat more strongly at the modern than at the traditional schools. There were few consistent differences, however, between the two types of schooling in terms of the student's ideas of right and wrong and in terms of whether students perceived adults as accepting-benevolent or as controlling-disapproving.

3. The third area of investigation entailed the child's self-views (for example, self-knowledge). Although the investigators write as if their data support the distinction between modern and traditional schools, inspection of the results by and large suggest that the type of school attended made for little difference in the child's self-view. Thus, despite the investigators' contention that the outcomes of this study were broadly consistent with their expectations, the actual data appear more largely to support the conclusion that the types of school environment, as implemented and evaluated in this study, had minimal impact on the child's cognitive processes, social attitudes, or views of himself (Wallach, 1971).

How typical are the above findings? In general, other studies of British and American free schools lead to basically similar conclusions. There is no difference of any educational significance with respect to mastery of conventional subjects. Students of free schools do show up better than formally taught students in those characteristics that progressive schools value—initiative, critical thinking, ability to express oneself in writing, capacity to work independently, and so on (Featherstone, 1971a). The meaning of this latter finding may be confounded, however, by differences in home backgrounds between those in progressive schools and those in traditional schools.

Unresolved Issues

The free schools, for all their merits, must face and overcome some difficult challenges if they are to realize their potential in America. First of all, we have not yet learned that the British model cannot be transported across the Atlantic from Great Britain in one giant step. There is obviously much to be learned from this model but circumstances necessarily alter our situations. In the British free schools, the headmistress works closely with her staff, often teaching alongside a teacher in a classroom. By contrast, the principal in American schools is not cast in the role of a master teacher. English children are still "traditionally obedient, soft-spoken and mannerly," and they are encouraged to help one another. Moreover, students typically spend several years with one teacher so that she can better meet their needs. A further difference is the outstandingly good relationship that a number of British schools have with parents.

Another major problem centers around teacher training. We cannot produce a master teacher by having her attend a summer institute. In fact, the New School of Behavioral Studies at the University of North Dakota has estimated that it takes a teacher 5 years in the classroom to become a first-rate open school teacher (Hapgood, 1971). Although some practitioners in the field seem to have expertise about how an informal classroom might best be run, their knowledges and skill often remain at an implicit, nonverbal, idiosyncratic, and private level. If open schools are to have a widespread impact, practitioners and teacher trainers must make their methodologies explicit and more public in a way that permits skills to be communicated and learned by prospective teachers (Ginsburg, 1972).

Another difficulty of no small magnitude is providing continuity from the primary to senior high school years. Only about one third of British schools are working along informal lines, and the approach has spread furthest in the infant schools that take youngsters between the ages of five to seven or eight. In general, the higher up the educational ladder, the less well the open school has fared. Partly, this state of affairs is a chronological matter, in that reform started with young children and is working its way upward. Partly, too, it reflects a genuine difficulty experienced in organizing active learning for older youth (Featherstone, 1971a). It is harder to know the older student's background and how to capitalize on it. Despite severe criticism, there seems to be an absence of any work on the secondary level to compare favorably with the emerging vision of what a good primary school should be. It is not yet clear what forms open high schools should take.

For whom is the open school most appropriate? Although the open school approach has its merits, it is not the only effective way to teach. Nor is it necessarily the method of choice for all students, as indicated by the follow-up study of Summerhill's graduates. One would suspect that anxious and dependent students, for example, would fare better under more structured classroom conditions. Even those who did well in the open setting might have been more productive if assisted to develop greater self-discipline.

Perhaps a traditional school is more appropriate for children from homes that emphasize such values as order, discipline, hard work, and thrift. On the other hand, the open school may better meet the needs of youth from homes valuing openness, feelings, creativity, spontaneity. At this stage of the game, we simply do not know which "types" of students will benefit most from an informal educational setting. Assuming that the values of the home play a significant role in determining student receptiveness to a given type of educational atmosphere, the policy of allowing parents and/or students to choose a classroom climate that is congruent with family atmosphere might well have a certain merit.

As noted elsewhere in the text, the notion of accountability looms large today. Open schools, like their traditional counterparts, must ask themselves if they are doing an effective and efficient job. This demand for accountability may prove even more troublesome for open schools than it has for regular schools. The vagueness of educational objectives (e.g., to influence students to become thinking, autonomous, sensitive individuals) together with the difficulty and expense of developing assessment techniques designed to measure the benefits of individualized instruction pose formidable obstacles to adequate evaluation. The use of standardized tests and informal evaluation will help in assessing educational outcomes, but these techniques may lack in sensitivity and objectivity respectively. Disentangling the effects of school atmosphere, child-rearing practices in the home, and community influence will not be easy.

The above difficulties by no means represent the totality of problems to be overcome, for there are others (e.g., the possibility of conflict in values between the community and the open school). But if this new brand of humane education can surmount these

shortcomings, it might yield impressive results.

PEER RELATIONS AND THE SCHOOL

Children are responsive to the behavior of their peers as early as infancy. Peer influences on behavior increase with development, peaking during the adolescent period. Compared to the associations of students with their teachers, those with peers are more frequent, intense, and varied (Schmuck, 1971). The basic notion in this section is that to be most effective teachers must work within the context of the peer group.

The Preschool Years

The first important period for contacts with peers comes when the child is three to four years of age when he leaves his parents to engage in daily neighborhood play groups, preschool classes, or day care centers.

Clearly, the years two through five are rich in social development. The striking proliferation of social behaviors is documented by Murphy's (1937) observation that all kinds of social interactions are on the increase between two and four years of age. Sympathy, leadership, and friendships increase as do resistance, aggression, and negativism. Although the early peer groups exert a less substantial influence than do the gangs of middle childhood or adolescent cliques, they are already playing a vital role as an extrafamilial influence even at the preschool period. Friends, for instance, give one another emotional support as they engage in activities that run against adult standards.

Although the inventory of early peer relations is impressive, the child's short attention span, his limited ability to use language to communicate, and his crude techniques for controlling others all place realistic limits on his ability to sustain social interactions. Thus by age six, despite a strong interest in making friends, having friends, and being friends, friendships readily come apart at the seams as an outcome of conflicts. The preschooler knows the label "friend" but not the concept, and his friendly relations give way to his egocentric needs to win, to be first, and the like (Wenar, 1971). Let us now examine a second significant developmental period for peer contacts—the child's introduction to formal schooling.

Middle Childhood

Considerable continuity exists in peer relations between the preschool years and middle childhood. Indeed, the bases for acceptability remain basically the same in middle childhood as they were in the earlier years (Wenar, 1971). Yet the latter period is sharply different in several important ways. "First, patterns of interaction and preference become more stable in middle childhood. Second, norms become a much more salient feature of group behavior. Finally, responsiveness to peer influences in the form of conformity, suggestibility and modeling all become much more common than in early childhood." (Hartup, 1970, p. 271) While both the preschooler and his school-aged counterpart are influenced through peer reward and peer modeling, it is the latter who is more sensitive to group norms. For peer groups of older students are bound together by a complex network of shared standards, values, and rules. Young children do comply with rules, but compliance is largely to rules imposed by adult authority. In contrast, the peer group itself tends to generate guidelines in the case of the older child. This is not to say that the child sets aside family values as he becomes more peer oriented. Indeed, there is a striking similarity between peer values and family standards from the preschool period through high school. Conformity to peer influence is simply increasing.

The transition from preschool group to what some psychologists call the "gang age" follows a gradual course between six and eight years of age. The rules governing gang behavior are few and there is a rapid turnover in membership. When groups are formed, participation is based to a great extent on expediency. Children join in group activities to satisfy specific interests, such as playing soldier. They leave the group when their interest wanes. Attention to one's own needs still predominates and the "spirit is one of 'my' rather than 'our' activity." (Wenar, 1971, p. 294)

Only when children reach later elementary school, roughly eight to twelve years of age, does the gang meet Sherif's (1961) criteria of a true group, namely, a social unit consisting of individuals who have interdependent status and role relationships with a set of norms or standards that regulate the behavior of individuals in matters of importance to the group. At around age nine, the gang takes precedence over the self. "We" becomes more important than "I." The student begins to subordinate his interests and desires to the demands of the group, conforms to group values, and criticizes those who fail to do so. Competence in skill valued by the group now assumes added importance. To gain respect from the group, the child is compared with other group members in terms of his courage, athletic prowess, intellectual skills, sociability, and so forth. These and other social developments all occur when children begin formal schooling—a time when peer relations come into their own.

Adolescent Groups

As the student enters high school, the high point of group involvement is reached. The *gang*, with its emphasis on adventure and excitement, may persist into the adolescent years. Often its orientation is hostile to adult society. Its goals are specific, for example, sexual, athletic, and, at times, delinquent. Gang names, dress codes, and initiation rites continue. Although the gang is one type of adolescent group, the preadolescent gang is more commonly replaced by the *clique* or the *crowd* among middle-class youth. The clique is a small, closely knit group whose members are constantly together sharing interests, concerns, hopes, and secrets. Although lacking in the trappings of the formal organizational characteristics of the gang, the clique is bound together by an intense affective bond that renders it unresponsive to adult influence. The adolescent *crowd* is not characterized by the intense personal involvement true of the clique. The crowd differs from the gang in that it requires less loyalty and solidarity. Typically, the crowd is a larger social unit.

Why do groups assume added importance during this period? The answer is not difficult to understand. The sense of belonging is never more crucial than in this transitional period when the individual has outgrown the status of childhood, but has not yet achieved the status of adulthood. Adolescence is a time of rapid change. Physical changes occur. Variations in body build become a source of concern, and the youngster must develop a new body image. Social expectations are also different. New roles with the opposite sex must be mastered. Thoughts about one's vocational future come to mind. The peer group helps to resolve these various dilemmas by providing an arena for social encounters, reducing uncertainty through the provision of clear guidelines for behavior, and supporting the individ-

ual in his opposition to parental dominance.

What kinds of changes in peer group relationships occur following adolescence? We will not answer this question in detail, because our emphasis is on the school years. We do want the reader to be aware, however, that significant advances are to be achieved in the years following adolescence. These advances have been clearly and concisely stated by Wenar (1971), who notes, "Perspective and flexibility, a realization that people should be evaluated in terms of personal worth, loyalty to the group without chauvinism, social commitments which transcend immediate group interests—all these lie in the future." (p. 301)

Peer Relations and the School

BIG SCHOOL, SMALL SCHOOL, AND STUDENT INVOLVEMENT

One of the most striking features of a school (peer group) is its size. Students seem particularly aware of how large or small the class or school is. When young, children leave their parents and small neighborhood groups to enter a class of 25 to 30 students. Sooner or later they enter larger classes. A question commonly asked is, "What effects, if any, does peer group size have on the behavior and kinds of experiences that the youngster has with his peers?" Barker and Gump (1964) found some striking differences with regard to the involvements of students in small high schools and large high schools. Students in small schools, for instance, participated in twice as many school and extracurricular activities during their high school careers as students from large schools did, despite the greater availability of such activities at the big schools. Contact with peers was greater among students in small schools. Moreover, a much larger percentage of small-school students held central positions of importance and responsibility in the behavior settings they entered, and they assumed positions of this nature in a greater variety of settings than big-school students.

Peer group relations wielded a more significant influence on students from small schools. Students from small schools reported greater satisfaction in developing a sense of competence, in being challenged, in becoming involved in important actions and decisions, in participating in group activities, and in acquiring moral and cultural values. In contrast, students from large schools reported greater satisfaction from vicarious forms of enjoyment, large-school affiliations, learning about other individuals and affairs, and gaining "points" for participation. Youngsters from large schools probably develop intimate relations with peers, but tend to do so outside of school activities. Students having academic difficulty in the large schools were a group apart, a group of outsiders, whereas their counterparts in small schools felt just as identified with school as the average or good students.

Studies of college environments indicate that students from small schools perceive their campuses as more friendly, cohesive, and supportive than students from large institutions do (Pace, 1967; Astin, 1968). In the larger colleges, there was less concern for the individual, lack of involvement in classes, greater competitiveness, and lower cohesiveness. One point seems clear—it is the quality of the use, not the number and variety of facilities, that is important in promoting student involvement and participation.

These findings strongly suggest that small-school students are more fully involved in their relations with peers and the school—a point worthy of interest given the concern over alienation. Conceivably, it is possible to have the best of both worlds in a large insti-

tution by developing small units within the larger context. Universities can be divided into living-learning complexes and smaller colleges. Classrooms can be divided into committees, buzz groups, and reaction panels. Large lectures can be supplemented with small group seminars, individualized instruction, and small helping groups. Many large schools have attempted this, but how successful they have been is questionable. In general, the larger the group, the more skilled the leader must be, the more difficult it is to achieve consensus, the more members feel that their opinions are insignificant, and the greater the danger of group incohesiveness (Hartup, 1970). If student involvement in a number of activities—curricular and extracurricular—is considered educationally valuable, we must strive to achieve a certain degree of smallness.

IMPACT OF PEER GROUP NORMS

Group Conformity and Educational Achievement. Peer group norms can either facilitate or impede the achievement of educational objectives. Peer norms can alter adolescent aspirations about college attendance. Wilson (1959), for instance, reported that sons of manual workers are more likely to have middle-class aspirations if they attend a predominantly middle-class school. On the other hand, the aspirations of sons of professional workers are lower if they attend a predominantly working-class school. Other studies show that a student is more apt to aspire to a higher education and actually go to college if his best friend also plans to go to college (Alexander and Campbell, 1964).

Unfortunately, peer group norms are not always consistent with school goals. In his investigation of teenage values, Coleman (1961) discovered that the aspirations and actions of American adolescents were primarily determined by the "leading crowd."

For boys in this leading crowd, the hallmark of success was glory in athletics, for girls, the popular date. Intellectual achievement was, at best, a secondary value. Even bright, college-bound students are strong conformists to a peer group culture that emphasizes athletics and social life. The influence of classmates is also evident in higher education. For example, medical students receive support from peers for acting in ways contrary to faculty values. The peer culture determines which lectures are to be attended, which faculty members are most knowledgeable, which experiences are most desirable, and which goals are to be pursued (Hughes et al., 1962).

How important is peer influence compared to other factors that bear on school achievement? The most comprehensive study relevant to this issue was the survey by Coleman (1966) in which data were obtained from over 600,000 youngsters in grades one to twelve in 4000 public schools. Four sets of factors were studied in terms of their relative contribution to school achievement.

1. Family background: parents' education, family size, presence in the home of reading materials, and so on.

2. School characteristics: per pupil expenditure, classroom size, laboratory and library facilities, and so on.

3. Teacher characteristics: background, training, years of experience, verbal skills, and so on.

4. Characteristics of other pupils in the same school: their background, career plans, academic achievement, and so on.

Among the many findings of this study, two were particularly impressive. The first, which was expected, indicated that home background was the most important factor in determining how well the child did at school. The second conclusion was somewhat surprising. Of all the factors concerned with aspects of school environment itself, the characteristics (abilities, interests, and aspirations) of the other children attending the same school were by far the most important. Specifically, it a poor child had classmates who came from advantaged homes, he did reasonably well. But if all the other schoolmates came from impoverished backgrounds, he did poorly in school.

In summary, we can predict that group norms will be most influential when:

1. The group is highly cohesive, that is, when group members are actively involved with one another, care about one another, and help one another.

2. When the norm is highly relevant or intense, that is, when the group feels strongly about a particular issue.

3. When the group has "jelled," that is, has shared opinions and a sense of direction.

4. When the group experience is satisfying to the individual.

5. When the situation facing the group is ambiguous, that is, when two influential individuals or subgroups disagree on an issue (Schmuck and Schmuck, 1971).

Modifying Peer Influence. Perhaps peer norms are more amenable to change during the elementary school years than during the adolescent years when peer group membership cuts across several individual classrooms and is practically inaccessible in its entirety to the individual instructor (Schmuck, 1971). If this is true, what course of action is open to elementary school teachers who encounter antischool norms in the peer group? One strategy that has proven helpful in several instances involves the following steps. (1) Determine and appoint the five or six most popular and influential peers to represent the group on an initial steering committee. (2)

Have the group meet with the teacher once a week to discuss classroom problems and to develop appropriate guidelines. (3) Have the committee present the rules (class constitution) for their appraisal and commitment. (4) Encourage the initial committee to appoint another committee that will serve for 3 or 4 weeks. (5) Set aside a certain time of the week to review the class behavior during the week and to revise regulations when necessary. By developing and formulating their own guidelines under the subtle direction of the teacher, opposition to school norms can be decreased. Furthermore, the teacher can devote more time to instruction and less time to control functions (Schmuck, 1971).

CROSS-AGE ASSOCIATIONS

Youngsters have a strong tendency to imitate those who are older and perceived as more competent and prestigeful. In fact, many of our skills and values are the outcomes of our identification with older youth and adults. We learn a lot by watching others. "The behavior of others is contagious." (Bronfenbrenner, 1970, p. 124)

Given the above facts, it would seem that peers constitute an untapped instructional resource. Because of the variety of role demands made on today's teachers, they cannot possibly be all things to all people. The advantages of cross-age tutoring include the possibilities that (1) a younger child will more readily identify with an older student than with the teacher; (2) an older child's self-esteem would be enhanced from assuming teacherlike responsibilities; (3) both the older and younger child would increase their academic competencies; and (4) both would develop more realistic notions of their own capacities and be more highly motivated to learn new skills (Lippitt and Lohman, 1965).

Simply allowing children of different ages to interact will not automatically produce effective cross-age helping. At least four parties—the teachers, the administrators, the tutors, and those to be tutored—must be involved in an effective cross-age helper's program. The administrators must give their blessing to the program so that teachers will feel free to go ahead with it. Teachers who agree to the project must understand its purposes and the unique contribution students can make. The tutors are led to understand that they will be forming a partnership with the teacher in setting goals, planning instructional methods, and providing feedback to those tutored. Care must be taken in selecting tutors to guard against exploitation and domination of younger students. Preferably students with high peer status will be used as tutors. Role-playing experiences as well as special training in the subject-matter area constitute essential parts of the training program. Similarly, it is desirable that at least some of the younger students being tutored have high status in order to avoid any stigma being attached to the tutoring relationship. Projects of this nature must still be thoroughly evaluated but, if conducted properly, they seem to hold considerable promise as a means of providing for individual differences, increasing motivation for learning, and developing an attitude of caring about others. It must be noted, however, that some students work more effectively alone and that certain assignments may be more readily solved in isolation than through student interaction. Like any strategy, the use of cross-age tutoring must be used judiciously.

Bronfenbrenner (1972) favors a pattern of cross-age helping in which groups in the school adopt another group. That is, each class would take responsibility for the care of a class of younger students. For example, a third-grade class might adopt a first-grade class in the same school. The older students could escort the younger children to school, teach them new games, read to them, and help them learn. Moreover, the older students would be evaluated on the way in which they fulfilled this civic responsibility as a regular part of the curriculum. The type of cross-age program envisioned by Bronfenbrenner would differ from similar programs in its focus on the child as an individual and as a member of his community. This program would not be restricted to the development of academic skills and subject matter.

TEACHER POWER AND ACCEPTANCE

Social Structure in the Classroom. As background to a fuller understanding of the teacher's impact on student-student relations, let us briefly review certain findings about classroom social structure. When we use this term, we are referring to three aspects of classroom groups: emotional acceptance (who likes whom?); perceived competence (who is good at doing the things you do in school?); and social power (who is good at getting you to do things in school?). We know that these three features of classroom groups

1. Develop early in the school year.

2. Remain relatively stable.

3. Produce reasonably accurate perceptions by individuals of their own position in the class structure.

4. Result in stable pairs and subgroups of children who like and respect each other plus a few socially isolated youngsters.

5. Reflect for any given individual or subgroups a position in the social pecking order.

6. Depend, in part, on teacher behavior, particularly the teacher's use of emotional acceptance and social power (Glidewell et al., 1966).

It makes a difference whether the social structure is central or diffuse. In centrally structured peer groups, many of the students pick only a small cluster of their schoolmates as pupils they like. Many students are neglected entirely. In diffusely structured peer groups, on the other hand, there is a more equal distribution of friendship choices. There are no distinct subgroups and fewer students are entirely neglected. Diffusely structured peer groups have a more positive and supportive emotional climate. Pupils are more accurate in estimating their own status in the centrally structured classroom. Almost every student knows who is liked and not liked in these classrooms, with low-status youngsters being particularly aware of their positions. The significance of these findings is heightened by the further finding that the perception of having low status is related to the incomplete use of one's abilities and to negative attitudes toward the self and toward the school. Classroom peer groups with diffuse friendship structures have greater cohesiveness and positive norms regarding the goals of the school.

Teacher Influence. How much influence can the teacher as a social-emotional leader have on friendship and power relations in the classroom peer group? The teacher can have marked effects on classroom social organization by delegating social power to some extent to the students and by dispersing emotional acceptance. In general, dispersion of the teacher's social power and emotional acceptance has been found to (1) promote greater student-to-student contact; (2) enhance mutual respect, rapport, and self-esteem; (3) induce a greater tolerance for divergent opinions in the initial phases of decision making and greater convergence of opinion in the later stages of decision making; (4) reduce anxiety and conflicts between students; (5) increase self-initiated school work, responsibility, and the prevalence of adult-oriented moral values (Glidewell, 1966).

How does the teacher go about dispersing

social power and emotional acceptance? There is no set prescription, but the following techniques have proved helpful. (1) Obtain an accurate picture of the distribution of liking and influence choices in the classroom. Who chooses whom? Are some always included and some rarely, if ever, included? Who gets the leadership roles? (See the discussion of sociometric techniques in Chapter 17.) (2) Examine your own behavior to see how you are dispersing classroom rewards and punishments. Whom do you favor? Whom do you pick on? Whom do you neglect? (3) Create a cooperative study group consisting of high- and low-status students working together toward a common unifying goal. This technique can be particularly helpful in correcting inaccurate perceptions and stereotypes. (4) Provide opportunities for low-status students to participate in high-status roles, such as a position on a steering committee. (5) Provide information about individual differences as part of the subject matter. (6) Train the class in empathy and in taking the role of other students. This technique is often effective in reducing tensions between students. In one study, the teacher used a chair to represent a fictitious person with certain characteristics. First, the low-status students were asked to sit in it and display behaviors that would "turn other people off." Then high-status students were asked to sit in the chair and display understanding, acceptance, and inclusion of others. After training in separate groups and having discussed the relevance of their sessions for the classroom, the entire class met to role play classroom situations of acceptance and rejection. (7) Encourage strength-building exercises. In this approach, each student is to write in large letters on a large sheet what he considers to be his strengths as a person. Every student is to have at least three items. These sheets are then hung up around the classroom, and other students are given the chance to add to this list of strengths. Later, the sheets are mimeographed and various ways to use these strengths in the classroom are discussed (Schmuck and Schmuck, 1971).

PREJUDICE AND EDUCATION

The Origins and Development of Prejudice

Children are not born with prejudices. Like other attitudes, ethnic and racial attitudes are learned. By age three or four, children are aware of racial differences and usually exhibit a sense of curiosity and interest—nothing more. By this early age, youngsters are also conscious of ethnic group distinctions and know that people are clustered into such groups. Interestingly, racial awareness does not depend on being in racially mixed neighborhoods or integrated situations. Studies, for instance, show no differences in racial awareness between youngsters who attended racially mixed or segregated nursery schools (Goodman, 1964).

Between the ages of four to eight, children acquire a general orientation to racial relations. At this time, they use many words and concepts to express their stereotypes of other racial groups, but few know the precise derogatory implications of their language. While not wholly understanding, they use "power words" such as "nigger" and "wop" to upset others. Thus, the emotional meaning of power words are learned prior to becoming attached —specifically and exclusively—to the referent. With advancing age, the child's ethnic attitudes and behavior become increasingly consistent with those held by adult society.

We know that racial attitudes are learned. But we must move beyond this truism and ask what specific factors influence the development of ethnic attitudes in our society. As with most complex phenomena, there is no simple answer to this question. Many factors help to shape ethnic attitudes. We will examine three major factors: child-rearing practices, cultural norms, and cognitive development.

CHILD-REARING PRACTICES

The role that a child's parents play in his becoming prejudiced is well documented. Clark (1963) cites Frenkel-Brunswick's studies describing parents who are apt to foster pathological prejudice in their children as conventional, anxious concerning their status, socially conforming to the point of rigidity, and discouraging of spontaneous expression of feeling. Allport (1958) notes that a style of parenthood that is suppressive, critical, and relatively rigid puts the child on his guard. He must watch and control his impulses and watch carefully for signs of parental approval or disapproval, since love may be withdrawn if parental displeasure is evoked, leaving the child, in his own eyes, alone and exposed. The result of such parent-child interactions, in Allport's view, is the child's learning that power dominates human relations. He learns, too, to mistrust his own impulses and to fear evil in himself. Through projection, he comes to fear evil impulses in others, and thus learns that others are not to be trusted—that they are different and fearsome. "Outsiders" become scapegoats—convenient targets for their own self-discontent and frustrations.

CULTURAL TRANSMISSION

While there is evidence to support the more pathological type of prejudice based on the projection of forbidden traits to certain outgroups whom it is "proper" to despise and to reject, this explanation does little to account for the more frequently encountered *normal* prejudices that are transmitted through one's culture. Most prejudice probably results from one's learning in a culture that holds prejudicial attitudes. Thus, we see that cultural norms and values are also of relevance to the development of prejudice. Prejudice grows not only out of a single parent's nurturance of prejudiced attitudes in a child, but also out of the societal support that the child senses among peers and other significant adults and in various social institutions. If brought up in a community where black inferiority is taken for granted, one is apt to accept this view without questioning it.

COGNITIVE FACTORS

Cognitive factors also play a role in the formation of ethnic attitudes. As the child's cognitive capacities develop, he becomes aware of and curious about racial and other physical differences, and associates certain attributes with these differences. Rokeach (1965) has argued vigorously for the importance of "belief congruence" as a determinant of ethnic attitudes. Certainly, religious wars and political ideologies that have resulted in conflict are partly based on perceived dissimilarity of beliefs. For certain individuals, the perceived similarity or dissimilarity of beliefs may be more important than ethnic differences in developing and maintaining prejudices.

The origins of prejudice thus lie in child-rearing practices, the broader norms of society that touch on one's day-to-day living, and in the child's own expanding intellectual capacities.

The Effects of Prejudice

THE EFFECTS OF PREJUDICE ON MINORITY GROUP CHILDREN

The major and overriding effect of prejudice on minority children has been devaluation of one's own race, and its concomitant effects: preference of other race children to children of one's own race, unhappiness and anxiety over one's own racial characteristics, and, particularly among young children, a wish not to be a member of one's own race. Studies detailing such effects were being made at least as early as the late 1930s.

Several studies in the late 1960s and early 1970s yielded similar results, but seemed to detect some decrease in the universality and depth of such effects, that is, some minority children were found who expressed some degree of own-race acceptance if not outright preference. Durret and Davy's (1970) findings are representative of recent research in this area. In their study of Anglo, black and Mexican-American preschoolers in California, it was found that while blacks expressed the least own-group preference of any of the three racial groups studied, this lack of own-group preference was not universal among the black children. The investigators, after examining prior research, concluded that there had been a decrease in own-race rejection on the part of black children since 1960, and a decline in the expression of racially hostile attitudes among both black and white children.

Another effect, which becomes increasingly pronounced as minority group students grow older, lies in the preference not to attend a desegregated school if they have never been to such a school before. The 1967 Report of the U.S. Commission on Civil Rights notes this effect. Similarly, a study by Bolner and Vedlitz (1971) documents the preference of black high school students, attending a black high school, to continue attending that black high school instead of integrating into a formerly white high school, in spite of their expressed approval of the principle of desegregation. The students' preference for the black high school did not, they said, grow out of fear of social or physical harm, but simply out of the fact that they preferred "their own" school.

One particularly damaging effect of prejudice is that it provides an all-embracing rationalization for personal shortcomings. The objective facts of racial discrimination provide an excuse for apathy, lack of striving, personal deficiencies, and antisocial behavior (Ausubel and Ausubel, 1963). Blaming the past may make one feel better, but it hinders the development of the personal responsibility that is needed for self-improvement and self-direction.

THE EFFECTS OF PREJUDICE AND RACIAL ISOLATION ON MAJORITY GROUP MEMBERS

A basic effect of prejudice on the white majority seems to lie in a pronounced narrowing of awareness and tolerance for persons different than themselves. When one speaks of the effects of prejudice on majority group members, one must speak directly to the effects of racial isolation. A major response to prejudice among the majority group has been the placement of itself into virtual racial isolation (or the placement of the minority into such isolation).

The most definitive study of the effects of racial isolation on the majority was reported by Meil (1967). Covering a period of 4 years, the study examined a "representative" suburban white community and found in general that the suburban white child was characterized by a striving toward academic success and competition; a passion for conformity (confinement to a narrow view of what people are and should be like); a major interest in oneself, without concern for others; and a strong valuation of cleanliness and order. The investigators found that the suburban, racially isolated child's life and social contacts were almost totally circumscribed, inclusive of people only like himself and his parents (in terms of race, age, income, aspirations, etc.). They also found that the children, at very young ages, were very deeply prejudiced, but uncomfortable about this fact when confronted with it. These children knew, for example, that its "not nice" to say that black children are dirty, but nevertheless indicated strong feelings of that nature. This fact sometimes led to high and overt anxiety on the part of the children when questioned concerning black or other "different" children. Meil concludes that "there is little in their education, formal or otherwise, to familiarize them with the rich diversity of American life."

Programs for Changing Racial Attitudes

In addition to efforts to remedy academic deficiencies among the disadvantaged, the schools may be able to reduce social and racial conflict to some degree by bringing about attitude change. Because of the urgency of this problem, it is advisable that we study the potential that the schools have as a vehicle for modifying racial attitudes through educational encounters.

INTERGROUP CONTACT

Helpful or Harmful. Social psychologists have relied on a variety of ways to alter attitudes. One of the two main tactics used by the school to date has consisted of "induced" (as contrasted with "natural") contact between members of different social and racial groups. This strategy for change is, in large measure, a by-product of the U.S. Supreme Court Decision of 1954 on school desegregation. Let us sample some of the findings on this topic.

A report of the United States Commission on Civil Rights (1967) cited evidence supporting the effectiveness of intergroup contact in altering racial attitudes. Of black pupils attending integrated schools, 70% stated that they planned to live in integrated neighborhoods, whereas only 50% of black pupils

attending segregated schools expressed such plans. A trend toward desegregation or segregation preference seemed discernible and was related to previous experiences; that is, attendance in desegregated elementary schools fostered enrollment in a desegregated high school and encouraged residence in a desegregated neighborhood. Initial experiences of segregation seemed to favor choosing a continuation of segregated situations. Moreover, it was reported that the absence of interracial education perpetuates in whites the feelings that both blacks and "black schools" are inferior.

A recent analysis on the effects of busing in five northern cities by research sociologist David Armor (1972) has attracted considerable attention. The studies reported all had control groups consisting of nonbused students for comparison purposes and a longitudinal research design in which the same tests were administered at different points in time. Conclusions for each of the major areas studied are as follows:

1. Academic achievement. None of the studies demonstrated conclusively that integration had an effect on academic achievement as measured by standardized tests.

2. Aspiration and self-concept. Bused students did not raise their aspirations with regard to college attendance or occupational level. Integration does not seem to influence measures of self-esteem in any consistent or significant way.

3. Race relations. Under conditions of induced busing, integration tends to heighten racial consciousness, enhances ideologies that promote racial segregation, and reduces opportunities for actual contact between the races.

4. Long-term educational effects. Bused students were much more likely to start college than nonbused students. The drop-out rate in college for bused students is higher, however, with the result that bused students near the end of the sophomore year were not much more likely to be enrolled full-time in college than the control group.

Conclusions. In light of the conflicting evidence, prospects for attitude changes as a result of school contacts remain largely speculative. The following points seem noteworthy.

1. The only warranted conclusion is that racial contact in a school setting has an indeterminate effect on racial attitudes. In some instances of integration, contact has led to the development of positive attitudes. In other instances, the change has been intensely negative. Of one thing we can be certain: "interracial contact is not apt to be a neutral event for either racial party." (Jones, 1972, p. 104)

2. Biracial contacts and the interpersonal experiences possible in integrated classes seem to be a necessary but not sufficient condition for the development of favorable racial attitudes.

3. As noted above, attendance in integrated schools can influence interracial experiences either favorably or unfavorably in some situations and under certain conditions, but not in other situations and conditions. No one knows for sure what these important conditions and situations are, but consideration should be given to such factors as community atmosphere, teacher attitude, and racial distribution in the classroom. Watson and Johnson (1972) conclude that, for favorable ethnic attitudes to develop, at least one of five major conditions must be present. "The different ethnic groups must have common goals, whose accomplishment does not involve intergroup competition. Cooperative independence must exist between the groups. . . . Status of both groups must be equal. Furthermore, either custom, law or authority must support the

reduction of intergroup prejudice. Finally, the members of neither ethnic group must be perceived as acting in ways which confirm existing stereotypes." (Watson and Johnson, 1972, p. 325) These are indeed difficult conditions to meet.

First of all, intergroup competition does occur. And when minority group students are at a disadvantage in their competition with middle-class students for grades, class offices, homecoming queen, cheer leader positions, and so on, increased contact seems less likely to have a positive effect on racial relations. Moreover, integrating black and white students does little, in the short term, to reduce the academic and social status differences between them. Integration must be backed up with programs of equal education. Finally, conditions of unequal footing between various races probably increase prejudices to the extent that stereotypes are reflected by actual group differences (Armor, 1972). For black students, initial stereotypes about white students as snobbish, intellectual, and "straight" may be partially confirmed by actual experience. Similarly white students may partially confirm their stereotypes of blacks as intellectually dull, hostile, and having different values. Unguided contacts are not the answer. The Protestant-Catholic conflict in Northern Ireland and the Israeli-Arab battles in the Middle East are two cases in point. We are quickly learning that desegregated schools do not always become integrated schools and that the *type* of contact be more critical than the *amount* of contact.

4. Future research must, in addition to considering the relevant variables mentioned above, conduct longitudinal studies to ascertain the long-term (versus short-term) effects of enforced racial contacts, investigate other approaches to attitude change (e.g., giving accurate information regarding racial and ethnic stereotypes), determine if projects for changing attitudes are more successful with younger children than with older students whose attitudes may be more deeply ingrained, seek more modest goals initially (e.g., achieving favorable nonintimate racial relations, such as working together, versus intimate racial relations, such as dating), and ascertain the optimal percentage of middle- and low-income youngsters to be integrated.

PROVIDING INFORMATION AND PERSUASION

If integration by no means necessarily ensures the appearance of equalitarian and friendly cross-racial orientations, how are we to reduce prejudice? One way, as noted above, is to continue striving toward the conditions that do make for more favorable intergroup contact. How about those school districts that remain segregated? As important as integration is to racial harmony, it is not the only means available for beginning to deal with the effects of prejudice. A number of alternative suggestions have been proposed by various writers. Providing information about minority groups might well aid in the reduction of prejudices transmitted by the culture. There is evidence to suggest that a great deal of interracial conflict results from the fact that people have no prior knowledge of the attitudes, values, and behavior of other groups, thereby basing their decisions on stereotypes. If prejudice can be learned without direct contact with minority groups, it should be theoretically possible to learn new racial attitudes indirectly through the provision of favorable information about target groups. Let us at this point turn to some of the studies in this area.

Clark (1963) suggests that textbooks be examined for (and if necessary, replaced with books exemplifying) positive treatment of minority races and ethnic groups, as well as "simple" positive human relations. While many textbooks since the middle 1960s have

moved away from a thoroughly homogeneous (white, upper-middle class) portrayal of life in the United States, charges of stereotyping and inferior treatment even within the context of minority-race depiction have been heard. Textbooks have improved in this regard, however, and the situation in the areas of literature for children is probably more diverse and less stereotyped, at least in recent years. The applicability of Clark's suggestion for both the integrated and the racially isolated school is obvious.

One curricular innovation administered not on a one-shot basis, but as an integral part of the regular school curriculum, was studied by Roth (1969) in Michigan. Roth, in studying the effects of a black studies program in both segregated and integrated elementary schools in Michigan, found positive own-race attitudes among fifth-grade blacks in both integrated and segregated settings. He also found that these attitudes were more uniformly positive in schools of both types receiving the black studies program than in the schools not receiving the program. Roth's research examined the effects of the black studies program only on black students; it would be interesting to replicate the study with an examination of the effects of the program on white students.

In what is perhaps a classic study, Litcher and Johnson (1969) compared the ethnic attitudes of second-grade students who used a multiethnic reader that included characters from several ethnic groups with the ethnic attitudes of similar students who used a reader that included only whites. Use of the multiethnic readers resulted in marked changes in the children's attitudes toward black Americans.

Harding and his associates (1969) believe that school courses may produce positive changes in ethnic attitudes of students if (1) a favorable balance of information about an ethnic group is presented; (2) the teacher conveys to the students that his own attitude toward the ethnic group is more favorable than theirs; and (3) a positive relationship between teacher and student exists.

The practical aspects of dealing with prejudice in the schools have been addressed in both general and specific ways by various writers and researchers. Some of the ingredients of a good integrated school program seem at this time rather obvious, if not always simply implemented. There are also, however, a number of steps that can be taken in regard to the nonintegrated school. It would seem that lessening the effects and occurrence of prejudice is a function not so much of integration *per se*, as a function of school acceptance and support of human differences as well as human similarities, manifested in both specific programs and in positive interpersonal relations.

CHANGING THE SCHOOLS

In this and other chapters, ideas have been suggested regarding the directions in which schools might change. Yet there has been little if any discussion about *how* schools might be changed. How do those who want to improve student mental health, to make schools more "open," to increase racial harmony, to use peer groups more effectively, achieve these changes? How does it happen that modern math, foreign language laboratories, the use of teacher aids, programmed instruction, team teaching, behavior modification programs, or Head Start programs spring up throughout the country? On the other hand, what accounts for resistances to change? Are all resistances irrational? How is change implemented? Who controls the powers to promote or resist change? What are the major obstacles to change? How effective have educational changes been? Regardless of the type of change sought, these are among the

major concerns that one should consider if change is to be successfully implemented. In this section, we will discuss factors that impede change, common methods for promoting change, and the need to evaluate educational innovation. Our discussion will be limited primarily to those forces within the school that promote or impede change.

Problems in Change

Schools, like other institutions, are characterized by a set of standardized role behaviors, norms and values, and a division of labor. The special mission of this particular institution is to prepare people for roles in other organizations and for participation in society at large. Although sharing the basic characteristics of all other organizations, schools have special features that set them apart from other organizations and bear on the issue of change. These distinguishing characteristics have been aptly delineated by Johnson (1970) as follows.

1. Having a monopoly on formal education, their existence is guaranteed. Because the public school is protected and cared for much like a pet, it has been called a "domesticated" institution.

2. The economic and noneconomic rewards for the staff are given on the basis of criteria such as seniority, amount of formal education, and so on, instead of for the quality of one's job performance. Rewards given students are in the distant future and sometimes ineffective because of peer norms and values.

3. The goals of the public school are ambiguous—a feature that impedes measuring any teacher's or district's success.

4. There is a wide variation in input of students and personnel. The school accepts children regardless of motivation and ability.

Teacher variability prompts the development of methods and curriculum materials that are teacher proof.

5. The manner in which a teacher performs his job is generally not observed by colleagues or supervisors.

6. Compared to economic institutions such as those involved in manufacturing or transportation, schools have a low interdependence of parts, so that the failure of one teacher to perform his duties does not directly effect the behavior of any other teacher. As a consequence, the behavior of any teacher can become routinized in unproductive ways.

7. Public schools are subject to control and criticism from the community and school board. This means that nonprofessionals often determine educational policy and that the school can initiate only those changes that do not elicit strong opposition from the community.

The most disquieting consequences of the above characteristics are twofold. Schools feel a restricted need for and interest in change and a relative lack of concern for quality performance. Nevertheless, change is needed in any organization from time to time, but *when* should we change, *what* should we change, and *how* can we produce change?

Implementing Change

WHEN TO CHANGE

How does one know *when* change is needed? There is no easy answer to this question, but it may prove instructive to examine three dimensions of organizational health in attempting to reach a decision about change. For present purposes, organizational health can be divided into the task-accomplishment dimension, the internal integration dimension, and the growth and change dimension.

If unhealthy, with respect to task area, the school would have unclear or inappropriate goals, distorted communication, and an authoritarian power base. In the internal-integration area, it would be unhealthy if resources are used in ways that school personnel could not grow professionally and personally, if the members no longer wanted to be identified with the school, and if the morale of teachers and/or students was low. Finally, with respect to the growth and change area, a school would be unhealthy if innovativeness were at a low ebb, if the impetus to change has to come largely from the outside, and if its ability to detect and solve pressing problems is poor. When many of these problems are noted, a school organization might be said to be unhealthy and in need of modification (Johnson, 1970).

WHAT TO CHANGE

One of the first things in implementing change is to decide what to change. Johnson (1970) has identified five possible targets for organizational change.

1. The personalities, skills, and attitudes of the individual members, for example, consulting with a fifth-grade teacher about her need to provide emotional support and low vocabulary-high interest materials to a disabled reader in her class.

2. The roles, norms, communication patterns, and power relationships of the *work team;* for example, providing a workshop for those involved in team teaching, conferring with the pupil personnel team (counselors, social workers, and school psychologists) about the value and need for removing unnecessary sources of stress on pupils, and having sensitivity training sessions for the top decision-making team.

3. The roles, norms, communication patterns, and influence structure of the organization as an entity; for example, unionizing teachers, giving more control of schools to the community, and stressing the need for accountability.

4. The technology of the school; for example, modifying the curriculum, introducing educational hardware, altering methods of grouping students, and suggesting modular scheduling.

5. The task objectives of the institution; for example, increasing the emphasis on career education, valuing self-direction on the part of students, and focusing on creative thinking.

There is no easy recipe detailing the order in which various aspects should be attacked. The choice as to what to change and in what order, if any, is undoubtedly a complex one involving such particulars as the nature of the problem in question, one's resources for change, the faculty's receptiveness to change, and the like.

HOW TO CHANGE

Having decided on what to change, one has to address himself to methods of change. The methods that follow have been identified by a number of authorities (Johnson, 1970; Guskin and Guskin, 1970) as among the most common ways to enact organizational change.

Administrative Order. A directive from someone in authority, such as the superintendent or school board, seems to be the most common vehicle for attempting to produce change. This approach is impersonal, formal, and task oriented. Because the decision-making authority is usually unrepresentative of all those who will be affected by its decision, lack of commitment to involvement in and a resistance to the change are common reactions.

Replacement of Key Personnel. This strategy assumes that these are certain key positions of influence, and if filled with the "right"

individuals, change will result. This approach has much in common with the use of administrative directives, for example (change from above, formal, impersonal), and accordingly, shares similar disadvantages.

Providing Information. This is an intellectual approach that assumes that the individual will be motivated to change in a direction that is in his best interest. This rather traditional means often seems to be unsuccessful. The messages conveyed by books or audiovisual aids too frequently fail to involve the reader or viewer in a meaningful, personal way. The result is that teachers and administrators still view the problems in an abstract, intellectualized manner.

Survey Feedback. This technique involves the collection of data by questionnaires or interviews usually conducted by outside researchers about various aspects of the organization's functioning. Once the data are gathered, analyzed, and summarized in a meaningful way, the information is fed back into the system. The "head" of the institution is typically the first person to receive the results. Because this approach gives a factual basis to organizational problems, the data cannot be easily ignored. There is some evidence to indicate that the survey feedback method can be used effectively in altering institutional functioning.

Sensitivity Training. This process, which is usually carried out in an unstructured group setting, is designed to increase one's awareness and sensitivity to the emotional and behavioral reactions in oneself and in others, to promote understanding of the factors that enhance or impair group functioning, to clarify and develop new goals, and to try out new styles of behavior. By exposing the individual's behavior, by giving and receiving feedback, and by trying out new behavior, the individual develops an awareness and acceptance of self and others, thereby facilitating effective group functioning. For example, a school district might try to deal with conflicts between old-timers and new teachers, between school and community, between boy and girl students, and between faculty and administrators through sensitivity training sessions that encourage direct, intimate, and power-free communication. Sensitivity group training, which is now widely used as a method of organizational change, can have the individual members, the work team, or the organization as a whole as its target for change.

One difficulty is that the factors that purportedly make a sensitivity training group very powerful — the release from job requirements, the unstructured situation, reduction in outside support for one's beliefs and attitudes — quickly vanish once school personnel return to their jobs. In an effort to promote longer lasting results, proponents of this technique have tried to bring together organizational families in the same group (e.g., all principals from a school district) and have added more structured techniques, such as role playing and skill practice.

Use of this approach seems to imply that communication and interpersonal problems are most important causes of problems in the school culture. Sarason (1971) insightfully points out that communication and interpersonal problems are more apt to be symptoms than causes and that this approach neglects such important causes as role dilemmas, the effects of tradition and routine, life in the classroom, irrelevant preparation of personnel, and the ways in which teaching and learning are conceptualized. There are two other cautions regarding the use of this technique. First, sensitivity training seems to have become an end in and of itself instead of a means to an end. Sensitivity training is an "in-thing" now. Second, many authorities believe that this technique is being oversold,

resulting in a disservice to those who receive sensitivity group training and to the technique itself.

Visiting a Successful Program. Nothing seems to persuade like a visit to and observation of a successful program in action. Administrators and teachers are particularly influenced to adopt educational innovations through seeing them succeed in everyday, run-of-the-mill situations in schools similar to their own. Situations that appear too dissimilar or too artificial are rejected.

Other methods for promoting change include confrontation (the presentation of an externally imposed problem), simulation or the use of gaming, individual counseling, and skill training.

Evaluation of Change

Solutions to urgent educational problems will not wait until researchers have validated the worth of innovations; however, eventual evaluation is essential if we are to know the value of the changes that have been implemented. As reasonable as this last assertion might sound, few educational innovations are ever evaluated. In fact, evaluation of educational innovation is rare. Based on Miles' book, *Innovation In Education* (1964), less than one half of 1% of nationally financed experimental programs in one large state were systematically evaluated. This situation is hopefully changing as the era of accountability is ushered in. The Coleman Report (Coleman, 1966) and the Westinghouse Report (1969) are illustrative of what may be an increased trend of program evaluation at the national level. The majority of innovations at the local level, however, are not made on the basis of empirical evidence but on the salesmanship of the promoter and current fads in educational circles (Johnson, 1970).

Summary

1. The educational process does not take place in a vacuum. Instead, it occurs within the elaborate organizational structure of an institution called the "school."

2. Each student must learn to master the hidden curriculum if he is to make his way through the school. Mastery of the organizational curriculum is often more heavily rewarded than mastery of the academic curriculum.

3. The choice between authoritarian and democratic classroom climates appears to have little effect on subject-matter achievement, but it might have profound effects on attitudes toward school, on social behavior in the school, and on the acquisition of adult values. Within a democratic society such as ours, it seems reasonable to liberalize progressively authoritarian controls as the student advances toward maturity.

4. Most open schools are committed to the objective of educational excellence, but strive to achieve the goal through more flexible, individually geared, and noncoercive learning. There is no evidence that reducing the amount of formal control over students impairs conventional academic skills. The capacity to work independently and to think critically may be enhanced in progressively taught students, but the evidence on this point is not firm and cause-effect relationships have not been established.

5. Much of the significant interactions in the classroom center around student-student relations. Children become increasingly responsive to peer influence, with the high point occurring during the adolescent years. Educators must be particularly alert to the effects of school size, peer group norms, the potential of cross-age programs, and the influence of teacher power in student-student relations.

6. Three determinants of prejudice were presented: the roles played by child-rearing practices, by the socializing influences of cultural institutions, and by the child's increasing cognitive capacity, which enables him to become aware of the differential social valuations attached to various racial and ethnic groups.

7. The effects of prejudice are manifold. Prominent among minority group members is a negative self-image. Fortunately, recent studies suggest a lessened amount of ego devaluation among minority group members. For the majority groups, prejudice is associated with a pronounced narrowing of awareness and an intolerance of persons different than themselves.

8. Integration is no panacea for the problem of racial prejudice. Racial contact under nonoptimal conditions (e.g., active competition for the desirable, but scarce resources available in school) can have

adverse effects. Yet integration is an important and perhaps indispensable first step in overcoming the effects of prejudice. Many authorities still believe that the school is the most strategically located social institution for achieving more egalitarian and harmonious racial relations.

9. Preliminary findings suggest that the use of multiethnic readers and the inclusion of black studies programs hold promise as ways to produce positive changes in ethnic attitudes.

10. Because of certain unique organizational characteristics, the school may be one of the more difficult institutions to modify. Those who want to change schools must be aware of the factors that block change, methods for promoting change, and the need to evaluate change. The problem of school change is a complex one that does not yield to simple solutions.

CHAPTER 13
Mental Health in the Schools

"Let's plead insanity!"
(Drawing by Ford Button
from NEA Journal, 1964)

The schools are probably the most strategically placed institution to deal with the mental health of youth. The schools have tremendous potential for improving the mental health of youth. The teacher is the only trained professional person who has regular contact with so many youngsters. Moreover, teachers have access to youth for a prolonged period of time at a stage in life when personality is still presumed to be malleable. To get an even fuller appreciation of the potential impact that a school can have on mental health, you have only to consider the estimate that a pupil will spend approximately 14,000 to 16,000 hours in a classroom setting during the course of his 12 years of schooling. Can you imagine the number of healthy and/or unhealthy experiences that a student experiences over such an extended period of time?

Fortunately, as mental health programs have moved out of the therapist's private office and into the community, there has been a definite movement in the direction of greater teacher involvement in the mental health of children. Professional workers now realize that all problems do not stem from factors inside the individual and that we must carefully consider the child's life conditions, for example, the school, as factors in producing adjustment or maladjustment. During the past decade, the push toward a more reality-based mental health approach has become more and more evident, and, as the mental health team continues to expand in keeping with this new outlook, it may be the teacher, not the mental health specialist, who assumes the primary role in the promotion and protection of our youth's mental health.

WHO IS THE NORMAL CHILD?

What is normal behavior in children? How long must a child manifest abnormal behavior to warrant the label "emotionally disturbed"? What criteria are to be used in deciding what is abnormal and what is normal? How does one distinguish between the child who has problems and the child who is maladjusted? Various approaches have been made to the definition of normality in children, although none has proven entirely satisfactory. As Scott (1968) notes "The question 'What constitutes normality?' is best understood not as a question of fact, but rather as a question of conventional definition."

The issue of normality in children is more than an academic question to those who must render judgments regarding the behavior of children. This question also has ethical and practical ramifications, for the child usually does not seek help, but is referred for treatment by the adults in his life. The child may not need treatment, even though his parents and teachers believe he does. His referral may be simply a result of the parents' or teachers' low annoyance threshold. Shephard,

Oppenheim, and Mitchell (1966) found, for instance, that referral to a child-guidance clinic is as closely related to parental characteristics (anxious, easily upset, lacking in ability to cope with children) as it is to the child's problems. Teachers with 3 to 10 years of experience view undesirable acts as more serious than teachers with 10 years of experience do (Dobson, 1967).

The Statistical Approach

One of the most commonly discussed approaches to normality employs a statistical criterion. According to this standard, normal behavior is defined as what the majority does. The more an individual is like the average, the more normal he is considered to be. For example, the average five-year old may have five arguments with friends a month. If so, this condition would be considered normal. We could also calculate what percentage of five-year olds have as many as ten or as few as two arguments a month. If a child deviated markedly from the average, he would be considered abnormal from a statistical viewpoint in this aspect of his behavior. Similar estimates could be established for other aspects of behavior, such as the number of fears, the frequency of truancy, and the extent of aggressive attacks for children of various age levels.

There are some rather noticeable shortcomings in this approach, however. First, the statistical concept of normality implies that what is common is normal. Colds are very common, but are not regarded as desirable. Similarly, 95% of boys have masturbated by age fifteen or sixteen, yet masturbation is not necessarily regarded as healthy. Although a sizeable segment of the adolescent population may take drugs, we do not regard this as desirable. Second, abnormality in a statistical sense is not always unhealthy. Take the case of a very creative youngster. His performance may be statistically infrequent and therefore deviate markedly from the average. Are we to say that this youngster is abnormal when his very talent may lend itself to self-actualization on his part and to benefits for society? A third problem centers around the complexity of personality. It may be possible to gather norms on certain characteristics, for example, the amount of nailbiting, but it is difficult to isolate and quantify many of the subtle or more elusive characteristics of personality. Still another problem exists with the statistical approach; the norms are frequently based on maladjusted populations, such as delinquents. Evidence derived from the incidence of problem behavior in the general population strongly suggests that the use of general standards based on a study of deviant groups can be misleading. Finally, there is the question of cutoff points. Just how many times does a seven-year old have to be truant to be considered a problem child? What percentage of the school population must he exceed with regard to truancy? It is difficult to give definitive answers to such questions.

A variation or subtype of the statistical approach is the use of adjustment to social expectations as the criterion of normality. Normality thus becomes defined relatively, according to a given set of cultural values, which are comprised of both laws and customs. The socialization process itself has as its aim the inculcation of social values and the development of behaviors congruent with environmental expectations. Definitions of normality in terms of adherence to social expectations, and abnormality in terms of violations of these expectations are, therefore, not unexpected.

Although it may seem reasonable to judge deviancy by comparing behavior against social norms, this approach also has its limitations. For example, to what degree does one have to deviate from social norms to be judged "culturally deviant"? How many times does one have to steal to be considered maladjusted? Most of us have stolen or cheated at times, but we do not consider ourselves to be delinquent. Cutoff points between the conformer and the habitual offender are difficult to determine and would probably have to be at least somewhat arbitrary in nature.

Another difficulty occurs when a society or institution is dominated by a particular set of social-political values. Is compliance, then, a sign of normality or of personal maladjustment? Who were the maladjusted Germans — those who fought the Nazi system or those who went along with it? Also consider the lower-class youngster or the college student who rebels against school. Is he to be considered deviant because of his objections to being forced into a situation in which he experiences demands and expectations he does not regard as relevant? Or are some of the institutions in the society irrelevant?

We must recognize that children and adults can suffer from overconformity. The problem of normality does not seem to be resolved by a strict adherence to conformity since, eventually, conformity reaches a point beyond which normality is apt to be threatened. Compliance to the point that one's personal integrity is sacrificed is conducive neither to personal nor societal harmony. Furthermore, as Havighurst (1966) argues, it is important that a society educate for certain forms of deviancy, for example, creative behavior. On occasion, a good adjustment demands that we rebel and express dissatisfaction with social mores and institutions. The value for the individual and for society of certain expressions of nonconformity are, unfortunately, often overlooked. Finally, we must ask whose norms we are going to use in judging normality. One group in society often judges behavior by a different set of expectations than other groups. For example, how would ministers, teachers, social workers, doctors, cultural anthropologists, and laborers as separate groups view a child who habitually curses? In all probability, there would be widely differing views regarding the acceptability and desirability of such behavior.

The Idealistic Approach

The other major approach might be termed the "idealistic" model. Whereas the statistical approach describes the frequency or typicality of given behaviors, the use of the ideal criterion by definition implies evaluation of desirability. Whereas comparison with social norms involves relativity, an ideal criterion is based on absolute standards assumed to be worthy of emulation. The statistical approach is concerned with "what is"; the idealistic approach is concerned with "what should be." An ideal of behavior is posited for each individual, and a determination is made as to whether the individual is functioning at this level. Maslow's hierarchy of basic human needs illustrates this approach. His hierarchy lists, in ascending order, physiological needs,

safety needs, needs for affection and belongingness, esteem needs, cognitive needs, such as a search for knowledge, aesthetic needs, such as a longing for beauty, and self-actualization needs. When the needs at the lower levels have been met, the needs on the next step in the hierarchic structure seek satisfaction. Only self-actualizing people are seen as operating at an optimal level. According to Maslow (1954), anything that detracts from the course of self-actualization is pathological.

The equating of normality with perfection has an undeniably positive air about it, but this approach is also fraught with difficulties. Ideal criteria, for one thing, have little practical meaning and, therefore, are of limited value to the educator in his decision-making process. Guidelines derived from such criteria as self-actualization do not aid the teacher in deciding whether the child is normal or in need of professional help. Second, few people can ever attain the ideal; even those who do seem to qualify have other human frailties and weaknesses. Finally, since ideal criteria are in terms of what *ought* to be, we run the risk of assuming that we *know* what the ideal attributes are and that these are supracultural in character, equally valid for child and adult, man or woman, socialite and slum dweller.

Toward a Definition of Mental Health

While there is no universally acceptable definition of normality, there are certain ingredients that a suitable definition must include. It should take into account the child's *developmental level*, since what is regarded as normal at one age may be viewed as abnormal at a later age, for example, physical aggressiveness or chewing on the carpet. The student's *sex* is another factor that influences the teacher's judgment about the appropriateness of a student's behavior. Consideration must also be extended to a child's particular *cultural background*. Since judgments concerning the desirability of a specific behavior vary from one group to another, the relativity of any particular behavioral pattern becomes an important consideration (Havighurst, 1966). Allowances for *individuality* must be made also. Finally, the definition of normality must be *multidimensional* in nature, that is, it must take into account how the child functions in various representative areas of development.

After reviewing several definitions, Ringness (1968, p. 12) lists the following attributes as characteristic of the mentally healthy child.

1. Is self-acceptant and has reasonably high self-esteem, feels generally adequate, but recognizes his own shortcomings and seeks to improve.

2. Has a realistic evaluation of himself and sets his aspirations accordingly.

3. Accepts responsibility for managing his own life and making his own decisions and does not vacillate or lean on others.

4. Is well-balanced, flexible, and consistent in his attitudes, goals, and ideals.

5. Can withstand stress, tolerate some anxiety, and overcome the effects of trauma and frustration.

6. Can relate well to others and has the good of society at heart.

7. Seeks independence, autonomy, and self-direction and is neither completely conforming nor completely selfish.

8. Attempts to solve his problems, instead of to escape them or to employ defense mechanisms excessively.

What would the mentally healthy child look like in the school setting? Bower (1970) expects the following characteristics.

1. *Managing Symbols.* A mentally healthy child is one who is able to deal with and manage the symbols of our society. Such symbols include language symbols, mathematical symbols, sound symbols as in music, and art symbols. Without such symbolic skill the child is virtually unable to function in school and later on in the adult society.

2. *Coping With Authority.* A mentally healthy child must be able to deal with rules, manage rapid and sometimes arbitrary changes in rules, and be able to accept penalties for breaking rules. It is highly significant that no society of adults or children can go on without goals, rules by which one reaches goals, and penalties for those who do not play by the rules. In the case of children, those who do not play by the rules are often not permitted to play. In adult society, those who continually break the rules are sent to institutions that prevent them from functioning in our society. A child has little alternative; he must learn how to deal with authority.

3. *Living With Peer Groups.* As part of the skill of dealing with rules, one must learn how to be an individual and yet function in his peer group. The mentally healthy child has learned how to deal with the "give and take" nature of daily associations with his classmates and friends.

4. *Regulating Emotions.* The mentally healthy child is able to control and manage his impulses. This does not mean that a child must give up his impulses or inner life in order to become a mentally healthy person. The ability to control one's impulses must also include the ability to loosen controls when such freedom is appropriate and desirable. It suggests freedom to be imaginative, to be spontaneous, or to be emotional when such behavior is enhancing and productive for the individual. Inhibited behavior can be just as irrational in some contexts as impulsive behavior often seems to be. A mentally healthy child needs to have access to his impulse life and must be able to utilize each success appropriately. One can say that a mentally healthy individual has achieved an integrative balance between his emotional and rational capabilities.

THE PREVALENCE OF BEHAVIOR DISORDERS

It is difficult to determine with any degree of accuracy the incidence of behavior disorders in children, because estimates of maladjustment vary with the definition of disturbance, the agencies sampled (school, child-guidance clinics, juvenile court, resident hospitals), and the identification methods employed (referrals to professional specialists, rating scales, self-report inventories, and sociograms).

The most thorough review of incidence studies on maladjustment in elementary school pupils is contained in a report prepared for the Joint Commission on the Mental Health of Children by Glidewell and Swallow (1968). Their data, which are based on 27 studies reported between 1925 and 1967, indicate that 30% of the elementary school youth show at least mild adjustment problems, 10% are in need of professional clinical assistance, and 4% would be referred to clinical facilities if such services were available. These findings are consistent with those reported by Bower (1960) in that they, too, indicate that three youngsters in the average classroom (10%) have moderate to severe mental health problems. Using this 10% figure, Bower (1970) estimated that there are 5.5 million youth from kindergarten through college who have moderate to severe problems of adjustment. Regrettably, the vast majority of disturbed youngsters do not receive the assistance they need.

Whether or not the incidence of childhood disturbance in the United States is on the rise is a difficult question to answer, since the statistics pertaining to this matter do not lend themselves to unequivocal interpretations. It may well be, however, that the increase in cases seen by child-guidance clinics reflects a heightened concern over childhood disorders instead of an actual increase in such problems. Regardless of whether or not mental illness is on the increase, we do know that emotional disturbance in children is not randomly distributed throughout the childhood population. Instead, it is commonly associated with certain variables, the discussion of which follows.

Factors Related to Prevalence

EDUCATIONAL MALADJUSTMENT

There is considerable evidence to show that educational maladjustment is associated with personal maladjustment in school-age children. Burke and Simons (1965), using a questionnaire technique with institutionalized delinquents, reported that more than 90% of the sample had records of truancy and poor school adjustment, nearly three fourths had failed two or more grades, more than 75% had left school at or before the legal age of sixteen, two thirds were reading below the sixth-grade level, and 60% had IQ scores in the average range. One large-scale investigation of public school classes for emotionally disturbed children of normal intellectual ability revealed that a significant degree of academic retardation accompanied the emotional maladjustment characteristic of this population (Morse, Cutler, and Fink, 1964). Turning to the regular classroom setting, we find similar results. Students, for instance, who are the same age or younger than their classmates receive greater peer acceptance than students who are older than their classmates (Bedoian, 1954).

It is often very difficult to distinguish between educational maladjustment and personal maladjustment in school-age youth. Finding a close relationship between the two is expected for at least two reaons. (1) Accomplishment in school-related activities constitutes perhaps the major developmental task of youth in our society. Hence, if something interferes with the achievement of a reasonable mastery of this developmental task, such failure probably affects other aspects of the child's personal adjustment. Developmental tasks are interrelated, so that success or failure in one task tends to increase the likelihood of success or failure in others. (2) School maladjustment and personal maladjustment have many common determinants, such as low intelligence, low socioeconomic status, poor peer relations, and a variety of ego factors (distractibility, an inability to delay reward, and poor moral character). We are not equating educational and personal maladjustment, however. Broader and more nonacademic criteria must be considered or applied in arriving at a definition of emotional disturbance in children. We are, however, stressing the notion that adjustment to school is related to the child's mental health during the school years.

SEX DIFFERENCES IN ADJUSTMENT

The Plight of Boys. The variable of sex is the one most clearly related to differences in adjustment among children. Emotional disturbance in children is primarily a male phenomenon. Indeed, practically every major study reports sex differences in adjustment. In general, the sex ratio for male adjustment among elementary school students is about 3:1. That is, for every three boys labeled as maladjusted by teachers, there is only one girl so labeled. Applying this 3:1 sex ratio to the 10% prevalence rate for moderate to severe forms of maladjustment among the elementary school population indicates that about 15% of boys and about 5% of girls are in need of professional attention. School adjustment difficulties for boys typically center around problems of acceptance of authority, concentration, cognitive achievement, speech, and reading (Glidewell and Swallow, 1968). Their difficulties are reflected in the following facts: there is a higher percentage of failure among boys in every grade and in every subject; boys comprise the bulk of early school leavers; boys dislike school more than do girls; on achievement tests, boys score from 6 to 18 months below girls at the elementary and secondary school levels.

Like the evidence emanating from the public schools, child guidance clinics, and juvenile courts, admissions data on inpatient or residential psychiatric facilities reflect a sex differential for children under age fifteen (U.S. Department of Health, Education, and Welfare, 1965). Interestingly, this sex differential seems to disappear with increasing age. For example, the clinic termination rates for males dropped approximately one third after late adolescence. By contrast, the rates for females increased 22% during this period.

The findings on sex differences in mental health raise a number of interesting questions. Is emotional disturbance, for boys at least, primarily a childhood or school-related phenomenon, or does it persist into adulthood? Do female rates rise because of role conflicts experienced in the years following graduation from high school? Does maladjustment in males really decrease with age or are older males simply less willing to admit to having problems than females? What is there about society's basic institutions, namely, the home and the school, that affect boys adversely? Firm answers to all these questions are unfortunately not yet available.

What Can the School Do? Four basic approaches have been advanced to cope with

"You'd better go to school tomorrow and see how things are . . . he prayed
for his teacher tonight!" *(Drawing by Joe E. Buresch from* Today's Education/
NEA Journal, 1971)

problems of sex differences in school adjustment. First, efforts have been made to hire more *male teachers* at the elementary school level. With the general increase in teacher salaries and with scarcity of jobs at the secondary level, it is reasonable to anticipate an upsurge in the number of male teachers available for younger students. Whether male teachers will affect boys differently than their female counterparts remains to be seen. Recent evidence suggests that the sex of the teacher, as such, appears to be of little or no importance (Brophy and Good, 1973). Furthermore, as Garai and Scheinfeld (1968) note, the mere addition of male teachers to the staff is not likely to have any permanent effect if they are unaware of the importance in the educational process of the sex differences that exist in abilities, cognitive styles, interests, and motivations.

Administrative provisions have also been proposed. Foremost among these are separate classes for the sexes and the postponing of school entrance by 1 year for boys because of their maturational lag. While these proposals are not without merit, they, too, have drawbacks. The most serious of these stems from the fact that most boys (approximately 85%) are able to achieve a satisfactory adjustment under current administrative plans. Certainly, many educators and parents would object to holding back the large majority of boys 1 year when there is no apparent advantage in doing so. Moreover, if we did change the age requirements for school entrance, we might find that when seven-year-old boys are taught with six-year-old girls, the boys benefit from the equalization of language skills but the girls are handicapped in arithmetic. Maturational differences and sex-related abilities, interests, and motivations interact to make this a very complex problem that will not yield to such simple solutions. A more promising approach is to identify those students, females as well as males, who are likely to encounter difficulty in school and provide various special arrangements for them.

Differences in cognitive style and noncognitive traits have been cited as possible rationales for *single-sex education*.[1] Although the findings are far from conclusive, there is some evidence to suggest that in certain subjects, males learn better in all-male classes (Garai and Scheinfeld, 1968). Yet it would also seem that males as well as females benefit in ways not yet measured from association with the opposite sex. Total segregation of the sexes seems unjustified in the light of current information, but the use of single-sex classes might be warranted in certain areas, not only to improve the adjustment of the male student, but to enhance the achievements of females in areas in which they are ordinarily not encouraged to excel (e.g., mathematics).

A third proposal centers around *changes in curriculum and teaching strategies*. Many basal readers are now beginning to include stories that hold more appeal for boys (e.g., racing stories). The use of programmed teaching also deserves further attention. One of the few studies that ever reported superior reading of boys over girls involved the use of programmed reading materials (McNeil, 1964). The gadgetry or technologized instruction involved might have appealed to these young male students.

Finally, it is imperative that teachers develop *an appreciation of the differences between the sexes* with regard to abilities, interests, and motivations. Understanding these differences can form a basis for new modes of dealing with this problem. We must do more than simply supply teachers with additional information. We have to help them develop favorable attitudes toward the sexes. The elementary school teacher, for instance, must see the boy's activity orientation as desirable because it helps promote a masculine sex identity, although it may be disruptive to classroom conformity on occasion. Providing information and changing attitudes can perhaps be best accomplished through discussions in teacher-training courses and through in-service workshops conducted by school counselors and psychologists.

SOCIOECONOMIC STATUS AND RACE

Mental health specialists are becoming more aware of and concerned about the role played by social and cultural factors in childhood difficulties. Data based on 579 of 682 clinics in 25 states indicate that nonwhite rates of disturbance are higher during most of adolescence and adulthood, although lower in early childhood (ages three to eleven) except for mental deficiency. Moreover, non-

[1] Each sex appears to have its own cognitive style in approaching mechanical, spatial, mathematical, and scientific problems, with women using narrower categories, paying more attention to detail, and relying on fewer spatial cues, and men using broader categories, paying greater attention to global configurations, and relying on a wider variety of spatial cues. Noncognitive differences exist with regard to achievement motivation with males appearing to be more concerned with the intrinsic satisfaction found in successful completion of a task and females more concerned with satisfaction derived from their affiliative needs, that is, their needs for social acceptance and recognition.

whites tend to be seen for more serious disorders (Rosen, Bahn, and Kramer, 1964).

Racial differences at the elementary school level have not been carefully studied, but problems of classroom management are more common in the black slum school (Glidewell and Swallow, 1968). The incidence of deviant behavior may run as high as 70% in inner-city schools (Kellam and Schiff, 1967). Although there is probably class bias involved in the definition of deviant behavior, this finding is consistent with the observation that teachers of inner-city youth do spend an inordinate amount of time on matters of discipline.

The higher incidence of behavior disorders in blacks than in whites can be attributed to the debilitating influence of such factors as prejudice, discrimination, segregation, an unstable and matriarchal family structure, restricted educational and vocational opportunities, and possibly a negative self-image (Ausubel and Ausubel, 1963). According to Douglas (1959), the frustrations resulting from such conditions has resulted in a juvenile delinquency rate in blacks that surpasses that of whites by at least 2 to 1. Not surprisingly, suppressed feelings of aggression (Karon, 1958) and a high level of anxiety (Palermo, 1959) have been identified as common features of maladjustment among blacks. Though the need for mental health services appears to be greater for blacks than for whites, clients from impoverished backgrounds have a relatively shorter length of clinic stay (Bahn, Chandler, and Eisenberg, 1962). Our mental health services are not always closely related to the needs of people.

When socioeconomic status, regardless of race, is examined, the picture remains basically unchanged. For example, Bower (1961), in his California study, reported a higher incidence of disturbed children among certain occupational groups. The group whose fathers' occupations were categorized as "service" or "semiskilled" produced more than twice as many emotionally handicapped pupils as would be anticipated on the basis of their percentage of the state's total population. Fathers in the "unskilled" occupation category also produced more than their share of emotionally disturbed children. Pupils of fathers who were employed in professional or managerial positions, on the other hand, produced far fewer emotionally disturbed children than was expected.

AGE

Maladjustment among students seems to attract the greatest attention during the preadolescent and middle adolescent periods. We know, for example, that the highest percentage of emotionally handicapped pupils are in the elementary and junior high grades, with the lowest percentage of emotionally handicapped children in the early primary grades and later high school years (Bower, 1961). Approximately two thirds of classes for emotionally disturbed children in the public schools are at the later elementary and junior high levels (Morse, Cutler, and Fink, 1964).

Glidewell and Swallow (1968) report, however, that age differences *per se* in the prevalence of maladjustment are probably not great. Many of the problems experienced by kindergartners and first graders are often viewed as merely temporary symptoms of normal process of accommodation to school. Delayed reporting of these problems may partly explain the higher incidence of referrals to clinics and special classes during the elementary and junior high years. The lower referral rates during the adolescent years might be related to the fact that many students with a long history of maladjustment drop out of school.

MALADJUSTMENT IN CHILDREN AND YOUTH: SIGNS AND STABILITY

Recognizing Signs of Maladjustment

The difficulties associated with the definition of normality and deviancy were discussed earlier in this chapter. One definition that can help teachers to identify "emotionally disturbed" children is advanced by Bower (1970). He notes that the emotionally handicapped child has one or more of the following characteristics.

1. *An unexplained inability to learn.* The child's difficulty cannot be explained adequately or primarily by intellectual deficits, specific learning disabilities, physical difficulties, or differences in cultural or ethnic background. This characteristic is regarded as the most significant in spotting students with mental health problems. The inability to use one's intelligence efficiently as manifested by an appreciable discrepancy between actual and expected academic performance carries considerable importance as a criterion of emotional disturbance in children.

2. *An inability to achieve satisfactory social relationships* with children or adults. The child is unable to show warmth and sympathy toward others, to stand alone when necessary, to have close friends, to be assertively constructive, and so forth.

3. *An inability to behave at a level commensurate with one's developmental status.* The child operates at a more immature level, in terms of his interests and behavior, than do most youngsters his age.

4. *An inability to display confidence and belief in one's self* or to overcome feelings of sadness. This child's unhappiness and feelings of inadequacy may manifest itself in his expressive play, art work, written assignments, or discussion periods. Any kind of *joie de vivre* is missing in his school work and social relations.

5. *An inability to cope with stressful personal or school situations* without developing fears, physical symptoms, or pains, such as headaches or stomachaches.

While all children may at some point in life exhibit some of the above inabilities, Bower argues that a child, in order to be considered emotionally handicapped, must exhibit these characteristics to a marked extent and over a prolonged period of time before the designation of "emotionally handicapped" is justified. In other words, we must also consider the frequency, intensity, and duration of the behavior in determining if maladjustment exists.

The Stability of Deviant Behavior

Most children experience problems in the course of development; the resolution of these tasks leads to differential modes of adjustment. The question arises, however, as to whether childhood problems and maladaptive modes of behavior are transient or permanent in nature. In other words, does a child grow out of his problems with advancing age, or does he become increasingly disturbed? The answer to this question is of interest to both theorists and practitioners. For the theorist, knowledge pertaining to the stability of deviant behavior furthers understanding of both normal and abnormal personality development. For the practicing educator, such knowledge would better enable him not only to predict the course and outcome of various behavior problems, but also to focus treatment on the cases most in need of professional intervention.

What can we conclude in the light of available evidence? Conclusions must be tentative, because there has been no study specifically designed to measure the stability of deviant behavior over time and because of the methodological shortcomings of past studies. Still, we will advance some tentative conclusions, first for the school years, then for post-school adjustment.

THE SCHOOL YEARS

In contrast to the results of long-term follow-up studies on clinic populations, follow-up studies of behavior disorders among school children suggest that school maladjustment does persist. For instance, one follow-up study (Zax et al., 1968) reported that students identified early in their school careers as emotionally disturbed were as seventh graders more negatively perceived by teachers and peers, required more attention from the school nurse, and achieved less well in comparison with a group of normal youngsters. Stringer and Glidwell (1967) likewise reported that 87% of students markedly deficient in both achievement and mental health during the early grades maintained the same status throughout elementary school.

The research literature is not entirely consistent, however. In studies in Onondaga County, New York, for example, it was reported that of 515 students rated as disturbed in 1961 by their teachers, only 160 were so perceived in 1963. In 1965, only 9 of the original group were so perceived. Approximately three fourths of the 515 students were designated as disturbed only once (Mental Health Research Unit, 1964, 1967). More rigorous research will be needed, however, before we can draw any firm conclusions about the stability of school maladjustment. Even if school maladjustment is found to persist throughout

one's school years, it might not prove a good predictor of later adult adjustment.

POSTSCHOOL ADJUSTMENT

How does the deviant youngster fare once he has left school and home?

1. The population of disturbed children appears to contribute more than its share to the population of adults with psychiatric disabilities. About 30% of disturbed children will continue to have moderate to severe problems as adults.

2. While it is commonly assumed that adult behaviors and personality are established in early life experiences, and while there is a body of research demonstrating the stability of personality over time, there is nonetheless a real danger in overgeneralization. For it appears that 70% of those with childhood disorders grow up to be normal adults.

3. In large measure, the stability of the deviant behavior depends on the child's environment. This is a major factor in his total adjustment. A dependent adult, for instance, may achieve an adequate adjustment if he has a supportive employer who will take time to give him the attention and direction he needs. Similarly, an individual who has problems with authority may not experience adjustment difficulties if he has a job in which he is able to work under conditions of minimal supervision and has an easygoing, nondirective wife. Thus, even if personality characteristics remained perfectly constant, we could expect some change in an individual's behavior as a consequence of environmental factors.

4. Aggressive, antisocial, acting-out behavior of a severe nature is most predictive of later disturbance as an adult and most deserving of treatment efforts. For example, Roff (1961) found that reliable group predictions of military adjustment could be made on the basis of earlier social adjustment in school. Children who were mean and disliked by their classmates typically had bad conduct records in military service.

5. Although two out of three "incorrigibly" delinquent youngsters continue in their antisocial ways, it must not be assumed that the majority of young norm violators become adult criminals. It is widely agreed that much juvenile delinquency does not inevitably terminate in adult criminal activity.

6. Shyness and withdrawn behavior tend to disappear with advancing age. At worst, these problems are less incapacitating and socially disruptive than those of the antisocial child. Moreover, there is little evidence to suggest that shyness is predictive of later serious disturbance, despite the fact that introverted behavior is often viewed as having dire consequences for mental health.

7. Neurotic symptoms (fears, hypersensitiveness, tics), often presumed to be the precursors of adult neurotic disturbances, have also been found lacking in predictive power. The findings of current research challenge the long-held assumptions that adult neurotic behaviors result from disturbances in parent-child relations or from parental loss in childhood (Robins, 1966).

8. The probability of improvement in childhood schizophrenia, a very severe but infrequent condition, is indeed low. Approximately one in four of those so diagnosed apparently achieve a reasonably adequate adjustment (Eisenberg, 1957).

9. Generally speaking, it is very difficult to postulate any direct causal relationship between early childhood maladjustment and later specific psychiatric disability. We still do not fully understand the effects of later experiences on personality adjustment. Also, we must not overlook the possibility that

many adult disturbances arise independently of childhood problems.

In our present state of knowledge, we can conclude that there is at best only mild or or moderate evidence to support the notion that disturbed children turn into seriously disturbed adults. Since the less noxious childhood disorders are more common than the more severe disorders, it would seem that, all in all, change appears to characterize the course of behavior deviations in children more than chronicity or stability. The conception of emotional disturbance in children as a condition that deteriorates into dramatic and bizarre varieties of mental disorders in later life is thus called into question.

Undoubtedly, some of the improvement in mental health with age can be attributed to different standards of adjustment for children and adults. In the case of children, the ability to learn academic tasks constitutes a primary yardstick for normality. If the child is unteachable, he is often considered maladjusted. In the case of adults, however, the ability to learn academic tasks no longer constitutes a basic criterion of adjustment. The basic yardstick has become vocational and social adequacy. If the adult can adapt reasonably well to his environment, he is apt to be seen as normal. We must also remember that the adult has much greater choice in selecting suitable or more psychologically comfortable surroundings than the child does. The child cannot change his home, his teacher, his school, or his neighborhood. The adult can change his job, his spouse, his boss, his friends, and his residence. In other words, the adult is freer than the child to select a setting more compatible with his style of life. In a sense he can choose his own norm group, while for a child, there is essentially one set of norms—the school's.

We are not implying that certain behaviors, such as stealing and seclusiveness, are not indicative of serious emotional disturbance in children. Furthermore, we do not want to leave the impression that children's problems are unimportant and therefore should be left to self-resolution. These problems are in need of alleviation, since they can distress both children and the adults who must deal with them. Finally, although most maladjusted youth do not develop *severe* pathologies as adults, it is still an open question as to whether disturbed children eventually develop life-styles characteristic of *mild* personality disturbance (aloofness, insensitiveness, oversensitiveness, obsequiousness, flightiness, snobbishness, mistrust, hostility, narrow-mindedness, compulsiveness, indecisiveness, impatience, pessimism, and so forth). Regrettably, no investigations of this possibility have been reported.

IMPLICATIONS FOR EDUCATIONAL PRACTICE

Guidelines for Referral

Assuming that professional help is available, when should a teacher refer a youngster for professional help? There are no rules that permit a definite answer to this issue, but Bower's description of the emotionally handicapped child should prove helpful in reaching a decision as to whether the child needs professional assistance. The list of questions advanced by Kessler (1966) can also serve as guideposts for referral. If the answers to the questions that follow suggest more than the usual amount of adjustment difficulties, consideration should then be given to a search for outside consultation.

1. *Age discrepancy.* Is there a significant difference between actual chronological age and the behavioral age?

2. *Frequency of occurrence* of the symptom. How often are the problem behaviors manifested?

3. *The number of symptoms.* Is it an isolated problem area or does the child have a number of problems?

4. *The degree of social disadvantage.* How much do the behaviors influence the child's interpersonal relations, and how much influence do they have on the behaviors of others?

5. *The child's inner suffering.* Does the problem "hurt" the child, that is, cause anguish, or is he quite content in and with himself?

6. *Intractability of behaviors.* Does the problem persist even after others have tried to bring about change?

7. *General personality appraisal.* Since the most important thing is general adjustment, does the problem cause a significant disruption in the child's general psychosocial behavioral functioning?

The teacher with a problem pupil might consider three basic criteria in reaching a decision about referral. He might first ask himself if the child's social, emotional, and intellectual needs are being reasonably met within the classroom setting. If the child is unable to benefit academically or achieve relatively satisfying interpersonal relations despite adjustments in the school program designed to promote such development, professional consultation may be indicated.

Consideration for the rights of normal children must also be undertaken. American public education is based on group methods of instruction and has established its goals for normal pupils. Not infrequently, emotionally disturbed youngsters demand so much of the teacher's time and energy that the education of the group suffers. As any experienced educator will testify, a teacher can spend as much or more time with one emotionally disturbed pupil as he does with the rest of the class. When the teacher believes that the group's needs are being sacrificed for one child's needs, it is time to seek professional assistance.

The teacher must also take his own mental health into account. Behaviorally disordered students are often quite skillful at irritating other people. They have mastered a variety of techniques and have had years of experience in antagonizing others. One kindergarten boy so distressed his teacher that he became obsessed with thoughts regarding the daily management of this child and actually dreaded coming to work. As the teacher recognizes that his own mental hygiene is suffering and that his teaching effectiveness is being impaired, he would do well to request an evaluation for the child so that additional therapeutic or corrective measures may be planned. The teacher should also remember that he can receive advice regarding the desirability of referral from such co-workers as the school counselor, other teachers, and the principal.

Services Needed

Because students vary widely in their mental health needs, it is important that schools provide a variety of services. Reynolds (1962) has presented a hierarchy of services that is particularly applicable to the mental health needs of children. (See Figure 13-1.)

REGULAR CLASSES

What might not be obvious from the discussion of stability of deviant behavior is that approximately 70% of disturbed adults come from the population of "normal" children. This finding strongly indicates that a battery

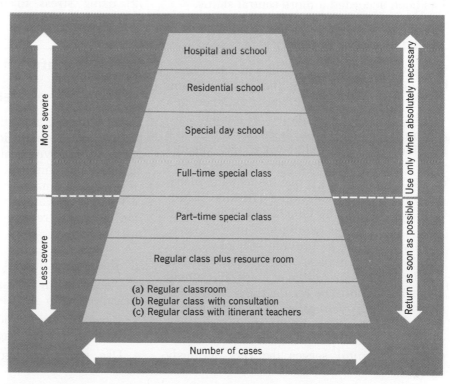

Figure 13-1.
Hierarchy of services for special education programs for children with behavior disorders. *(Adapted from M. C. Reynolds, "A Framework for Considering Some Issues in Special Education," Exceptional Children, 28, March, 1962)*

of school mental health services should first and foremost include a sound program of prevention for all students. Healthy teacher-pupil relationships coupled with a curriculum that is broad and flexible enough to encompass individual differences in ability, interests, and cultural background can go far in providing a sound base for a school mental health program. Redl and Wattenberg (1959) list four specific ways in which learning can assist development. (1) Learning builds and supports the child's feeling of self worth. (2) Learning can help to satisfy the needs for belonging. (3) Learning builds confidence, which in turn increases the drive for further learning. (4) Achievement in learning helps a child to set realistic goals for himself.

In the past we have neglected the preventive aspects of a school mental health program in favor of the treatment aspect. In recent years, however, the concept of prevention has been accorded a more central status.

ADDITIONAL PROVISIONS

Some youngsters require other forms of help. One popular provision is the *resource room*. Under this plan, the student is assigned to a regular class, but spends part of the day with a resource teacher who diagnoses the child's problem, offers remedial work, and consults with the regular classroom teacher. If the above arrangements prove inadequate, placement in a *special class* on a part-time or full-time basis might be considered. The special *day school* serves youngsters in a separate facility in order to provide special services not available in most school districts. The children continue to live at home, but attend a special school. The *residential school* is designed to help youngsters (e.g., delinquents) whose needs cannot be met in the community, and who require 24-hour care. The *psychiatric hospital* serves the very seriously disturbed youth. Most psychiatric hospitals now have residential schools, but some youngsters are too disturbed to attend and must remain on the wards.

The school cannot become a panacea for all of the ills afflicting youngsters, since many forces influencing psychological robustness are beyond the control of educational institutions as they are presently constituted. It would be extremely difficult for even the best school mental health program to counteract the impact of such extraschool influences as geographical mobility, changing value systems in the culture at large, and undesirable child-rearing practices. Moreover, many of the formative influences may well have exacted their toll by the time youngsters enter school. Despite these limitations, the school does have a large number of specific and practical options available for (1) reducing pupil stress when it might have a destructive impact and (2) using stress to foster positive mental health.

Stress: Harmful and Helpful

ACTIVITIES FOR REDUCING STRESS

Stress-reducing activities fall into three basic categories: (1) modification or elimination, (2) isolation of vulnerable children from stress that cannot be modified, and (3) interception of problems at an early stage (Lambert, 1964).

There are several ways in which the school can modify or reduce stress. Some examples are:

1. Shorten the pupil's school day.

2. Place him in a smaller group within the classroom or in another class.

3. Have a home-school conference to elicit parental understanding and help.

4. Use new teaching techniques in areas

where a child has previously failed. For example, the use of counters in building arithmetic concepts, kinesthetic (tracing-sounding) approaches in spelling, and/or programmed learning materials may offer the child new opportunities for success.

5. Have a morning nutrition period to forestall hunger pangs that interfere with concentration in school work.

In many cases it is difficult to reduce the causes of stress. Under such circumstances the following kinds of activities have proven helpful.

1. Assign the child to a resource room for part of the day.

2. See if medication is needed.

3. Use cubicles or "offices."

4. Excuse the student from stress-producing activities.

5. Eliminate grading for the time being, substituting charts of the child's progress.

Schools can also do much to intercept problems early in an attempt to prevent further difficulty. Some activities involving early identification and treatment of stress are listed below.

1. Provide screening programs for locating children with potential physical, emotional, and social difficulties. Follow up with diagnosis and recommendations for specific interventions.

2. Have an orientation program for parents and children when the children are beginning a new grade sequence or a new school.

3. Check pupil progress regularly for students who may fail or have difficulty.

4. Use remedial education as soon as the help is indicated.

5. Refer the pupil to other professional workers to obtain additional assistance.

ACTIVITIES TO STRENGTHEN PERSONALITY

While massive stress can be harmful and lead to unhealthy patterns of behavior, stress, when properly managed, can also stimulate growth and maturity. Here are some examples of ways in which the school can help build personality strength in students who experience stress.

1. Help students through minor traumas by role playing.

2. Get youngsters together in some type of nonacademic activity such as crafts, music, and field trips to emphasize mutual interests and development of special skills and talents.

3. Assist the child in his ability to relate to others by establishing a "mother," "father," or "big-brother" bank in the school.

4. Increase the youngster's motivation to cope actively with his shortcomings by finding areas of interest. For example, help adolescents learn to read to pass the examination for a driver's license.

5. Hold group problem-solving meetings in order to teach students to apply their intelligence to personal and social dilemmas.

Curriculum Approaches

Some workers believe that one of the most effective ways to promote the mental health of students entails the incorporation of psychological concepts into the curriculum. Such incorporation would not only insure a definite place for mental health instruction, but also accomplish this instruction in a systematic manner. Curriculum approaches fall into one of three basic types (Kaplan, 1971): (1) incidental instruction, (2) separate courses, and (3) units. Each approach has advantages and disadvantages.

INCIDENTAL INSTRUCTION

Incidental instruction has in its favor the fact that instruction occurs at a time when problems are immediate and real and motivation and interest are maximal. Drawbacks to this approach center around the need for teacher sensitivity and teacher sophistication in child developmental and mental health.

SEPARATE COURSES

Separate courses have also been used. Outstanding among these are the Bullis Project and Roen's behavioral-science curriculum. In the Bullis Project (Kaplan, 1971), the teacher is provided with a basic textbook containing lesson plans and stimulus stories. These stories, which center around emotional problems similar to those that preadolescents and early adolescents might be experiencing, are read to the class. After a discussion of the stories, the teacher summarizes the mental health principles involved and the students record the conclusions in a daily log. Sample topics include "How Emotions Are Aroused," "Overcoming Personal Handicaps," and "Submitting to Authority." Kaplan contends that this approach is too didactic and moralistic. To our knowledge, there has been no research evaluation of this approach.

Roen (1965, 1967) developed a behavioral-sciences course that he taught to fourth graders. The class met for 40 minutes once a week over the school year. Roen reports that it was not difficult to recast concepts into terms the students could comprehend. A seminar entitled "Teaching the Behavioral Sciences to Children" was used to assist teachers. The course content included such topics as the influences of heredity and en-

vironment on development, psychosocial stages of development, the self-concept, various learning-theory concepts, the concept of intelligence, institutional influences on development, and sociological analysis of the classroom. At the end of the course, each student was asked to write an autobiography discussing his uniqueness as a person and the particular forces producing that uniqueness. It is still too early to determine the effectiveness of this behavioral-science teaching program. Preliminary evaluation indicates, however, that these elementary school students mastered the course content satisfactorily. Furthermore, the children reportedly responded enthusiastically to the course, and there were no complaints from the adult community.

UNITS

The third approach, the use of mental health units, is viewed by Kaplan (1971) as a compromise between the other two approaches. These units, which are built around problems at various stages of development, become an integral part of courses already in the curriculum and provide consistent and systematic mental health instruction. The Ojemann Projects, which used special units in addition to revised basic text material, serve as an example of this approach.

Since 1941, Ojemann and his associates have developed and evaluated a curriculum approach to mental health that emphasizes a causal orientation to the social environment. By incorporating behavioral-science concepts into a curriculum that focuses on the causes or motivations of human behavior — as opposed to the surface or behavioral aspects — Ojemann hoped that the student would be better prepared to solve problems confronting him at the time and in the future. The basic rationale is that a person who becomes more fully aware and appreciative of the dynamics of human behavior in general and of his own in particular is better able to cope with personal and social crises.

A dynamic approach involves an awareness of the probabilistic nature of human behavior, an attitude of flexibility and tolerance, and an ability to view a given situation from another's perspective. A causal approach, in short, seeks to foster a greater sensitivity to interpersonal relationships so that more effective interaction with the environment is facilitated. Many adults are capable of solving impersonal problems, but fail to "use their heads" in coping with personal and social anxieties. Ojemann (1967) contends that a sensible arrangement would be to lay a foundation in the causal or motivational approach to behavior in children starting in kindergarten. Then, as the child passes into adulthood, he can add to this foundation and apply such a base to the study of marriage and family relationships, employer-employee interactions, and so forth. This approach not only enables the child to surmount current crises, but establishes a foundation for the solution of crises in later development.

How does Ojemann hope to establish a causal approach? For one thing, he stresses the need to educate the teacher "to live a causal approach in the classroom." As a modeling procedure, daily associations with a teacher who handles situations in an understanding way can go far in developing a causal approach to life.

One teaching strategy used during the primary grades consists of narratives in which the surface and causal approaches are contrasted. In kindergarten and first grade, the teacher reads the narratives. In the later grades, the child reads them by himself. Each narrative depicts a situation in which a character in the story responds in a surface way initially, but in a causal way after he has thought through the situation again. Realistic stories are used. To promote a more generalized approach, stories are described involving children older and younger than himself as well as those from different environments. Discussion focusing on the meaning and causes of the behavior in question follows each narrative.

At the elementary and secondary levels, the social sciences and English literature offer numerous opportunities to study the forces influencing the behavior of people. Even in areas such as math and science, the teacher can serve as a model for this type of approach.

Evaluations of this approach to date have been promising. The results of more than a dozen research studies indicate that an "appreciation of the dynamics of behavior is accompanied by significant changes in such dimensions as manifest anxiety, tendency to immediate arbitrary punitivensss, antidemocratic tendencies, conception of the teacher and tolerance of ambiguity." (Ojemann, 1967) There is some evidence, then, that education in the behavioral sciences can produce youngsters who are less anxiety ridden, less arbitrary, and less authoritarian in handling personal problems. Unfortunately, this curriculum has had very little impact on school procedures (Roen, 1967).

TEACHER MENTAL HEALTH

Impact on Students

Teaching can offer numerous opportunities for an altruistic, beneficient, and constructive kind of self-fulfillment (Peck and Mitchell, 1969). Not only can teachers derive a sense of personal competence from fulfilling their roles effectively, but they have the added benefit of knowing that they have helped others advance both cognitively and emotionally. In a genuine sense, the competent teacher grows personally and professionally as he helps students to develop.

The well-adjusted teacher is free to concentrate on the needs of his students. He is free because he is "not laboring under the burden of his own personal problems which could sap his emotional strength and leave little time or energy for anything else." (Peck and Mitchell, 1969) Moreover, he serves as a model of good mental health by communicating his own satisfaction with life, by exemplifying his own enthusiasm for learning, by accepting the challenges of his job, and by inspiring confidence.

Unfortunately, teaching does not always satisfy constructive motivations, and poor mental health is also contagious. For some, teaching provides an outlet for hostile or neurotic kinds of gratification. Illustrative of exploitive need fulfillment are the "mother-hen complex" and "the habit of command" complex (Peck and Mitchell, 1969). In the former, the teacher fosters the dependency needs of her students. This teacher takes every opportunity to suffocate students, and expects their devotion in return for her help. When this exploitive pattern does not work, the teacher overreacts and becomes deeply hurt. This reaction is not surprising, since such teachers have a neurotic need to be liked and accepted by their students. They derive strength from the dependency of their pupils. They are gratified to see their students cry as they say good-bye at the end of the year (Kaplan, 1971). Nurturance and acceptance are, of course, desirable characteristics of teachers. However, developing total reliance, both emotionally and intellectually, is undesirable, because it stunts development. Students must become more self-reliant and independent in both the personal and academic spheres of their lives. The mother-hen is rarely aware of the real purpose of her actions. In fact, she typically assumes that her motivations are of the highest order because of her extensive contacts with students and the amount of nurturance she provides them.

The "habit of command" complex refers to teachers who become overly impressed with their own sense of importance, wisdom, and power. The classroom becomes their arena for ego income. Every teacher needs self-esteem, but it should not come at the expense of student needs. Regrettably, student initiative and responsibility are commonly squelched under such teacher domination. Because of his own needs for self-aggrandizement, this teacher is not free to develop a classroom atmosphere that fosters the students' best interests. This kind of teacher is often unaware of his own needs for power and status. Furthermore, when appreciable portions of a teacher's time and energy are absorbed in gratifying their own neurotic needs, it cannot be expended in preparation of lessons, in individualizing instruction, or in promoting the student's well-being.

The pervasive influence of the teacher's role is reflected in the fact that a teacher's mental health can strongly influence his relationship with students, his disciplinary tactics, his evaluation procedures, and his style of teaching. As Witty (1955) pointed out, there is a very high incidence of personality disturbance among students in classes taught by unstable teachers.

To set the matter of teacher mental health and its influence on students in perspective, however, two points should be noted. First, although reliable evidence is difficult to find, it appears that the incidence of emotional disturbance among teachers is no higher than among other professional groups. As Kaplan (1971) notes, "the fragmentary data available points to the existence of a relatively small group of teachers whose presence in the classroom is a sore spot in education." Second, as Ausubel (1969, p. 28) notes:

"Within fairly broad limits, many different kinds of teacher personality structure and ways of relating to children are compatible with normal mental health and personality development in pupils. This principle applies when either mildly undesirable classroom practices prevail over an extended period of time, or when more serious deviations from optimal standards occur occasionally. In general, children are not nearly as fragile as we profess to believe, and do not develop permanent personality disabilities from temporary exposure to interpersonal practices that fall short of what the experts currently regard as appropriate."

Stresses and Frustrations of Teachers

In this section, we will limit discussion to some of the occupational hazards that threaten teacher mental health. This focus on pressures emanating from one's professional role does not constitute a denial of the importance of personal problems, such as feelings of inadequacy, marital difficulties, and financial problems, which can influence how one discharges his professional duties. In actuality, stresses from the personal and professional sectors of life interact and intensify one another. As educators, our present concern will be, however, with certain occupational hazards—their identification and amelioration.

INCREASING CURRICULAR DEMANDS

Demands on the teacher have increased to the point that it is very difficult for the average person to meet them satisfactorily without experiencing excessive stress and strain. Teachers are to disseminate information of the effects of alcohol, tobacco, drugs; they must discuss environmental pollution; they must be able to spot the signposts of emotional disturbance in their students, cope with behavior problems, serve as a moral model,

"When they said the hours were from 9 to 3, I didn't know they meant 3 A.M." *(Drawing by Mal Gordon from NEA Journal, 1965)*

understand psychological test results, and yet not jeopardize instruction in subject matter areas (Kaplan, 1971). Then there is the new math, new science courses, foreign languages, and other curricular innovations that have put additional pressures on teachers. If nothing is done about such heavy demands on the teacher's time and energy, his job may cease to be a rewarding experience. It is practically impossible to acquire all the skills a teacher needs within the years spent in a teacher-training institution. Yet when teachers realize that they are not adequate for the task, there is often an ensuing threat to their own sense of personal and professional confidence. At times, this threat is handled by developing feelings of inferiority. In other instances, the teacher may cope with such feelings by finding deficiencies in his students. That is, he might come to believe that it is solely or primarily the students' fault that they do not learn as much as they should. The knowledge that one cannot perform his job adequately, especially after 4 to 5 years of training, can serve to impair teacher mental health and pedagogical effectiveness. Other teachers deny the existence of problems, perhaps to the point of ignoring students' needs for referral. Some teachers become perfectionists, driving their students toward unreasonable goals; in so doing, they threaten students' mental health.

DEMANDS FOR PROFESSIONAL ADVANCEMENT

As curricular demands have increased, so have the demands for professional improvement (Kaplan, 1971). Now many states require credit hours beyond the bachelor's degree for permanent certification. Some states even require the master's degree. In addition to formal course work requirements, there are a variety of workshops, building meetings, grade level meetings, PTA meetings, district meetings, and in-service meetings. One teacher estimated that she spent an extra 8 work weeks because of such meetings (Kaplan, 1971). Attending these meetings can be particularly fatiguing after having taught 30 youngsters all day. Even worse from the standpoint of teacher mental health is the fact that most of these meetings are not perceived as meaningful by many teachers.

COPING WITH MALADJUSTED CHILDREN

Having to work with emotionally disturbed children can also generate a sense of despair and helplessness in the teacher (Long and Newman, 1969). Some disturbed students are well versed in knowing how to antagonize teachers. Others may leave teachers frustrated and bewildered because of their withdrawal tendencies. Then there are the nonlearners who disturb a teacher's self-confidence. Al-

though many school systems now have specialists who consult on such cases, it is still the teacher who must live with the maladjusted student.

DIFFICULTIES WITH PARENTS

Parents can also be a source of difficulty for teachers. As one teacher complained, "I have a parent who calls me every night to complain about her child's behavior. At first I tried to be nice and tell her what to do but nothing is enough. Can't she see that I have a right to my evenings and can't she handle her own child? But I can't seem to cut her off and I feel helpless to do anything. I've told the principal, and he doesn't seem interested in helping me. 'Oh, she'll stop,' says he. But when?" (Long and Newman, 1969, p. 286)

Tensions between parents and teachers persistently center around three main sources: relationships to children, personal-professional differences, and counseling problems (Kaplan, 1971).

Relationships to Children. A teacher's relationship with a student differs from the parents' relationship with their child. Teachers have relatively temporary relationships with students and view them as members of a group situation. Furthermore, their relationship is a task-oriented one, and they are apt to take a more objective view of students. By contrast, parents view their child first as an individual, and their emotional involvement is considerable. Accordingly, their perceptions of the child's scholastic progress and affective behavior are inclined to be quite subjective and biased. Naturally enough, these differences in perspective do not foster effective communication between parents and teachers. What one party may view as reasonable, the other party may perceive as unreasonable.

Personal-Professional Differences. There are

also differences in viewpoint regarding changes in educational practices that cause tensions between parents and teachers. Parents, for example, might feel quite differently than educators regarding courses on sex education or the use of team teaching arrangements at the elementary school level. Some parents may be suspicious of innovations. Others may openly oppose them. In upper-middle class districts, the parents may feel that the schools are not sufficiently innovative and apply pressure to force changes in educational practice. Teachers, on the other hand, may feel that as professionals they are in a better position to judge the desirability of various instructional strategies and kinds of curriculum than parents are. Whenever any of the above disagreements occur, it usually poses a barrier to effective cooperation between the schools and the community.

Counseling Parents. Counseling with parents can often be an exasperating and threatening experience for teachers, especially since they receive no formal training in the art of interviewing. Parents may not be ready to accept the facts about their child's adjustment in school or they may regard the advice given as impractical in light of their own circumstances. For example, it may be impossible for parents to change such conditions as poor housing, working hours, domestic tensions, or unacceptable behavior patterns in the child. It is especially difficult for teachers to present negative information in an honest, yet kind considerate way. Usually we try to "soft-pedal" things so as not to hurt the parents and/or have them blame us for the child's shortcomings. Just as teachers feel uncomfortable about being the bearers of sad tidings, parents often find it difficult to accept unpleasant news. What usually happens is that both parties blame one another, and this only serves to increase the guilt and anguish of all concerned.

ISOLATION FROM THE ADULT WORLD

The teacher lives in a world of youth. There are many advantages that stem from association with young people, but there are also disadvantages. Foremost among these is an isolation from people his own age. The teacher not only spends his day with youth, but he often finds himself involved in other roles outside of the school setting that enforce contact with children and adolescents. For instance, he may find himself in community service roles, such as Sunday school teacher, scout leader, playground supervisor, athletic coach, or camp counselor. Because dedicated teachers are characterized by a high social service drive, and because they have had experience with young people, they often find themselves immersed in youth work (Wilson et al., 1969). This leaves little time for contact with other adults.

ADDITIONAL THREATS TO TEACHER MENTAL HEALTH

Other job conditions that can place the teacher under strain include

1. Restrictions on one's personal and social life (e.g., one teacher was told that he would have to live in the small town in which he taught).

2. Heavy work load (preparing lesson plans, correcting assignments, page work, sponsoring after school activities, various meetings, parent conferences, etc.).

3. Overcrowded classrooms (some teachers still have 40 students in a class—dull ones, bright ones, noisy ones, and shy ones).

4. Administrative practices (not supporting teachers when they are in the right, an emphasis on public relations, which comes at the expense of the teachers' and students' psychological welfare, failure to provide leadership, etc.).

5. Interpersonal difficulties with other staff (e.g., the formation of factions such as the progressive teachers versus the traditional ones, or the division into groups along pro- or antiadministration lines).

6. Lack of professional status and social isolation are also mental health hazards.

Toward Better Mental Health

A SENSE OF COMPETENCE

If teachers are to achieve a sense of professional and personal accomplishment, they must set goals that they can realistically achieve, they must recognize that all pupils will not, for a variety of reasons, function at grade level, that all deviant pupils cannot be "cured," and that all units will not be highly successful. By adopting a realistic level of aspiration, teachers can lessen their sense of guilt and despair (Ringness, 1968).

There are other ways in which teachers can develop a feeling of competence besides the setting of realistic goals. Attacking problems constructively is helpful. Doing something about problems is much healthier in the long run than habitual indecisiveness, withdrawal, and denial. Cultivating self-acceptance is still another way of promoting feelings of adequacy. Everybody has strengths and weaknesses. Concentrating on one's shortcomings and competition with other staff members should be avoided. Instead, one should focus on his successes, be himself, and remember that no human has ever achieved perfection.

ASSISTANCE WITH DIFFICULT STUDENTS

Coping with a severe learning disability case, an emotionally disturbed child, or one indifferent to school, can take as much teacher time and energy as the other 25 students in the class. As one teacher remarked: "There is a child in the classroom who suffers from an emotional problem. He is withdrawn, sensitive and nervous. . . . I try to work with this child, giving him projects that will display his self-worth, encourage him to join in the play activities of other children, give him extra 'slaps on the back' for work well done, etc. . . . After school he goes home, back into the same surroundings that have caused him to be emotionally disturbed in the first place. My work, seemingly, becomes undone; the child enters the classroom the next day in the same condition as he entered the day before. . . . I cannot help but sense a feeling of failure and helplessness."

Effective handling of a difficult student requires appreciable skill on the teacher's part. Because of the importance of effective classroom discipline, we have included a separate chapter on this topic (Chapter 14). In addition to the training provided by training institutions, the mental health specialists in the public schools might well offer workshops, institutes, and in-service programs on the management and instruction of difficult students, particularly for beginning teachers. Support from administrators would also ease the teacher's burden. A principal might, for example, seek additional personnel (learning disabilities specialists, counselors, teachers aides, etc.) or special materials to facilitate the adjustment of problem students. Administrative support is critical also when suspension from school is indicated as the method of choice for coping with a student.

In short, the teacher cannot be expected to go it alone. He must be given additional training on how to teach and manage students who are different, and he must be backed administratively in his exercising of legitimate sanctions.

A VOICE IN DECISION MAKING

Few professionals enjoy having to perform their roles in a manner dictated by others, especially when these others (nonteachers) do not have to experience the outcomes or consequences of their decisions on a daily basis. Teachers definitely want a voice in such matters as job conditions (class size, equipment), salary, fringe benefits, tenure provisions, curriculum change, and arranging the classroom learning environment. Indeed, without open channels of communication and participation of this sort, teachers will have difficulty achieving professional status and the kind of job conditions conducive to sound mental health.

RELIEF FROM NONTEACHING CHORES

One way of achieving better work conditions centers around relief from nonprofessional duties (Kaplan, 1971). One of the most common complaints of teachers is that they have to spend too much time in such menial chores as collecting the milk money, taking attendance, and completing records. All of these noninstructional chores detract from the amount of time teachers can spend fulfilling their primary teaching role. Much of the frustration attendant upon nonteaching obligations could be alleviated through added secretarial help and use of nonprofessionals. Students can also help if teachers are willing to delegate certain responsibilities to them. Trying to do everything in the classroom alone taxes both physical and mental stability. Aside from the issue of teacher mental health, it makes little sense to use professional educators to perform tasks that less well-trained people can easily do. We must free the teacher to teach, especially if we expect him to individualize instruction and master his many professional tasks.

HELP IN DEALING WITH PARENTS

As we noted earlier, working with parents is a common source of strain. Supervised experiences in counseling parents are sorely needed in teacher training programs. School counselors, psychologists, and social workers should be available to conduct in-service training programs to develop teachers' conference skills. Observation of parent conferences involving the above specialists and/or master teachers and role-playing experiences can also help the teacher. The objective is not to make teachers professional counselors, but to sharpen their skills to the point that they can communicate effectively with parents regarding common problems about the school adjustment difficulties of students.

The following guidelines for conducting parent conferences should help improve relationships between the home and the school.

1. Be friendly and try to put the parent at ease. This can be best accomplished in an informal atmosphere.

2. To initiate the conference, ask questions that focus on the child and his school work. Be careful not to convey the impression that the parent is a failure. See to it that the parent talks at least half of the time. And do not downgrade previous teachers or schools.

3. Start the conference with a discussion of the child's good points. You can talk about his needs later. Talk in a manner that you would appreciate a teacher using if she were talking to you about your own child.

4. Do not mislead the parent by downplaying the child's difficulties. Realism and constructive criticism are essential to good parental conferences.

5. Since the parents know the child better than you do, elicit suggestions from them as to ways the child's needs might best be satisfied (Kaplan, 1971).

More will be said about parent conferences in Chapter 16.

NEW INTERESTS

It is important that teachers develop interests outside of the school setting. Preoccupation with one's self and work is unhealthy. *Contact with other adults* is especially needed. Many of a teacher's adult contacts with other adults involve, unfortunately, other teachers (e.g., a teacher bowling team). The danger in this is that the teachers will talk shop and, in effect, take their jobs home with them. They should try to avoid associating with the same people over and over again. They must learn to converse with people from various walks of life, to take an interest in their pursuits, and to enjoy their companionship.

Because teachers spend so much time in contact with other people, some teachers may do well to develop interests which they can explore alone. Following a hectic day or week, nothing can be as relaxing as being alone—reading a book, playing a musical instrument, working in the garden, or taking a hike. By having our solitary moments, we can be more considerate when we do deal with others.

TIME FOR RECREATION

Because teachers live such busy, active lives, they are apt to use their "spare" time in other ways unless they set aside specific times for leisure. They must resist temptation to "catch up on things" during their free time. The healthy individual can play as well as work. Everyone needs a hobby or avocational pursuit. One has less time to dwell on petty personal and professional problems when he becomes engrossed in leisure time activities. Participation in leisure time activities should be given as much priority as household and professional duties. Every teacher owes himself this much.

Summary

1. There are two basic approaches used in defining normality—the statistical and the idealistic.

2. A mentally healthy student is one who (a) has mastered the symbols of society, (b) accepts reasonable authority, (c) can function well in groups, and (d) controls his impulses without loss of spontaneity.

3. Approximately 10% of school youth have moderate to severe emotional problems.

4. The incidence of emotional disturbance is not randomly distributed. Instead, it is associated with factors such as sex, educational maladjustment, socioeconomic status, and age.

5. Emotionally disturbed children will manifest some of the following characteristics to a marked extent and over an extended period of time: (a) an unexplained inability to learn, (b) poor social relationship, (c) immaturity, (d) feelings of sadness, and (e) an inability to cope with stress.

6. Maladjustment tends to be persistent during the school years, but it is not necessarily predictive of adult adjustment.

7. The majority of disturbed adults appear to come from the population of "normal children."

8. In trying to reach a decision about referral, the teacher should consider the welfare of the child, the group, and herself.

9. The school is not a mental health institution but it does have a role to play in this regard.

10. The school can reduce unnecessary stresses by modifying or eliminating them, isolating the vulnerable student, and intercepting the problem at any early stage.

11. The school can also strengthen a student's personality through strategies such as assisting him in group interactions, corrective learning experiences, and motivational development.

12. The mental health of teachers is probably comparable to that of individuals in other professions.

13. Within fairly broad limits, many different kinds of teacher personalities are compatible with the development of pupil mental health.

14. The occupational demands of teaching include increased curricular demands, demands for professional advancement, coping with difficult students, tense relationships with parents, social isolation, and a lack of voice in decisions regarding classroom life.

15. Teachers' mental health can be promoted through development of a sense of competence, assistance with maladjusted pupils, help in dealing with parents, relief from nonteaching chores, and the development of nonschool interests.

CHAPTER 14
Toward Positive Classroom Discipline

"Personally, I think these stories about classroom misbehavior are greatly exaggerated." *(Drawing by Derek Eastoe from Teacher's World, © 1973 by Evans Brothers Limited, London)*

Classroom management is one of the foremost problems for teachers. Adequate control of the class is a prerequisite to achieving instructional objectives and to safeguarding the psychological and physical well-being of students. Control techniques are also of vital concern to students, parents, and administrators. The student's attitudes toward school as well as the extent of his learnings are influenced to an appreciable degree by the disciplinary procedures used by the teacher (Kaplan, 1971). Parents also express considerable interest in the kinds of disciplinary practices employed in the schools, with some parents advocating the use of more stringent controls and others contending that the schools are already too severe and restrictive in their handling of students. School administrators regard maintenance of discipline as the greatest problem of inexperienced teachers.

The problem of discipline is by no means limited to the inexperienced; even seasoned teachers can be pushed to their wits' end in coping with deviant behavior. Many veteran teachers readily admit a need for more practical information about classroom discipline. Furthermore, they complain about finding themselves caught in a double bind in that they are told to maintain order and then subjected to criticism when they do. It is little wonder that many teachers, particularly beginning teachers and those on the secondary level, leave the field because of an inability to cope with problem students.

OBJECTIVES FOR CHAPTER 14

1. Identify the three phases involved in classroom discipline.
2. Define each of the four major techniques of changing behavior and list the advantages and disadvantages of each technique.
3. Explain the importance of frequency, timing, and type of rewards in modifying behavior.
4. Define the characteristics of a good rule and distinguish between good rules and poor rules.
5. Give examples of how the peer group can change behavior.
6. List the three outcomes of observational learning.
7. List ways that will enhance the effectiveness of extinction procedures.
8. Describe guidelines that will make for the positive use of punishment procedures.
9. Illustrate how disciplinary techniques can be applied to the solution of actual discipline cases.

A NEW APPROACH TO CLASSROOM DISCIPLINE

While traditional views on personality development and treatment have not yielded much in the way of value to the classroom teacher, there has developed an increasingly popular approach, called behavior modification, that has helped to narrow the gap between theory and classroom disciplinary practices. As the name of this approach suggests, it is more directly concerned with the modification of actual behavior (e.g., hitting others) than with deep-rooted psychological explanations. Accordingly, greater emphasis is devoted to the teaching or training of specific behaviors (e.g., getting history assignments completed) than to the development of a sophisticated insight into the remote causes of the maladaptive behavior (e.g., failing in school to punish his parents). Behavior modification techniques can be used effectively not only to help problem students, but to prevent problems from arising in the first place.

Four Steps in Behavior Modification

TARGET SELECTION

The first step involves the selection of specific target behaviors to change. In many cases, there are several target behaviors that the teacher might like to change. In these instances, it is necessary to establish priorities by deciding which behaviors are most important to the child's academic and social functioning.

Targets must be specific, observable, countable, and measurable. By selecting targets with these characteristics, we can tell whether the strategies being used are having the intended effect.

Be sure not to bite off more than can be chewed. Too frequently we choose goals that are too broad and ambitious. Instead of attempting to correct a global personality defect, we recommend a piecemeal approach. Take small steps at a time. The molecular approach will prove more effective in the long run.

Finally, identify behaviors that are to be increased as well as those to be decreased. When possible, choose behaviors that are incompatible (e.g., paying attention and unnecessary noise making).

EXAMINING THE ANTECEDENTS AND CONSEQUENCES

It is frequently helpful to see under what conditions the target behaviors are most apt to occur. For instance, once the teacher notes that Jim completes structured assignments accurately, but whines and dawdles when given unstructured assignments, he is in a position to modify Jim's behavior by providing more concrete and specific directions for the completion of assignments. *Gradually,* Jim can be helped to map out the steps necessary for completion of unstructured tasks.

To illustrate the value in identifying the consequences of a behavior, consider the case of Sam, the class clown. When Sam's teacher stopped to remember what happened after Sam acted up, it became apparent that the clowning was being kept alive by peer group laughter and teacher scolding. Armed with this knowledge, the teacher was able to decrease the frequency of clowning by getting the peer group and himself to ignore such unacceptable behavior. Remember, looking to see what happens *before* and *after* behavior can be invaluable in decreasing undesired behavior and in increasing desired behavior.

CHOOSING STRATEGIES

Now it is time to select the techniques that you will use to encourage acceptable performance and to discourage unacceptable performance. For the learning and maintaining of appropriate behaviors, positive reinforcement and modeling techniques are indicated. We will refer to these two techniques as *behavior formation* techniques. With re-

gard to discouraging behavior, extinction and punishment techniques are commonly used. These are referred to as *behavior elimination* techniques.

RECORDING RESULTS

It is essential that both teacher and student have feedback on what is happening to the target behavior. The data let both of them know if the procedures are taking effect. Remember that the behavior in question is always right. Only the data on the behavior can tell if the program was effective.

Three Significant Questions

If a positive approach to classroom discipline is to be realized, we must ask the following questions regarding the disorderly student when we plan our strategies for modifying his behavior.

1. Does he know what is expected of him, that is, does he clearly understand what the rules are? Directions can be clear to the teacher, but the information they provide to students might be incomplete, inaccurate, or conflicting. If there is some confusion about the ground rules, then it is necessary to make them as explicit as possible. Listing the rules on the board, having the student explain in his own words what the rule means, minimizing distractions while giving directions, and keeping rules short are all ways to help the student understand the rules. The teacher should also be careful to relate the student's behavior to the rule so that he knows exactly what he is being rewarded or punished for (e.g., "Now, you're *paying attention.*").

2. If the student knows the rules but still misbehaves, then you should consider the second question. Does he have the skills and abilities to do what I asked him to accomplish? Much misbehavior probably occurs as a result of demands that exceed the student's current level of readiness. When behavior problems stem from skill deficits and are secondary to the learning problem, it is necessary to teach the academic and social skills needed to assume the role of a student. The four techniques discussed in this chapter should help teachers to overcome deficits in the skill area. Providing greater freedom regarding choice in the curriculum also deserves serious consideration in such cases. One high school, for instance, listed more than 50 different English and social studies courses from which the students could choose. In short, one can change the student and/or change his environment to better suit his present skills by gearing instruction to his abilities and interests.

3. When the student knows what the rules are and when he has the competencies to perform in an acceptable way, and yet continues to misbehave, then we must ask a third question. Is he motivated to do what is expected of him? On many occasions the disruptive student finds his deviant ways more satisfying than conventional ways. In such cases, we must increase the reward value of the school setting so that students move toward it instead of away from it or by striking out at it. Again, the techniques to be presented should prove relevant to the solution of motivational problems. Let us at this point turn to the various techniques that can be used in a positive approach to classroom discipline.

POSITIVE REINFORCEMENT

If a behavior has the effect we want, then we are inclined to repeat it. Behavior, in other words, is determined in large measure by its consequences. For instance, if a student can attract attention by blurting out answers in class, he will probably not raise his hand and wait his turn. All behaviors must have a payoff of some kind, or we discontinue them. Among the most common payoffs for misbehavior are attracting attention, gaining power, getting revenge, and being left alone.

Giving rewards constitutes one of the most valuable tools teachers have at their disposal. Teachers have long recognized the importance of rewards and often use them to change behavior. Thus, the teacher who says, "I see that Johnny is ready to begin his math now that recess is over," is rewarding Johnny by giving him recognition for his attentiveness and studiousness.

One of the merits of this approach stems from its applicability to all students. It is not for just the antisocial student or just for the educationally disadvantaged or for the brain injured or for the emotionally disturbed or for the normal child. Every student, regardless of the label attached to him, needs ample rewards if he is to behave and achieve in school. To be effective, the teacher must answer questions relating to the frequency of reward, the timing of reward, and the type of reward to be used.

How Often Should I Be Rewarding?

With respect to the frequency of rewards, a distinction must be made between the acquisition (i.e., learning or building) of a behavior and its maintenance. When the teacher wants a student to behave differently, he should ideally reward the student *every time* the given behavior occurs. (In actual practice, it is not always possible to reward a behavior every time it occurs. The student's actions should be rewarded as often as possible, however. Remember, the greater the frequency and amount the reward, the faster the learning.) Thus, for example, the habitually hostile child who makes a friendly or cooperative or nonaggressive response toward a classmate should be rewarded *every time* he does so. Rewarding him once or twice is not enough. We must do it again and again on a *regular* basis until his cooperative behavior toward others had been securely acquired. Then, it is no longer necessary to give frequent rewards. In fact, it would then be best that the teacher reinforce such behavior every now and then (intermittent reinforcement) instead of 100% of the time, since intermittent reinforcement renders the behavior less subject to forgetting. Once the new behavior has been acquired, the problem centers around the maintenance of behavior, that is, with how long the student will remember to behave this way once you are occupied with other students or activities and cannot reward him regularly. After all, to get along in the classroom, the student has to behave appropriately without the teacher paying attention to him all the time. Having established the desirable behavior, we should reward the student every now and then for appropriate behavior.

When Should I Be Rewarding?

Timing is especially critical in giving rewards. Sometimes teachers give rewards before the child has complied with demands. This is a mistake, since there is little incentive to put forth effort once the payoff has been received. This is why we customarily pay people *after* they do the job.

How much time should elapse between performance of the desired behavior and giving the reward? Initially, the delay factor may have to be quite short when dealing with acting-out youngsters in that they typically have difficulty postponing gratification. Step by step, however, the interval can be lengthened as the child acquires more ade-

quate behavioral controls. Hence, the teacher may, initially, have to reward the conduct-disordered child immediately after his good behavior at recess time or in the laboratory. Eventually, if all proceeds well, the student will develop greater ability to postpone gratification. One teacher was able to lengthen the time interval by asking the student if he would mind waiting until tomorrow to get his Lifesaver as she was fresh out of them. Another teacher, who had been using art activities for some time as a potent reward, asked the student if it would be all right if they skipped art this afternoon, since other class activities had run behind schedule.

The delay interval may also have to be short with youngsters whose self-esteem and self-confidence are severely impaired. A seriously disabled reader may, for example, need a reward such as the teacher's praise or encouragement immediately after he has sounded out a single word. Later, as he gains in reading skills and personal confidence, he may not need to be rewarded until he has completed a whole page or story. In fact, once the student's frustration tolerance increases, the reward need not even be given during the school day or in the school setting. The accumulations of a certain number of points may be used to earn him a fishing trip with his dad on the weekend or entitle him to the school picnic coming up next month or to watch his favorite TV program that night or to go horseback riding.

What Type of Reward Should I Use?

There are a wide variety of rewards that teachers can use. For purposes of exposition, the rewards listed in Table 14-1 are arbitrarily divided into four categories: tangible rewards, people rewards, activity rewards, and intrinsic rewards. Although listed separately, the effective classroom teacher will use dif-

Table 14-1
Examples of Different Types of Reward

Tangible Rewards	People Rewards	Activity Rewards	Intrinsic Rewards
Candy	Praise	Going on field trip	Overcoming a problem or handicap
Popcorn	A smile	Choosing your own seat	Success experiences
Whistles	A wink	Reading a favorite story	A sense of pride in accomplishment
Stars	Expressing interest	Putting head down and resting	Allowing student to plot his progress
Trinkets	Physical nearness	Doing cross word puzzle	Using content that is humorous, dramatic or surprising
Points	Approval	Drawing	Letting the student catch teacher mistakes
Money	Picking teacher as a playmate	Cleaning erasers	Providing for repetition by converting drills into games
Comics	Showing respect	Tutoring	Allowing student to explore his curiosity about a topic
Baseball cards	Having parents sign note of good behavior	Having a "rap" session	Developing a sense of mastery
Athletic passes	Membership in "Who's Who Club"	Getting extra recess	Allowing student to vary methods he learns, for example, use of slides
			Writing creative short stories

ferent kinds of rewards instead of overworking a single reward. Even mature adults require the kinds of rewards presented in Table 14-1.

What if Appropriate Behavior Does Not Occur?

One frequent problem is the student's failure to display rewardable behavior. The teacher cannot reinforce acceptable behavior when there is none. In many instances there would be an endless wait if rewards were restricted to only perfect performance. In everyday practice, it is necessary to reward successive approximations of the desired behavior. Gradually, the student has to perform closer and closer to the target behavior before the reward is given. At the outset, it may be necessary,

for example, to reward a disabled reader after he recognizes the letters in a given word. Gradually, as his skills improve, he will be expected to recognize words before being rewarded. Then we might demand that he complete a sentence, or a paragraph, or a page, or a whole lesson in order to earn his reward. You will recognize this strategy as the one called "shaping" in Chapter 6.

A good rule to follow is to *start small* and to reward the first signs of appropriate behavior. Consider the youngster who refuses to complete arithmetic assignments even though instruction is geared to his level. The teacher might reward him for the following successive approximations.

1. Being in his seat even though he is not working.

2. Taking out his arithmetic book.

3. Opening the book to the assignment.

4. Looking at it.

5. Picking up his pencil.

6. Doing one problem.

7. Doing two or three problems.

8. Doing a short row of problems.

9. Doing the two rows of addition problems.

10. Doing the two rows of subtraction problems.

11. Completing arithmetic assignment.

12. Finally completing assignment at higher levels of accuracy.

On each of these occasions, rewards should be given for his approximation of the ultimate performance required. For example, upon noticing him looking at the assignment, you might say in a pleasant tone something similar to, "Good, I'm glad to see you've got the right book today and that you're ready to go." Eventually, rewards will be given only when he completes his assignment satisfactorily. Note that successful completion of this sequence must be undertaken over a period of time, so guard against the tendency to expect too rapid a change. Also remember that the steps appropriate for one youngster may be either too large or too small for other activities or other students.

With the negativistic child, you might want to start with situations in which he is generally cooperative (e.g., sending him on an errand) and gradually introduce those situations in which he is uncooperative. Since cooperative behavior is a habit he has yet to acquire, rewards must be given as often as possible in this situation. One hundred percent reinforcement would be ideal. By rewarding his cooperative efforts, we are strengthening behavior that competes with

negativistic behavior. The student cannot do both at the same time. If the student fails to become more cooperative, consideration should be given to the use of smaller steps in the shaping process.

Increasing incentives is another way of facilitating the onset of desired behavior that we want to reward. Increasing the payoff makes the teacher's way of doing things more attractive to the student and thus increases the probability that he will engage in behavior we seek. Contingency contracts (discussed in Chapter 7) and/or modeling procedures are also helpful in getting desired behavior to occur.

STUDENTS LEARN FROM WHAT THEY SEE

Effective as positive rewards are for strengthening old behaviors, they often demand arduous and ingenious changes in classroom procedures to produce appropriate *new* behaviors that can then be rewarded. As we noted earlier, the new behavior or some approximation thereof must first occur before appropriate rewards can be applied. In addition to being time consuming, the rewarding of trial and error learning can prove hazardous in many natural settings. For example, if we waited for an individual learning to swim to exhibit spontaneously a proper stroke or an approximation thereof and then rewarded him, few of us would live long enough to become adept swimmers.[1] Modeling procedures (which refer to such processes

---

[1] Reward procedures can be used alone to evoke new patterns of behavior when (1) the individual already has the available component skills, (2) environmental conditions exist that are capable of arousing actions similar to the desired behaviors, and (3) the student and teacher possess sufficient endurance to employ such time-consuming methods (Bandura, 1969).

as imitation, observational learning, role playing, vicarious experience, and emotional contagion) can circumvent these difficulties, thereby offering us a short cut to the learning of complex tasks. The importance of learning by watching has been stressed by Bandura (1969), who notes, "It would be difficult to imagine a culture in which the language, mores, vocational and avocational patterns, familial customs, and educational, social and political practices were shaped in each new member through a gradual process of differential reinforcement without the response guidance of models who exemplify the accumulated cultural repertories in their own behavior." Under most natural learning conditions, social behaviors are typically learned through imitation in large segments or in toto instead of acquired in a piecemeal, trial and error manner. The sheer simplicity of learning through imitation often justifies its use in preference to or in combination with positive reward. Modeling procedures are an economical means of transmitting new appropriate behaviors, especially when telling the student what to do (verbal modeling) is combined with demonstrations. In actual classroom situations these two ways of encouraging behavior—positive reward and modeling—are typically combined with the student obtaining a reward when he imitates an act performed by the model. Once acquired, the behavior can often be maintained without external support, since human beings learn to reward themselves for behaving appropriately. Bandura emphasizes that the combination of modeling and reward procedures is probably the most effective method of transmitting, eliciting, and maintaining social response patterns.

Teachers who are aware of the importance of observational learning realize that we often teach by example. Since the learning and regulation of human behavior can be strongly influenced through examples of socially acceptable behavior, teachers are often able to influence student behavior through the use of modeling. Although much remains to be learned about modeling procedures, these techniques are, as we will see, well suited for use by educators with withdrawn students, antisocial youngsters, and those who simply are lacking in adequate social and scholastic skills.

Despite having distinct practical value, this technique has been neglected in helping students to behave more constructively. Training institutions have long recognized the importance of the preventive value of modeling procedures in the preparation of future teachers, and therefore have attempted to provide adequate models in the form of critic teachers; however, less attention has been devoted by training institutions to use the modeling procedures as a means of influencing the behavior of the pupils with whom the teachers will have to work. The reader will recall from Chapter 7 that all models are not equally effective and that differences in the model, the observer, and the consequences of the imitated behavior can determine the outcomes of modeling.

Learning to Behave in New Ways

Simple reflection and observation indicate that much of our behavior is learned through imitation instead of through direct instruction. Indeed, practically all learnings can be acquired on a vicarious basis through observation of other people's behavior and its consequences for them. Students can acquire *complex intellectual and social competencies* merely by observing the performance of suitable models. Speech, foreign languages, vocational skills, hobbies, specialized technical skills, athletics, dancing, love making, and the art of social conversation can all be learned through this technique.

Emotional reactions can also be acquired simply by witnessing the pleasurable and painful experiences of others. Approach and avoidance behaviors (i.e., learning to like or dislike) can be learned in this way. Barnwell and Sechrest (1965), for example, found that both first- and third-grade students selected a task on which they observed their classmates receiving praise and avoided a task on which they witnessed other children receiving disapproval. Likewise, learning to fear a teacher can be established simply by observing a classmate being scolded. Similarly, a student can learn to like his teacher by watching his classmates having pleasant interactions with him. Aggressive behaviors can also be learned through exposure to persons who behave aggressively. In contrast, it is possible to teach aggressive and domineering children new ways of handling frustrating situations. For example, Chittenden (1942) had a group of acting-out children observe and discuss a series of eleven 15-minute plays in which dolls representing preschool children exhibited an aggressive and a cooperative solution to childhood quarrels similar to those they were likely to encounter in their daily associations. The consequences of aggression were shown to be unpleasant and those of cooperativeness were shown to be pleasant. Two boys fighting over a wagon, for example, were both depicted as unhappy because they broke the wagon during their struggle. By contrast, the two boys who took turns with the wagon wound up feeling happy and enjoying themselves. Acting-out children who viewed these two different reactions and consequences showed a decrease in dominative aggressiveness. Of even greater interest is the finding that these changes in behavior carried over to the actual nursery school and were still evident a month later. The effectiveness of similar procedures has also been demonstrated with older children (Gittelman, 1965). In brief, the point to be underscored is that emotional responsiveness of many varieties can be learned on a vicarious basis.

The Ripple Effect

Imitation not only promotes the learning of new behaviors, but it also can encourage or discourage the performance of previously learned responses. Generally, we become more inhibited when we see others punished for engaging in behavior similar to ours. In other words, vicarious punishment (i.e., simply watching others being punished) can produce suppressive effects. In fact, Benton (1967) found that vicarious punishment results in the same amount of inhibition as directly experienced punishment.

By contrast, we tend to be less inhibited when we see others being rewarded for engaging in behavior similar to ours. That is, positive reward can also be experienced on a vicarious basis with the result that we become more and more open in the expression of previously punished behaviors. This result is fine if the teacher wants to encourage a given behavior. It may not be so good, however, if the teacher wants to discourage a certain behavior. It is interesting to note that an observer's misbehavior increases when he sees somebody misbehave and get away with it.

The Triggering Effect

So far we have discussed the effects of modeling on (1) learning to behave more appropriately and (2) discouraging old maladaptive behaviors. But modeling has yet another effect—the triggering effect. It differs from the two effects discussed earlier in that the imitated behavior is neither new nor previously punished. In other words, the triggering effect refers to the elicitation of behavior that is either neutral or socially approved. In this type of modeling effect, watching the teacher's or peer's behavior helps the student to understand how to respond and behave in more acceptable ways. The right word or cue from the teacher might, for example, encourage a student to volunteer to clean up the blackboards, to help fellow students who are having trouble with an assignment, to settle down to finish his own work, or to persuade others to follow the example of a prestigeful peer. In short, the triggering effect refers to a process in which the frequency of existing desirable behaviors is increased.

The following case illustrates the triggering effect. Mr. Andy Septic was concerned about the mess left after each class in his woodshop. Students "forgot" to pick up the scraps and to put the tools away. Conditions got to the point that he had to clean up the shop after every class. Naturally enough, he became irritated with the state of affairs. He decided that near the end of each period, he would start to put away certain materials and tools of his own and remind others that they should do likewise. By setting a good example and by telling others to follow his example (verbal modeling), he was able to keep his shop orderly and productive. Note that the behavior triggered (cleaning up) was a socially approved one that the students had already learned. The teacher's intention was simply to make it occur more frequently.

CONSTRUCTIVE USE OF EXTINCTION PROCEDURES

Just as there is a substantial body of research demonstrating that the presentation of rewards can facilitate the learning and maintenance of given behaviors, there is a growing body of literature demonstrating that extinction—which refers to a process of discouraging certain specific behaviors by not re-

warding them—can reduce or eliminate troublesome behaviors. If a behavior is learned through the giving of rewards, it can be unlearned by taking the rewards away. If a given behavior no longer has its intended effect, its frequency tends to diminish.

As Hunter (1967) points out, "We don't keep on doing something that doesn't work." If the troublesome student acts out and nothing happens, he soon gets the message and abandons the particular maladaptive way. In short, simply removing the rewarding consequences of an act constitutes an effective way of discouraging it. As you will see, this technique has been found effective with a wide variety of behavior.

Despite the simplicity and potency of this principle, teachers often fail to use it to its best advantage. Hopefully, a fuller understanding of the cautions and guidelines regarding the use of this technique will enable us to apply it to better advantage.

Use of a Combination of Techniques

Although unacceptable behavior can be weakened by simply removing the rewards that keep it alive, extinction, if used as the sole method, is not always the most economical and effective means to produce behavioral change. For this reason it is wise to use extinction in conjunction with other techniques. One particularly effective combination involves the simultaneous use of extinction and reward. The teacher might, for example, ignore the child when he talks out of turn in class, but make a favorable comment about his answer when he speaks out in ways consistent with classroom ground rules, for example, "That's a good point, Jim," or "Jim, thank you for waiting your turn," whenever he raises his hand to answer or otherwise waits his turn. If the youngster has not yet learned to raise his hand, the teacher might assist him. For instance, whenever she notices him about to blurt something, she might say in a friendly voice something like, "Jim, did you want to raise your hand to say something?" Or the teacher might say something like, "Jim, I know you have something you want to say. We'll get to you in just a bit." Then the teacher might call on him in 20 to 30 seconds (gradually this interval could be increased) and say, "Thank you for waiting, Jim. Now, let's hear what you have to say."

When Old Habits Recur

It should be noted that the term extinction is probably a misnomer, because extinguished behavior is displaced, not permanently lost. If the original undesirable misbehavior is again reinforced, it is often easily reinstated. This difficulty can be overcome through the use of additional extinction trials. For example, one teacher had, for all practical purposes, eliminated tantrum behavior in Jane, a third-grade student, by ignoring her temper outbursts. The teacher took ill for a week. Upon her return she found that Jane was up to her old tricks again. The teacher later confirmed her suspicions that the substitute teacher had inadvertently strengthened tantrum behavior by attending to it. The regular teacher was able, nevertheless, to reduce these episodes to a minimal frequency again through reinstatement of her ignoring policy.

One of the primary factors in the reappearance of undesirable behavior is occasional or intermittent reward. As noted earlier, behaviors, whether troublesome or otherwise, once established can be maintained or even strengthened despite being only occasionally rewarded. What sometimes happens is that many undesirable behaviors, for example, talking out loud in class, are occasionally reinforced either directly or vicariously and are thereby set up on an intermittent rein-

forcement schedule. Therefore, instead of abolishing the behavior through extinction as intended, there is a rise in the frequency and intensity of deviant responses through irregular rewards. On some occasions, a given teacher might be inconsistent in her ignoring of a certain behavior. He might, for instance, become angry when the disorderly student talks out loud in class and consequently pay attention to the behavior by scolding. On other occasions, there might be inconsistency between teachers. This type of inconsistency is most likely to occur in elementary schools in conjunction with team taught courses and in junior and senior high schools where students typically have several teachers. Remember that any rewards given during the extinction process by teachers or by others will reinstate the misbehavior, and frequently at a higher level than if extinction had not been attempted (Bandura, 1969).

What should the teacher do when old habits recur after they had been supposedly eliminated? Although you may be inclined to blow your top and thereby reinforce the misbehavior, you should simply lay the unwanted behavior to rest once again by withholding reinforcement, that is, you should undertake another series of extinction trials. Fortunately, the unwanted behavior can ordinarily be more readily extinguished on the second series of extinction trials.

Ignoring Is Difficult—But Can Work

This leads us to a related point: it is especially difficult for teachers to ignore behavior deviations. We are good detectives and we quickly spot (and attend to) rule violations. It is as though we are compelled to respond to misbehavior. "George, get back to your seat." "Mary, you've been at the pencil sharpener long enough." "Bob, stop pestering your neighbors and get back to work." "Tom, do

"I don't get as much mileage out of a tantrum as I used to." *(Drawing by Joe E. Buresch from Today's Education/NEA Journal, 1969)*

you always have to be moving around in your desk?" "Barry, how long are you going to keep tapping that pencil?" "Carol, sit up straight." "Bill, watch your feet." "Steve, scoot your chair over." As you know now, teacher attention can often strengthen the undesirable behavior. Although teachers have little difficulty in grasping the value of ignoring (and thereby removing the reward for the deviant behavior), they have considerable difficulty in implementing this idea. As one teacher related, "As a practice teacher, I vowed that I would not harp like my supervising teacher but found myself doing it too once I got on the job." Being aware of the value of ignoring is one matter, and practicing to ignore is quite another. Ignoring requires rigorous self-control.

If teachers are to derive maximum benefit from extinction procedures, they must learn not to respond to all undesirable behavior.[2] Many classroom transgressions could probably be safely ignored. Motor behaviors such

---

[2] Because it is unlikely that a teacher will ignore all instances of a given misbehavior, extinction procedures should be combined with positive reinforcement of acceptable behaviors.

as getting out of the seat, standing up, wandering around the room, and moving chairs could probably be ignored. Irrelevant verbalizations or noises such as conversations with others, answering without raising one's hand, crying, whistling, and coughing also can fall into the category of behaviors to which the teacher should not respond. Oppositional tactics, for example, negativism, should also be ignored (Madsen, et al., 1968). The teacher, even though she might initially feel uncomfortable, will manage classroom behavior better if she can learn to avoid responding to certain misbehaviors. Remember that teacher disapproval can encourage deviant behavior, whereas ignoring can discourage such behavior by removing the payoff. The student must learn that unacceptable behavior is not worth anything.

Should a teacher ignore all undesirable behavior? If not, how will he know what behaviors to ignore? The following general guidelines may help teachers to answer these questions. There are certain types of behavior that the teacher cannot ignore. These include behaviors injurious to self or others, and inappropriate behaviors for which the teacher cannot for various reasons remove the reward, that is, self-rewarding behaviors and behaviors rewarded by the peer group. Hunter (1967) suggests that if a given misbehavior is is relatively new, you can probably ignore it. On the other hand, if the misbehavior occurs consistently and for a long period, extinction procedures might prove inadequate. If the misbehavior happens frequently and is of long standing, one can be reasonably sure that it is being rewarded. Either other social agents, such as the peer group, are making such deviances worth his while, or the individual's behavior is rewarding in and of itself, for example, sleeping in class, laughing, and hitting. As you will read later, it may be necessary to use some form of punishment to deal

effectively with behavior that is intense and/or frequent. For now, remember that ignoring works only when the reward is attention.

Enlist Peer Group Support

We will now comment on peer group extinction. Conversations with and observations of teachers indicate that they frequently do not come to grips with the problem of the peer group. More often than not, teachers allow the peer group to reinforce undesirable behavior. For instance, if a boy clowns in class and three to four other students generally respond with laughter, teachers rarely enlist the assistance of these students in extinguishing the undesired behavior. Just as peer group rewards can serve as a powerful strengthener of behavior, group extinction procedures can also serve as powerful weakeners of behavior. More will be said later in the chapter regarding peer groups and discipline.

Self-Rewarding Behaviors Call for Other Tactics

Sometimes the reward for the misbehavior comes from the act itself. Consequently, it is sometimes extremely difficult to keep maladaptive behaviors from being reinforced. For instance, the aggressive pupil who kicks the teacher or a classmate cannot help but be reinforced by the look of pain on the victim's face. Furthermore, even if the victim somehow manages to keep a straight face, the kicker knows that he has inflicted pain, and this knowledge in itself can be reinforcing. Looking out the window, having a good laugh, or a conquering-hero daydream are all intrinsically rewarding. When dealing with behavior that contains its own satisfactions, it is necessary to punish the undesirable behavior to suppress it temporarily and to reward incompatible positive behaviors. For example, the aggressive student might have to relinquish certain classroom privileges, such as playing with his peers, when he acts out. Yet every effort would be made to reward his cooperative or friendly interactions.

Do Not Wait for the Worst to Happen

There are also situations in which we cannot wait for a behavior to fizzle out through repeated nonreward. This limitation is particularly characteristic of situations wherein the dangers of emotional contagion and severe injury to self or others are distinct possibilities. In such cases, immediate action is necessary, and some form of punishment (e.g., isolation or physical restraint) is probably the method of choice.

Things May Get Worse Before They Get Better

The teacher should fully expect that misbehavior, if it does not increase in frequency or intensity, will remain at a high level during the initial stages of the extinction process. The old adage that things will get worse before they get better certainly pertains here. Temper tantrums may soar to frightening intensities, initially mild dependency demands may culminate in a sharp kick in the shins, and negative attention-getting behavior may assume more and more ludicrous forms (Bandura, 1969). This state of affairs should not discourage the teacher; as this vigorous misbehavior proves unsuccessful, it will gradually taper off, and alternative ways of behavior will emerge.

New Misbehaviors Sometimes Emerge

The extinction of a given maladaptive behavior constitutes no guarantee in and of itself that desirable behavior will automatically appear. As dominant modes of behavior are extinguished, the student will use alternative courses of action that have proved successful on previous occasions in similar circumstances. The use of extinction alone poses no special problems provided that students' alternative behaviors are acceptable to the teacher. A problem does arise, however, when the new behaviors are also maladaptive. The teacher can avoid the problems associated with extinguishing a long succession of inappropriate behaviors by combining extinction procedures with other methods that foster more effective modes of adjustment.

Because teachers have not always taken the above cautions and guidelines into account, they have sometimes become discouraged in their use of this technique. We have seen many teachers become disheartened in trying to implement the school counselor's advice to not reward maladaptive behaviors. What commonly happens, unless the above precautions are taken, is that the teacher's efforts to extinguish unacceptable student behaviors themselves undergo extinction.

PUNISHMENT: A NEW LOOK

Objections to the Use of Punishment

Punishment is as old as human history. It is an inevitable part of everyone's learning history. Indications are that punishment is here to stay. And by the usual standards of scientific merit—efficiency and effectiveness—the research findings on the use of punishment as a means of modifying troublesome behavior should evoke admiration (Baer, 1971). The use of negative consequences has been disavowed, however, on both moral and scientific grounds.

MORAL OBJECTIONS

From a moral viewpoint, the word punishment connotes inhumane treatment, negative attitudes, and hostile acts. If successful, punishment forces the person to do something against his will. Baer suggests that much of our revulsion regarding punishment is based on our reactions against the snake-pitlike conditions found many years ago in our state hospitals and prisons. Advocating the use of punishment is, in the minds of many people, tantamount to asking them to forego years of progress in human reform. However, it is actually probably much more humane to subject people to a small number of brief painful experiences in exchange for the interminable pain of a lifelong maladjustment. Society must ask itself a basic question, namely, which punishment is tougher on the individual and which one lasts longer (Baer, 1971).

SCIENTIFIC OBJECTIONS

Traditionally, certain specific objections have been raised on scientific grounds against the use of punishment as a behavior modification technique. The cautions to be discussed suggest that if punishment is to be used as a means of changing behavior, its use should be judiciously applied. As Bandura (1969) notes, "Because of the varied and complex effects of punishment particularly when socially mediated, it must be employed with care and skill in programs of behavioral change." Let us at this point consider five of the most common scientific criticisms leveled against punishment.

Short-Term Effects. Laboratory studies that have been conducted on animals suggested that punishment does not eliminate the maladaptive response. Instead, it merely slowed down the rate at which the troublesome behaviors were emitted. How many times have you scolded a student, kept him in from recess, retained him after school, put him out in the hall, threatened to lower his grade, or sent him to the principal's office, only to find that he engages in the very same misbehavior after a short while?

Lack of Direction. Punishment simply serves notice to stop inappropriate behaviors. It does not indicate to the student what behaviors are appropriate in the situation. How often do we catch ourselves saying things such as, "George, stop that and do what you're supposed to be doing." "Sally, quit that fooling around and do it right." "Pete, do you have to do that? Settle down!" "Don, get with it!" Our verbal reprimands make it painfully clear to students what we want them to do. Consequently, the student may frequently not know exactly how he is to remedy the situation.

Escape and Avoidance Behaviors. Foremost among the unfavorable side effects of punishment is the development of avoidance behaviors. We have a strong tendency to avoid contact with individuals and situations that we find unpleasant. Often these resulting escape and avoidance behaviors (truancy, lying, cheating, etc.) may be more unwholesome than the behavior that the original punishment was designed to eliminate. Moreover, once these escape behaviors become established, they can be difficult to eliminate. One especially unfortunate consequence of escape behaviors is an avoidance of teachers and/or other change agents. This can be a particularly serious hindrance, since it deprives the student of the opportunity to learn both attitudes and behaviors normally acquired through unforced modeling.

Constricted Behavior. There are two other consequences that can stem from the use of punishment: the inhibition of socially desirable behaviors and the development of personal rigidity. The effects of punishment are not always confined to the behaviors that we want eliminated. Harsh punishments, especially those applied over lengthy periods of time, can also lead to the inhibition of socially desirable behaviors and to a loss of spontaneity. In other words, the punished student may come to suppress socially acceptable patterns of behavior that are not in need of censor. As a consequence of overgeneralization to other aspects of behavior, the student may also become less flexible in his adjustment.

Setting a Bad Example. On many occasions, the teacher's words or direct teachings say one thing to the student, while his actions or indirect teachings say something contradictory. Unwittingly, parents and teachers provide a clear-cut model of the very behavior from which they want their children or students to refrain.

Despite the limitations associated with this technique, many psychologists now contend that certain negative sanctions, if properly applied, can assist in eliminating detrimental patterns of adjustment. As we will see shortly, the undesirable by-products are not necessarily inherent in punishment, but stem from the faulty fashion in which they are applied. Indeed, considerable human behavior is changed and maintained by natural aversive consequences without any ill effects. To avoid painful consequences, we put on warm clothes to protect against the cold, we walk along the side of the road, we run from falling objects, we try not to fall down, we drive properly so that we do not lose our driver's license, we guard ourselves in various ways so that we do not get jilted by girl friends, we try to be careful in our business transactions

so that we do not lose money, we work industriously and get along with our superiors to avoid the unpleasant consequences of losing our jobs, and so forth. We engage in a great deal of behavior simply to avoid pain, and our personalities do not become warped as a result. Few would criticize the use of punishment in teaching young children to stay out of busy streets, to keep their hands off of hot stoves, or to refrain from inserting metal objects in electric wall sockets (Bandura, 1969).

The use of punishment as an intervention technique is necessary because it is impossible to guide children effectively through the use of only positive reinforcement and extinction. Ausubel (1961), among others, rejects the idea that only "positive" forms of discipline are beneficial. He points out that a child does not come to regard rudeness as an undesirable form of behavior simply by reinforcing respect for others. As Ausubel (1961) asserts, ". . . it is impossible for children to learn what is not approved and tolerated simply by generalizing in reverse from the approval they receive for the behavior that is acceptable."

Guidelines Toward a More Effective Use of Punishment

1. Punishment should be used in a corrective way. It is designed to help the student improve now and in the future. It is not to retaliate for wrongdoing in the past. Punishment prompted by teacher mood has no place in the classroom. Moral indignation may make the teacher feel better, but it will not change student behavior. Punishment is to be used in a rational, systematic way, designed to improve student behavior, not to provide a cathartic effect for the punishment agent.

2. Ideally, punishment should be inherent in the situation instead of an expression of the

power of one person over another. In other words, punishment should express the reality of the social or physical situation. The idea is to let the child experience the unpleasant but natural or logical result of his own actions. Used in this way, we can minimize or avoid the dangers associated with one human being's delivering punishment to another.

3. The role of the teacher is to be that of a friendly, interested, and objective bystander. Note that it is the tone of the teacher's voice that provides a true barometer of the teacher's attitudes toward the child.

4. On the occasions that it is necessary for one human being (e.g., teacher, principal, peer group) to punish another human being (e.g., student), it should be done in an impersonal, matter-of-fact way. The punishing agent must guard against the tendency to yell or scold, since this often reinforces unacceptable behavior and indicates that your attitude is one of revenge.

5. Once a good rule has been agreed on, the youngster who violates it should experience the unpleasant consequences of his misbehavior. Excuses and promises are not accepted. There is to be no escape from the unpleasant consequences of his actions. Acceptance of rationalizations only serves to promote social and personal irresponsibility. Insist on performance.

6. A youngster should be given one warning or signal before punishment is delivered. The warning may eliminate the need for punishment. Even when the warning proves ineffective, it adds an element of fairness to

"With the crisis condition of the schools today, Miss Carrington, how can you be concerned with spitballs. . . . ?" *(Drawing by Short and Weaver Cartoons)*

what follows. On the occasions when the warning fails to deter unacceptable behavior, extended discussion or "reasoning" is contra-indicated, since teacher attention tends to strengthen unacceptable behavior.

7. The nature of the punishment and the manner of presenting it should avoid the arousal of strong emotional responses in the person punished. The use of a behavioral contract in which the student has a choice in consequences (as well as goals) can prove helpful in this regard.

8. The teacher must be consistent in his use of punishment. Ideally, the target behavior should be punished each time it occurs. Once the student has learned the habit of not responding in a particular way, intermittent punishment should be used.

9. Administer the punishment in full force. The greater the intensity, the greater the reduction of misbehavior.

10. Avoid extended periods of punishment, especially where low intensity punishments are used. Letting the youngster experience the maximum intensity of the punishment is more humane and effective than exposing him to a prolonged series of lesser punishments. A firmly presented time-out period is more effective than several "no's" of increasing loudness.

11. One strategy designed to promote a durable elimination involves the combined use of punishment and reward. Various research studies indicate that this combination is much more effective and efficient than the use of punishment alone. Punishment reminds the student what not to do. The reward of appropriate alternative behaviors tells the student what he should do.

12. Timing plays an important role in determining the effectiveness of punishment. Available evidence indicates rather consistently that children who are punished early in a given sequence of misbehavior de-

velop greater resistance to temptation than those who are punished only after completion of the misdeed. Punishing a child after he has stolen something leaves the initial phases of interest, intention and approach relatively unaffected.

13. To guard against behavioral constriction we must reward acceptable behaviors that are related or similar in nature to the ones being punished. For instance, hitting others may be punished, but desirable assertiveness may be rewarded. This sort of selective reinforcement greatly assists the student to discriminate what behaviors are acceptable for a given situation.

14. Remove or reduce the *magnitude* and *frequency* of the rewards that are maintaining misbehavior. Punishment works much more effectively and efficiently once the rewards that maintain misbehavior are eliminated or decreased.

15. Be certain that the delivery of punishment is not associated with the giving of reinforcement. For example, if removal from the group is a rewarding experience, then it will not be effective in modifying the target behavior.

16. Punishment should be used to foster self-direction. The use of behavior contracts is helpful because it promotes self-direction by having the student assume responsibility for his own behavior. The basic rationale is to provide opportunities for some degree of choice in determining one's goals and to let him experience the consequences of his actions. Allowing the student to end the punishment when his behavior improves also facilitates self-direction.

17. It is important that the use of punishment requires little of the teacher's time and energy. If delivery of the punishment fatigues the teacher, he is apt to stop the delivery of punishment because he is tired, not because the misbehavior has improved.

THE PEER GROUP AND CLASSROOM DISCIPLINE

The teacher is not the sole source of reward, nor is she always the primary source of reward in the classroom. The effective classroom manager realizes these facts of classroom life and will make use of other sources of reward, such as the peer group. In many instances, the teacher will have at his disposal a ready tool in peer group support, because other students are often annoyed by unacceptable behavior and are as anxious as the teacher to see it cleared up. Group praise, recognition, and rejection, although commonly overlooked as methods of classroom management, can be very effective tools for building and maintaining desirable behavior.

One study demonstrating the potency of the peer group as modifiers of troublesome behavior was conducted in a class for educationally handicapped elementary school students (Stiavelli and Shirley, 1968). In this study, the Citizenship Council (CC), a group procedure using group pressure and positive rewards, was established in an effort to lighten the teacher's disciplinary burden. Pupils met each day at 12:30 P.M. to nominate and vote on which students had earned or had lost their citizenship on the basis of their performance on the playground, in the cafeteria, and in the classroom. The class, teacher, and the two aides met as a group and established by unanimous vote the criteria for citizenship, rewards, privileges, and disciplinary consequences. The following four lists were established.

I. Rules of Conduct for Citizenship — A Citizen.
   1. Respects the rights of others.
   2. Respects the property of others.
   3. Hands in assignments on time.
   4. Does not tattle.
   5. Does unto others as he would have them do unto him.
   6. Does all his work neatly and accurately.
   7. Raises his hand to talk or ask a question and does not interrupt others.
   8. Lines up quietly.
   9. Helps others.
   10. Tries to understand others' behavior.

II. Rewards.
   1. A gold pin with the inscription "Citizenship." (The principal pinned on the pin the first time earned and the student was allowed to take the pin home to show his parents. Thereafter, he was pinned by the teacher and kept it through the school day.)
   2. A gold plaque with the inscription "Citizen of the Month." (This was given to the student who had received the most stars on the progress chart and was hung in the student's cubicle.)
   3. A gold star. (This was placed on the progress chart for each day of citizenship earned. The students were acutely aware of the chart and it proved to be an effective reinforcer.)

III. *Privileges.*
   1. The citizens are to be allowed to come and go from the room to the lavatory or for a drink and move about the room as they wish without asking for permission as the noncitizens are required to do. The citizen is only required to inform the teacher or aides as to what he plans to do or where he is going.
   2. The citizens are to be allowed to leave for lunch 5 minutes earlier than the noncitizens. (This placed them first in the cafeteria line and out on the playground 5 minutes early.)
   3. During recess and P.E. the citizens are

to be allowed first choice of playground equipment and be first in line to go out and come into the room.

4. Only the citizens are to be chosen as class helpers and messengers.

5. The citizen of the month and his two closest competitors on the progress chart are to be taken bowling during school hours. (One game lasting approximately 1 hour.)

IV. Disciplinary Measures.

1. A spanking of two to five swats administered by the principal.

2. Loss of citizenship for an extended period of time, with a maximum of 2 weeks.

3. Isolation during lunch, P.E., and recess either in the room or in principal's office (Stiavelli and Shirley, 1968, p. 150).

Observations made by school personnel indicated the effectiveness of this technique. Group cohesiveness increased, the students' frustration tolerance rose, self-control improved, and teaching became more enjoyable. Interestingly, the parents of a neurologically handicapped child, although initially opposed to this group process, became its staunchest defenders as their son's behavior improved both at school and at home. One caution to bear in mind is that with the use of this technique, peers tend to be too severe in setting standards for behavior. It is perhaps wise to suggest a trial period before drafting a more permanent set of guidelines, since initial guidelines are generally too demanding to live with comfortably over any extended period of time.

Another application of the use of the group for managing behavior is the "Social Problem-Solving Meeting." (Glasser, 1961) Students are seated in a circle, and individual as well as group problems are discussed. These prob-lems for discussion can be proposed by the students, the teacher, the principal, or the counselor. The meetings are conducted once a week or as the situation warrants, and are designed to give students an active voice in finding solutions to individual or group problems. Discussions are to be held in a constructive, nonjudgmental way, without fault finding or punishment. Glasser, a psychiatrist, reports that when students discover that their classmates do care about them (a social reward), they can make intelligent plans for solving disciplinary problems. This approach might prove even more effective in changing behavior if guidelines for behavior were charted and enforced through the use of rewards and punishment.

The power of peer group rewards has been noted frequently in the research literature related to classroom discipline. What is surprising, at first glance, is the suggestion that approval from a disliked or unpopular peer has greater reward value than does approval from a liked peer. Teachers, however, have long recognized that having two friends work together often interfered with completion of a given task or assignment. Students are apparently challenged more by peers who are negatively perceived than by close friends. Then again, it may be that positive recognition is more potent when it occurs in a situation in which it is not expected. The teacher might do well, therefore, to have the disorderly student sit at a table with nonfriends for at least certain assignments or during troublesome times of the day, for example, late afternoon when his ability to resist temptation is lowered. The peers at his table could easily be taught to reward his academic and/or social progress.

Teachers must make more effective use of group dynamics in promoting the social and academic adjustment of their students. To facilitate self-control on the student's part, the teacher must reduce dependence on himself and offer the class opportunities for self-management. Classroom management should not and need not be the responsibility of the teacher alone. This is especially true at the secondary level, when students feel a need for greater self-determination. The teacher who arbitrarily and unilaterally imposes standards in a high-handed fashion is inviting trouble (Kaplan, 1971). On the other hand, a cohesive group with a high degree of morale can go far in preventing disciplinary problems. A teacher cannot afford to ignore the power and persuasiveness of the group in establishing and enforcing class rules.

RULES AND CLASSROOM DISCIPLINE

All teachers use rules in their attempts at classroom management. For our purposes, we will define a rule as any task the student must perform, or as any decision regarding what he may or may not do. A good rule should have three properties. It must be definable, reasonable, and enforceable (Smith and Smith, 1966). Instead of telling a student, "From here on in, you behave yourself in my class," it would be better if the teacher spelled out one or two specific rules to guide the student's conduct. For instance, the teacher might state, "You are to work on your algebra assignment for the rest of this period. There will be no talking during this time." Rules can also be unreasonable at times. The teacher might, for example, expect the student to accomplish a task for which his skills are deficient or for which the time limits are too demanding. A sense of fairness and justice is essential. Finally, if a rule cannot be enforced through rewards and/or punishment, it will be ineffective in guiding behavior. Teachers often invite difficulty by establishing unnecessary and impractical rules. One useful procedure, is to start with a limited number of rules. With extremely unsocialized youngsters, it may be best to start with just one rule. Which rule(s) should be selected? One that will most effectively promote significant academic and personal skills in the child, one that is of major concern to you as a teacher, and definitely one that is enforceable. A rule forbidding chewing gum would probably not be a good one with which to start. Although well defined, it is difficult to enforce as the student can swallow it or chew it when you are not looking. Furthermore, compliance with this rule does little to develop important scholastic or social achievements. It would be better to state that the student must satisfactorily complete a given assignment before he can turn to other activities that he enjoys. This rule would be clear, enforceable, and beneficial.

There are several reasons why we should start with a very small number of rules. Foremost among these are the following.

1. Too many rules amounts to nagging. Students feel that the teacher is always on them, if not for one thing, then for another.

2. If the teacher has been inconsistent in the past, the student's testing of this first rule will be more intense and prolonged than for later rules. Briefly, enforcement of your first rules will probably demand all the energy you can summon. When he learns that you are firm and mean business, there will be less testing of later rules.

3. The student will often focus his misbehavior on established rules. Other kinds of misbehavior may be abandoned as he concentrates his energies on breaking the few rules you have established. This knowledge is useful. By selecting a rule you know to be enforceable, you have at your disposal a clear plan by which consequences can be implemented. This is one way of stacking the deck in your favor.

4. Finally, you will see that things will change around the classroom following the enforcement of just a very few rules. This change in behavior will lessen the need for rules that seemed warranted earlier (Smith and Smith, 1966).

In closing, remember the following guidelines for establishing rules[3] (Madsen and Madsen, 1970).

1. Be sure to involve the class in making up the rules.

2. Rules should be short and to the point.

3. Try to phrase the rules in a positive way.

4. Call attention to the rules at times other than when someone has misbehaved.

5. Rules should differ for varied activities.

6. Let the student know when the different rules are in effect.

7. Post the rules in a conspicuous location and review them regularly.

8. Keep a personal record of the number of times that you review the rules.

Positive Classroom Discipline in Action

Problem: **"Smarting Off" in Class**

Technique: **Ripple Effect**

Mr. M., who taught a required course on U.S. history, ordinarily ignored sly or sarcastic remarks from students because of their infrequent occurrence. Ignoring seemed to work well with most students; however, one fellow in the class, a popular member of the football team, would make wisecracks at every opportunity during class discussions. Realizing that he was being tested and that this "smarting-off" could easily be contagious, Mr. M. decided to take a firm stand with respect to this disturbing behavior. The next time discourteous remarks were made, Mr. M. acted without hesitation. "Bob, you will have to leave the room and go to the office." Bob's reaction and that of the entire class was one of surprise—"you can't possibly do this" to one of our heroes. Bob was readmitted to the class following a brief apology to his classmates and Mr. M. Bob was not the only one to learn a lesson. His classmates quickly realized that if Mr. M. dared to set limits for such a popular student as Bob, they certainly would not be immune to similar sanctions. The class respected Mr. M. for his display of strength and fairness in not overlooking the rule infraction of a student who was so popular with other students and teachers.

Comment. This incident shows how the correction of a prestigious leader can become a vicarious learning experience for those who witnessed the punishment. The value of "firmness" and an "I mean what

[3] These guidelines seem most applicable to the elementary school level.

I say" approach is also seen in this example. As teachers, we commonly warn too often, thereby showing the student that we really do not mean what we say. Finally, this case illustrates the value of judicious punishment, whether experienced directly or vicariously in coping with misbehavior that occurs with a high frequency.

Problem: **Aggressiveness and hyperactivity**

Techniques: **Extinction by teacher and peers, use of rewarded models**

Danny was a five-year old enrolled in a Head Start class. After remaining on the fringes of the group for a week, he became more aggressive and hyperactive. He would spill another child's orange juice, knock over another's tower made of blocks, throw the ball over the playground fence, throw away clean napkins to be used for snacks, and engage in a variety of other impulsive and destructive behaviors. He was always promptly scolded for his misbehavior.

A case conference was held and the teachers, although reluctant, agreed to ignore his inappropriate behaviors. In keeping with this strategy, the teachers ignored Danny when he would run in the opposite direction instead of coming indoors. As you might suspect, the teachers wondered if he would come back. At first, he would run outside the fence, laughing and yelling in an effort to attract attention. Initially, some children would try to call the teacher's attention to Danny's tactics. On such occasions, the teacher would simply change the topic of conversation. She might, for example, express curiosity about what their snack for the day might be and continue on into the classroom. After a few seconds, Danny would appear at the door and shout, "Teacher, look at me!" Some of the students turned to look at him, but the teacher continued talking about the subject at hand as they munched their snacks. The teacher, for purposes of imitation, provided the students with a model who does not pay attention to inappropriate behavior. A combination of both teacher and peer extinction procedures was now underway. The next day, Danny came indoors with the other youngsters, even though he was the last one in. He did not wash his hands or eat his snack, but instead went to the back of the room to build high towers of blocks, only to send them tumbling to the floor. He would look at the teacher each time he smashed a tower. Both the teacher and the other children ignored him.

On the third day, Danny was again the last one to come in, but this time managed to arrive at the table just before the end of snack time. The cookies had been eaten, but the teacher offered him some juice, which he drank. He forgot to put his napkin in the basket, but this "oversight" was ignored.

On the fourth day, Danny came indoors, washed his hands, and went to the snack table. The head teacher seated him and included him in the conversation, but did not make a big affair of his joining the others for a snack for fear that any form of conspicuous reinforcement might call more attention to his usual misbehavior than to his acceptable behavior. Danny's behavior became more constructive, and the teacher rewarded his efforts by paying attention to him. She encouraged him, for example, by such statements as "I like the colors you are using," or "Your picture is interesting, Danny. Tell me about it." Within 2 weeks, Danny's behavior changed from disruptive to cooperative and from destructive to constructive (Vance, 1969).

Comment. This case study, in addition to illustrating the effectiveness of extinction procedures, also highlights the benefits that can accrue from a combination of techniques, in this case, extinction, positive reward and punishment (missing the snack), and the provision of appropriate models.

Problem: **Chronic fighting with other boys on the playground**

Agent: **Child himself**

Techniques: **Extinction combined with reinforcement of a competing response.**

Jimmy was referred to the school social worker for being a chronic fighter on the playground. He was ten years and seven months old and in the sixth grade. Jimmy's fighting was so habitual that he was suspended from school on four occasions during a 5-month period (to be suspended, a student had to receive five misconduct slips for fighting in 1 week). Every misconduct slip that Jimmy received was for fighting on the playground. Because the fights were always provoked by the other boys calling him names, the teacher felt that if Jimmy would ignore these remarks, the name calling would decrease and his fighting would be curtailed.

It was decided that Jimmy himself should be the agent who would be actively involved in extinguishing the name-calling behavior. Instead of reacting with anger, Jimmy was told to ignore the taunts instead, to act as if he never heard them. Jimmy had already been told that the other boys would probably not call him names if he would not pay attention to them, but he was still unable to control his temper. It was decided that he could not adhere to the extinction procedure unless he were to make an active response that was incompatible with his usual response (fighting) to name calling. Accordingly, he was asked to write the name caller's name on a sheet of paper that he carried in his pocket. This procedure was to serve as an incompatible response to fighting and to give him a record of who was doing the most name calling.

Data collected for 8 consecutive weeks after the initiation of extinction procedures showed that Jimmy's fighting behavior had completely disappeared. The name-calling responses dropped gradually, and within 2 weeks they had been completely extinguished (Goens, 1969).

Comment. The question arises as to why Jimmy was able to ignore name calling at this time when he had been unable to do so in the past. Two possible explanations were advanced. (1) He was now required to perform a response that competed with fighting. One cannot fight and write at the same time. (2) This time he was told that name calling would not disappear immediately, but that it would die out gradually if he continued to ignore it consistently.

Problem: **The use of foul language in class**

Technique: **Use of a fine**

The problem in this particular high school class had to do with the habitual use of abusive language. The more bad words the student used, the higher his status in the peer group. It was clearly a case whereby peer group values conflicted with values of the school. Realizing that the peer rewards had to be broken down or changed, the teacher enlisted student support in developing a class code. One of the rules that was mutually agreed on called for the use of proper language in the classroom. This rule was to be enforced by assessing a fine of 15 cents per violation. Since the fines were to be spent on suitable activities that the entire class enjoyed (sports events, class picnics, special field trips), the peer group did an outstanding job of policing foul language.

Comment. Note the use of punishment to cope with a frequent misbehavior, the importance of involving the peer group in the formation of rules, and the use of presenting painful stimulation, in this case, fines, as a sanction to back up the rule. It is especially interesting to observe that the teacher by sharing his authority actually strengthened his position.

In giving the peer a voice in disciplinary matters, it is important that the teacher does not legalize scapegoating or clique domination. Furthermore, the peer group must not get the impression that punishment is the only or best technique for dealing with problems. The teacher must gently remind the group of ways to change behavior through rewards and good example.

Problem: **The "naughty finger"**

Technique: **Removal of a reward**

This classroom consisted of 14 mentally retarded students—seven girls and seven boys between the ages of six and ten. A not uncommon gesture that disturbs others is the "naughty finger" (the fist raised with middle finger extended). This gesture not only upsets middle-class teachers, but disrupts classroom activities as well, since some students return the gesture, others laugh about it, others become angry, and some report this misbehavior to the teacher.

To cope with this problem, the teacher placed 10 cards, numbered 1 to 10, on a bracelet in front of the room and made the following announcement.

"From now on there will be a special 10-minute recess at the end of the day. However, if I see the naughty finger or hear about it, I will flip down one of these cards, and you will have 1 minute less of recess whenever this happens. Remember, every time I flip down one of these cards, all of you lose a minute from your recess."

Use of this simple tactic reduced this undesirable behavior from an average of 16 occurrences per day to about 2 (Sulzbacher & Houser, 1968).

Comment. This is a technique that can be easily put to effective use in classrooms whether they consist of mentally retarded children or normal ones. In this instance, the technique promoted group cooperation and also eliminated a behavior disruptive to classroom activities. One variation of this approach would be for the class to establish a rule prohibiting use of the "naughty finger" and then to let the group select a representative to flip down the card when violations occur. In this way, the teacher could assume the role of an interested bystander and not be directly associated with the punishment. Another possibility might involve some automatic flipping of cards to impersonalize the punishment and to make it appear as a natural consequence of one's misbehavior.

Summary

1. Discipline is one of teachers' foremost concerns. Prevention of problems is as important or more so than their treatment.

2. There are three phases of classroom discipline—identifying specific target behaviors for attack, finding ways of weakening undesirable behaviors, and planning ways to encourage positive behaviors.

3. Positive reward and social modeling are two major techniques for strengthening desirable conduct. Extinction, punishment, and desensitization procedures are designed primarily to weaken unacceptable acts.

4. Teachers must consider the frequency, timing, and nature of rewards.

5. Rewards must be earned.

6. Make sure *you* are not rewarding unacceptable behavior.

7. Shaping and/or modeling procedures should be considered when the disorderly student does not engage in acceptable behaviors for the teacher to reward.

8. Rules must be definable, reasonable, and enforceable.

9. The peer group is often a very potent source of reward, particularly during preadolescent and adolescent years.

10. Students learn a great deal from observing others.

11. Observational learning can result in learning of new behaviors, in discouraging old maladaptive ways, and in triggering existing acceptable behaviors.

12. Teachers should make use of both live and symbolic models.

13. Whether a student will imitate what he sees depends in large measure on the characteristics of the model, attributes of the observer, and the consequences associated with modeling.

14. Removing the reward that keeps a behavior alive (extinction) can be an effective way of reducing deviant behavior.

15. The effective teacher will use a variety of disciplinary strategies.

16. Do not blow up if old habits crop up again. Remember that extinction procedures generally work faster the second time around.

17. Ignoring misbehavior is effective when the reward is personal attention.

18. Enlist the support of the peer group in extinguishing unwanted behaviors.

19. Behaviors that carry their own built-in rewards call for techniques other than extinction.

20. Extinction procedures are not the method of choice when there is danger of physical injury or emotional contagion.

21. Do not be disheartened if troublesome behaviors increase in frequency and/or intensity when extinction procedures are first applied. It is a sign that extinction procedures are beginning to take hold.

22. Combine extinction procedures with reward so that new misbehaviors do not replace the behavior just extinguished.

23. Punishment is often needed to cope with deviant behavior that is frequent and/or intense.

24. Most of the drawbacks associated with punishment are not inherent in the technique itself, but in its faulty use.

25. Combine reward with punishment to decrease the likelihood that the punished behavior will come back.

26. Early punishment appears to be more effective than punishment after the misbehavior.

27. It is not sufficient to tell students what not to do. Tell students what is right to do.

28. Harsh and repeated punishments can alienate students.

29. Psychologists prefer the type of punishment that involves the removal of rewards over punishments that entail the infliction of pain.

30. Do not set a punitive example.

31. The wise teacher will make greater use of rewards than punishment.

PART V
STATISTICS, MEASUREMENT, AND EVALUATION

CHAPTER 15
Quantitative Methods in Education

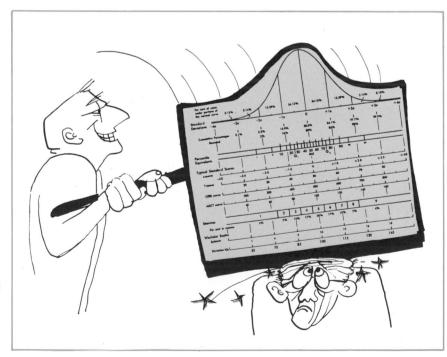

The Statisticion. (From
*THE GREAT TEACHING
MACHINE by Jim Crane,*
© *M. E. Brather 1966.
Used by permission of
John Knox Press)*

Most of the information presented in this book was first obtained and/or verified through research. Research competency is obviously essential for the professional educational psychologist. However, some basic knowledge of quantitative methods is also important to the classroom teacher.

One of the areas in which some knowledge of basic statistics is important is in educational evaluation. Evaluation, for reasons to be discussed in Chapter 16, is an important activity for the professional educator. To be knowledgeable, for example, about how to build, analyze, improve, and interpret classroom tests, and to be aware of meaningful ways to combine data about individuals or groups, a teacher needs some working knowledge of descriptive statistics. Another task that requires knowledge of statistics is in the interpretation of standardized test scores. Administering such tests is standard practice in most schools, and teachers are expected to be able to interpret the scores they yield. To obtain full use of data from tests (and to avoid misusing them), teachers should also have some basic understanding of methods of summarizing and interpreting the results.

Teachers not only have to know some basic statistics to help in their evaluation processes, they also must know something about statistics and research for other purposes. Perhaps the most important reason why teachers should have a grasp of basic research is so that they are better able to understand and critically evaluate the professional literature. The reading of research should keep teachers up to date and increase their enthusiasm for the improvement of instructional procedures and education in general. Ideally, teachers will be able to communicate an appreciation of the role scientific investigations play in advancing our society to their pupils.

A final reason teachers should understand statistics and research is so that they can *do* research. Teachers should continually be on the lookout for methods of improving classroom instruction. By doing small research projects within the classroom, they can often determine which of several procedures works best for them. This book, however, does not present nearly enough material to make the readers really competent *producers* of research. A basic course or two in educational research would be necessary to accomplish that objective.

This chapter presents the kinds of material in statistics and research that educators need for competency in the evaluation of educational objectives and in so doing introduces the reader to the basics that would start him on the road to becoming a competent consumer of research. Hopefully, the material in this chapter will convice the reader that to be a really professional educator instead of a technician, he should continue his studies in this important field.

OBJECTIVES FOR CHAPTER 15	1. Tabulate and graph data, interpret data depicted in such formats, and be aware of when and how such procedures are useful to the educator.
	2. Compute and interpret three different "averages" and state their similarities and differences.
	3. Compute two indices of the variability among student scores.
	4. Interpret and understand uses of derived or "transformed" scores, such as percentile ranks, z and T scores, stanines, grade equivalents, and deviation IQs.
	5. Recognize the advantages and limitations of the various derived scores.
	6. Understand the concept of relationship and the ways in which the correlation coefficient might be useful to educators.
	7. Discuss the nature and purposes of educational research.

METHODS OF DESCRIBING EDUCATIONAL DATA

Statistics serves two major functions, description and inference. *Descriptive statistics* serves the purpose of organizing and presenting data so that it is more readily interpreted. For example, preparing a frequency distribution and computing the arithmetic average for the test scores of our pupils aids them and us in interpreting how well they did on the test. *Inferential statistics* allows us to infer from a particular sample of data to a larger domain,

for example, to reach conclusions about all teachers' mental health from information on a much smaller number of teachers. Descriptive statistics is covered in this section; the concept of inferential statistics will not be discussed further in this book.

Many of the examples of this section use the data (or portions of it) presented in Table 15-1. This table depicts the scores of 50 students on a classroom English test and their previous grade point average and scholastic aptitude (IQ) test scores.

Table 15-1
Scores of 50 Students on a Classroom English Exam and Their Previous Grade Point Average and IQ Scores

Student	Test Scores	GPA	IQ
1	83	3.5	120
2	72	3.4	121
3	53	2.4	105
4	35	2.3	104
5	39	2.8	106
6	53	2.7	110
7	17	1.8	85
8	19	2.0	93
9	64	2.3	112
10	24	2.4	107
11	42	2.4	111
12	31	2.4	108
13	45	2.7	109
14	77	2.6	106
15	76	3.2	115
16	80	3.0	114
17	70	2.9	117
18	58	2.8	116
19	68	3.1	118
20	86	3.1	117
21	50	2.5	113
22	34	2.1	110
23	64	3.3	111
24	42	2.6	109
25	21	2.2	100
26	71	2.5	111
27	29	2.6	109
28	93	3.4	118
29	45	3.0	120
30	88	2.9	115
31	82	2.8	113
32	75	2.8	112
33	40	2.0	103
34	31	1.9	100
35	59	2.5	111
36	61	2.6	110

Student	Test Scores	GPA	IQ
37	34	2.7	103
38	66	2.7	109
39	95	3.6	119
40	49	2.1	105
41	54	3.0	113
42	93	3.2	111
43	36	2.5	103
44	55	2.2	103
45	49	2.8	112
46	63	2.9	115
47	83	3.3	118
48	55	3.2	110
49	47	2.3	100
50	92	3.0	118
Totals	2848	135.0	5498

Presenting Data Succinctly: Tabulating and Graphing

Imagine that you, a teacher, have just given a final examination to the 50 pupils in your class. You have obtained the results shown in Table 15-1. How can you arrange the data to make it easier to interpret? One way, of course, is to *order the test scores*, as shown in Table 15-2. By looking at this table one can immediately see that the scores ranged from a high of 95 for individual 39 to a low of 17 for individual 7. You will note that several individuals had identical scores. For these individuals, it does not matter which one is listed first. For example, individual 28 could have been listed before individual 42.

At times teachers will want to present these data in other tabular or graphic forms. Table 15-2 gives one a pretty clear picture of how the students performed, but a *frequency* dis-

Table 15-2
*The English Test Scores in Table 15-1
Ordered from Highest to Lowest*

Student	Test Score
39	95
42	93
28	93
50	92
30	88
20	86
47	83
1	83
31	82
16	80
14	77
15	76
32	75
2	72
26	71
17	70
19	68
38	66
23	64
9	64
46	63
36	61
35	59
18	58
48	55
44	55
41	54
6	53
3	53
21	50
45	49
40	49
49	47
29	45
13	45
24	42
11	42

Student	Test Score
33	40
5	39
43	36
4	35
37	34
22	34
34	31
12	31
27	29
10	24
25	21
8	19
7	17

tribution, a *histogram*, a *frequency polygon*, or a *cumulative frequency* or *percent curve* would make the data even more interpretable. Even if a teacher deems it unnecessary to prepare one of these for his own ease of interpretation, he may wish to prepare such an aid for his students, or at times for presentation at a teachers' meeting or PTA. A frequency distribution, frequency polygon, or histogram would be particularly beneficial if there were many more scores, as might be the case if a teacher gave the same exam to, for example, five different sections of freshman English. Whether or not a teacher would ever tabulate data in any of the methods to be discussed, every teacher will read literature where such tabulation is presented, so it is vital that one understand the procedures.

FREQUENCY DISTRIBUTIONS

One way to reduce the size of Table 15-2 (and thereby make it easier to interpret and/or graph) would be to list every unique score, and to the right of each score list the number (or frequency) of times that score occurred in the distribution. Since there are 40 unique

English scores in Table 15-2, that would reduce the number of entries in the test score column from 50 to 40. A way to reduce the number in the column still further would be to combine different scores into *class intervals*. Table 15-3 shows a frequency distribution using a class interval of five. There are some general guidelines for preparing class intervals.

1. The size of the class interval should be selected so that between 10 and 18 such intervals will cover the total range of observed scores.

2. The size of the class interval should be an odd number so that the midpoint of the interval is a whole number (see Table 15-3, column 5). This makes some types of computation easier and facilitates graphing.

3. It is generally considered good style to start the class interval at a value that is a multiple of that interval. For example, the interval in Table 15-3 is 5, so the lowest class interval started with a value (15) that was a multiple of 5.

Notice the cumulative frequency column in Table 15-3. It is obtained by summing the entries in the frequency column, starting with the lowest class interval. The cumulative

Table 15-3
Frequency Distribution of the English Test Scores of Table 15-1

(1) Class Interval	(2) Frequency (Number) in Interval	(3) Cumulative Frequency (Number at or Below Interval)	(4) Cumulative Percent	(5) Midpoints
95-99	1	50	100	97
90-94	3	49	98	92
85-89	2	46	92	87
80-84	4	44	88	82
75-79	3	40	80	77
70-74	3	37	74	72
65-69	2	34	68	67
60-64	4	32	64	62
55-59	4	28	56	57
50-54	4	24	48	52
45-49	5	20	40	47
40-44	3	15	30	42
35-39	3	12	24	37
30-34	4	9	18	32
25-29	1	5	10	27
20-24	2	4	8	22
15-19	2	2	4	17

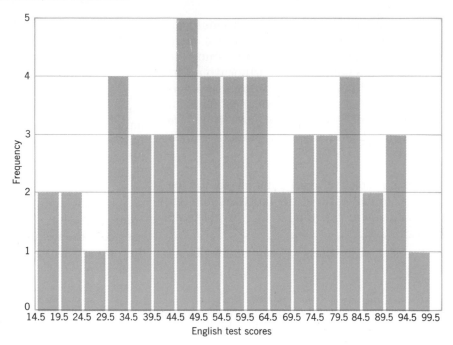

Figure 15-1.
Histogram of the English
test scores.

percent column is obtained by dividing the number in the cumulative frequency column by the total number of scores and converting that value to a percent. For example, the last number in the cumulative frequency column is a 2. Dividing 2 by the total number of scores (50) gives us .04. Converting this value to a percent gives us the 4th percent.

It should be recognized that when grouping occurs, some information is lost. For example, the scores of 80, 82, 83, and 84 have all been put in the interval 80-84. When one computes certain statistics or prepares graphs from frequency distributions, it is necessary to make an assumption regarding the values within the intervals. One typically assumes either that (1) the observations are uniformly distributed over the limits of the interval or (2) all scores fall on the midpoint of the interval. The degree to which such assumptions affect the accuracy of the graphs and statistics computed from the class intervals depends on

the size and number of class intervals and the total frequency of scores.

HISTOGRAMS

The data displayed in Table 15-3 may also be graphed. Graphic representation greatly helps us to understand the data of frequency distributions and in comparing different frequency distributions to each other. A *histogram* is a graph in which the frequencies are represented by bars. Figure 15-1 displays the data of Table 15-3 in the form of a histogram. Notice that frequencies are along the vertical axis and the scores along the horizontal axis. This is not mandatory, but is the most usual procedure. In making a histogram one assumes that the scores are evenly distributed within the class interval, thus giving rectangular bars. The numbers on the horizontal axis are always listed as halfway between the two intervals. It is difficult to superimpose more than one histogram on the same graph. Therefore comparisons of several frequency distributions cannot readily be made by using histograms. Frequency polygons are much better suited to that purpose.

FREQUENCY POLYGONS

A frequency polygon is shown in Figure 15-2. In constructing a frequency polygon one assumes that all the scores within a class interval fall at the midpoint of that interval. Notice that the midpoints of the class intervals just above the highest actual interval and below the lowest actual interval are also marked on the horizontal axis and are given a frequency of zero. This is typically done. If a teacher had frequency distributions for other classes that he wished to compare with this one, he could plot them on the same graph by using colored lines, broken lines, dotted lines, or some other differentiating procedure and labeling the lines appropri-

ately. Of course, if class sizes differed, it would be better to change all frequencies to proportions and plot proportion polygons.

CUMULATIVE FREQUENCY OR PERCENT POLYGONS

Columns 3 and 4 of Table 15-3 give the data necessary to construct a cumulative frequency polygon and a cumulative percent polygon. The cumulative percent polygon is frequently used graphically to display percentiles (see the section on measures of relative position). Both curves can be represented on the same graph, as shown in Figure 15-3, or a separate graph could be constructed for each. When plotting the cumulative polygons, we plot the values halfway between the top of one class interval and the beginning of the next on the horizontal axis. Thus, the first value is plotted at 19.5, which is halfway between 19 and 20. There are two scores below this value (both

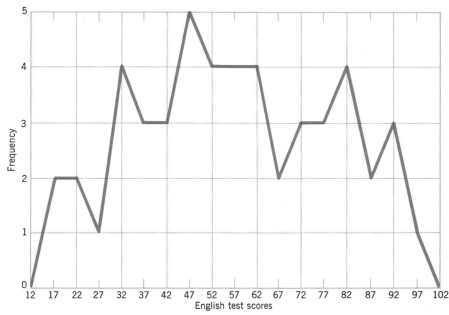

Figure 15-2.
Frequency polygon of the English test scores.

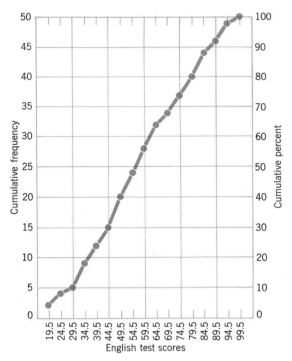

Figure 15-3.
Cumulative polygon of the English test scores.

in the first interval), so we put a dot at 2 above 19.5.

Typical Performance: Measures of Central Tendency

Given an ordered set of scores, or a frequency distribution, it is often of value to use numbers or score values to summarize certain characteristics of this distribution. One characteristic that is of particular interest is a *measure of central tendency* that gives some idea of the average or typical score in the distribution. As a student, you wish to know not only how you performed on an examination, but also how well, in general, the other students performed. When you teach, your students will want the same information.

Three measures of average performance or "central tendency"—the *mean, median,* and *mode*—all present this type of information.

MEAN

The mean $(\overline{X})$ is the arithmetic average of a set of scores. It is found by adding all the scores in the distribution and dividing by the total number of scores (N).[1] The formula is written as follows.

$$\overline{X} = \frac{\Sigma X}{N} \qquad (15\text{-}1)$$

where $\overline{X}$ = the mean
X = the score for a person
N = the number of scores
and Σ = a summation sign indicating that all the Xs in the distribution are added

The mean for the English test scores given in Table 15-1 would be:

$$\overline{X} = \frac{\Sigma X}{N} = \frac{2848}{50} = 56.96$$

For most practical purposes we would round this number to 57.0. Another example of computing the mean is given in Table 15-4.

MEDIAN

The *median* (Mdn) is the point below which 50% of the scores lie. It is obtained from *ordered* data by simply finding the score in the middle of the distribution. For an odd number of scores, such as 55, the median

---

[1] The statistics described in this section can also be obtained for grouped data such as those displayed in Table 15-3. However, the grouped data methods are somewhat more difficult to understand, and for the number of scores teachers ordinarily deal with, if a person has access to a desk calculator or an adding machine, it is easier to use the methods given in this book. Also, as mentioned earlier, statistics computed from class interval data are not quite as precise because of the assumptions made.

would be the middle score, or the score below which and above which 27 scores lie (actually 27½ if one splits the middle score and considers half of it to be above the midpoint and half below). That is, the median is considered to be the 28th score. For an even number of scores, the median would be the point that lies halfway between the two middle scores. For the data in Table 15-2 the median would be 55 since both the 25th and 26th scores are 55. The median for the data in Table 15-4 is 80, halfway between the 10th and 11th scores.

MODE

The *mode* is the most frequently occurring score in the distribution. However, it can be greatly influenced by chance fluctuations and is seldom used. For the data in Table 15-4, the mode is 75.

COMPARISONS OF MEAN, MEDIAN, AND MODE

The mean takes into account the actual numerical value of every score in the distribution and is generally preferred by statisticians. The median is preferred if one wants a measure of central tendency that is not affected by a few very high or low scores. Since the median is easier to determine, it is sometimes preferred by those who do not have access to desk calculators or other computational aids. Table 15-4 presents a *hypothetical* distribution of IQ scores where the median would be considered a better indicator of central tendency than the mean. The mean of 90 is a misleading figure, greatly influenced by two students with very high scores. Note that the mean is six points above the third highest score! The median of 80 is a much more representative figure. (In this case the mode of 75 is a very nonrepresentative measure of central tendency. It is the lowest score in the distribution!)

Table 15-4
A Hypothetical Distribution of IQ Scores

IQ Scores	
186	
186	
84	
84	$\Sigma X = 1800$
83	$N = 20$
82	
82	$\bar{X} = \dfrac{\Sigma X}{N} = \dfrac{1800}{20} = 90$
81	
81	Mdn $= 80$
81	Mode $= 75$
79	
79	
79	
78	
78	
77	
75	
75	
75	
75	

For normal distributions (see Figure 15-4 for an example of a normal distribution) the mean, median, and mode all coincide.[2] The distributions obtained from most standardized test results are fairly normal, so in those cases it would matter little which measure of central tendency was used.

How Much Do Individuals Differ: Measures of Variability

Another statistical characteristic of a distribution that is of interest is a measure of variability that gives an indication of how much

[2] Actually this is true for all distributions that are symmetrical about the mode.

the scores vary (or spread of scores). The three measures of variability most often used are the range, variance, and standard deviation. The standard deviation is a statistic used in computing some of the various derived scores discussed in the next section.

RANGE

The *range* is the difference between the highest and lowest theoretical limits. For the English test scores of Table 15-2, the range would be $95.5 - 16.5 = 79$. The same value would be obtained if one subtracted the lowest obtained score from the highest obtained score and added one. (For the English test scores: $95 - 17 + 1 = 79$.) The range is easy to compute, but can be influenced considerably by a change in the highest or lowest score.

VARIANCE AND STANDARD DEVIATION

The variance (S^2) and standard deviation (S) are the two measures of variability most often used. The standard deviation is the square root of the variance. This relationship is indicated by use of the exponent 2 with the symbol for variance. The variance can be computed by using either of the following two formulas.

$$S_x^2 = \frac{\Sigma(X - \overline{X})^2}{N} \qquad (15\text{-}2)$$

$$S_x^2 = \frac{\Sigma X^2}{N} - \frac{(\Sigma X)^2}{N^2} \qquad (15\text{-}3)$$

where all the symbols on the right side of the equations have been previously defined and the subscript x on the S_x^2 identifies the distribution whose variance is being computed.

Equation 15-2 is a definitional formula. The $X - \overline{X}$ is known as a deviation value showing the distance between a person's

score (X) and the mean $(\overline{X})$. Equation 15-2 is easier to use if one is computing by hand. (Rounding $\overline{X}$ to the nearest whole number, while destroying accuracy somewhat, makes hand computation quite easy.) In other words, this formula tells us the variation is the mean of the squared deviation values: square each deviation value, add all the squares, and divide by the number. Equation 15-3 is the easier one to use if a desk calculator is available.

The standard deviation is obtained by taking the square root of the variance. The square root of equation 15-2 would be

$$S_x = \sqrt{\frac{\Sigma(X - \overline{X})^2}{N}} \qquad (15\text{-}4)$$

The square root of Equation 15-3 is written

$$S_x = \sqrt{\frac{\Sigma X^2}{N} - \frac{(\Sigma X)^2}{N^2}} \qquad (15\text{-}5)$$

Two examples of computing the variance and standard deviation using Equations 15-2 and 15-4 are illustrated in Table 15-5. This table illustrates the practical value of knowing something about a measure of variability as well as a measure of central tendency. Although the two IQ score distributions have the same mean, they have quite different variances and standard deviations. A teacher would hardly use the same procedures in teaching a group of students distributed like those in Table 15-5a as he would in Table 15-5b.

How Do We Compare Students: Measures of Relative Position

To know a person's observed score (often called a raw score) on a measuring instrument gives us some information about his performance. To know how that person's score

Table 15-5
Two Distributions of IQ Scores with Equal Means but Unequal Variances

	a			b	
X	$X - \overline{X}$	$(X - \overline{X})^2$	X	$X - \overline{X}$	$(X - \overline{X})^2$
119	9	81	195	85	7225
118	8	64	157	47	2209
117	7	49	131	21	441
115	5	25	118	8	64
115	5	25	116	6	36
113	3	9	114	4	16
112	2	4	113	3	9
111	1	1	113	3	9
111	1	1	112	2	4
111	1	1	111	1	1
109	−1	1	109	−1	1
109	−1	1	106	−4	16
107	−3	9	101	−9	81
107	−3	9	93	−17	289
106	−4	16	92	−18	324
105	−5	25	90	−20	400
105	−5	25	84	−26	676
104	−6	36	84	−26	676
103	7	49	81	−29	841
103	−7	49	80	−30	900
$\Sigma = 2200$		$480 = \Sigma(X - \overline{X})^2$	$\Sigma X = 2200$	$\Sigma(X - \overline{X})^2 = 14{,}218$	

$$N = 20 \qquad \overline{X} = \frac{\Sigma X}{N} = \frac{2200}{20} = 110$$

$$S_x{}^2 = \frac{480}{20} = 24$$

$$S_x = \sqrt{24} \doteq 4.9$$

$$N = 20 \quad \overline{X} = \frac{\Sigma X}{N} = \frac{2200}{20} = 110$$

$$S_x{}^2 = \frac{14{,}218}{20} = 710.9$$

$$S_x = \sqrt{710.9} \doteq 26.66$$

compares to the mean score of an identifiable group (often called a "norm group") is of more value. If one has an indication of the variability of the distribution of scores in the comparison or norm group as well, much more information is obtained. If a person's raw score is changed into a score that *by itself* gives normative or relative information, we can present the information more efficiently, since the mean and standard deviation need

not also be reported. Such expressions as *kinds of scales*, *kinds of norms*, *types of scores*, and *derived scores* all refer to those scores obtained from various procedures that transform raw scores into scores that have relative meanings.[3]

[3] We are not suggesting that relative data provide the only meaningful information obtained from test performance. Content standard test scores are meaningful also. They will be discussed briefly in Chapter 16.

Derived scores are useful, then, in comparing a person's score to those of others, that is, in making interindividual comparisons. A second use is in making intraindividual (within individual) comparisons. It is not possible, for example, to compare the test score, GPA, and IQ measures as the values are currently listed for individual 1 in Table 15-1. It is first necessary to transfer all the data into comparable units.

Assume Robert, a ninth-grade boy, has received the following *raw scores* on the Differential Aptitude Tests (DAT).

	Verbal Reasoning	Numerical Ability	Abstract Reasoning	Clerical S & A
Raw Score	32	29	32	42

	Mechanical Reasoning	Space Relations	Language Usage I: Spelling	Language Usage II: Grammar
Raw Score	42	36	64	30

Do these data, in and of themselves, tell us anything about how Robert compares with others his age? No, since we have no idea how other children score. Do they tell us anything about whether Robert is better in one subtest area than another? No, since we do not know the total number of questions on each subtest or whether some subtests have easier questions than the others. Some type of derived score is necessary for both types of interpretation.

A third value of derived scores is that they enable one to combine data. At times one wants to combine various pieces of information to make a single decision about an individual. An example would be to combine results of term papers, quizzes, and examinations to arrive at a final grade. The question is, how does one weight the various pieces of data? By converting all scores to derived scores with the same units of measurement a weighting scheme can be carried out.

The types of derived scores that teachers are most apt to use themselves and/or find used in reporting standardized test results are percentiles, z scores, T scores, stanines, grade equivalents, and deviation IQ scores. These will be explained and advantages and disadvantages will be discussed briefly. First, however, we will briefly discuss the normal curve.

THE NORMAL CURVE

The normal curve is a bell-shaped curve, as shown in Figure 15-4. It is symmetrical about the mean and, as already mentioned, the mean, median, and mode coincide. Also, a specified percent of scores fall within each standard deviation from the mean. As can be seen from Figure 15-4, about 68% of the scores fall between $\pm 1S$, 95% fall between $\pm 2S$, and 99.9% fall between $\pm 3S$.

There has been considerable discussion in the past about whether all human characteristics are normally distributed. Whatever the truth about this, classes of 30 to 50 students are *not* apt to be distributed normally with respect to any characteristic. On the other hand, the test results from the large norm

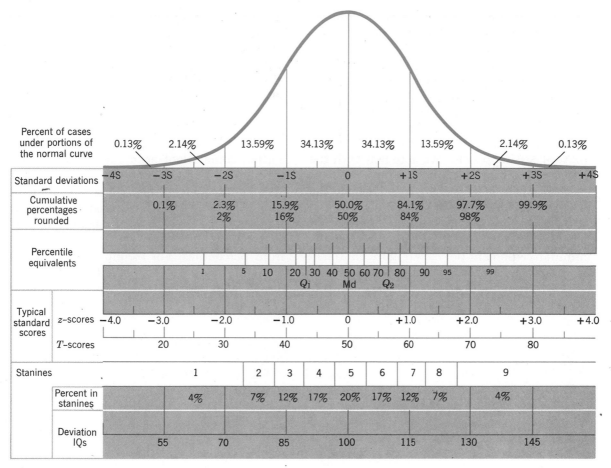

Figure 15-4.

Chart showing the normal curve and its relationship to various derived scores. *(Adapted and reproduced with the permission of The Psychological Corporation)*

groups used for standardized tests are apt to be approximately normally distributed. Therefore the derived scores from standardized tests are often interpreted as if the raw score distribution were normal. This should not be done for teacher-made tests.

PERCENTILES AND PERCENTILE RANKS

A *percentile* is defined as a point on the distribution below which a certain percent of the scores fall. A *percentile rank* is a person's

relative position or the percent of students' scores falling below his obtained score.[4] To illustrate the computation of percentiles, consider the data in Table 15-2. There are 50 scores. If one wanted to compute the 80th percentile (P_{80}) for our sample distribution, he would want to find a point below which 40 (80% of 50) of the scores lie and above

---

[4] Statisticians differ somewhat in the precise definitions of these terms, but these differences are minor and need not concern us.

which 10 of the scores lie. We see that 40 scores lie below 77.5 (halfway between 77 and 78) and 10 scores lie above 79.5. P_{80} falls somewhere in the range 77.5 to 79.5. Convention suggests we designate P_{80} as falling halfway between these two points, so $P_{80} = 78.5$. For one more example, let us compute the 50th percentile (P_{50}). We wish to find the point below which and above which 25 (50% of 50) scores lie. We note that both the 25th and 26th scores are 55. Thus $P_{50} = 55$. (Note that this value is the same as the median, which it should be.)

If the grouped frequency distribution (Table 15-3) had been constructed and the cumulative percent polygon (Figure 15-3) had been drawn, we could obtain percentiles directly from Figure 15-3. To obtain P_{80} one would look for the 80 on the right side of the graph and look in the figure to see the point at where the drawn line crosses the line for P_{80}. Going down from that point we see the value for the English test score to be 79.5. This would be the estimate of the 80th percentile. Note that it is not quite the same as the value obtained by computation in the paragraph above. This is because Figure 15-3 is based on grouped data and, as pointed out earlier, some slight accuracy is usually lost when the data are grouped.

Percentiles have the advantage of being easy to compute and fairly easy to interpret. As with other derived scores, both intra- and interindividual comparisons can be made from percentiles. For example, looking at a percentile norm table for the DAT values for Robert given earlier, we find the following percentiles.[5]

	Verbal Reasoning	Numerical Ability	Abstract Reasoning	Clerical S & A
Raw Score	32	29	32	42
Percentile	90	85	45	30

	Mechanical Reasoning	Space Relations	Language Usage I: Spelling	Language Usage II: Grammar
Raw Score	42	36	64	30
Percentile	45	75	60	70

We can now see how Robert's scores in each subtest compare with other ninth-grade boys (interindividual comparison) as well as see how his scores in the different subtests compare with each other (intraindividual comparison). For example, Robert is at the 90th percentile in verbal reasoning and at the 45th percentile in mechanical reasoning. The 90 and 45 each compare Robert to others. The comparison between the 90 and 45 shows Robert to be relatively better in verbal than mechanical reasoning. As can be seen, the magnitude of the raw scores by itself was meaningless information.

Percentiles have a disadvantage in that the size of the percentile units is not constant in terms of raw score units. For example, if the distribution is normal, the raw score differences between the 90th and 99th percentiles is much greater than the raw score difference between the 50th and 59th percentile (see Figure 15-4). Thus, a percentile difference does not really represent the same amount of

[5] Some would call these percentile ranks. The DAT manual refers to them as percentiles.

raw score difference in the middle of the distribution as it does at the extremes. Any interpretation of percentiles must take this fact into account. We can be more confident that differences in percentiles represent true differences at the extremes than at the middle of the distribution.

z AND T SCORES

A type of derived score that does not have the disadvantage just mentioned is a *standard score*. The z score is the basic standard score. The formula for a z score is

$$z = \frac{\text{raw score} - \text{mean}}{\text{standard deviation}} = \frac{X - \overline{X}}{S_x} \quad (15\text{-}6)$$

where all the symbols except z have been previously defined. As can be seen from the formula, a person whose raw score was equal to the mean would have a z score of zero. If a

person has a raw score one standard deviation above the mean, his z score would be +1.0. Thus, z scores are standard scores with a mean of zero and a standard deviation of one.

The formula for a T score is

$$T = 10z + 50 \quad (15\text{-}7)$$

Thus, T scores are derived scores with a mean of 50 (the T score if z = 0) and a standard deviation of 10.

There is no theoretical advantage for the T score over the z score, or vice versa. One is a simple transformation of the other. Practitioners often prefer T scores because negative numbers can generally be avoided. (Doesn't it seem easier to tell a parent that their child had a score of 20 instead of a −3?)

Table 15-6 shows the computation of the z and T scores for individual 1 in Table 15-1.

Table 15-6
Computation of z and T Scores for Individual 1 in Table 15-1

	Raw Score	Mean	Standard deviation	z	T
Test score	83.0	56.96	21.4	1.2	62
GPA	3.5	2.70	.4	2.0	70
IQ	120.0	109.96	7.0	1.4	64

Test score: $z = \dfrac{83 - 56.96}{21.4} = \dfrac{26.04}{21.4} = 1.2$

Test score: $T = 10(1.2) + 50 = 12 + 50 = 62$

GPA: $\quad z = \dfrac{3.5 - 2.7}{.4} = \dfrac{.8}{.4} = 2$

GPA: $\quad T = 10(2) + 50 = 20 + 50 = 70$

IQ: $\quad z = \dfrac{120 - 109.96}{7.0} = \dfrac{10.04}{7.0} = 1.4$

IQ: $\quad T = 10(1.4) + 50 = 14 + 50 = 64$

(The means and standard deviations are provided. Computation of all of these values has not yet been demonstrated in the text. As practice you may want to verify these values.)

When scores are normally distributed, there is a precise mathematical relationship between z and T scores and other derived scores. Recall that in a normal distribution, approximately 68% of the scores fall between $\pm 1 S_x$, 95% fall between $\pm 2 S_x$, and 99.9% fall between $\pm 3 S_x$. Since a z score has a standard deviation of one, approximately 68% of the z scores will be between ± 1, 95% will be between ± 2, and 99.9% will be between ± 3 in a normal distribution. As Figure 15-4 illustrates, when a person scores one standard deviation above the mean, he has a z score of one (T = 60), and is at about the 84th percentile.

As mentioned earlier, most norm groups for standardized tests are quite large, and the distribution of their scores approaches normality.[6] Thus, z and T scores for most standardized tests can be interpreted as if they relate to percentiles, as shown in Figure 15-4. Classrooms of 50 pupils, however, *do not* typically present normal distributions, and the relationship depicted in Figure 15-4 would not be accurate.

STANINES

Stanines are standard scores with a mean of 5 and a standard deviation of 2. Only the integers 1 to 9 can occur. In a normal distribution, stanines are related to other scores as is shown in Figure 15-4. As can be seen, the percentage of scores at each stanine is 4, 7, 12, 17, 20, 17, 12, 7, and 4, respectively. Whether or not the original distribution is normal, stanine scores are typically assigned so the resultant stanine distribution is the 4, 7, 12,

---

[6] Some test authors use statistical procedures to transform their z and T scores into a normal distribution if the original distribution is not normal. This normalization procedure is beyond the scope of this textbook.

17, 20, . . . 4 one mentioned earlier. This is done by (1) ordering the scores, (2) finding the median, (3) assigning 10% of the scores on each side of the median a stanine of 5, (4) assigning the next lowest 17% of the scores a stanine of 4 and the next highest 17% a stanine of 6, and so forth. Table 15-7 shows an example of stanine computation for the English test scores of Table 15-2.

There is no particular advantage of stanines over other types of derived scores. They do represent the finest discrimination that can be made on one column of an IBM card. The major reason we present them in this book is that they are frequently used in reporting the results on standardized tests, and a competent teacher should be able to interpret such scores.

GRADE EQUIVALENTS

Grade equivalents can best be explained by an example. If a student obtains a score on a test that is equal to the median score for all the beginning seventh graders in the norm group, then that student is given a grade equivalent of 7.0. If a student obtains a score equal to the median score of beginning sixth graders, then he is given a grade equivalent of 6.0. If a student would score between these two points, linear interpolation would be used to determine his grade equivalent.

Grade equivalents suffer from at least four major limitations. One of these limitations is the problem of "extrapolation." When a test author standardizes his test, he normally does not use students of all grade levels in his normative sample. Suppose a particular test is designed to be used in grades 4 to 6. Often the norming would be done on only these three grades. Now, if the median sixth grader receives a grade equivalent of 6.0, then half the sixth graders must have a grade equivalent higher than this. How much higher? 7.0, 7.8, 9.0, 12.0? We do not know. Since the test was not given to students beyond the sixth grade,

Table 15-7 *Stanine Computation for The English Test Scores of Table 15-2*		

English Test Scores	Stanines	Steps
95	9	1. Find the median (see line marked Median).
93		
93	8	2. Count off 5 scores (10% of 50) on each side of the median. These values all have a stanine of 5.
92		
88		
86		3. Since 17% of 50 is 8.5, we can count off either 8 or 9 more scores on each side and assign values of 4 and 6. (We chose 9.)
83		
83	7	
82		
80		
77		4. Count off 6 more scores (12% of 50) on each side and assign values 3 and 7.
76		
75		
72		
71		5. Since 7% of 50 is 3.5, we can count off either 3 or 4 more scores (we should choose 4 to avoid splitting the two 93s into different stanines) on each side and assign values of 2 and 8.
70	6	
68		
66		
64		
64		
63		6. The two end values receive stanines of 1 and 9, respectively.
61		
59		7. Due to rounding, this distribution does not give the exact proportions found in a stanine distribution, but it is close enough.
58		
55		
55 ← Median	5	
54		
53		
53		
50		
49		
49		
47		
45		
45	4	
42		
42		
40		
39		
36		
35		
34		
34	3	
31		
31		
29		
24		
21	2	
19		
17	1	

there is no way to know how they would have scored. The test maker has to estimate what the students of other grades would have received, and we cannot be sure that he is right. There are many chances for error.

A second limitation of grade equivalents is that they give us little information concerning the percentile standing of a person within his class. A fifth-grade student may, for example, because of the differences in the grade equivalent distributions for various subject matter, have a grade equivalent of 5.9 in Word Meaning and 5.7 in Arithmetic Computation and yet have a higher fifth-grade percentile rank in the latter.

The third limitation of grade equivalents is that (contrary to what the numbers indicate) a fourth grader with a grade equivalent of 7.0 does *not* necessarily know the same amount or the same kinds of things as a ninth grader with a grade equivalent of 7.0. For example, a bright fourth grader who can do very well on an arithmetic test involving speed and accuracy may perform equally as well as the average seventh grader. A weak ninth grader may be poor in speed and accuracy and perform at the seventh-grade level on a test demanding those skills. Yet those two respective students, receiving equal scores on an arithmetic test, do not know the same things about mathematics in a more general sense.

A fourth limitation of grade equivalents is that they are particularly prone to misinterpretation by the critics of education. By the very definition of grade equivalents, one half the beginning sixth-grade students in the nation *must be* below a grade equivalent of 6.0. Yet the critics of education despair that not

"But you have to remember, dad, that below average is a lot higher than it used to be." (Drawing by Short and Weaver Cartoons)

everyone is "reading up to grade level!" This is *exactly* the same as taking the irrational position that everyone should be at or above the 50th percentile.

Grade equivalents remain popular in spite of their serious inadequacies. Teachers believe that such scores are easily and correctly understood by both children and parents. This is unfortunate. It is probably not too dogmatic to suggest that grade equivalents, although useful if used in conjunction with other kinds of scores, such as percentiles, should never be used alone.

DEVIATION IQs

The intelligence quotient (IQ) is one of the most misunderstood concepts in measurement. Much of this confusion exists because of a lack of understanding of intelligence tests. (In Chapter 17 we will consider what an aptitude or intelligence test supposedly measures, and how the scores can be usefully interpreted.) Part of the confusion, however, exists because people do not understand a type of score often used to report the results of intelligence tests, that is, the IQ. Originally the IQ was actually a quotient (a ratio). It was found by dividing a person's mental age by his chronological age and then multiplying by 100 (IQ = MA/CA × 100). The problem was in determining a person's mental age. This was accomplished differently on various tests, but essentially the process was similar to obtaining grade equivalents. Thus, if a student obtained a raw score equal to the median raw score of all ten-year olds, he would be given a mental age of ten years.

The ratio IQ had many inadequacies. One weakness was that the standard deviations of the IQs were not constant for different ages, so that an IQ score of 110, for example, would be equal to a different percentile at one age than another. A second problem was that opinions varied concerning what the maximum value of the denominator should be. When does a person stop growing intellectually—at twelve years, sixteen years, eighteen years? Because of these various inadequacies of the ratio IQ, test constructors now report deviation IQs. Deviation IQs are computed separately for each age group within the norm sample. These are not literally intelligence quotients. They are transformations much like the z or T values discussed earlier. Typically these derived IQs have a mean of 100 and a standard deviation of 15 or 16, but not all do, and this is one of the reasons why we cannot compare two individuals' IQ scores unless they have taken the same test. A person who scores 128 on a test with a standard deviation of 12 scores higher relative to other persons than one who scores 130 on a test with a standard deviation of 16.

Measures of Relationship

If we have two sets of scores from the same group of people, it is often desirable to know the degree to which the scores are related. For example, we may be interested in the relationship between the English test scores and GPA for the 50 individuals whose scores are given in Table 15-1. Or we may be interested in either or both of the other relationships: test score and IQ or GPA and IQ. We are also interested in relationships between two sets of scores when we are studying the reliability or validity of a test. (See Chapter 16 for a discussion on reliability and validity.)

The Pearson product moment correlation coefficient (r) is the statistic most often used to give us an indication of this relationship. The value of r can change from +1.00 to −1.00. When an increase in one variable tends to be accompanied by an increase in the other variable (such as aptitude and achievement), the correlation is positive. When an increase in one tends to be accompanied by a decrease in the other (such as speed and accuracy), then the correlation is negative. A perfect positive correlation (1.00) or a perfect negative correlation (−1.00) occurs when a change in the one variable is always accompanied by a commensurate change in the other variable. A zero (.00) correlation occurs when there is no relationship between the two variables.

How high (positively or negatively) an r must be in order to indicate that a significant relationship exists is difficult to specify. It depends on how one defines significance. Significance can be considered in either a statistical or practical sense. For example, a correlation coefficient of .08 (say between teaching method and grades) will be statistically significant if the number of cases used to compute the correlation is sufficiently large. But this correlation is so low that it has no practical significance in educational decision making.

Obviously we do not expect different sets of variables to all have equal degrees of relationship. Correlations vary considerably in size, and the value of a given correlation must be interpreted in part by comparing it to other correlations obtained for similar variables. For example, a correlation of .80 would be considered low if one were correlating two equivalent forms of an aptitude test. However, a correlation of .60 between scholastic aptitude test scores and college grade point averages would be interpreted as quite high. Table 15-8 gives some typical correlation coefficients for selected variables. The more experience you obtain, *the more you will know* what degree of relationship is expected between different variables.

Two cautions should be mentioned concerning the interpretation of a Pearson product moment correlation coefficient.

1. It is not an indication of cause and effect. One can find all sorts of variables that are related, but have no causal relationship. For

Table 15-8
Typical Correlation Coefficients for Selected Variables

Variables	r
Equivalent forms of a test	.95
Intelligence of identical twins	.90
Height and weight of adults	.60
High school and college GPA	.50
Intelligence of siblings	.50
Height versus intelligence	.05

example, for children, the size of the big toe is slightly correlated with mental age—yet one does not cause the other. They are correlated simply because they are both related to a third variable: chronological age.

2. It is a measure of linear (straight line) relationship. If one suspects that two variables have a relationship other than linear, a different index of correlation should be computed.

EDUCATIONAL RESEARCH

We indeed live in a world of fantastic scientific accomplishments. Men have walked on the moon. Organ transplants are becoming more and more common. We can destroy most of the earth's inhabitants by pushing a few buttons. These and many other scientific accomplishments (most beneficial, some potentially very harmful) have been obtained through the processes of research. While research is not the only way of acquiring new knowledge, it appears to be one of the most productive. In fact, we live in a research-oriented world.

Research, or the scientific method, is based on the following steps: (1) stating a problem; (2) forming tentative hypotheses about the problem; (3) collecting and analysing the data; (4) interpreting the data; and (5) drawing conclusions and implications from the data.

Definition of Educational Research

Educational research has the same general goals as other types of research: to advance the understanding, prediction, and control of our environment. It is, of course, restricted in scope to the study of educational issues. Travers (1964, p. 5) states that, "The scientific goal of educational research is to discover laws or generalizations about behavior which can be used to make predictions and control events within educational situations."

Tyler (1965, p. 2) has defined educational research as "disciplined inquiry into questions relating to the processes of education and the enterprises conducted for educational purposes." The terms "processes of education" and "enterprises conducted for educational purposes" as Tyler uses them include the study of educational objectives, learning, curriculum, and evaluation, as well as studies of all types of educational institutions. Thus, although "restricted" to educational concerns, educational research is still very broad in scope and expanding every year.

Expansion of Educational Research

For every existing social ill there exists someone who strongly advocates that the responsibility for the solution lies with education. (It is even quite popular to blame education for the original causes of many social ills.) Since educators do not have the repertoire of skills necessary for these solutions and in many instances do not even know what caused the problems or what skills are needed to alleviate them, much more research is necessary.

As Bloom (1966, p. 212) points out: "Education is looked to for solutions to problems of poverty, racial discord, crime and delinquency, urban living, peace, and even for the problems arising from affluence. The new tasks thrust on education require new approaches, new understandings, and a closer relation between theory, research, and practice than has ever existed before."

To help in finding solutions to education's new task, more and more disciplines become involved in educational research. Anthropologists, biologists, communications experts, economists, geneticists, political scientists, psychologists, and sociologists are all doing educational research.

Problems in Educational Research

In spite of an expansion in quality and quantity of educational research, it has obviously fallen short of its goals. It has not given educators many of the answers they need. Why has this happened?

Many of the problems confronting educational researchers are of the same type as those confronting other researchers. Obtaining knowledge through research is an arduous task. But it should be obvious that the giant advances made in biological and physical sciences have not been equaled in the social sciences. This is partly because education is a more complex field to research. Because of the difficulty in controlling the relevant variables, many feel that it is amazing that we have learned as much as we have about the educational process.

Society seems to have a much different attitude toward natural science research than toward social science research. As Remmers (1949) pointed out more than two decades ago, our thinking is quite different in the areas of natural and social sciences. In natural science the public has an experimental attitude. Old ideas are held as invalid and the past is viewed with amusement. Change is welcomed as progress. In social science there is more of a stand pat attitude. Cherished traditions, beliefs, and loyalties are hard to give up. New ideas are viewed as unsound and the future is viewed with alarm. Change, having been identified with cultural decay, is opposed. With public attitudes such as these it is no wonder that so little time and money has been expended in research, that so little has been accomplished, and that the public has resisted new findings.

There has been another problem in educational research that is just the opposite of that mentioned above. There is far too often an unwarranted and uncritical acceptance of research findings. All scientists realize that the public cannot evaluate their research procedures. But it seems that the public, having more and stronger biases about social science, is more gullible in accepting "findings" that agree with their biases (and, as mentioned, will reject those that do not). This is natural, and a problem that educational researchers will have to live with. A problem that does seem solvable, however, is the gullibility of professional educators. Professional physicists can critique physical research. Professional biologists can critique biological research. Why can't professional educators be critical of educational research? Glass (1968, p. 148) suggests that educators' gullibility stems from two causes.

1. An insensitivity—which is a venial sin in the layman, but a mortal one in the professional—to the nature of empirical evidence.

2. A commitment by professionals to "help" the child rather than understand him or his circumstances, a commitment which engenders an uncritical wish to believe that the latest educational nostrum . . . is miraculously effective.

Glass reports several examples of this will to believe and how the desire to help children renders people irrational and gullible. Sipay (1965) wrote a report of a fictitious research project entitled "The Effect of Prenatal Instruction on Reading Achievement." It was a satire on the attempts to teach reading to younger and younger children. In this imaginary study lessons were broadcast to unborn children in an experimental group by means of a fetoscope. At the end of the first grade these children could read better than control groups. Sipay, as reported by Glass (1968), has received serious letters requesting more information about his fetoscope and his techniques!

What seems unfortunate to us is the fact that many educators accepted reported results without looking critically at the *research*. Hopefully teachers (and certainly professors of education), in the near future, will have enough research sophistication so that they can accept or reject research findings on their merit instead of on their emotional appeal.

The commitment by professionals to help children is good, not bad. However, when this commitment blinds us to the fallacies of poor research (or causes us to reject good research), then the commitment itself can hinder the desired outcomes. This problem is made more serious by the fact that so much poor research is published (see Dunnette, 1966).

Another suggested reason why educational practice has advanced more slowly than other areas (for example, medical practice) is that there has been an overemphasis on the wrong types of research. A great deal of research has been applied instead of basic. Many feel this has left us knowing too little about the theoretical aspects of education.

Whether or not there has been too little emphasis on basic research, most educators agree that there is a gap between theory and practice. Some have suggested that the lag between the publication of research findings and the implementation of those findings is as long as 50 years. This lag is partly due to distrust of research, the inability of educators to read and understand research reports, and insufficient funds for implementing change. Unfortunately, we suspect the lag in educational practice is partly due to the human tendency toward laziness. We are reminded of the farmer who, when the government agent offered him free pamphlets that would explain better farming practices replied, "Why bother, I ain't farming half as good as I know how to now."

In summary, it is apparent that educational research has not advanced the practice of education to the degree hoped for, or indeed even to the degree necessary in this complex society. There are many possible reasons for this: lack of public support, distrust of social science research, poorly trained researchers, and even more poorly trained practitioners of education. One of the more promising solutions to the problems of educational research is to improve our training for both producers and consumers of research. As mentioned, one goal of this chapter is to make at least a start in giving you some competency as consumers of research. An equally important goal is to make you aware of the actual and potential value of educational research, so that you will desire and obtain further growth in research consumer competency.

Some Contributions of Educational Research

The previous section may have left you with a pessimistic feeling about educational research. Educational research has had its problems, but most of them are curable by better education of the public and professional educators concerning research. But educational research has also made many major contributions in the past. As mentioned at the beginning of this chapter, most of what we have learned in educational psychology has been learned through research. Bloom (1966) has listed some areas in which research studies have contributed to our understanding.

1. The development of the individual.

2. The predictability of human characteristics.

3. The modifiability of human characteristics.

4. Teaching machines and instructional strategies.

5. Individual differences in learners.

6. Principles of learning.

7. Sequencing in learning.

These and others have been discussed throughout this book. They are mentioned here to impress on you the important role research plays in the field of education.

Summary

1. Knowledge of some basic statistics is important in evaluation processes.

2. Knowledge of research procedures is important if teachers wish to understand and critically evaluate the professional literature.

3. Descriptive statistics organize and present data so that it is more readily interpreted.

4. Tabulating and/or graphing data aids in its ease of interpretation.

5. The mean, median, and mode are measures of central tendency. They give an idea of the average or typical score in the distribution.

6. The mean is generally the preferred measure of central tendency.

7. For distributions that are fairly normal (such as those obtained from most standardized tests results), it matters little which measure of central tendency is used.

8. The range, variance, and standard deviation are measures of variability. They give an indication of the spread of scores in a distribution.

9. The standard deviation is the square root of the variance.

10. It is valuable to know how a person's score compares to the scores of an identifiable (norm) group. Measures of relative position (derived scores) provide this information.

11. Derived scores are also useful in making intraindividual comparisons and in combining data from different sources.

12. Percentile ranks, z scores, T scores, stanines, grade equivalents, and deviation IQ scores are the types of derived scores most frequently used.

13. A percentile is a point on the distribution below which a certain percent of the scores fall. A percentile rank is a score representing a person's relative position. Percentile ranks are easier to compute and interpret than other derived scores.

14. z and T scores are linear transformations of raw scores. z scores have a mean of zero and a standard deviation of 1. T scores have a mean of 50 and a standard deviation of 10.

15. Stanines are standard scores with a mean of 5 and a standard deviation of 2.

16. Grade equivalents, while frequently used, have several major limitations. They should not be used as the sole method of reporting data.

17. Deviation IQs are derived scores. Generally the mean is 100 and the standard deviation around 15 or 16. They have replaced the inadequate ratio IQs as a method of reporting scholastic aptitude test results.

18. The Pearson product moment correlation coefficient is the statistic most often used to provide a measure of relationship. The values of the coefficient can range from -1.00 and $+1.00$, indicating perfect negative and perfect positive relationships, respectively. A value of 0(zero) indicates no relationship.

19. There are two major cautions in interpreting a Pearson product moment correlation coefficient.

a. It is not an indication of cause and effect.

b. It is only a measure of linear relationship.

20. The purpose of educational research is to advance our understanding, prediction, and control of the educational phenomenon.

21. It is more difficult to conduct research in education than in many other fields. The independent variables in educational research are difficult to control.

22. In the past, professional educators have not been competent critics of educational research.

CHAPTER 16
Measurement and Evaluation:
Purposes, Principles, and Issues

"It's nice to see a cheerful headline for a change."
(Drawing by Bill O'Malley from Today's Education NEA Journal, 1973)

Definitions: Test, Measurement, and Evaluation
The Purposes of Measurement and Evaluation
Criteria of Good Measurement Procedures
General Considerations and Issues in Evaluation Programs
Reporting the Results of Measurement

At the beginning of Chapter 15 we indicated that one reason prospective teachers should learn some basic statistical concepts was to enable them to do a better job of evaluating. Chapters 16 and 17 are devoted to a closer examination of evaluation principles and procedures. Chapter 16 is largely devoted to the purposes and principles of measurement and evaluation; Chapter 17 is devoted to techniques of evaluation.

OBJECTIVES FOR CHAPTER 16

1. Define the terms test, measurement, and evaluation.
2. Understand the relationship between evaluation and decision making.
3. List three major categories of purposes of evaluation and discuss ways that evaluation helps both the teacher and student.
4. Define reliability and list some sources of error in pupils' scores.
5. Differentiate between the types of validity.
6. Define objectivity and discrimination and discuss why they are relevant criteria for a measuring instrument.
7. Recognize the philosophical and measurement concerns of accountability programs.
8. Understand the similarities and differences between curriculum and student evaluation.
9. Recognize the importance of affective evaluation and know some reasons for its neglect among teachers.

10. Recognize the distinctions between normative and criterion-referenced measurement.
11. Recognize the necessity for reporting procedures and discuss how experts can be useful for different groups of people.
12. Know the advantages and limitations of various reporting procedures.

DEFINITIONS: TEST, MEASUREMENT, AND EVALUATION

The terms "test," "measurement," and "evaluation" are sometimes used interchangeably, but some distinctions do exist. Test, the narrowest of the three terms, connotes the presentation of a standard set of questions through which we obtain a measure (i.e., a numerical value) of a characteristic of a person. *Measurement* is a broader concept. We can measure characteristics without tests. Using observations, rating scales, or any other device that allows us to obtain information in a quantitative form is also measurement. *Evaluation* is ". . . the process of delineating, obtaining, and providing useful information for judging decision alternatives." (Stufflebeam et al., 1971, p. xxv) Some define evaluation as a process that allows one to make a judgment about the desirability or value of a measure. Thus, evaluation encompasses but also goes beyond the meaning of the terms test and measurement. Two students may obtain the same score when we measure them, but we might evaluate those measures differently. Suppose, at the end of sixth grade, we have two students who are both reading at the sixth-grade level. However, at the beginning of the year one was reading at the fourth-grade level, and the other was reading at the fifth-grade, sixth-month level. Our evaluations of those outcomes are not the same. One student progressed at an above average rate and the other at below average rate. One is a desir-

able outcome, the other is not.

Also, it is important to point out that we never evaluate people. We evaluate characteristics or properties of people—their scholastic potential, knowledge of algebra, honesty, perseverance, ability to teach, and so forth. This is *NOT* to be confused with evaluating the worth of a person. Teachers, parents, and students do not always seem to keep this distinction clearly in mind.

THE PURPOSES OF MEASUREMENT AND EVALUATION

Why evaluate? For one reason, taxpayers are beginning to demand an accounting. If they spend money, they want to know what the results are. Another reason is that students, teachers, administrators, and parents all work hard toward achieving educational goals, and it is only natural that they should want to ascertain the degree to which those goals have been realized. Just the satisfaction of knowing, the removal of ignorance, is an important reason for evaluation. But these reasons must take second and third place to the more important reason. *Measurement and evaluation are essential to sound educational decision making.*

There are many decisions that educators must continually make, and countless more that they must assist individual pupils, parents, taxpayers, and governmental agencies in making. Should Susan be placed in an advanced reading group? Should Johnny take algebra or general mathematics next year? Should the school continue using the mathematics textbook adopted this year, revert back to the previous text, or try still another one? Is grammar being stressed at the expense of pronunciation in first-year German? Am I doing as well in my chemistry as I should? Have I been studying the right material? Should I go to college? These are just a few of the questions and decisions facing educators, parents, and students. As discussed in Chapter 1, the more accurate and relevant the information on which a decision is based, the better that decision is likely to be. In fact, many decision theorists define a good decision as one that is based on *all* the *relevant* information. To reiterate, educational decisions need to be made, these decisions should be based on relevant and accurate information, and the responsibility of gathering and imparting that information belongs to educators.

A general purpose of evaluation, then, is to aid in decision making. This general purpose, however, can be subdivided. We can talk of administrative, guidance, and instructional decisions. Teachers or prospective teachers are likely to be most interested in instructional decisions. We will briefly mention the other two types, also, however, since it is often quite appropriately the task of the classroom teacher to obtain the data necessary for, and indeed sometimes to make, administrative and guidance decisions.

Administrative Purposes

Administrators must often make decisions about such things as the selection of pupils, placement of pupils, and curriculum offerings. Some questions, to be answered properly, demand knowledge of various characteristics of the student body in general. What should be the ratio of algebra to general math sections in ninth grade? Does the school system need another remedial reading teacher? Should the school district be offering more college preparatory courses, or should it be emphasizing vocational education? Should the work-study program be expanded?

Other decisions depend on knowledge concerning specific students. Should Billy be admitted to kindergarten this year, or should he wait until he is one year older? Will Beth profit from a remedial reading program? Whatever the question, the administrator often depends on the teacher to obtain the necessary data, and at times to actually make the decision.

Guidance Purposes

Students need to be guided in their vocational choices, their educational programs, and their personal problems. For students to make sound decisions in these areas it is crucial that they have accurate self-concepts. A student must depend, in part, on the school to help him form a self-concept. The classroom teacher can be particularly helpful in providing the student with information concerning his mastery of subject matter. Standardized tests of aptitude, achievement, interest, and personality inventories also provide information useful in guiding the student.

Instructional Purposes

The primary role of the school and the individual classroom teacher, is to facilitate certain types of student learning. Activities that interfere with this student learning should be shunned—activities that promote it should be conducted. Sometimes teachers feel that measurement and evaluation are the antitheses of instruction—that somehow the role of evaluator is at odds with the role of a stimulator and promoter of learning. This is not necessarily true. Evaluation incorrectly done is at odds with the promotion of learning. Evaluation correctly done greatly enhances learning. It aids both the teacher in teaching and the student in learning.

EVALUATING HELPS THE TEACHER

There are several ways in which evaluation procedures aid the teacher: (1) they provide him with knowledge of what a student can do, his "entry behaviors"; (2) they aid him setting, refining, and clarifying realistic new goals; (3) they help him to evaluate the degree to which the objectives are achieved; and (4) they help him in determining and evaluating his instructional techniques.

We have discussed in this book the importance of readiness for learning. To teach effectively we must find out where a student is and start from there. We should have estimates of the students' capacities for learning, as well as estimates of what they currently know. We cannot, for example, teach long division to a student who cannot subtract. To be effective teachers we must be aware of what our students already know.

There are many ways to obtain data regarding entry behavior. (Some of these have been discussed previously, for example, in the section in Chapter 11 on individualized instruction.) Aptitude test results provide general information concerning the speed and ease with which a student can be expected to learn. General achievement tests provide information on whether a student is generally weak or strong in a subject matter area. For more specific information on any deficiencies, diagnostic instruments are useful. Reports from previous teachers are another source of information regarding entry behavior.

Measurement and evaluation also aid the teacher in setting, refining, and clarifying realistic goals. Knowledge of entry behavior obviously helps in the setting of realistic goals. The acts of building measurement devices and carefully looking at the outcomes help in refining and clarifying these goals. Nothing is quite as helpful in forcing a teacher to think through his goals as the act of constructing or choosing measurement devices. To determine what behaviors will be observed in order to ascertain whether goals have been reached requires careful consideration of those goals.

After administering a measuring instrument, one can make some judgment about how realistic the goals were and the effectiveness of the instructional procedure. For example, if a third-grade teacher used the Cuisenaire method for teaching arithmetic, knowledge about the degree of student success would be necessary to evaluate the efficacy of that method.

EVALUATING HELPS THE STUDENT

Evaluation aids the student by (1) communicating the goals of the teacher; (2) increasing motivation; (3) encouraging good study habits; and (4) providing feedback regarding his strengths and weaknesses.

Of course, the goals of instruction should be communicated to students well in advance of any evaluation. Students are much more apt to learn what we deem important if they know our thinking. However, if we never evaluated to find out whether our objectives were being achieved, the students might become cynical about what our goals really are, or indeed whether we have set any. Advance information about the nature of an examination is one of the most effective ways of communicating our objectives to students. Occasionally people will criticize testing (one form of evaluation) because the student tries to "psych out the teacher" and learn what the teacher thinks is important. This criticism seems to assume that it is better if students do not bother trying to ascertain the teacher's objectives!

As you have read in previous chapters, performance requires motivation. Knowing that one's performance is to be evaluated increases motivation. Some have argued that we should not have to resort to evaluative techniques (such as testing) in order to motivate students. They maintain that learning should be fun and that the intrinsic joy of learning is more desirable than extrinsic motivation. However, as Ebel (1972, p. 42) has pointed out, ". . . no choice need be made between extrinsic and intrinsic motivation." Learning should be enjoyable, but this does not mean that evaluation is bad. In fact, learning is apt to be more enjoyable if students realize that their efforts and achievements are being recognized. Realists, though, are aware that striving toward excellence in any endeavor is not all fun. The professional baseball player does not play ball just for fun. The professional singer does not practice just for fun. The extrinsic factors of money, fame, and fear of losing a job exist in real life. Without extrinsic motivation many people would not work so hard or accomplish so much. The same is true of students. This may not be an ideal aspect of the world, but it is a realistic one.

One aspect of good study habits is frequent review. By frequent evaluation this study habit is encouraged. We have known for more than 30 years (Ross and Henry, 1939) that students favor frequent tests and feel they learn more because of them.

Another important aspect of learning is that the student must be aware of his strengths and weaknesses. Evaluation and subsequent feedback to the student regarding the evaluation can play a big role in guiding the student's future efforts. The importance of feedback to students, as well as teaching students self-evaluation skills, should be recognized. Also, the very taking of a test is a learning experi-

ence. A student learns while studying for the test, while taking the test, and while going over the test after it is completed.[1]

CRITERIA OF GOOD MEASUREMENT PROCEDURES

There are certain general criteria that any measurement procedure should meet. These criteria are relevant regardless of the particular measuring procedure employed or the purposes for which the measurement takes place. Only general ideas, not complete detail, are presented in this section. Students desiring more information should consult a textbook devoted solely to measurement, such as that by Mehrens and Lehmann (1973).

Reliability

Reliability can be defined as the degree of consistency among different measures of the same thing. If we wish to infer something about a student's knowledge of mathematics, foreign language ability, or interest in mechanical activities, it is important to have some knowledge concerning the degree of consistency of our measurement.

Measurement of psychological variables, such as those mentioned above, are not always reliable. Psychological measurement is indirect and is conducted with imprecise instruments on traits that are not always stable or well defined. There are many reasons why a pupil's score may vary. A partial listing follows.

1. Trait instability.
2. Sampling error.

[1] It is essential that the teacher discuss the test with the students. Just informing the pupils of the results or even returning their papers will not suffice.

3. Administrator error.

4. Scoring error.

5. Health, motivation, and/or degree of fatigue.

6. Good or bad luck in guessing.

Any of these can, under certain conditions, affect the consistency of a measurement. While it is difficult to determine which factors influence any single score, there are different methods of estimating reliability that can give us some information not only about the degree of consistency, but also some clues as to the reasons for inconsistency. We will discuss the six reasons listed above as well as various methods of estimating reliability.

1. TRAIT INSTABILITY

The characteristic we are measuring may not be stable. The degree to which a measuring instrument gives consistent results across time can be determined by giving the same test to the same group of pupils on two different occasions and determining how closely the two sets of scores agree or correspond by correlating (see Chapter 15) the results. This procedure gives us an estimate of reliability typically called the *coefficient of stability*. If the correlation is relatively high we can conclude that the characteristic being measured is relatively stable. If the correlation is low we do not know for sure whether it is because of actual *trait instability* or for reasons such as points 3 to 6 mentioned above. But we would know that the *scores are inconsistent* or unreliable across time.

If we wish to use data to help us make long-range decisions and/or predictions, we would want the data to be stable. To the extent that the data are unstable, their usefulness in long-range decisions or predictions is lessened. For example, in order for a scholastic aptitude test given in grade 10 to be useful in predicting college grade-point average, the char-

acteristic, must be fairly stable.

We do not always need or even expect scores to be stable across time. It depends on how we wish to use the data. For example, if we are measuring knowledge of mathematics we would not expect a group of students to score the same at the end of grade seven as they did at the beginning. Nor would we necessarily expect the students to maintain their original ranks in class on this variable. Thus, not only the amount, but also the relative amount each student has of this characteristic may change across time. Knowing the degree of stability of the students' relative positions in knowledge of mathematics allows one to determine how accurately (if at all) one can predict each pupil's end of year achievement from knowledge of his achievement at the beginning of the year.

2. SAMPLING ERROR

As mentioned, it is not necessary for a score to be stable over time to be useful. We might have good reasons for wanting to obtain a measure of a person's knowledge (or attitude, interest, or degree of open mindedness) at a particular point in time. The typical uses of a classroom achievement test are good examples of this. However, we are *not* only interested in concluding whether a student knows the answers to a *specific* set of items, but whether he knows the area those items sample. The items in an exam typically serve as a *sample* from a population of similar items that cover the whole domain of relevant subject matter. What we would like to do is to infer knowledge of the whole domain from observing the performance on a limited sample of questions. For example, if you wish to measure second graders' competence in a certain aspect of addition, you might ask them to add 10 examples of two single-digit numbers (e.g., $3 + 5$). What you probably wish to conclude, however, is not whether a student knows those 10 particular combinations, but instead, something about his competence in adding *any* combination of two single-digit numbers. To determine how confident one can be in drawing such an inference, one would need to find out whether the scores would have been different had another set of 10 combinations been used. To obtain this type of information the students could be given an equivalent form of the test at approximately the same time.[2] Computing a correlation coefficient between the two sets of results gives us an estimate of reliability called the *coefficient of equivalence.* If the correlation is relatively high between the two equivalent forms, we can conclude that the score a person gets on either form of the test does give us information concerning how well the student has mastered the domain that the test sampled. The lower the correlation, the less confident we should be about inference to the domain from the sample. (Although, again, the low correlation could be due to reasons 3 to 6 mentioned above).

An estimate of sampling error can also be obtained with just one administration of one test. For scoring, the test can be split into two halves (e.g., odd versus even items). The correlation between the scores on the two halves gives an estimated reliability of a test half as long as the original and therefore must be corrected using the Spearman-Brown Prophecy formula.[3] This whole procedure is called the *split-half reliability estimate.*

3. ADMINISTRATOR ERROR

Scores could be inconsistent because an error is made in the administration of the test. If

too much time is allowed in a speed test, or if the directions are not clearly stated, scores are influenced. This type of error can be minimized, if not alleviated, by careful administration.

An area that is receiving more attention is the influence on scores that may arise due to interactions between administrator and test taker. Unless one varies the administrators from one setting to the next (e.g., have a black administrator for one form and a white administrator for an equivalent form), this influence would not show up as inconsistency or unreliability. It would influence the validity of the score instead.

4. SCORING ERROR

Occasionally unreliable results are obtained because of scoring inconsistencies or errors. These kinds of errors are most likely to occur with instruments that do no have precise, objective, scoring rationales. Essay tests and themes are notorious examples of procedures that arc not scored reliably. Estimates of scorer reliability can be obtained by having different people score the same set of measures (essay tests, themes, oral examinations, observations, or whatever) and correlating the results. An alternate procedure would be to have the same person score the set of measures at two different times.

Obviously, if scorer reliability is low we would not want to put too much faith in a single score.

5. OTHER SOURCES OF ERROR

There are many additional reasons why scores may be somewhat unreliable, such as health and motivation of the examinee and good or back luck. Attempts should be made to control these factors as much as possible. They cannot, however, be completely controlled, and we must recognize that every score has an error component, and that had existing

---

[2] An equivalent form of a test is one that samples from the same domain of knowledge in the same proportions as the original test. An equivalent form should have the same mean and standard deviation as the original test.

[3] No computational procedures are discussed in this section. See texts such as Mehrens and Lehmann (1973) for computational procedures.

conditions been somewhat different the scores would also have varied.

CONTROL OF RELIABILITY

Teachers cannot control for many of the sources of unreliability on standardized instruments. They should, however, be careful in administering and scoring such instruments. Also, they should try to get their students motivated to perform well. Teachers should choose standardized tests partly on the basis of reported reliability estimates, and any use of a test score should be governed by the type and degree of reliability demonstrated.

In deriving their own measuring procedures, teachers should realize that poorly constructed items, biased or inadequate sampling, and inadequate scoring methods all lower reliability. These aspects will be discussed further in Chapter 17 in the section on teacher-constructed evaluative procedures.

LEVEL OF RELIABILITY

How reliable a test should be depends on the purposes for which the test is to be used. If it is to be used to help make decisions about individuals, then it should be more reliable than if it is to be used to make decisions about groups of people. Although there is no universal agreement, it is generally accepted that tests used to assist in making decisions about individuals should have reliability coefficients of at least .85. For group decisions, a reliability coefficient of about .65 may suffice. These are only guidelines. There are no absolutes; one should use the best test available. A more relevant factor is the consideration of how good a decision can be made without the help of the test data. If there is very little other information on which to base a decision, and a decision must be made, it may be helpful to use a test with low reliability instead of none at all. (A test with low reli-

ability can still have some validity and can therefore be useful.) On the other hand, if a good decision (or accurate prediction) can be made without any test data, it may not be worthwhile to give a test even though it is reliable.

Validity

Validity is the single most important aspect of a measuring procedure. It can best be defined as the degree to which a measuring instrument is capable of achieving certain aims. Since a single measuring procedure (e.g., test) may be used for many different purposes, there is no single validity index for it. A test that has some validity for one purpose may not be at all valid for another. Validity is also sometimes defined as truthfulness. Does the instrument measure what it purports to measure? The truthfulness aspect refers only to content and construct validities, not to criterion-related validity (see below).

For a measure to be valid it must first be reliable. If we cannot get consistent measures of a person's height, we can hardly claim that any one of them is an accurate, or valid, measure of his height. Note, however, that a measure might be very consistent (reliable) and not accurate (valid). For example, if a bathroom scale consistently shows you weigh 10 pounds more than you do, it is a reliable measure, but it is invalid. In other words, reliability is a necessary but not sufficient condition for validity.

KINDS OF VALIDITY

While different authors have used many different terms for validity (Ebel, 1972, p. 437), the *Standards for Educational and Psychological Tests and Manuals* (French and Michael, 1966) delimits only three kinds of validity.

Content validity is related to how adequately the content of the test samples the domain of subject matter about which inferences are to be made. It is particularly important in measuring educational achievements. There is no numerical expression for content validity. It is determined by a thorough inspection of the items. An achievement test that may have good content validity for one teacher may prove to have low content validity for another teacher. Not all teachers (even those teaching the same course titles in the same grade) are teaching exactly the same domain of subject matter.

Classroom teachers should take care to insure that the tests they construct have content validity. Using a test blueprint (see Chapter 17) when constructing a test helps to insure adequate content validity. In selecting standardized achievement tests, careful attention should be given to the content of the test. One of the main reasons teachers should help in such selection is that they are best able to judge the content validity of a test for their particular course.

Criterion-related validity pertains to the techniques of studying the relationship between one set of scores and a set of independent external measures. We might be interested in doing this because we want to substitute an easier measuring device for a more complex one. If we could devise, for example, a 20 minute, group administered, objectively scored test that correlated perfectly with the scores obtained through 1-hour individualized interviews, it is obvious that the test could replace the interviews as an evaluative device.

Or we may be interested in predicting some future behavior from knowledge of present performance, for example, predicting college GPA from a high school scholastic aptitude test. The degree of relationship between the two variables tells us how valid the scholastic aptitude test is for the purpose of predicting college GPA. Notice that the relationship indi-

cates the degree of validity *for a particular purpose*. A test may be quite valid for predicting college GPA and worthless at predicting success as a teacher.

Construct validity is the degree to which test scores can be accounted for by certain explanatory constructs in a theory. If a test has construct validity, peoples' scores will vary, as the theory predicts. Construct validity is of more importance to theoretical psychologists than practicing educators, so we will not discuss it further. Interested readers may wish to consult the classic article by Cronbach and Meehl (1955) on this topic.

LEVEL OF VALIDITY

Just as for reliability, the type and extent of validity one should expect depend on the purposes for which the test is to be used. Naturally, one should select the best possible test. Suppose, however, that no test is very valid for our purpose. Does that mean we should not test? To decide, we must answer the question, How much better decision can we make using the test information in addition to all other information than we could make just from the other data alone? Once that question is answered, we must inquire whether this increase in accuracy of prediction is sufficiently greater to justify the use of the test. This could theoretically be answered by analyzing the cost of the procedures in relation to the savings if we could specify the cost of faulty decisions.

Objectivity

There are two aspects to objectivity. First, can experts agree as to the correct answers. That is, can a scoring key be determined? Second, once the key is determined, will different scorers agree on what score should be assigned to a test paper? Multiple choice, true-false, and other objectively scored tests are, by definition, objective in the second sense. Such measurement procedures as essay tests, oral examinations, and observations are less objectively scored. No type of test is necessarily objective in the first sense. Interest and personality inventories often do not have factually right and wrong answers. Aptitude and achievement tests should. Poorly written aptitude or achievement items can be so ambiguous as to lead to expert disagreement. Also, an item can be asking for knowledge on such a minute, picky point that the experts actually do not know the answer. If a question is not based on substantiated knowledge, but on opinions or hypotheses not shared by all experts, the item will not be objective.

To determine whether a measurement procedure has objectivity it is necessary to give it to some experts who took no part in developing it. Ebel (1972, p. 373) suggests that the mean score of these experts should be at least 90% of a perfect score. All questions on which there is less than perfect agreement should be carefully scrutinized to see if they can be made more objective.

Discrimination

Many, but certainly not all, measurement devices are for the purpose of discriminating among people on the basis of degrees of the characteristic being measured. Discrimination is often desired along the whole range of the characteristic. Thus, we not only want to discriminate among those lowest on the characteristic, or among those medium or highest on the characteristic. We want to do all of those things. Given this goal of discrimination, a measuring instrument should have certain characteristics.

First, if an instrument is to be discriminating it should be neither too easy nor too hard. If most people get a perfect score on a test, it

probably does not mean that those people have all mastered the subject to the same extent. It more likely means that the test was too easy to discriminate among those people. Likewise, if most people score around zero (or chance on a test where guessing can occur) it does not mean that these people are all equally ignorant. It simply means that the test was too difficult. In general, the mean score should be about 50% of the highest possible score. Where guessing can occur, the average difficulty index (percent correct on the test) must necessarily be higher. (For example, on a true-false test, 50% is just a chance score.) A very general rule of thumb is that the mean should be halfway between a chance and perfect score (e.g., 75% on a true-false test or 60% on a five-option multiple choice). However, Lord (1952) has shown that for tests where guessing can occur, more reliable results will be obtained if the test is just a little bit easier. This cuts down on chance guessing and increases the reliability of the test.

In constructing a test so as to obtain difficulty levels as mentioned above, one could vary the item difficulties (making some easy, some of middle difficulty, and some hard), or make all items of about the same difficulty. For purposes of discrimination, reliability, and validity, the latter approach is definitely preferable. The value of minimizing the range of item difficulties has been studied by a number of investigators and all arrive at essentially the same conclusion: items should all be of about equal difficulty *if one wants a discriminating test.* (See, for example, Cronbach and Warrington, 1952; Gulliksen, 1945; and Lord, 1952.)

Thus, both test difficulty and range of item difficulties affect test discrimination. Another important consideration is the discriminating ability of each item. A discrimination index can be computed for each item. This index tells us whether that item helped in differentiating among the individuals. This index will be covered in more detail in Chapter 17 when we discuss methods of analyzing and evaluating teacher-constructed tests.

GENERAL CONSIDERATIONS AND ISSUES IN EVALUATION PROGRAMS

Accountability

The 1970s are being referred to as the decade of accountability in education. The concept of accountability has become a major controversial topic of discussion. Accountability means different things to different people and it has been defined in a myriad of ways. Some typical components of accountability are *setting correct goals, determining whether they have been achieved* and at what *price, presenting* and *interpreting* this information to the public, and *accepting responsibility* for any results that are perceived to be inadequate. While accountability is related to every aspect of education, we discuss the concept in this chapter because any accountability program is absolutely dependent on good measurement and the correct use of the data gathered. We will briefly discuss two philosophical and two measurement concerns to which educators should be alert.

"Miss Fischer really gives the taxpayers their money's worth." *(Drawing by Reg Hider from Today's Education/NEA Journal, 1973)*

PHILOSOPHICAL CONCERNS

Basically the philosophical concerns center around who is accountable and for what they are accountable. We are not suggesting that we have the answers to these questions, but we can present some of the issues.

Who is accountable? There is certainly no current agreement on either who is presently being held accountable in education or who should be. Deterline (1971, p. 16) feels that educators operate so that "... all failures and ineffective aspects of our instruction are slyly laid on the students, in the form of a grade or rating, [and] we never really have to face the facts of our own incompetence in the field of instruction." He suggests that students are held accountable if they do not learn—in spite of any failures, deficiencies, and incompetence in our teaching—and welcomes educational accountability as a countervailing force.

Campbell (1971, p. 176) feels Deterline is guilty of fighting yesterday's wars instead of today's.

"There was a time when teachers were scarcely held accountable for their shortcomings as instructors, but this has not been the state of affairs I have noted in my 20 years of education. Rather, there has been a drumfire of extramural criticism and intramural breast-beating rising to the present crescendo. Through every possible medium, including his professional journals, the teacher receives the same message: 'You are a failure. You are incompetent at best and probably insensitive, unimaginative, lazy, and cruel as well.' His grade is a straight F/U.

By contrast, 'failure' for students is like the death penalty—still legal, but seldom applied."

Whether or not it has, it does seem to us that the pendulum can swing too far toward holding educators accountable for lack of pupil learning in spite of any failures, deficiencies, and incompetence in the students, parents, and/or society. The definition of teaching for many educational critics has changed from an activity *intended* to induce learning to an activity that *does* induce learning. Although it seems condescending to assume students have no responsibility for their own learning, most writers on educational accountability do not mention students' (or parents') accountability. Yet, "... substituting the teacher ... for the pupil as the *only* accountable party is an example of reactionary thinking." (Campbell, 1971, p. 177) Educators *alone* cannot be held accountable for a product when they have virtually no control over their resources or raw material.

The foregoing paragraph is not meant to let educators off the hook. Just because educators are not accountable for everything does not mean they are not accountable for anything. But we must be somewhat moderate in any approach to accountability. We have to recognize that "Each participant [including students and teachers] in the educational process should be held responsible only for those educational outcomes that he can affect by his actions or decisions and only to the extent that he can affect them." (Barro, 1970, p. 199)

In summary, educators should be held accountable for some aspects of children's learning. But there is no easy way to discern which portions are under their control, and accountability programs must keep this in mind. The "who is accountable" question cannot at present be answered and until (and if) it can, we must remember that the purpose of accountability programs should not be punitive in nature, but instead for the purpose of quality control. We should not use educators as the whipping boys of society.

Accountable for What? Perhaps even more difficult than the question of who should be held accountable is the question of "accountable for what." The simple-minded answer is that we should be held accountable for the pupils' attainment of our educational objectives. But although there does exist a general consensus about many desired outcomes, there are diverse goals or objectives held by our educational systems. Some people feel "good citizenship" or "healthy self-concepts" are more important than reading skills. Others feel just the opposite. This difference of opinion causes considerable difficulty when it comes to instituting accountability programs. And, since we can measure some objectives more readily than others, there may be a tendency for accountability programs to focus in on these easily measured objectives. We will discuss this further in the section on measurement problems related to accountability.

Not only are there differences of opinion regarding what our outcome objectives should be, there are differences of opinion regarding what the distribution of these results should be. Downs (1968) discusses four diverse goals regarding distribution.

1. The *minimum-citizenship (level) goal,* which means that all students should be brought up to some basic minimum level of proficiency.

2. The *maximum-system-output-goal,* which means that the total capabilities of all students considered as a group (perhaps best measured by their total resulting productivity) should be made as large as possible.

3. The *equal opportunity (really equal outcome) goal,* which means that all students emerging from the system (say, upon high school graduation) should have approximately the same capabilities for entering into the postschooling portion of their lives.[4]

---

[4] This would coincide with the definition Colemen (1966) gives of equal opportunity as the equality of outcome.

4. The *maximum-individual-advancement goal,* which means that each student should be given as much development of his individual potential as possible.

As Downs points out, ". . . pursuing each of the above goals exclusively, without regard to the others, would result in very different allocations of publicly-supplied educational inputs. At one extreme, the equal-opportunity goal would require a heavy concentration of resources among the poorest and most culturally-deprived students. They would receive much higher inputs than children from higher-income and more advantaged homes. . . . In contrast . . . the maximum system output goal would concentrate publicly-supplied inputs on the best qualified students. This would result in the greatest total gain in technical proficiency per dollar invested." (1968, p. 16, 17)

Other writers (e.g., Dyer, 1970; Harmes, 1971) approach "accountability for what" in a different way. Dyer, for example, emphasizes, ". . . that staff members are to be held accountable for keeping themselves informed about the diverse needs of their pupils and for doing the best they can to meet those needs. In light of what we know about the teaching-learning process, this is the most we may reasonably expect. To hold teachers, or anybody else, accountable for some sort of "guaranteed pupil performance" is likely to do more harm than good in the lives of the children" (1970, p. 206). Thus, Dyer is talking about a process accountability, not a *product* accountability. This seems more in agreement with the definition of teaching that states that the *intent* of teaching is to induce learning.

Educators must measure student outcomes in order to make wise educational decisions. However, this position is not analogous to blaming teachers for any specified lack of pupil performance. Whether one wishes to say they are *accountable* for pupil outcomes partly depends on how one wants to define accountability and partly on philosophical/political considerations. We are inclined to agree with Dyer, rather than with those proselytes of accountability who would hold educators *accountable for specified pupil performance.*

Thus, there are considerable differences of opinion on the "what" issue. Whether we should assess basic cognitive skills or affective objectives, what is the ideal distribution of educational results, and whether we should have process or product assessment are the three we have discussed.

MEASUREMENT CONCERNS

The measurement problems in accountability include the traditional problems of measurement, for example, validity and correct interpretation, but they seem in many respects to be even more difficult. We do not intend to discuss all these problems in detail. That would be an unrealistic goal in a basic text. Instead, we wish to introduce the reader to a few key concerns. As a professional educator, you almost invariably will be subject to some accountability programs and therefore should be alert to some of the more pressing measurement problems involved.

Establishing Causal Relations. This concern is directly related to the philosophical issue of *who* is to be held accountable. The abstract answer was that one should only be held responsible for those outcomes he can affect. As we stated, concrete details of how to determine that are at best incomplete. But even if we determine that a teacher can and should affect reading skills, how can we determine that a student who reads well does so *because* of the teacher's efforts?

Specialists in educational measurement and evaluation have historically concentrated their efforts on determining "what is," rather than who is *responsible* or accountable for

"what is." Establishing causal relationships between school outcomes and input and process variables requires something more than measurement.

It is extremely difficult to take all the variables that may affect student achievement into account. Thus, for example, there is a danger that schools (and teachers) in those districts where surrounding conditions are poor will be unduly chastised for low student achievement. Some critics of education naively believe that the school can and should be held accountable for overcoming any and all deficiencies of the student and the community. Yet research sources such as the Colemen report (1966) and the Jenck's review (1972) show quite clearly that a large proportion of the variation in student performance is accounted for by out-of-school variables, such as pupils' socioeconomic status and home environments.

Validity. Just as the measurement problem of establishing causal relations is related to the philosophical issue of who is to be held accountable, the measurement problem of validity is related to the "what is to be assessed" concern. Since most accountability programs only focus on outcome variables, we will limit our discussion of validity to that area.

Because "basic skill" areas are very important as well as being the easiest areas to assess, many accountability programs focus only on these areas. The school's objectives are ordinarily much broader than the basic skills, so the assessment tools have inadequate content validity. While poor content validity is always deplorable, it is particularly troublesome when the results of an assessment device are used to hold the schools accountable.

We have discussed in Chapter 2 such topics as whether the performances observed on an assessment instrument are indeed the school's goals or only indicants of the school's goals, and under what circumstances teaching for the test is a harmful educational practice. Anytime the performance tested is only a sample (or indicant) of our objectives, teaching directly for the test, that is, teaching for those specific questions on the test, is inappropriate. If a test indeed covers accepted objectives, it is appropriate to teach for the general topics covered by the test. But when the objectives covered on the test are much narrower in focus than the objectives of the school, it would be inappropriate to stress *only* the general objectives covered by the test.

Thus, there are two dangers in teaching for a test used to determine accountability. There is a strong temptation for a teacher to teach for the specific questions in the test. If this is prevented by having secure tests (or secure teachers!), the danger still persists of the general curriculum becoming disproportionately weighted in favor of the narrow set of objectives sampled on the assessment instrument. This is of considerable concern to those educators who feel that such goals as good citizenship are the most important ones to stress in the schools.

CONSEQUENCES OF ACCOUNTABILITY

Since educational accountability is defined in so many different ways, there are many different approaches to it. Operationalizing a construct as complicated as this is more of a building process than simply adopting some complete and adequate accountability program. We tentatively predict that as a result of accountability (1) schools will be forced to do a better job of specifying and evaluating objectives; (2) there will be an increased focus on the relationship between outcomes, input, and process variables; (3) schools will work toward adopting better management tech-

niques and fiscal controls; and (4) there will be more concerted efforts to keep the public informed of educational objectives, expenses, processes, and results. All of this seems commendable. We hope that accountability programs will *NOT* hold educators accountable for that which they cannot control.

Curriculum Evaluation and Student Evaluation

Within the past decade educators have rapidly increased the rate of curriculum and instructional change. Math, science, and social studies curriculums, for example, have all changed considerably. Not only have the curricular goals changed, but so have the particular instructional methods for achieving the goals. Many schools that have jumped on new curricular bandwagons have been very lax in evaluating the effectiveness of these new programs. However, governmental and private agencies have provided a substantial proportion of the funds for some innovative curriculum programs, and these funds are usually provided with the stipulation that a careful evaluation of the program be conducted to ascertain its effectiveness.

The accountability demands have brought about a rapid increase in an awareness of the need for curriculum evaluation, but the procedures for curriculum evalation have not been well developed. The professional scholars in curriculum and evaluation as well as the local school personnel have been caught somewhat unprepared.

Although school personnel have always made implicit evaluations of their curriculum (i.e., they have made decisions about their curriculum), current school personnel have typically had no training in more formal, explicit aspects of curriculum evaluation. They are unsure what the term encompasses, how curriculum evaluation differs from student evaluation, and what procedures are appropriate. The next generation of educators will hopefully be much better equipped to engage in curriculum evaluation. This section presents a general introduction to some aspects of curriculum evaluation and how it compares with student evaluation.

Several writers have discussed the distinctions between and similarities of curriculum and student evaluation. (See, for example, Cronbach, 1963; Popham et al., 1969; Stake, 1967.) The basic distinction between curriculum and student evaluation is related to the decisions that are to be made. When we ask whether Susan should take advanced algebra, or how she did in first-year French, we are concerned with student evaluation. When we wonder whether nongraded classrooms such as those in operation in elementary school A should be effected in school B, we are concerned with curriculum evaluation.[5] The decision of whether to continue any experimental program (such as using the Initial Teaching Alphabet) requires curriculum evaluation.

Student evaluation is actually a subset of curriculum evaluation. Student evaluation involves the determination of whether a student is making appropriate progress toward stated goals. Curriculum evaluation is considerably broader. Students progress toward goals is only one dimension of curriculum evaluation, although probably the most important. Curriculum evaluation involves evaluating whether the stated goals are appropriate as well as evaluating the extent to which those goals are achieved. As Scriven (1967, p. 52) pointed out, ". . . it is obvious that if the goals aren't worth achieving then it is uninteresting how well they are achieved."

Other questions for curriculum evaluation that are not aspects of student evaluation are the effects on teachers, effects on students not in that particular program or curriculum, and effects on parents and taxpayers. Is a teacher's knowledge updated with a new curriculum? Does the teacher suffer from more fatigue? Has he become more enthusiastic about teaching? Scriven (1967, p. 77), for example, has pointed out that some programmed texts have left teachers feeling less significant. Are other teachers in the system forced to teach less attractive courses, or increase their work load as a result of the new curriculum program? Is there jealousy, or are the other teachers stimulated through contact with the teachers in the new program? Do students not in the new program feel discriminated against? Are there positive side effects such as improved library facilities or an improved teacher/pupil ratio? How does the community at large react to the new program? The controversy on sex education in the schools is a good example to illustrate the importance of considering public attitudes.

Process and Product Evaluation

The terms process and product have not been used with complete consistency by educators. It seems clear that there are at least two aspects to a student's performance—the process (or procedure) and the product—but the dividing line between the two is not always clear cut. (Is singing a song a process or a product?) There are some differences between having knowledge about music and being a good musician, between knowing about the technique of arc welding and being

---

[5] Popham (1969, p. 34) differentiates between *curriculum* and *instructional* questions. Curriculum questions revolve around considerations of *ends*, that is, the objectives an educational system hopes its learners will achieve. Instructional questions revolve around the *means* used to achieve those instructional ends. Since most major revisions in means are accompanied by changes in hoped-for ends, we will consider all such questions as curriculum questions in this section. Popham's distinction would be useful, however, in a more detailed presentation of the issues.

able to weld a good bead. In fact, not all people who can teach creative writing are creative writers. If we want to evaluate a student on such tasks as welding or creative writing, we can best do so by having the student perform and assess the quality of the performance. Sometimes it seems more appropriate to evaluate the process engaged in by the pupil, at other times it is more appropriate to evaluate the displayed product. The importance of evaluating process can be illustrated by using typing as an example. A student who has "played around" on the typewriter prior to his first formal course, may, by the end of the second week, outperform all his peers in terms of a product—typing faster and more accurately. However, he may be using such a poor process (e.g., hunt and peck) that his chances of any further product improvement are severely limited. Similar examples exist in most subject matters. Music, art, home economics, physical education, shop, and science all require correct processes in order for the products to achieve real excellence.

Tests are most often used to evaluate products and rating scales are often employed to evaulate both products and processes. Observational techniques are particularly valuable in assessing processes. Both of these techniques will be discussed more fully in Chapter 17.

Cognitive and Affective Evaluation

Cognitive objectives are those "which emphasize remembering or reproducing something which has presumably been learned, as well as objectives which involve the solving of some intellective task for which the individual has to determine the essential problem and then reorder given material or combine it with ideas, methods, or procedures previously learned." (Krathwohl et al., 1964, p. 6) Affective objectives are those "which em-

phasize a feeling tone, an emotion, or a degree of acceptance or rejection." (Krathwohl, et al., 1964, p. 7)

Not all educators take the same stance regarding the relative importance of these two types of objectives. However, most educators would agree that affective objectives are of some concern in education, and most would agree that we do an even poorer job evaluating these affective objectives than we do cognitive ones.

Perhaps one reason teachers do not try harder to measure affect is that they simply do not value affect highly enough. Demands for increased intellectual competence may push out some of the concern for student affect. Thus, for example, if students can learn to read at age five, it may be assumed that they should.

Another reason that keeps teachers from trying harder to measure affect is the implicit belief of many that if cognitive objectives are attained, there will be a corresponding change in appropriate affective behaviors. The somewhat simplistic notion that if a person is good at something he will grow to like it holds wide appeal. Nevertheless, research does not support this position. Adkins and Kuder (1940), for example, have shown that there is really very little relationship between aptitudes and interests. Mayhew (1958) reports little relationship between attitude changes and growth of knowledge in a college course. While a skillful teacher can use the development of cognitive skills to increase motivation, and increased motivation to strengthen cognitive skills, neither follow automatically from the other. In fact, it is entirely possible that the development of cognitive behaviors may inhibit the development of (or indeed destroy) desired affective behaviors. Inappropriate methods of teaching multiplication facts, geometric proofs, history, or poetry may develop cognitive skills, but inhibit positive affect. Many students learn the skill of reading, but not the joy or excitement in reading. Therefore they seldom read. A teacher interested in accomplishing both types of objectives must evaluate both separately, and not assume one follows from the other.

Other reasons that affect is underevaluated in school is that it is hard to change, and even when changed, hard to measure accurately. The instructional techniques of attitude change are not nearly as well developed or as successful as techniques for attaining cognitive objectives. Certainly results are not usually so immediately apparent. The measurement of affect is difficult because affect can so easily be faked. It is much easier to fake an interest in something than it is to fake knowledge or skill.

Even if one disregards the faking problem, measurement in the affective domain is difficult. One of the major problems centers around the lack of behavioral objectives. As mentioned in Chapter 2, specific behaviors are not always our actual goals when dealing in the affective domain. Behaviors are occasionally only indicants that the goals have been achieved. Yet we can only measure behavior, and educators have done far too little in stating affective objectives behaviorally (see Chapter 7).

The first step in improving affective evaluation is to do a better job of specifying our objectives in behavioral terms. Examples of behavior related to attitudes toward learning were given in Chapter 7. Fraenkel (1969) provides an illustration for the affective goal, "recognizes the dignity and worth of others." How can we tell when our students have achieved this goal? Only by specifying certain behaviors that we would accept as evidence. Fraenkel (1969) lists the following types of behaviors as such evidence.

1. *Waits* until others have finished speaking before speaking himself (does not interrupt others).

2. *Encourages* everyone involved in a discussion to offer his opinions (does not monopolize the conversation with his arguments).

3. *Revises* his own opinions when the opinions of others are more solidly grounded in, and supported by, factual evidence than his own (does not blindly insist on his own point of view).

4. *Makes statements* in support of others no matter what their social status (does not put others in embarrassing, humiliating, or subservient positions).

As Fraenkel goes on to say, these behavioral statements do not "totally capture the essence of the more general goal." It is literally impossible to do this. However, we can specify examples of behaviors "which we will accept as specific manifestations of the general concept." This position is obviously consistent with the one we have taken in Chapter 2 on behavioral objectives.

Gall (1967) reports another example of measuring some less tangible goals. He built a series of checklists using characteristics, such as the ones listed below, designed to measure "respect for others."

1. Is completely unconcerned with the welfare of others (defaces school property, strikes others, shoves in line, takes personal property of others, uses abusive language).

2. Is beginning to demonstrate some awareness that others have rights.

3. Cooperates in small groups in which only his friends are involved.

4. Is beginning to show some acceptance of others—new children or nonmembers of his group.

5. Will work cooperatively with children of different backgrounds when directed.

6. Listens to and judges opinions of others without bias.

7. Respects race, creed, color, or national origin of others.

8. Treats everyone equally and participates readily in democratic procedures.

9. Has warm regard for the ways and contributions of others regardless of class, color, religion, or other differences from himself.

10. Actively fosters harmonious intergroup relations.

One can argue that these terms are not completely behavioral or completely objective and, of course, they are not. But they are moving in the right direction and these statements are probably as behavioral as teachers are likely to formulate.

Norm-Referenced and Criterion-Referenced Measurement

There has been considerable discussion in education concerning the distinctions between and the advantages and disadvantages of, "norm-referenced" and "criterion-referenced" measurement. The basic issue concerns interpretation or how we derive meaning from a score, but related to this are questions of the purposes of measurement and techniques of constructing tests.

The distinction between the interpretation of *scores* seems clear enough. If we interpret a score of an individual by comparing his score to those of other individuals (called a norm group), this would be norm referencing. If we interpret a person's performance by comparing it to some specified behavioral criterion of proficiency, this would be criterion referencing (some prefer to call this content referencing). To polarize the distinction we could say that the focus of a normative score is on how many of Johnny's peers do not perform (score) as well as he does, and the focus of a criterion referenced score is on

what it is that Johnny can do. Of course, we can and often do interpret a single test score both ways. In norm referencing we might make a statement that "John did better than 80% of the students in a test on addition of whole numbers." With a criterion reference interpretation we might say that "John got 70% of the items correct in a test on addition of whole numbers." Ebel (1962, p. 19) has pointed out that "to be meaningful any test scores must be related to test content *as well as* to the scores of other examinees."

Depending on the decision we wish to make, one of the above ways of interpreting the score will likely be more useful than the other; many have suggested that tests should also be constructed and analyzed differently for each purpose.[6]

Classical measurement theory originated and developed from an interest in measuring the aptitudes of individuals. Thus the emphasis has been on devising measures that differentiate or discriminate among individuals at all points along the continuum. That is, a test is devised so that individuals who have more aptitude will score higher on the test than those who possess less. The interpretation of "how much" aptitude a person possesses is a normative one. The same test theory, and this tendency to construct tests that discriminate among individuals, has carried over to achievement testing. There are times, however, when it is not necessary, and perhaps not even advisable, to differentiate individuals at all degrees of achievement. We may simply want to find out whether individuals have achieved a specific set of objectives. In other words, we reference a person's score against a criterion. Thus, there are really two different goals or objectives in *achievement*

---

[6] In fact, some writers define criterion-referenced tests as those deliberately constructed to yield scores directly interpretable in terms of specified performance standards. (See Glaser and Nitko, 1971; Jackson, 1970.)

testing: (1) to discriminate among all individuals according to their degrees of achievement and (2) to determine whether a person has achieved a specific set of objectives.[7]

USES FOR CRITERION-REFERENCED MEASUREMENT

The recent support for criterion-referenced measurement seems to have originated largely from the emphases on behavioral objectives, the sequencing and individualization of instruction, the development of programmed materials, a learning theory that suggests that most anybody can learn most anything given enough time, and a belief that norm referencing promotes unhealthy competition and is injurious to low-scoring students' self-concepts.

If we can specify important objectives in behavioral terms then, many would argue, the important consideration is to ascertain whether a student obtained those objectives rather than his position relative to other students. Traditionally criteron-referenced measurement has been used principally in "mastery tests." A mastery test is a particular type of criterion-referenced test. Mastery, as it is typically used, connotes an either-or situation. The person either has achieved (mastered) the objective(s) satisfactorily or he has not. Criterion-referenced testing in general could also apply to degrees of performance. Mastery tests are used in programs of individualized instruction such as the individually prescribed instruction program discussed in Chapter 11. Recall that such instructional programs are composed of units or modules, usually considered hierarchical, each based on a number of instructional

objectives. Each individual is required to work on the unit until he has achieved a specified minimum level of achievement. This is accepted as evidence that he has "mastered" the unit. In such programs, the instructional decision of what to do with a student is not dependent on how he compares with others. If he has performed adequately on the objectives, then the decision is to move on to the next unit of study. If he has not, then he should restudy the material (although perhaps using a different procedure) covered in the test until he has performed adequately or "mastered" the material. If instructional procedures are organized so that time is the dimension that varies and degree of mastery is held constant, then we should use a greater proportion of mastery tests than educators do at present.

Criterion-referenced measures may also be used to evaluate (make decisions about) instructional programs. In order to determine whether specific instructional treatments or procedures were successful, it is necessary to have data regarding the outcomes on the specific objectives the program was designed to teach. A measure comparing students to each other (norm referencing) may not give as effective data as a measure comparing each student's performance to the objectives.

Also, criterion-referenced measures offer certain benefits for instructional decision making within the classroom. The diagnosis of specific difficulties accompanied by a prescription of certain instructional treatments is necessary in instruction, whether or not one uses a mastery approach to learning.

USES FOR NORM-REFERENCED MEASUREMENT

As stated in the beginning of this section, most testing and testing theory has been based on the norm-referenced approach. There is

---

[7] Of course, one could discriminate with a criterion-referenced measure, but that is not the primary purpose of such a measure.

little argument that such an approach is useful in aptitude testing where we wish to make differential predictions. It is also often very useful in achievement testing. Many educators would agree with Gronlund (1971, p. 139) when he states:

"In measuring the extent to which pupils are achieving our course objectives, we have no absolute standard by which to determine their progress. A pupil's achievement can be regarded as high or low only by comparing it with the achievement of other pupils."

Accepting this view, the role of a measuring device is to give us as reliable a rank ordering of the pupils as possible with respect to the achievement we are measuring. Knowing what we do about individual differences, it is obvious that students will learn differing amounts of subject matter even under a mastery learning approach. It may be that all students, or at least a high percentage of them, have learned a significant enough portion of a teacher's objectives to be categorized as having "mastered" the essentials of the course or unit. But some of these students have learned more than others, and it seems worthwhile to employ measurement techniques that identify these pupils. In the first place, students want and deserve recognition for accomplishment that goes beyond the minimum. If we would continually give only mastery tests, those students who accomplish at a higher level would lose one of the important extrinsic rewards of learning, that is, recognition for such accomplishments.

Perhaps a more important reason for discrimination testing than student recognition is in its benefits for decision making. If two doctors have mastered surgery, but one has mastered it better, which one do you wish to have operate on you? (For that matter, even if two doctors had equally mastered their training program, one would probably want some norm-referencing information regarding time to completion. If one doctor is such a slow learner that it takes him five times as long to learn the material as the other one, it is probably safe to assume that after he has been on the job 10 years he will not be as up to date on current medical practices as the fast learner.) If two teachers have mastered the basics of teaching, but one is a much better teacher, which do we want to hire? If two students have mastered first-semester algebra, but one has learned it much better (or faster, time being norm referenced), which should receive the most encouragement to continue in mathematics? We probably all agree on the answers to the above questions. However, if we have not employed evaluation techniques that allow us to differentiate between the individuals, we cannot make these types of decisions. Certainly norm-referenced measures are the most helpful in fixed-quota selection decisions. For example, if there are a limited number of openings in a pilot training school, the school would want to select the best of the applicants, even though they were all above some "mastery level."

Comparing the Uses of Norm-Referenced and Criterion-Referenced Measurement

When to use norm-referenced measurement and when to use criterion-referenced measurement depends on the kind of decision one wishes to make. In achievement testing it depends mostly on the instructional procedures employed. If instruction is structured so that time is the variable, and a student keeps at a task until he has mastered it, then we should use mastery testing. This type of instruction is often employed in individualized instruction. If instruction is structured so that time of exposure is constant, then students will achieve at different levels, and we should attempt to discern this differential achievement with a test that discriminates, although we might well want to attach both normative and criterion-referenced meaning to the score. Which instructional procedure should be used depends on the structure and importance of the subject matter being taught.

There surely are some subjects so hierarchically structured that it is futile to teach higher concepts until basic ones have been mastered. For example, a student cannot do long division until he can subtract and multiply at some basic level (although precisely what that level is, is unknown). This is certainly not true of all subjects, however. We do not really need to have mastered (or even have read) *A Tale of Two Cities* before reading *Catcher in the Rye,* or vice versa.

Likewise, there may be some skills or knowledge so important that all students should master them, regardless of how long it takes. Knowing how to spell one's name fits into this category. But again, this is not true of all subjects. With regard to this point, Ebel (1969 (a) p. 12) states:

"We might be willing to allow one student a week to learn what another can learn in a day. But sum these differences over the myriads of things to be learned. Does anyone, student, teacher, or society, want to see one person spend 16 or 24 years getting the same elementary education another can get in eight? Should it be those least able to learn quickly who spend the largest portion of their lives in trying to learn? Our present practice is quite the reverse. Those who are facile in learning make a career of it. Those who are not find other avenues of service, fulfillment and success."

Gronlund (1970, p. 32) makes a distinction between objectives that are considered as *minimum essentials* and those that encourage *maximum development.* For the former, one would want to employ mastery testing, for the latter, discrimination testing.

Thus, there is a place for both mastery (criterion-referenced) and discrimination (norm-referenced) testing. The way most schools are currently organized, with time of instruction constant for all individuals and degree of learning the variable, discrimination testing should be more prevalent. However, as more individualized instructional processes are used, and as more is learned about how various subject matters should be sequenced, mastery testing may increase in importance. Mastery testing is likely more important in the early elementary grades than later in school. Table 16-1, while an oversimplification, summarizes the polar positions.

CONSTRUCTING CRITERION AND NORM-REFERENCED ACHIEVEMENT TESTS

As mentioned earlier, traditional test theory and techniques of test construction have been developed on the assumption that the purpose of a test is to discriminate among individuals. If the purpose of a test is to compare each individual with a standard, then it is irrelevant whether or not the individuals differ from each other. Thus, some of the criteria of a measuring instrument considered essential for a norm-referenced measure are not important for criterion-referenced measures. (See Popham and Husek, 1969.) What one looks for in reliability and in some types of validity are different in a criterion-referenced measure.

However, for many aspects of test construction—for example, considering the objectives, preparing test blueprints, and actually word-

Table 16-1
Summary Position Statements on The
Mastery-Discrimination Controversy.

Beliefs of advocates of discrimination testing	Beliefs of advocates of mastery testing
1. Mastery can only be arbitrarily defined and there are important decisions to be reached from knowledge of degrees of achievement.	1. Mastery is definable, in a meaningful, useful way and degrees of mastery for many subjects either do not exist or are unimportant.
2. Most subject matter is not so structured that understanding one concept requires "complete mastery" of a previous concept.	2. Most subject matter is hierarchically structured.
3. Varying time instead of amount learned is not the most beneficial or efficient instructional strategy.	3. For hierarchically structured subjects it is an unwise pedagogical decision to attempt to teach higher concepts if the basics have not been mastered.
4. All students need not and probably should not learn many—if any—things to the same degree of proficiency.	4. Therefore, it is better to allow variations in the time spent in learning than in the amount learned (i.e., it is better for a student to learn fewer things more thoroughly).
5. Even if that were a reasonable goal, what we know about individual differences suggests that even making time a variable, student proficiencies are not likely to be very homogeneous.	
6. If differential learning exists, it is wasteful not to measure it, since it is a potential aid in decision making.	

ing the items—there are more similarities than differences in the preparation of norm-referenced and criterion-referenced tests. There is a healthy emphasis, for example, on making sure items measure certain specified objectives in criterion-referenced tests. However, this same characteristic should hold for a norm-referenced instrument.

REPORTING THE RESULTS OF MEASUREMENT

Few, if any, professional educators doubt the wisdom of determining how much or how well students have learned. Not to do so would mean that we could never evaluate the job schools are doing or the progress students are making. However, whether we need to record what students have learned and, if so, in what fashion, is a more debatable issue. To us it seems self-evident that some record keeping of student progress is necessary. Not all decisions that depend on level of student achievement can be made at the time the achievement level is observed. Thus, the data should be recorded. Furthermore, information regarding student progress needs to be systematically reported.

Necessity for Reporting Procedures: Who Needs Them?

Many people make or help the student make decisions based partly on how the student has done in school. A particular decision may depend on highly specific information (e.g., how well can the student type?) or upon much more general data (e.g., is the student a good writer?) Thus we obviously need a variety of reporting procedures. Before discussing these we should take a look at what people need information and how they use it.

STUDENTS

Feedback to students serves at least one major purpose, that of guidance. Students need information to guide them in their immediate decision making. Should I study more this weekend? Was the review session with Joe and Ted helpful enough to be repeated? Do I need to review the division of fractions? They also need guidance in their long-range plans; Should I go to medical school? A second possible purpose of reporting to students is to enhance motivation. The motivating dimension of feedback is more debatable than the guidance dimension. It is possible for feedback to either reduce or enhance motivation, and the same reporting scheme may have differential motivating impact on different students. Teachers should take this into account. Some students need friendly encouragement, some need mild chastising, others may need to be motivated through fear.

Nevertheless, many educators and students firmly believe that feedback (and recording grades) does have the effect of inducing students to apply themselves to learning things that they would not otherwise learn (Katz et al., 1968; Sparks, 1969; Stallings and Lesslie, 1970). Some educators may feel this is bad and that students should feel free to learn what they wish. Probably more would agree with Feldmesser (1971). He suggests that teachers are obliged ". . . to exert some pressure on the student to get him to learn material whose importance he is not yet in a position to perceive." (1971, p. 7)

Regardless of the stand our readers may take on Feldmesser's quote, it seems obvious that all students should receive accurate reports of how they are doing. Since teachers and students interact with each other every day, students receive ongoing feedback and probably have fairly good knowledge about the quality of their achievements. Nevertheless, regular marking periods can be a helpful means of further communication.

PARENTS

Parents also need to know how their children are doing in school and *good* reporting practices *should* result in improved relations between school and home. Unfortunately, many schools do not do an effective enough job in this respect. Parents often do not even know what the school's objectives are, let alone whether or not their children are accomplishing these objectives. Many parents would be willing to help their children in weak areas, but without knowledge of what those weak areas are, it is impossible to do so.

Also, since parents' opinions play a major role in a child's emotional and vocational planning, it is important for them to be as knowledgeable as possible in the area. Parents do not have daily contact with the school, so the quality of the formal periodic reporting scheme is very important.

ADMINISTRATORS AND TEACHERS

Curriculum and instructional decisions should be based primarily on student outcomes. Administrators must make decisions regarding the proportion of "college prep" courses, whether new curricula innovations should be continued, whether Johnny should be placed in a special class, whether Susan should be encouraged to take trigonometry, and countless other decisions that are made more rationally with some knowledge of how the students are achieving.

Reporting can also help a teacher evaluate his own strengths and weaknesses. If students are doing well in some aspects of a course but poorly in others, a teacher should examine his instructional procedures to formulate possible hypotheses as to why that is so. Teachers, like students, are not as dependent on a periodic reporting scheme for their feedback information, but the task of preparing a formal report may cause a teacher to look more carefully at student achievements than they would otherwise.

PROSPECTIVE EMPLOYERS

While many people may justifiably feel that how a student achieves should be private information between that student and the school, it usually does not work that way. If Donna applied for a secretarial job after high school, it is unreasonable to suppose that the prospective employer will not ask the school personnel what courses Donna took related to secretarial training and how well she did in those courses. If Donna did not agree to let the school release such data, her application might be rejected. Certainly if Sean applied for a government job requiring security clearance, a part of that clearance will involve a search of the school records. To not have available or to withhold appropriate school records from employers would require that they greatly expand their own personnel department and/or make poor selection and classification decisions.

COLLEGE ADMISSIONS OFFICERS

There is a growing debate about whether records of high school achievement should play a role in college admissions. It is generally recognized that high school grades are the best predictor available for middle-class students, but not necessarily for disadvantaged youth (Thomas and Stanley, 1969). Thus the debate is not primarily based on the empirical question of whether high school achievement can predict college success. Instead, it seems to center on the philosophical question of whether anyone should be denied the right to a higher education. If colleges move toward admitting all high school graduates on a "first come, first serve" basis, then it is obvious that high school grades would become irrelevant for *selection* decisions. However, in such a case they would become very important data to assist in placement decisions. Thus, either way, records and reports of high school achievement are valuable to college personnel.

Marking and Reporting Procedures

We have suggested in the previous section that there are a variety of people who have good reason for desiring information regarding student achievement. Since their needs differ somewhat, the schools may need to consider different reporting procedures to communicate adequately with all. Reporting schemes may also vary, depending on the grade level of the student. For example, a single summary mark may not be necessary or even advisable for early elementary grades, whereas such a score may be almost mandatory for reporting high school students' scores to colleges.

We should also stress that comparing differing reporting schemes should not be on an either-or basis. It is certainly possible, and usually advantageous, to use more than one procedure simultaneously. As the data in Table 16-2 show, many schools do use more than one.

In this section we will discuss a variety of marking and reporting procedures and point out some advantages and disadvantages of each. We will discuss symbols, checklists, letters, and conferences. The most important requirements of any scheme are that (1) those using it, both in terms of giving and interpreting the reports, understand the system and (2) the reports are based on the major objectives the school is striving to reach.

Table 16-2
Types of Pupil Progress Reports. (From "Reports to Parents," NEA Research Bulletin, May 1967, p. 51.)

Type	Kindergarten	Grade 1	Grade Grade 4	Junior High	Senior High
Classified scale	16.8%	73.1%	85.8%	82.3%	79.5%
Pass or fail	5.7	11.6	9.0	8.2	8.1
Written description	33.2	30.2	20.0	12.5	9.1
Conference with parents	38.5	52.2	44.7	26.3	18.5
Other	0.6	0.1	. . .	. . .	. . .
Not applicable or not indicated	42.1	3.6	3.6	10.9	13.2

SYMBOLS

By symbols we mean the systems that use summary marks of some type. These marks may be A, B, C, D, F; O, S, U; 9 to 1; pass-fail; or most any other set of symbols. Whether or not these marks serve any useful function depends on how a teacher decides which mark to give a child and whether the meaning the teacher has for the mark is the one interpreted by whomever it is reported to.

There are several points to consider when using symbols. One must decide if the grades should represent achievement or attitude. If they represent the former, should it be achievement relative to an individual's own ability, relative to a set standard, or relative to peer performance? Should we grade on the basis of status or growth? What percent of the students should fail?[8]

Achievement or Attitude? Most educators believe that if only a *single* mark is given, it should represent achievement in the subject matter rather than in attitude. There are several reasons for this. (1) Achievement is easier to measure accurately; attitudes can be faked. (2) Most people interpret scores as if they indicate degree of competency instead of degree of effort. (3) Students must learn to realize that in real life, achievement is more important than effort or interest. (How hard surgeons or pilots try is not nearly as important as whether they do the job for which they are hired.

Teachers are often tempted to let a single symbol represent some combination of achievement and attitude. This is poor practice, because it makes the symbol impossible to interpret. There is no way to know how much of the symbol was caused by each factor or in which of the two the student was deemed better. Teachers, however, should have the de-

velopment of good attitudes as one of their objectives. It is important to evaluate the degree to which that objective is met and to report on it in some fashion, at least to students and parents. If the student's general attitudes are to be reported by a single symbol, it should be a separate mark from the one reporting achievement level. Many schools use symbols A to F to represent achievement level and 1 to 3 to represent general attitude. Thus, one student may get a B-1 and another student a B-3. This dual system communicates more effectively than just reporting on achievement or, worse yet, raising the first student's mark to an A and/or lowering the second student's mark to a C because of respectively good and poor attitudes. Actually, some sort of expanded report form such as a checklist would be a much better system for reporting attitudes, since they are not likely undimensional.

Achievement relative to a set standard, a norm group, or one's own ability level. Historically, marks were dependent on a set "standard" or they were criterion referenced. A student had to achieve a 94% for an A, an 88% for a B, and so on. However, the percent right on a test is as dependent on test characteristics as student characteristics. Thus, there is simply no mathematical, psychological, or educational basis for such things as equating 94% or above with an A and 69% or below with F. The major problem with standards is that all teachers just do not hold the same standards for student performance.

Recognizing the fallacies of such set standards, many educators moved to a norm-referenced system of assigning marks. Thus, a student's grade would be dependent on how others achieve. But there seems to be considerable reaction by teachers and students against such norm referencing. People mistakenly think it means "grading on the normal curve," and therefore failing 5% (or 7%)

[8] See Terwilliger (1971) for a more extended discussion of these considerations.

and giving As to 5% (or 7%) of every class. Marking on a normative basis does not necessarily mean that each class will have a normal distribution of grades or that any one will necessarily fail. It simply means that the symbol used indicates how a student achieved relative to other students.[9]

Certainly there are dangers of using a normative basis for assigning marks if the norm group is too small. However, if teachers would all try to keep in mind the performance level of students in general and grade on a normative basis, there likely would be more consistency in grading among teachers than if every teacher graded on the basis of their arbitrary standards.

Actually, the debate between norms and standards is, in a sense, a false one. Sometimes those who argue for standards maintain that experienced teachers know what the standards should be and that inexperienced teachers can quickly learn these. But this means that "standards" are derived from observing students' performances, so they are actually norms!

Of course, if schools adopt more mastery-learning approaches to instruction, then educators should use criterion-referenced measurement as opposed to norm-referenced measurement, and therefore the reporting system should be based on criteria or standards. However, under such an instructional procedure, the teachers should have the same set of standards. Thus the "grade" a person receives might well be a statement regarding his position in the sequence of materials. (For example, if Johnny has finished Unit IVA in arithmetic, his grade is IVA.) Although this grade would be a standard rather than norm based, there is nothing to prevent the report

from *also* including some normative data. (For example, about 85% of the students who have been in school 3 years have finished Unit IIIC, 40% have completed IVA, and the top 15% have finished Unit VD.)

A criticism occasionally made of marking systems based on either a norm or set standard is that such systems ignore individual differences. Of course, that is not true. In fact, such systems explicitly *report* individual differences in achievement. Yet a question that often arises in education is whether one should hold different standards for students of different ability levels and let the set of symbols used in marking take on variable meaning for students of differing abilities. Of course we should hold different standards in one sense of the word. We should expect more from some students than others. And we should report—at least in formative evaluations—whether a student is doing as well as we expect. This should certainly be communicated to students and parents in some fashion. But it is most confusing to give a "low-ability" student an "A" because his low achievement comes up to a level we would expect and to give a "high-ability" student a "B" when he achieves well, because we know he could do better still. Any reporting of achievement relative to one's own ability should not be accomplished through a system that obscures information regarding actual level of achievement. Also, when one compares two fallible measures—level of achievement with level of aptitude—any "difference" between them is likely to be quite unreliable. Thus, only reasonably large discrepancies should be noted.

Status or Growth. Some instructors and students think grades would be more fair if based on the level of improvement (growth) that a student makes instead of on the final level of achievement (status). Marking on the basis of growth introduces difficulties similar to those

---

[9] Interestingly enough we once heard a person discussing marks at a school board meeting say that ". . . my children are different and I don't want them compared to anyone." We wondered how he knew they were different if he had not compared them to someone!

of marking on effort or in comparison to aptitude. (1) Growth is hard to measure. Change scores are notably unreliable. There is an advantage to students with initially low scores. Also, students soon learn to fake ignorance on pretests to present an illusion of great growth. (2) Most score interpretation is of status instead of growth. (3) In the long run, competence is more important than growth.

Of course, no teacher should ignore growth and there should be communication of that growth (as well as it can be measured) to students and parents. This is particularly true in elementary school. However, reporting growth should not be a replacement for reporting status.

To Fail or Not to Fail. As Mouly (1968) indicated, a distinction, at least on whether to pass or fail, must be made between what he terms the public school and professional school philosophy.

"In a professional school, e.g., the medical school, grades serve to protect society from professional incompetence. In teacher training, the college sets certain standards of attainment, and, for the protection of the children who might be harmed by having an incompetent teacher, fails any prospective teacher unable to meet these standards. Here grades are a screening device and the welfare of society takes precedence over that of the individual aspiring to professional status. In the public school, on the other hand, the primary purpose . . . is to determine the student's status as a prerequisite for planning his further growth. Presumably, then, a student would be failed only when his teacher is convinced that his growth can be promoted more effectively in his present grade than in the next." (Mouly, 1968, pp. 436-437)

If the guideline is not to fail a person unless it is in the best interests of that person, then we should fail very few students. Research shows quite conclusively that repeating a grade, or even a specific course, seldom results in improved performance (e.g., Goodlad, 1952). What is called automatic or social promotion is becoming more and more common. This is probably best for the students in elementary and secondary schools. It does mean, however, that employers should not interpret the possession of a high school diploma as indicative of any minimum level of knowledge. Instead, it should be interpreted as saying "the holder of this diploma attended school for 12 years."

The Pass-Fail System. In spite of the higher reliability of a grading system with five or more categories (Ebel, 1969(b), 1972), there has been a considerable move toward a more restrictive two category (pass-fail) system. The pass-fail system has been adopted, at least for a few courses, by about two thirds of American colleges and universities (Burwen, 1971). Many high schools are also adopting a modified form of the pass-fail system. There has been considerable discussion in the literature about whether this is good or bad.

The most common justification for the pass-fail plan is that it encourages students to take courses they would otherwise not take because of a fear of lowering their grade-point average (GPA). Other stated purposes are that such a system reduces student anxiety, gives students greater control over the allocation of study time, and shifts students' efforts from grade getting to learning. (See, for example, Feldmesser, 1969; Milton, 1967; Quann, 1970.)

Questionnaires and empirical studies on the results of the pass-fail system suggest that:

1. Roughly 75 to 85% of the students who elect to take a course pass-fail would have taken the course anyway (e.g., Karlins, 1969; Morishima and Micek, 1970).

2. Students report they feel less anxious in

pass-fail courses (Cromer, 1969; Karlins, 1969; Melville and Stamm, 1967).

3. Students do use the pass-fail option to reduce study time in that area and concentrate on other courses (Feldmesser, 1969; Karlins, 1969; Milton, 1967; Morishima and Micek, 1970).

4. The motivation to learn in a pass-fail course is about the same or *less* for 85% of the respondents in one study (Hales, et al., 1971).

5. Students do not perform as well in pass-fail courses as in regular courses (Karlins, 1969; Stallings and Smock, 1971).

Whether these studies in general support or refute the advantages of a pass-fail system is debatable. Since the evidence suggests that students neither learn nor feel as motivated to learn in pass-fail courses as they do in graded classes, we might consider the evidence as negative. It appears that when excellence is not recognized or rewarded, there is no external motivation to do more than just get by. Indeed, 31% of the respondents in one survey admitted that in a pass-fail course they attempt to earn a grade just high enough to pass (Hales et al., 1971). On the other hand, we do wish to encourage students to explore different areas, and a few more probably do this when we offer a pass-fail option. Also, if students reallocate their study time and learn less in the pass-fail courses, they may be learning more in their other courses.

In general we think there is more to be gained than lost in initiating a *partial* pass-fail system. This could be initiated at any point in junior or senior high school. A school probably should not allow a pupil to take more than 20% (10 to 15% might be better) of his course work under such a plan for the following reasons:

1. It appears that study effort may be reduced.

2. A two-category system of reporting is less reliable and certainly less informative. It reduces the data either a student or others have available for decision making. This is upsetting to many who have to make decisions about further study (Dale, 1969; Hassler, 1969; Law School Admission Test Council, 1970; Rossmann, 1970).

3. A pass-fail system does not allow for compensation. We might decide, for example, that if a medical student received a C average he should graduate. Ds in some subjects could be counterbalanced by Bs in others. However, if one went to a pass-fail system and defined a score equivalent to "C" as passing, excellence in some areas could not compensate for minimal performance (Ds) in others. If "D" is defined as passing, standards have been lowered from the original scheme.

If adopting a 20% or less pass-fail option, schools may wish to consider a slight deviation of this scheme and use a pass-no record grade where, in the event of a nonpass, no record at all would be entered on the transcript. Some faculty object to this because the "no pass" would not count in the GPA and a student could continue going to school indefinitely until he finally accumulates enough credits to graduate. But this would not necessarily be bad. As Warren (1970, p. 19) suggests, "The basic argument is whether students taking courses in which they can fail without penalty would constitute an inefficient use of the institution's resources. No one knows."

Disadvantages of Symbols. The most often-mentioned disadvantages of using a single symbol to represent the degree to which a student has achieved certain objectives are as follows (see Anderson, 1966).

1. Marks are inaccurate measures of competence and are not used in a comparable way from school to school, or even instructor to instructor. To one teacher, B may be average, while to another teacher C— may be average. One teacher may mark on effort, another on results. One may fail 30% of the class, another none. These types of inconsistencies are very harmful and destroy the interpretability of such marking schemes.

2. Marks are not related to the important objectives of the school.

3. Marks are inadequate in communicating between the home and school.

4. Marks produce side effects detrimental to the welfare of the child. The side effects usually mentioned are:

a. The debilitating impact of failure.

b. Excess competitiveness.

c. Cheating.

d. A distortion of educational values that makes marks, not learning, the important criterion of success.

These objections need not necessarily apply to marks, nor are they unique to the symbol system. Both points 1 and 2 above are often relevant criticisms of existing practices, but the symbol system does not force these disadvantages. Marks *could* and *should* be comparable; they *could* and *should* be related to important objectives. They will always be somewhat inaccurate, but no more so than any other system of recording evaluations. Point 3 above is true. However, the implication of recognizing that truth could just as well be to *supplement* the marks with additional means of communication instead of to eliminate marks. Every other single system is inadequate also. Point 4a may be true. Certainly many social psychologists have gathered data that they maintain supports that claim. But it is really an irrelevant criticism of symbols. None of the symbols need to represent failure in the sense of not receiving credit for the course. And failure, however defined, could be reported through any sys-

tem. One does not have to use *symbols* to communicate inadequate performance. And if inadequate performance unduly affects self-concept, let us remember that it is the inadequate performance that is the problem, not the reporting of it. Points 4b and 4d above are made with little solid evidence to support them. If they are true, however, it is because of an overemphasis on reporting instead of any inherent limitation of the method of reporting by symbols instead of by check lists, letters, or conferences.

Advantages of Symbols. Before listing the advantages of symbols we remind the reader that we are not comparing the reporting systems on an either-or basis. The use of symbols in no way precludes the use of other methods. Some of the advantages of marks are as follows.

1. Symbols are the least time consuming method of reporting.

2. Symbols can be converted to numbers. Thus GPAs (and high school ranks) can be computed. These GPAs are useful in many types of selection, placement, and classification decisions. If an organization has to make many decisions, an actuarial approach using GPA as one of the input variables is much more efficient and results in a greater number of accurate decisions than if clinical decisions were made on the basis of letters of recommendation.

3. Symbols not only relate to one's chances to obtain good grades in future courses, they also relate somewhat to achievements beyond school. This relationship is not often very high for a number of reasons. Nevertheless Tilton (1951), for example, found that the highest tenth in college marks had three times as many people elected to the National Academy of Science as the other $9/10$ combined!

4. A symbol serves as an overall summary

	O	S	U	NB
READING 1. Hears differences in sounds				
2. Sees differences in shapes, words and letters				
3. Reads orally with accuracy and expression				
4. Reads with understanding				
5. Uses word-attack skills				
6. Reads for enjoyment				
ENGLISH LANGUAGE 1. Expresses ideas well in writing				
2. Expresses ideas well in speaking				
3. Listens with understanding				
HAND-WRITING 1. Forms letters and numbers correctly				
2. Writes legibly and neatly				
SPELLING 1. Spells the assigned lists of words correctly				
2. Spells correctly in written work				
3. Uses dictionary				
MATHE-MATICS 1. Understands basic concepts				
2. Knows mathematical processes				
3. Reasons well in problems				

Figure 16-1.
Rating scale for various subjects.

	O	S	U	NB
SCIENCE 1. Understands scientific concepts				
2. Experiments to find answers				
3. Values and uses science in everyday life				
SOCIAL STUDIES 1. Shows understanding of his world				
2. Participates in group activities				
3. Shows interest in everyday events				
4. Uses globes and maps				
5. Uses reference materials				
MUSIC 1. Participates in music class				
2. Sings in tune				
3. Reads music				
4. Enjoys listening to music				
ART 1. Enjoys art activities				
2. Uses tools purposefully				
3. Uses own ideas				
HEALTH AND PHYSICAL EDUCATION 1. Observes good health habits				
2. Participates in games				
3. Skillful in games				

O = Outstanding
S = Satisfactory
U = Unsatisfactory
NB = No basis for judgment

		O	S	U	NB
WORK HABITS	1. Listens carefully				
	2. Follows directions				
	3. Uses time wisely				
	4. Works independently				
	5. Works well with others				
	6. Takes pride in work				
SOCIAL HABITS	1. Is courteous and considerate				
	2. Respects authority				
	3. Respects personal and other's property				
	4. Assumes responsibility for his own actions				
	5. Plays well with others				
	6. Uses self-control				
O = Outstanding S = Satisfactory U = Unsatisfactory NB = No basis for judgment					

Figure 16-2.

Rating scale for work and social habits.

index and students want and need to know how they did on the whole—all things considered—as well as how they did on each separate subobjective.

CHECKLISTS OR RATING SCALES

Perhaps the major limitation of a single mark is that it does not provide enough specific information to be helpful in diagnosing a student's strengths and weaknesses. The feedback to the pupil, his parents, and other teachers is just too limited for them to plan diagnostic or remedial help. One solution is to provide more detailed checklists or rating scales. These rating scales or checklists should include the major cognitive (or psychomotor) objectives for each subject-matter area. Also, checklists or rating scales on affective objectives should be developed. These scales may be common across all subject-matter areas.

Subject-matter rating scales appropriate to early elementary school pupils are shown in

Figure 16-1. Major objectives are listed and the teacher is to mark an O, S, U, or NB column for each objective. A school may wish to use more specific and detailed rating scales than this. If so, it may be necessary to use a different set of objectives for each grade level. This would be commendable in a graded school, but hard to do in a nongraded school. Examples in the work habits and social areas are shown in Figure 16-2.

If general instructional objectives have been written out for each course, these could serve as the basis for a checklist or rating scale. For example, the objectives listed at the beginning of this chapter could be used. The teacher could check each one according to whether the objective had been achieved or rate the degree to which the objectives had been achieved on a three- or five-point scale.

If rating scales are to be useful, it is absolutely mandatory that they accurately reflect the school's objectives and that teachers gather sufficient data (through observations, tests, etc.) so that they can be completed accu-

Table 16-3
Guide to Performance Appraisal. (Author unknown.)

Performance Factors	Performance Degrees				
	Far Exceeds Job Requirements	Exceeds Job Requirements	Meets Job Requirements	Needs Improvement	Does Not Meet Minimum Requirements
Ability	Leaps tall buildings in a single bound.	Must take running start to leap over tall buildings.	Can leap over short buildings only.	Crashes into buildings when attempting to leap over them.	Cannot recognize buildings at all.
Speediness	Is faster than a speeding bullet.	Is as fast as a speeding bullet.	Not quite as fast as a speeding bullet.	Would you believe a slow bullet?	Wounds self with bullets when attempting to shoot.
Initiative	Is stronger than a locomotive.	Is stronger than a bull elephant.	Is stronger than a bull.	Is full of bull.	Smells like a bull.
Stability	Walks on water consistently.	Walks on water in emergencies.	Washes with water.	Drinks water.	Passes water in emergencies.
Communication	Talks with God.	Talks with the angels.	Talks to himself.	Argues with himself.	Loses those arguments.

rately. Using rating scales such as are in Figures 16-1 and 16-2 *in conjunction with* a summary symbol that gives some relative information as to progress toward the school's objectives can provide a very meaningful report.

LETTERS

Letters can be used to report school progress to parents, prospective employers, and college admissions officers. They are used in a repetitive systematic fashion only with parents. An advantage of a letter is that it can emphasize many different aspects of a child's school experiences. Physical, social, and emotional development along with subject-matter achievement can be reported. A major limitation of letters is that, if done adequately, they are very time consuming. Although not an inherent disadvantage of the method, most letters are very monotonous, stereotyped and not very informative. The following letter would not be too atypical.

> Johnny is a very likable child. He appears to be adjusting well to school and his emotional development is proceeding at a normal rate. He seems to enjoy his classes and is achieving satisfactory progress in all his subjects.

In order to write a good letter, a teacher must not only have adequate time, but must also have a good grasp of the objectives. While we are certainly not suggesting a teacher can assign correct symbols without having established some objectives, the lack of objectives may be less noticeable under such a system. Any vagueness in objectives *will* probably be noticeable in a letter. An example of a reasonably good letter follows.

> Dear Mr. and Mrs. Smith:
>
> Johnny is a very likable child. He is friendly and outgoing with his fellow classmates. He has two classmates who are quite close friends and he gets along well with the other students. This observation is in agreement with the results of a questionnaire given to the students this fall.
>
> Johnny appears to like school as well as the average fourth-grade boy. He is polite and attentive during discussion periods and works well independently during study time. He does have a slight tendency to "goof off" when working in small groups, but I interpret this more as being due to his vivacious manner than due to any dislike or disinterest in the task.
>
> Although Johnny did not show up on our routine school physical as having any disabilities I have noticed him frowning and/or squinting while reading. You might wish to have his eyes examined.
>
> Johnny is progressing satisfactorily in all subject-matter content. He is at or above grade level on all the subtests of Iowa Test of Basic Skills with the exception of spelling, where he is just slightly below average. He did particularly well in the arithmetic portions of the test. If you wish more complete details on what the Iowa Test of Basic Skills measures or how well Johnny did on it, please feel free to stop in and see me.
>
> Johnny is presently reading at a level comparable to the average fifth grader. He is in the second from the top reading group in my class. He should be

particularly commended for this since, as you know, he was reading slightly below average last year. He tells me that he read a lot last summer and this activity apparently was very helpful.

Johnny did an outstanding job on his social studies project. His talk on Korea and the display map he built were very well received by his classmates. Johnny also seemed to enjoy and learn from the reports of his classmates.

In summary, Johnny is getting along very well in school. His social-emotional development is above average. He likes others and they like him. He has a favorable attitude toward school work and is learning the types of things expected of fourth graders. If you wish to discuss any aspect of Johnny's progress please feel free to make an appointment.

Sincerely,
Mrs. Angela Brown

CONFERENCES

Conferences are certainly a good idea in theory. Misunderstandings and miscommunications between home and school would be much less frequent if parents and educators meet face to face than if all communication is written. Unfortunately, the beneficial results of actual conferences are not as great as they should be. There are several reasons for this.

1. Typically there are two conferences per year. The first is often scheduled too soon—before the teacher really knows the child. The second one is scheduled too late to do much good.

2. Teachers do not prepare well enough for conferences.

3. Parents often do not show up.

4. Parents and teachers are often defensive.

5. The excessive time necessary for preparing for and conducting conferences may keep a teacher from performing other important tasks.

The task of holding a successful, meaningful dialogue with a parent about a child is not an easy one. A teacher needs considerable preparation for such a task. Many schools

"Has tremendous energy if channeled properly." (*Drawing by Charles D. Saxon from* Family Circle, *October, 1962. Used by permission of the artist*)

hold workshops to help teachers improve their skills in this area. Helpful guidelines to such conferences are given below (Romano, 1959).

1. Establish a friendly atmosphere free from interruption.

2. Be positive; begin and end the conference by enumerating favorable points.

3. Be truthful, yet tactful.

4. Be constructive in all suggestions to pupils and parents.

5. Help parents to achieve better understanding of their child as an individual.

6. Respect parents' and childrens' information as confidential.

7. Remain poised throughout the conference.

8. Be a good listener; let parents talk.

9. Observe professional ethics at all times.

10. Help parents find their own solutions to a problem.

11. Keep vocabulary simple; explain new terminology.

12. If you take notes during the conference, review them with parents.

13. Invite parents to visit and participate in school functions.

14. Base your judgments on all available facts and on actual situations.

15. Offer more than one possible solution to a problem.

SELF-EVALUATION

An aspect of evaluation that is receiving increasing emphasis is the value of student self-evaluation. Self-evaluation is particularly important if a student is to be engaged in self-directed learning. Self-directed learning is essential both in school and after the student leaves school. Unfortunately, research does not indicate clearly how teachers can improve students' abilities in self-evaluation (Sawin, 1969, pp. 194 ff).

Self-evaluation should not be used as a *replacement* for the marking and reporting done by teachers. Students are not always very accurate or honest in self-evaluations. However, allowing a student to fill out a report both to be sent home and filed in the school's cumulative record may assist in the development of self-evaluation skills.

"Brings new information to class." *(Drawings by Charles D. Saxon from* Family Circle, *October, 1962. Used by permission of the artist)*

"He's good with his hands." *(Drawings by Charles D. Saxon from Family Circle, October, 1962. Used by permission of the artist)*

CRITERIA FOR A MARKING-REPORTING SYSTEM

The following criteria should be helpful to educators who wish to evaluate their own marking system.

1. Is the system based on a clear statement of educational objectives?

2. Is the system understood by both those making the reports and those to whom they are sent?

3. Does the system desirably affect the students' learning?

4. Is the system detailed enough to be diagnostic and yet compact enough to be practical?

5. Does the system involve *two*-way communication between home and school?

6. Does the system promote desirable public relations?

7. Is the system reasonably economical in terms of teacher time?

Any single method of reporting may not achieve all of these criteria. We recommend a combination of procedures to be most effective; which procedures to use depends on the school's objectives, the grade level of the student, and the recipient of the reports.

Summary

1. To test means to present a standard set of questions to be answered. Measurement is a broader concept. We can measure characteristics by procedures other than tests. Evaluation is the process of delineating, obtaining, and providing useful information for judging decision alternatives.

2. Measurement and evaluation are essential to sound educational decision making.

3. The purposes of evaluation can be subdivided into administrative, guidance, and instructional purposes.

4. Evaluation aids both the teacher in teaching and the learner in learning.

5. A good measuring instrument should have the following properties: reliability, validity, objectivity, and discriminability.

6. Reliability is the degree of consistency among different measures of the same thing with one group of subjects.

7. Many factors operate to decrease reliability. Some of these are trait instability, sampling error, administrator error, scoring error, motivation, and luck.

8. There are several methods of estimating reliability. The method to be used depends on which factors affecting reliability we wish to influence our estimate.

9. Validity is the degree to which a measuring instrument is capable of achieving certain aims.

10. Content validity is related to how adequately the content of the test samples the domain of subject matter about which inferences are to be made. Content validity is extremely important in achievement testing.

11. Criterion-related validity pertains to the technique of studying the relationship between one set of scores and a set of independent external measures. Knowledge of the degree of criterion-related validity is important if we wish to predict one type of behavior from knowledge of previous behavior.

12. Construct validity is the degree to which test scores can be accounted for by certain explanatory constructs in a theory.

13. Objectivity in a test refers to whether (a) experts can agree on the correct answers and (b) once a key is determined different scorers will agree on what score should be assigned to a test paper. Both types of objectivity are important if we wish to obtain meaningful and reliable data.

14. For tests to discriminate the test should be of about medium difficulty and all the items should have about that same difficulty level.

15. Accountability includes setting correct goals, determining whether they have been achieved and at what price, presenting and interpreting this information to the public, and accepting responsi-

bility for any results which are perceived inadequate.

16. Curriculum evaluation includes, but is broader than, student evaluation.

17. It is important to evaluate both products and processes.

18. Educators have typically done a poor job of measurement in the affective domain. Techniques such as observations and anecdotal records can help in the evaluation of affect.

19. Norm-referenced test interpretation compares a person's score to that of other individuals.

20. Criterion-referenced test interpretation compares a person's score to some specified behavioral criterion.

21. As schools are presently organized with time a constant and degrees of achievement the variable, norm-referenced testing should be used. When using programmed materials in structured subject matter and individualized instruction, criterion-referenced testing is more appropriate.

22. Evaluation is necessary for wise educational decision making. Since all decisions are not made at the time of evaluation, it is necessary to keep a record of student progress.

23. Since many people make, or help the student make, decisions based on school achievement, we must consider what reporting schemes can best communicate the student's achievements.

24. Students, parents, administrators, teachers, prospective employers, and college admissions officers all need information from the school to assist them in decision making.

25. Some of the most common methods of reporting school achievement are by use of symbol systems, checklists, letters, and conferences.

26. The most important requirements of any marking-reporting procedure are that (a) those using it understand the system and (b) the reports are based on the objectives the school is striving to teach.

27. If only a single mark is given, it should represent achievement in a subject matter, not attitude; status, not growth; and it should be based on a norm, not a standard.

28. It is generally not beneficial to fail a student, that is, to make the student take the same course (or grade) a second time.

29. The major faults of grading are not inherent faults of the marking system, but are caused by teachers not using the system correctly.

30. Checklists or rating scales provide more detailed information than symbol systems.

31. Letters could be a very effective method of communicating with parents. Unfortunately, most letters are stereotyped and not very informative.

32. Parent-teacher conferences are used primarily in the elementary grades. If a teacher prepares properly they can be a very effective method of presentation.

CHAPTER 17
Techniques of Measurement and Evaluation

This is One Test Those Kids Won't Get Their Hands On! (© College Media Services, Box 9411, Berkeley, Ca. 94709)

In Chapter 15 we discussed some of the basic statistical concepts used in evaluation. Chapter 16 covered some purposes and principles of evaluation. In this chapter the specific techniques of measurement and evaluation will be discussed.

OBJECTIVES FOR CHAPTER 17

1. Understand the differences between essay and objective tests; know the limitations and advantages of each; know the guidelines to follow in constructing such tests.
2. Understand the assembling and administering aspects of testing.
3. List, define, and discuss the uses of four nontesting methods of evaluation: observational techniques, rating scales, anecdotal records, and sociometric methods.
4. List four major purposes of standardized tests.
5. Recognize what factors should be considered in selecting standardized tests.
6. Explain the differences between standardized and teacher-made achievement tests.
7. Understand the differences between survey batteries, specific subject-matter tests, and diagnostic tests, and specify when one might use each type of test.
8. Understand the various types and uses of aptitude, interest, personality, and attitude inventories.
9. Discuss some of the public concerns about testing.

TEACHER-CONSTRUCTED EVALUATION PROCEDURES

Teachers obtain data concerning their students' attainments mostly by their daily contacts with the students. Teacher observations of daily behavior and test results are the major contributions to teacher impressions of student achievement. It is important that teachers form correct impressions. To do so they must be trained in classroom evaluation techniques. This section covers some of the basic aspects of teacher-constructed evaluation procedures. While reading this section, keep in mind the criteria of evaluative instruments covered in Chapter 16.

Planning for Classroom Evaluation

A major mistake that educators make in evaluation is inadequate planning. Evaluation should not be a spur-of-the-moment affair. The why, what, how, and when of evaluation deserve careful consideration. Continuity and integration of the standardized testing program (to be discussed in the next section) and the classroom evaluative program are important. Educators should plan total evaluation programs as a group instead of individually to minimize the gaps and overlaps in the evaluation. Individual teachers must also plan carefully the evaluations they do in their classrooms.

SPECIFYING PURPOSES: DETERMINING THE WHY OF EVALUATION

When planning either an evaluative program or a specific evaluative technique, one's purposes have to be considered in detail. The kinds of evaluative techniques most helpful in administrative decision making are not likely to be those most appropriate for guidance or instructional decisions. Will the data be used to make decisions about the students as a group or about each individual student? Is a teacher interested in finding out which students are achieving above a minimum level of competency, or is he interested in differentiating levels of competency among the students? Will a test be used for diagnostic or grading purposes?

What we are suggesting is that evaluation will not be very effective if only *general* purposes of evaluation are recognized. One should determine specifically what decisions are to be made with the help of each evaluative procedure. It is only through this specific planning that one can expect effective and efficient evaluation.

SPECIFYING CONTENT: DETERMINING THE WHAT

The objectives to be evaluated are highly dependent on the purposes of evaluation. The why determines the what to a large extent. However, it seems helpful to consider them as separate aspects in planning the evaluation program. One *may* use the same data to help make many different decisions, and one may use many different types of data to help make a single decision. Thus, the why of evaluation may be to provide data that will assist in a decision about retaining the present seventh-grade mathematics text. A variety of measures may be obtained to help in this decision. The mathematical knowledge obtained by the students is one appropriate measure. Their attitudes toward the text as well as the teacher's attitudes are other appropriate measures. Each of these measures, though, is likely to be useful for other decisions as well.

Specifying the what by stating that one is going to measure the student's knowledge of mathematics is not sufficient, however. One should actually build an evaluation blueprint or table of specifications. This topic will be discussed in more detail after a brief consideration of two more aspects of planning for evaluation.

SPECIFYING METHOD: DETERMINING HOW TO EVALUATE

There are many procedures one can use to evaluate. Objective and essay examinations, oral examinations, rating scales, observations, anecdotal records, and sociometric methods are some of the most common methods of teacher-constructed evaluation. The pros and cons of each of these methods will be discussed in a forthcoming section of this chapter.

SPECIFYING TIMING: DETERMINING WHEN TO EVALUATE

Determining when and how often to evaluate also depends on the purposes of evaluation. Formative evaluation is that done while building a curriculum; summative evaluation is the process of evaluating a completed curriculum (Scriven, 1967). A similar distinction may be made in student evaluation. Given a period of time (such as a semester or a year), a teacher will want to evaluate his students within that period to aid in the instructional process. Such techniques as short quizzes, work samples, and observations can aid in this formative evaluation. In most educational situations a final summative evaluation is also performed. This summative evaluation (perhaps in conjunction with the formative evaluations) is used for decisions regarding promotion, grading, future curricular choices for the student, and even eligibility for various extracurricular activities.

Evaluation should be (and is) a continuous process if one considers all aspects of it. A teacher does observe his pupils every day. Work samples are available in some classes every day. These everyday evaluations are worthwhile and are particularly helpful in formative evaluation. However, the informal

and perhaps even cavalier nature of these evaluations demand that they be supplemented with more formal techniques. These more formal methods have the disadvantage of being periodic instead of continuous, but they have the decided advantage of being more carefully planned.

There are no particular guidelines as to when an evaluation should occur. It seems preferable, in general, if it follows the completion of a content unit instead of a time unit, but school policy may dictate the latter procedure. If summative evaluation is required at a particular time in a school system, then a teacher should strive to organize his content so that the completion of content units coincides with the time units.

Whenever a test is given, we take the position that it be announced to the student in advance. We hold to this same position for short quizzes. Some teachers like to give unannounced quizzes to "keep the students on their toes." While there do appear to be some positive arguments supporting such a practice, the negative affect on the part of the students more than offsets any motivational learning or evaluative advantages.

CONSTRUCTING A TEST BLUEPRINT

In developing a specific measuring instrument the first task is to review the instructional objectives. This task clarifies what variables should be evaluated, but it will not tell us in what proportion to evaluate these variables. A table of specifications or test blueprint is necessary to insure that various aspects are evaluated in the proper proportions.

Suppose a teacher were to give a final examination covering this text. What proportion of the test should come from each chapter? That, of course, is a value judgment and depends on the teacher's objectives. Some teachers may stress Part II, others Part III. Still others may feel that either Part IV or

Table 17-1
Proposed Test Blueprint for a Final Examination Over This Book

Chapter	Recall	Understanding	Application	Total
1	2	2	2	6
2	3	4	5	12
3	3	5	4	12
4	3	3	4	10
5	3	4	3	10
6	3	5	6	14
8	3	6	5	14
8	3	5	5	13
9	3	5	5	13
10	3	5	5	13
11	3	5	5	13
12	3	5	4	12
13	3	5	5	13
14	3	5	5	13
15	3	2	3	8
16	3	4	5	12
17	3	5	4	12
	50	75	75	200

Part V is more important. Whatever the objectives of the teacher, they should be made known to the student in advance of the test.

If there are to be 200 questions on the final, the teacher may decide that those 200 questions are to be divided among the 17 chapters as shown in the first and last columns of Table 17-1. These two columns provide a blueprint concerning the content to be covered, but not for the types of behavior one wishes to measure. The behavioral dimensions (or kinds of abilities) one wishes to measure can be classified in many different ways (Bloom, et al., 1956; Krathwohl, et al., 1964). Some of these procedures are more elaborate than others. For the professional test constructor, these more elaborate schemes have much to recommend them. For the practicing teacher, a simple scheme should suf-

fice. We suggest a test blueprint such as shown in the two-way grid of Table 17-1.

Once a table like this is constructed it serves as a guide to the teacher in constructing a test balanced in accord with his objectives. It also serves as a guide to the students. Without such a table the teacher is apt to construct a test that is not at all balanced. Some areas are easier to write questions about than others. Recall questions, for example, are easier to construct than ones that demand student understanding and application. Unless conscious effort is made to avoid constructing a test overemphasizing recall (such as by following a blueprint), a teacher may very well do just that.

Teacher-Constructed Tests

There are many techniques, both formal and informal, used by teachers in evaluating student progress. Written paper and pencil tests probably are the most frequently used formal procedures and everyday observation in the classroom is the most frequent informal procedure. We believe that many different evaluation procedures should be used, but that each method should be made as formal (*not* unnatural) as possible. (Increasing formality usually increases reliability and validity.) We classify, for example, observations and rating scales under teacher-constructed evaluation procedures, because a teacher should plan carefully when using these methods of evaluation. Building observation schedules and preplanning what observations are to be recorded do, in a sense, constitute the development of an evaluative procedure. However, these methods are not usually considered tests.

For years educators have argued over the relative values of various types of evaluative procedures. Some feel essay tests are superior to objective tests, and some feel the opposite.

Some prefer observations to paper and pencil exams while others prefer the paper and pencil examinations. We feel that it is short-sighted to laud one procedure as always being superior to others. Which method is to be used depends on the specific decision one wishes to make. We will point out the advantages and limitations of each procedure as we discuss it.

KINDS OF TESTS: ESSAY AND OBJECTIVE

Classroom tests have often been classified into either essay or objective tests. The former includes tests in which the questions require the student to plan his own answer and express it in his own words. The most frequently used item formats in the second category are short answer, matching, true-false, and multiple choice questions. Some authors have objected to the term objective as applied to these latter types of questions. They are objective in that they can be scored fairly objectively once a key is constructed, but subjectivity is involved when any test is originally constructed. The determination of what questions to ask and how to ask those questions does involve subjective judgment. Also, the terms essay and objective imply that essay tests are scored subjectively. Reader or scorer reliability is much lower in essay type exams but, as we will see, there are techniques that allow essay scoring to become somewhat objective. At any rate, convention has suggested the dichotomy of terms and, in general, the two types of tests do differ quite considerably in the degree to which they are amenable to objective scoring.

Some teachers (and students) strongly prefer essay tests while others prefer objective tests. Many times these affective reactions are based on misconceptions, not truths. Specialists in test construction (who supposedly have fewer misconceptions) seem to favor objective testing. Without necessarily trying to change your attitudes (but perhaps your reasons for them), let us consider some differences in the two methods and when each type of test will be most appropriate.

Ebel (1972, pp. 123–138) has noted the following differences between the two types of exams.[1]

1. Essay tests require an individual to organize and express his answer in his own words. Objective tests require an individual to fill in a brief (one or two word) answer or to choose among several alternatives. Many people seem to think that admitting this difference implies the superiority of essay exams, but this is not necessarily so. As Ebel (1972, p. 126) points out: Producing an answer is not necessarily a more complex or difficult task, or one more indicative of achievement, than choosing the best of the available alternatives. ". . . if the populace had a clear choice between a man good at making statements but weak on decisions and another weak on making statements but good at making decisions, is there any doubt which they should choose?" Nevertheless we do occasionally wish to measure ability to organize, and essay tests are superior for that purpose.

2. An essay test consists of fewer questions, but ones that call for more lengthy answers. Objective tests would have more questions, but ones taking less time to answer. Adequacy of sampling, efficiency, and reliability therefore are likely to be superior in objective tests.

3. The quality of an essay test depends largely on the skill of the person grading the exam, and that of an objective test on the skill of the test constructor.

4. Essay tests are relatively easy to prepare

---

[1] For further discussion of these differences, see Ebel's text.

and hard to score accurately. The opposite is true for objective tests.

5. Objective tests permit guessing and essay tests permit bluffing. The seriousness of both of these problems has often been overemphasized. Blind guessing seldom occurs on objective tests, and when it does it is not likely to result in a large change in a student's position with respect to the norm group. Bluffing is relatively easy to detect if the reader has some skills in reading essay exams and knows what answer he is seeking.

ESSAY TESTS

As Coffman (1971) points out, ". . . essay examinations are still widely used in spite of more than a half century of criticism by specialists in educational measurement." In constructing and scoring essay exams, though, one should be aware of these limitations and attempt to minimize them.

The two most serious limitations of essay questions are their poor content sampling and their low reader reliability. Not surprisingly, some students do better on some questions while others do better on others (Godshalk, Swineford, and Coffman, 1966; Gosling, 1966; Young, 1962). Thus, a student's raw score (and relative score) will depend on the questions asked. The more questions (assuming they do not all cover the same content), the less likely that a student's score will suffer because of inadequate sampling of content by the test items, and the more reliable the test will be. Therefore, essay tests that contain several questions requiring short answers are preferable to a test that only asks one question requiring a lengthy answer.

The second major problem, reader reliability, can be minimized both by careful construction of the questions and by setting up specified scoring procedures. The study of Falls (1928) shows the extent of the problem. Although it is a study of reader reliability of an actual essay, it gives results highly similar to results of essay tests. In 1928, Falls had 100 English teachers grade copies of an essay written by a high school senior. The teachers were required to assign both a numerical grade to the essay and to indicate at what grade level they thought the essay was written. The grades varied from 60 to 98%, and the grade level varied from fifth grade to college junior! With this type of variation across readers, it is no wonder that measurement specialists are concerned about the adequacy of essays (or essay tests) as evaluation procedures. If a score is so dependent on who reads the paper, it is probably not a very accurate reflection of the achievement of the student.

Two commonly used methods have been developed for scoring essay questions: the *analytical* method and the *global* method. In both procedures the ideal answer to a question is specified in advance. In analytical scoring this answer is then analyzed, and its component parts are specified and assigned points. As each pupil's response is read, he receives points for those component parts of the ideal answer that he includes in his answer. In general, analytical scoring is considered more reliable than global scoring. Its major danger, as Diederick (1967, pp. 582–583) has noted, is that in attempting to identify the elements, undue attention may be given to superficial aspects of the answer.

In global scoring the ideal answer is not divided into component parts; it simply serves as a standard. The rater is to read a question rapidly, form a general impression, and then rate the response. Four or five rating categories are probably sufficient for most purposes. With global reading, each set of responses should be read and classified at least twice, preferably by a different reader the second time. This is not an undue hardship, since global rating is considerably faster than analytical scoring. For professionally trained readers, global scoring seems preferable (see Godshalk, et al., 1966); for teachers, analytical scoring probably gives more reliable scores.

Whether analytical or global scoring is used, a rater should read the answers to one question on all students' papers before going to the next question. This reading should all be done at one sitting. If possible, each paper should be scored without knowledge of who the writer was.

A third problem or limitation of essay test questions is that the student does not always understand what the question is asking and therefore is not sure how to respond. (This problem also occurs in objective testing, but to a much less extent.) To minimize this problem, the examiner should write the question so that the student's task is defined as completely and specifically as possible.

Given the potential disadvantages of essay tests mentioned in the above paragraphs, why are they still in use? Several reasons can be suggested.

1. Many teachers are unaware of the problems of essay testing.

2. Teachers who are aware of the problems of poor sampling, reader unreliability, and vagueness of questions can do much to overcome these problems.

3. Essay tests are probably the best procedures for measuring some characteristics, such as writing ability.

4. Even when an essay test turns out to be a poor measuring instrument, the testing experience can be a valuable learning experience.

5. As we will see, objective tests are not without their faults, either.

In constructing essay test questions, the following guidelines should be considered.

1. Restrict the subject matter to be covered by the question.

2. Define the students' task as completely as possible.

3. Provide generous time limits for the test.

4. Check the adequacy of the question by seeing if you and "other experts" can agree on an ideal answer.

OBJECTIVE TESTS

While there are many minor variations of objective testing, the most popular formats are short answer, matching, true-false, and multiple choice questions. As mentioned all types are objectively scored once a key has been determined. Also, since it generally takes only a short while to answer each question, many questions can be asked during an examination period and more adequate content coverage can be assured.

Short-Answer Items. A short answer item consists of a question or incomplete statement that the pupil is to answer with a word or phrase. This type of item is somewhat of a compromise between an essay item and the other types of objective items. Sloppy phrasing and/or an imprecise key could result in questions that cannot be scored with complete objectivity. For example, suppose one presents the following item.

The capitol of New York State is _____.
One correct answer is "much smaller than New York City." Another correct answer would be "east of the Rockies." If the key specifically states that Albany is the *only* answer to be counted correct, then the scoring would be objective, but the determination of the key would be very subjective, indeed. Would "Allbany" or "Alabany" be counted correct? We do not wish to make too big a point of this lack of objectivity. Proper wording can alleviate most problems of this type. (Write the name of the city that is the capitol of New York State.)

Another aspect of short answer items that

makes them somewhat of a cross between essay and other objective items is that like essay items, they require recall rather than recognition. While recalling a correct answer and recognizing a correct answer are two different behaviors, studies have indicated that correlations between scores on two tests differing in recall versus recognition format are extremely high. (See Cook, 1955.)

The chief limitation of short answer items is that they tend to cover details and measure knowledge of facts instead of understanding or application. Exceptions would be math and/or science questions demanding numerical answers or chemical compounds.

When short answer items are used, the teacher should strive to word the item in such a way that only one answer is correct. If the item is a sentence completion type, the blank(s) should be toward the end of the sentence, and excessive blanks should be avoided. (For example, The _____ of _____ is _____.) In computation problems, the degree of precision expected should be stated.

Matching. A matching exercise consists of a list of stimuli and a list of responses. The pupil is to match one of the responses to each stimulus. The major advantage of matching type items is that they require relatively little reading time, and many questions can be asked in a small amount of time. Also, they, like true-false and multiple choice exercises, are amenable to machine scoring.

When constructing matching items, the following suggestions should be kept in mind.

1. The lists of stimuli and responses should be as homogeneous as possible.

2. Keep the lists relatively short—no more than 10 or 12 in a list.

3. The number of items in the response list should exceed the number in the stimuli list. (This cuts down on guessing.)

4. Arrange the lists in some meaningful order (such as alphabetical or chronological).

5. State in the directions the basis on which the matching is to be done.

True-False Items. True-false items, while popular in the early days of objective testing, have lost much of their popularity. They are seldom used in standardized tests, and most authors of measurement texts speak disparagingly of them. (See, e.g., Ahmann and Glock, 1971.)

The two major disadvantages to true-false items are that (1) they often measure trivial pieces of information (similar to many short answer items) and (2) pupils' scores on true-false tests can be influenced considerably by good or poor luck in guessing. Other frequently mentioned disadvantages are that (3) true-false items are often ambiguous and (4) the exposure of students to false statements is pedagogically a poor procedure. (This fourth disadvantage is certainly debatable. Experimental studies do not support this contention.)

The major advantages of true-false exercises are that: (1) a true-false test can satisfactorily cover a large amount of subject matter in a small amount of testing time, (2) true-false questions are relatively easy to construct, and (3) they are particularly suitable to testing beliefs in popular misconceptions and superstitions.

When constructing true-false items the following suggestions should be kept in mind.

1. Try to use statements that are clearly true or false without exceptions or qualifications.

2. Avoid the use of specific determiners such as all, always, and never.

3. Restrict each statement to a single idea.

4. Use an approximately equal number of true and false items.

5. Avoid negative statements if possible, particularly double negatives.

6. Avoid the exact wording of the textbook.

Multiple Choice Items. A multiple choice item consists of a direct question or incomplete statement (stem) followed by two or more possible answers (responses), only one of which is to be chosen.[2] Multiple choice items are the most popular of the objective test item formats. There are two types, those that call for the best answer and those that call for the correct answer.

There are several major advantages to multiple choice items. First, they are versatile. Multiple choice questions can measure recall as well as understanding, applications, and other "higher-order" processes. They can also be built for any subject-matter area. Second, they are relatively efficient. True-false and matching questions are slightly more efficient, but essays are far less efficient. Third, the difficulty level of the test can be controlled by changing the degree of homogeneity of item foils. If, for example, one is giving a test for purposes of discrimination, then one desires items that are neither extremely easy or hard. Knapp (see Womer, 1968) conducted a study that compared three versions of a multiple choice exercise. The choice of the foils often drastically affected the difficulty of the item. A fourth advantage is that, compared to true-false questions, they have a relatively small susceptibility to score variations due to guessing.

In spite of their popularity, multiple choice items are not without their critics. (See Hoffmann, 1961.) These critics are not opposed to multiple choice exercises alone.

They object to all objective-type items, suggesting that such formats almost invariably lead to the asking of trivial, ambiguous questions that may handicap the really able students. Two serious limitations detract from their critics' credibility. First, the critics supply no empirical evidence supporting their contentions, and second, they offer no alternative methods of assessment and appear unaware of the serious limitations of essay testing. There are, however, some agreed on disadvantages or limitations to multiple choice items. First, they are not easy to construct. Teachers can not always think of plausible-sounding distractors (incorrect alternatives). If only one good distractor is listed, we end up with a multiple choice item with as large a guessing factor as a true-false item. Second, there is a tendency for teachers to write multiple choice items demanding only factual knowledge. This tendency is probably less for multiple choice items than other objective items, but it still persists.

When writing multiple choice items, the following suggestions should be followed.

1. Choose relevant, important topics from which to develop the item.

2. Write the stem first. Try to make it as short as possible and use clear, simple language.

3. Try to make all of the distractors equally plausible to the poorly prepared student, but obviously wrong to the well-prepared student (or obviously "less good" when using a best-answer type).

4. Make all alternatives about equal in length.

5. Place the correct answer equally often in each possible position.

6. Arrange the responses in a logical order.

7. Make sure all responses fit grammatically with the stem.

8. "None of these" should be avoided as a distractor in best-answer situations. It is

---

[2] A possible variation is to have multiple choice questions where the students choose as many options as are correct. This method is generally not preferred. It leads to problems in scoring, and probably allows personality factors to play too large a part in a student's final score.

acceptable in correct-answer situations such as where a numerical answer is required. Overuse, however, can make it ineffective. If used, it should be the correct answer in the proper proportion of questions.

ASSEMBLING, ADMINISTERING, AND SCORING TESTS

There are other aspects to consider in teacher test construction besides those mentioned under planning and the techniques of item writing. The methods of administration and scoring should be decided in advance. In general, the best administrative procedure is to reproduce enough copies of the test so that each student can have his own copy. Such techniques as writing questions on the blackboard or reading them aloud are clearly less desirable. (However, for some age groups reading aloud in *addition* to handing out copies of the test may be the best procedure.)

In preparing the test for typing and duplication, the following suggestions should be kept in mind.

1. If more than one item format is used (e.g., essay and multiple choice), all items of the same format should be grouped together.

2. Within format type the items should generally be ordered from easiest to most difficult. (Remember, however, that tests used for discrimination purposes should be composed of items fairly homogeneous with respect to difficulty.)

3. Complete directions should precede each set (type of format) of items. For younger subjects sample and/or practice exercises should be included.

4. If points vary from item to item (or item type to item type), the total amount of credit possible for each question should be stated.

5. The test should be typed neatly and accurately. A question should not be split between two separate pages.

When administering the test the teacher should make sure that the students understand the directions and that they are kept informed of the time remaining (e.g., through writing on the blackboard). Careful proctoring should take place so that cheating is eliminated, discouraged, and/or detected. Considering the prevalence of cheating on exams, it is apparent that many teachers do not take their proctoring responsibilities seriously enough. Students should be made to realize that cheating is dishonest and, if detected, will result in no credit being given the student for that exam.

Some educators have suggested the honor system as a deterrent to cheating. However, as most educators now realize, the honor system really does not work very well. And, as Ebel (1972, p. 241) remarks, this is not surprising since "the honor sought by the honor system . . . must be purchased at the price of another kind of honor, that of loyalty to one's close associates."

One final point should be made in this section. Some people advocate the use of scoring formulas that "correct for guessing" on objective tests. Such formulas are sometimes misunderstood. They do *not* eliminate the effects of chance on the test scores. The lucky guesser, after his score is corrected, is still far better off than the unlucky guesser. While there is nothing wrong in applying guessing formulas, most educators do not feel it worth the bother on classroom tests. We concur.

Other Teacher-Constructed Procedures

Teacher-constructed tests are only one of the methods of evaluation available to educators. Standardized tests, to be discussed in the next section, constitute another type of tool. Tests, both teacher constructed and standardized, can be very effective evaluative devices, but they should not be the only methods of evaluation. They must be supplemented with other procedures. Tests periodically measure certain outcomes of instruction (primarily those in the cognitive domain) under contrived conditions. These and many other instructional outcomes should be measured continuously in more natural settings. (One could argue that the normal classroom, and even the playground, are not completely natural settings, but they are much less restricted than test-taking situations.) Learning outcomes in the psychomotor and affective domains are particularly difficult to measure through tests.

This section will cover methods of evaluation other than testing. These methods depend on observations of pupil behavior or the product of that behavior. In general the methods discussed here will be less able than tests to meet the criteria of measurement procedures discussed in Chapter 16. However, as observation becomes more systematized and less like everyday perception, the evaluation can become quite accurate. The topics to be discussed in this section are (1) observational techniques, (2) rating scales, (3) anecdotal records, and (4) sociometric methods. These topics are related both to methods of observing and methods of recording behavior.

OBSERVATIONAL TECHNIQUES

Classroom teachers continuously observe their students. These observations however, are typically informal and unsystematic, carried on without benefit of particular planned procedures. Since so much of what teachers "know" about children is based on their observations, it is important that these observations be as accurate and reliable as possible.

Observational techniques are not to be considered a completely different procedure than rating scales. In fact, an individual may use a rating scale (or checklist) to record an observation. However, rating scales typically ask the rater to synthesize and integrate evidence (behaviors) in order to determine the degree to which a person possesses a characteristic (e.g., cheerfulness). The observational technique requires the observer to be completely objective and to come as close as possible to being a mechanical recording device — recording the actual behaviors (e.g., laughed) without attempting to synthesize or interpret the behavior.

There are several limitations, difficulties, and/or potential problems in observations. Some of these can be overcome by trained observers using appropriate techniques. One of the major difficulties is in determining a meaningful and productive set of behaviors to be observed. This determination, like deciding what content to put in an achievement test, must depend on the objectives one wishes to evaluate and the decisions one hopes the data will help determine. However, it is often somewhat harder to specify what observed behaviors are relevant than it is to specify what questions should be asked on a test or what general characteristics should be judged on a rating scale. What we observe and what it signifies are two different things. Yet, we are ultimately interested in the significance of an isolated piece of behavior if we are observing it. This may be easy enough to determine in a psychomotor skill area (the significance of a person watching the typewriter keys or looking at the basketball while dribbling are obvious enough), but the significance of isolated bits of behavior in the affective domain is more difficult to determine. One way to avoid this problem is not to specify in advance what categories of behavior to observe, but this takes us back to an unsystematic procedure and could lead a teacher to say something like "the students were using class time for independent study so there was no behavior for me to observe!" Of course, the students were behaving. It's just that the teacher had no idea what to look for. Behaviors that could be observed would include such things as chewing nails, looking out the window, pushing a fellow student, and talking.

In addition to the problem of specifying what behaviors to observe, an observer must be concerned with sampling errors. If we observe an individual at 9:20 A.M., we cannot necessarily infer from his behavior at that time to how he would behave at other times. To minimize errors that may occur due to sampling, a technique called time sampling is often employed. In time sampling a teacher determines either systematically or randomly a schedule for observations, insuring that each individual is observed at many different times during a day, week, or semester. Thus, an observation schedule may call for an observation of individual A from 9:15 to 9:20 A.M. on Monday, 10:20 to 10:25 A.M. on Tuesday, 2:30 to 2:35 P.M. on Wednesday, and so on. Individual B would be observed on a different, but comparable, schedule.

In spite of the difficulties in obtaining accurate and significant data from observations, teachers do observe continually. Specifying what behavior to observe and determining a time schedule for such observations will improve the data considerably.

RATING SCALES

Any judgment based on an observation of either a process or product involves a rating. Rating scales provide systematic procedures for obtaining, recording, and reporting these judgments. Rating scales may be filled out while the observation is going on; immediately after the observations are made; or as is often the case when teachers fill out forms for students, they are filled out long after the

observation and are really based on remembered behavior.

Uses of Rating Scales. Since rating scales, like the other methods discussed in this section, tend not to be as reliable, valid, and so on, as tests, they should not be used to evaluate outcomes that can more easily be assessed by the testing procedure.

Rating scales are most helpful in evaluating procedures, products, and personal-social development. (See Gronlund, 1971, pp. 421–425.) Such procedures as those necessary in typing, working in a lab, shop work, or athletic skills, cannot easily be measured by paper and pencil tests. Yet for instructional purposes, it is often important that these procedures be evaluated. If the procedures result in a product, it is often advisable to evaluate that product. As Gronlund (1971, p. 422) suggests: "In some areas . . . it might be most desirable to rate *procedures* during the early phases of learning, and *products* later, after the basic skills have been mastered."

Probably the most common use of rating scales in education is in the evaluation of personal-social development. It is not uncommon for teachers to rate their students periodically on various characteristics such as punctuality, enthusiasm, and cheerfulness. One of the problems of such evaluations is that, although supposedly based on observations, the observations have been spread over a long period of time. Such ratings are often on "remembered" behavior, not on actual behavior. That is, they are apt to reflect a teacher's biases concerning a student instead of the student's actual behavior.

Types of Rating Scales. The most popular rating scales can be classified into three broad categories: numerical rating scales, graphic rating scales, and comparative rating scales. A similar technique (checklists) is also often considered as a type of rating scales.

In the numerical rating scale the rater

simply marks a number that indicates the degree to which a characteristic is present. Graphic rating scales are similar, except the rater checks a position anywhere along a continuous line. Examples of both are shown in Table 17-2. For classroom use, neither has any particular advantages over the other, although the numerical scale may be somewhat easier to construct. The important point for either type is that either the numbers or periodic points on the line be described sufficiently so that the rater understands their meaning.

The comparative rating scale provides the rater with several standard samples of different degrees of quality with which to compare the sample he is rating. This type of rating scale is used chiefly for products and is often called a product scale. The rater's task is to compare the pupil's product to the carefully selected series of samples of the product. The pupil's product is assigned the scale value of the sample product it most closely resembles. (As you will recognize, this procedure is similar to the global procedure in scoring essays.)

Checklists are similar to rating scales, except the rater makes only a judgment of whether or not a characteristic is present instead of judging the degree of existence. Checklists are easier to use than rating scales and are useful in evaluating those objectives that are based on the presence or absence of a behavior, event, or characteristic.

Sources of Error in Rating Scales. There are several common sources of error in rating scales. Errors due to ambiguity, halo effect, leniency or severity effects, and errors of central tendency are some of the most common. By "ambiguity" we refer to the uncertainty by the rater concerning what trait he is really rating. Two teachers rating their students on aggressiveness may be making ratings on quite different characteristics. To one

teacher aggressiveness may be a positive trait suggesting the student is appropriately self-assertive. To the other teacher aggressiveness may connote hostility. The "halo effect" occurs when the rater's general impression of a person influences how he rates him on individual characteristics. If we like a person and think he is attractive and studious, we are apt to rank him high on other traits that may be quite unrelated to good looks and studiousness. Or, if we have a generally unfavorable attitude toward a person, we are apt to rank him low on all traits. The "leniency," "severity," and "central tendency" errors all arise because raters do not have uniform standards. Three raters may know a set of students equally well and indeed perceive them about the same. Yet one rater, on a five-point scale, may give the students a mean rating of 4.3, another rater a mean of 1.7, and the third a mean of 3. The first rater is likely too lenient and the second too severe. The third may be about right. However, if the third rater gave practically all 3s, only a few 2s and 4s, and no 1s and 5s, he is probably committing the error of central tendency. That is, he is not differentiating the students as much as he should.

More serious than any of the errors mentioned in the previous paragraph are the errors a rater makes because of not knowing the person he is rating well enough. The only reasonable thing to do is to refuse to rate the person on those characteristics about which you have no knowledge.

Ways To Improve Rating-Scale Data. Rating-scale data can be improved either by improving the rating scale or improving the raters. The following suggestions are helpful:

1. Carefully define the characteristics you wish rated. Make sure they are educationally significant.

2. Define the response options (points along

Table 17-2*a*
Numerical Rating Scale.
Directions: Indicate by circling a number the degree to which this pupil is characterized by the following.

	Very Uncharac- teristic	Somewhat Uncharac- teristic	Neither Charac- teristic nor Uncharac- teristic	Somewhat Charac- teristic	Very Charac- teristic
1. Is self-reliant	1	2	3	4	5
2. Works well with others	1	2	3	4	5
3. Plays well with others	1	2	3	4	5
4. Respects authority	1	2	3	4	5
5. Makes good use of free time	1	2	3	4	5
6. Seems happy and cheerful	1	2	3	4	5

the scale) so that a more uniform standard is adopted by all raters.

3. Choose qualified raters who know the individuals being rated.

4. Motivate the raters to do as accurate a job as possible.

5. Allow raters to omit ratings on those characteristics and/or individuals where they feel unqualified to judge.

6. Combine (or average) judges' ratings.

ANECDOTAL RECORDS

Another procedure for recording behavior is through the use of anecdotal records. These are records of specific incidents of student behavior. These records are typically less formal than those obtained through observational techniques. Time sampling is not employed. For this reason the data from anecdotal rec-

ords is ordinarily not as reliable. However, anecdotal records do have some advantages. They are not as time consuming, they record critical incidents, and they describe the behavior more thoroughly. The information provided goes beyond the rating of an ambiguous trait or the tally of any particular miniscule piece of behavior. Many teachers consider these more complete descriptions of behavior better suited to understanding and guiding students than the other procedures discussed. A single anecdote is not particularly helpful, but if a response is fairly typical of a child, it will recur. Little interpretive significance should be placed on a *single* anecdote.

A good anecdotal record should have the following features.

1. It should provide an accurate description of a specific event.

Table 17-2*b*
Graphic Rating Scale.
Directions: Indicate by placing a check anywhere on the line the degree to which this pupil is characterized by the following.

	Very Uncharac- teristic	Somewhat Uncharac- teristic	Neither Charac- teristic nor Uncharac- teristic	Somewhat Charac- teristic	Very Charac- teristic
1. Is self-reliant					
2. Works well with others					
3. Plays well with others					
4. Respects authority					
5. Makes good use of free time					
6. Seems happy and cheerful					

2. It should describe the setting sufficiently to give the event meaning.

3. Any interpretation or evaluation should be separated from the description of the behavior and clearly identified.

4. The event described should be identified as either representative or strikingly different from the child's usual mode of behaviors.

PEER APPRAISAL

A teacher's observation of pupil behavior is valuable but limited. He observes the pupil in a special setting where the student may be behaving somewhat differently than in other settings. Also, the teacher is necessarily observing from a certain frame of reference. Peer appraisal can be a very good supplement in the evaluation program. In evaluating such characteristics as popularity, leadership ability, power, and concern for others, fellow students are often better judges than teachers.

Peer appraisal could be obtained by using any of the rating-scale methods already discussed. If each student filled out a rating form for every other student, considerable data would be available. However, a more simplified task is the *guess-who* or *nominating* technique.

In the guess-who technique each pupil is presented with a list of descriptions and asked to name the pupil who best fits each description. The descriptions one uses depend on what characteristics one wishes to measure. If one wished to assess cheerfulness, the description might be as follows.

"This person is always happy."

If one wished to assess leadership qualities, a possible description is:

"This person is an effective leader."

The particular wording of the questions is important. The vocabulary should be appropriate to the age of the students.

In guess-who techniques, one simply tallies the number of times each person was named for each description. Data regarding who named which people are also available, but it is seldom used in the guess-who technique.

The nominating technique is a very similar procedure, except that the questions are slightly different. Instead of choosing a name to fit a description, the student is asked to nominate the person (or persons) with whom he would most like to work, sit by, or play. Again, what one wants to measure determines what particular question is asked. We could, for example, measure perceived competence, power, or social acceptance. Occasionally, students are asked to nominate who they would *least* like to sit by, play with, and so on. This is not generally recommended and could hurt group morale. The nominating technique provides data relevant to the social relationships of the class. With this technique we are interested in who made the nomination as well as who was nominated. Reciprocal relationships are looked for.

Suppose we have asked fourth-grade students to list their first and second choice of fellow students with whom they would most like to play. The results can be tabulated in a matrix like the hypothetical one shown in Table 17-3. (We have assumed a small class for convenience of illustration.) The pupils' names are listed both on the side and on the top. The names along the side represent the person doing the nominating. The two people chosen are indicated by placing a one under the name of the first choice and a two under the name of the second choice. The totals along the bottom of the table indicate the number of times each person was nominated. Mutual choices are circled, ignoring the distinction between first and second choices. Notice that mutual choices are always an equal number of cells from the main diagonal. Another way of depicting the data would be by way of a sociogram. We will not cover that method in this book. See Gronlund (1959) for a good source on sociometry.

The data displayed in Table 17-3 can be looked at in a variety of ways. Robert is a *star*. He received the most nominations. (Three of the four were for first choice.) Bill, Harvey, Judy, Lori, and Machell all received three nominations—one more than the average. Diana, Fred, and Jake were *isolates*, receiving no nominations. Carol received only one. Notice that there were 14 mutual choices out of the 24. There is a suggestion of a clique between Bill, Harvey, and Robert. There were no opposite sex choices. (This is a typical finding for fourth graders.) By using similar matrices for other nominations, such as choices for seating or work companions, the teacher can obtain some valuable insights into the group relationships.

There are several points to keep in mind when interpreting nominating data.

1. The group relationships depicted depend on the questions asked. (A student may wish to play with some peers and work with others.)

2. The relationships are not necessarily stable. They may vary during the school year. (Maybe Jake has just moved into the school. In another 3 months he could be a *star*.)

3. Nominating techniques only reveal relationships, they do not tell why the relationships exist.

As we have stressed before, one gathers evaluative data to aid in decision making. The obtaining of peer appraisals is no exception. Although the reasons behind the nominations are unknown, teachers can use the results to organize classroom groups and to improve the social structure of the group by

Table 17-3
A matrix showing students choices of play companions.

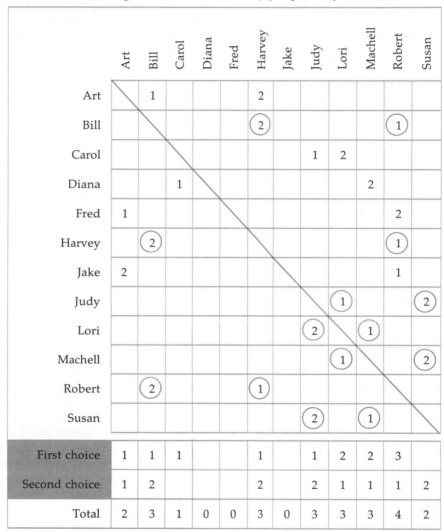

	Art	Bill	Carol	Diana	Fred	Harvey	Jake	Judy	Lori	Machell	Robert	Susan
Art		1				2						
Bill						(2)					(1)	
Carol								1	2			
Diana			1								2	
Fred	1										2	
Harvey		(2)									(1)	
Jake	2										1	
Judy									1			(2)
Lori								(2)		(1)		
Machell								1				(2)
Robert		(2)				(1)						
Susan								(2)		(1)		
First choice	1	1	1			1		1	2	2	3	
Second choice	1	2				2		2	1	1	1	2
Total	2	3	1	0	0	3	0	3	3	3	4	2

breaking up cliques and/or helping the isolates become more accepted. Further study may be necessary to determine why some students are isolates. Often teachers can assist isolates in becoming integrated into the group by providing them with more opportunity for social contact with the group and improving their social skills.

Analyzing, Evaluating, and Revising Teacher-Constructed Instruments

If classroom evaluation results are to be used for decision-making purposes, it is important that these procedures give as accurate information as possible. If they do not provide accurate data, we would want to know that so we would place less emphasis on the data in decision making and so we could improve the measuring instruments for use in future evaluations and decision making. Ebel (1972, p. 93) suggests that one of the common mistakes of teachers is that they do not check on the effectiveness of their tests. This is probably due to several reasons. (1) Teachers do not always understand the importance of accurate evaluation. (2) Teachers are not aware of methods of analyzing tests. (3) Teachers feel that test analysis is too time consuming. We certainly hope that by now you realize that important decisions are often based on a teacher's evaluation and that accuracy is therefore important. This section should dispel the validity of the second two reasons.

EVALUATE WITH RESPECT TO MEASUREMENT CRITERIA

As we have discussed in Chapter 16, there are several criteria (reliability, validity, objectivity, and discrimination) that evaluation processes should possess. Teachers do not have time to check all aspects of these characteristics for all evaluative instruments, but many of them can be checked for most instruments without consuming a great deal of teacher time. For example, reliability can and should be checked for major evaluative instruments, such as the end of semester exams. The scorer reliability of essay exams and rating scales can be checked by comparing the values given by two or more teachers.

On achievement measures, the validity of most concern to educators is content validity. As mentioned under the section on planning, a blueprint should be constructed for every test, so that the content in the test is appropriate to the objectives of the course. With other teacher-constructed instruments, such as rating scales or observational techniques, teachers are, in a sense, checking for content validity when they rethink whether the characteristics rated or the behaviors observed are really relevant to their educational objectives and decision making. Other teachers and students can be valuable resource people in examining the validity of any measuring instrument.

Objectivity can be easily examined on any instrument. Discrimination is the only other criteria for effective evaluation mentioned. This (and a related variable, item difficulty) can be checked by a procedure known as item analysis. While something analogous to item analysis can be performed on any instrument, it is most useful for objective tests. We will limit our discussion of item analysis to the most typical case, objective tests using multiple choice questions.

ITEM ANALYSIS

Item analysis is the process of examining the students' responses to each item. Specifically what one usually looks for is the difficulty and discriminating ability of the item as well as the effectiveness of each alternative. Item analysis has several values. (1) It helps one judge the worth of a test. (2) It helps in test revisions. (3) It leads to increased skill in test construction. (4) It provides diagnostic value and helps in planning future learning activities. (5) If students assist in or are told the results of item analyses, it is a learning experience for them.

There are a variety of different item-analysis procedures. (See, e.g., Davis, 1964, Chapter 10; Englehart, 1965). In general, the simpler procedures are as effective as the more statistically complicated for purposes of analyzing classroom tests. In conducting an item analysis one should follow the steps listed below.

1. Arrange the test papers from the highest to the lowest score.

2. From the ordered set of papers, choose two

groups; put those with the highest scores in one group and those with the lowest scores in the other group. There are some statistical reasons (Kelley, 1939) why one should place the best 27% of the papers in one group and the poorest 27% in the other group, but for classroom purposes, it really is not very important what percentage is used. If the class is small (say 40 or fewer students), there would be too few papers in the top and bottom 27% to obtain very reliable item-analysis indices. In this typical type of classroom situation it is quite appropriate simply to divide the total group into the top half and the bottom half.

3. For each item, count the number of students in each group who chose each alternative.

4. Record the count as follows for each item (assume a total of 40 papers—20 in each group—for this example).

	Alternatives				
	A	B	C*	D	E
Upper group	0	0	20	0	0
Lower group	4	2	8	3	3

* = the correct answer

5. For each item compute the percentage of students who get the item correct. This is called the *item difficulty*. In the above table this is the total number of students who answered C (28) divided by the total number of students (40). Convert this fraction into a percent.

$$\frac{28}{40} = 70\%$$

If one did not divide the total group into two halves but put the top 27% in the upper and the bottom 27% in the lower group, one could obtain an estimate of the item difficulty by dividing the number of people in those two groups who answered the item correctly by the total number of people in those two groups. Recall that for purposes of discrimination items should be of about middle difficulty. In a five-option multiple choice question where a person has a 20% chance of

getting the item right by guessing, a 70% difficulty level would be appropriate. (See Chapter 16.)

6. Compute the *item discrimination index* for each item by subtracting the number of students in the lower group who got the item right from the number in the upper group who got the item right and dividing by the number of students in either group (i.e., half the total number of students). In our sample,

$$\frac{U - L}{N} = \frac{20 - 8}{20} = .60$$

This value is usually expressed as a decimal fraction. If this value is positive, the item has positive discrimination. This means that more knowledgeable students (as determined by total test score) got the item right than poor students. If the value is zero the item has zero discrimination. This can occur because the item is too easy or too hard (if everybody got the item right or everybody missed the item, there would be zero discrimination) or because it is ambiguous. If more of the poor students got the item right than good students, one would obtain a negative discriminator. With a small number of students this could be a chance result, but it may indicate that the item is ambiguous or miskeyed. In general, the higher the item discrimination index, the better. For classroom tests, where one divides the class into upper and lower halves as we have done, one would hope that most of the items would have discrimination indices above .20. (If one uses the upper and lower 27% one should expect higher values, since there is more difference between the two groups.)

7. Look at how the distractors (incorrect alternatives) worked by using the same process specified above. For the distractors we hope to get negative values. That is, more poor students than good students should choose incorrect answers.

USING ITEM-ANALYSIS RESULTS

While item difficulty, item discrimination, and the response frequency of the distractors are useful in judging the adequacy of the test already given, they probably are more useful in helping revise the test (or the items) for future occasions. Very poor items should be discarded or better yet rewritten. Lange, et al. (1967) have shown that items can be improved, without too much effort, through using item-analysis data. Revising these poor items is probably more economical than simply discarding them and attempting to write new ones. By keeping a record of the item analysis data on subsequent revisions, one can determine the effectiveness of the revisions. This continual revising and rechecking process leads to increased skill in test construction; a teacher gradually learns what methods of wording and what type of

distractors will work best.

Another use of item-analysis data relates to its impact on instructional procedures. If students all did poorly on some items it may be due to poor teaching of that content. By carefully looking at the content of the hard items, a teacher can pick up clues concerning what the students are not learning and, in future classes, attempt to do a more effective job in that area.

PROFESSIONALLY CONSTRUCTED (STANDARDIZED) EVALUATION PROCEDURES

Standardized evaluation procedures are those for which uniform procedures for administering and scoring have been developed. They are typically constructed by subject-matter specialists in conjunction with experts on testing. National and subnational norm data are provided for most standardized instruments that allow performance comparisons to be made on other than just local norms. A variety of derived scores (such as the percentiles, stanines, and grade equivalents discussed in Chapter 15) based on the norm groups are provided to aid in the interpretation of scores.

There are many ways in which standardized inventories can be classified. The most popular broad classification is according to what is measured. In our discussion we will employ the following classification.

1. Achievement tests.

2. Aptitude tests (general, multiple, and special).

3. Interest, personality, and attitude inventories.

Educators have found that standardized inventories can be very helpful in the complex decisions educators face. Table 17-4 displays some of the purposes of standardized instruments. These will be discussed in more detail when we discuss each kind of test. Note that only aptitude and achievement tests serve many instructional purposes. Interest, personality, and attitude inventories are most useful in the guidance functions of the school.

Selecting Standardized Tests

One of the questions that always arises when schools are planning a testing program is, "Who should select the tests?" One way to stimulate test use is to have all the professional staff who will ever use the tests help in the test selection process. If teachers are expected to use test information, then they should assist in selecting the tests; if guidance personnel will be using tests results, then they should be involved; and if the principal also plans to use the test results to help him in certain decisions, then he should assist in the test selection. Test selection should be a cooperative venture by all the professional staff who intend to use the test information.

There are many different factors to consider when selecting a test, such as the purposes, reliability, validity, administrative ease, scoring ease, interpretability of the scores, cost, and format. Prior to consideration of these, however, we wish to discuss briefly some sources of information about tests.

SOURCES OF INFORMATION

There are many sources of information that will assist in test selection, such as Buros' *Mental Measurements Yearbook* (1972), publishers' catalogs, specimen tests, professional journals, measurement texts, and bulletins published by testing corporations.

A good place to start is the latest edition of the *Mental Measurements Yearbook*. The seventh edition lists most of the published standardized tests that were in print at the time the yearbook went to press. Those tests not reviewed in earlier editions (and those previously reviewed that have been revised) are described and criticized by educational and psychological authorities. Each school district should own a copy of this book and use it extensively in the test selection process.

Test publishers' catalogs are a particularly good source for locating new and recently revised tests. These catalogs provide basic information about the purpose and content of the test, appropriate level, working time, cost, and scoring services available. An important piece of information that is not provided in all publishers' catalogs is the copyright date (or norm date).

After locating some promising tests by searching the *Mental Measurements Yearbooks* and the publishers' catalogs, it is essential that the tests be examined before you make a final selection and order large quantities. Most publishers will send, for a very nominal price, specimen sets of tests. These sets usually include the test booklet, answer sheet, administrator's manual, and technical manual, as well as complete information on cost and scoring services. Careful study of the set is essential in determining whether or not that test will meet the specific purposes you have in mind.

Other sources of information are the test reviews found in the professional periodicals. Journals such as *Educational and Psychological Measurement*, the *Journal of Educational Measurement*, the *Journal of Counseling Psychology*, and *Measurement and Evaluation in Guidance* typically carry reviews of some of the more recently published or revised tests. *Educational and Psychological Measurement* also publishes a validity studies section twice a year. The bulk of the articles in this section are reports of studies using

Table 17-4
Purposes of Standardized Tests[a]

	Purposes	Kinds of Tests				
		Achievement	Aptitude	Interest	Personality	Attitude
Instructional	Evaluation of learning outcomes	X	X	?	?	
	Evaluation of teaching	X	X			
	Evaluation of curriculum	X	X	?		?
	Learning diagnosis	X	X			
	Differential assignments within class	X	X	?	?	?
	Grading	?	?			
	Motivation	?				X
Guidance	Vocational	X	X	X	X	X
	Educational	X	X	?	?	X
	Personal	?	?	X	X	X
Administrative	Selection	X	X	?	?	
	Classification	X	X	X	X	
	Placement	X	X	?		
	Public relations (information)	X	X	?		
	Curriculum planning and evaluation	X	X	?		
	Evaluating teachers	?	?	?	?	
	Providing information for outside agencies	X	X			
Research		X	X	X	X	X

[a] An X indicates that a test can and should be used for that purpose. A ? indicates that there is some debate concerning whether or not a test can serve that purpose.

various standardized instruments for predictive purposes. Textbooks on measurement also typically include information on various tests.

It should be obvious by now that there is an abundance of sources of information about tests. Using these sources makes test selection both easier and better.

PURPOSES OF TESTING

When deciding which test(s) to select, the first consideration should be a detailed examination of the purposes for which the testing is to be done.

If specific uses are anticipated, then test selection can occur in a more sensible and systematic fashion. Quite often one can decide easily what general kind of test is most desirable. Aptitude, achievement, interest, and personality tests are not used for exactly the same specific purposes. Although Table 17-4, for example, shows that all kinds of tests can be used for vocational guidance, they obviously do not all serve the same *specific* purpose. *Many* purposes could fall under the heading of vocational guidance, and adequate test selection demands more specific preplanning. Knowing that a test is to be used for the purpose of comparing Johnny's interests to the interests of people in various professional occupations would make the selection much easier.

Even knowing precisely the purpose for which one is testing does not necessarily make selection automatic. Suppose you are a seventh-grade mathematics teacher and you wish to measure the achievement of your students in mathematics so you can help evaluate (1) whether or not they have learned enough material to undertake the eighth-grade math curriculum and (2) whether you have been an effective teacher. Furthermore, suppose you wish to use a standardized test in addition to your own classroom test to help make the evaluations. How do you decide which of the many standardized seventh-grade mathematics tests to administer? To make this decision you must be precise in considering your purposes. One difference in all the tests you might choose from is that they do not all cover the same mathematics content. Some of the tests will cover "modern math." Others will cover the content taught in traditional courses. To make a decision among these tests you have to decide what your specific objectives are and exactly what area of mathematics you wish to test. Although this is a problem of content validity, it is also a problem of determining just exactly why you wish to use the test. It cannot be emphasized too strongly that the first and most important step in test selection is to determine exactly why you are giving the test, what type of information you expect from it, and how you intend to use that information once you have it.

RELIABILITY AND VALIDITY

Reliability and validity have been introduced in Chapter 16. When selecting tests, both concepts should be considered. As mentioned, how reliable a test should be depends on the purpose for which the test is to be used. If it is to be used to help make decisions about individuals, then it should be more reliable than if it is to be used to make decisions about groups of people. Although there is no universal agreement, it is generally accepted that tests used to assist in making decisions about individuals should have reliability coefficients of at least .85. For group decisions, a reliability coefficient of about .65 may suffice. These are only guidelines. There are no absolutes; one should use the best test available.

Validity is a matter of degree, and a test has many validities, each depending on the specific purposes for which one uses the test.

Thus, just as for reliability, the kinds and extent of validity data that one should expect to find in a test manual depend on the type of test and on how one wishes to use it. For achievement tests, content validity is by far the most important type of validity. Naturally, one should select the best test possible. Suppose, however, that no test is very valid for our purpose. Does that mean we should not test? To decide, we must answer the question raised in the section on validity in Chapter 16: "Can we make a better decision using the test information in addition to all other information than we could make just from the other data alone?" Once that question is answered, we must inquire whether this increase in accuracy of prediction is sufficiently greater to justify the use of the test.

In addition to reporting the type(s) of validity evidence, the manual must also provide other relevant information. The characteristics of the group(s) from which the evidence was obtained must be reported in detail. Tables of specifications and their rationale should be given in support of content validity claims and standard errors of estimates should be reported for validity coefficients.

OTHER SELECTION CONSIDERATIONS

Naturally when one selects a standardized test such aspects as ease of administration, ease of scoring, interpretability of the scores, cost and format are all worthy of consideration. With the exceptions of score interpretability, which is dependent on the adequacy of the norms, these are of secondary importance.

Standardized Achievement Tests

Achievement tests are used more often in the educational setting than any other type of evaluative instrument. The major differences between standardized achievement tests and teacher made achievement tests are in the prescribed directions for administration and scoring, the sampling of content, the method of construction, the norms, and the purpose and use. Table 17-5 displays these major differences.

SURVEY BATTERIES

Standardized achievement tests can be subclassified into three types: survey batteries, specific subject-matter tests, and diagnostic tests. Survey batteries measure pupils' knowledge in many diverse areas. If we wish to assess and/or to compare a pupil (or a class as a whole) in various subject matter areas, such a battery is quite useful. Survey batteries are most useful at the primary and elementary levels where there is a fairly common core of subjects and objectives for all students. They are less useful in high school where only some students take physics, foreign languages, advanced algebra, and so on. The many survey batteries appropriate for the primary and elementary school have considerable similarities in terms of subtests. Spelling, language usage, reading knowledge, vocabulary, arithmetic reasoning, and arithmetic fundamentals are typical subtests. Some of the more popular survey batteries are the *California Achievement Tests*, the *Iowa Test of Basic Skills*, the *Metropolitan Achievement Tests*, the *Iowa Test of Educational Development*, the *Sequential Tests of Educational Progress*, and the *Stanford Achievement Test*. Typically, schools administer a battery every year (or at least every other year) from grades four to eight. High school batteries are used less frequently.

Although the survey batteries are similar, there are some important differences, and teachers should carefully consider how these differences will affect the quality of the particular decisions the test data will help deter-

Table 17-5
Comparisons between Classroom and Standardized Achievement Tests

	Classroom Achievement Tests	Standardized Achievement Tests
Directions for administration and scoring	Usually no uniform directions specified.	Specific instructions are provided that standardize the administration and scoring procedures.
Sampling of content	The content and the sampling of it are both determined by the classroom teacher.	Content determined by curriculum and subject matter experts. Involves extensive investigations of existing syllabi, textbooks, and programs. Sampling of content done systematically.
Method of construction	May be hurried and haphazard. Often no test blueprints, item tryouts, item analysis, or revision. Quality of test may be quite poor.	Meticulous construction procedures are employed that include constructing objectives and test blueprints, employing item tryouts, item analysis, and item revisions.
Norms	Local classroom norms are all that are available.	In addition to local norms, standardized tests typically make available national, school district, and school building norms.
Purposes and use	Best suited for measuring particular objectives set by teacher and for intraclass comparisons.	Best suited for measuring broader curriculum objectives and for interclass, school, and national comparisons.

mine. These tests differ more on content than on technical aspects. For example, some emphasize reading comprehension considerably more than others. Some place emphasis on the measurement of factual material, others emphasize the analysis, synthesis, and interpretation of knowledge. If teachers have a thorough knowledge of their curriculum and what information they wish to obtain from the survey battery, they can carefully look at the contents of the various tests and choose one that most closely serves their purposes.

SPECIFIC SUBJECT-MATTER TESTS

Standardized achievement tests are available for nearly every subject-matter area and grade level. Reading and reading readiness tests are the most popular of these. A reading readiness test is typically administered late in the kindergarten year or early in the first grade. The purpose of such a test is to help identify those youngsters who need more prereading types of learning experiences. Such tests usually include items measuring motor skills, auditory and visual discriminations, vocabulary, and memory. Some teachers feel they do not need the results from reading readiness tests to help make decisions regarding reading or prereading instruction. This may be true. We are committed to the idea that alert, dedicated teachers can obtain much valuable information about a child's reading readiness by other methods (primarily classroom observation). Nevertheless, reading is such an important skill that teachers should not rely on their judgment alone concerning the child's readiness in this area. Reading readiness tests provide valuable supplementary information.

Reading tests are typically given in grades two and three in the school districts that do not administer survey batteries until fourth grade. Again, reading is of such importance that data supplementary to teachers' judg-

ments seems necessary for effective instructional decision making.

Teachers in junior and senior high schools may wish to administer standardized achievement tests in their particular subject-matter areas. A teacher of chemistry, physics, foreign language, or advanced algebra may wish to know how his pupils are progressing compared to others in the nation. If an achievement test can be found that assesses the objectives of the teacher, such a test can provide useful normative data.

DIAGNOSTIC TESTS

A diagnostic test is designed to assess a student's particular strengths or weaknesses within a given subject-matter area. Diagnostic tests are used most frequently in the area of reading. Subtest scores in such areas as reading rate, comprehension, vocabulary, visual and auditory discrimination, and motor skills are provided. These subtests help to pinpoint a child's problem. Needless to say, if no educator within the school building knows enough about reading instruction to use these data to improve the child's instruction, there is no point in giving the test. Hopefully all elementary teachers will know something about remedial reading instruction and at least one educator in the building will be expert enough in the area to obtain solid instructional guidelines from the diagnostic information.

USING STANDARDIZED ACHIEVEMENT TEST RESULTS

Table 17-4 refers to instructional, guidance, administrative, and research purposes of achievement tests. Correct use of standardized tests mandates that they not be the sole criteria for any educational decision, but the data can serve as useful adjunct information in many ways. For example, standardized achievement test results can aid in setting and evaluating learning outcomes. They can suggest the need for differential treatments of individuals; by looking at class or school profiles the curriculum and/or teaching effectiveness can be assessed. They are useful in placing new students in the school.

Scholastic Aptitude (Intelligence) Tests

There are many types of tests that could be classified under the general rubric of aptitude tests. Not all psychologists agree as to what intelligence or aptitude is. Since there is so much disagreement among psychologists attempts to measure the construct have varied. General, multifactor, and special aptitude tests have all been constructed.

In this section we will discuss those tests that give a measure of general aptitude. We will briefly discuss both individually and group-administered tests of general aptitude.

Although the term "intelligence" historically has been used in place of aptitude, that term is slowly being replaced. To some, the word intelligence connotes something completely innate. Since it is widely recognized that scores on our present aptitude tests can be affected by environmental variables, using a term without the innateness connotation seems preferable. Actually, many educators and psychologists think the term scholastic aptitude tests is the most descriptive. No doubt that what these tests do best is to predict future school performance.

INDIVIDUALLY ADMINISTERED APTITUDE TESTS

For the most part, educational institutions make use of group tests. However, occasionally it is more appropriate to administer an individual test to a person. Individual administration allows the psychologist to more closely observe and control the behavior of the individual. The major advantages of individual tests are that (1) they are generally slightly more reliable; (2) they are more useful in clinical settings; (3) they can be used with individuals who for either physical or psychological reasons cannot perform validly on a group test; and (4) although highly verbal they require considerably less reading ability than most group tests. The major disadvantages are that (1) they are time consuming and require a highly trained administrator and (2) being less dependent on reading ability and less designed to specifically predict school success, they sometimes are less predictive of school success than the group tests.

The most popular of the individual tests are the Stanford-Binet and the three Weschler Scales (WAIS, WISC, WPPSI). The Stanford-Binet provides a total score, and the three Weschler scales provide both verbal and performance scales as well as a total score.

Since teachers are not trained to give individually administered aptitude tests, we will not discuss them further. Teachers should realize that such tests are available and that trained personnel are willing to test those youngsters that a teacher can identify as unlikely to perform validly on group tests.

GROUP-ADMINISTERED APTITUDE TESTS

Group-administered aptitude tests are used far more extensively than individually administered tests. They are much less expensive and time consuming and generally provide comparable results. Although in many schools the actual test administration may be performed by a counselor or someone else with special advanced training, most group tests are designed so that any teacher, with a minimum of training, should be capable of the administrative task.

Many of the group tests provide three scores: verbal, nonverbal (or performance or numerical), and total. Some of the more popular tests at the elementary and secondary school levels are the *Analysis of Learning Potential*, *Kuhlmann-Anderson Intelligence Tests*, the *Otis-Lennon Mental Ability Tests*, the *Henmon-Nelson Tests of Mental Maturity*, the *Cooperative School and College Ability Tests*, *Series II*, and the *Cognitive Abilities Test*.

USES OF SCHOLASTIC APTITUDE TESTS

The average child will probably take at least three scholastic aptitude tests between kindergarten and twelfth grade. In some schools aptitude tests are even given with greater frequency than standardized achievement tests. In spite of (or perhaps partly because of) their common usage, aptitude tests have come under considerable criticism. Several of the nation's largest school systems have banned the use of scholastic aptitude tests in early elementary school. There are certainly some limitations and even some dangers (to be discussed later) in using scholastic aptitude tests, but at times the criticisms of and hostility toward aptitude tests have been irrational.

A basic assumption of scholastic aptitude tests is that individuals do differ in scholastic ability and that these differences are of practical importance in making educational decisions. Opposed to this is the position that all people are equal (misinterpreted to mean identical), are entitled to equal (identical) treatment, and that any test showing that people have unequal aptitudes must be un-American! Of course, as has been pointed out elsewhere (see Chapters 3, 5, and 11), people are not identical (although all people should have equal rights). Some do have more potential for schooling than others. Opposing apti-

tude tests for revealing those differences is as irrational as opposing tape measures for revealing differences in height.

As Table 17-4 indicates, aptitude tests can be used for almost all the same general purposes (but in different ways) as achievement tests. Knowledge of the level of aptitude test scores of a class helps a teacher make more appropriate decisions about the kinds and level of class material to present. Also, teachers can determine whether students are learning as much as one would predict as judged by ability level. While some people object to the term underachievement (since it is really overprediction), it is helpful to know whether or not a person is performing as well as could be predicted on the basis of his scholastic aptitude test scores.

Aptitude tests are also useful in making selection, classification, and placement decisions. Who should be admitted to kindergarten early, who should be placed in enriched and remedial classes, and who should be admitted to college are examples of potential decisions that can be made more effectively by using test data.

We mentioned earlier that there were some potential dangers in using scholastic aptitude tests. Let us discuss those.

The misuse that has received the most attention is giving a scholastic aptitude test to subgroups for which the test is inappropriate and then ignoring the inappropriateness of the test when making decisions based on the test score. An obvious misuse would be to give a typical test to a first grader who has been raised in a Spanish-speaking environment and then conclude that he is mentally retarded if he scores at a low level. It would not be a misuse to give the test if the *only* conclusion drawn (prediction made) is that he will likely have some academic difficulties in early elementary school. The decision as to whether a youngster is or is not from an appropriate subgroup is not clear cut. Some would rule out tests for all members of certain minorities.

Another argument that has occasionally been voiced against the use of aptitude tests for instructional purposes is that teachers will use low aptitude scores as an excuse for not attempting to teach the students ("The students can't learn anyway" attitude). Unfortunately, it is probably true that some teachers do this. Aptitude test scores should be used in helping teachers form realistic expectations of students; they should not be used to help teachers develop fatalistic expectations.

However, in agreeing that this potential danger of testing exists, we do not think it should be overemphasized. The teachers in inner-city schools who do not try their hardest because of preconceived ideas that their students can not learn have not obtained their ideas of student deficiency primarily from aptitude scores. Such factors as the students' achievement in class, the parents' educational level, socioeconomic status, race, and occupation all help teachers form their opinions concerning a child's aptitude (Goslin, 1967).

Knowing that Denny has a measured IQ of 80, that his father is an unemployed alcoholic, and that his mother entertains men to pay for the groceries, the teacher may conclude (correctly or incorrectly) that Denny will have trouble in school learning. If the teacher accepts these factors in the spirit of a challenge and does his best—fine. If the teacher adopts a fatalistic attitude toward Denny—bad. However, there is no more compelling reason to blame the test for the improper attitude of the teacher than to blame his knowledge of all the other facts.

Let us make this point clear. Aptitude tests can help teachers develop realistic expectations for their students. While we, in no way, condone, in, fact, do condemn, teachers who develop fatalistic attitudes toward the learning abilities of their students, we do not think

aptitude tests should be made the scapegoat. One must remember, however, that if we use any kind of data (including aptitude tests) to label children, we must be careful not to misuse the labels. Labels must be treated as descriptions, not as explanations, which too often happens.

A problem related to educators becoming fatalistic is the development of a fatalistic attitude in the children. A popular topic of conversation these days is the importance of developing a good self-concept in the students. There is no doubt that students should be self-accepting and feel that others accept them also. If a counselor interprets a low test score so that the student feels unworthy, then that is, indeed, unfortunate. However, as with other possible misuses of test results, we feel this problem of low aptitude scores resulting in poor self-concepts can be overemphasized. Just as test scores are not the major factors in forming teachers' opinions about the learning ability of children, low aptitude test scores are also probably much less influential than other factors in contributing to an undesirable (inaccurately low) self-concept. Tests often seem to be blamed for educational problems that were not really caused by the tests.

There are also potential misuses of test scores in administrative decisions. Some persons charge that the major misuse of tests in administrative functions is that decisions made on the basis of test scores are often treated as if they were permanent, irreversible decisions. If a child is put into a remedial class in third grade, for example, there is often too much of a tendency on the part of the administration, having made a decision once, to forget about it. The child then gets lockstepped into a curriculum.

Although we in no way support administrative inflexibility in the reconsideration of decisions, we should consider whether the use of test scores is really the causative factor of this inflexibility. We must admit that in some cases, it is. Some people simply place too much faith in test scores, and this unwarranted faith results in too much trust in the correctness of decisions—so they are made and then forgotten. However, not all, or even most inflexibility can be charged to test score misuse. Many of the decisions made would be incorrectly treated as permanent, even if there were no test score data on the students. It is worth noting that, if a decision must be made, it should be based on as much evidence as possible.

Other Aptitude Tests

As mentioned, psychologists do not all agree as to the structure of intellect or aptitude. Some contend that aptitude is a general characteristic, and that one (or two) scores can represent adequately that aptitude. Others subscribe to a multifactor theory and argue that many factor scores are needed to represent a person. Still others suggest that aptitudes are very specific and that separate aptitude tests are needed for the various subject matter fields (or indeed the different courses within a field) for which performance is being predicted. Consequently psychologists have developed, and educators find useful, batteries referred to as multifactor tests as well as special aptitude tests. These will be discussed briefly, although space does not permit extended discussion of the types and uses of these aptitude tests. Texts such as Anastasi (1968) or Mehrens and Lehmann (1973) can be referred to for more information.

MULTIFACTOR TESTS

Multifactor aptitude tests are considered useful in counseling. Most schools administer such a test somewhere between the eighth and tenth grades. The *Differential Aptitude Tests* (DAT) is the most popular multifactor battery. It provides scores on the following eight factors: verbal reasoning (VR), numerical ability (NA), abstract reasoning (AR), clerical speed and accuracy (CSA), mechanical reasoning (MR), space relations (SR), Spelling (SP), and Language Usage (LU). The authors of the test also report a ninth score. It is simply VR + NA. This combined score correlates highly with, and is interpreted the same way as many general scholastic aptitude tests.

SPECIAL APTITUDE TESTS

Aptitude tests have been developed for particular school subjects such as algebra, geometry, foreign language, music, and art. These tests have found some use in helping individual pupils with their curricular choice. Knowing what we do about intraindividual differences, we should not be surprised to find that the best student in foreign language is not necessarily the best mathematician or musician. Typically, however, specific aptitude tests do not do a much better job of predicting school success than the relevant subscores on multifactor aptitude tests or survey achievement batteries. Consequently they are not routinely administered in most schools. If a teacher finds them useful they should certainly be used, but it is dangerous to generalize their usefulness from one school setting to another.

Some psychologists would classify creativity tests as a type of special aptitude test. It is generally believed that creativity is a distinct concept, not identical to general scholastic aptitude, although the two are certainly correlated. While there are some standardized creativity tests, such as the *Torrance Tests of Creative Thinking*, these tests are still in the research stage and are not particularly useful to the classroom teacher. This statement should not be interpreted to mean that we think creativity unimportant. That is not so. Creativity is important, and there are many potential benefits available to society if one could effectively measure and teach for creativity. In Chapter 10 we have discussed some ways to encourage creativity. The importance of creativity, however, should not delude our appraisal of our limitations in measuring it.

Interest, Personality, and Attitude Inventories

As mentioned in several places in this book, objectives in the affective domain have a definite place in educational institutions. Since educators do have certain affective objectives, there should be some attempt to measure student affect to see if the objectives are being realized. Not only is affect important as a goal, but knowledge of affect can influence educational decision making about such questions as "how to teach" and "what to teach." It is generally agreed that one must have an understanding of a child's interests, personality, and attitudes in order to provide optimal learning conditions.

However, one must obtain data before it can be used. As we have mentioned before, educators do not have as much success in measuring noncognitive characteristics as they do cognitive. This is particularly true when "paper and pencil" tests are employed as the measuring instruments, and we have urged educators to make use of other processes such as observations, rating scales, and anecdotal records for measuring affect.

As can be seen from Table 17-4, we contend that the noncognitive measures have less *instructional* value than achievement and aptitude measures. Nevertheless, psychologists have expended considerable energy in devising interest, personality, and attitude

inventories, and educators can use them profitably. Standardized inventories do have the advantage of being uniformly administered and objectively scored. Typically they also provide normative data. While their interpretations typically require greater psychological sophistication than the average classroom teacher has, a teacher should be aware that such tests exist and that counselors are available to assist teachers in understanding and using the data from such tests in instructional decision making. Counselors, of course, find such tests useful in guiding the students in educational, vocational, and personal decision making.

Public Concerns About Standardized Instruments

The use of standardized tests in education has increased tremendously in the last two decades. With such an increased use of tests, it is natural and appropriate that the public show interest in and concern about this use. However, too often the interested and concerned individuals have made little use of the cognitive process, and criticisms have tended to be emotional blasts instead of well thought out, valid criticism. Written criticisms of testing have tended toward the unscholarly journalistic exposé fashion. (See Black, 1963; Gross, 1962; Hoffmann, 1962.)

MISUSE OF TEST SCORES

Although many of the criticisms against testing have not been well founded, it is obvious to any measurement expert that there are severe faults in many existing tests, and that other high-quality instruments have been severely misused.

Probably the most frequently suggested misuses of tests are the following.

1. Depending too much on test results for decision making, for example, using test scores as the sole basis for selection or placement.

2. Making inflexible decisions based on test results.

3. Teachers forming fatalistic low expectations of pupil performance on the basis of test data.

4. Students forming low self-concepts because of test results.

5. Using tests that are inappropriate for some groups, for example, minority groups.

6. Invading one's privacy by asking irrelevant questions on a test.

We have discussed the first four of these points earlier. More should be said about the final two points.

FAIRNESS OF TESTS TO MINORITY GROUPS

Aptitude tests have often been severely criticized for their "cultural biases." People of different nations as well as people in different subcultures within the United States place different values on verbal fluency, speed, and other variables that influence aptitude test scores. As has already been pointed out (See Chapters 5 and 11), some subcultures in the United States perform less well on typical aptitude tests than others. Does this mean they have less aptitude, or are the tests biased against them, or both? Can one build an aptitude test so that the relative positions of subcultures are reversed? Should one strive to build a test so that the mean scores for all subcultures are equal? These kinds of questions have been raised most often with a group called the culturally disadvantaged.

Psychologists have attempted to develop tests that are equally fair to members of all cultures. Examples of such tests are the *Cattell Culture Fair Intelligence Test* and the *Davis-Eells Test of General Intelligence* or *Problem Solving Ability*. In attempting to achieve this cultural fairness these tests include tasks that involve nonsense material or tasks that should be equally familiar or unfamiliar to all cultures. Figure 17-1 presents some sample items from the *Cattell Culture Fair Intelligence Test*. Oral directions are given to the subject so that even non-readers will understand the task. The content of the items do not appear to be unfair to any one culture. However, research evidence suggests that these tests are still culturally unfair in that different subgroups have different means. It seems to be almost impossible to construct a test where all the different identified subgroups obtain equal means.

And, as Anastasi (1968, p. 588) points out: "To criticize tests because they reveal cultural influences is to miss the essential nature of tests." Discrimination can be defined as either (1) making a distinction; using good judgment or (2) making a difference in treatment or favor on a basis other than individual merit.

Tests can and do help make distinctions. That is the whole purpose of testing. If there were no differences in test scores (i.e., if tests did not discriminate), they would be worthless.

If, however, a test does tend to discriminate (differentiate) between races or other subcultures and if the differential scores are not related to what we are predicting (such as on-the-job success), then the test is being used unfairly. This can (and does) occur for many reasons. For example, the test may demand knowledge that depends on having been raised in a certain cultural environment, whereas the criterion may not depend on this knowledge. Or, perhaps some subgroups do not do as well on tests, not because they do not know the material, but because they lack test-taking skills. This lack of test-taking skills may well not affect the performance on the criterion at all. Thus, it can be seen that the question of fairness of test use is really one of test validity. A test may differentiate blacks from whites and be fair (valid) for some purposes and not for others. Differentiation alone is not what makes a test unfair. (See Cleary, 1968; Darlington, 1971; Thorndike, 1971 for further discussions of this point.)

There are some who charge that college admissions tests are unfair because they are not valid predictors for culturally disadvantaged minority groups, and that the tests are biased against such students. Considerable research has been done on this topic. Anastasi, in summarizing the research up to 1968, states that: "Several studies with college admission tests have thus far yielded no evidence that such tests are biased against students with culturally disadvantaged backgrounds" (1968, p. 560). Cleary (1968), in

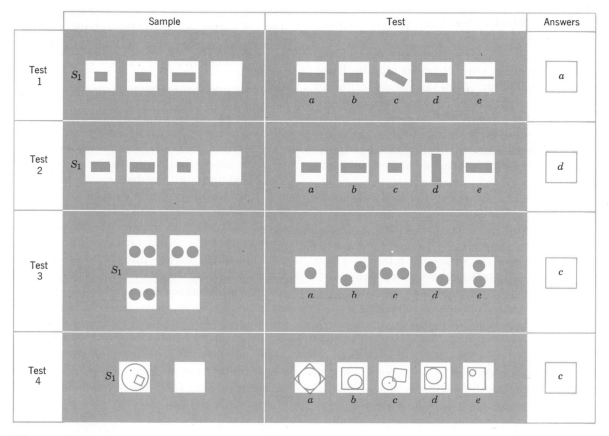

Figure 17-1.

Sample items from Scale 2, Form A of the Cattell Culture Fair Intelligence Test. *(Copyright © 1949, 1957 by the Institute for Personality and Ability Testing, 1602 Coronado Drive, Champaign, Illinois, U. S. A. All rights reserved. Reprinted with permission)*

an investigation comparing actual and predicted grades of black and white students in three integrated colleges, found that in two of the colleges there were no differences between blacks and whites in the degree to which the SAT (a scholastic aptitude test) overpredicted or underpredicted grades. However, in the third college, blacks' grades were overpredicted from SAT scores. The test was biased in favor of black students. Thomas and Stanley (1969), in a review of many studies, have found that academic aptitude scores "are often (relative to high school grades) better predictors of college grades for blacks than they are for whites" (1970, p. 217).

Judging, then, from research evidence, it seems that tests are not unfair standards for college admission, given the present criterion (grades) for success. Making decisions on the basis of objective measures is actually more fair, and results in more valid decisions, than making them on affective feelings (positive or negative) we have toward different subcultures.

Of course, the data reported in the previous studies are for present programs and the present criteria of success. The data may differ for new programs devised for students with special needs or different talents. There has been a definite move away from tests as the sole data for decisions on college admission. (Actually, very few colleges ever used such a narrow data base, although the critics would have us believe otherwise.) The broadening of the basis for college admission is probably a wise decision, but to rule out scholastic aptitude test scores as one of the variables would be unwise.

INVASION OF PRIVACY

The invasion of privacy issue as it relates to standardized tests is primarily concerned with the use of personality inventories. Since the typical classroom teacher is not apt to use such instruments, there is no need to go into detail on this topic. Many of the concerns of the public on this issue are related to the relevancy of the information gathered, the qualifications of the gatherer, the use to which the information is put, and what is done about the confidentiality (and storage) of such data. These are real and worthy concerns, and educators should not use personality inventories until they have thought through such concerns and have arrived at adequate answers.

CONCLUSIONS ABOUT PUBLIC CONCERNS

There are many concerns about testing. We maintain that in most cases the issues of concern are associated with test use instead of with psychometric properties of the tests. It is our hope that educators will become better users of tests, and that criticism due to test misuse will thereby diminish. However, we should point out that some of the negative affect of the public toward tests is precisely because tests are used as they should be, to help make decisions. In our society, decisions must be made. These decisions are not always pleasant for the people involved. Because tests help make decisions, they have been attacked. There are some people who seem to assume that by doing away with tests, we could avoid making decisions. That of course, is not the case.

Summary

1. Most educators do not adequately plan their evaluation procedures.

2. The purposes of evaluation must be clearly specified prior to evaluation.

3. In developing a specific measuring instrument the first task is to review the instructional objectives. Following this, a table of specifications or test blueprint should be constructed.

4. Paper and pencil tests are the most frequently used formal evaluation procedure.

5. Classroom tests can be classified as either essay or objective.

6. Essay tests are probably preferable for measuring such characteristics as writing ability.

7. The two most serious limitations of essay questions are their poor content sampling and their low reader reliability.

8. The most popular formats for objective questions are short answer, matching, true-false, and multiple choice.

9. A short answer item consists of a question or incomplete statement that is to be answered with a word or phrase.

10. A matching exercise consists of a list of responses that are to be matched to a list of stimuli. The chief advantage of such exercises is that they require little reading time and many questions can be asked in a small amount of time.

11. Multiple choice items are the most popular of the objective test item formats.

12. Exams should be carefully proctored so that cheating is eliminated, discouraged, and/or detected.

13. Tests should not be the only means of evaluation. They must be supplemented by other procedures such as observational techniques, rating scales, anecdotal records, and sociometric methods.

14. Classroom observations are typically too informal. Teachers should attempt to systematize their observations. The least they should do is to specify what behaviors they are to observe and determine a time schedule for such observation.

15. Rating scales are most helpful in evaluating procedures, products, and personal-social development.

16. There are several sources of error in rating scales. Errors due to ambiguity, halo effect, leniency or severity effects, and errors of central tendency are the most common.

17. Ancedotal records are recorded incidents of specific student behavior. Good records describe events, they do not evaluate them.

18. Peer appraisal can be a very good supplement in an evaluation program. In evaluating such characteristics as popularity, leadership

ability, and concern for others, fellow students are often better judges than teachers.

19. The nominating or "guess who" technique is frequently used for peer appraisal.

20. Teachers should obtain the difficulty and discrimination indices for their test items. This is helpful in selecting and revising items. The data are also useful in judging the effectiveness of instructional procedures.

21. Standardized aptitude and achievement tests are helpful in instructional, guidance, and administrative decision making. Interest, personality, and attitude inventories are used most for guidance purposes.

22. In selecting standardized tests attention must be given to one's purposes for testing as well as the psychometric characteristics of the test.

23. Reliability and validity are the two most important psychometric qualities of a standardized test.

24. Standardized achievement tests can be subclassified into survey batteries, specific subject-matter tests, and diagnostic tests.

25. Survey batteries measure pupils' knowledge in many diverse areas. They are most useful at the primary and elementary levels, where there is a fairly common core of subjects and objectives for all students.

26. Reading achievement and reading tests are the most popular specific subject-matter tests.

27. A diagnostic test is designed to assess a student's particular strengths or weaknesses within a given subject-matter area. Diagnostic tests are used most frequently in the area of reading.

28. Scholastic aptitude tests are the second most popular type of standardized test used in the school.

29. Both individual and group administered aptitude tests are available. Group tests are used far more extensively than individual tests.

30. Scholastic aptitude tests have been, and continue to be, misused. Although there are dangers and misuses of these tests, it seems wiser to try and correct misuses and minimize dangers instead of not using such tests.

31. Multifactor aptitude tests are particularly useful in counseling.

32. There are, quite appropriately, some public concerns about standardized tests. These revolve around issues such as the misuse of test scores, the fairness of tests to minority groups, and tests as an invasion of privacy.

33. Most of the public's concerns are associated with test use instead of with the psychometric properties of the test. If educators become more highly skilled in test use, public concerns should diminish.

References

Ablon, J., Rosenthal, A., and Miller, D. (1967). An overview of the mental health problems of Indian Children. (Prepared for Joint Commission on Mental Health of Children, Inc.)

Adams, J. A. (1967). *Human memory.* New York: McGraw-Hill.

Aderman, M. (1958). The effect of differential training upon the relative strength of place vs. response habits. *Journal of Comparative Physiological Psychology,* 51:372-375.

Adkins, Dorothy C., and Kuder, G. Frederic (1940). The relation of primary mental abilities to activity preference. *Psychometrika,* 5:251-262.

Adler, M. (1965). Jean Piaget, school organization and instruction. *Principal's Journal,* 6:32-51.

Ahmann, J. Stanley, and Glock, Marvin D. (1971). *Evaluating pupil growth: principles of tests and measurement (4th ed.).* Boston: Allyn & Bacon.

Albrecht, G. (1960). A survey of teacher opinions in California. *Phi Delta Kappan,* 42:103-108.

Alexander, C., and Campbell, E. (1964). Peer influences on adolescent aspirations and attainments. *American Sociological Review,* 29:568-575.

Allport, G. (1958). *The nature of prejudice.* New York: Doubleday.

Allport, G. (1955). *Becoming: Basic consideration for a psychology of personality.* New Haven, Conn.: Yale University Press.

Almy, M., Chittenden, E., and Miller, P. (1966). *Young children's thinking.* New York: Teachers College, Columbia University.

A look at problems in prenatal service programs (1966). *Currents in public health,* 5:1-4.

Alschuler, A. S., Tabor, D., and McIntyre, J. (1970). *Teaching achievement motivation.* Middletown, Conn.: Education Ventures.

Ammons, Margaret (1964). An empirical study of progress and product in curriculum development. *Journal of Educational Research,* 27(9):451-457.

Anastasi, Anne (1968). *Psychological testing (3rd ed.).* New York: Macmillan.

Anderson, R. (1959). Learning in discussions: a resume of the authoritarian—democratic studies. *Harvard Educational Review,* 29:201-215.

Anderson, R. C. (1970). Control of student mediating processes during verbal learning and instruction. *Review of Educational Research,* 40:349-369.

Anderson, R. C., and Hidde, J. L. (1971). Imagery and sentence learning. *Journal of Educational Psychology,* 62:526-530.

Anderson, R. C., and Kulhavy, R. W. (1972). Imagery and prose learning. *Journal of Educational Psychology,* 63:242-243.

Anderson, R. C., and Kulhavy, R. W. (1972). Learning concepts from definitions. *American Educational Research Journal,* 9:385-390.

Anderson, R. C., Kulhavy, R. W., and Andre, T. (1971). Feedback procedures in programmed instruction. *Journal of Educational Psychology,* 62:148-156.

Anderson, R. H. (1966). The importance and purposes of reporting. *National Elementary School Principal, 45*:6-11.

Armor, D. J. (1972). The evidence on busing. *The Public Interest, 28*:90-126.

Astin, A. W. (1968). *The college environment*. Washington, D.C.: American Council on Education.

Atkinson, J. W. (1965). The mainsprings of achievement oriented activity. In J. D. Krumboltz, ed., *Learning and the educational process*. Skokie, Ill.: Rand McNally, pp. 25-66.

Atkinson, J. W. (1953). The achievement motive and recall of interrupted and completed tasks. *Journal of Experimental Psychology, 46*:381-390.

Atkinson, R. C., and Shiffrin, R. M. (1968). Human memory: a proposed system and its cognitive processes. In K. Spence and J. Spence, eds., *The psychology of learning and motivation: Advances in research and theory*, Vol. II. New York: Academic Press.

Ausubel, D. P. (1969). Some misconceptions regarding mental health functions and practices in the school. In H. F. Clarizio, ed., *Mental health and the educative process: Selected readings*. New York: Rand McNally, p. 26.

Ausubel, D. P. (ed.) (1969). *Readings in school learning*. New York: Holt, Rinehart and Winston.

Ausubel, D. P. (1968). *Educational psychology: A cognitive view*. New York: Holt, Rinehart and Winston.

Ausubel, D. P. (1963). *The psychology of meaningful verbal learning*. New York: Grune and Stratton.

Ausubel, D. P. (1961). A new look at classroom discipline. *Phi Delta Kappan, 43*:25-30.

Ausubel, D. P. (1951). Prestige motivation of gifted children. *Genetic Psychology Monographs, 43*:53-117.

Ausubel, D. P., and Ausubel, P. (1963). Ego development among segregated Negro children. In A. H. Passow, ed., *Education in depressed areas*. New York: Teachers College Press, pp. 109-141.

Ausubel, D. P., and Robinson, F. G. (1969). *School learning, An introduction to educational psychology*. New York: Holt, Rinehart and Winston.

Ausubel, D. P., Schpoont, S. H., and Cukier, L. (1957). The influence of intention on the retention of school materials. *Journal of Educational Psychology, 48*:87-92.

Ausubel, D. P., and Sullivan, E. (1970). *Theory and problems of child development* (2nd ed.). New York: Grune and Stratton.

Ausubel, D. P., and Youssef, M. (1963). The role of discriminability in meaningful parallel learning. *Journal of Educational Psychology, 54*:331-336.

Baer, C. J. (1958). The school progress of underage and overage students. *Journal of Educational Psychology, 49*:17-19.

Baer, D. (1971). Let's take another look at punishment. *Psychology Today, 5*(5):32-34, 36-37, 111.

Bahn, A., Chandler, C. A., and Eisenberg, L. (1962). Diagnostic characteristics related to services in psychiatric clinics for children. *Milbank Memorial Fund Quarterly*, pp. 289-318.

Balzer, L. (1970). Teacher behaviors and student inquiry in biology. *American Biology Teacher, 32*:27-28.

Balzer, L. (1969). Nonverbal and verbal behaviors of biology teachers. *American Biology Teacher, 31*:226-229.

Bandura, A. (1969). *Principles of behavior modification*. New York: Holt, Rinehart and Winston.

Bandura, A. (1969). Social-learning theory of identificatory processes. In D. A. Goslin, ed., *Handbook of socialization theory and research*. Chicago: Rand McNally.

Bandura, A., and Walters, R. H. (1959). *Adolescent aggression*. New York: Ronald Press.

Barbe, W. B. (1967). Identification and diagnosis of the needs of the educationally retarded and disadvantaged. In P. A. Witty, ed., *The educationally retarded and disadvantaged*. National Society for the Study of Education Yearbook. Chicago: University of Chicago Press, Part I, p. 106.

Barbe, W. B., and Frierson, E. C. (1967). Analysis of topics in selected comprehensive bibliographies. In P. A. Witty, ed., *The educationally retarded and disadvantaged*. The Sixty-Sixth Yearbook of the National Society for the Study of Education. Chicago: University of Chicago Press, pp. 363-373.

Barber, T., Calverley, D., Forgione, A., McPeake, J., and Chavez, J. (1969). Five attempts to replicate the experimenter bias effect. *Journal of Consulting Psychology, 33*:1-6.

Barker, R., and Gump, P. (1964). *Big school, small school: High school size and student behavior*. Stanford, Calif.: Stanford University Press.

Barnwell, A., and Sechrest, L. (1965). Vicarious reinforcement in children at two age levels. *Journal of Educational Psychology, 56*:100-106.

Barro, S. M. (1970). An approach to developing accountability measures for the public schools. *Phi Delta Kappan, 52*(4):196-205.

Bartlett, F. C. (1932). *Remembering*. Cambridge University Press.

Bayley, N. (1949). Consistency and variability in the growth of intelligence from birth to eighteen years. *Journal of Genetic Psychology, 75*:165-196.

Becker. W. C. (1964). Consequences of different kinds of parental discipline. In M. L. Hoffman and L. W. Hoffman, eds., *Review of child development research*, Vol. I. New York: Russell Sage Foundation, pp. 169-208.

Becker, W. C., Engelmann, S., and Thomas, D. R. (1971). *Teaching: A course in applied psychology*. Chicago: Science Research Associates.

Bedoian, U. H. (1954). Social acceptability and social rejection of underage, at-age, and overage pupils in the sixth grade. *Journal of Educational Research, 47*:513-520.

Benton, A. (1967). Effects of the timing of negative response consequences on the observational learning of resistance to temptation in children. *Dissertation Abstracts, 27*:2153-2154.

Bentzen, F. (1963). Sex ratios in learning and behavior disorders. *American Journal of Orthopsychiatry, 33*:93-98.

Berlyne, D. E. (1966). Curiosity and exploration. *Science, 153*:25-33.

Berlyne, D. E. (1960). *Conflict, Arousal and Curiosity*. New York: McGraw-Hill.

Berlyne, D. E. (1954). A theory of human curiosity. *British Journal of Psychology, 45*:180-191.

Bernstein, B. (1964). "Social Class Speech Systems and Psychotherapy." In F. Riessman, J. Cohen, and A. Pearl, eds., *Mental health of the poor.*

Glencoe, Ill.: Free Press of Glencoe.

Bernstein, E. (1968). What does a Summerhill old school tie look like? *Psychology Today, 2*(5):37-70.

Bickel, A. M. (1967). Skelly Wright's sweeping decision. *New Republic, 157,* 11-12.

Biehler, R. F. (1971). *Psychology applied to teaching.* Boston: Houghton-Mifflin.

Biggs, J. B., and Lyman, J. (1971). *Information and human learning.* Glenview, Ill.: Scott, Foresman.

Binet, A., and Simon, T. (1916). *The development of intelligence in children.* Vineland, N.J.: Training School Publication #11, p. 192.

Biological Sciences Curriculum Study (1965), Joseph J. Schwab, Supervisor, *Biology Teacher's Handbook.* New York: Wiley.

Birch, H. G., and Rabinowitz, H. S. (1951). The negative effect of previous experience on productive thinking. *Journal of Experimental Psychology, 41*:121-125.

Black, Hillel (1963). *They shall not pass.* New York: Morrow.

Block, J. H., ed. (1971). *Mastery learning: Theory and practice.* New York: Holt, Rinehart and Winston, 152 pp.

Bloom, B. S. (1971). Mastery learning and its implications for curriculum development. Chapter 1 in Elliot W. Eisner, ed., *Confronting curriculum reform.* Boston: Little, Brown.

Bloom, B. S. (1968). Learning for mastery. *Evaluation Comment,* Vol. 1, No. 2. Los Angeles: Center for the Study of the Evaluation of Instructional Programs, University of California.

Bloom, B. S. (1966). Twenty-five years of educational research. *American Educational Research Journal, 3*:211-221.

Bloom, B. S. (1964). *Stability and change in human characteristics.* New York: Wiley, pp. 210 and 215.

Bloom, B. S., ed. (1956). *Taxonomy of educational objectives. Handbook I. The cognitive domain.* New York: David McKay.

Bloom, B. S., Englehardt, M. D., Furst, E. J., and Krathwohl, D. R. (1956). *A taxonomy of educational objectives: Handbook I. The cognitive domain.* New York: Longmans, Green.

Bloom, B. S., Hastings, J. T., Madaus, G. F. (1971). *Handbook in formative and summative evaluation of student learning.* New York: McGraw-Hill.

Boesel, F. F. (1960). *Effects of nonpromotion on reading achievement and behavior problem tendencies in the primary grades.* Unpublished doctoral dissertation, University of Michigan.

Bolner, J., and Vedlitz, A. (1971). The affinity of Negro pupils for segregated schools: Obstacle to desegregation. *Journal of Negro Education, 40*:313-321.

Borg, Walter R. (1964). *An evaluation of ability grouping.* U.S. Department of Health, Education, and Welfare. Office of Education, Cooperative Research Project No. 577, Logan: Utah State University, 441 pp.

Bourne, L. E., and Haygood, R. C. (1960). Effects of intermittent reinforcement of an irrelevant dimension and task complexity upon concept identification. *Journal of Experimental Psychology, 60*:371-375.

Bourne, L. E., and Pendleton, R. (1958). Concept identification as a function of completeness and probability of information feedback. *Journal of Experimental Psychology, 56*:413-420.

Bower, E. M. (1970). Mental Health. In R. Ebel, ed., *Encyclopedia of educational research* (4th ed.). New York: Macmillan, pp. 811-828.

Bower, E. M. (1961). *The education of emotionally handicapped children.* Sacramento: California State Department of Education.

Brenner, A. (1967). Readiness for school and today's pressures. In the *12th Interinstitutional seminar in child development.* Waldenwoods Conference Center. Edison Institute.

Briggs, L. J. (1970). *Handbook of procedures for the design of instruction.* Pittsburgh: American Institutes for Research.

Briggs, L. J. (1968). *Sequencing of instruction in relation to hierarchies of competence.* Pittsburgh: American Institutes for Research.

Bronfenbrenner, U. (1970). *Two worlds of childhood.* New York: Russell Sage Foundation.

Bronfenbrenner, U. (1972) Childhood: The roots of alienation. *National Elementary Principal, LII*(2):23-29.

Brophy, J., and Good, T. (1973). Feminization of American elementary schools. *Phi Delta Kappan, LIV*(8):564-566.

Brown, B. F. (1963). The non-graded high school. *Phi Delta Kappan, 44*:206-209.

Brownell, W. A. (1960). Observations of instruction in lower-grade arithmetic in English and Scottish schools. *Arithmetic Teacher, 7*:165-177.

Brumbaugh, F. M. (1955). Our youngest intellectuals thirteen years later. *Exceptional Children, 21*:168-170.

Bruner, J. S. (1966). *Toward a theory of instruction.* Cambridge, Mass.: Belknap Press of Harvard University Press.

Bruner, J. S. (1960). *The process of education.* Cambridge, Mass.: Harvard University Press.

Bruner, J. S., Goodnow, J. J., and Austin, G. A. (1956). *A study of thinking.* New York: John Wiley.

Bryan, G. L., and Rigney, J. W. (1956). An evaluation of a method for shipboard training in operations knowledge, *Technical Report No. 18.* Los Angeles: Department of Psychology, University of Southern California.

Bryan, J. A., and Locke, E. A. (1967). Goal setting as a means of increasing motivation. *Journal of Applied Psychology, 51*:274-277.

Bryan, J. H. and Schwartz, T. (1971). Effects of film material upon children's behavior. *Psychological Bulletin, 75,* pp. 50-59.

Bugelski, B. R. (1964). *Psychology of learning applied to teaching.* Indianapolis, Ind.: Bobbs-Merrill.

Burke, N. S., and Simons, A. E. (1965). Factors which precipitate dropouts and delinquency. *Federal Probation, 29*:28-32.

Burns, R. A. (1972). *New approaches to behavioral objectives.* Dubuque, Iowa: William C. Brown.

Buros, O. K., ed. (1972). *The seventh mental measurements yearbook.* Highland Park, N.J.: Gryphon Press.

Burt, C. E. (1958). The inheritance of mental ability. *American Psychologist, 13*:1-15.

Burtt, H. E. (1941). An experimental study of early childhood memory. *Journal of General Psychology*, 58:435-439.

Burwen, L. S. (1971). Current practices: a national survey. Paper presented at the annual meeting of the American Educational Research Association, New York.

Calfe, R. C. (1970). Information-processing models and curriculum design. *Educational Technology*, 10:30-38.

Campbell, C. M. (1967). Community programs and adult education. In P. A. Witty, ed., *The educationally retarded and disadvantaged*. The Sixty-Sixth Yearbook of the National Society for the Study of Education. Chicago, Ill.: University of Chicago Press, pp. 260-277.

Campbell, R. E. (1971). Accountability and stone soup. *Phi Delta Kappan*, 53(3):176-178.

Carmichael, L., Hogan, H. P., and Walter, A. A. (1932). An experimental study of the effect of language on the reproduction of visually perceived forms. *Journal of Experimental Psychology*, 15:73-80.

Carroll, J. B. (1971). Problems of Measurement Related to the Concept of Learning for Mastery. Chapter 3 in James H. Block, ed., *Mastery learning: Theory and practice*. New York: Holt, Rinehart and Winston, p. 152.

Carroll, J. B. (1967). Instructional methods and individual differences. Pp. 40-44 in Robert M. Gagne, ed., *Learning and individual differences*. Columbus, Ohio: Merrill.

Carroll, J. B. (1964). Words, meanings and concepts. *Harvard Educational Review*, 24:178-202.

Carroll, J. B. (1963). A model for school learning. *Teachers College Record*, 64:723-733.

Carroll, L. (1916). *Alice's adventures in wonderland*. Chicago: Rand McNally.

Cartwright, W. J., and Burtis, T. R. (1970). Race and Intelligence: Changing opinions in social science. In J. L. Frost and G. R. Hawkes, eds., *The disadvantaged child* (2nd ed.). Boston: Houghton Mifflin, pp. 125-138.

Cellura, A. R. (1969). The application of psychological theory in educational settings: an overview. *American Educational Research Journal*, 6:349-382.

Chansky, N. M. (1960). Learning: A function of schedule and type of feedback. *Psychological Reports*, 7:362.

Charlesworth, R., and Hartup, W. W. (1967). Positive social reinforcement in the nursery school peer group. *Child Development*, 38:993-1002.

Chilman, C. (1966). *Growing up poor*. U.S. Dept. of Health, Education and Welfare. Washington, D.C.: Government Printing Office.

Chittenden, G. (1942). An experimental study in measuring and modifying assertive behavior in young children. *Monographs of the Society for Research in Child Development*, 7, 1, No. 31.

Citizens' board of inquiry into hunger and malnutrition in the United States. (1968). *Hunger, U.S.A.* Washington: New Community Press, pp. 85-86.

Clarizio, H. F., Craig, R. C., and Mehrens, W. A., eds., (1974). *Contemporary issues in educational psychology* (2nd ed.). Boston: Allyn & Bacon.

Clark, D. C. (1971). Teaching concepts in the classroom: a set of teaching prescriptions derived from experimental research. *Journal of Educational*

Psychology, 62:253-278.

Clark, K. (1963). *Prejudice and your child*, (2nd ed.). Boston: Beacon Press.

Clark, K. B. (1965). *Dark ghetto: Dilemmas of social power*. New York: Harper and Row, p. 131.

Clark, P. M. (1970). Psychology, education and the concept of motivation. *Theory into practice*, 1:16-22.

Cleary, T. A. (1968). Test bias: Prediction of grades for Negro and white students in integrated colleges. *Journal of Educational Measurement*, 5:115-124.

Coffman, William E. "Essay Examinations." In R. L. Thorndike (ed.), *Educational Measurement*. Washington, D.C.: American Council on Education, 1971.

Cogan, M. L. (1958). The behavior of teachers and the productive behavior of their pupils. *Journal of Experimental Education*, 27:89-124.

Cohen, A. R. (1964). *Attitude change and social influence*. New York: Basic Books.

Cole, M., and Bruner, J. (1972). Preliminaries to a theory of cultural differences. In I. Gordon, ed., *Early childhood education. The Seventy-First Yearbook of the National Society for the Study of Education*, Part II. Chicago: University of Chicago Press, pp. 161-180.

Coleman, J. (1961). *The adolescent society*. Glencoe, Ill.: The Free Press.

Coleman, J. S., et al. (1966). *Equality of educational opportunity*. Washington, D.C.: U.S. Government Printing Office.

Combs, A. W., and Snygg, D. (1959). *Individual behavior: A perceptual approach to behavior*. New York: Harper.

Commission on the Reorganization of Secondary Education (1918). The seven cardinal principles of secondary education. Washington, D.C.: Bureau of Education, Government Printing Office.

Committee on Agriculture, House of Representatives (1968). *Hunger study*. Washington, D.C.: U.S. Government Printing Office, p. 1.

Conant, James B. (1959). *The American high school today*. New York: McGraw-Hill.

Cook, Desmond L. (1955). An investigation of three aspects of free-response and choice-type tests at the college level. *Dissertation Abstracts*, 15:1351.

Cook, Walter W. (1941). *Grouping and promotion in the elementary schools*. Series on Individualization of Instruction, No. 2, Minneapolis: University of Minnesota Press.

Cook, W. W., and Clymer, T. (1962). Acceleration and retardation. Chapter XI in *Individualizing Instruction. The Sixty-First Yearbook of the National Society for the Study of Education*, Part 1. Chicago: NSSE.

Cormany, R. B. (1970). Returning special education students to regular classes. *The Personnel and Guidance Journal*, 48(8):641-646.

Cormier, W. H. (1970). Effects of approving teaching behavior on classroom behavior of disadvantaged adolescents. University of Tennessee, Department of Educational Psychology and Guidance. Project No. 9-D-017, Grant No. 520017-0029-057 USOE Bureau of Research.

Corsini, R. J., and Howard, D. D., eds., (1964). *Critical incidents in teaching*. Englewood Cliffs, N.J.: Prentice-Hall.

Craig, R. C. (1969). Recent research on discovery. *Educational Leadership*, 26:501-505.

Craig, R. C. (1968). Psychological theories and classroom learning. In V. H. Noll and R. P. Noll, eds., *Readings in educational psychology* (2nd ed.). New York: Macmillan, pp. 171-183.

Craig, R. C. (1966). *The psychology of learning in the classroom.* New York: Macmillan.

Craig, R. C., and Holsbach, Sr., M. (February 1964). Utilizing existing interests to develop others in general science classes. *School, science and mathematics*, pp. 120-127.

Cram, D. (1961). *Explaining "teaching machines" and programming.* San Francisco: Fearon.

Crockenberg, S. B. (1972). Creativity tests: A boon or boondoggle for education. *Review of Educational Research*, 42:27-45.

Cromer, W. (1969). An empirical investigation of student attitudes toward the pass-fail grading system of Wellesley College. Philadelphia: Paper presented at Eastern Psychological Association.

Cronbach, L. J. (1971). Comments on mastery learning and its implications for curriculum development. Pp. 49-55 in Elliot W. Eisner, ed. *Confronting Curriculum Reform.* Boston: Little Brown.

Cronbach, L. J. (1969). Heredity, environment and educational policy. *In environment, heredity and intelligence.* Harvard Educational Review, Reprint Series No. 2.

Cronbach, L. J. (1967). How can instruction be adapted to individual differences? Chapter 2 in Robert M. Gagne, ed., *Learning and individual differences*, Columbus, Ohio: Merrill.

Cronbach, L. J. (1963). Course improvement through evaluation. *Teacher's College Record*, 64:672-683.

Cronbach, L. J., and Meehl, P. E. (1955). Construct validity in psychological tests. *Psychological Bulletin*, 52:281-302.

Cronbach, L. J., and Warrington, W. G. (1952). Efficiency of multiple-choice tests as a function of spread of item difficulties. *Psychometrika*, 17:127-147.

Crosby, M. (1967). Elementary-school programs for the education of the disadvantaged. In P. A. Witty, ed., *The educationally retarded and disadvantaged. The Sixty-Sixth Yearbook of the National Society for the Study of Education.* Chicago, Ill.: University of Chicago Press, pp. 168-183.

Crovitz, H. F. (1970). *Galton's walk: Methods for the analysis of thinking, intelligence and creativity.* New York: Harper & Row.

Cunningham, D. J. (1972). Retention of connected discourse. *Review of Educational Research*, 42:47-71.

Cunnington, B. F., and Torrance, E. P. (1965). *Imagi/Craft.* Boston: Ginn.

Dale, W. (1969). Concerning grading and other forms of student evaluation. Washington: Paper presented at the Council of Graduate Schools in the United States, ED 036 260.

Darlington, R. B. (1971). Another look at cultural fairness. *Journal of Educational Measurement*, 8(2):71-82.

Davis, F. B. (1964). *Educational Measurements and their Interpretation.* Belmont, Calif.: Wadsworth Publishing.

Davis, G. A., and Houtman, S. W. (1968). *Thinking creatively: A guide to training imagination.* Madison, Wisc.: Wisconsin Research and Development Center for Cognitive Learning.

Davis, R. H., Alexander, L. T., and Yelon, S. L. (1974). *Learning system design.* (Prepublication edition). East Lansing: Michigan State University. New York: McGraw-Hill, 1974.

DeCecco, J. P. (1972). High schools: Decision making in a democracy. In J. P. DeCecco, ed., *The regeneration of the school,* Holt, Rinehart and Winston, pp. 229-235.

DeCecco, J. P. (1968). *The psychology of learning and instruction: Educational psychology.* Englewood Cliffs, N.J.: Prentice-Hall.

Deese, J. (1969). Behavior and fact. *American Psychologist, 24:*515-522.

Dennis, W. (1941). Infant development under conditions of restricted practice and of minimal social stimulation. *Genetic Psychological Monographs, 23:*143-189.

Dennis, W. (1940). *The Hopi child.* New York: Appleton-Century Crofts.

Derr, Richard L. (1973). *A taxonomy of social purposes of public schools: A handbook.* New York: McKay.

Deterline, W. A. (1971). Applied Accountability. *Educational technology, 11*(1):15-20.

Deutsch, M. (1960). Minority group and class status as related to social and personality factors in scholastic achievement. P. 3. Ithaca, New York: Society for Applied Anthropology.

Dewey, J. (1929). *Sources of a science of education.* New York: Liveright, pp. 13-14.

Dewey, J. (1910). *How we think.* Boston: D. C. Heath.

Dickie, J. P. (1968). Effectiveness of structured and unstructured (traditional) methods of language training. In M. A. Brottman, ed., *Language remediation for the disadvantaged preschool child.* Monographs of the Society for Research in Child Development, *33*(8):62-79.

Diederick, P. B. (1967). Cooperative preparation and rating of essay tests. *English Journal, 56:*573-584.

Dienes, Z. P. (1964). Insight into arithmetical processes. *School Review, 72:*183-200.

Dobson, R. L. (1967). The perception and treatment by teachers of the behavioral problems of elementary school children in culturally deprived and middle class neighborhoods. Doctoral thesis, University of Oklahoma, 1966. Dissertation Abstracts, 27, 1702 A-03 A, No. 6.

Dolbear, A. E. (1908). Antediluvian education. *Journal of Education, 68:*424.

Douglas, J. H. (1959). The extent and characteristics of juvenile delinquency in the United States. *Journal of Negro Education, 28:*214-229.

Downs, A. (1968). Competition and Community Schools. Mimeograph.

Drews, E. M. (1961). *The effectiveness of homogeneous and heterogeneous ability grouping in the 9th grade english classes with slow, average, and superior students, including the investigation of attitudes, self-concept, and critical thinking.* Michigan State University. Mimeographed.

Duncan, C. P. (1959). Recent research on human problem solving. *Psychological Bulletin, 56:*397-429.

Dunlap, J. M. (January 1955). Gifted children in an enriched program. *Ex-*

ceptional Children, 21:135-137.

Dunn, L. M. (September 1968). Special education for the mildly retarded — is much of it justifiable? *Exceptional Children*, 5-22.

Dunnette, M. D. (1966). Fads, fashions, and folderol in psychology. *American Psychologist*, 21:343-352.

Dunnette, M. D., Campbell, J., and Jaastad, K. (1963). The effect of group participation on brainstorming effectiveness for two industrial samples. *Journal of Applied Psychology*, 47:30-37.

Durr, W. K. (1964). *The gifted student*. New York: Oxford University Press.

Durrett, M. E., and Davy, A. (1970). Racial awareness in young Mexican-American, Negro and Anglo Children. *Young Children*, 26:16-24.

Dyer, H. S. (1970). Toward objective criteria of professional accountability in the schools of New York City. *Phi Delta Kappan*, 52(4):206-211.

Dyer, H. S. (1967). The discovery and development of educational goals. *Proceedings of the 1966 Invitational Conference on Testing Problems*. Princeton, N.J.: Educational Testing Service, pp. 12-24.

Ebbinghaus, G. H. (1913). *Memory, 1885*. (Translated by H. A. Ruger and C. E. Bussenius.) New York: Teachers College, Columbia University.

Ebbinghaus, H. (1913). Memory: a contribution to experimental psychology. (Translated by H. A. Ruger.) New York: Teachers College, Columbia University.

Ebel, R. L. (1972). *Essentials of educational measurement*. Englewood Cliffs, N.J.: Prentice-Hall.

Ebel, R. L. (May 1970). Curriculum and achievement testing. *Educational Technology*, 10(5):22-23.

Ebel, R. L. (1969). Relation of scale fineness to grade accuracy. *Journal of Educational Measurement*, 6:217-221, (b).

Ebel, R. L. (1969). The relation between curricula and achievement testing. Michigan State University: Mimeograph, (a).

Ebel, R. L. (1962). Content standard test scores. *Educational and Psychological Measurement*, 22:15-25.

Edling, J. V. *Individualized instruction*. PREP Kit No. 16. National Center for Educational Communication. Office of Education.

Edwards, A. L. (1941). Political frames of reference as a factor influencing recognition. *Journal of Abnormal Social Psychology*, 36:34-50.

Edwards, M. D., and Tyler, L. E. (1965). Intelligence, creativity and achievement in a nonselective public junior high school. *Journal of Educational Psychology*, 56:96-99.

Eichenwald, H. F., and Fry, P. C. (1969). Nutrition and learning. *Science*, 163:644-648.

Eisenberg, L. (1957). The course of childhood schizophrenia. *Archives of Neurology and Psychiatry*, 78:69-83.

Eisner, E. W. (1969). Instructional and expressure educational objectives: Their formulation and use in curriculum. In W. James Popam, et al., eds., *Instructional objectives*. Chicago: Rand McNally, pp. 1-18.

Eisner, E. W. (1964). Instruction, teaching, and learning: An attempt at differentiation. *Elementary School Journal*, 65:115-119.

Ekstrom, R. B. (April 1959). *Experimental studies of homogeneous grouping*. Princeton, N.J.: Educational Testing Service, p. 26.

Elkind, D. (1971). Early childhood education. *The National Elementary Principal*, 51:48-55.

Elkind, D. (1970). *Children and adolescents.* New York: Oxford University Press.

Elkind, D. (1969). Preschool education—enrichment or instruction? *Childhood Education*, 45:321-328.

Elkind, D. (May 26 1968). Giant in the nursery—Jean Piaget. *New York Times Magazine*, pp. 25-80.

Ellinger, B. D. (1965). Nonpromotions: A review essay. *Theory into Practice*. 4:122-128.

Ellis, H. D. (1972). *Fundamentals of human learning and cognition.* Dubuque, Iowa: William C. Brown.

Engelhart, M. D. (1965). A comparison of several item discrimination indices. *Journal of Educational Measurement*, 2:69-76.

Engelmann, S., and Engelmann, T. (1968). *Give your child a superior mind.* New York: Simon and Schuster.

Entwisle, D., and Higgins, W. (1964). Interference in meaningful learning. *Journal of Educational Psychology*, 55:75-78.

Eron, L., Banta, T., Walder, L., and Laulicht, J. (1961). Comparison of data obtained from fathers and mothers on childrearing practices and their relations to child aggression. *Child Development*, 32:457-472.

Estes, W. K. (1950). Toward a statistical theory of learning. *Psychological Review*, 42:94-107.

Evans, E. D. (1971). *Contemporary influences in early childhood education.* New York: Holt, Rinehart and Winston.

Falls, J. D. (1928). Research in secondary education. *Kentucky School Journal*, 6:42-46.

Farb, P. (1970). The American Indian: A portrait in limbo. In J. L. Frost and G. R. Hawkes, eds., *The disadvantaged child.* Boston: Houghton Mifflin, (2nd ed.), pp. 39-46.

Featherstone, J. (September 11, 1971). Open schools—the British and Us. *The New Republic*, 165, (a).

Featherstone, J. (September 25, 1971). Open schools—Tempering a Fad. *The New Republic*, 165, (b).

Federal Programs Assisting Children and Youth (1968). Department of Health, Education and Welfare, Social and Rehabilitation Service, Children's Bureau, Inter-departmental Committee on Children and Youth. Washington, D.C.: Government Printing Office.

Feldmesser, R. A. (1971). The positive function of grades. Paper presented at the annual meeting of the American Educational Research Association, New York.

Feldmesser, R. A. (1969). *The option: Analysis of an educational innovation.* Hanover, N.H.: Dartmouth College.

Ferguson, F. R. (1970). Dependency motivation in socialization. In R. Hoppe, et al., eds., *Early experiences and the processes of socialization.* New York: Academic Press.

Ferster, C. S., and Skinner, B. F. (1957). *Schedules of reinforcement.* New York: Appleton-Century Crofts.

Festinger, L. (1957). *A Theory of Cognitive Dissonance.* Evanston, Ill.: Row,

Peterson.

Fiedler, F. E. (1967). The effect of inter-group competition on group member adjustment. *Personnel Psychology*, *20*(1):33-44.

Findley, W. G., and Bryan, M. M. (1971). *Ability grouping: 1970, status, impact, and alternatives.* University of Georgia, Athens: Center for Educational Improvement.

Flanagan, J. C. (January 1971). The PLAN system for individualizing education. *Measurement in Education*, *2*:2.

Flanagan, J. C., Shanner, W. M., and Mager, R. (1971). *Behavioral objectives: A guide for individualizing learning.* New York: Westinghouse Learning Press.

Flanagan, J. C., et al. (1964). *The American high school student.* Pittsburg: University of Pittsburg Press.

Flanders, J. P. (1968). A review of research on imitative behavior. *Psychological Bulletin*, *69*, pp. 316-337.

Flescher, I. (1963). Anxiety and achievement of intellectually and creatively gifted children. *Journal of Psychology*, *56*:251-268.

Fowler, H., Jr. (1965). *Curiosity and exploratory behavior.* New York: Macmillan.

Fowler, W. (1962). Teaching a two-year-old to read: An experiment in early childhood learning. *Genetic Psychological Monograph*, *66*:181-283 (b).

Fox, D. (1967). The more effective schools. *Evaluation of New York City Title I Educational Projects 1966-67.* New York: Center for Urban Education, September.

Fox, L. (1962). Effecting the use of efficient study habits. *Journal of Mathetics*, *1*:75-86.

Fraenkel, J. R. (1969). Value education in the social studies. *Phi Delta Kappan*, *50*:457-461.

Frase, L. T. (1970). Boundary conditions for mathemagenic behaviors. *Review of Educational Research*, *40*:337-347.

French, J. L., ed. (1964). *Educating the gifted* (2nd ed.). New York: Holt, Rinehart and Winston.

French, J. W., and Michael, W. B. (1966). *Standards for educational and psychological tests and manuals.* Washington, D.C.: American Psychological Association.

French, J., and Associates (1957). *Behavioral goals of general education in high school.* New York: The Russell Sage Foundation.

Freud, S. (1953). *A general introduction to psychoanalysis.* New York: Permabooks.

Friedman, N. L. (August 1967). Cultural deprivation: a commentary in the sociology of knowledge. *Journal of Educational Thought*. *1*:88-89.

Frierson, E. C. (1969). The Gifted. *Review of Educational Research*, *39*(1):25-37.

Frost, J. L., and Hawkes, G. H. (1970). *The disadvantaged child* (2nd ed.). Boston: Houghton Mifflin.

Frost, J., and Hawkes, G. (1966). *The disadvantaged child.* Geneva, Ill.: Houghton Mifflin.

Frost, J. L., and Payne, B. L. (1970). Hunger in America: scope and consequences. In J. L. Frost and G. R. Hawkes, eds., *The disadvantaged child—*

Issues and innovations (2nd ed.). Boston: Houghton Mifflin, 70-83.

Frymier, J. R. (1960). Motivation, the mainspring and gyroscope of learning. *Theory into Practice, 9*(1):23-32.

Furneaux, W. D. (1962). The psychologist and the university. *University Quarterly, 17*:33-47.

Furth, H. (1970). *Piaget for teachers.* Englewood Cliffs, N.J.: Prentice-Hall.

Gage, N. L. (1964). Theories of teaching. In *Theories of learning and instruction,* E. R. Hilgard, ed., Part 1 of the 63rd Yearbook of the National Society for the Study of Education, pp. 268-85, Chicago: University of Chicago Press.

Gagne, R. M. (1973). Learning and instructional sequence. In F. N. Kerlinger, ed., *Review of research in education I.* Itasca, Ill.: F. E. Peacock, pp. 3-33.

Gagne, R. M. (1971). Instruction based on research in learning. *Engineering Education, 61*:519-523.

Gagne, R. M. (1970). *The conditions of learning* (2nd ed.). New York: Holt, Rinehart and Winston.

Gagne, R. M. (1968). Learning hierarchies. *Educational Psychologist, 6*:1-9.

Gagne, R. M. (1967). *Learning and individual differences.* Columbus, Ohio: Charles E. Merrill.

Gagne, R. M. (1966). The learning of principles. In H. J. Klausmeier and C. W. Harris, eds., *Analyses of concept learning.* New York: Academic Press, pp. 81-95.

Gagne, R. M. (1962). The acquisition of knowledge. *Psychological Review, 69*:355-365.

Gagne, R. M., et al. (1965). Some factors in learning non-metric geometry. *Monographs of the Society for Research in Child Development, 30*(1):42-49.

Gagne, R. M., and Bassler, O. C. (1963). Study of retention of some topics of elementary non-metric geometry. *Journal of Educational Psychology, 54*:123-131.

Gagne, R. M., and Brown, L. T. (1961). Some factors in the programming of conceptual learning. *Journal of Experimental Psychology, 62*:12-18.

Gall, M. (April 1967). They learn more than you teach them. *Grade Teacher Magazine, 84*:105-106.

Gallagher, J. J. (1969). Gifted children. In Robert L. Ebel, ed., *Encyclopedia of educational research,* (4th ed.). Toronto: Macmillan, pp. 537-542.

Gallagher, J. J. (1960). *Analysis of research on the education of gifted children.* Springfield, Ill.: Office of the Supt. of Public Instruction, pp. 107-114.

Garai, J., and Scheinfeld, A. (May 1968). Sex differences in mental and behavioral traits. *Genetic Psychology Monographs, 77*, Second Half, pp. 227-279.

Gardner, J. W. (1961). *Excellence: Can we be equal and excellent too?* New York: Harper.

Garry, R., and Kingsley, H. L. (1970). *The nature and conditions of learning* (3rd ed.). Englewood Cliffs, N.J.: Prentice-Hall.

Gates, A. I., and Taylor, G. A. (1925). An experimental study of the nature of improvement resulting from practice on a mental function. *Journal of Educational Psychology, 16*:583-592.

Getzels, J. W. (1969). A social psychology of education. In E. Lindzey and E.

Aronson, eds., *The handbook of social psychology*, Vol. 5. Reading, Mass.: Addison—Wesley, pp. 459-537.

Getzels, J. W., and Jackson, P. W. (1962). *Creativity and intelligence: Explorations with gifted students.* New York: Wiley.

Gibson, E. J. (1941). Retroactive inhibition as a function of degree of generalization between tasks. *Journal of Experimental Psychology,* 28:93-115.

Gilmore, J. V. (1968). The factor of attention in underachievement. *Journal of Education,* 150:41-66.

Ginsburg, H. (1972) *The Myth of the Deprived Child.* Englewood Cliffs, N.J.: Prentice-Hall.

Ginsburg, H., and Opper, S. (1969). *Piaget's theory of intellectual development.* Englewood Cliffs, N.J.: Prentice-Hall.

Gittelman, M. (1965). Behavior rehearsal as a technique in child treatment. *Journal of Child Psychology and Psychiatry,* 6:251-255.

Glaser, R. (1969). Learning. In R. L. Ebel, ed., *Encyclopedia of educational research* (4th ed.). New York: Macmillan, pp. 706-727.

Glaser, R. (1968). Adapting the elementary school curriculum to individual performance. *Proceedings of the 1967 Invitational Conference on Testing Problems.* Princeton: Educational Testing Service.

Glaser, R. (1968). Concept learning and concept teaching. In R. M. Gagne and W. J. Gephart, eds., *Learning research and school subjects.* Itasca, Ill.: F. E. Peacock, pp. 1-36.

Glaser, R. (1962). Psychology and instructional technology. In R. Glaser, ed., *Training, Research and Education.* Pittsburgh: University of Pittsburgh Press, pp. 1-30.

Glaser, Robert and Anthony J. Nitko. "Measurement in Learning and Instruction." In Robert L. Thorndike (ed.) *Educational Measurement (2nd ed.).* Washington D.C.: American Council on Education, 1971.

Glass, G. V. (1968). Educational piltdown men. *Phi Delta Kappan,* 50:148-151.

Glasser, W. (1961). *Mental health or mental illness?* New York: Harper.

Glidewell, J., and Swallow, C. (1968). *The prevalence of maladjustment in elementary schools.* Chicago: University of Chicago Press.

Glidewell, J., Kantor, M., Smith, L., and Stringer, L. (1966). Socialization and social structure in the classroom. In L. Hoffman and M. Hoffman, eds., *Review of child development research,* Vol. 2. New York: Russell Sage Foundation, pp. 221-256.

Glover, L. E. (1965). *A review and summary of the literature on pupil retention and promotion.* Research Report No. 2, Los Angeles County Supt. of Schools, Division of Research and Guidance. January, 31 pp. Mimeograph.

Glueck, S., and Glueck, E. (1950). *Unraveling juvenile delinquency.* Cambridge: Harvard University Press.

Godshalk, F. I., Swineford, F., and Coffman, W. E. (1966). *The measurement of writing ability.* New York: College Entrance Examination Board.

Goens, B. (1969). The effects of teaching a physically aggressive child operant techniques. *School Applications of Learning Theory,* 1:17-21.

Goldberg, M. L. (1970). Issues in the education of the disadvantaged. In J. R. Davitz and S. Ball, eds., *Psychology of the educational process.* New York: McGraw-Hill, pp. 260-298.

Goldman, M. (1965). A comparison of individual and group performance for varying combinations of initial ability. *Journal of Personal & Social Psychology*, 1:210-216.

Goodlad, J. I. (1955). Ungrading the elementary grades. *NEA Journal*, 44:170-171.

Goodlad, J. I. (November 1952). Research and theory regarding promotion and nonpromotion. *Elementary School Journal*, 53:150-155.

Goodlad, J. I., and Anderson, R. H. (1960). *The Non-Graded Elementary School*. New York: Harcourt.

Goodman, M. E. (1964). *Race awareness in young children* (2nd ed.). New York: Collier Books.

Gordon, I. J. (1969). Early child stimulation through parent education. Report of Research. PHS-R-306, PHS-R-306 (1)m.

Goslin, D. A. (1967). *Teachers and testing*. New York: Russell Sage Foundation.

Gosling, G. W. H. (1966). *Marking english compositions*. Victoria, Australia: Australian Council for Educational Research.

Gossett, T. F. (1963). *The history of an idea in america*. Dallas:Southern Methodist University Press, p.6.

Graubard, A. (1972). The free school movement. *Harvard Education Review*, 42:351-373.

Grimes, J. W., and Allinsmith, W. (1961). Compulsivity, anxiety and school achievement. *Merrill-Palmer Quarterly*, 7:247-71.

Gronlund, N. E. (1971). *Measurement and evaluation in teaching* (2nd ed.). New York: Macmillan.

Gronlund, N. E. (1970). *Stating behavioral objectives for classroom instruction*. Toronto, Ontario, Canada: Macmillan.

Gronlund, N. E. (1965). *Measurement and evaluation in teaching*. New York: Macmillan.

Gronlund, N. E. (1959). *Sociometry in the classroom*. New York: Harper and Row.

Gross, M. L. (1962). *The brain watchers*. New York: Random House.

Grost, A. (1970). *Genius in residence*. Englewood Cliffs, N.J.: Prentice-Hall.

Guilford, J. P. (1969). *Intelligence, creativity and their educational implications*. San Diego, Calif.: Educational & Industrial Testing Service.

Guilford, J. P. (1967). *The nature of human intelligence*. New York: McGraw Hill.

Guilford, J. P. (1966). *Intelligence: 1965 model. American Psychologist*, 21:20-26.

Guilford, J. P. (1962). Factors that aid and hinder creativity. *Teachers College Record*, 63:380-392.

Gulliksen, H. (1945). The relation of item difficulty and inter-item correlation to test variance and reliability. *Psychometrika*, 10:79-91.

Guskin, A., Guskin, E. (1970). *A social psychology of education*. Reading, Mass.: Addison-Wesley.

Guthrie, E. R. (1942). Conditioning: A theory of learning in terms of stimulus, response and association. In N. B. Henry, ed., *The psychology of learning. Forty-First-Yearbook of the National Society for the Study of Education*, Part II. Chicago: University of Chicago Press, pp. 17-60.

Guthrie, J. T. (1967). Expository instruction versus a discovery method. *Journal of Educational Psychology,* 58:45-59.

Hales, L. W., Bain, P. T., and Rand, L. P. (1971). An investigation of some aspects of the pass-fail grading system. Mimeograph.

Hall, A. (1965). Ability grouping is democratic. *The Clearing House,* 40:159-160.

Hall, C. V. (1963). Does entrance age affect achievement? *Elementary School Journal,* 63:391-396.

Hall, E. (December, 1970). Bad education—a conversation with Jerome Bruner. *Psychology Today,* 51-74.

Hall, R. V., Axelrod, S., Foundopoulos, M., et al. (1971). The effective use of punishment to modify behavior in the classroom. *Educational Technology,* 11(4):24-26.

Hallworth, H. J. (1969). Computer simulation of cognitive processes. *Educational Technology,* 9:60-63.

Hamachek, D. E. (1968). *Motivation in Teaching and Learning. What Research Says to the Teacher.* No. 34. Washington, D.C.: National Education Association.

Hapgood, M. (September 18, 1971). The open classroom: protect it from its friends. *Saturday Review, 21.*

Harding, J., Proshansky, H., Kutner, B., and Chein, I. (1969). Prejudice and ethnic relations. In the *Handbook of social psychology,* Vol. 5. G. Lindzey and E. Aronson, eds. Reading, Mass.: Addison-Wesley, pp. 1-77.

Harlow, A. H. (1950). Learning and satiation of response in intrinsically motivated complex puzzle performance by monkeys. *Journal of Comparative & Physiological Psychology,* 43:289-294.

Harlow, H. F. (1959). Learning set and error factor theory. In S. Koch, ed., *Psychology: A study of a science,* Vol. 2. New York: McGraw Hill, pp. 492-537.

Harlow, H. F. (1953). Mice, monkeys, men and motives. *Psychological Review,* 60:23-32.

Harmes, H. M. (1971). Specifying objectives for performance contracts. *Educational Technology,* 11(1):52-56.

Harrow, Anita J. (1972). *A taxonomy of the psychomotor domain: A guide for developing behavioral objectives.* New York: David McKay.

Hart, F. W. (1934). *Teachers and teaching.* New York: Macmillan.

Hart, J. T. (1965). Memory and the feeling of knowing experience. *Journal of Educational Psychology,* 56:208-216.

Hartshorne, H., and May, M. A. (1928-1930). *Studies in the nature of character.* Vol. 1, *Studies in Deceit,* Vol. 11, *Studies in Self-Control,* Vol. 111, *Studies in the Organization of Character.* New York: Macmillan.

Hartup, W. (1970). Peer relations. In T. Spencer and N. Kass, eds., *Perspectives in child psychology.* New York: McGraw-Hill.

Hartup, W. W. (1963). Dependency and independence. In H. Stevenson, ed., *Child psychology. Yearbook of the National Society for the Study of Education,* Vol. 62, Part I, pp. 333-363.

Hassler, W. W. (1969). *Results of pass-fail questionnaire sent to graduate school deans.* Indiana, Penn.: Indiana University of Pennsylvania, HE 001 388.

Havighurst, R. J., and Moorefield, T. E. (1967). The disadvantage in industrial cities. In P. Witty, ed., *The educationally retarded and disadvantaged.* Sixty-sixth Yearbook of the National Society for *the Study of Education,* Part I, pp. 8-20.

Havighurst, R. J. (1966). Social deviancy among youth: types and significance. In W. W. Wattenberg, ed., *Social deviancy among youth: types and significance. Yearbook of the National Society for the Study of Education,* Vol. 65, Part I, pp. 59-77.

Heathers, E. (1953). Emotional dependence and independence in a physical threat situation. *Child Development, 24*:169-179.

Heathers, G. (February 6, 1971). A definition of individualized education. Paper presented at the 1971 AERA annual meeting in New York City.

Heathers, G. (1955). Emotional dependence and independence in nursery school play. *Journal of Genetic Psychology, 87*:37-57.

Heathers, O. (1966). School organizations, nongrading, dual progress, and team teaching. In John I. Goodlad and H. O. Richey, eds., *The changing american school, Sixty-Fifth Yearbook of the National Society for the Study of Education,* Part II, pp. 110-134.

Heider, F. (1960). The gestalt theory of motivation. In M. R. Jones, ed., *Nebraska symposium on motivation.* Lincoln: University of Nebraska Press, pp. 145-172.

Herman, D. T., Lawless, R. H., and Marshall, R. W. (1957). Variables in the effect of language on the reproduction of visually perceived forms. *Perceptual Motor Skills, 7*:171-186.

Herron, M. D. (1971). The nature of scientific inquiry. *School Review, 79*:171-212.

Hewett, F. M. (1968). *The emotionally disturbed child in the classroom.* Boston: Allyn and Bacon.

Highet, G. (1950). *The art of teaching.* New York: Vintage Books.

Hilgard, E. R. (1964). The place of gestalt theory and field theories in contemporary learning theory. In E. R. Hilgard, ed., *Theories of learning and instruction.* Sixty-third Yearbook of the National Society for the Study of Education. Part I. Chicago: University of Chicago Press, pp. 54-77.

Hilgard, E. R., and Bower, G. H. (1966). *Theories of learning* (3rd ed.). New York: Appleton-Century Crofts.

Hilgard, J. R. (1933). The effect of early and delayed practice on memory and motor performances studied by the method of co-twin control. *Genetic Psychology Monographs, 14*:493-567.

Hill, K. T., and Sarason, S. B. (1966). The relation of test anxiety and defensiveness to test and school performance over the elementary-school years: A further longitudinal study. *Monographs of the Society for Research on Child Development. 31*(2).

Hill, W. F. (1964). Contemporary developments within stimulus-response learning theory. In E. R. Hilgard, ed., *Theories of learning and instruction. Sixty-third book of the National Society for the Study of Education.* Chicago: University of Chicago Press, pp. 27-53.

Hill, W. F. (1956). Activity as an autonomous drive. *Journal of Comparative and Physiological Psychology, 44*:15-19.

Hitt, W. D., and Stock, J. R. (1965). The relationship between psychological characteristics and creative behavior. *Psychological Record, 15*:133-140.

Hoffmann, B. (1962). *The tyranny of testing.* New York: Crowell-Collier-Macmillan.

Hoffmann, B. (1961). The tyranny of multiple-choice tests. *Harper's Magazine,* 222:37-44.

Hoffmann, M. L. (1970). Moral development. In P. H. Mussen, ed., *Carmichael's manual of child psychology,* Vol. II (3rd ed.). New York: Wiley, pp. 261-360.

Homme, L., Csanyi, A. P., Gonzales, M. A., and Rechs, J. R. (1969). *How to use contingency contracting in the classroom.* Champaign, Ill.: Research Press.

Honzik, M. P., Macfarlane, J. W., and Allen, L. (1948). The stability of mental test performance between two and eighteen years. *Journal of Experimental Education,* 17:309-324.

Hopkins, K. D., and Bibelheimer, M. (1971). Five-year stability of intelligence quotients from language and non-language group tests. *Child Development,* 42:645-649.

Hoppe, F. (1930). Erfolg und misserfolg. *Psychologische Forschung,* 14:1-62.

Hosford, R. E. (1969). Overcoming fear of speaking in a group. In J. D. Krumboltz and C. E. Thoresen, eds., *Behavioral counseling: Cases and techniques.* New York: Holt, Rinehart and Winston, pp. 80-82.

Houston, S. H. (1970). A re-examination of some assumptions about the language of the disadvantaged child. *Child Development,* 41:947-963.

Hovland, C. I. (1960). Computer simulation of thinking. *American Psychologist,* 15:687-693.

Howe, M. J. A. (1969). *Introduction to human memory.* New York: Harper & Row.

Hughes, E. C., Becker, H. S., and Geer, B. (1962). Student subculture and academic effort. In N. Stanford, ed., *The american college,* New York: Wiley, pp. 515-530.

Hull, C. L. (1943). *Principles of behavior.* New York: Appleton-Century-Crofts.

Hunt, J. McV. (1961). *Intelligence and experience.* New York: Ronald Press.

Hunter, I. M. L. (1964). *Memory.* New York: Penguin.

Hunter, M. (1967). *Reinforcement.* El Segundo, Calif.: TIP Publications.

Husen, T. (1967). *International study of achievement in mathematics,* Vol. 2. Uppsala, Sweden: Almquist and Wiksells.

Hyman, R. T. (1970). *Ways of teaching.* Philadelphia: J. B. Lippincott.

Hymes, J. (1958). *Before the child reads.* Evanston, Ill.: Row, Peterson.

Ilg, F. L., and Ames, L. B. (1965). *School readiness: Behavior tests used at the Gesell Institute.* New York: Harper and Row.

Jackson, P. (1968). *Life in the classroom.* New York: Holt, Rinehart and Winston.

Jackson, P. (1966). The student's world. *The Elementary School Journal,* 66:357.

Jackson, P. (1962). The teacher and individual differences. Chapter V in *Individualizing Instruction, The Sixty-First Yearbook of the National Society for the Study of Education,* Part 1. Chicago: NSSE.

Jackson, P., and Wolfson, B. (September 1968). Varieties of constraint in a nursery school. *Young Children XXIII*(6).

Jackson, R. (June 1970). Developing criterion-referenced tests. ERIC Clearing-house on Tests, Measurement and Evaluation.

Jencks, C., et al. (1972). *Inequality: A reassessment of the effect of family and schooling in america*. New York: Basic Books.

Jenkins, J. G., and Dallenbach, K. M. (1924). Oblivescence during sleep and waking. *American Journal of Psychology*, *35*:605-612.

Jenkins, J. R., and Deno, S. L. (1971). Influence of knowledge and type of objectives on subject-matter learning. *Journal of Educational Psychology*, *62*:67-70.

Jensen, A. R. (1969). How much can we boost I.Q. and scholastic achievement. *Harvard Educational Review*, *39*:1-123.

Jensen, A. (1969). How can we boost I.Q. and scholastic achievement. In *Environment Heredity & Intelligence. Harvard Educational Review*, Reprint Series No. 2.

Jensen House subcommittee hears Jensen. (July 8, 1970). *Report on Educational Research*.

Jersild, A. T., and Tasch, R. J. (1949). *Children's interests*. New York: Teachers' College Press, Columbia University.

Johnson, D. (1971). Students against the school establishment: Crisis intervention in school conflicts and organizational change. *Journal of School Psychology*, *9*:84-92.

Johnson, D. M., and Stratton, R. P. (1966). Evaluation of five methods of teaching concepts. *Journal of Educational Psychology*, *57*:48-53.

Johnson, D. W. (1970). *The Social Psychology of Education*. Holt, Rinehart and Winston.

Johnson, G. O. (1967). The education of mentally retarded children. In William M. Cruickshank and G. Orville Johnson, eds., *Education of exceptional children and youth* (2nd ed.). Englewood Cliffs, N.J.: Prentice-Hall, pp. 194-237.

Johnson, G. O. (1962). Special education for the mentally handicapped — a paradox. *Exceptional Children*, *29*:62-69.

Johnson, G. O. (1950). A study of the social position of mentally handicapped children in the regular grades. *American Journal of Mental Deficiency*, *55*:60-89.

Johnson, G. O., and Kirk, S. A. (1950). Are mentally handicapped children segregated in the regular grades? *Journal of Exceptional Children*, *17*:65-68, 87-88.

Jones, J. (1972). *Prejudice and racism*. Reading, Mass.: Addison-Wesley.

Kagan, J. (1965). Impulsive and reflective children: Significance of conceptual tempo. In J. D. Krumboltz, ed., *Learning and the educational processes*. Chicago: Rand McNally, pp. 133-161.

Kagan, J., and Moss, H. A. (1960). The stability of passive and dependent behavior from childhood through adulthood. *Child Development*, *31*:577-591.

Kamii, C. K., and Radin, N. L. (1970). A framework for a preschool curriculum based on some Piagetian concepts. In I. J. Athey and D. O. Rubadeau, eds., *Educational implications of Piaget's theory*. Massachusetts: Ginn-Blaisdell, pp. 89-100.

Kaplan, L. (1971). *Education and mental health*. New York: Harper & Row.

Karlins, M. (1969). Academic attitudes and performance as a function of differential grading systems: An evaluation of Princeton's pass-fail system. *Journal of Experimental Education*, 37:38-50.

Karnes, M., et al. (in press). Educational intervention at home by mothers of disadvantaged infants. *Child Development*.

Karon, B. P. (1958). *The Negro personality*. New York: Springer.

Katz, J., and Associates (1968). *No time for youth: Growth and constraint in college students*. San Francisco: Jossey-Bass.

Kaufman, R. A. (January, 1971). Accountability, a system approach and the quantitative improvement of education—an attempted integration. *Educational Technology*, 11:21-26.

Kearney, N. C. (1953). *Elementary school objectives*. New York: Russell Sage Foundation.

Keister, B. V. (1941). Reading skills acquired by five-year old children. *Elementary School Journal*, 41:587-596.

Kellam, S., and Schiff, S. (1967). Adaptation and mental illness in the first grade classrooms of an urban community. *Psychiatric Research Report*, 21:79-91.

Kelley, T. L. (1939). The selection of upper and lower groups for the validation of test items. *Journal of Educational Psychology*, 30:17-24.

Kennedy, B. J. (1968). Motivational effect of individual conferences and goal setting on performance and attitudes in arithmetic. ERIC: ED 032113

Kessler, J. W. (1966). *Psychopathology of childhood*. Englewood Cliffs, N.J.: Prentice-Hall.

Kibler, R. J., Barker, L. L., and Miles, D. T. (1970). *Behavioral objectives and instruction*. Boston: Allyn and Bacon.

Kidd, J. W. (1964). Toward a more precise definition of mental retardation. *Mental Retardation* II, pp. 209-212.

Klausmeier, H. J., Harris, C. W., and Wiersma, W. (1964). *Strategies of learning and efficiency of concept attainment by individuals and groups*. U.S. Office of Education, cooperative research project no. 1442. Madison, Wis.: University of Wisconsin.

Kohlberg, L. (January 9, 1969). The moral atmosphere of the school. Paper delivered at Association for Supervision and Curriculum Development Conference on the "Unstudied Curriculum," Washington, D.C.

Kohlberg, L. (1968). Early education: A cognitive-developmental view. *Child Development*, 39:1013-1062.

Kohlberg, L. (1964). Development of moral character and moral ideology. In M. L. Hoffman and L. W. Hoffman, eds., *Review of child development research*, Vol. I. New York: Russell Sage Foundation, pp. 383-432.

Kohler, W. (1925). *The mentality of apes*. (Translated by E. Winter.) New York: Harcourt.

Kolstoe, O. P. (1972). Programs for the mildly retarded: A reply to the critics. *Exceptional Children*, 39:51-56.

Kozol, J. (April 1972). Free schools fail because they don't teach. *Psychology Today*, p. 33.

Krathwohl, D. R., Bloom, B. S., and Masia, B. (1964). Taxonomy of educational objectives. Handbook II. *The affective domain.* New York: David McKay.

Kumar, V. K. (1971). The structure of human memory and some educational implications. *Review of Educational Research, 41*:379-417.

Labov, W., Cohen, P., Robins, C., and Lewis, J. (1968). "A study of the non-standard English of Negro & Puerto Rican speakers in N.Y. City." Final Report, U.S. Office of Educ. Cooperative Research Project No. 3288. Two volumes. New York: Columbia University. Mimeograph.

Lambert, N. (1964). *The protection and promotion of mental health in schools.* Washington, D.C.: Government Printing Office.

Lange, A., Lehmann, I. J., and Mehrens, W. A. (1967). Using item analysis to improve tests. *The Journal of Educational Measurement, 4*:65-68.

Law school admission test council: Statement on pass-fail grading systems (October 27, 1970). HE 001 881.

Lehman, H. C. (1954). Men's creative production rate at different ages and in different countries. *Scientific Monthly, 78*:321-326.

Lehman, H. C. (1953). *Age and achievement.* Princeton, N.J.: Princeton University Press.

Lennenberg, E. (1967). *Biological foundations of language.* New York: Wiley.

Lesser, G. S. (1972). Learning, teaching, and television production for children: The experience of Sesame Street. *Harvard Educational Review, 42*(2).

Lesser, G. S., Fifer, G., and Clark, D. H. (1964). *Mental abilities of children in different social and cultural groups.* Cooperative research project No. 1635; Washington, D.C.: U.S. Office of Education.

Levine, J., and Murphy, G. (1943). The learning and forgetting of controversial material. *Journal of Abnormal and Social Psychology, 38*:507-517.

Levy, D. (1943). *Maternal overprotection.* New York: Columbia University Press.

Lewin, K., Lippitt, R., and White, R. (1939). Patterns of aggressive behavior in experimentally created social climates. *Journal of Social Psychology, 10*:271-299.

Lewin, R. (1942). Field theory and learning. In N. B. Henry, ed., *Psychology of Learning. Forty-First Yearbook of the National Society for the Study of Education.* Part II. Chicago: University of Chicago Press, pp. 215-242.

Liebert, R. M., and Naele, J. M. (1972). TV violence and aggression. *Psychology Today, 11*(11):38-39.

Lindgren, H. C. (1967). Brainstorming and the facilitation of creativity expressed in drawing. *Perceptual Motor Skills, 24*:350.

Lindgren, H. C., and Lindgren, D. F. (1965). Brainstorming and orneriness as facilitators of creativity. *Psychological Reports, 16*:577-83.

Lindquist, E. F. (1951). Preliminary consideration in objective test construction. In E. F. Lindquist, ed., *Educational measurement.* Washington: American Council on Education, pp. 119-158.

Lindvall, C. M., and Bolvin, J. O. (1967). Programmed instruction in the schools: an application of programming principles in "individually prescribed instruction." Chapter VIII in *Programmed instruction. Sixty-Sixth*

Yearbook of the National Society for the Study of Education, Part II. Chicago: NSSE.

Lindvall, C. M., and Cox, R. C. (1970). *The IPI evaluation program.* AERA Monograph Series on Curriculum Evaluation, #5. Chicago: Rand McNally.

Lindvall, C. M., and Cox, R. C. (1969). The role of evaluation in programs for individualized instruction. Chapter VIII in *Educational evaluation: New roles, new means. Sixty-Eighth Yearbook of the National Society for the Study of Education,* Part II. Chicago: NSSE.

Lipe, D., and Jung, S. M. (1971). Manipulating incentives to enhance school learning. *Review of Educational Research,* 41:249-280.

Lippitt, R., and Lohman, J. (1965). Cross-age relationships: an educational resource. *Children,* 12(3):113-117.

Litcher, J., and Johnson, D. (1969). Changes in attitudes toward Negroes of white elementary school students after use of multiethnic readers. *Journal of Educational Psychology,* 60:148-152.

Long, N. J., and Newman, R. G. (1969). The straws that break the teacher's back. In H. F. Clarizio, ed., *Mental health and the educative process: Selected readings.* New York: Rand McNally, pp. 282-288.

Lord, F. M. (1952). The relation of the reliability of multiple-choice tests to the distribution of item difficulties. *Psychometrika,* 17:181-194.

Loretan, J. (1966). *Alternatives to intelligence testing.* Proceedings of the 1965 invitational conference on testing problems. Educational Testing Service.

Lovitt, T. C., and Curtiss, K. A. (1969). Academic response rate as a function of teacher and self-imposed contingencies. *Journal of Applied Behavioral Analysis,* 2:49-53.

Luchins, A. S. (1961). Implications of gestalt psychology for AV learning. *Audio-Visual Communications Review,* Supplement IV, pp. 7-31.

Luchins, A. S. (1942). Mechanization in problem-solving: The effect of einstellung. *Psychological Monograph,* 54(6).

Lumsdaine, A. A. (1964). Educational technology, programmed learning, and instructional sciences. In E. R. Hilgard, eds., *Theories of learning and instruction. Sixty-Third Yearbook of the National Society for Study of Education,* Part I. Chicago: University of Chicago Press, pp. 371-401.

Maccoby, E. E. (1966). Sex differences in intellectual functioning. *The development of sex differences.* Stanford, Calif.: Stanford University Press, p. 25.

MacKinnon, D. W. (1962). The nature and nurture of creative talent. *American Psychologist,* 17:484-495.

Madsen, C. H., Jr., and Madsen, C. K. (1970). *Teaching Discipline.* Boston: Allyn and Bacon.

Madsen, C. H., Becker, W. C., and Thomas, D. R. (1968). Rules, praise and ignoring: Elements of elementary classroom control. *Journal of Applied Behavioral Analysis,* 1:139-150.

Mager, R. F. (1968). *Developing attitude toward learning.* Palo Alto, Calif.: Fearon.

Mager, R. F., and Pipe, P. (1970). *Analyzing performance problems.* Belmont, Calif.: Fearon.

Maller, J. B. (1929). *Cooperation and competition: An experimental study in motivation.* New York: Teachers College Press.

Marquardt, D. A. (1955). Group problem solving. *Journal of Social Psychology,* 41:103-113.

Martorella, P. H. (1972). *Concept learning: Designs for instruction.* Scranton, Pa.: Intext.

Maslow, A. (1954). *Motivation and personality.* New York: Harper.

Mathis, B. C., Cotton, J. W., and Sechrest, L. (1970). *Psychological foundations of education,* New York: Academic Press.

Mayhew, L. B. (1958). And in attitudes. Chapter 4 in Paul L. Dressel, ed., *Evaluation in the basic college at Michigan State University.* New York: Harper & Row.

McAllister, L. W., Stachowaik, J. G., Baer, D. M., and Conderman, L. (1969). The application of operant conditioning techniques in a secondary school classroom. *Journal of Applied Behavior Analysis, 2:*277-285.

McCandless, B. (1967). *Children-behavior and development* (2nd ed.). New York: Holt, Rinehart and Winston.

McClelland, D. C. (1972). What is the effect of achievement motivation training in the schools? *Teachers College Record, 74:*129-145.

McClelland, D. C. (1965a). Toward a new theory of motive acquisition. *American Psychologist, 20:*321-334.

McClelland, D. C., Atkinson, J. W., Clark, R. A., and Lowell, E. L. (1953). *The achievement motive.* New York: Appleton-Century Crofts.

McConnell, T. R. (1942). Reconciliation of learning theories. In N. B. Henry, ed., *Psychology of learning. Forty-First Yearbook of the National Society for the Study of Education,* Part II. Chicago: University of Chicago Press, pp. 243-286.

McCord, W., McCord, J., and Zola, I. (1959). *Origins of crime: A new evaluation of the Cambridge-Somerville youth study.* New York: Columbia University Press.

McCord, W., and McCord, J. (1956). *Psychopathy and delinquency.* New York: Grune & Stratton.

McGeoch, J. A., and Irion, A. L. (1952). *The psychology of human learning* (rev. ed.). New York: Forgmans.

McGuire, W. J. (1964). Inducing resistance to persuasion. In L. Berkowitz, ed., *Advances in experimental social psychology,* Vol. I. New York: Academic Press, pp. 191-229.

McLoughlin, W. P. (1972). Individualization of instruction vs. nongrading. *Phi Delta Kappan, 53*(6):378-381.

McLoughlin, W. P. (1968). The phantom nongraded school. *Phi Delta Kappan,* 49:248-250.

McNassor, D. (1967). This frantic pace in education. *Childhood Education,* 44:148-154.

McNeil, J. (1964). Programmed instruction vs. usual procedures in teaching boys to read. *American Education Research Association,* pp. 113-119.

McNeill, D. (1970). The development of language. In P. H. Mussen, ed., *Carmichael's Manual of child psychology.* New York: Wiley, pp. 1061-1163.

McNemar, Q. (1964). Lost: Our intelligence? Why? *American Psychologist,* 19:871-882.

McNulty, J. A. (1966). A partial learning model of recognition memory. *Canadian Journal of Psychology, 20:*302-315.

McNulty, J. A. (1965). An analysis of recall and recognition processes in verbal learning. *Journal of Verbal Learning and Verbal Behavior*, 4:430-436.

Mehrens, W. A., and Lehmann, I. J. (1973). *Measurement and evaluation of education and psychology.* New York: Holt, Rinehart and Winston.

Mehrens, W. A., and Lehmann, I. J. (1969). *Standardized tests in education.* New York: Holt, Rinehart and Winston.

Meil, A. (1967). *The shortchanged children of suburbia: What schools don't teach about human differences.* American Jewish Committee. Institute of Human Relations Press.

Melville, G. L., and Stamm, E. (1967). The pass-fail system and the change in the accounting of grades on comprehensive examinations at Knox College. Galesburg, Ill.: Office of Institutional Research, Knox College, ED 014 788.

Mental Health Research Unit (December 1967). *Behavior patterns associated with persistent emotional disturbance of school children in regular classes of elementary grades.* Syracuse: N.Y. State Dept. of Mental Hygiene.

Mercer, J. R. (1972). The lethál label. *Psychology Today*, 6(4):44-47, 95-97.

Mercer, J. R. (1971). Sociocultural factors in labeling mental retardates. *The Peabody Journal of Education*, 48(3):188-203.

Merrill, M. D. (1971). Necessary psychological conditions for defining instructional outcomes. *Educational Technology*, 11(8):34-39.

Metfessel, N. S., Michael, W. B., and Kirsner, D. A. (1969). Instrumentation of Bloom's and Krathwohl's taxonomies for the writing of educational objectives. *Psychology in the Schools*, 6:227-231.

Meyer, S. R. (1960). A test of the principles of "activity," "immediate reinforcement," and "guidance" as instrumented by Skinner's teaching machine. *Dissertation Abstracts*, 20:4729-4730.

Miles, M. (1964). *Innovation in education.* New York: Teachers College Press.

Miller, D. R., and Swanson, C. E. (1960). *Inner conflict and defense.* New York: Holt, Rinehart and Winston.

Miller, G. A. (1968). *The psychology of communication.* Harmondsworth, Middlesex, England: Penguin Books.

Miller, G. A. (1956). Information and memory. *Scientific American*, 195(2): 42-46.

Miller, G. A. (1956). The magical number 7 ± 2. *Psychological Review*, 63:8-97.

Miller, G. A., Galenter, E., and Pribram, K. (1960). *Plans and the structure of behavior.* New York: Holt, Rinehart and Winston.

Miller, N. E., and Dollard J. (1941). *Social learning and imitation.* New Haven, Conn.: Yale University Press.

Miller, S. M., Rein, M., Roby, P., and Gross, B. M. (1967). Poverty, inequality, and conflict. *Social Goals and Indicators for American Society*, Vol. 2, The Annals of the American Academy of Political and Social Science, Vol. 373, pp. 16-52.

Milner, B. (1959). The memory defect in bilateral hippocampal lesions. *Psychiatric Research Reports*, 11:43-58.

Milton, O. (1967). *Teaching-Learning Issues*, No. 5. Knoxville, Tenn.: Learning Resources Center, The University of Tennessee.

Minuchin, P., Biber, B., Shapiro, E., and Zimiles, H. (1969). *The psychological impact of school experience.* New York: Basic Books.

Morishima, J. K., and Micek, S. S. (1970). Pass-fail evaluation: Phase II. Questionnaire analysis. Seattle: Office of Institutional Educational Research, University of Washington.

Morrison, H. C. (1926). *The practice of teaching in the secondary school.* Chicago: University of Chicago Press.

Morse, W. C., Cutler, R. L., and Fink, A. H. (1964). *Public school classes for the emotionally handicapped: A research analysis.* Washington, D.C.: Council for Exceptional Children.

Morse, W. C., and Wingo, G. M. (1969). *Psychology and teaching.* Glenview, Ill.: Scott, Foresman.

Moss, H. A., and Kagan, J. (1961). Stability of achievement and recognition seeking behaviors from early childhood through adulthood. *Journal of Abnormal Psychology,* 62:504-513.

Mosteller, F. and Moynihan, D. (1972) *On equality of educational opportunity.* New York: Random House.

Mouly, G. J. (1968). *Psychology for effective teaching.* New York: Holt, Rinehart and Winston.

Mowrer, O. H. (1960). *Learning theory and behavior.* New York: Wiley.

Moynihan, D. (1965). *The Negro family: The case for national action.* Washington, D.C.: Office of Policy Planning and Research, U.S. Dept. of Labor.

Mukerji, N. F. (1940). Investigation of ability to work in groups and in isolation. *British Journal of Psychology,* 30:352-356.

Murphy, L. B. (1937). *Social behavior and child personality.* New York: Columbia University Press.

Mussen, P. H., Conger, J. J., and Kagan, J. (1969). *Child development and personality.* (3rd ed.). New York: Harper & Row.

Mussen, P., Conger, J., and Kagan, J. (1963). *Child development and personality.* New York: Harper and Row.

Myers, R. E., and Torrance, E. P. (1965). *Invitations to speaking and writing creatively.* Boston: Ginn.

National Assessment of Educational Progress. *Objectives in Ten Subject Matter Areas.* 822 Lincoln Tower, 1860 Lincoln Street. Denver, Colorado.

National Education Association (1967). Reports to parents. *NEA Research Bulletin,* 45:51-53.

National Society for the Study of Education. Thirty-ninth Yearbook, 1940, Part II-Intelligence: Its Nature and Nurture-Original Studies and Experiments. G. D. Stoddard.

Neill, A. S. (1960). *Summerhill: A radical approach to child rearing.* New York: Hart Publishing.

Newell, A., Shaw, J. C., and Simon, H. (1958). Elements of a theory of human problem solving. *Psychological Review,* 65:151-166.

Newell, A., and Simon, H. (1963). Computers in psychology. In R. D. Luce, R. R. Bush, and E. Galanter, eds., *Hardbook of mathematical psychology,* Vol. I. New York: Wiley, pp. 421-423.

Newman, E. B. (1939). Forgetting of meaningful material during sleep and waking. *American Journal of Psychology,* 52:65-71.

Newsfront (1969). *Phi Delta Kappan,* 51:223-224.

Newsnotes (1972). *Phi Delta Kappan,* 54(2):140.

Newsom, R. S. Eischens, R., and Looft, W. R. (1972). Intrinsic individual differences: A basis for enhancing instructional programs. *Journal of Educational Research, 65*:387-392.

Newsweek (May 22, 1972). Never too young to learn. pp. 96-99.

Niesser, U. (1967). *Cognitive psychology.* New York: Appleton-Century-Crofts.

North, A. F. (1969). Research issues in child health: An overview. In E. Grotberg, ed., *Critical issues in research related to disadvantaged children.* Princeton, N.J.: Educational Testing Service.

Novak, J. D. (1966). The role of concepts in science teaching. In H. J. Klausmeier and C. W. Harris, eds., *Analyses of concept learning.* New York: Academic Press, pp. 239-254.

O'Connor, K. (1971). *Learning: An introduction.* Glenview, Ill.: Scott, Foresman.

Ojemann, R. Incorporating psychological concepts in the school curriculum. *J. Sch. Psychol.,* 1967, 5, 195-204.

Okey, J. R., and Gagne, R. M. (1970). Revision of a science topic using evidence of performance on subsequent skills. *Journal of Research Science Teaching, 7*:321-325.

Osborne, A. F. (1957). *Applied imagination: Principles and procedures of creative thinking.* New York: Scribner.

Osgood, C. E. (1968). Toward a wedding of insufficiencies. In R. T. Dixon and D. L. Norton, eds., *Verbal behavior and general behavior theory.* Englewood Cliffs, N.J.: Prentice-Hall.

Otto, H. J. (1954). *Elementary school organization and administration.* New York: Appleton-Century-Crofts.

Ovsiankina, M. (1928). Die wiederaufnahme unterbrachener handlungen. *Psychologische Forschung, 11*:302-379.

Pace, C. R. (1967). *Analysis of a national sample of college environment.* Final report, Cooperative Research Project No. 50764, Washington, D.C.: Office of Education, U.S. Dept. of Health, Education and Welfare.

Page, E. B. (1958). Teacher comments and student performance: A seventy-four classroom experiment in school motivation. *Journal of Educational Psychology, 49*:173-181.

Palermo, D. S. (1959). Racial comparisons and additional normative data on the children's manifest anxiety scale. *Child Development, 30*:53-57.

Parnes, S. J., and Meadow, A. (1963). Development of individual creative talent. In C. W. Taylor and F. X. Barron, eds., *Scientific creativity: Its recognition and development.* New York: Wiley, pp. 311-320.

Pasamanick, B., and Knobloch, H. (1966). Retrospective studies on the epidemiology of reproductive casualty: Old and new. *Merrill-Palmer Quarterly of Behavior and Development, 12*:7-23.

Passow, A. H. (1962). The maze of the research on ability grouping. *The Educational Forum, 26*:281-288.

Pavlov, I. P. (1927). *Conditioned reflexes.* London: Oxford Press.

Peck, R. F., and Mitchell, J. V. Jr. (1969). The mental health of the teacher. In H. F. Clarizio, ed., *Mental health and the educative process: Selected readings.* New York: Rand McNally, pp. 273-277.

Peddiwell, J. A. (1939). *The saber-tooth curriculum*. New York: McGraw Hill.

Piaget, J. (1932). *The moral judgment of the child*. N.Y.: Harcourt, Brace.

Pinard, A., and Sharp, E. (1972). I.Q. and point of view. *Psychology Today*, *6*, pp. 65-68, 90.

Pines, M. (July 6, 1969). Why some three-year-olds get A's and some get C's. *New York Times Magazine*, pp. 4-17.

Pines, M. (May 1963). How three-year-olds teach themselves to read and love it. *Harpers*, *226*:58-64.

Popham, W. J. (1970). The instructional objectives exchange: New support for criterion-referenced instruction. *Phi Delta Kappan, 52*(3):174-175.

Popham, W. J. (1969). Objectives and instruction. In W. J. Popham, et al., *Instructional Objectives*. AERA Monograph Series on Curriculum Evaluation, No. 3. Chicago: Rand McNally, pp. 32-64.

Popham, W. J. (1968). *Probing the validity of arguments against behavioral goals*. Paper presented at the annual convention of the American Educational Research Association, Chicago.

Popham, W. J., et al. (1969). *Instructional objectives*. AERA Monograph Series on Curriculum Evaluation, No. 3. Chicago: Rand McNally.

Popham, W. J., and Husek, T. R. (1969). Implications of criterion-referenced measurement. *Journal of Educational Measurement*, 6:1-10.

Premack, D. (1965). Reinforcement theory. In D. Levine, ed., *Nebraska symposium on motivation*. Lincoln: University of Nebraska Press, pp. 123-180.

President's Commission on Higher Education, The (1947). *Higher Education for American Democracy, Vol. I. Establishing the Goals*. Washington, D.C.: U.S. Government Printing Office.

Quann, C. J. (1970). Pass-fail grading: What are the trends? Paper presented at the meeting of the American Association of Collegiate Registrars and Admissions Officers, New Orleans.

Quay, H. (1963). Some basic considerations in the education of emotionally disordered children. *Exceptional Children, 30*:27-31.

Rambusch, N. M. (1962). *Learning how to learn: An American approach to Montessori*. Baltimore: Helicon.

Raulerson, J. D., Jr. (1971). The human as an information processor: A guide for instructional design. *Educational Technology, 11*(12):12-16.

Read, M. S. (1972). The biological bases: Malnutrition and behavioral development. In *NSSE Yearbook, LXXI*, Part II, pp. 55-71.

Ream, M. A. (1968). *Ability grouping: Research summary 1968-5-3*. Washington, D.C. National Educ. Association Research Division.

Redl, F., and Wattenberg, W. (1959). *Mental hygiene in teaching*. New York: Harcourt.

Reed, H. B. (1961). Teacher variables of warmth, demand, and utilization of intrinsic motivation related to pupils' science interests: A study illustrating several potentials of variance-covariance. *Journal of Experimental Education, 29*:205-229.

Reitman, W. R. (1965). *Cognition and thought: An information processing approach*. New York: Wiley.

Remmers, H. H. (April 1949). The expanding role of research. *North Central Association Quarterly, 23*:369-376.

Report of the Joint Commission on Mental Health of Children (1970). *Crisis in child mental health: Challenge for the 1970's.* New York: Harper & Row.

Reynolds, M. C. (1969). Special education. In Robert L. Ebel, ed., *Encyclopedia of educational research* (4th ed.). Toronto: Macmillan, pp. 1254-1263.

Reynolds, M. (1962). A framework for considering some issues in special education. *Exceptional Children, 28,* p. 368.

Rife, D. C., and Snyder, L. H. (1931). Studies in human inheritance. *Human Biology, 3:*547-559.

Ringness, T. (1968). *Mental health in the schools.* New York: Random House.

Robins, L. N. (1966). *Deviant children grow up.* Baltimore: Williams & Wilkins.

Robinson, D. (1965). Scraps from a teacher's notebook. *Phi Delta Kappan,* 47:157.

Rock, R. T. Jr. (1929). A critical study of current practices in ability grouping. *Educational Research Bulletin, Catholic University of America,* Nos. 5 and 6.

Rockefeller Report V. (1958). *The pursuit of excellence: Education and the future of America.* Garden City, N.Y.: Doubleday.

Roen, S. R. The behavioral sciences in the primary grades. *Amer. Psychologist,* 1965, 20, 430-432

Roen, S. Primary prevention in the classroom through a teaching program in the behavioral sciences. In E. L. Cowen, E. A. Gardner, and M. Zax (Eds.), *Emergent approaches to mental health problems.* New York: Appleton-Century-Crofts, 1967. Pp. 252-270.

Roeper, A., and Sigel, I., eds. (1968). *Logical thinking in children.* New York: Holt, Rinehart and Winston.

Roff, M. (1961). Childhood social interactions and young adult bad conduct. *Journal of Abnormal and Social Psychology, 63:*333-337.

Rogers, C. R. (1969). *Freedom to learn.* Columbus, Ohio: Charles E. Merrill.

Rogers, C. R. (1963). Actualizing tendency in relation to "motives" and consciousness. In M. R. Jones, ed., *Nebraska symposium on motivation.* Lincoln, Neb.: University of Nebraska Press.

Rohwer, W. D. Jr. (1972). Decisive research: A means for answering fundamental questions about instruction. *Educational Researcher,* 1(7):5-11.

Rohwer, W. D. Jr. (1970). Images and pictures in children's learning: Research results and educational implications. *Psychological Bulletin, 73:*393-403.

Rohwer, W. D. (1970). Implications of cognitive development for education. In P. H. Mussen, ed., *Carmichael's manual of child psychology.* New York: Wiley, pp. 1379-1455.

Rokeach, M., and Rothman, G. (1965). The principle of belief congruence and the congruity principles as models of cognitive interaction. *Psychological Review, 72:*128-142.

Rollins, S. P. (1968). *Developing nongraded schools.* Itasca, Ill.: F. E. Peacock Publishers.

Romano, L. (1959). The parent-teacher conference. *National Education Association Journal,* 48:21-22.

Rosen, B. C. (1959). Race, ethnicity and the achievement syndrome. *American Sociological Review,* 24:47-60.

Rosen, B. C. (1956). The achievement syndrome: A psychocultural dimension of social stratification. *American Sociological Review*, 21:203-211.

Rosen, B. M., Bahn, A. K., and Kramer, M. (1964). Demographic and diagnostic characteristics of psychiatric clinic outpatients in the U.S.A. 1961. *American Journal of Orthopsychiatry*, 34:455-468.

Rosenhan, D., and White, G. M. (1967). Observation and rehearsal as determinants of pro-social behavior. *Journal of Personality and Social Psychology*, 5:424-431.

Rosenthal, R. L., and Jacobson, L. (1968). *Pygmalion in the classroom*. New York: Holt, Rinehart and Winston.

Rosenzweig, S. (1943). An experimental study of "repression" with special reference to need-persistive and ego-defensive reactions to frustration. *Journal of Experimental Psychology*, 32:64-74.

Ross, C. C., and Henry, L. K. (1939). The relation between frequency of testing and progress in learning psychology. *Journal of Educational Psychology*, 30:604-611.

Rossman, J. E. (Summer 1970). Graduate school attitudes to S-U grades. *Educational Record*, 51:310-313.

Roth, R. (1969). The effects of Black studies on Negro fifth grade students. *Journal of Negro Education*, 38:435-439.

Roughead, W. G., and Scandura, J. M. (1968). 'What is learned' in mathematical discovery. *Journal of Educational Psychology*, 59:283-89.

Ruebush, B. K. (1963). "Anxiety." In H. Stevenson, ed., *Child psychology. Yearbook of the National Society for the Study of Education*, 62, Part I, pp. 460-516.

Ryans, D. G. (1961). Some relationships between pupil behavior and certain teacher characteristics. *Journal of Educational Psychology*, 52:82-90.

Ryans, D. G. (1960). *Characteristics of teachers*. Washington, D.C.: American Council in Education.

Sadker, M., and Sadker, D. (October 1972). Sexual discrimination in the elementary school. *The National Elementary Principal*, LII(2).

Sarason, S. (1971). *The culture of the school and the problem of change*. Boston: Allyn and Bacon.

Sarason, S. B. (1960). *Anxiety in elementary school children*. New York: Wiley.

Sassenrath, J., and Garverick, C. M. (1965). Effects of differential feedback from examinations on retention and transfer. *Journal of Educational Psychology*, 56:259-263.

Sawin, E. I. (1969). *Evaluation and the work of the teacher*. Belmont, Calif.: Wadsworth.

Sax, G. (1960). Concept acquisition as a function of differing schedules and delays of reinforcement. *Journal of Educational Psychology*, 51:32-36.

Sax, G., and Ottina, J. (1958). The arithmetic reasoning of pupils differing in school experience. *California Journal of Educational Research*, 9:15-19.

Scheerer, M. (1971). Problem solving. In R. C. Atkinson, ed., *Contemporary psychology: Readings from scientific american*. San Francisco: W. H. Freeman, pp. 241-248 (originally published 1963).

Schmuck, R. (1971). Influence of the peer group. In G. Lesser, ed., *Psychology and educational practice.* Glenview, Ill.: Scott, Foresman.

Schmuck, R., and Schmuck, P. (1971). *Group processes in the classroom.* Dubuque, Iowa: Wm. C. Brown.

Science — A Process Approach (1967). New York: Xerox Corporation.

Scott, W. (1968). Concepts of normality. In E. Borgatta and W. Lambert, eds., *Handbook of personality theory and research.* Chicago: Rand McNally.

Scriven, M. (1967). The methodology of evaluation. In Ralph Tyler, et al., *Perspectives of curriculum evaluation.* AERA Monograph Series on Curriculum Evaluation, No. 1. Chicago: Rand McNally, pp. 39-83.

Seagoe, M. V. (1970). *The learning process and school practice.* Scranton, Penn.: Chandler.

Sears, P. S. (1963). *The effect of classroom conditions on the strength of achievement motivation and work output in children.* Stanford, Calif.: Stanford University Press.

Sears, P. S. (1940). Levels of aspiration in academically successful and unsuccessful children. *Journal of Abnormal and Social Psychology,* 35:498-536.

Sears, R., Maccoby, E., and Levin, H. (1957). *Patterns of child rearing.* New York: Row and Peterson.

Shane, H. G. (1970). A curriculum continuum: Possible trends in the 70's. *Phi Delta Kappan,* 51:389-392.

Shaw, M. E., and Wright, J. M. (1967). Scales for the measurement of attitudes. New York: McGraw-Hill.

Sheffield, F. D. (1961). Theoretical considerations in the learning of complex sequential tasks from demonstration and practice. In A. A. Lumsdaine, ed., *Student response in programmed instruction.* Washington, D.C.: National Academy of Sciences-National Research Council. Publication 943, pp. 13-32.

Scheerer, M. (1971). Problem-Solving. In Atkinson, R. C., (ed.), *Contemporary Psychology.* San Francisco, Cal.: W. H. Freeman.

Shephard, M., Oppenheim, A. N., and Mitchell, S. (1966). Childhood behavior disorders and the child-guidance clinic: An epidemiological study. *Journal of Child Psychology and Psychiatry,* 7:39-52.

Sherif, M., et al. (1961). *Intragroup conflict and cooperation: The robbers cave experiment.* Norman: University of Oklahoma Book Exchange.

Shuey, A. M. (1966). *The testing of Negro intelligence* (2nd ed.). New York: Social Science Press.

Shulman, L. E., and Keislar, E. R., eds. (1966). *Learning by discovery: A critical appraisal.* Chicago: Rand-McNally.

Silberman, M. L. (1971). *The experience of schooling.* New York: Holt, Rinehart and Winston.

Simon, H. A., and Newell, A. (1964). Information processing in computer and man. *American Scientist,* 52:281-300.

Simon, S. A., Howe, L. W., and Kirschenbaum, H. (1972). *Values clarification.* New York: Hart.

Simpson, E. J. (1966). The classification of educational objectives: Psychomotor domain. *Illinois Teacher of Home Economics,* 10(4):110-144.

Singer, R. D., and Singer, A. (1969). *Psychological Development in Children.* Philadelphia: W. B. Saunders.

Sipay, E. R. (April 1965). The effect of prenatal instruction on reading achievement. *Elementary English*, pp. 431-432.

Skeels, H. (1966). Adult status of children with contrasting early life experiences. *Society for Research in Child Development Monographs*, 31.

Skinner, B. F. (1971). *Beyond freedom and dignity*. New York: Alfred A. Knopf.

Skinner, B. F. (1969). *Contingencies of reinforcement: A theoretical analysis*. New York: Appleton-Century Crofts.

Skinner, B. F. (1968). *The technology of teaching*. New York: Meredith.

Skinner, B. F. (1957). The experimental analysis of behavior. *American Scientist*, 45:343-371.

Skinner, B. F. (1954). The science of learning and the art of teaching. *Harvard Educational Review*, 24:86-97.

Skinner, B. F. (1948). *Walden II*. New York: Macmillan.

Skinner, B. F. (1938). *The behavior of organisms: An experimental analysis*. New York: Appleton-Century-Crofts.

Slamecka, N. J. (1962). Retention of connected discourse as a function of interpolated learning. *Journal of Experimental Psychology*, 63:480-486.

Smith, B. O. (1960). A concept of teaching. *Teachers College Record*, 61:229-241.

Smith, J. M., and Smith, D. (1966). *Child management: A program for parents*. Ann Arbor, Mich.: Ann Arbor Publishers.

Snow, R. E. (1968). Unfinished Pygmalion. *Contemporary Psychology*, April 1969 XIV(4):197-199. Reviews book of R. Rosenthal and L. Jacobsen. *Pygmalion in the Classroom: Teacher Expectation and Pupil's Intellectual Development*. New York: Holt, Rinehart and Winston.

Solomon, D., Rosenberg, L., and Bezdek, W. E. (1964). Teacher behavior and student learning. *Journal of Educational Psychology*, 55:23-30.

Solomon, R. L. (1964). Punishment. *American Psychologist*, 19:239-253.

Sonquist, H., Kamii, C., and Derman, L. (1970). A Piaget-derived preschool curriculum. In I. J. Athey and D. O. Rubadeau, eds., *Educational implications of Piaget's theory*. Massachusetts: Ginn-Blaisdell, pp. 101-114.

Sparks, D. S. (1969). Grading and student evaluation. Washington, D.C.: Paper presented at the Council of Graduate Schools in the United States, ED 036 261.

Spaulding, R. (1968). Classroom behavior analysis and treatment. San Jose: San Jose State College.

Spence, K. (1956). *Behavior theory and conditioning*. New Haven, Conn.: Yale University Press.

Spiegler, C. G. (1967). Provisions and programs for educationally disadvantaged youth in secondary schools. In P. A. Witty, ed., *The educationally retarded and disadvantaged. The Sixty-Sixth Yearbook of the National Society for the Study of Education*. Chicago, Ill.: University of Chicago Press, pp. 184-210.

Stagner, R. (1931). The redintegration of pleasant and unpleasant and experience. *American Journal of Psychology*, 43:463-468.

Stake, R. E. (1967). Countenance of educational evaluation. *Teachers College Record*, 68:523-540.

Stallings, W. M., and Lesslie, E. K. (Winter 1970). Student attitudes toward grades and grading. *Improved College and University Teaching*, 18:66-68.

Stallings, W. M., and Smock, H. R. (1971). The pass-fail grading option at a state university: A five semester evaluation. *Journal of Educational Measurement*, 8(3):153-160.

Stephens, T. (1970). *Directive teaching*. Columbus, Ohio: Charles Merrill.

Stiavelli, R. S., and Shirley, D. T. (1968). The citizens' council: A technique for managing behavior disorders in the educationally handicapped class. *Journal for School Psychology*, 6:147-153.

Stoddard, G. D. (1943). *The meaning of intelligence*. New York: Macmillan, p. 4.

St. John, N. A. (1970). Desegregation and minority group performance. In E. Gordon ed., Education for socially disadvantaged children. *Review of Educational Research*, 40(1):111-134.

Stringer, L. A., and Glidewell, J. C. (1967). *Early detection of emotional illnesses in school children: Final report*. Clayton, Mo.: St. Louis County Health Department.

Stufflebeam, Daniel L., et. al. *Educational Evaluation and Decision Making*. Bloomington, Inc.: Phi Delta Kappa, 1971.

Stulurow, L. M. (1964). Social impact of programmed instruction: aptitudes and abilities revisited. In J. P. DeCecco, ed., *Educational technology*. New York: Holt, Rinehart and Winston, pp. 348-355.

Suchman, J. R. (1966). *Inquiry Development Program: Developing Inquiry*. Chicago: Science Research Associates.

Suchman, J. R. (1962). The elementary school training program. *Scientific Inquiry*. Urbana: University of Illinois Press.

Sulzbacher, S., and Houser, J. (1968). A tactic to eliminate disruptive behavior: Group contingent consequences. *American Journal of Mental Deficiency*, 73:88-90.

Suppes, P. (1966). Tomorrow's education? Computer based instruction in the elementary school. *Ed Age 2*.

Sweet, R. C. (1966). *Educational attainment and attitudes toward school as a function of feedback in the form of teachers' written comments. Technical Report No. 15*. Madison, Wisc.: Wisconsin Research and Development Center for Cognitive Learning.

Sweigert, R. L. (December 1968). The discovery of need in education: Developing a need inquiry system. *Journal of Secondary Education*, (b).

Sweigert, R. L. (1968). Need assessment—The first step toward deliberate rather than impulsive response to problems. California State Department of Education, (a).

Swenson, T. L., Hesse, K., and Hansen, L. (1971). *A unipac on dialect*. Madison, Wisc.: Madison Public Schools (Title III Language Arts Project).

Taylor, D. W., Berry, P. C., and Black, C. H. (1958). Does group participation when using brainstorming facilitate or inhibit creative thinking? *Administrative Science Quarterly*, 3:23-47.

Telford, C. W., and Sawrey, J. M. (1967). *The exceptional individual*. Englewood Cliffs, N.J.: Prentice-Hall.

Temple, R., and Amen, E. (1944). A study of anxiety in young children by means of a projective technique. *Genetic Psychology Monographs*, 30:59-113.

Tennyson, R. D., and Merrill, M. D. (1971). Hierarchical models in the development of a theory of instruction: A comparison of Bloom, Gagne and Merrill. *Educational Technology,* 11(9):27-31.

Terman, L. W. (1917). The intelligence quotient of Francis Galton in child-hood. *The American Journal of Psychology,* 28:208-215.

Terman, L. W. (1916). *The measurement of intelligence.* Boston: Houghton Mifflin.

Terman, L. M., and Oden, M. H. (1959). *The gifted group at mid-life.* Stanford, Calif.: Stanford University Press.

Terte, R. (September 2, 1965). Enriched schools short on results. *New York Times,* p. 33.

Terwilliger, J. S. (1971). *Assigning grades to students.* Glenview, Ill.: Scott, Foresman.

Thelen, H. A. (1967). *Classroom grouping for teachability.* New York: Wiley.

Thomas, C. L., and Stanley, J. C. (1969). Effectiveness of high school grades for predicting college grades of black students: a review and discussion. *Journal of Educational Measurement,* 6(4):203-216.

Thomas, R. M., and Thomas, S. M. (1965). *Individual differences in the class-room.* New York: David McKay.

Thomas, S., and Knudsen, D. D. (1965). The relationship between non-promo-tion and the dropout problem. *Theory Into Practice,* 4:90-94.

Thompson, G. G., and Hunnicutt, C. W. (1944). The effect of repeated praise or blame on the work achievement of introverts and extroverts. *Journal of Educational Psychology,* 35:257-266.

Thompson, J. (1941). Development of facial expression of emotion in blind and seeing children. *Archives of Psychology,* 37:264.

Thorndike, E. L. (1932). *The fundamentals of learning.* New York. Teachers College.

Thorndike, E. L. (1913). *The psychology of learning.* New York: Teachers College.

Thorndike, E. L. (1898). Animal intelligence: An experimental study of the associative processes in animals. *Psychological Review Monograph Sup-plement,* II, No. 8.

Thorndike, R. L. (1971). Concepts of cultural fairness. *Journal of Educational Measurement,* 8(2):63-70.

Thorndike, R. L. (1968). Review of R. Rosenthal and L. Jacobsen. Pygmalion in the classroom. *American Educational Research Journal,* 5:708-711.

Thorndike, R. L. (1963). Some methodological issues in the study of creativity. In E. F. Gardner, ed., *Proceedings of the 1962 Invitational Conference on Testing Problems.* Princeton, N.J.: Educational Testing Service, pp. 40-54.

Thorndike, R. L. (1950). How children learn the principles and techniques of problem-solving. In N. B. Henry, ed., *Learning and instruction. Forty-Ninth Yearbook of the National Society for the Study of Education,* Part I. Chicago: University of Chicago Press, pp. 192-216.

Thurstone, L. L. (1933). *The theory of multiple factors.* Author.

Tilton, J. W. (1951). *Educational psychology of learning.* New York: Macmillan.

Tolman, E. C. (1959). *Principles of purposive behavior.* In S. Koch, ed., *Psy-chology: A study of a science.* Vol. 2. New York: McGraw-Hill, pp. 92-157.

Tolman, E. C. (1932). *Purposive behavior in animals and men.* New York: Appleton-Century-Crofts.

Tolman, E. C., and Honzik, C. H. (1930). Introduction and removal of reward and maze performance in rats. *University of California Publications in Psychology*, *14*:257-75.

Tolman, E. C., Ritchie, B. F., and Ralish, D. (1946). Studies in spatial learning, II: Place learning vs. response learning. *Journal of Experimental Psychology*, *36*:221-229.

Torrance, E. P. (1970). *Encouraging creativity in the classroom*. Dubuque, Iowa: William C. Brown.

Torrance, E. P. (1962). *Guiding creative talent*. Englewood Cliffs, N.J.: Prentice-Hall.

Torrance, E. P. (1961). Priming creative thinking in the primary grades. *Elementary School Journal*, *62*:34-41.

Trabasso, T. (1970). Pay attention. In J. P. DeCecco, ed., *Readings in educational psychology today*. Del Mar, Calif.: Communications Research Machines. pp. 105-109.

Trabasso, T., and Bower, G. H. (1968). *Attention in learning: Theory and research*. New York: Wiley.

Travers, R. M. W. (1970). *Man's information system*. Scranton, Penn.: Chandler.

Travers, R. M. W. (1967). *Essentials of learning* (2nd ed.). New York: Macmillan.

Travers, R. M. W. (1964). *An introduction to educational research* (2nd ed.). New York: Macmillan.

Turiel, E. (1969). Developmental processes in the child's moral thinking. In P. Mussen, J. Langer, and M. Covington, eds., *Trends and issues in developmental psychology*. New York: Holt, Rinehart and Winston, pp. 92-133.

Tyler, F. (1964). Issues related to readiness. In E. Hilgard, ed., *Theories of learning and instruction. Sixty-third Yearbook of the National Society for the Study of Education*, Part I. Chicago: University of Chicago Press.

Tyler, F. T., and Brownell, W. A. (1962). Facts and issues: A concluding statement. Chapter XVII in *Individualizing instruction. The Sixty-first Yearbook of the National Society for the Study of Education*. Part I. Chicago: NSSE.

Tyler, R. W. (1965). The field of educational research. In Egon Guba and Stanley Elam, eds. *The Training and Nurture of Educational Researchers, Sixth Annual Phi Delta Kappa Symposium on Educational Research*. Bloomington, Ind.: Phi Delta Kappa, Inc., pp. 1-12.

Tyler, R. W. (1950). *Basic principles of curriculum and instruction*. Chicago: University of Chicago Press.

Tyler, R. W. (1934). Some findings from studies in the field of college biology. *Science Education*, *18*:133-143.

Underwood, B. A. (1967). Forgetting. In R. C. Atkinson, ed., *Contemporary psychology: Readings from scientific american*. San Francisco: W. H. Freeman.

Underwood, B. J. (1964). Laboratory studies of verbal learning. In E. R. Hilgard, ed., *Theories of learning and instruction. Sixty-third Yearbook of the National Society for the Study of Education*, Part I. Chicago: University of Chicago Press, pp. 133-152.

Urevick, S. J. (1965). Ability grouping: Why is it undemocratic? *The Clearing House*, *39*:530-532.

U.S. Commission on Civil Rights (1967). Racial isolation in the public schools. Washington, D.C.: U.S. Government Printing Office.

U.S. Department of Health, Education and Welfare (1965). *Patients in Mental Institutions in U.S.A.* 1964. Washington, D.C.: Government Printing Office.

U.S. House of Representatives Subcommittee on the war on poverty program (1965). Hearings held in Washington, D.C. April 12–15 and 30.

Vance, B. (1969). Modifying hyperactive and aggressive behavior in J. Krumboltz and C. Thoresen, eds., *Behavioral counseling: Cases and techniques.* New York: Holt, Rinehart and Winston, pp. 30-33.

Vernon, P. E. (1958). Education and the psychology of individual differences. *Harvard Educational Review,* 28:91-104.

Verville, E. (1967). *Behavior problems of children.* Philadelphia: W. B. Saunders.

Voeks, V. W. (1950). Formalization and clarification of a theory of learning. *Journal of Psychology,* 30:341-363.

Wagner, J. A. (December 1960). Talented high-school students. *Education,* 81:232-234.

Wallach, M. (1971). Essay review. The psychological impact of school experience by Minuchin, et al. *Harvard Educational Review,* 41(2):230-239.

Wallach, M., and Kogan, N. (1965). *Modes of thinking in young children.* New York: Holt, Rinehart and Winston.

Warren, J. R. (1970). College grading practices: An overview. Princeton, N.J.: Educational Testing Service.

Washburne, Carleton W. "Educational Measurements as a Key to Individualizing Instruction and Promotions." *Journal of Educational Research,* 1922, 5, 195-206.

Washington Report (1972). *Phi Delta Kappan,* 53(6):391.

Watson, G., and Johnson, D. (1972). *Social Psychology—Issues and Insights* (2nd ed.). Philadelphia, Penn.: J. B. Lippincott.

Watson, J. B. (1930). *Behaviorism* (2nd ed.). Chicago: University of Chicago Press.

Webb, L. N. (May 1965). *Nongraded Schools.* National Education Association.

Weiner, B. (1968). Motivated forgetting, and the study of repression. *Journal of Personality,* 36:213-234.

Weiner, B. (1966). Motivation and memory. *Psychological Monographs,* 80 (18, Whole No. 626).

Weiner, B. (1969). Motivation. In R. L. Ebel, ed., *Encyclopedia of educational research* (4th ed.). New York: Macmillan, pp. 878-888.

Weiner, B., and Reed, H. (1969). Effects of the instructional sets to remember and to forget on short-term retention: Studies of rehearsal control and retrieval inhibition (repression). *Journal of Experimental Psychology,* 79: 226-232.

Wenar, C. (1971). Personality development—from infancy to adulthood. Geneva, Ill.: Houghton Mifflin.

Wertheimer, M. (1959). *Productive thinking* (enlarged ed.). New York: Harper & Row.

Westinghouse and Ohio University (1970). *The impact of Head Start: An evaluation of the effects of Head Start on children's cognitive and affective development.* In J. L. Frost and G. R. Hawkes, eds., *The disadvantaged child—issues and innovations* (2nd ed.). Boston: Houghton-Mifflin, pp. 325-343.

Westinghouse (June 1969). The impact of Head Start: An evaluation of the effects of Head Start on children's cognitive and affective development. Westinghouse Learning Corporation and Ohio University.

Wheeler, R. H., and Perkins, F. T. (1932). *Principles of mental development.* New York: Crosswell.

White, R. W. (1959). Motivation reconsidered: The concept of competence. *Psychological Review,* 66:297-333.

Williams, R. J. (1967). *You are extraordinary.* New York: Random House.

Williams, R. J. (1956). *Biochemical individuality.* New York: Wiley.

Williams, R. J. (1953). *Free and unequal.* Austin: University of Texas Press.

Williams, R. J. (1946). *The human frontier.* New York: Harcourt.

Wilson, A. (1959). Residential segregation of social classes and aspirations of high school boys. *American Sociological Review, 24,* pp. 836-845.

Wilson, J. A. R., Robeck, M. C., Michael, W. B. (1969). *Psychological foundations of learning and teaching.* New York: McGraw-Hill.

Winder, C., and Rau, L. (1962). Parental attitudes associated with social deviance in pre-adolescent boys. *Journal of Abnormal and Social Psychology,* 64:418-424.

Wise, A. E. (1969). The constitutional challenge to inequities in school finance. *Phi Delta Kappan, 51*(3):145-148.

Wittrock, M. C. (1963). Set applied to student teaching. In J. P. DeCecco, ed., *Human learning in the school.* New York: Holt, Rinehart and Winston, pp. 107-117.

Wittrock, M. C., Keislar, E. R., and Stern, C. (1964). Verbal cues in concept identification. *Journal of Educational Psychology, 55*:195-200.

Witty, P. A. (1955). Introduction. In N. B. Henry, ed., *Intelligence: Its nature and nurture. Fifty-fourth Yearbook of the National Society for the Study of Education.* Part II. Chicago: University of Chicago Press.

Witty, P. A. (1951). *The gifted child.* New York: Heath.

Witty, P. A. (1947). An analysis of the personality traits of the effective teacher. *Journal of Educational Research, 40*:662-671.

Wolfle, D. (1960). Diversity of talent. *American Psychologist, 15*:535-545.

Wolfson, B. J. (1967). The promise of multiage grouping for individualizing instruction. *The Elementary School Journal, 67*:354-362.

Womer, F. B. (1968). Research toward national assessment. *Western Regional Conference on Testing Problems.* Proceedings, pp. 34-49.

Worcester, D. A. (1956). *The Education of Children of Above-Average Mentality.* Lincoln: University of Nebraska Press.

Working Paper 20 (February 1971). *Comprehensive achievement monitoring (CAM): A project to develop longitudinal classroom evaluation using item sampling.* A symposium presented at the Annual Meeting of the National Council of Measurement of Education, New York.

Working Paper 21 (February 1971). *Monitoring and managing student outcomes by using new computer technology.* A symposium presented at the Annual Meeting of the American Educational Research Association, New York.

Worthen, B. R. (1968). Discovery and expository task presentation in elementary mathematics. *Journal of Educational Psychology, Monograph Supplement, 59*(1), Part 2.

Wright, D. (1971). *The psychology of moral behavior.* Baltimore: Penguin Books.

Yamamota, K. (1964). Role of creative thinking and intelligence in high school achievement. *Psychological Reports,* 14:785-789.

Yarrow, L., and Pederson, F. (1972). Attachment: Its origins and course. In W. Hartup, ed., *The young child,* Vol. II. Washington, D.C.: National Association for the Education of Young Children.

Yee, A. H. (1968). Source and direction of causal influence in teacher-pupil relationships. *Journal of Educational Psychology,* 59:275-282.

Young, D. (1962). Examining essays for eleven plus classification. *British Journal of Educational Psychology,* 32:267-274.

Zax, M., Cowen, E., Rappaport, J., Beach, D., and Laird, J. (1968). Follow-up study of children identified early as emotionally disturbed. *Journal of Consulting and Clinical Psychology,* 32:369-377.

Zeignarnik, B. (1938). On finished and unfinished tasks. In W. D. Ellis, ed., *A sourcebook of gestalt psychology.* New York: Harcourt, pp. 300-314.

Zeller, A. F. (1950). An experimental analogue of repression: II. The effect of individual failure and success on memory measured by relearning. *Journal of Experimental Psychology,* 40:411-422.

Zigler, E. (1970). Social class and the socialization process. Education for socially disadvantaged children. *Review of Educational Research,* 40(1):87-110.

Zigler, E. (1970). *The environmental mystique: Training the intellect. Child-hood Education,* 46:402-412.

AUTHOR INDEX

SUBJECT INDEX